Why You Need This New Edition

If you're wondering why you should buy this new edition of *Psychology for Living: Adjustment, Growth, and Behavior*, here are 8 good reasons!

1. This edition features a new author, **Steve Kirsh**, who brings to this edition his exciting experiences as a seasoned book author, a human development specialist, and an insightful scientist and teacher.

2. There are nearly **500 new references** as well as **new glossary terms**.

3. A **How to Study** section at the beginning of the book provides suggestions for studying and test taking.

4. **Chapter outlines** at the beginning of each chapter give students an overview of what will be covered.

5. **End-of-chapter summaries** help the reader to grasp the main points of the chapter and **end-of-chapter exercises** heighten the student's involvement in the material.

6. **World Wide Web sites** and additional readings are listed at the end of each chapter along with recommended additional readings.

7. **Self-tests**, consisting of 10 multiple-choice questions, help students to assess their understanding of the material covered. **Questions for self-reflection** encourage students to relate the material in the text to themselves.

8. **Cases** intertwined throughout the chapter demonstrate the information to readers.

PEARSON

Tenth Edition

Psychology for Living

Adjustment, Growth, and Behavior Today

Karen Grover Duffy
State University of New York–Geneseo

Steven J. Kirsh
State University of New York–Geneseo

Eastwood Atwater

Prentice Hall

Boston   Columbus   Indianapolis   New York   San Francisco   Upper Saddle River
Amsterdam   Cape Town   Dubai   London   Madrid   Milan   Munich   Paris   Montreal   Toronto
Delhi   Mexico City   Sao Paulo   Sydney   Hong Kong   Seoul   Singapore   Taipei   Tokyo

Executive Editor: Susan Hartman
Project Editor: Kara Kikel
Editorial Assistant: Laura Barry
Marketing Manager: Nicole Kunzmann
Marketing Assistant: Amanda Olweck
Production Project Manager: Claudine Bellanton
Manufacturing Buyer: Debbie Rossi
Cover Administrator/Designer: Kristina Mose-Libon
Editorial Production and Composition Service: Laserwords Maine

Credits appear on page 443, which constitutes an extension of the copyright page.

Library of Congress Cataloging-in-Publication Data

Duffy, Karen Grover.
   Psychology for living : adjustment, growth, and behavior today / Karen Grover Duffy, Steven J. Kirsh, Eastwood
Atwater. — 10th ed.
       p. cm.
   ISBN-13: 978-0-205-79036-4
   ISBN-10: 0-205-79036-4
   1.   Conduct of life—Textbooks. I.   Kirsh, Steven J. II.   Atwater, Eastwood, 1925- III.   Title.
   BF335.A88 2010
   158—dc22

                                                                                                 2010012904

10 9 8 7 6 5 4 3 2 1 EB 14 13 12 11 10

**Prentice Hall
is an imprint of**

www.pearsonhighered.com

ISBN 10:   0-205-79036-4
ISBN 13: 978-0-205-79036-4

Dedicated to the rescuers and caregivers of people and animals all over the world.
~KGD

Dedicated to my sister, Janice Zalk, for her love, support, and friendship.
~SJK

Brief Contents

Contents

PART 4 BEING SOCIAL

CHAPTER 8

CHAPTER 9

Preface

This book is intended for readers interested in applying psychological insights and principles to their own lives as a way of achieving a better understanding of themselves *and* of living more effectively. To this end, we have included material from the major perspectives of psychology, including the psychodynamic, cognitive-behavioral, and humanistic viewpoints. Since a well-rounded text cuts across several branches of psychology, we have included contributions from clinical, personality, social, and developmental psychology, as well as from the important fields of cognitive, biological, and health psychology. Throughout the book, we've presented differing views on the same issue, along with questions that are designed to stimulate readers' critical thinking. Our aim is to increase readers' understanding as well as their knowledge about personal adjustment, in order that they may continue learning on their own.

Major features of this tenth edition are explained in the following sections.

ORGANIZATION

The chapters of this book stand alone; that is, you can read them out of order and still understand all of the material even though you have not read a preceding chapter.

The introductory chapter on self-direction and social change remains at the beginning, of course. The second large unit is about development or the state of "becoming." The chapters on childhood and adulthood can be found here. The third large unit pertains to the individual in the present or in a state of "being." Here you will find the chapters on self-concept, health, personal control, and decision making, as well as on emotion and motivation.

The next large unit is about the social side of adjustment and growth. Here are located the chapters on friends, groups (leaders and followers), and work and leisure. This unit is followed by an apt unit about closer intimate relationships. This short unit contains two chapters, one each on sexuality and on committed or intimate relationships.

Finally, any book about personal growth and adjustment would be incomplete without including material on the challenges each of us faces. The last unit contains chapters on stress, mental disorders, therapy, and death and dying. Please let us know how you feel about this organization, and remember that the chapters are self-contained so they can easily be read in any order you wish. We can be reached at duffy@geneseo.edu and kirsh@geneseo.edu.

NEW CONTENT

We have made some changes to the content of the book to reflect changes in the field of psychology in addition to world events. First, the book features a new author, Steve Kirsh, who brings to this edition exciting experiences as a seasoned book author, a human development specialist, and an insightful scientist whose research has helped enhance our understanding of the effects of various media and technologies on everyday life. Second, there are nearly 500 new references as well as new glossary terms. Third, you will also find new or additional information on the following topics:

- Technology and how it is benefiting yet at the same time perplexing our lives.
- The ecological perspective on human development.
- The impact and proliferation of hand-held devices such as PDAs and cell phones.
- The malleability versus fixedness of personality.
- Updated U.S. census figures (and world population growth) throughout the book.
- The neuroscience of self-control.
- Recent research on body image and the influence of the media.
- New research on post-decision regret, including hindsight bias.
- Women in management positions and their experience with the glass cliff.
- Updated research on the impact of electronic communication at work.
- The resurgence of interest in the trait approach to leadership.
- Inclusion of information on post-traumatic stress syndrome in Iraq war veterans.
- The prominence of resilience in everyday life and in coping with stressors.
- The influence of the media in promoting eating disorders.
- Data on the prevalence of personality disorders.
- The concept that well-being is different from the mere absence of disorder and stress.
- The controversies swirling around evidence-based therapies.
- The movement away from theories of stages of bereavement and toward interest in growth theories of bereavement.
- The continuing threat of terrorism and how it has changed the way we live and cope.
- Expanded critiques of the concepts of individual and collective societies.
- Changes in the American family and how they affect individual members.
- The effects of the baby boomers on society as they enter later adulthood.
- Thoughtful analysis of the role ethnicity and race play in health care, psychotherapy, and other areas.
- More coverage on cultural effects of nonverbal communication (and miscommunication).
- Additional information on child pornography and sexual assault.

LEARNING AIDS

Several features have been included to assist the student in making the best use of this book:

- A How to Study section at the beginning of the book provides suggestions for studying and test taking.
- Chapter outlines at the beginning of each chapter give students an overview of what will be covered.
- Learning objectives identify what students are expected to attain in regard to knowledge, understanding, and application.
- Terms that may be new to students are boldfaced and are followed by an italicized definition that is repeated in the glossary. Each time the term is used, regardless of the chapter, it is highlighted so that no matter in what order the chapters are read, the term will be familiar to the reader.
- Special-interest boxes, figures, and tables contain interesting and important material supplemental to the text.
- A glossary at the end of the book defines key, boldfaced terms in the text.
- End-of-chapter summaries, arranged by major headings, help the reader to grasp the main points of the chapter.
- Self-tests, consisting of 10 multiple-choice questions, help students to assess their understanding of the material covered.

APPLICATIONS

- Cases intertwined throughout the chapter reify the information for readers. These are *real* cases based on Dr. Atwater's (founding author of this text) or our experiences. The cases have been fictionalized and modified to protect the identity of the people in them.
- One or two self-scoring inventories in each chapter enable students to apply the concepts and principles covered in the text. These inventories are designed by us, so please note that they have no scientifically derived validity or reliability. They are merely meant to be tools for self-exploration and self-understanding and should be interpreted as such.
- End-of-chapter exercises heighten the student's involvement in the material.
- Questions for self-reflection encourage students to relate the material in the text to themselves.

SUPPLEMENTS

Instructor's Manual with Tests (0–205–79037–2)　The instructor's manual is a wonderful tool for classroom preparation and management. Each chapter in the teaching aids section includes a chapter overview, lecture suggestions, discussion questions, class activities, and media resources. Each chapter contains a set of tests, containing representative multiple-choice, true-false, short-answer, and essay questions, each with a page reference, difficulty rating, and type designation. The tests are also available in the MyTest (0–205–79057–7) computerized version for ease in creating tests for the classroom.

PowerPoint Presentation (0-205-79038-0)   Completely revised, the PowerPoint presentation is an exciting interactive tool for use in the classroom. Each chapter pairs key concepts with images from the textbook to reinforce student learning.

MyPsychKit, www.mypsychkit.com (0-205-79058-5)   MyPsychKit provides a wealth of study tools for students looking to clarify and deepen their understanding of *Psychology for Living: Adjustment, Growth, and Behavior,* 10th Edition. Each chapter includes learning objectives, animations and simulations, flash-card glossary terms, online practice tests with multiple-choice questions, and survey questions in the survey tool.

FOR FURTHER INFORMATION

A special feature at the end of each chapter is a list of ways to explore topics electronically or in print. One of the points the text establishes is that we have moved into a technological information age. Therefore, World Wide Web sites are listed at the end of the chapter along with recommended additional readings. These websites and additional readings are provided with a brief description of their contents and are intended for those who wish to pursue a given topic in greater depth.

ACKNOWLEDGMENTS

Many thanks to Dr. Eastwood Atwater for providing us with the opportunity to take over this well-established book. While he is no longer with us, we hope that he would approve of our continued efforts at producing the same high-quality book he wrote. Many thanks to the professors who adopted past editions and provided feedback to us. We really DO appreciate your comments and take them to heart. Special thanks goes to LeeAnn Doherty at Pearson Education for all of her patience and excellent guidance in the past and for bravely taking on our project this time. To our friends and family, a big thank you for nudging us along when we got discouraged about getting this and other books completed, especially given the vicissitudes of daily life and the distracting tug at our heart strings of the sun, moon, stars, spouses, children, and many critters who needed petting.

Many thanks to the following reviewers for their insightful comments and helpful suggestions:

Norma Caltagirone
Hillsborough Community College

Linda Fayard
Mississippi Gulf Coast Community College

Carie Forden
Clarion University

Stan Mazur-Hart
Linn-Benton Community College

Patrick Saxe
State University of New York–New Paltz

How to Study

Students give many excuses about why they haven't done well on a test. Occasionally, they will admit outright, "I just didn't study." But more often they will say, "I really studied for that test. I can't understand why I did so poorly." A common problem is waiting until the last minute to study. But in many instances, students just don't know how to study. Regardless of whether you fall into this category, chances are you could improve your studying habits by applying one of the following time-honored methods of studying.

THE PQ4R METHOD

The PQ4R method gets its name from the six overlapping stages for studying material such as textbook chapters—preview, question, read, reflect, recite, and review.* Extensive experience has shown that this method can improve your understanding and memory, and thus your test performance.

PREVIEW

It's a good idea to look over the chapter as a whole before you begin it. When you read a novel, you usually start at the beginning and read straight through so as not to spoil the surprise ending. But with concepts and factual material, it's just the opposite. Here, it's important to get an idea of the material as a whole so you can put the details in context as you read.

- First, look over the table of contents.
- Next, skim through the chapter, looking at the headings and subheadings.
- Then, read the chapter summary.
- Finally, decide how much you want to read at a sitting.

*E. L. Thomas and H. A. Robinson, *Improving memory in every class: A sourcebook for teachers* (Boston: Allyn & Bacon, 1972).

QUESTION

Once you've looked over the chapter, you may be curious about the material. A helpful technique is to ask yourself questions about the material. Then read the chapter with the aim of finding the answers to your questions. One way to do this is to turn each bold-faced heading and subheading into a question. For example, the first major heading and subheadings in Chapter 1 on self-direction are

- Social Change
- Living in a Technological World
- Living with Other Social Changes
- How Certain Is Our Future?

Now use these headings and subheadings to think up some questions. Here are some examples: What is social change? I know I live in a technological world, but how does that relate to social change and self-direction? What are some of the other social changes that I have witnessed? With terror alerts and other dramatic changes, just how certain is my future? Your use of such questions may prove even more effective if you jot them down, and then, as you read, write down your answers.

READ

Make it a point to understand what you're reading, digesting the material in one section before proceeding to the next. Skimming through material without compre-hending it leads to superficial understanding at best, but more often, to downright con-fusion. In contrast, when you take the time to understand what you read, you'll also retain it better. If you're not clear about the meaning of a word, check the glossary of terms at the end of the book. If you can't find the word in the glossary, look it up in one of the better dictionaries such as *Webster's New World Dictionary*. Also, feel free to make explanatory notes to yourself in the margins of the pages of your textbook.

REFLECT

A good way to improve your understanding of something is to pause periodically and reflect on it. Ask yourself: Do I really understand this material? Could I explain it to someone else? If the answer is no, reread the material.

It's also helpful to mark or underline key passages in the chapter. This makes you an active participant in reading and provides you with key passages to review for tests. Some students prefer to mark or underline as they read. Others prefer to read through the material and then go back and highlight the most important points. Experts prefer the latter approach, because we usually have a better idea of the key passages after we've read through the material. Here are some suggestions for marking or underlining:

- Read through each section before marking or underlining.
- Mark only key passages or ideas.
- Use a marker or pen. Pencil often smears.

RECITE

Perhaps you've had this experience: You look up someone's telephone number, but no sooner have you closed the phone book than you've forgotten the number. You reopen the book and find the number again. But this time as you close the book, you repeat the number to yourself, either silently or audibly. You're improving your memory through recitation—the act of repeating or speaking aloud. Recitation improves your memory in several ways. First, by focusing your attention on the page a bit longer, you can encode the material better, thereby ensuring accurate storage of the material. Repeated practice may also help you to retrieve the material when you need it.

There are several ways to use recitation. First, the act of reflection, or asking questions about the material, mentioned earlier, is itself a form of recitation. Second, you may also recite by closing the book and mentally recalling what you've just read. A third way is to recite aloud, either by discussing the material with a classmate or by sharing your reactions or asking questions about it in class. A fourth way is to make a written outline of what you've read. We highly recommend this method because it forces you to select the main ideas in the material. Occasionally, students attempt to escape the thinking process by simply copying down the headings and subheadings, including little else. Others include too much detail, which becomes distracting. Instead, be selective. You should be able to outline an entire chapter of this book in just several written pages, depending, of course, on how large you write. The entire process of selecting the major ideas and writing them down is an excellent form of recitation. It also provides you with a handy guide to review for the test.

The amount of time spent on recitation depends on the material covered. When you're trying to remember isolated bits of information, like names or numbers, up to 80 percent of your time should be spent in recitation. But when you're learning ideas or concepts that are highly meaningful and well organized, perhaps you would spend only 20 percent of your time in recitation. Personal experience will help you to determine which method of recitation works best for you.

REVIEW

When you're ready to review, reread the summary at the end of the chapter to give yourself a sense of the material as a whole. Then look back over the material in the chapter, paying special attention to the key ideas you've marked or underlined under each heading and subheading. If you've made a written outline of the chapter, review this, too. Ideally, you should review the material periodically, to offset the rapid decline in retention once you've learned something. It's recommended that you review the material within 24 hours of the initial reading, and then again 72 hours later. After this, it's a good idea to review the material about once a week until you're tested on it.

When you're ready, do the self-test at the end of each chapter. Then check your responses against the list of correct answers provided in the back of this book. When you miss a question, it's important to go back and look up the correct answer. Otherwise, you may make the same mistake again. You may observe that the order of test items parallels the sequence of material in the chapter, thus facilitating your use of the self-test for study purposes.

WHERE AND WHEN TO STUDY

Once the semester is under way, you're ready to plan your study schedule. Consider your class schedule, the workload in each course, and other commitments, such as a part-time job or family responsibilities. Be realistic. Don't try to study too much material at one time.

First, it's important to find a place to study that is free from distractions. Then use this place only for studying. In this way, you'll develop a set of associations that will strengthen your study habits. One of the worst places to study is on your bed. The bed is associated with fatigue; thus, you may find yourself falling asleep rather than studying. When you find yourself daydreaming or worrying about something else, take a short break and return when you're ready to study. When you finish studying, leave this place. By consistently doing so, you'll associate this place with studying and feel more like studying only there.

It's also important to set aside particular times for study. You may wish to study for a given block of time and quit at the end of this period regardless of how much you've read. Or you may want to study until you've covered a certain amount of material. Either way, it's best to study in reasonable blocks of time, about one to three hours. After a long stretch, you may have difficulty concentrating on the material at hand. That's why it's a good idea to take a short break at least once an hour, or even on the half-hour when you're covering very difficult material. Also, you might select other things you enjoy doing and make them contingent on completing your study goal for a given time slot. For instance, if you'd like to call a friend or watch television, do your studying first. Then make your call or watch TV as a reward to yourself.

Above all, don't procrastinate. Distribute your study times realistically so you don't try to absorb too much material at a time. For instance, if you must cover four chapters in this book for a test, plan to read no more than one chapter in a given time slot. Spacing out your study time cuts down on boredom and fatigue and also allows your memory time to consolidate the material. Your mind may continue absorbing the material in the intervals between study periods. This is especially important to keep in mind when you're learning complex or difficult material.

TAKING TESTS

When taking a test, stay calm and reasonably relaxed. By keeping your anxiety at a mild to moderate level, you minimize its interference with your thinking process. If you encounter a question that makes you especially anxious, note this on the question sheet or test itself. Then proceed to do the remaining questions before returning to tackle the difficult question(s). Realizing that you've completed most of the test helps you to concentrate on the more difficult items.

Regardless of the type of test, take time to read the questions carefully. Make certain you understand what the instructor is asking. Don't read things into a question, making it more complicated than it is. If the item looks particularly confusing, raise your hand and ask the instructor to rephrase the item. Be sure also to read every single choice for multiple-choice questions before selecting the correct one.

Before answering an essay question, take a few moments to jot down a brief outline on the back of a page. This helps to keep your thoughts on the subject while you write. If your test includes both multiple-choice and essay questions, first outline the essay question. Then complete the multiple-choice questions before writing out the essay answer.

After you've read a multiple-choice question and selected an answer, it's best to reread the question to make certain your answer matches the question. This helps to avoid simple "forgetting" mistakes, because material stays in our short-term memory for only about 30 seconds. By the time you've decided on the correct answer, chances are you've forgotten the exact wording of the question. Consequently, it's helpful to reread the question before marking your answer. This time, read the answer choices in reverse order.

Learn to eliminate incorrect answers before settling on the correct one. For instance, if there are four possible answers, eliminate the two that are the least plausible. With only two remaining answers to choose from, you have a 50–50 chance of selecting the correct one. Answers containing words like *always*, *never*, *only*, *must*, and *totally* often imply sweeping assertions and can usually be eliminated early on.

Should you ever change your answer? It all depends. If you have studied reasonably well and feel good about your answer, stick with it. If you have strong doubts about an answer, however, especially if you're not well informed on the subject, it might pay to reconsider. At the same time, a lot depends on the individual. In going over tests with students, we've found that anxious, impulsive students may initially choose an incorrect answer and would benefit from taking another look at their answer. On the other hand, students who lack self-confidence will often change a correct answer to an incorrect one because they distrust their own abilities. As a result, we suggest keeping track of the answers you change. Then go over each test, recording the number of answers you changed from wrong to right, and vice versa. Take this information into consideration throughout future test taking.

Finally, there are other ways you can learn from your test results. If your instructor goes over the test in class, make it a point to attend that day. Find out what you missed and, equally important, why. Were the questions different from what you expected, requiring, say, the understanding of concepts rather than factual information? If you didn't do well on an essay test, ask your instructor how you can do better next time. Try not to waste time making excuses or blaming your instructor or yourself. Find out what you need to do in order to improve your test performance next time. Then modify your study habits and test taking accordingly. Good luck!

About the Authors

Karen Duffy is a Distinguished Service Professor–Emerita, at the State University of New York at Geneseo. She received her Ph.D. in social and personality psychology from Michigan State University. Dr. Duffy served as a family mediator for the New York Unified Court System. She has also served on the executive committee and as the chief instructor for the training institute for the New York State Employee Assistance Program (EAP), as well as on the board of directors for a shelter for domestic violence and on an educational committee for a family planning agency. She has consulted to a variety of work settings on stress management, EAPs, and other work issues. She is a member of the American Psychological Society. Dr. Duffy has written several other books, including *Community Mediation: A Handbook for Practitioners and Researchers* and *Community Psychology*. She has also edited several hard-copy and web-based annual editions for another publisher, on topics including psychology of personality, social psychology, introductory psychology, and adjustment. She has held two Fulbright Fellowships to St. Petersburg State University, St. Petersburg, Russia. While in Russia, she worked with AIDS International, several children's shelters, and other community agencies. More recently, she completed two humanitarian aid trips to Mongolia.

Steven J. Kirsh is a Professor of Psychology at The State University of New York at Geneseo. Dr. Kirsh's primary areas of research focus on the influence of violent media on emotion recognition and social information processing. He has published *Children, Adolescents, and Media Violence: A Critical Look at the Research* (2006) and *Media and Youth: A Developmental Perspective* (2010) as well as numerous scientific articles and book chapters.

CHAPTER 1

Self-Direction in a Changing World

Learning Objectives

After completing this chapter, you should be able to

1. Explain how technology is changing the way we communicate and live.
2. Describe several characteristics of our postindustrial society.
3. Discuss other recent social changes unrelated to technology.
4. Explain Fromm's notion of human freedom, why freedom causes us anxiety, and how freedom relates to personal growth.
5. Discuss what it means to take charge of your life and give examples of various aspects of taking charge.
6. Understand several personal traits and which ones are likely to change throughout adulthood, if at all.
7. Describe the three-phase cycle by which we experience personal growth.

Change has always been an important part of our American way of life. To understand the impact of change, let's meet two college students, Zachary and Karen, related by blood but separated by over 100 years. Zachary is a freshman in college in the late 1800s. He is among the privileged few to attend college, mostly because his family is sufficiently well off to send him to school. Zachary travels to college by train, passing through miles of farmland and forests along the way. He keeps in touch with his family by letters. Zachary hopes to be a physician, an occupation pretty much closed to women in the 1800s. A few women do attend Zachary's college but major in home economics, teacher education, and more traditional female majors. Zachary lives at a boardinghouse for male college students. He takes his meals there but studies at the library, where he reads by gaslight. There are no computers or other technology such as photocopiers in the library. Zachary goes to the librarian to find what he needs. He hand-copies everything and also writes papers by hand. No one, absolutely no one, is using a mobile phone in Zachary's library.

Karen, Zachary's great-granddaughter, is a first-year college student of the twenty-first century. Since her parents' divorce, she has lived with her mother and sister. She is able to attend college mostly because of financial aid from private lenders and the government. Karen travels back and forth to college by plane several times a year, passing over the megalopolis on the East Coast that covers several hundred miles. To keep in touch with her family, she has only to pick up her walkie-talkie enabled phone or send a text message. Electricity lights up the room in which Karen reads and powers the computer she uses for term papers and correspondence. She is very glad that the computer checks her spelling and grammar. Karen lives in a coed dormitory, something absolutely taboo in Zachary's day. Karen is accustomed to mingling with students from different ethnic and racial groups on campus, and about half of them are women. In Karen's dining hall, genetically engineered tomatoes are occasionally served along with chicken and beef that have been infused with flavor enhancers. Karen uses the library as Zachary did, but she is fortunate to have an electronic card catalog, photocopiers, electronic article downloads, and access to the information highway known as the World Wide Web. Karen hopes to be a physician, as did Zachary. She, however, wants to specialize in gynecology, something Zachary would never dream of. Zachary planned to be a general practitioner who would visit the homes of his patients. Zachary knew some patients could not give him money, so he would take produce, wool, or other products in payment. Karen, on the other hand, wants a posh office, working hours from 9 a.m. to 5 p.m., and an answering service so she can enjoy her private life. She knows she will set up her financial accounting system to accept credit cards, not eggs and bacon.

SOCIAL CHANGE

Living in a Technological World

Both Zachary and Karen have lived in periods of rapid social change. **Social changes** are *changes in social patterns and institutions in society*. Social change can occur in any time period and be planned in advance or totally unplanned (Moritsugu, Wong, & Duffy, 2010). Planned changes are those created and engineered by humans, for example, building a new housing development wired for the most current technology. Unplanned changes are created by nature or by social accident, such as tsunamis and hurricanes or unexpected shifts in the population of a country due to disease or famine.

In Zachary's lifetime, America slowly transformed from an agrarian society to an urban one, and numerous inventions of the industrial revolution made transportation, farming, and manufacturing better and easier. Shortly, America was transformed from a frontier society to an industrial giant. Karen, in turn, takes technological change for granted. She believes that medical advances will soon have a cure for many life-threatening illnesses, including AIDS and cancer. She worries that the shortages of fossil fuels in addition to increased **greenhouse gases** are changing the world she knows. Greenhouse gases *are gases that are naturally occurring or man-made and that trap heat in the earth's atmosphere.* Meanwhile, she has learned that spiraling social change is normal and inevitable, although she occasionally wonders what lies ahead. Karen knows that social change is not always planned or positive.

All of us now realize that the galloping rate of technological, scientific, and social change occurs worldwide and has far-reaching (global) consequences. Social change seems to be a pervasive condition of our time (Moritsugu, Wong, & Duffy, 2010), and technology has expanded interconnectedness of peoples and increased awareness of a common, global humanity (Stepinsky, 2005). Figure 1–1 reveals the steep increase in computer and Internet use in U.S. households.

Technology makes relationships among people more fluid, flexible, and portable and has freed us from the constraints of being in only one place. Technology connects us to more people more of the time; it also equips us to work both at home and at our job sites, blurring the boundaries between them (Jackson, 2005). Technology, in fact, may be the most powerful engine of change in today's world (Sood & Tellis, 2005). People in almost every country are growing up in a world of greater interdependence because of technology. The revolution in communication, in particular, is re-creating the world in the image of a "global village," in which every aspect of life—every thought, act, and institution—is being reconsidered in light of what is happening to people in other parts of the world (Alterman, 1999; Shah, 2007).

Although people recognize the fact of change, they often disagree on the direction (better or worse) in which we're headed ((Kohut & Wike, 2008; Shah, 2007). Some assume that the world as we know it will last indefinitely and that all the changes around us will not shake the familiar social, economic, and political structures that hold our society together (Moen & Roehling, 2005). A larger proportion of people, however, fed by a steady diet of bad news about crime, economic problems, world crises, the threats

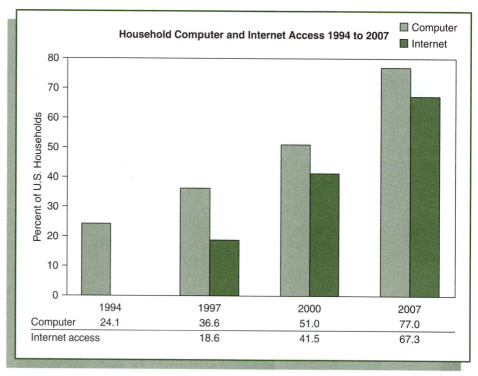

FIGURE 1–1

Household computer and Internet access in the United States: 1984 to 2007.
SOURCE: NTIA and ESA, U.S. Department of Commerce, using: U.S. Bureau of the Census Population Survey supplements, www.ntia.doc, and U.S. Bureau of the Census, *Internet Access and Usage 2007*, www.census.gov/compendia/statab/tables/0951120.pdf and Nielsen Ratings. Huge room for Internet service suppliers to drive Internet use http://kr.en.nielsen.com/news/20071004a.shtml

SELF-DIRECTION IN A CHANGING WORLD **5**

of terrorism, natural disasters, and possible nuclear destruction, have adopted a bleaker view (Huddy, Khatib, & Capelos, 2002). And yet others worry that digitalization and technology will damage or threaten local cultures and economies (Shah, 2007). Additionally, many forms of employment will be affected by automation and computerized systems. The increasing need for technical solutions places a premium on intellectual and technical knowledge. In turn, educated, middle-class workers will make up a larger proportion of the workforce in comparison to blue-collar workers, at least in the United States.

One major problem related to increasing people's knowledge and use of technology, however, is that *some people fear technology. Such fear is called* **technophobia** (Moritsugu, Wong, & Duffy, 2010). For example, some people are apprehensive about using computers because they fear they will break the computers, make costly errors, or look stupid. The gap between use of computers by men and women seems to have narrowed (Cooper, 2006; Popovich, Gullekson, Morris, & Morse, 2008; Wasserman & Richmond-Abbott, 2005). Other marginalized individuals, however, who are uneducated, poor, elderly, disabled, Hispanic or African American (Karavides, Lim, & Katsikas, 2005; Mehra, Merkel, & Bishop, 2004; Moritsugu, Wong, & Duffy, 2010; National Science Foundation, 2003; Wasserman & Richmond-Abbott, 2005), or live in rural areas (U.S. Department of Commerce, 2002) are less likely to use computers.

This has created a seeming digital divide. As mentioned above, except for women whose frequency of use of technology has recently become more similar to men's (Cooper, 2006; Popovich, Gullekson, Morris, & Morse, 2008; Wasserman & Richmond-Abbott, 2005) but whose anxiety about technology remains higher than men's (Zeidner & Matthews, 2005) and whose types of use (e.g., email versus web searches) is different from men's (Pierce & Boekelheide, 2008), those individuals who are already less powerful use technology least; they are perhaps the very individuals who could benefit from knowledge about technology in order to improve their jobs, social standing, and economic conditions (Mehra et al., 2004).

Interestingly, however, the overall technology picture is changing. Horrigan (2008) reports that mobile or "on the go" technology (cell phones and other wireless handhelds) is reducing this digital divide. Specifically, Horrigan reports that more and more senior citizens, economically disadvantaged individuals, African Americans, and Hispanics, who have generally lagged behind White men in usage, have cell phones. In fact, for use of non-voice applications (e.g., texting, photographing, and emailing) on handhelds, Hispanics and African Americans lead the way relative to White Americans. Can you think of some reasons for these new trends in technological use? These technological changes, along with other scientific discoveries, are moving Americans, Canadians, Koreans, Swedes, and other technologically advanced societies away from manufacturing and industry to service-oriented and technological employment just as the Industrial Revolution moved Zachary's generation from agricultural to manufacturing jobs. For an interesting summary of other ways in which technology has changed our world, see Table 1–1 (page 6).

Living with Other Social Changes

The world seems much smaller to Karen than it did to Zachary. Karen can zip an email to a college friend who resides in Ireland. Karen can view the news about Iran, Russia, Peru, and Kenya on television or even on her mobile phone. Karen also hears about the cloning of animals and stem cell research, which interests her immensely because it relates to medicine. Karen can visit the supermarket and watch the scanned price of each item rapidly appear. Karen can take digital photos with her mobile phone, edit them, and zap them in

TABLE 1–1

THE SOCIAL/CULTURAL DIMENSION OF THE INFORMATION REVOLUTION: HOW THE WORLD HAS CHANGED

- More information flowing among people and countries with less obstruction and fewer delays
- Information flowing *regardless* of distance
- Increased opportunities for economic cooperation across borders
- Greater opportunities for businesses and individuals to profit globally
- The erosion or difficulty of censorship in certain countries with a history of censorship
- People being inundated with vast quantities of information
- The democratization of information [i.e., people voicing their opinions more freely (e.g., blogging)]
- Greater awareness of prosperity and poverty in our own country or elsewhere in the world
- A growing information gap between wealthy and poor individuals and nations

SOURCE: Alterman (1999).

an instant to multiple friends. Zachary had no such abilities or knowledge. In Zachary's day, word traveled via itinerate workers such as doctors and blacksmiths or by rural dwellers visiting town to obtain provisions they could not grow or make themselves.

What other changes can we expect in today's global village? One additional change will be continued population expansion and attendant worries about the health of our environment, including sufficient water and arable land, increased pollution, poverty, unemployment, and a plethora of related problems. The world population stands at over 6.7 billion (as of May 1, 2009; see the World POPClock at the U.S. Census Bureau website), with almost 150 new people born every minute. Furthermore, pollution as well as exhaustion of natural resources are problems for all countries and are contributed to by our increasing population. As mentioned above, another dramatic change will be the increase in the diversity of the population in the United States. Table 1–2 documents some of these historic changes. Beyond the data in the table, the U.S. Census Bureau

TABLE 1–2

CHANGES IN OUR POPULATION

As you can determine from this table, the percentage of the population made up by minorities as identified by the U.S. Census Bureau is increasing.

Population	1990—% of total	2007—% of total
White	75.6	66
Black or African American	11.7	12
Hispanic*	9.0	15
Asian	2.8	4
American Indian or Alaska Native	0.7	1
Race other than above	0.1	1
Two or more races	Not available	1

*Hispanics are the fastest growing segment of our population.
SOURCES: U.S. Census Bureau, Census 2000, Summary File, Tables PL1 and PL2, http://www.census.gov/main/www/cen2000.html, and U.S. Census Bureau American Community Survey Data Profile Highlights (2004), http://quickfacts.census.gov/qfd/states/00000.html. U.S. and Census Bureau, Fact Sheet; *2005-2007 American Community Survey 3-Year Estimates.* http://factfinder.census.gov/servlet/ACSSAFFFacts?_submenuId=factsheet_1&_sse=on. Kaiser Family Foundation. (2008). *Distribution of the United States population, Race/Ethnicity,* 2007. http://facts.kff.org/chart.aspx?ch=362.

projects that by 2042 minorities will no longer be "minorities" and that by 2050 they collectively will represent 54 percent of the population (U.S. Bureau of the Census, 2008). An increasing number of immigrants from various regions of the world are entering this country, too. They bring a wealth of cultural ideas, languages, and customs. Accommodating these individuals will not be easy (Lamb, 2009), in particular because some Americans are closed-minded and rather ignorant of, insensitive to, or bigoted about people from other cultures. Because of increasing **cultural diversity** in this country, that is, *the increase in the number of cultures*, this book offers information about various racial and ethnic groups in America and how they uniquely cope with problems of adjustment. Where possible, information about other countries and cultures is also introduced. Similarly, we will also include valuable information on men and women.

How Certain Is Our Future?

How each of us understands the changes and trends in today's world is somewhat like the proverbial question of whether we perceive a partly filled glass as half empty or half full. Pessimists tend to see the glass as half empty; optimists see it as half full. Social forecasters, who speculate on our long-term future, admit that we live in uncertain times— both good and bad (Kohut & Wike, 2008). They nevertheless project a fairly optimistic future. Although they do not necessarily agree on what the future holds for us (Kohut & Wike), they typically see it as promising.

Social forecasters view many of the problems of our time as the growing pains of success rather than the harbingers of doom. While the problems of overcrowding, unemployment, environmental pollution, social inequality, and poverty cannot be dismissed, such issues perhaps should be seen as temporary phenomena with which society must deal rather than the inevitable foreshadowing of the end of civilization. Societies can and do rebound from problems that at the time appear to be insurmountable (Moritsugu, Wong, & Duffy, 2010).

THE CHALLENGE OF SELF-DIRECTION

Self-Direction and Society

These rapid social changes and the growing importance of information and access to technology heighten the challenge of **self-direction**, which is *the need to learn more about ourselves and our world as a means of directing our lives more effectively*. Self-direction helps us respond to many life events—such as technological advances—as either a threat or a challenge. For example, like Karen, the young woman you met in the opening vignette, some individuals find using computers to be exciting and challenging; they purposely seek them out and try to learn more about them. Others view computers as a threat or complain about having to use them.

Another issue is that the world is seemingly changing and shrinking, in large part due to the technological changes discussed earlier. Given this, there are bound to be cultural clashes, disputes, and sometimes out-and-out warfare. On a daily basis, people from one society are bound to conflict with or misunderstand others from a different society (Mortisugu, Wong, & Duffy, 2010). Here's a specific cultural example. Park, Lee, and Song (2005) studied SPAM (electronic advertising) sent to U.S. and Korean citizens. The Korean SPAMs included apologies for the unsolicited advertising; the U.S. ones did not. Koreans, therefore, might well think Americans rude for complaining about any unsolicited American advertisements Koreans receive.

We are increasingly exposed to other cultures due to the diversity of the U.S. population and to technological change (e.g., the Internet) which seemingly brings the rest of the world closer.

The study of culture, then, is extremely important to our understanding of one another; thus, you should try to better understand cultural differences (Bucher, 2009). To that end, one commonly used system for classifying cultures is via the orientation taken toward the individual in that culture. **Individualistic societies**, referred to throughout this text, are *societies in which individual gain is appreciated more than general societal gain*. Individualistic societies are sometimes referred to as *independent or autonomous* cultures, where the sense of self is developed based on privately held attitudes, preferences, and judgments (Kitayama & Uchida, 2005; Matsumoto, 2007). Another term for individualistic culture is *individual-level* culture (Matsumoto, 2003, 2007). Individualistic societies can be contrasted to **collectivist societies**, *in which collective or societal gain is cherished over individual advancement*. Collectivist societies are also known as *interdependent* societies (Matsumoto, 2007), where the sense of self is based on attitudes, preferences, and judgments held by others (Kitayama & Uchida, 2005). Another way to refer to collectivistic cultures is as *consensual-level* (or *group-level*) or embedded cultures (Matsumoto, 2003, 2007). Thus, the pressure to conform to group or cultural pressures in collectivist societies is far greater than in individualistic societies.

In contrast to U.S. and Canadian society, many Eastern and Asian cultures remain collectivist societies. Some contemporary scientists argue, however, that the contrasts are not as sharp between individualistic and collectivistic societies as once thought (Oishi, Hahn, Schimmack, Radhakrishan, Dzokoto, & Ahadi, 2005; Oyserman, Coon, & Kemmelmeier, 2002). Ask yourself whether this could be because of the technological revolution we are experiencing today. In the same vein, it is important to remember that any label applied to a culture *cannot and does not* capture the individual variations that exist within that culture (Matsumoto, 2003, 2007). For example, there is culture-level consensus in the United States about the value of egalitarianism, but in reality, life for many Americans is not very egalitarian (Matsumoto, 2003). Another case in point is that at the societal level we agree that democracy and voting is important. Most of-age Americans are entitled to vote, including the elderly in nursing homes, but often residents of nursing homes do not vote if no one makes voting or going to a polling place easy for them.

You may well be familiar with individualistic societies but may be unfamiliar with collective societies if you have only lived in the United States. Describing his childhood in a collectivist society, Joseph Lemasolai Lekuton, born Maasai in Kenya, said about his childhood in this nomadic society, "In my tribe, the village is you, and you are the village. . . . Everyone older than you will tell you what to do. And you never defy their orders" (Court, 2003, p. 5). As adults, in mainstream U.S. culture, we enjoy personal freedom, independence from others, and take greater pride in personal achievements than do people in collectivist cultures. By the same token, we as Americans may be more vulnerable to insecurity, confusion, and loneliness. Rest assured that there are many other dimensions along which societies and cultures vary (Cohen, 2009; Nair, 2001), for example, masculine–feminine, respect for authority figures, and uncertainty avoidance (Matsumoto, 2007). You will read about some of these concepts in other chapters of this book.

The above discussion brings us to another issue related to self-direction—freedom. Americans assume that freedom is a wonderful thing, but is it?

The Ambiguity of Personal Freedom

Nobody has written more eloquently about the ambiguity of human freedom than Erich Fromm (1963), the distinguished psychoanalyst. His experience of growing up in Germany during the Nazi regime and his subsequent move to the United States gave him tremendous insight into the problems of totalitarianism and human freedom. For example, especially in individualistic societies, we have freedom to direct our lives—from the details of daily life to the more crucial choices such as what career to choose. On the other hand, the challenge of freedom can make us feel more anxious, insecure, and isolated. Fromm contends that such isolation may be so unbearable that many people are inclined to escape from the burden of freedom into new dependencies, such as looking to experts and the government for assistance or in our modern society, people are also becoming dependent on (sometimes addicted to) the Internet for assistance, for example, for health-related information (U.S. Department of Commerce, 2002) or to find new romantic partners.

The ambiguity of human freedom is especially evident when making important life choices, for example, *who* we want to be and *how* we want to live our lives. We may find ourselves coping by becoming anxious and "freezing up" in the face of important decisions. Another common strategy is *drifting*. Instead of choosing how to live, people simply drift along, either by living according to the status quo or by dropping out, becoming people whose lives are guided by no ties, codes, traditions, or major purposes. Another strategy is based on *shared decision making*, as in committee work, marriage, and family life, and assumed agreements among friends. Instead of really making a decision, people just talk until something happens. They presume a consensus, often never questioning it, but if things turn out badly, no one feels responsible: Each merely goes along. Another frequently used strategy for making choices is based on an *appeal to some type of authority*—an expert, a movement, a religion, the government, or some institution. Truly autonomous people rely on none of these strategies. Some psychologists call such autonomous, optimal people "self-actualized" individuals. (Self-actualization is described in more detail in several other chapters.) Autonomous or **self-actualized** individuals *accept responsibility for their lives and carefully scrutinize the alternatives available to them. They also keep their eyes open and have the courage to admit when they are wrong and need to change.* For example, many Russian writers working under communist rule in Soviet times, such as Alexander Solzhenitsyn, were examples of truly autonomous persons who made one decisive choice after another in order to maintain their personal integrity. They often made these decisions in the face of overwhelming criticism and the threat of severe punishment from their oppressive governments.

Taking Charge of Our Lives

Today, many people the world over are pursuing a similar odyssey of freedom. Much of the dissatisfaction that occurs in other countries reflects people's desire for the greater freedom and economic opportunity they see in the more economically advantaged societies. Many of the people who immigrate to the United States seek the very freedoms we take for granted—freedom of speech, freedom of religion, and freedom of movement, for instance.

Indeed, surveys indicate that the majority of Americans feel they have more freedom and control over their lives than their parents did. With regard to the two individuals in our opening vignette, Karen probably experiences more freedom (e.g., mobility) than did Zachary, as well as more control (e.g., more laws). Most people today feel their parents' lives were hemmed in by all kinds of social, educational, and economic constraints that they themselves have escaped. For example, most of today's middle-aged Americans did not face the Great Depression and World War II, which delimited their parents' options. They believe they have more options in the important areas of education, work, sex, marriage, religion, family, friends, travel, possessions, where to live, and how to live.

Before you proceed further, make an honest assessment of whether you are actively taking charge of your life by completing the survey in Activity 1–1.

ACTIVITY 1–1

DO YOU TAKE CHARGE OF YOUR LIFE?

INSTRUCTIONS: *For each statement below, circle T if the statement is generally true of you; circle F if the statement generally is not true of you.*

1. I enjoy being interconnected to others—both friends and family members.　T　F

2. Sometimes I have difficulty making the choices that make the most sense for my life.　T　F

3. I have many options from which to select in terms of my education, career, social circle, etc.　T　F

4. My friends are better than I am at making efficient and sound decisions.　T　F

5. I get a great deal of satisfaction out of helping others less fortunate than I.　T　F

6. If I have a choice, I much prefer to do the safe rather than the risky thing.　T　F

7. I strongly feel that a promise is a promise and should not be broken.　T　F

8. Difficult decisions daunt me because I have little confidence in my decisional abilities.　T　F

9. No matter where I am (e.g., at work or at college), I accept my responsibilities. T   F

10. Sometimes I call in sick when I am healthy because I do not want to work or study. T   F

11. I'd invest my money in a risky but challenging venture. T   F

12. During times of stress, I feel as if my life is out of control. T   F

13. I am fully aware of who, where, and what I am as well as my personal goals. T   F

14. I am disturbed that some charities call me for donations and invade my privacy. T   F

15. When and if I ever borrow money, I make sure that I pay it back. T   F

16. I do not like it when others expect me to be the one to choose our leisure activity. T   F

SCORING: These items are intended as a self-assessment to stimulate you to think about how much you take charge of or direct your life. The *even-numbered items* are phrased in a negative direction, so if you answered "F" (false), you may have a "take-charge" attitude or exercise self-direction. The *odd-numbered items* are phrased such that a "T" (true) indicates agreement with an item demonstrating that you probably have self-direction.

Total number of _____ "Fs" for even numbered items _____
+ Total number of _____ "Ts" for odd-numbered items _____

_____

= Grand total for self-determination _____

The higher your grand total, the more self-direction you may have. Now return to the regular reading with your score in mind. Pay attention to how and in what areas of self-direction you can improve.

Freedom, however, has its downside. Exercising our positive freedom means facing up to the necessity of decision making in our lives, especially the life choices that shape our destinies. At the same time, the fear of making the wrong decision in front of others is so great that many youths speak of "keeping my options open," living in an "extended holding pattern," and being "leery of commitment." Much of this reaction is understandable in light of the uncertainties of our times; however, research has demonstrated that individuals extrinsically motivated by financial success, an appealing appearance, or social recognition have lower vitality and lower self-actualizing potential and report more physical (health) symptoms than individuals who are more intrinsically or internally inspired. Intrinsically motivated, autonomous, self-actualized individuals appear to be healthier, more self-accepting, and more community-minded (Kasser & Ryan, 1996) as well as better adjusted and less distressed (Baker, 2004).

Taking charge of our lives means that we *can and must choose for ourselves*, that is, we must be self-directed. A lack of decisiveness, by default, becomes its own decision. Also, we must make choices in a timely fashion so that our choices do not make us miss opportunities that lead to **personal growth**, which includes change or development in a desirable direction, including the fulfillment of one's inborn potential. On the other hand, it is for-tunate that not all decisions are cast in stone. We can and often do change many decisions as we grow and mature—for example, change our college majors or our careers. Mean-while, the realization that our decisions are only as good as the information they are based on reminds us again of the value of continuous learning and critical thinking.

Acting on our *positive* freedom also means *assuming responsibility for our choices*, with-out blaming others or fate for what happens to us. In fact, those who are self-actualized or internally directed experience less interpersonal distress (Baker, 2004) and more interpersonal closeness (Sheffield, Carey, Patenaude, & Lambert, 1995), perhaps because they are less likely to blame others. Interestingly, self-actualization correlates with **altruism**, or *the desire to help others at cost to the helper* (Sharma & Rosha, 1992).

Admittedly, we had no choice about being thrust into the world, but we have a great deal of choice in the manner in which we live. However, we often hear people say things such as "I can't help it because that's the way I am" or "Naturally I'm this way because of the way I grew up." These people fail to realize that free choice and responsibility go hand in hand. As a constant reminder of this fact, Viktor Frankl (1978) suggested that the Statue of Liberty on the East Coast be supplemented by the Statue of Responsibility on the West Coast.

Self-realization also involves taking calculated risks and making commitments in spite of uncertainty. Where would the world be without the risks taken by, for example, Thomas Edison, Mikhail Gorbachev, the Dalai Lama, and Bill Gates? Personal growth involves stepping into unfamiliar and potentially risky situations, thereby leaving us more vulnerable to hurt and disappointment. Perfectionists are especially prone *not* to take risks and to be satisfied with low levels of actualization. Self-actualizers are more tolerant of failure (Flett, Hewitt, Blankstein, & Mosher, 1991). With regard to these issues, it is important to ask yourself the following questions: How self-directed are you? How does perfectionism interfere with your taking risks? How actualized are you? How open are you to new experiences?

The decision to grow or actualize our potential often has to be made in spite of risks and therefore requires courage. This is the "courage to be," that is, the courage to affirm ourselves and our possibilities in spite of risks. On the other hand, we run a risk whenever we avoid growing. Each time we pass up an opportunity to develop a new skill or when we value security over challenge, we run the risk of becoming stagnant or succumbing to boredom. When we habitually suppress or deny the inherent growth tendency of humans, we risk becoming maladaptive, sometimes in obvious ways, sometimes in subtle ways, sometimes immediately, or sometimes later in life. Fortunately, higher education and con-tinual learning, mechanisms for growth that you as well as Zachary and Karen are taking advantage of, help individuals self-actualize (Barnes & Srinivas, 1993; MacKay & Kuh, 1994). One of the fathers of humanistic psychology, Abraham Maslow (1968), once observed that many of the characteristic disorders of our time such as the "stunted person," the "amoral person," or the "apathetic person" result from the fundamental failure to grow.

Living in Today's Individualistic Society

Interestingly, the times in which we live afford us a more supportive environment because of the technological advances that bring friends and family on the other side of the continent "closer" to us. In fact, we can twitter a whole group of supportive people at once by merely pressing a few buttons on our handheld devices. Just as important, though, is the increased number of hazards in our social and physical environments: We meet more people, some of whom are highly critical of us and judgmental; we become bewildered by the increasing number of available consumer choices; and we worry about the proliferation of hazards in our environment, from threats of child victimization on the World Wide Web to pandemics such as H1N1 (Swine) flu and AIDS. These, in turn, heighten the challenge of self-direction.

The cumulative impact of these social changes has given rise to newer social values and newer rules by which people live in comparison to those of Zachary's generation. Generally, these changes mean greater interest in shaping the environment to meet *our* needs (i.e., increased personal control) rather than society's needs and goals. To you it may appear true that many people are preoccupied with themselves today. Especially to our international visitors, Americans appear to be rather self-absorbed in several ways.

There is often great impatience in Westerners to satisfy one's own goals. Individuals scoff when told they need to "pay your dues" through hard work to achieve success in a career or happiness in a marriage. They want success and happiness NOW. Or to paraphrase the more self-centered seekers, "I want it all—right now!" The "future" orientation of earlier generations like Zachary's—with the assumption that things need to get better for future generations—appears to have been superseded by a "now" orientation, by living solely in the present, where the collective future is merely a lurking shadow in the back of our minds.

Still another change is the greater assertiveness of individuals, who seem more concerned with their personal rights than with social responsibilities. As a result, more individuals today appear to be relentlessly pursuing their own interests and goals, at the risk of violating the rights of others. When conflicts of interest do arise, individuals are less willing to deny themselves anything to accommodate or compromise with others, as if adhering to some new moral principle—"I have a duty to myself, not to you or society." Road rage is an apt example of obstinately pursuing one's own needs at the expense of others. Luckily, Zachary never experienced road rage, but Karen has.

THEMES OF PERSONAL GROWTH

Living with Contradictions and Uncertainty

Not just Zachary and Karen, but all of us face the challenge of reconciling old rules with new rules and old values with new values. Many of us feel we must honor the old values of hard work, frugality, and moderation to complete an education and secure our careers and, thus, the means to enjoy the new values associated with personal pleasure and freedom (Moen & Roehling, 2005). In many ways these two sets of values contradict each other, making it difficult to reconcile them. For example, we know we must work to support our families, but we also want to drive an expensive convertible car and experience the thrill of the wind blowing through our hair—a symbol of independence and freedom. This task of reconciling the old and the new is hard enough for reasonably well-educated and well-informed individuals. It is even more confusing and unsettling to the less educated, who anticipate more dramatic and negative social changes than do college-educated people.

Those of us who seek guidance about personal growth from popular self-help books, television shows that entertain more than they educate, and movements that blend pop psychology with quasi-religious thought do not always fare well. Many of these sources oversimplify the process of personal and social change, generating grossly unrealistic and disappointing results. In contrast, a good textbook on scientific psychology can provide sound principles of personal development and growth as well as guidance related to self-direction and social responsibility. Throughout this book we attempt to show how the principles and findings of contemporary psychology can help us better understand ourselves and others and, thus, to cope more effectively with our environment and fulfill more of our potential.

This statement does not mean that personal growth can be achieved by simply reading a book on the subject. Neither does mere exposure to scientific knowledge or interesting examples guarantee that you will use the information. Now, let's look further at some other issues related to seeking self-direction.

Continuity and Change

A key issue for psychologists and the public alike is the extent to which people change over a lifetime. Do our personalities really change, or do they remain stable? Or do we simply and naturally mellow with age? Do we change in fits and starts or gradually? What makes us change—many small experiences or cataclysmic events?

A generation ago psychologists and the public assumed that genes and early experiences were the decisive influences on development, so that once we reached adulthood we tended to remain the same. Then, during the 1960s and 1970s, new findings as well as social trends suggested that people tend to continue growing throughout their adult lives. Today, professionals acknowledge that *both continuity and change* are important to development.

Robert McCrae and Paul Costa (1994, 2003) have discovered some evidence for the stability of personality throughout the life span. The highest degree of stability was found in the domain of introversion–extroversion, which reflects gregariousness, warmth, and assertiveness. There is almost as much stability in the area of "neuroticism," which includes such traits as depression and hostility. Thus, individuals who were expressive and outgoing in their teens are apt to remain that way in adulthood; those who were inhibited and shy in their teens tend to remain inhibited and shy. Similarly, **longitudinal studies**, *which follow the same individuals over a long time period*, indicate only slight decreases over the course of adulthood in anxiety, hostility, and impulsiveness.

Psychologists supporting the stability thesis state that even when individuals do change because of personal maturation or life experiences, the unique differences among people remain. This means that a rather impulsive 20-year-old like Karen may be a bit less impulsive by the time she is 55, but she is still likely to be more impulsive than her agemates at any given time. In addition, as people grow older, the stability of their personalities becomes more evident. Thus, there is more stability of personality from 30 to 40 than there is from 20 to 30 years of age (Pfaffenberger, 2005). Part of the reason for increased stability with age is that we tend to select and stay in environments and marry people that help sustain our traits (Caspi & Herbener, 1990).

Other researchers, while acknowledging the importance of stability, emphasize the variability or change that occurs with development (Pfaffenberger, 2005). They point out that *only certain traits* have been shown to be relatively stable, most notably introversion–extroversion, anxiety, and depression. These researchers suggest that people are more likely to change in other respects, especially self-esteem, sense of personal mastery or control over their environment, and values. Recently, Dweck (2008) argued that personal beliefs (e.g., about the malleability of personality) can play a significant role in altering personality across the life span. Individuals who believe that they can change (e.g., have a malleable view of personality), are more open to learning, more willing to confront challenges, and are better able to bounce back from failures. Those who believe that their traits are fixed have a more difficult time facing challenges such as stressful business tasks or conflict-laden relationships. The emphasis on the potential for change has been embraced by those who want to foster change, from weight watchers to social watchers, all of whom stress openness to change throughout the course of adulthood.

The tension between continuity and change is found not only in academic debates but also in each of us. How much personal growth or change in a desirable direction we want depends greatly on the different priorities we assign to stability or change, that is, *how much we want to change* and *how differently we want to live our lives*. Thus, people with traditional values tend to exhibit a high degree of stability in their lives unless something happens to make them change. For them, the events most likely to cause change are usually quite dramatic, such as an unwanted divorce, the death of a child, failure in one's career, or witnessing a traumatic event In contrast, those who put more value on personal growth may continue changing to a greater extent throughout their lives unless they become stuck at a particular developmental milestone. For instance, a coal miner who spends 10 hours a day under the earth for 30 years may have little opportunity for personal growth. If you, on the other hand, value change, you probably have ample opportunities to experience change and personal growth.

The Experience of Personal Growth

To believe we can change is one thing. To *pursue and actively achieve personal change* is something else. Think about all the times you have vowed to exercise but didn't or vowed to quit smoking cigarettes and failed. These are but small instances of attempts to change.

Like all patterns of development, our inner experience of growth tends to be uneven, with spurts and plateaus. We may be willing to try out something new one minute and retreat to the familiar the next. Because we experience our inner world more as a continuous flow of ideas, feelings, and meanings, we are more apt to realize that we've grown *in retrospect* than while we're in the midst of a particular growth cycle.

The experience of growth tends to follow *a three-phase cycle*:

1. Acknowledging change. Growth usually begins with the acknowledgment of change. Actually, changes occur all the time, but we're not always aware of them. A constant awareness of change would be too disrupting to our daily lives. Instead, we strive to construct an image of ourselves and our world that pictures reality as under our control and more stable than it really is. As a result, we become more acutely aware of changes at some moments than at others. Sometimes, we become aware of change rather suddenly, for example, by receiving an unexpected compliment or criticism. Taking on new responsibilities, such as a new marriage, parenthood, or a promotion at work, forces us to acknowledge change, too. Karen's graduation from college and her entry into medical school will force her to acknowledge change. The common denominator in all these experiences is *the realization that things are different from what they were*—or what we believed or expected they would be.

2. A sense of dissonance or dissatisfaction. Whether the awareness of change leads to growth depends on how we react. Sometimes we may respond to change defensively, with little awareness of our real feelings—positive or negative. In contrast, when someone feels disappointment, he or she actually may be aroused or motivated to seek further change or confront the challenge of disappointment. Thus, the growth cycle can often be triggered by disappointment and failure as well as by success.

This phase of growth (dissonance) is inevitably accompanied by a certain degree of anxiety and discomfort. When our motive for growth proceeds out of a sense of challenge or mastery, we may be more stimulated and less apprehensive about the outcome, as when Zachary, Karen's ancestor, decided to break in his own horse—out of a need for accomplishment but with some trepidation—rather than let his older brother do it as was usual. But when our motive springs from profound dissatisfaction with ourselves, our feelings tend to be more agonizing.

3. Reorganizing our experience. In conventional psychological terms, *reorganizing* is often defined as acquiring new ideas and then altering our attitudes, behaviors, and values in response. In some instances, such as the discovery that most students like Karen, Zachary, and you feel anxious about examinations, additional insight may alter our understanding of ourselves or others. The additional insight may be that we are aware of our own largely unconscious processes, such as realizing that our chronic sense of anxiety during tests really masks an undue fear of criticism and failure. Or we may adopt a new attitude toward another person, becoming more willing to listen to someone's criticism because we know that the person wants to help rather than hurt us. Growth may also take the form of new self-perceptions, such as increased self-acceptance and confidence from an achievement like Karen's earning a medical degree, which made her feel that she was indeed smarter than she thought. The main point is that each inner adjustment or change we make affects the whole of our experience, so that growth consists of the continuous reorganization of that experience.

Beyond Individualism

There still exists in America a language of individualism that limits the way people think. For example, we have long celebrated "independence" on July 4, but we are only now slowly recognizing our interdependence on others via "Make a Difference Day." Being responsible to the self alone, many Americans still act independently of any cultural or social influence. As a result, we are still somewhat less committed to the common purposes of society than we are to the self. This is in sharp contrast to collectivist societies or earlier periods of American life—say, in Zachary's lifetime—in which self-orientation was held in check by strong ties to the family, church, and community. We are, however, very good at "coming together" with others in times of crisis. Witness how the whole nation pulled together when the World Trade Center was bombed.

Terrorist acts and national disasters sometimes stimulate collectivism in Americans who are otherwise fairly individualistic.

A major reassessment of the search for self-fulfillment may be giving rise to a more realistic view of life and personal fulfillment. Millions of Americans are discovering, often through such painful experiences as terrorist attacks or watching their adult children or parents become unemployed, that preoccupation with their own personal needs is not a direct path to fulfillment. Americans are learning that they cannot disregard the rest of the world. The heart of this new outlook is the realization that *personal fulfillment can be achieved only in relation to others*—through a web of shared meanings that transcend the isolated individual. Personal fulfillment in the deeper sense requires commitments that endure over long periods of time and perhaps require self-sacrifice. The term *commitment* shifts the focus away from unduly individualistic notions of the self, either self-denial or self-fulfillment, toward the more inclusive "self connected to others." This is a positive change, because almost all of our activity occurs in relationships, groups, and community, structured by institutions and interpreted by cultural meaning. Activity 1–2 is designed to help you discover the extent of your own individualism in our interdependent world. When you have finished the activity, ask yourself if you need to be more interconnected with your community and the rest of the world.

As we've seen, human fulfillment is more complex than popularly thought and requires a better balance between the interests of self and of society.

ACTIVITY 1–2

How Individualistic Are You?

Psychologists have figured out some very clever ways to research people's behaviors and attitudes without directly asking or observing them. Once a person is approached by a psychologist, the study and data can become contaminated by virtue of the very fact that people know they are being studied. For example, if you knew I wanted to know about your individualism (e.g., selfish tendencies), you might try to guess the answers to my questions rather than give me an honest assessment of your individualistic tendencies.

Psychological scientists, then, turn to indirect methods. One indirect method is the **archival method**, *where scientists examine existing data such as historical documents that were fashioned without anyone knowing they are the subject of study*. You have created many such historical documents that have never been studied. Go back to your email account, your diary, letters you have written to your friends and family, or some other written document developed by you. Count how many times pronouns related to yourself such as *I*, *my*, *me*, *mine*, etc. occur and how many times pronouns such as *you* or *we* or *they* (or pronouns indicating that you were taking into account another's feelings, needs, or desires) occur.

PRONOUNS RELATED TO SELF _____

PRONOUNS RELATED TO OTHERS _____

Which type of pronouns prevailed? Are pronouns indicating the importance of others more predominant or are pronouns related to you more predominant? In terms of individualism and social connectedness, what do your results suggest about you?

SUMMARY

SOCIAL CHANGE

We began the chapter by describing how rapid technological and social changes are having far-reaching effects throughout the world. The revolution in communication, in particular, is giving rise to a global outlook in which people in many countries are influenced by what they see happening in other countries.

Economically advantaged nations, such as the United States, are moving into a postindustrial era in which the service industries are becoming dominant, and there is a premium on intellectual and technical knowledge. Similarly, the information age drives us to create, process, and distribute information in different ways and with a wider variety of people. Social forecasters admit we live in uncertain times, but they tend to have an optimistic view of the future. The biggest challenge is how to prepare people to live and work in the new information-driven society that demands high-tech skills and more education.

THE CHALLENGE OF SELF-DIRECTION

Living in a rapidly changing society poses an even greater challenge to the self-direction of individuals than was the case in the past. As Fromm reminds us, we have been more successful in achieving freedom "from" traditional authorities than in using this freedom "for" actualizing our individual destinies. The challenge of self-direction is so great that we tend to escape from it by looking to the experts for decisions on important choices or conforming to the crowd or simply drifting. In contrast, taking charge of our lives means facing up to the importance of decision making, taking calculated risks for the sake of growth, and assuming full responsibility for our lives.

The new rules in today's individualistic societies accentuate the challenge of self-direction. As a result, people are increasingly questioning the old rules that emphasize social conformity and self-denial. Instead, individuals are busily pursuing their individual rights and, in varying degrees, self-fulfillment. A major change is that people want and expect more out of life in return for their efforts.

THEMES OF PERSONAL GROWTH

The search for self-fulfillment creates a predicament for the individual as well as the nation, challenging us to reconcile old and new values. People looking to self-help books for advice tend to find an oversimplified idea of self-fulfillment, leading to unrealistic expectations that end in disappointment. In contrast, the field of psychology offers sound principles and tested knowledge that may help to achieve realistic self-direction and growth.

According to psychology, the tendencies toward both continuity and change are present in each of us. How much you and others change depends greatly on the different priorities you assign to stability or change and whether you, in fact, believe you can change. At the same time, we live in an era in which personal growth occurs more widely than before.

The subjective experience of growth involves a three-phase cycle: (1) the acknowledgment of change within ourselves or our environment, (2) a sense of dissonance or dissatisfaction within, which in turn leads to (3) reorganizing our experience in some way, such as adopting a new attitude toward ourselves or others. Today, however, a major reassessment of the self-fulfillment movement is under way, giving rise to a more realistic view of life and personal fulfillment. The core of this new approach is the call for a realignment of the interests of self and society so that personal fulfillment can be realized in relation to others—through a web of shared meanings that transcend the isolated individual.

SELF-TEST

1. Early American society can be described as
   a. ruggedly individualistic.
   b. agrarian and collective.
   c. self-directed.
   d. materialistic.

2. Who suffers most from technophobia?
   a. mid-level managers.
   b. white-collar workers.
   c. children.
   d. minorities and women.

3. What statement is true?
   a. Minorities generally tend to avoid all forms of technology.
   b. Computers are still the technology of choice for connecting with others.
   c. African Americans and Hispanics are taking advantage of mobile technologies at higher rates than Whites.
   d. There are still large numbers of Americans without some form of technology at their disposal.

4. An individualistic society
   a. is consensual.
   b. looks upon societal gain as important.
   c. is exemplified by American culture.
   d. is the same as a collectivist society.

5. Which group is increasing fastest in the United States?
   a. Hispanics
   b. African Americans
   c. Asians
   d. Whites

6. Which of the following characteristics is the least likely to change throughout adulthood?
   a. Extroversion
   b. Anxiety
   c. Depression
   d. Neuroticism

7. A subjective experience of growth begins with
   a. a sense of dissonance.
   b. acknowledging change.
   c. a commitment to change.
   d. reorganizing experiences.

8. The second stage of personal growth is
   a. a sense of dissonance.
   b. acknowledging change.
   c. a commitment to change.
   d. reorganizing experiences.

9. American society is typified by
   a. inattention to societal needs.
   b. a need for relatedness.
   c. personal inability to make decisions.
   d. slower rates of social change than in the past.

10. The contemporary reassessment of the self-fulfillment movement suggests that personal fulfillment can be realized only
    a. by educated people.
    b. during middle or late adulthood.
    c. in relation to others.
    d. by perfectionistic people.

EXERCISES

1. *Social change.* What two or three societal changes are having the greatest impact on your life (e.g., changes in technology, the economy)? Write a page or so about how your life is affected by these changes. For example, think about how a computer has altered your academic, business, and personal life. Are most of the societal changes having a negative or positive impact on your life? Are you coping with the changes appropriately? Are the changes helping you grow?

2. *Change as a challenge or threat.* Select some change that has occurred in your environment recently, such as a new professor, a marital engagement, or layoffs at work. Then write a page or so describing how you feel about this change, especially whether you see it as a challenge or a threat and why.

3. *Identify your level of interdependence.* Identify at least one important aspect of your life, such as a job, a friendship, or marriage. Then describe in a few paragraphs how much you're prepared to give to this relationship and how much you expect in return. Are your expectations fair? If the give and take is unbalanced, how do you think your expectations will affect your relationships?

4. *How important is self-fulfillment to you?* Think about what you do that is fulfilling. What are your life goals? Are they generally other-centered or self-centered, and is this adaptive and growth-oriented? What do you do to actively meet these goals?

5. *Self-fulfillment and personal and social involvement.* Select some area of your life that has been very gratifying to you (an accomplishment, relationship, etc.) and describe the extent to which your sense of fulfillment depended on involvement with others.

QUESTIONS FOR SELF-REFLECTION

1. Are you more optimistic about your own personal future than that of our society or the world?

2. Are you so concerned about keeping your options open that you may suffer from the inability to make decisions? Are you too perfectionistic?

3. How much control do you feel you have over your life? How much control do you think you need? Are you a self-directed person?

4. Would you agree that many of the ground rules in our society have changed from one century to the next? How so?

5. Have you met people who act as if there are no rules—that anything goes? What are such people like?

6. How important are self-fulfillment values to you?

7. Do you expect more out of life than your parents did?

8. Can you remember a difficult time in your life and, in retrospect, realize it was a time of growth?

9. Would you agree that personal fulfillment is achieved mostly in and through our relationships with others?

FOR FURTHER INFORMATION

RECOMMENDED READINGS

BUCHER, D. (2009). *Diversity consciousness: Opening our minds to people, cultures and opportunities.* Upper Saddle River, NJ: Prentice Hall. This is a readable book that incorporates current research and works by other authors to help the reader move to better understanding and respect for diversity.

FREDRICKSON, B. (2009). *Positivity: Groundbreaking research reveals how to embrace the hidden strength of positive emotions, overcome negative, and thrive.* New York: Crown Publishing Group. A leading researcher shares her insights on this new school of thought in psychology that is turning psychologists' attention from negative concepts to more positive concepts about the self and the world.

LECHNER, F. J., & BOLI, J. (Eds.). (2008). *The globalization reader.* Hoboken, NJ: John Wiley & Sons. This edited book is a comprehensible compendium of ideas on globalization. It turns a complex and important topic into a thoughtful set of essays from various vantage points.

JOHNSON, D. W. (2005). *Reaching out: Interpersonal effectiveness and self-actualization.* Upper Saddle River, NJ: Prentice Hall. An expert on group behavior and interpersonal relationships examines the relevancy of other people to the concept of self-actualization and vice versa.

MOEN, P., & ROEHLING, P. (2004). *The career mystique: Cracks in the American Dream.* Lanham, MD: Rowman & Littlefield. The authors review the American dream of hard work and frugality turning into success. Given the changing world and the many uncertainties of modern life, the authors claim that today the dream is a myth.

WEBSITES AND THE INTERNET

http://www.apa.org/psychnet A site designed to provide lots of information about psychology on a wide range of topics.

http://www.culturalstudies.net A location where popular American culture in its ever-changing forms is tracked. There are links to other cultural studies sites as well as information on other countries and cultures. The site is designed to celebrate diversity.

http://www.cpsr.org A site supported by computer professionals concerned about the responsible use of technology in society. Their motto is apt: Technology is driving the future; it is up to us to do the steering.

http://www.wfs.org Interested in the future or what the world will look like in several years? This site has predictions and other information that will interest, motivate, and sometimes startle you.

http://www.sierraclub.org America's oldest, largest, and most influential grassroots environmental organization.

The Puzzle of Childhood

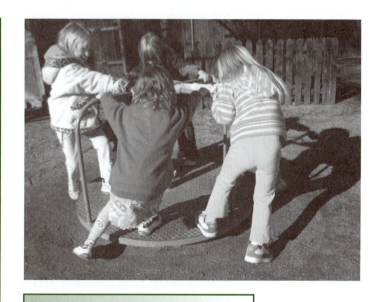

Learning Objectives

After completing this chapter, you should be able to

1. Understand why a perspective approach to understanding development is important.
2. Discuss the relative importance of genetic influences on development.
3. Discuss how youth are both directly and indirectly influenced by their surrounding environments.
4. Explain Bronfenbrenner's theory of ecological development and the four contexts of the environment that comprise it.
5. Understand the developmental tasks of Erikson's eight stages of psychosocial development.
6. Explain Bandura's concept of modeling and social learning.
7. Understand the importance of self-efficacy to youth.
8. Explain Maslow's concept of self-actualization as it relates to development.
9. Identify three key foundational elements of childhood.

Three-year-old Sara was having the time of her life. This was her first trip to the zoo, and she was excited to be near the animals that she had only previously seen on TV. Sara especially liked the black bears because they looked just like Teddy, the stuffed animal she was carrying under her arm. But then her parents told her it was time to go. Sara, having been in this situation before, knew just what to do . . . she became enraged, refusing to get back into the stroller. She yelled and screamed, and even tossed her beloved Teddy to the ground. Sara's parents knew this was coming, as she frequently had outbursts in public. Exasperated, her parents gave up trying to get Sara into the stroller, and let her walk around the zoo until she was tired. At preschool the next day, Sara told her friends what a great time she had at the zoo. All the students started talking about their favorite animals; even the teacher joined in on the fun. When she was 14, Sara found herself smiling as she remembered this event, as well as other times she had gotten her way by having a huge hissy-fit. She had plenty of time to think about these sorts of things, as she was grounded in her room for doing *something* her parents did not like, even though she wasn't quite sure what it was.

PERSPECTIVES ON CHILD DEVELOPMENT

Development can be defined as *the relatively enduring changes in people's capacities and behavior as they grow older because of biological growth processes and people's interaction with their environment, including their social environment.* From infancy through adolescence, the ways in which youth think, feel, and interact with others is dramatically transformed. For example, whereas infants cry when left alone, adolescents desire solitude; while 4-year-olds believe that monsters live under beds, teenagers believe no such thing, rather, they are afraid of their parents embarrassing them in front of their peers; and for young children "friends" are people you play with, in contrast, for older youth friendship requires trust, intimacy, and being "friended" on Facebook.

Psychologists approach development from different viewpoints or perspectives. Although there are dozens of different theories of development, most of them generally can be grouped into five basic types: biological, ecological, psychodynamic, social-cognitive (including behavioral), and humanistic perspectives. Each perspective emphasizes certain aspects of development, while minimizing, if not overlooking, others. What *each* view offers us, then, is a limited understanding of how children grow, think, feel, and interact with others over time. When looked at as a whole, however, a more complete picture of childhood emerges. So, rather than attempting to prove which view of development is more correct, it is more helpful to learn the best that each perspective has to offer (Slater, Hocking, & Loose, 2003). Think of each perspective as a piece in the puzzle that is child development.

Historically, children were once thought to be miniature versions of adults. That is, children had the *same* thoughts, feelings, and capabilities as adults, only they were a lot smaller (deMause, 1974). When children and adults are alike in every meaningful way, childhood becomes unimportant. Today, not only are children and adults viewed as having different physical and psychological characteristics, but childhood is looked upon as one of the most important contributors to a healthy adulthood. For instance, the quality of the relationships between infants and their mothers has been shown to influence friendships during elementary school, self-esteem during adolescence, and interactions with spouses and children decades later (Cassidy & Shaver, 2008).

Psychologists liken child development to the building of a house. Childhood is the foundation upon which the remainder of development rests, just as the house's foundation is the support for the rest of the home—the floors, walls, roof, and so forth. If the foundation is weak, the future of the house is in jeopardy as problems, such as cracks in the walls or sticky windows, develop when the foundation sags. If the foundation of the house is sound, however, the house may well withstand duress such as floods and high winds. If not, it can certainly be easily rebuilt. Many perspectives on development take this same tack—that a healthy childhood can create resiliency that helps the person overcome problems later in life. Before proceeding further, look at Box 2–1 (page 26), which presents some interesting and often startling statistics about childhood in America. Ask yourself whether today's children have a solid foundation on which to develop into happy and healthy adults.

THE BIOLOGICAL PERSPECTIVE ON CHILD DEVELOPMENT

Today, the rapid increase in knowledge about brain functioning and **genes** (*the biochemical units by which characteristics are inherited*) provides scientific evidence for a biological basis for some aspects of development. Although the exact proportions remain unknown, genetic influences probably account for between 25 percent and 75 percent of the differences in characteristics among the general population (Bouchard, 2004). For instance, genetic factors have been cited for a wide range of psychological outcomes in adulthood, including alcoholism, depression, and phobias. During childhood, the evidence seems strongest for such characteristics as intelligence, sociability, emotionality, and activity level (Plomin & Rende, 1991).

Box 2–1

AMERICA'S CHILDREN: WILL THEY MAKE IT?

Most perspectives on development suggest that children need a positive start—physically and psychologically—in order to become well-adjusted adults. Here are some revealing statistics—both positive and negative—about America's children. Decide for yourself whether you think today's children have a good start on a happy and productive life:

AMERICAN FAMILIES

- The number of children in the United States is projected to increase to 77.2 million by 2020. In 2007, 70 percent of our children lived with two parents. Of the 25 million who live with only one parent, one-third will not see their father over the course of a year.

- Nearly 40 percent of U.S. children are born out of wedlock.

CHILDREN'S HEALTH

- Over 13 percent of pregnant women smoke. Smoking is detrimental to the unborn child.

- Several federal agencies estimate that about three children die of maltreatment (abuse and neglect) every day in the United States.

- Fifty-eight million children (82 percent of the total) enjoy excellent or very good health; 2 percent are in fair or poor health.

- Almost one-third of all twelfth-graders report having five or more alcoholic drinks per week.

- Nearly 40 percent of youth had tried marijuana at least once in their lifetime.

EDUCATION

- Recently, about one-quarter of U.S. schoolchildren attended school without missing a day. Six percent of school-age children missed more than 10 days of school due to illness or injury.

- The overall high school completion rate for young adults is about 85 percent.

- The number of children 5 to 7 years of age who spoke a language other than English and who had difficulty speaking English has increased to over 2.5 million.

- Boys earn 70 percent of the Ds and Fs teachers assign. Boys make up two-thirds of the students labeled "learning disabled."

Some psychologists argue that biology influences almost all of our personal qualities and development (e.g., Bouchard, 2004). Biological aspects of development include heredity (*the transmission of traits from parents to offspring*), aspects of the nervous system related to behavior, and the influence of hormones. For instance, preschool children's preference for arousing or sedentary activities is affected by the amount of the hormone testosterone (which is typically found in greater quantities in males than females) they are exposed to during prenatal development (Cohen-Bendahan, van de Beek, & Berenbaum, 2005). However, in most arguments about development, heredity comes to the forefront as the most important biological determinant of who we are and how we develop.

Applying It to Yourself

According to the **biological perspective**, *many of our personal attributes and much of our personal development may be attributable to genetic and other biological influences.* As we've seen, characteristics like intelligence and sociability may have a marked genetic influence. Even these characteristics are determined not so much by a single gene as by a

Are only children really pampered, spoiled, self-centered, and uncooperative? Do first-born children strive to please others and have the highest IQs? Are they controlling of others but conforming to parental desires? Do second-born children always rebel and feel as if they are in a constant race to catch up to their other sibling? Surely middle children always view life as unfair, feel unloved, and become the "problem child." In thinking of your own family, or those of your friends, supporting cases easily come to mind. Whether the portrayal involves Jan and Peter from *The Brady Bunch* or Malcolm from *Malcolm in the Middle,* television and movies often portray siblings along the lines of the birth order stereotypes mentioned above. Nevertheless, psychologists have had great difficulty finding consistent support for the idea that personality, social relationships, and intelligence systematically vary by the order of one's birth (Wichman, Rodgers, & MacCallum, 2007). At this point, birth order effects are more myth than reality!

complex combination of genes that gives rise to a range of potential responses. How much or how little of our potential we develop, however, depends largely on our interaction with the environment. For instance, a first-born girl might earn high grades and go on to become a physician. Her younger sister, who is equally smart but impatient about waiting to start her career, may choose a career as an emergency medical technician. The schooling required is less demanding and time-consuming and therefore may appeal to her impatient tendencies. While both sisters may continue to get similar scores on the same intelligence test, they have different perceptions about their futures and interests. Do such sibling differences occur in reality? Absolutely, but are such differences characteristic related to birth order, such as being a first- or second-born child? Take a look at Box 2–2 for a discussion of the myth of birth order effects.

Have you ever considered the dominant traits in your family tree? At the next family gathering, observe your relatives for a while. You might notice that a favorite uncle or aunt exhibits the same warmth and sociability that you do. How is it possible that you are more similar to this more distant relative than to your siblings on this trait? The answer may be heredity; you may simply share more genes with this person than with your brothers and sisters.

THE ECOLOGICAL PERSPECTIVE ON CHILD DEVELOPMENT

Although biology is an important influence on development, so too are the environments in which development takes places. For instance, Sara's parents took her to the zoo because they felt that real-life encounters with interesting animals would provide Sara with valuable experiences. Each year, youth encounter hundreds, if not thousands, of different environments, such as school, church, and the zoo. Although the settings for each of these environments differ, they all have one thing in common: The child experiences the environment *directly.* However, children can also be *indirectly* influenced by environments they are not in, and therefore, did not experience. For instance, the *No Child Left Behind Act* of 2001, requires that children in grades 3 through 8 take standardized tests every year. Although children were not involved in the legislation of this act, they are still influenced by it every time they take a mandated test! Urie Bronfenbrenner's (1993) **ecological perspective** emphasizes the role of such environmental *contexts* on children's development. Bronfenbrenner organized the environments that children come across (either directly or indirectly) into four inter-related contexts (or systems) of development: microsystem, mesosystem, exosystem, and macrosystem. Let's take a look at each.

A **microsystem** *refers to the setting that the child is currently in, such as the home or day-care center.* Typically, the first microsystem that youth encounter is the hospital in which they are born. Within each microsystem, youth engage in activities (e.g., playing, eating) and interact with others (e.g., talking, fighting). Some of these activities/interactions are initiated by the child and some are initiated by other individuals. As such, microsystems are dynamic contexts of interaction. Over time, children are influenced by the different microsystems that they encounter, and the types of experiences had within. For instance, children and adolescents with TVs in their bedrooms watch more TV, get less sleep, and report feeling more tired than youth without TVs in their bedroom (Eggermont & Van den Bulck, 2006; Paavonen, Pennonen, Roine, Valkonen, & Lahikainen, 2006).

As mentioned above, while at preschool Sara told her classmates about the great time she had at the zoo and they responded positively. Thus, what happened to Sara in one microsystem (the zoo) influenced her, a short time later, in a *different* microsystem (preschool). *In the ecological environment, the linking of microsystems* is referred to as a **mesosystem.** It is important to remember that mesosystem influences take place over time, as the child is directly involved in each microsystem. The concept of the mesosystem is extremely important to the understanding of child development, for it states that not only are the experiences within each microsystem important to the child in that particular setting, but other settings as well! For instance, children experiencing sensitive, responsive care at home are better liked by their peers at school (Cassidy & Shaver, 2008); and for adolescents, watching multiple hours of music videos per week at home increases the odds of drinking alcohol when going out by 239 percent (Van den Bulck, Beullens, & Mulder, 2006).

In the third context of development, the **exosystem,** *children and adolescents are influenced by social settings that they do not take part in.* How is it possible that children can be affected by a context that is unknown to them? The answer is simple: Someone the child knows was in that setting and what happened to *him or her* causes a change in how he or she acts toward the child in a *different* setting. For example, when single mothers are stressed due to work-related conditions, the home environment (e.g., parent less sentitive, more hostile) of their preschool children suffers (Lleras, 2008). In this case, a context unfamiliar to the child (mom's workplace) influenced the child's life.

The last of Bronfenbrenner's systems, the **macrosystem,** refers to the larger socio-cultural context in which development takes place, including cultural (e.g., American or French), sub-cultural (e.g., gender, race, religion) and social-class (e.g., weathly or poor) distinctions. Essentially, the macrosystem refers to *the set of shared values, goals, practices, and attitudes that characterizes a group of people.* In turn, these values, goals, etc. influence all other systems within the ecological environment, which in turn affects the child's development. As an example, youth brought up in a culture that is more accepting of real-life violence tend to be more violent themselves (Tolan, Gorman-Smith, & Henry, 2003).

Another study found that adolescents who were raised to believe that religion was important were less likely than other youth to have initiated alcohol use, be a current drinker, or to have engaged in binge drinking (Dunn, 2005).

Applying It to Yourself

Because of macro- and exosystem influences, each of us plays a role in the development of children, even those that we do not know. By reinforcing cultural ideology, attitudes, and values (macrosystem influences) and by our interactions with coworkers, siblings, and strangers (as part of an exosystem), we indirectly influence the children around us. Of course, whenever we encounter children directly, we have entered into a microsystem, and therefore become a direct influence in their lives. And the lessons learned in these microsystem can be taken by children to other environments, affecting a whole new group of children (via the mesosystem). Thus, the welfare of children is influenced by environments both big and small. Not only can improvements in society, such as the Civil Rights Movement, positively affect children for generations to come, but so too can *personal* growth lead to benefits for numerous others. In line with this, a relatively new theme in psychology has emerged—**positive psychology.** Positive psychology is *an umbrella term for the study of positive emotions, positive character traits, and enabling institutions* (Seligman, Steen, Park, & Peterson, 2005). Individuals are now being viewed in the light of their potential for health and fulfillment as well as in terms of their vulnerabilities and maladjustments. As the ecological environment demonstrates, the health and fulfillment of one individual has the potential to influence many children.

THE PSYCHODYNAMIC PERSPECTIVE ON CHILD DEVELOPMENT

Psychodynamic theory consists of a *group of related theories that view personality and behavior in terms of the dynamics, or interactions, of driving forces of personality and development such as desires, anxieties, conflicts, and defenses.* According to this viewpoint, individuals are inevitably caught in the clash between conflicting forces of life, such as between impulses and inhibitions or between individuals and society. For the child, the conflict occurs between the child's own desires and the demands of parents and society. Although different psychodynamic theories emphasize different aspects of development, most psychodynamic theorists agree that basic dynamics include conflict between two opposing forces: anxiety (which results from the clash between desires and inhibitions) and defenses against the desires that arouse anxiety. Although Sigmund Freud's theory introduced the psychodynamic perspective to the world and revolutionized the field of psychology (see Box 2–3 on page 30 for Freud's stages of psychosexual development), it does not encompass a *realistic* view of child development. As such, we focus on Erik Erikson's psychosocial perspective, which details *key* issues that individuals face during specific periods of development.

Box 2–3

FREUD'S PSYCHOSEXUAL STAGES OF DEVELOPMENT

Since Freud regarded **libido,** or *psychic energy related to sexuality,* as fundamental, he interpreted development on the basis of the *sequential process* of **psychosexual stages.** In each stage, *the child seeks to gratify the drive for pleasure in the various body zones: the mouth, the anus, and the genitals. The manner in which children handle the conflict* between their impulses and environmental restrictions is decisive for development. Too little or too much gratification at a certain stage may result in **fixation,** *by which the person becomes emotionally fixed at a particular anxiety-ridden stage and continues to act out symbolically the wishes that were overly inhibited or indulged.*

Stage	Approximate Age	Major Characteristics
Oral	Birth–1 year	The mouth is the primary means of gratification. Fixation may result in either a passive personality associated with addictive eating, smoking, or drinking or in sarcasm in a person who is always criticizing everyone else's ideas without offering any of his or her own.
Anal	1–3 years	The major source of physical pleasure becomes the releasing or retaining of feces. Fixation in the early phase of this stage may result in adult tendencies toward disorderly, messy behavior. By contrast, fixation in the later phase of this stage would give rise to the stubborn, compulsively orderly personality in adulthood.
Phallic	3–5 years	The child experiences sensual pleasure through handling of his or her genitals. Too little or too much gratification sets the stage for later difficulties, such as the individual who feels guilty about his or her sexuality or engages in sex to reduce anxiety. Children develop an **Oedipus** (boys) or **Electra** (girls) **complex**, in which they *are sexually attracted to the opposite-sex parent* and envy the same-sex parent. Resolution of these complexes results in children identifying with the same-sex parent, thus incorporating their parent's sexual orientation, mannerisms, and values.
Latency	5–12 years	Early sexual feelings are forgotten and sexual urges lie relatively dormant. Children focus on sports, schoolwork and same-sex friendships.
Genital	12 years onward	Sexual interests are reawakened and focus on gratification through genital or sexual activity. The well-adjusted adult experiences genital strivings so that he or she is capable of genuine love and adult sexual satisfaction. Most adult problems with sex derive from fixations at the earlier oral, anal, or phallic stages.

Erikson's Eight Stages of Psychosocial Development

Erik Erikson (1964) has widened the potential application of psychodynamic theory by transforming Freud's psychosexual theory of development into a more inclusive view of personality development. Whereas Freud focused on the child's psychosexual development with the family, Erikson takes into account the individual's psychosocial relationships within the larger society. And whereas Freud's stages covered only the years between birth and puberty, Erikson's stages extend throughout adulthood into old age. Each of the eight psychosocial stages is presented as a polarity (or crisis), with a positive ability to be achieved along with a related threat or vulnerability. At every stage of development, key social agents help the individual resolve the current crisis, with the resolution (be it successful or unsuccessful) influencing the outcome of the next crisis encountered. Thus, human development is thought to be both sequential *and* cumulative, with one's overall personality composed of the strengths and weaknesses acquired during each psychosocial stage.

The first year of life corresponds to the first psychosocial stage, *Trust Versus Mistrust.* Being completely helpless, infants must rely on others to meet (1) their physical needs for food, clothing, diaper changes, bodily comfort, etc.; and (2) their psychological desires for affection, emotional sensitivity, and timely responsiveness to their signals for care. When infant's physical and emotional needs are *consistently* met, the world seems like a safe place and the infant learns to trust the people around him or her. If, however, their needs are not met, infants become anxious and mistrustful, for the world has proven to be unresponsive to their needs and therefore dangerous to be in. During this stage, the key social agent (whose *behavior* creates in the infant a sense of trust or mistrust) is the primary caretaker, typically the mother.

Erikson's second psychosocial stage, *Autonomy Versus Shame and Doubt,* which occurs between 1 and 3 years of age, focuses on the toddler's increasing desire to be independent and self-reliant. As parents (the key social agents of this stage) encourage children to walk, talk, and do things for themselves, children will develop age-appropriate autonomy. However, as Sara's behavior at the zoo illustrated, autonomy can quickly turn into defiance, and if parents are coercive or overprotective, children will experience self-doubt and feel ashamed of themselves.

Erik Erikson's theory asserts that an infant's primary caregiver provides the child with a sense of trust or mistrust.

From 3 to 6 years of age, children are faced with the crisis of *Initiative Versus Guilt*. During the third psychosocial stage, preschoolers readily roam about and attempt to plan new activities, make new friends, and develop a sense of judgment (e.g., knowing when it is appropriate to cross a road). Rather than simply imitating the actions of others, which is commonplace during the toddler period, youth are now initiating them. If such efforts are supported by family members, children will enjoy exploring their environment and trying new things, and consequently develop a sense of initiative. If such actions conflict with the goals of parents and siblings, and are thus unduly restricted or punished, children may become passive and guilt-ridden about taking the initiative. As this description illustrates, *all* family members have now become key social agents. Frequent conflicts with siblings and sibling rivalry (*jealousy and resentment between siblings*) are threats to the successful development of initiative.

Industry Versus Inferiority is the fourth crisis that children face. Taking place from about 6 to 11 years of age, children are tasked with mastering both academic and social skills. Aiding children during this crisis are newly developed cognitive skills that allow youth to not only compare themselves with their peers, but also consider how their peers view them! The resolution of this crisis is aided by teachers and peers, the key social agents of this stage. Industrious, self-assured youth succeed at developing various abilities at home, school, and play. The more competent youth become in dealing with their environment, the better they feel about themselves as persons. Undue frustration and failure evoke the sense of inferiority or worthlessness.

Throughout adolescence, roughly 12 to 18 years of age, individuals are busily redefining their identities in ways that incorporate the various changes occurring in their bodies, minds, and sexual development. Thus, during the fifth psychosocial stage, known as *Identity Versus Role Confusion,* the answer to the self-posed question, "Who am I?" changes. The more successful adolescents are in facing this identity crisis, the stronger their sense of personal identity. The more difficulty experienced, the more confusion adolescents feel about who they are and what they may become. During adolescence, identities are explored through real-world interactions with others, thus, it is not surprising that peers are the key social agents of this stage. For today's youth, however, the Internet also affords youth additional ways to explore their identities, ways that are not readily available in person. When online, adolescents can try out virtually any identity: smart or dumb, skinny or obese, young or old, rich or poor, nice or mean, etc. Outlets for identity exploration include social networking sites, Twitter, blogs, and online gaming. For instance, players in the popular Internet-based game *Second Life* can create any type of persona they would like, even if it is nothing like how they are in reality. One advantage of online identity exploration, over real-world ones, is that the relative anonymity of the Internet allows youth to try out identities with little concern about real-life negative social consequences. It is not surprising then, that more and more identity exploration is occurring online (Kirsh, 2010).

The remaining three psychosocial stages occur after the periods of childhood and adolescence have ended. Nevertheless, given that the outcomes of the crises faced during adulthood are influenced by the resolution of each crisis faced earlier in life, the final stages are presented here. The sixth stage, *Intimacy Versus Isolation,* occurs as family ties are loosened during early adulthood. Young adults (ages 20 to 40) attempt to establish close relationships with peers and loving, companion-based relationships with significant others. A successful resolution to this crisis will result in individuals forming satisfying, close relationships with peers of both sexes as well as an intimate relationship with another person. The inability to establish rewarding relationships with friends, including a lover or spouse, results in a painful sense of isolation or loneliness. Thus, the key social agents of this stage are friends and significant others.

Between 40 and 65 years of age, otherwise known as middle adulthood, individuals are faced with a new crisis, *Generativity Versus Stagnation*. Generativity refers to the ability to look beyond one's self, family, and job and to contribute to the welfare of others. The successful resolution of this stage results in an individual who is both happy and a productive member of society. However, for many individuals, especially those developing a sense of isolation during young adulthood, such societal responsibilities can be overwhelming. For those that fail to meet the challenges set forth for them by society, stagnation occurs, and the person becomes increasingly self-absorbed. In addition to family members (including children), the key social agents of this stage are cultural expectations regarding the care of others. For the first time, individuals are not only influenced by living, breathing people, but by a culturally based belief system as well.

During late adulthood, individuals are faced with the final crisis of their lives: *Integrity Versus Despair*. The final stage is a one of reflection, as individuals tend to look back upon their lives as a whole. To the extent individuals feel satisfied with who they used to be and who they have become, they will reflect upon a life fulfilled and feel happy with themselves in old age. But if they feel that their life has been disappointing, meaningless, and a failure, despair will be the result. There is no key social agent in this stage, only one's memories and expectations.

Applying It to Yourself

In the psychodynamic perspective, each of us is driven by motives, needs, and conflicts we're not fully aware of. Accordingly, at times we're beset by ambivalence and indecision, such as whether we really want to remain in a given relationship or job. However, much of the way we cope with life and relate to others depends on how we've grown up and, specifically, how we've resolved the various psychosocial crises that we have faced. Our adjustment to life, therefore, has evolved through a developmental process in which early experiences have had a significant bearing on our present or adult functioning, especially if our childhood experiences were marked by trauma or maladaptive relationships.

When thinking about your own past resolutions to Erikson's psychosocial stages and their potential influence in determining success during the next psychosocial stage, it is important to keep in mind that each stage brings with it new opportunities for success, not just failure. Even if one has had an unsuccessful resolution during the previous stage, the possibility of a positive outcome during the next stage is still there. Optimal adjustment, therefore, comes from figuring out what must be done to meet the challenges ahead. Essentially, this consists of increasing our self-understanding and self-mastery so that we can make meaningful accommodations between our deepest needs and desires and, on the other hand, the social demands made of us. Our goal should be to maximize the satisfaction of our needs while minimizing guilt, self-defeating tendencies, and harm to others and society. As Freud observed, and as Erikson's stages reveal, if we are able "to love and to work"—to establish satisfying relationships and find meaningful work—we are indeed fortunate.

THE SOCIAL-COGNITIVE PERSPECTIVE ON CHILD DEVELOPMENT

The **social-cognitive perspective** *is a broad term that includes behavioral and social learning theories* as well as **cognitive psychology.** *This perspective often assumes that learning and behavior involve higher-level cognitive functions or thinking.* The early behavioral psychologists relied on scientific laboratory methods to observe behavior. As such, they focused on how behavior is learned; hence, the terms *learning theory* and *behaviorism* are often associated with their approach. **Learning theory** is *the systematic statement of learning principles that explain* **learning,** *which is a relatively permanent change in behavior;* **behaviorism** (also known as behavior analysis) is *an objective science that studies external behaviors.* Most learning theorists, following the pioneering efforts of Ivan Pavlov, John Watson, and B. F. Skinner, focused on the mechanics of behavior, especially the importance of reinforcement, in a way that excluded (Slater et al., 2003) human consciousness. **Reinforcement** is *the addition of something that increases the likelihood of a behavior.* As a concrete example of this, let us again examine Sara's behavior at the zoo. Prior to her bad behavior at the zoo, Sara had a history of whining and fussing in order to get her way. In effect, each time her parents gave in to her tantrums (either out of exhaustion or fear of embarrassment), they were actually reinforcing her bad behavior—that is, increasing the likelihood of her tantruming in the future!

Many of the early findings of learning theory and behaviorism were based on animal studies and dealt with the more elementary types of learning and behavior rather than consciousness and cognition (Baars, 2003). In recent years, behavioral research has shifted to complex human behaviors and real-life problems. Learning concepts are being expanded and integrated with ideas and findings in other areas of psychology—especially cognitive psychology. As a result, there is more emphasis on the interaction between individuals and their environment, as well as on how their elaborate cognitive abilities affect learning and behavior (Zimmerman & Schunk, 2003). Such cognitive abilities include but are not limited to thinking, problem solving, decision making, and interpretation of events.

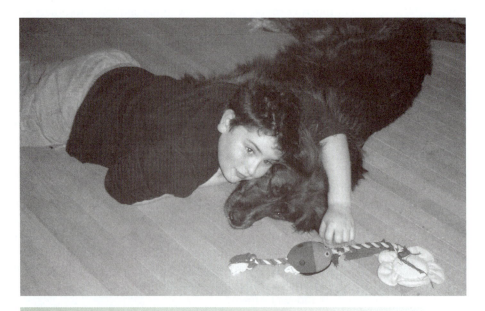

According to social learning theory, children who observe their parents interacting in positive ways with animals also learn to be kind and gentle to animals.

Social Learning Theories

Albert Bandura (1986) and others have demonstrated that much of what we know and do, especially as children, is acquired through the process of **observational learning**. This is *a process in which we learn by observing events and other people, or "models," without any direct reward or reinforcement*. For instance, after watching an episode of *The Power Rangers* (an action-adventure television show filled with martial arts violence), children in elementary school imitated the flying kicks, punches, and blocks that they had just seen (Boyatzis, Matillo, & Nesbitt, 1995). Such learning depends on four components: attention, retention, reproduction, and motivation. In other words, we must *pay attention* to what is going on around us, *retain* what we learn, *be motivated* to perform what we learn, and therefore *reproduce* the same behavior that we observed in others. Such learning is often combined with direct reinforcement (or "reward") to enhance learning.

Bandura (1973) has paid special attention to how aggressive behavior may be acquired through observational learning (Slater et al., 2003). In one of the most famous studies in all of psychology, Bandura (1965) found that after watching a short movie of an adult hitting, kicking, and yelling at an inflatable "Bobo" doll, preschoolers imitated these behaviors the most when the adult models were reinforced for their aggressive actions. In another study, Bandura (1973) found that the fathers of overly aggressive boys were more rejecting of their sons and also more likely to use harsh, physical punishment. In turn, their sons were more apt to imitate their parents' aggressive behavior rather than their verbal warnings to the contrary. Thus, the old adage said by many parents, "Do as I say and not as I do" does not appear to work! Additional information about the effects of physical punishment on youth can be found in Box 2–4.

Box 2–4

Spanking: Does It Work?

Spanking tends to be fairly prevalent among U.S. parents and their children. In the United States, it is an acknowledged and widespread method of aversive control of children's behavior. A full 94 percent of U.S. parents spank their toddlers and preschoolers (Larzelere, 2008; Straus & Stewart, 1999). A pertinent question therefore arises: Is spanking a good idea? In other words, does spanking eliminate or lessen undesirable behaviors in children, or does spanking actually make undesirable behaviors worse?

Most experts on learning and behavior strongly suggest that spanking should not be used (Durrant, 2008), although some argue that mild spanking or punishment may be effective (Larzelere & Kuhn, 2005). The reasoning is that spanking invariably *does not work to lessen* the undesirable behavior. In fact, new studies find that spanking not only *increases current undesirable outcomes* (including depression and conduct problems),

but years later, aggression toward significant others (Christie-Mizell, Pryor, & Grossman, 2008; Lahey et al., 2008).

Researchers have found that the primary *positive* outcome of spanking a child is rapid compliance with the parent's request to cease the undesired behavior (Owen, 2004). As much as spanking seems efficient, most psychologists far prefer that parents find some other means for managing the behaviors of their children (e.g., time-outs, removal of privileges), because the long-term consequences of spanking, as noted, are simply too serious. Instead, parents should use other methods, such as rewarding or reinforcing the positive behaviors of a child (e.g., praising a child for working hard to get good grades at school). The take-home message from these studies is clear: For a better-behaved and less aggressive child, avoid spanking and praise constructive behaviors.

Video games, television, comic books, the Internet, etc., all provide youth with ample opportunities for observational learning. Regardless of the type of media consumed, children and adolescents are constantly witnessing media-based characters being reinforced for their violent actions. Bandura and others in the social-cognitive camp contend that violence in films, television, video games, and other media not only desensitize us to violence (that is, make it less bothersome) but also induce aggressive thoughts, feelings, and behavior in children and adults (Anderson, Gentile, & Buckley, 2007; Kirsh, 2006). Unfortunately, the level of televised and other media aggression in our society remains high. For evidence of this, see Table 2–1.

In the social-cognitive tradition, once a given characteristic or behavior has been learned, it is not necessarily expressed uniformly in all situations. For example, not all aggressive children are aggressive in all situations. A lot depends on the extent to which the behavior is valued or rewarded in various situations. For instance, whereas pushing and shoving is deemed acceptable when children are playing in a rough-and-tumble manner during recess, the same behavior is clearly unacceptable when standing in the lunch line at the cafeteria. Current behavior is therefore best understood in terms of the interaction between a child's past learning and the demands of the present situation. In fact, according to the social-cognitive theorists, behavior is often shaped more by the requirements of the particular situation we happen to be in at the moment than by some unconscious dynamic. Thus, the same child may act aggressively in sports, compliantly in the classroom, and democratically when socializing with friends.

Recent Additions: Cognition and Behavior

In recent years, psychologists have begun exploring the impact of cognition on behavior. Essentially, **cognition** has to do with *the processing of information, and it involves a variety of processes such as selective attention, information gathering, memory, and motivation.* Psychologists are studying cognition as a means of understanding those processes that mediate between the environment and the individual's behaviors. They believe that the impact of a stimulus depends on more than its objective physical characteristics. It also depends on environmental or contextual clues such as *how* it is presented and *the meaning* it has for the

---

TABLE 2–1

HOW PREVALENT IS MEDIA VIOLENCE AND WHAT ARE ITS POSSIBLE CONSEQUENCES?

1. U.S. children between 8 and 18 years of age are exposed to an average of 8 hours and 30 minutes of various media each day.
2. Televisions, VCR/DVD players, radios, and CD players are found in 99 percent of homes in the United States.
3. Nearly 70 percent of elementary school-aged children have TVs in their bedrooms, with close to 50 percent of youth also having a video game console.
4. The average young person will see 200,000 acts of violence portrayed in the media by the age of 18.
5. Over 60 percent of media programs show some type of interpersonal violence.
6. Only 68 percent of parents report using television rating systems to determine and monitor program violence.
7. When teachers and parents help children lower their media usage, children use media less often, approximately 30 percent less.
8. When children interact with media less, verbal and physical aggression both decrease by about 25 percent.

child. In other words, many contemporary learning theorists recognize that the total stimulus complex or environment and its interpretation, and not just some single isolated stimulus, influence behavior.

The recognition that cognitive variables intervene between our behavior and the environment means that we are active, complex beings and that a host of complicating factors affects our behavior. Bandura (1986) refers to the mutual interaction between the various components of learning as "reciprocal determinism." That is, the internal personal-cognitive variables, environmental influences, and behaviors all operate as interlocking determinants of one another. For example, our eating habits are influenced by our family's eating habits (environmental factors), which are also influenced by our past personal preferences (a cognitive factor). All these influences are mutual. Consequently, learning more about nutrition (a personal-cognitive factor) should affect which types of restaurants we seek out (an environmental factor), which in turn should shape our present eating patterns (or behavior) (Grier, Mensinger, Huang, Kumanyika, & Stettler, 2007; Jenvey, 2007). Such a view gives us a richer, more realistic understanding of human existence than earlier learning theories.

More recently, Bandura has added another important concept to his theoretical notions, self-efficacy. **Self-efficacy** is *the belief in one's capacity to organize and execute the courses of action required to produce given attainments.* Our overall functioning is enhanced by high self-efficacy (Bandura, 1997). Self-efficacy as a cognitive process affects our achievement, our physical and mental health, our career development, and even our voting behavior. Rather than simply being a reaction to environmental experiences or internal drives, human adaptation and change is now considered a result of self-organizing, proactive, self-reflecting, and self-regulating behavior. Moreover, the influence of the environment (e.g., television show, video game, teachers, etc.) on the individual is thought to be at its greatest when there is an agreement between the self and the messages coming from the environment. As a result, media, and other environmental stimuli, should have the greatest influence on youth when there is a high degree of similarity between the internal motivations of the individual and the content of the behaviors being observed in the environment. For instance, adolescents desiring to become some of the toughest kids on the block should learn more and be affected by violent media to a larger extent, than their peers wishing to be on the chess team.

Applying It to Yourself

According to the social-cognitive perspective, much of a child's personality and behavior patterns have been acquired through interaction with the environment, especially the significant people in their lives and the messages they encounter in the media (Kirsh, 2010). Although past experience may affect present functioning, it need not determine the whole of life. That is, through the learning process, many of the same mechanisms that are involved in childhood can be used to improve adult adjustment. For instance, a teen who acquired a smoking habit by imitating parents or peers may give up this habit as an adult when sufficiently motivated and encouraged by positive role models at work.

Social-cognitive learning theorists emphasize the importance of the environment and the present situation. Thus, children often act the way they do because of specific influences in their immediate environment, whether at school or at home. As such, maladaptive behavior is often more attributable to inadequate circumstances and faulty learning than deficiencies in a child's psychological makeup. Conversely, the possibility of change involves providing youth with new, more positive models from which they can learn! Consider the following study as an example of this. In an attempt to reduce racial stereotyping in third-grade children, youth were shown a series of videos entitled, *Different and the Same: A Prejudice Reduction Video Series.* In this series, racially diverse puppets modeled racially unbiased behaviors (e.g., resisting peer pressure, problem solving), thought processes (e.g., challenging stereotypes), and attitudes. As a result of viewing these videos, children showed marked reductions in their racial stereotyped attitudes and beliefs. Additionally, these youth were more likely to make cross-race friendships, offer help to a child of a different race, and report knowing how to effectively handle inter-racial conflict (Graves, 1999).

Optimal adjustment consists of maximizing our competencies and coping skills, along with improving interactions with our environment. Problems and conflicts need not be considered inevitable. Instead, problems and conflicts may be dealt with through a lifelong learning process. Thus, changes in our personality and behavior not only are possible but actually occur fairly continuously throughout a lifetime, not just in childhood, especially in an environment conducive to growth. Accordingly, it's best to see ourselves as active creatures with a tremendous capacity to learn, especially when we make full use of our "minds" (cognitions) and continue to increase our range of problem-solving and relationship-enhancing skills (Hohwy, 2004).

THE HUMANISTIC PERSPECTIVE ON CHILD DEVELOPMENT

Psychologists in the humanistic perspective claim that other perspectives leave out much of what makes human existence distinctive, such as the meaning and richness of subjective experience, the holistic characteristics of experience, and our capacity to willfully choose and determine behaviors and thoughts for ourselves (Lenderking, 2005). **Humanistic psychology** consists of *a group of related theories and therapies that emphasize the values of human freedom and the uniqueness of the individual.* Humanistic psychologists, thus, have called our attention to the constructive side of psychology. Individuals are now being viewed in the light of their potential for health and fulfillment as well as in terms of their vulnerabilities and maladjustments.

The Phenomenal Self

Two of the main ideas in the humanistic perspective are the phenomenal self and self-actualization. The term *phenomenonal* here refers to that which is apparent to or perceived by the senses—in short, reality as experienced by the individual. Carl Rogers (1980), a leading humanistic psychologist, emphasized that it is this "perceived reality," rather than absolute reality, that is the basis of behavior. Essentially, human behavior is the goal-directed attempt by individuals to satisfy needs as they experience or perceive them. In other words, how a child sees and interprets events in the environment determines how the child reacts to them.

A key concept in Rogers's theory of personality is the **phenomenal self,** or *the individual's overall self-concept available to awareness.* Rogers assumed the existence of an actualizing tendency at the biological level—a human's tendency to develop and fulfill the self. In the course of actualizing, the individual engages in a valuing (evaluation) process. Experiences that are perceived as enhancing are valued positively and sought after (e.g., buying a vineyard); those that are perceived as blocking fulfillment are valued negatively and avoided (e.g., practicing law). The degree to which individuals trust this valuing process depends in a large measure on their self-concept, especially the self-image derived from one's experience with significant others (such as parents) during the formative years of childhood.

As children become aware of themselves, they automatically develop a need for **positive regard** or *acceptance by others*. Parental acceptance often comes with strings attached, however, and the child incorporates these "conditions of worth" into his or her self-concept. From then on, these extraneous valuing processes compete with the child's own valuing process. If the **conditions of worth** are few and reasonable, the child engages in a variety of experiences and, in cooperation with the valuing process, can judge independently which are enhancing and which are not. If the conditions of self-worth placed upon the child by the parents are many and severely limiting, however, they serve to screen out or prevent much of the child's experience, whereby the self distorts and denies much of its overall experience.

The resulting tension between the self-concept and the child's valuing tendency is the major source of maladjustment. The basic problem is the discrepancy between our human tendency to value experiences on the basis of what is good or desirable to fulfill basic needs and the self's tendency to value experiences selectively, screening out experiences that don't conform to conditions of worth set by parents or by society. In fact, research has shown that when a major discrepancy exists between what we would like to be and who we really are, depression results (e.g., Neff, 2003). In the context of child development, humanistic psychologists like Rogers believe that children reared in supportive environments are more creative, perhaps because they can be more fully functioning in these environments.

Self-Actualization

Still another idea in the humanistic perspective is the concept of **self-actualization,** *the process of fulfilling our inborn potential*. The term *self-actualization* is usually associated with Abraham Maslow, who gave it its fullest explanation (Hanley & Abell, 2002). Maslow, like Rogers, assumed the existence of an inborn actualizing tendency in the individual. Each child and adult has an inherent need to actualize his or her potentialities. However, in Maslow's conceptualization, the core of growth operates in relation to a hierarchy of needs. Only as the individual's most basic needs are met do the higher growth needs become a potent force in motivation. As long as the individual's needs of hunger, safety, and human companionship remain *un*satisfied, the person's existence is governed mostly by deficiency motivation. Once these needs are relatively satisfied, the individual becomes more aware of growth motivation and of the desire to fulfill needs such as autonomy and creativity. Development, especially of our self-actualizing potential, continues throughout childhood *and* adulthood (Reiss & Havercamp, 2005).

Maslow (1971) held that certain people have reached a healthier, more optimal level of functioning than the average person. He called them *self-actualizing* people and held that studying them may teach us much about our potential for growth. Such people are relatively free from major psychological problems and have made the best possible use of their talents and strengths. Compared to the average person, self-actualizing people have certain characteristics in common, such as a continued freshness of appreciation of everyday realities; greater acceptance of themselves and others; high creativity, though not necessarily in the arts; and high resistance to conformity. If self-actualization is indeed a positive process, we should seek out means by which to become more actualized. Activity 2–1 (pages 40–41) contains a questionnaire designed to assess how much you are moving toward your self-actualization.

Our inner core of growth needs may be relatively weak and undeveloped, making it easily stifled by discouraging circumstances. Many people fail to actualize themselves because of the lack of supportive circumstances. However, countless people have been significantly creative despite deprived circumstances, and Maslow acknowledged that it is something of a mystery why affluence releases some people for growth while stunting others. As a result, Maslow suggested that a favorable environment is not enough to ensure growth. Individuals must also have an intense desire to grow to offset the fear and resistance to growth.

Applying It to Yourself

Humanistic psychologists encourage us to see ourselves in terms of our positive potential, or what we can become. As such, they are more concerned with our personal growth than with sheer survival. Problems and conflicts are neither necessary nor inevitable. When these occur, it's likely to be the result of our restrictive self-images, faulty choices, or an unsupportive environment. We may improve ourselves by changing the way we see ourselves and achieving more of the potential control we have over our lives. Such changes occur more readily in an environment conducive to growth, whether a challenging job or a happy marriage, not simply in psychotherapy.

ACTIVITY 2–1

ARE YOU BECOMING MORE SELF-ACTUALIZED?

The following questionnaire is based on Abraham Maslow's work. It was specifically devised for this book and thus has no scientifically researched validity or reliability. Please complete this survey and use the results as a guide rather than as fact in determining how far you have progressed on the road to self-actualization.

Each statement is followed by a scale of 1 (disagree) to 7 (agree). Please mark the extent of your agreement by circling the appropriate number.

1. I experience life fully in the present moment rather than dwelling on the past or worrying about the future.

    Disagree   1   2   3   4   5   6   7   Agree

2. I make choices that will enhance my growth by taking reasonable risks that will develop my potential rather than keep me safe and secure.

    Disagree   1   2   3   4   5   6   7   Agree

3. I listen to my own needs and reactions rather than let others influence me.

    Disagree   1   2   3   4   5   6   7   Agree

4. I am honest with myself and with other people.

    Disagree   1   2   3   4   5   6   7   Agree

5. I strive to do my best in accomplishing tangible goals in everyday life.

    Disagree   1   2   3   4   5   6   7   Agree

6. I am assertive in expressing my needs, ideas, and values.

    Disagree   1   2   3   4   5   6   7   Agree

7. I recognize and live by the inspiration of special moments or peak experiences in which I feel especially close to fulfilling my potential.

    Disagree   1   2   3   4   5   6   7   Agree

8. I relish new experiences and new knowledge.

    Disagree   1   2   3   4   5   6   7   Agree

9. I can identify my defenses and am willing to put them aside in order to revise my expectations, ideas, and values.

    Disagree   1   2   3   4   5   6   7   Agree

10. I commit to concerns and causes outside of myself because I recognize that self-actualization comes as a by-product of unique experiences.

    Disagree   1   2   3   4   5   6   7   Agree

11. I remember that self-actualization is a lifelong process; it is never fully achieved.

    Disagree   1   2   3   4   5   6   7   Agree

12. I trust my own experiences to be my guides in life.

    Disagree   1   2   3   4   5   6   7   Agree

Now add up your scores. The higher the score, the more you may have progressed toward optimal being or self-actualization. Find topics (questionnaire items with low scores) that might need more work. Also, keep in mind that few people are truly self-actualized. Actualization is a process, not a final end state.

Source: Based on Maslow, A. H. (1971). *The farther reaches of human nature.* New York: Viking.

PIECING THE PUZZLE TOGETHER

Each of the five perspectives mentioned above places a piece in the puzzle that is childhood. Erikson's stages of psychosocial development illuminate some of the key issues that children face as they grow. The theory highlights the fact that individuals face different challenges across the lifespan and that previous life experiences influence future growth and adaptation. At each stage of development, influential elements in the environment are identified. Similarly, Bronfenbrenner's ecological perspective explains the numerous ways that the environment can influence youth, ranging from interpersonal interactions to societal values. The biological perspective highlights the role that genes, hormones, etc. play in facing the challenges of development. The social learning theory suggest through direct experience with others and by watching those around them, children learn how to interact with the world. Finally, the humanistic perspective emphasizes that the potential for health, fulfillment, and self-actualization begins in childhood.

In summary, child development is a product of both inherited or biological factors *and* environment or learning. Just how much or how little of our genetic potential we realize depends greatly on our interaction with the environment, especially our selection and reaction to particular environments. However, such determinations are difficult to make, for biology and environment interact to influence youth in what could be described as a dance of intertwined partners. While each partner is responsible for the elements of the performance to varying degrees, together they produce something beautiful that when looking at each partner alone, may not necessarily be apparent.

THREE MAJOR DEVELOPMENTAL TASKS IN CHILDHOOD

In addition to the various perspectives mentioned above, psychologists have documented several constructs and have highlighted certain developmental milestones that serve as important *foundational* elements of development. That is to say, each is present during infancy or early childhood and each has the potential to influence youth decades later. Included in this list are temperament, attachment, and self-concept.

Temperament

Temperament is defined as *an individual's characteristic pattern of emotional response and behavioral reactivity to situations and stressors.* When we describe an individual as "easy-going," "laid-back," or "intense," we basically are describing that individual's temperament. Sara's negative reaction after being told that it was time to leave the zoo, in part, resulted from her more intense temperamental style.

In a landmark study published in 1968, Chess, Thomas, and Birch observed and documented temperamental differences in 133 infants. The temperament of the majority of these infants could be categorized in one of three ways: 40 percent were described as "easy"—these children were happy and cheerful for the most part, had very regular biological rhythms, and they adapted to new situations well; 10 percent were described as "difficult"—irritable in their responses, unpredictable with regard to their eating and sleep habits, and intense in terms of their emotional expression; 15 percent were categorized as "slow-to-warm"—in novel situations, slow-to-warm children appear to be cautious and restrained, but as they "warm up" they become more open and playful in their responses. The remaining 35 percent of the infants in the sample could not be categorized as neatly. Their temperamental patterns seemed to consist of various combinations of the three primary patterns observed (Thomas & Chess, 1984).

The consensus among researchers is that temperament seems to be inborn, strongly based in our biology and surprisingly consistent over time—even through adulthood (Thomas & Chess, 1977, 1984). The notion of a biological element accounting for temperament is consistent with the biological perspective as presented earlier. Chess and Thomas tracked the original 133 infants into adulthood and found that individuals' temperaments, for the most part, remained consistent through the years. Other researchers, using measures derived from Chess and Thomas's original findings, have found that a child's temperament at age 3 is highly correlated with personality, interpersonal functioning at home, work, and with friends, and romantic partners in late adolescence and young adulthood (Caspi & Silva, 1995). Think of Sara, who frequently got into trouble as a preschooler and was still getting into trouble for her high level of reactivity as a teenager.

Temperament is not necessarily the sum total of whom you are and how you adjust—most certainly the experiences that we have and the interactions we have with others throughout our lifetimes affect our personality in a number of ways. But based on the fact that temperamental patterns can be observed in infants, we can say that temperament serves as one of the building blocks for our social and emotional functioning.

Attachment

Attachment is often defined as *a close, emotional tie with another person*. Throughout our lives we develop attachments to various individuals—parents, grandparents, siblings, friends, boyfriends, girlfriends, spouses (Cassidy, 1999). Across child development, attachment is characterized by the tendency to seek out caregivers (referred to as attachment figures) for comfort and support in times of stress. During infancy, children typically require physical contact to derive a sense of comfort. However, with increasing age children can feel comforted by sight of their caregivers or the sound of their voices. Even pictures of caregivers can make children feel safe and secure. Feeling comforted by an attachment figure without actual contact has been termed by attachment researchers as "felt security" (Greenberg, Cicchetti, & Cummings, 1993).

The concept of felt security can also be used to explain a very commonplace behavior of childhood: namely, the carrying around of blankets, stuffed animals, and other special objects by young children. As you recall, Sara went everywhere with her stuffed animal, Teddy. As another example, think of the cartoon character Linus, from *Peanuts,* who not only has his blanket with him at all times, but also cuddles and squeezes it whenever he is feeling insecure. Over 60 percent of U.S. children derive comfort and felt security from such objects (Hobara, 2003).

Teddy bears, blankets, pacifiers and the like are referred to as **transitional objects** by psychologists because they *help the child transition from dependence on a caregiver for comfort and support to more independent forms of coping*. Even thumb sucking fits into this category. Recent research suggests that transitional objects do, in fact, allow children to feel secure and self-sooth during times when the caregiver is not available to meet their needs (Green, Groves, & Tegano, 2004). Does the use of transitional objects mean that children cannot derive comfort from their mothers and other attachment figures? Absolutely not! In fact, it has been argued that children cannot develop an emotional connection with an *object* unless they've developed an even stronger relationship with their mother first (Winnicott, 1953).

Back in the 1960s and 1970s, when research on attachment burgeoned, the primary caregiver in most children's lives was the mother and, thus, most research examined the relationship between mother and child. In addition to mothers, fathers are now considered to be important attachment figures in the lives of youth, a finding echoed by current research (Rohner, 1998). See Box 2–5 (page 44) for an understanding of the role that fathers play in the lives of their children.

Box 2–5

RECOGNIZING THE IMPORTANCE OF FATHERS

Psychologists have long recognized the significant impact parents have on their children. For generations, however, researchers mainly focused on mothers, resulting in a lack of reliable information about the role fathers play in their children's lives (Stolz, Barber, & Olsen, 2005). Collecting information on fathers could help parents, social service agencies, and government policymakers meet the needs of children and families. Without such information, the stereotype of fathers remains that of a clueless dad stumped by his eye-rolling and sometimes sarcastic offspring (Dickenson, 2002).

Statistics support that fathers are very important in the lives of their children. More than 2 million children in the United States are raised primarily by their fathers, and fathers now provide three-fourths of the day-to-day child care that mothers provide; this is contrary to the stereotype of modern American fathers providing little care for their children (Abrams & Lamb, 2002). Additionally and contrary to popular opinion, most unmarried fathers in their twenties and thirties maintain close contact with at least one of their children.

Researchers (e.g., Stolz et al., 2005) are finding, in fact, that fathers *are* significant in their child's development:

- When fathers are involved in their children's schooling, the children complete more years of school and have higher wages as adults than children whose fathers were uninvolved.

- When both the mother and the father are present in the family, the children have fewer behavioral problems and earn better math and reading scores in school.

- When no father is present in a son's life, the son is more likely to become a father as a teenager and to live apart from his children.

- When fathers are present and have warm relationships with their daughters, the daughters are less likely to engage in early sexual activities.

- The more sons and daughters report feeling supported by their fathers, the more likely they are to show initiative in engaging in prosocial activities outside the home.

Fathers indeed make a difference; thus, researchers are pushing for more research on fatherhood. In the meantime, all parents—whether fathers or mothers—need to do the best parenting job they can in order to raise well-adjusted, healthy children. A few parents (as well as some observers of parental behavior) may well guess that there are many "bad" parents. The National Mental Health Information Center (2003), however, suggests that this is a myth. There are *no* dysfunctional families, the Center suggests; there are only distressed and undersupported families.

It is believed that the attachment one develops with the primary caregiver is strongly based on biology. For human infants, who are particularly vulnerable from an evolutionary standpoint, attachment has survival value (Bowlby, 1977). Although there may be a genetic basis for attachment, the quality of that attachment is very much determined by the early interaction one has with the primary caregiver.

How is attachment with the primary caregiver studied? Back in the 1970s, Mary Ainsworth and her colleagues developed an experimental procedure now referred to as the "Strange Situation." The procedure involves observing the interactions between mother, child, and stranger in an unfamiliar playroom filled with novel toys. The quality of the attachment is gauged by how readily the child explores the room, how the child responds to the stranger entering the room, how the child reacts when the mother leaves the room, and, most important, how the child responds when mother returns.

After observing hundreds of mothers and infants, Ainsworth and her colleagues (1978) found the quality of a child's attachment to a caregiver could be categorized in one of three ways. Most children displayed *secure* attachments. They were very comfortable exploring the new environment and interacting with the stranger as long as mom was present. When mom was coached to leave the room, these children became very distressed and sought out mom's comfort when she returned. In Ainsworth's thinking, mom is a secure base from which these children can explore the physical and social world. Some children in Ainsworth's sample displayed an *insecure-ambivalent* attachment. As the label implies, these children were very anxious in the new environment and in interacting with the stranger, even in the presence of the mother. They became upset when mom left the room, but weren't necessarily comforted when she returned. Another portion of the sample displayed what was termed an *insecure-avoidant* attachment. These children did not often interact with their mothers, nor were they distressed when mother left the room. After years of research, it became quite clear that a small proportion of infants did not fit into any of Ainsworth's original attachment patterns. Upon the return of the mother to the room, such infants demonstrated bizarre actions (such as spinning in circles or remaining immobile), displayed a fearful expression, or showed a mixture of avoidant and ambivalent behaviors. Because these infants showed no clear-cut strategy for interacting with their mothers, they were classified as having an *insecure-disorganized* attachment (Main & Solomon, 1990). Collectively, the three latter classifications have been labeled "insecure" attachments.

Additional research has verified that a variety of positive cognitive and social characteristics seem to be related to and may develop as a result of secure attachment. Securely attached toddlers generally display more positive emotions, like joy, whereas insecurely attached toddlers often display more negative emotions such as anger, fear, and distress (Kochanska, Coy, & Murray 2001). Insecurely attached youth are also more likely to be aggressive and antisocial (Ranson & Urichuk, 2008). Children with secure attachments have larger vocabularies (Meins, 1998), are more sociable (Elicker, Englund, & Sroufe, 1992), and are better problem solvers (Frankel & Bates, 1990) than same-aged peers with insecure attachments. And securely attached children tend to have closer, more stable friendships at ages 10 to 12 (Schneider, Atkinson, & Tardif, 2001). This finding occurs, in part, because secure children have better social skills than insecure children (Elicker, Egeland, & Sroufe, 1992).

Patterns of attachment first apparent during infancy remain fairly stable across childhood and adolescence (Fraley, 2002). It is not surprising then, that early interactions with our caregivers help set the stage for our interactions with others later in life. In a study detailed more closely in Chapter 12, Cindy Hazan and Phil Shaver (1994) questioned adults about the quality of their attachments and the nature of their relationships with others as adults and found that security of attachment in childhood often predicted security in individuals' adult relationships.

Self-Concept

Self-concept refers to *the set of abilities, characteristics, and values that an individual believes defines who he or she is.* However, the development of a sense of self is contingent upon a *child's ability to differentiate him- or herself from others in the social environment,* or what is termed **self-recognition.** Of course, this differentiation is made possible by the natural progression of neurological and cognitive development. But when does an infant develop the ability to recognize him- or herself?

In an ingenious study, Michael Lewis and Jeanne Brooks-Gunn (1979) utilized the "rouge test," now more commonly referred to as the "surprise-mark" test to estimate the age at which children are able to recognize themselves. They asked mothers to gently and inconspicuously smudge a dab of rouge on their infants' noses and place their babies in front of a mirror. The researchers observed that infants between the ages of 18 and 24 months reliably touched their noses in a seeming attempt to rub off the strange marks! Infants younger than 18 months, although capable of touching their noses, rarely did so. Other researchers (Nielsen, Suddendorf, & Slaughter, 2006) placed stickers on toddlers' legs in a variation on the rouge test and discovered that even when sitting in a high chair with a tray obstructing their view, children between 18 and 24 months reliably attempt to remove the sticker from their legs when they see themselves in a mirror, indicating that self-recognition at this age extends beyond the face. Interestingly, the rouge test findings have been replicated in a cross-cultural study (Priel & deSchonen, 1986), and children with mental retardation and other developmental disabilities also display evidence of self-recognition as evidenced by the rouge test only when they achieve a mental age of 18 to 20 months (Hill & Tomlin, 1981).

Lewis (1997) noted that toddlers start to use first-person pronouns like "I" and "me" around 20 to 24 months—another indication of self-awareness at this interval in a child's life. Once a child can distinguish him- or herself from the others in the social environment, the stage is set for the development of self-concept. In answer to the question "Who are you?" most preschool-aged children define themselves by their physical characteristics ("I have brown hair") or by what they own ("I have a tricycle") (Keller, Ford, & Meacham, 1978). Self-concept during the preschool years is colored by the concrete, tangible characteristics that define a child's impressions of self. As a child progresses through the school years into adolescence, behavior-based characteristics and physical attributes gradually are replaced by more reflective, abstract, psychologically based qualities in self-descriptions (Damon & Hart, 1988). Examples of statements reflecting a more advanced sense of self include "I am trustworthy," "I am a good friend," and "When I can, I help others out."

Sense of self is a very important aspect of personal and social functioning that will influence us as we navigate the social world throughout our lives. The types of environments we seek out, the decisions we make, and the values we hold are all influenced by how we view ourselves. For instance, many adolescents will value abilities that they are good at (e.g., skateboarding) and devalue those that they are not (e.g., academic achievement), even if the latter are highly valued by society (Harter, 2006). As this example illustrates, once youth can differentiate the self from others, they start comparing themselves to others. This social comparison process, which starts around the time children enter kindergarten (about age 5 or 6), is a key component in determining whether children, as well as adults, will feel good or bad about who they are.

Applying It to Yourself

Are you an easy-going person or are you generally suspicious of others until you get to know them? When you look in the mirror, what do you see? If you were to describe yourself, what qualities would you identify as characteristic of you? Are you happy with the person you are, or do you have different ideas regarding who you want to be? Are you secure in your relationships with friends and lovers, or do you sometimes feel betrayed or suspicious of their actions or intentions? The answers to these questions all have their roots in some of the major concepts examined in early childhood by developmental psychologists.

SUMMARY

PERSPECTIVES ON CHILD DEVELOPMENT

Psychologists approach development, adjustment, and growth from differing perspectives, each of which offers an optimal range of explanations rather than a comprehensive truth. Thus, by examining the distinctive contributions of all four major perspectives, we may attain a more inclusive, balanced understanding of personality and behavior. The four major perspectives are biological, ecological, psychodynamic, and social-cognitive.

THE BIOLOGICAL PERSPECTIVE ON CHILD DEVELOPMENT

Extensive studies of twins and others have shown that genetic influences may account for between 25 and 50 percent of the differences in personal characteristics among the general population. At the same time, the extent of the way we develop depends greatly on the interaction with our environment. As a result, we should speak of nature *via* or *through* nurture or perhaps nature *and* nurture rather than nature *versus* nurture.

THE ECOLOGICAL PERSPECTIVE ON CHILD DEVELOPMENT

The ecological perspective highlights the importance of four distinct, but interrelated settings on children's development: the microsystem, mesosystem, exosystem, and macrosystem. Moreover, this perspective emphasizes the fact that what happens in one setting can influence youth in other settings, in both direct (microsystem, mesosystem) and indirect (exosystem, mesosystem) manner.

THE PSYCHODYNAMIC PERSPECTIVE ON CHILD DEVELOPMENT

According to Erikson's psychosocial theory, youth develop in a sequential process (via psychosocial stages) in which they are faced with a specific crisis to resolve at different points of development. From cradle to grave, the manner in which the individual handles these crises has a decisive influence on his or her current and future development. Key elements in the environment influence the outcome of each psychosocial stage.

THE SOCIAL-COGNITIVE PERSPECTIVE ON CHILD DEVELOPMENT

Learning theorists de-emphasize the biological basis of behavior and instead focus on how behavior is learned through interaction with the environment. They contend that most of our personality and behavior is acquired through such processes as observational learning, with or without direct reinforcement (or reward). Furthermore, their recognition of cognitive variables that intervene between the environment and our behavior suggests that learning is affected by more complex factors than an isolated stimulus, as was the belief in early behavioral theory. Bandura has characterized the mutual interaction among the various components of learning—personal-cognitive variables, environment, and behavior—as reciprocal determinism. In this view, humans have a tremendous capacity to learn and change, especially when they make full use of their minds and maximize their competencies in dealing with the environment. Self-efficacy is one means for accomplishing growth and change.

THE HUMANISTIC PERSPECTIVE ON CHILD DEVELOPMENT

Humanistic psychologists emphasize the holistic characteristics of human experiences, such as human freedom and self-actualization. Rogers's theory of the phenomenal self stresses the importance of perceived reality, especially the way individuals perceive and experience themselves in relation to their environment. Moreover, we begin to live authentically only as we affirm our inherent human freedom and take responsibility for our lives. Both Maslow and Rogers hold that each person has an inherent need to actualize his or her potentialities but that self-actualization is more of a lifelong process that enhances the meaning of life rather than being a readily attainable goal.

THREE DEVELOPMENTAL TASKS OF CHILDHOOD

Developmental psychologists study many factors emerging in childhood that set the stage for later personality and social functioning. Temperament, described as a person's characteristic reactivity, is apparent at birth and is remarkably consistent throughout a person's life. The quality of our early attachment to our caregiver tends to influence childhood outcomes related to emotional, cognitive, and social functioning, as well as frame the ways we relate to significant others later in our lives. Self-recognition, critical to the development of self-concept, emerges at around 18 months. Self-concept in young children is based on their concrete personal characteristics, but as a child develops cognitively, psychological attributes tend to color self-characterization.

SELF-TEST

1. According to the _____ perspective, shyness, assertiveness, and other personal attributes are attributable to genetic influences.
   a. ecological
   b. biological
   c. environmental
   d. transactional

2. The part of the ecological environment that operates cultural ideals and values is the
   a. microsystem.
   b. mesosystem.
   c. exosystem.
   d. macrosystem.

3. The key social agent in the development of initiative is
   a. the mother
   b. peers
   c. the family
   d. society

4. According to Erikson, youth try to figure out "who they are" during the stage called
   a. Trust vs. Mistrust.
   b. Autonomy vs. Shame and Doubt.
   c. Identity vs. Role Confusion.
   d. Integrity vs. Despair.

5. The process by which people may acquire new behaviors by watching others is called
   a. self-actualization.
   b. observational learning.
   c. the conditioned response.
   d. operant learning.

6. Bandura's research demonstrates that we should be very concerned about children's imitation of
   a. media violence.
   b. adult misconduct.
   c. adults eating the wrong diet.
   d. other people's religious attitudes.

7. From the social-cognitive perspective, optimal adjustment is achieved through maximizing the individual's
   a. management of inner conflicts.
   b. self-actualizing drive.
   c. competencies and coping skills.
   d. self-esteem.

8. A(n) _____ child is reticent at first and then becomes more open to others.
   a. difficult
   b. slow to warm up
   c. easy
   d. All three equally.

9. Children with a(n) _____ attachment do not seem to know how to act in the Strange Situation, and sometimes they show fear of the caregiver.
   a. secure
   b. insecure-ambivalent
   c. insecure-avoidant
   d. insecure-disorganized

10. When you ask someone, "Tell me about yourself," you are really asking him or her to describe his or her
    a. self-concept.
    b. self-recognition.
    c. self-efficacy.
    d. self-esteem.

EXERCISES

1. *Which of Erikson's stages are you in?* Write approximately a page explaining how well you're mastering the appropriate developmental task for your stage, according to Erikson's theory. How important do you consider this task for someone at your stage of life? If possible, comment on how your past development affects your experience in the present stage of development.

2. *Identifying ecological influences.* Think about the various ecological influences in your life. Identify two examples for each system in the ecological environment.

3. *Barriers to personal growth.* Each of the four major perspectives covered in this chapter offers a different view of the barriers to personal growth. The biological view reminds us of the importance of heredity to our temperament, the ecological perspective highlights the importance of the interrelated environments we face, the psychodynamic view stresses the cumulative effect of the crises we face across development, and the social learning view emphasizes faulty models, environments, and maladaptive behavior. Write a paragraph or so explaining how each of these views may help to account for the barriers to your own personal growth.

4. *What can you learn from watching violence on TV?* According to the social-cognitive theory, we learn by observing others. Watch a show containing real violence (such as that shown the evening news), realistic violence (e.g., a dramatic series), and

cartoon violence (makes sure it's a funny cartoon). What did you learn about violence when watching each of these shows? Write your experiences down so you can compare and contrast what you learned.

5. *Which major perspective most reflects your views?* Select one of the four major perspectives that is most compatible with your own thoughts on adjustment and development. Then write a page or so explaining why you prefer this viewpoint. To what extent are you receptive to viewpoints different from your own? Would you agree that no one perspective possesses the whole truth?

QUESTIONS FOR SELF-REFLECTION

1. Why is it important to take a perspective approach to the study of development?

2. Given what you now know about development, do America's children stand a reasonably good chance of being happy and well adjusted?

3. Are there personal characteristics that seem to run in your family tree?

4. Do you agree with Erikson that across development we are faced with specific crises?

5. How do you feel about Freud's psychosexual stages of development? Are they realistic?

6. Do you believe that much of the inconsistency in people's behavior can be explained by situational factors?

7. When psychologists label their perspective "cognitive," what does this term mean to you?

8. Have you experienced birth-order effects in your life? What might account for differences between siblings, other than the order that they were born?

9. Why is it that not everyone is securely attached? Do you think that if caregivers knew more about adjustment and child development, the world would be a different place? How so?

10. What is your self-concept like? Describe yourself and identify the different types of characteristics (e.g., appearance, race, intelligence, etc.) you believe capture who you are.

FOR FURTHER INFORMATION

RECOMMENDED READINGS

BERK, L. (2008). *Child development*. Boston: Allyn and Bacon. Berk reviews normal child development. This book includes more cross-cultural information than the usual child development text.

CRAIN, W. (2005). *Theories of development*. Upper Saddle River, NJ: Prentice Hall. This book introduces the reader to various theories of development and provides fairly extensive critiques of each theory.

DUNLAP, L. L. (2004). *What all children need: Theory and application*. Lanham, MD: University Press of America. Dunlap discusses important aspects of what children need, including experiencing love and being valued. She also discusses building positive self-esteem and teaching children how to value themselves.

GARBARINO, J. (2006). *Why girls are growing more violent and what we can do about it*. New York: Penguin Press. An important book about why U.S. girls turn to violence and other antisocial behaviors. This book is a follow-up to Garbarino's book on the same topic but with regard to boys.

KOHN, A. (2005). *Unconditional parenting: Moving from rewards and punishment to love and reason*. New York: Atria. Kohn discusses modes of parenting and relationships between parents and children. His book is sprinkled with anecdotes with which most parents can identify.

WESITES AND THE INTERNET

http://www.parentingivillage.com   A site dedicated to helping parents in all domains of child rearing. Chat rooms are also available so that parents can share their thoughts and concerns with other parents.

http://www.genome.gov   The website for the human genome project, which is trying to document all of the genes on human chromosomes. This site also contains information on the policy, medical, and ethical considerations of trying to understand more about human genetics.

http://www.positiveparenting.com   A website that has the main goal of making parenting a positive experience, for example, other ways to discipline children besides spanking.

http://www.esrb.org   A website that assists parents and others by rating websites and video games for appropriateness for children.

http://www.apa.org/ppo/issues/snichd.html   The American Psychological Association's main page for links to information on children, developmental psychology, and other relevant topics.

Affirmative Aging—Adulthood

Learning Objectives

After completing this chapter, you should be able to

1. Describe various emotional and social aspects of leaving home in young adulthood.
2. Explain the difference between age-related and non-age-related development.
3. Understand how becoming a parent affects job pay and relationships.
4. Describe the characteristic physical and cognitive changes accompanying late adulthood.
5. Identify different paths to successful aging.
6. Discuss differences between men and women with regard to the process of aging.
7. Describe how individuals cope with retirement.

Zena sat on the edge of her bed. She felt stiff this morning and did not know why. She thought, "The funny thing about aging is the way it sneaks up on you. One minute you're 30 or 40. Before you know it, you're 64, like I am." She continued her thoughts as she rubbed her sore, stiff hands. "I don't feel 64, but my birthdays betray me. So do my arthritic hands," she thought. Zena continued to think of herself as someone in her late 40s, though she was reminded otherwise each time she looked in the mirror. It usually came as a surprise when her body rebelled. She didn't feel older, except in those rash moments when she overexerted herself, such as walking too quickly up a steep hill, or when she awoke to morning hand stiffness. As had Zena at times in her life, virtually all of us have been hit with the admonishment "Act your age." As Zena sat on the edge of the bed she wondered, "But what if your chronological age isn't the age you feel?"

ADULT DEVELOPMENT

Adulthood refers to *the period of life from physical maturity on, consisting of a sequence of physical and psychosocial changes.* New tasks, different challenges, and new sources of happiness and frustration mark each new period of our lives. Thus, the process of personal growth continues throughout our life span. Perhaps more than ever before, people are

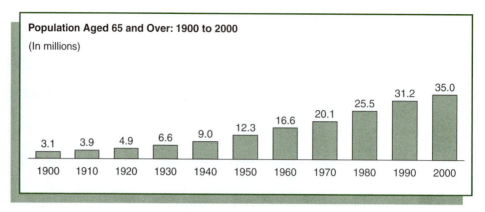

FIGURE 3–1

Population aged 65 and over: 1900 to 2000.

NOTE: The reference population for these data is the U.S. population.
SOURCES: 1900 to 1940, 1970, and 1980, U.S. Bureau of the Census, 1983, Table 42; 1950, U.S. Bureau of the Census, 1953, Table 38; 1960, U.S. Bureau of the Census, 1964, Table155; 1990, U.S. Bureau of the Census, 1991, Table QT-PI; 2000, U.S. Census Bureau, 2001, Table PCT12. For full citations, see references at end of chapter.

deliberately trying to change themselves, so that with age and experience they have greater coping skills and self-mastery. On the other hand, people often like to feel settled and connected to the familiar. Older adults, for example, much prefer to stay in their own homes rather than move to an assisted living facility or move in with their children (Administration on Aging, 2009). As Carl Rogers (1980), one of the pioneers of information on personal growth, grew older, he became convinced that the phrase "older but still growing" is a more apt description of adult development than the conventional cliché "growing old." With age, we all develop our own individual identities to a greater extent, feel more confidence in ourselves, and can achieve greater personal control and mastery over our lives (Pfaffenberger, 2005). Zena, our gracefully aging woman in the opening vignette, would heartily agree. Of note, the segment of the population known as "old" has been growing dramatically in recent years due to healthier lifestyles and medical advances. Figure 3–1 illustrates the dramatic rise in the number of older people through the year 2000.

From infancy through adolescence, much of our development is associated with **age-related changes**—*changes that occur at a given age,* such as learning to talk or walk and puberty. In contrast, adult development is increasingly influenced by **non-age-related changes,** or *events and influences that are unique to each of us and may occur at any age or not at all,* such as divorce or the decision to change careers. Nevertheless, because the physiological well-being, self-perceptions, emotional experiences, and social circumstances of adults vary with each additional decade of life, we'll examine adult adjustment and growth in terms of three broad stages across the lifespan: early, middle, and late adulthood. Keep in mind that the age boundaries between these stages are fuzzy and that people differ considerably in their own individual patterns of development. Before you read further, take the quiz in Activity 3–1 to examine how much knowledge you possess about the aging process.

ACTIVITY 3–1

How Much Do You Know About Aging?

Write either "true" or "false" by each of the following statements. Then check your responses with the answers at the end of this chapter.

_____   1.   All five senses tend to decline in old age.

_____   2.   People lose about one-third of their brain cells or neurons by late adulthood.

_____   3.   Drivers over 65 years of age have fewer traffic accidents per person than those under 30.

_____   4.   Most older people are pretty much alike.

_____   5.   Older adults become less susceptible to short-term illnesses, such as the common cold.

_____   6.   Recognition memory declines sharply with old age.

_____   7.   Reaction time generally becomes slower with age.

_____   8.   About one-fourth of those over 65 live in nursing homes.

_____   9.   People become more fearful of death as they grow older.

_____   10.   Widows outnumber widowers about three to one.

The answers can be found at the end of the chapter.

DECISIONS, DECISIONS, DECISIONS—EARLY ADULTHOOD

Early adulthood begins with an "early adult transition," *roughly from the late teens or early 20s and lasting well into a person's 30s.* Young adults are faced with many new challenges during this decade or so of life change, including leaving home, choosing and preparing for a career, establishing close relationships with friends and significant others (recall Intimacy vs. Isolation from the previous chapter), and starting a family of one's own. Because the decisions young people make will affect them for 50 years or more, this transition can be quite stressful. On the other hand, young adults' relationships with their parents become more positive and connected during early adulthood; after all, parents and adult-children now share increasingly similar roles in life (e.g., spouse, employee, voter; Masche, 2008). Thus, young adults often rely on their parents, and other family members, to help them with the difficult decisions that lie ahead.

Leaving Home

Leaving home involves more than just packing your things, loading up the car, and changing residences; as the old saying goes "Home is where the heart is." Of course, one aspect of leaving home does include moving out of the house or apartment that you grew up in. But there are other changes as well, such as becoming less dependent financially on parents, entering new, more adult-like, roles and responsibilities, and engaging in more autonomous decision making. It is this latter psychosocial transition that is essential for entering adulthood. Some individuals may run away from an unhappy home at an early age but take a long time before growing up emotionally; others may remain home well into their 20s (Strom & Strom, 2005). In both cases, it is the "symbolic" leaving from home that is so crucial to attaining emotional autonomy.

At the same time, a curious thing has been happening in the last decade. Like birds flying back to the nest, more young adults are moving in with their parents after years of absence from home. Nearly a third of young adults still live with their parents, and 50 percent of adult children will return to the nest for a brief stay at least once in their lifetime (Ward & Spitze, 2007). After experiencing emotional, psychological, and behavioral independence from parents, why would adult children return home? In large part, the increase in these "nesters" is due to both personal and economic situations. For example, Zena's only daughter, Jonelle, moved back with Zena after her divorce to "regroup," both emotionally and financially. It is often difficult for young people to maintain their own apartments or homes because housing prices generally continue to increase, and many young people are having a hard time finding a suitable job. In fact, the unemployment rate for 20- to 24-year-olds is about twice that of adults 25 and over (U.S. Bureau of Labor Statistics, 2009).

As you might expect, there are pros and cons to a "nesting" arrangement. For instance, food bills increase (though some young people pay board to offset these expenses), and parents may ask about their child's whereabouts and activities, such as, "Where were you last night?" Nevertheless, individuals and their parents often find that this is a satisfying time for sharing and strengthening their ties before a son or daughter leaves home again, usually for good (Strom & Strom, 2005).

Choosing a Career

In choosing a career, young adults must strike a balance between two somewhat contradictory tasks. One task is to explore the possibilities in the adult world, keeping their options open. The other task is to create a stable life structure with the aim of making something of themselves. Young adults often agonize over the important decisions they must make at this stage, whether they are making the right choice, and if not, how difficult it will be to change. If you experience some personal distress about career options as you progress through college, you are not alone!

Over the past several decades, earning potential has become an increasingly important issue when choosing an academic major and/or career, especially for men (Montgomery, 2004). Many students now plan to major in biology (for medical school), business, or economics, almost double the number several decades ago. Additionally, for the benefit of their careers, many young adults decide to delay (or forego altogether) starting a family. For women who choose to work *and* start a family, discrimination may soon follow. The **motherhood-penalty**, as it is called, *refers to the fact that working mothers are viewed as less competent and less committed to work than non-mothers.* As such, they are discriminated against when making hiring decision and determining salaries. In fact, working mothers are paid 5 percent less, *per child,* than non-mothers (Correll, Bernard, & Paik, 2007).

Starting a Family

Early adulthood is usually the time for starting a family. In today's world, however, starting a family occurs nearly as often for those who are married as for those who are not, as close to 40 percent of all childbirths in the United States occur out-of-wedlock (National Center for Health Statistics, 2009). When Zena and her husband married in their early 20s, they decided they wanted children right away and that Zena would delay her education and her career until the youngest began school. In comparison to couples of the 1950s, adults of the twenty-first century tend to wait longer before having children. Today, many couples do not have their first child until they are in their late 20s or early 30s (Abma & Martinez, 2006). Nevertheless, couples are giving more thought to whether they want children and if so, when to have them. One result is more voluntary childlessness. Nearly 10 percent of couples choose this option; however, few couples resolve this issue directly. Usually, couples decide to postpone having children until they eventually make the postponement permanent.

Having children may affect a couple's marriage in several ways. On the positive side, many couples report that having children makes them feel more responsible and adult. They also report increased satisfaction in sharing affection and experiences with their children, which enhances their sense of purpose in life. On the minus side, taking care of small children is an added stress on the marriage, leaving less time for the parents to do things on their own. Even without children, there can be a great deal of marital stress as individuals question their marriages and their relationships to their mates (Doss, Rhoades, Stanley, & Markman, 2009). For working couples, the stress increases; the couple may wish to spend lots of quality time with their children but cannot. Studies show that today's parents have 22 fewer hours per week to spend with their children (Kornblush, 2003). Many people have children before they realize how children can alter parents' lifestyles, sleep habits, and other matters of daily life. At times, raising children can be overwhelming, leaving parents unable or unwilling to cope with the financial, psychological, and emotional challenges of rearing youth. When such difficulties arise, other family members, especially the grandparents, take over child-rearing responsibilities. Demographers estimate today that close to 2.5 million children are raised by their grandparents. A similar number of elderly have both their adult children and their grandchildren living with them (U.S. Bureau of the Census, 2006).

SAME OLD, SAME OLD?—MIDDLE ADULTHOOD

Sometime between the late 30s and mid-40s, people make the transition from early adulthood to middle adulthood, often called midlife by many developmental psychologists. **Middle adulthood** may be defined as *that era between the late 30s and the 60s that is generally characterized by fulfillment of career and family goals.* Both men and women begin to see themselves differently, with new opportunities and tasks as well as new challenges. These individuals are going through the midlife transition. Today's middle-aged adults do not see themselves as old, whereas in earlier times, middle age *was* old age, when people were expected to die. In fact, middle-aged Americans nowadays identify more with younger adults than with the elderly (Elias, 2002). As a matter of fact, an intriguing and oft-repeated research finding is that adults *of all ages* tend to see themselves as younger than they really are (Furstenberg, 2002).

Midlife Transition or Midlife Crisis?

Essentially, the **midlife transition** is *a period of personal evaluation that comes sometimes with the realization that one's life is about half over.* The individual gradually pays less attention to the "time since birth" and starts thinking more in terms of "time I have left." Some people at this age may hide some of the more obvious changes of age or compensate by trying harder to appear young. For example, Americans spend several billion dollars each year on cosmetic surgery in an attempt to obtain a more youthful or pleasing appearance. It is sometimes difficult for middle-aged individuals to ignore other fundamental changes. For one thing, their parents retire, become ill, and die during these years. More of their friends and acquaintances are also lost through death, with death from all causes rising sharply at this time of life. Their children grow up and leave home, and middle-aged parents feel more aware of the mistakes they have made raising their children. Nevertheless, close to 75 percent of adults make it through midlife without experiencing a crisis, of any sort (Wethington, 2000).

As mentioned in Chapter 2, Erikson (1964) believed that the main task during this stage is to achieve a sense of generativity, which involves becoming less self-absorbed and more caring about others and future generations. As such, the realization that life is half over prompts many people to ask what they would like to do with the rest of their lives. Such self-questioning may lead to changes in their careers, marriages, or personal relationships (Helson & Soto, 2005; Lindgren, 2002). It often leads individuals to take up new interests or become active in community or national affairs as a way of making their world a better place in which to live. Zena thought to herself, "It's a time for becoming aware of the 'opposite,' unrealized side of my personality." Women sometimes may react to their midlife transitions differently than men, depending largely on whether their primary involvement has been in a career or the home. Professional women who have considered having children may realize that the biological clock is running down, and they may decide to have a child at this age. Single-mother adoptions and out-of-wedlock births also tend to increase. For women who had children as a young adult a need to fulfill themselves in other ways often develops. Many women return to school at this age, take a job outside the home, or do both simultaneously. Middle age, then, is a time for shifting gears and developing new interests and values. Research has shown that developing multiple interests is a great buffer against mental and physical illness in adults (Pfaffenberger, 2005).

These middle adult years can be particularly trying. Parents die, spouses take ill, grown children start families of their own. Sick family members may require constant care and attention, and grandchildren may demand the same. For Zena, not only did her mother die, but her father became ill, and her beloved husband died from cancer. When Zena cared for her husband and her father, she found what other middle-aged adult children discover: that there is a crisis in caregiving in America, as caring for loved ones is both expensive and time consuming (Carbonell, 2003). And if the aging parent has significant health issues (such as significant cognitive impairments), the health of the caregiver also tends to suffer (Di Mattei et al., 2008). The midlife transition, then, can become an uncomfortable time for some people. This need not be so, as recent research has discovered. Box 3–1 examines well-being in adulthood with information that may surprise you, because it indicates middle-aged people and older adults are remarkably happy.

Physical and Cognitive Changes

The most obvious signs of middle age are certain physical changes in appearance. People tend to gain weight around the waist, especially after 40 (Ziebland, Robertson, Jay, & Neil, 2002)—with women worrying most about their bodies (Saucier, 2004)—and head hair may turn gray. Zena's hair was good and gray, and she liked it just like that! Men's hairlines may begin to recede around their upper temples and make them wonder if they

Box 3–1

Well-Being Throughout Adulthood

Many people believe that life will become less satisfying as they move away from their 20s and 30s. They view midlife as an unstable period and old age as the worst of times. This negative image of aging, however, is at odds with some of the research on older people, and certainly at odds with how Zena felt about herself and her life. Aging research is focusing more and more on successful aging. Along this line, longitudinal research has found that life satisfaction tends to peak at about 65 years of age (Mroczek & Spiro, 2005). Despite the fact that health declines with age (Ross, 2005), other factors contribute to happiness in middle and late adulthood. Compared to younger adults, individuals at these older ages experience more autonomy in their lives and also feel that they are more likely to be doing their duty (e.g., voting or helping others). Thus, they experience a greater sense of well-being than younger adults (Sheldon, Kasser, Houser-Marko, Jones, & Turban, 2005). Additionally, older individuals are more likely than younger adults to experience memories of personal growth (e.g., successfully addressing challenges) (Bauer, McAdams, & Sakaeda, 2005). At the same time, well-being across the life span may be partly due to age-related emotional differences. Mather and Carstensen (2005) note that as people age, they experience more emotion regulation. They find themselves less often experiencing negative emotions and more often experiencing positive emotions than do younger people. Other factors also influence successful adaptation to aging. They include life course factors such as marital stability, religious beliefs, and health (Crosnoe & Elder, 2002).

---

are going bald. In fact, by middle-age close to 50 percent of Caucasian men will experience male pattern baldness (Ellis & Sinclair, 2008). All these changes reflect a gradual slowing down in the overall physical system, which can result in less physical energy and stamina. People typically get tired more easily and take more time to bounce back from fatigue or illness.

There is actually some improvement in general health in the sense that middle-aged adults get fewer colds, allergies, or minor illnesses, and they may experience fewer accidents. But they become more susceptible to chronic and serious illnesses, such as diabetes, heart attacks, strokes, and cancer. As a result, there is increasing concern over health and sometimes more attention placed on keeping fit (Malmberg, Miilunpalo, Pasanen, Vuori, & Oja, 2005). In fact, much research shows that greater overall activity level is related to greater happiness, function, and reduced mortality rate in adulthood. Even mild involvement in less strenuous activities, such as reading, can result in increased happiness, perhaps because it engages us in life (Menec, 2003).

Cognitive abilities may also change, depending on the person and the prior level of cognitive activity (Wilson et al., 2005). Starting around the age of 50, people begin to differ more and more from one another in terms of their intellectual capacity, as some, but not all, cognitive capabilities begin to decrease (Hedge, Borman, & Lammlein, 2006). If decline does occur, one of the first abilities to diminish is the ability to make sense of spatial relationships. Spatial ability helps us navigate through three-dimensional space; it allows us to remember where we parked our cars at the airport or how to drive to the shopping mall. Other abilities that may decrease include abstract reasoning (such as thinking about a hypothetical situation), memory, and the speed at which information is processed. Not surprisingly, across middle adulthood and beyond, people generally take longer to learn new and/or remember old information (Meijer, de Groot, van Gerven, van Boxtel, & Jolles, 2009).

Middle-aged individuals who stay active or take up new hobbies remain happier and healthier.

Box 3–2 discusses a debilitating cognitive disorder that may, in fact, begin to develop in midlife but is often associated with old age: **Alzheimer's disease.**

Sexual Changes

The biological and psychological changes that accompany the loss of reproduction contribute to the midlife transition in both sexes. Although these changes can pose new anxieties for men and women, they can present new opportunities for personal growth.

The most significant physical change in women is **menopause,** or *cessation of monthly menstrual cycles,* which signals the loss of childbearing capacity. Menopause in women is also sometimes called *the climacteric.* Menopause tends to occur sometime between 45 and 55 years of age in American women, which means that Zena had already passed this milestone. The physical effects vary from a certain degree of atrophy in the uterus, vagina, and breasts to a variety of other changes such as hot flashes. Some women find menopause mostly a negative experience, with adverse effects on their appearance and their physical, emotional, and sexual lives. Other women feel little or none of these effects. Some positive changes also occur during this period, thus evening out the quality of life between pre- and postmenopausal women (Özkan, Alatas, & Zencir, 2005). The lessened fear of pregnancy often leads to increased sexual responsiveness for many women. Other events of middle adulthood, such as changes in the marriage relationship, freedom from child-care responsibilities, and return to work outside the home, can be more important to women than the physical changes. Today, middle-aged women have the opportunity to address menopausal changes with hormone supplements, usually a combination of estrogen and progesterone. As a result of replacing these hormones, women experience a decline in post-menopausal symptoms, such as hot flashes, night

Box 3–2

Alzheimer's Disease: Will You Be a Victim?

Alzheimer's disease, a term that often strikes fear in our hearts, was not well known 100 years ago. Why? People simply did not live long enough for the disease to manifest itself.

Between now and 2050, the number of people with Alzheimer's will increase from an estimated 5.3 million up to 14 million, as the baby boomers enter the age of highest risk of the disease (Alzheimer's Association, 2009). Almost 10 million of these elderly live at home and are dependent on family caregivers. The caregivers, who are often adult children, find difficult the constant caring for a loved one who is confused, has trouble remembering the simplest of things such as whether to eat meat with a spoon or a fork, and whose behavior is often unpredictable.

Alzheimer's, at first blush, appears to be a degenerative brain disease of only the elderly. New research is shedding light on earlier memory problems that may forebode Alzheimer's disease. Scientists have found that they can sometimes predict who in midlife is at risk for Alzheimer's. A new diagnosis, **mild cognitive impairment (MCI),** *has been identified in a subgroup of people who have memory problems during the course of normal aging but are otherwise healthy and functional* (Alzheimer's Association, 2009).

When followed over a span of several years, such individuals develop Alzheimer's at a much higher rate than people in the general population. In MCI people have more trouble, for example, with the "tip of the tongue phenomenon," where information is at first difficult to recall but is eventually remembered by those without MCI. In other words, MCI sufferers have difficulty with everyday memory searches. An MCI diagnosis also hinges on problems with memory for tasks that involve a sequence of steps, such as the steps taken in baking a cake. MCI sufferers have more problems remembering things in a series than those with normal middle-aged memories.

Why would anyone want to know in advance that she or he might potentially develop this very disabling disease? Because help is on the horizon. Scientists appear to be on the brink of discovering much-needed treatments and even a preventive vaccine for Alzheimer's disease. One promising treatment involves the use of an enzyme that would block brain cell degeneration caused by Alzheimer's. The vaccine, which thus far has been tested with some success in humans and monkeys, might eventually immunize people if serious side effects are not found (Alzheimer's Association, 2009).

sweats, and dry skin. Additional benefits of hormone replacement therapy include a reduction in osteoporosis, colorectal cancer, and heart disease. However, this treatment is not without controversy because of such possible side effects as increased risk of certain cancers (Canderelli, Leccesse, & Miller, 2007). This particular risk induced Zena to refuse to take hormones after menopause when her doctor offered a prescription. "I'll get through this OK," she said aloud. Differences in the use of these drugs also exist, with African American and Hispanic women less likely to use replacement hormone therapy than White women (Elias, 1999a).

Although men are not subject to menopause, they do go through a male **climacteric,** defined technically as *the loss of reproductive capacity.* In men, the climacteric is accompanied by a gradual reduction in fertile sperm, a diminution of testosterone, and reduced sexual vigor, sometimes with increasing impotency in some men. However, men tend to reach their climacteric five to 10 years later than women reach menopause and do so in a much more gradual way, with fewer physiological consequences. The drug Viagra for men has added an interesting element to the aging male's sexuality, as revealed in Box 3–3 (page 62). Men and women who take these changes in stride often find their lives even more satisfying than before, including the sexual aspects of their lives. For one thing, the changes and anxieties of this period may make each individual more aware of the need for a spouse and the security of marriage. In fact, at middle age and older, men and women's friends and family are very important to their quality of life (Jaccoby, 1999). Perhaps nothing helps a man or woman through this stage as much as an understanding and supportive partner (Spotts et al., 2005). Actually, there is a rise in marital happiness among many couples as they age, with individuals in their late 40s and 50s reporting levels of marital happiness surpassing couples in their 20s (Bookwala & Jacobs, 2004).

Box 3–3

THAT LITTLE BLUE PILL . . .

Who would think a little blue pill would make such a big splash? The mass media tell us that there is a flourishing illegal trade in this supposedly magical sex cure and that people, both men and women, are flocking over the Mexican border to procure this blue aphrodisiac, this sexual enhancer, without a prescription.

Viagra (generically known as sildenafil), the little blue pill described here, was introduced in 1998 as a treatment for **male impotence** or **erectile inhibition**. This disorder is defined in the chapter on sexuality as *inability to experience an erection*. Scientists estimate that 52 percent of the men between the ages of 40 and 70 years old may suffer from erectile dysfunction (Cappelleri, Bell, Althof, Siegel, & Stecher, 2006). However, men who have regular intercourse are less likely to experience impotence (Ma & Qin, 2009). Clearly, this is a case of "use it or lose it!" Within months of the introduction of Viagra, sales reached 4.5 million prescriptions a month, breaking the all-time record for all new drug sales. Since its introduction on the market, Viagra has been tried by more than 30 million men in 120 different countries (Hill & McKie, 2008). Given its success, Viagra was quickly followed in the intimacy products market by Cialis (generically named tadofil) and Levitra (vardenafil) (Harder, 2005).

Collectively, these drugs are known as PDE5 inhibitors. They work by blocking an enzyme that impedes blood flow to the penis and that, in turn, impedes erection (Harder, 2005). Diminished blood flow is the most common cause of erectile inhibition. Many studies to date demonstrate that these drugs successfully treat erectile dysfunction (e.g., Rosen, Shabsigh, Kuritzky, Wang, & Sides, 2006). The drug itself does not cause erection.

These drugs do not work for every man; they don't take effect immediately either and have some unwelcome physiological side effects, such as a flushed face and, worse, sudden blindness (Harder, 2005). That is one reason why a

doctor's prescription is really important. There are other causes of sexual dysfunction for both men and women. Depression and some of the medications used to treat high blood pressure, diabetes, prostate cancer, and other factors affect general and sexual health. That is why a regular physician's checkup is also important.

Although medications for erectile dysfunction can have a positive effect on marriage by increasing sexual satisfaction and intimacy, such medications may lead to two additional side-effects: adultery and sexually transmitted diseases (STDs). According to newspaper reports, Viagra-fueled adultery has led to an increase in older women seeking divorces from their sexually meandering husbands (Hill & McKie, 2008). With regard to STDs, although the greatest number are contracted during late adolescence and early adulthood (15 to 24 years of age), the incidence of HIV and AIDS is growing faster among individuals 50 and older compared to those under 40 (Levy, Ding, Lakra, Kosteas, Niccolai, 2007).

Nevertheless, the true psychological and societal value of such drugs may be that they

- bring sexual dysfunction into the open.

- motivate more men to see physicians for physical exams.

- prompt researchers to search for a comparable sexual enhancer for women.

In the meantime, research on these drugs continues. Because they function as vasodilators, they may prove effective as treatments for a wide range of other health problems related to the circulatory system. Viagra has already been reborn as Revatio, a drug used to treat certain lung diseases (Sternberg, 2005). Other studies are attempting to examine whether the PDE5 inhibitors can successfully treat Raynaud's syndrome, diabetes-induced kidney problems, heart failure, and certain complications of pregnancy (Harder, 2005).

AGING GRACEFULLY—LATE ADULTHOOD

Late adulthood is *the final stage of adult development, from the mid-60s to death, and is characterized by adjustment to changing health, income, and social roles.* Today, more than 40 million men and women are 65 years of age or older. At 64 years of age, Zena is about to join this group. By the year 2050, there will be nearly 89 million Americans 65 or older and 19 million 85 and older (U.S. Bureau of the Census, 2008). The "graying of America" will alter every aspect of society—business, education, government spending, housing, medical care, and leisure. The elderly often discover that old people don't fit well into our society. Bottle caps are too hard to get off, restaurants are too noisy, and doors are hard to open. Older adults frequently report problems using everyday items, and sometimes such problems can negatively impact the health of the individual (Fisk & Rogers, 2002). For instance, because of poor eyesight the elderly are at risk for misreading over-the-counter medications, resulting in adverse drug reactions (Pawaskar & Sansgiry, 2006).

At the beginning of this chapter, you were asked to answer some questions on what it is like to be old. In comparing your answers to those in the back, how did you do? Younger adults tend to provide stereotypical answers to these types of questions, and these stereotypes tend to be quite negative (Pecchioni & Croghan, 2002). Significantly, age stereotypes sometimes translate into age discrimination, as evidenced by the number of age-bias suits that have surged in recent years (Baldas, 2007). Such discriminatory experiences have led gerontologists to coin the term **ageism,** which refers to *negative attitudes toward and treatment of older Americans.* Ageism can be seen in the readiness with which people attribute all sorts of negative qualities to the elderly, mostly because of their age. For example, many younger people assume that the typical older person is helpless and frail and resides in a nursing home, despite the fact that over 90 percent of older adults are not in need of custodial care. Another symptom of ageism is that the elderly are often **infantilized** or *treated like infants, as, for example, when other adults speak to them in baby talk.* Such instances of ageism perpetuate stereotypes—false generalizations—about the elderly, thereby restricting their opportunities, undermining their personal dignity, and alienating them from the larger society. We need to become more sensitive to ageism because as the largest cohort group, the baby boomers, moves through historic time (Teichert, 2002), the elderly American population will continue to grow.

Physical and Cognitive Changes

The literature on *aging* has identified two distinct groups of elderly: one group aged 65 to 74, known as *the young elderly,* and another group aged 75 and beyond, known as *the old elderly.* These two groups differ psychologically and physically. Many of the young elderly are free of infirmity, whereas those in the old elderly experience more disability.

With increasing age, the skin wrinkles and becomes thinner, the hair grays; there is a reduction in the sharpness of vision and hearing; and the reflexes slow down (Wingfield, Tun, & McCoy, 2005). Some older people eat less because their sense of taste diminishes, they exercise less, and they have less physical energy for life. They also sleep less restfully, although they spend more time in bed compensating for this lack of sleep. The old elderly sometimes have more trouble maintaining their sense of balance. Deaths from falls occur twice as frequently as deaths from other accidents. Deaths from high blood pressure, cancer, and heart disease are also more common among the old elderly. These changes, however, do not necessarily have to result in disability, especially in the young elderly and those older elderly who continue to exercise and adopt healthy lifestyles (Fries, 2002; Kolata, 2002).

Box 3–4

HEALTHY AGING

For traditionally aged college students, old age may seem far away. For less traditional students, old age may be approaching. Each of us can start NOW practicing healthy techniques that can ensure a healthier old age. The sooner we start, the longer our life is likely to be and the better the quality of our health as we age.

- Exercise, exercise, exercise. Study after study shows the benefits even for the very old. Exercise lowers the risk of heart attacks, results in fewer hip fractures, and promotes better mental health.

- Stop smoking. No matter how long you have smoked, when you stop your health improves. Avoid the use of drugs (other than medications), and if you drink alcohol, drink only in moderation.

- Eat well. In the chapter on health, the food pyramid is reviewed. Refer to this pyramid daily. Avoiding sugars and fats also improves overall health and helps ward off diabetes and arteriosclerosis.

- Avoid stress. This is easier said than done in today's modern world. If stress is overtaking your life, refer to the chapter on stress and stress management.

- Develop and maintain outside interests.

- See a physician regularly. Some of the infirmities of aging are silent, such as high blood pressure. Preventive checkups earlier in life can ensure healthier aging later in life.

- Find and maintain a social support system. Social support for the elderly increases their morale, buffers the effects of the loss of loved ones, and enhances their self-esteem.

Fortunately, with improved understanding of aging and of the importance of good health care and supportive environments, we are discovering that older people can remain in reasonably good health and function better at the same age than their parents and grandparents did (*Harvard Health Letter,* 2002). We're also learning that many of the negative changes associated with aging are due to stress, disease, and lifestyle rather than to the aging process itself. Box 3–4 discusses ways we can approach aging as healthy individuals.

Cognitive functions can also continue to be affected by the aging process (Wingfield et al., 2005), although rarely to the extent that justifies the stereotype of the absent-minded old person having a "senior moment." In fact, scientists now know that cognitive decline in late life is *not* inevitable, as is often assumed (Wright, Kunz-Ebrecht, Iliffe, Foese, & Steptoe, 2005). For instance, the ability to use accumulated knowledge to make judgments and solve problems often remains the same, and in many instances can improve with age! Individuals can also maintain their creativity well into late adulthood, depending on their type of work. Artists hit their peak in their 40s; scientists maintain their creativity well into their 60s; and those in the humanities (e.g., historians and philosophers) may show a steady increase in creativity through their 70s. For example, Benjamin Franklin invented the bifocal lens at age 78, and actress Jessica Tandy won acting awards well into her 80s. It may be that any decreased creativity ordinarily seen among older people is due more to their restricted environments than to aging. About 16 percent of America's elderly have some mobility limitations, especially elderly women, who are more prone to osteoarthritis than men. Such limitations restrict the types of environments in which the elderly find themselves.

However, cognitive declines do occur in late adulthood. For instance, older adults tend to have more difficulty remembering information related to time, such as the order of their occurrence or which event occurred more recently (Hartman & Warren, 2005). Moreover, the ability to process new information based on perceptual skills and memory does decline somewhat in middle age and even more sharply in late adulthood (Phillips, 2005). As a result, older people may exhibit slower mental reactions and are often less adept at processing new information. Perhaps these findings partially explain why the rate of car accidents for the elderly is second only to that for teenagers. Of note, because of their frailty, elderly drivers are also more likely to die in car accidents, relative to their younger counterparts (Skyving, Berg, & LaFlamme, 2009). Zena had not yet given up driving but was very worried about her elderly mother who still wanted her independence and mobility.

Box 3–5 showcases other individuals who seemed at their peak of achievement in their old age.

Personal and Social Adjustment

As you recall, Erikson (1964) suggested that integrity also brings successful aging. For example, the elderly who concentrate on what they *can* do rather than on what they cannot do age more gracefully and experience less anxiety about aging. Thus, if the elderly are resilient and motivated rather than bitter and passive, aging is more successful. Those people with positive attitudes toward aging also live longer. One of the most important ingredients of successful aging is the ability to maintain an **internal locus of control** such that *an individual believes that something within him- or herself controls life events* or, basically, such that a person possesses a sense of independence. When the elderly feel that they have control over their fates, they tend to live longer, healthier lives (Gruenewald, Karlamangla, Greendale, Singer, & Seeman, 2009). Due to significant losses, such as the death of loved ones, the elderly sometimes perceive less control than younger adults. Older adults who cope with loss of control by maintaining or enhancing their competencies or by shifting the subjective importance of their personal goals adjust better to the aging process (Schulz & Heckhausen, 1996). Zena knew this and was trying her best to be one of the better-adjusted older individuals after the death of her husband and her father.

An important area of psychosocial change and therefore control involves living arrangements for the elderly. The young elderly, those individuals from 65 to 74 years of age, are more likely to live at home, be in better health, and be more financially comfortable than the old elderly. Nearly twice as many older women as men live alone. Conversely and logically, more than twice as many men as women live with their spouses. As mentioned earlier, many

Box 3–5

A FEW OF THE LATE, GREAT ACHIEVERS

Sophocles wrote *Oedipus Rex* when he was 70 and *Electra* when he was 90.

Michelangelo began work on St. Peter's Basilica at age 70.

Anna Mary Robertson ("Grandma") Moses took up painting as a hobby at 76 and later staged 15 one-woman shows throughout Europe.

Pablo Picasso married for the second time at 77 and completed three series of drawings between 85 and 90.

Laura Ingalls Wilder didn't publish her first book until age 65 and wrote some of her best children's stories during her 70s.

Mother Teresa continued her missionary work around the clock, helping less fortunate people throughout the world, until her death at age 87.

Artur Rubinstein gave one of his greatest piano performances at New York's Carnegie Hall at age 89.

Golda Meir was named prime minister of Israel at age 71 and held that office for five years.

Mahatma Gandhi led India's opposition to British rule when he was 77.

Frank Lloyd Wright completed New York's Guggenheim Museum at 89 and continued teaching until his death.

elderly prefer to stay in their own homes, but a small number of older people find they are unable to care for themselves. These individuals generally are the frail or old elderly. In fact, 97 percent of nursing home residents have at least one disability. Contrary to stereotypes, however, only a small portion of individuals 75 and older (7.5 percent) reside in nursing homes (Administration on Aging, 2009).

By the age of 85, only about one-half of all the old elderly live alone. Unfortunately, a significant proportion of the old are at or below the poverty level, making any living arrangement difficult. Poverty is a special problem for elderly women (Administration on Aging, 2009), especially elderly women of color. A much smaller proportion of old elderly lives with others, such as with a grown child, because of a desire for independence (i.e., autonomy or control) and privacy not found in facilities for the elderly. Other older people live near a grown child who visits frequently. In some instances, as mentioned earlier, elderly parents can assist their children with childcare, and the latter can help their parents with finances and emotional support in times of illness.

Because most married women will outlive their husbands, as did Zena, there are more widows than widowers among the elderly. Half of the women in the United States are widowed by their early 60s, and 80 percent by their early 70s. Among those over 65, widows outnumber widowers three to one. Women tend to adjust to the loss of their spouse more readily than men. Although, as mentioned earlier, older men are usually better off financially than older women, they tend to have more difficulty coping with routine household tasks, are lonelier, and are less happy than widows and older women. People who have remained single throughout their lives often feel more satisfied in late adulthood than do widows or widowers the same age, possibly because they have chosen a single lifestyle and have become better adjusted to it.

Friendships are very important to the elderly and influence their survival (Giles, Glonek, Luszcz, & Andrews 2005). Women often have an easier time making and keeping friends in their old age, partly because of the way they have been socialized and partly because of the

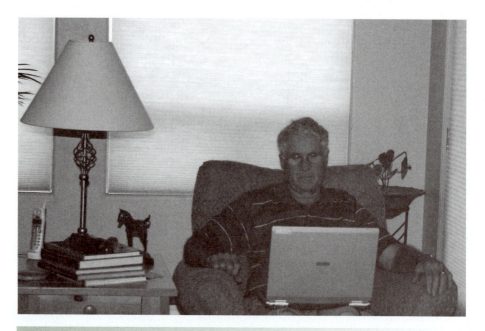

Cell phones and computers help maintain contact with friends and family. Widely embraced by teens and young adults, older adults are also adopting these technologies.

disproportionate number of older women. Yet with the reduction of social contacts at this age, friends become even more important to both sexes. People who continue to live in the same neighborhood as they get older, an increasingly frequent phenomenon, may keep in touch with their friends from the past. Other friends may be deceased, so the social networks of the old elderly are smaller, but they are just as close as those of younger people (Lang & Carstensen, 1994). Those who move elsewhere must make new friends. In both instances, friends can play as important a role as family members in preventing loneliness and disengagement from life among the elderly (Greenberg & Springen, 2001). This is perhaps why some people prefer to live in a retirement home or assisted living community, often in the Sunbelt of the South or Southwest. One such living facility found a unique but very modern method for keeping their elderly residents in contact with friends and family, no matter how distant—the Internet. In fact, such communications have been shown to ward off loneliness in the elderly. However, when older adults attempt to find *new* friends via the Internet, feelings of loneliness continue (Sum, Mathews, Hughes, & Campbell, 2008).

Retirement

The retirement experience, which varies considerably from one person to another, usually depends on several factors. Generally, the more voluntary the decision to retire is, the better the adjustment to retirement. Second, reasonably good health is also an important predictor for a satisfying retirement as well as for age of retirement; some people's retirements are related to poor health. Third, an adequate income is also very important at this age (Petkoska & Earl, 2009). It is the "perceived adequacy" of one's income rather than actual income that is the most crucial factor. Many seniors plan on living on Social Security after retirement, but the retirement age to receive this income is slowly rising. Social Security alone is generally not sufficient for the retired to maintain a reasonable standard of living (Moreau, 2002). Although retired people usually have a reduced income, they also have fewer major expenses such as mortgage payments or union dues, so their incomes may be sufficient for their present lifestyle. Those who have insufficient income after retirement are likely to continue to work, a phenomenon known as *bridge employment*. In fact, a "need for money" is the leading reason people continue to work after retirement from their primary jobs (Gobeski & Beehr, 2009). People from upper-level careers generally report a more favorable retirement experience, partly because they have ample income (Pinquart & Schindler, 2007).

Research on retirement demonstrates what Zena already knew—that retirees have the same levels of self-esteem as those who continue to work, and retirees are generally as well adjusted as non-retirees (Drentea, 2002); if anything, research demonstrates that retirement improves mental health (Mandal & Roe, 2008). Other factors that influence the decision to retire or continue to work include the need to be a caregiver, especially for women (Dentinger & Clarkberg, 2002), and whether the spouse will also retire (Pienta & Hayward, 2002). In retirement, volunteer work is the "work" most favored by retirees especially those who have sufficient funds (Carey & Ward, 2000).

Successful Aging

Which person does a better job of growing old gracefully—the individual who continues to work actively as a lawyer and keeps up an active social life or the person who retires to a rocking chair on the porch? Gerontologists who favor the **activity theory of aging** suggest that the more active a person remains, the more satisfied and better adjusted that person is likely to be, regardless of age. Those who adhere to the **disengagement**

theory of aging point out individuals tend to disengage from society with advancing age, with psychological disengagement usually preceding social withdrawal by about 10 years. Zena, for example, was content sometimes to sit in a chair, read, and listen to music. She also enjoyed doing volunteer work at her former place of employment, the community hospital. She was both active and disengaged, depending on the day.

As Zena's retirement demonstrates, there is no single way to age successfully, and different people adapt to old age in their own way. In her now classic research, Bernice Neugarten (1986) found that people tend to select a style of aging that best suits their personality, needs, and interests. Thus, an energetic, hard-working person will continue to tackle new projects, whereas a more contemplative person will probably do more reading. Neugarten found that some older people tend to benefit from activity more than others. For example, although those with a well-integrated personality generally adjusted better to old age regardless of how active they were, the less well-integrated exhibited better adjustment with higher levels of activity.

It's also important for individuals to feel an inner satisfaction with their lives as they grow older. Recall that in Erikson's theory (1964), the developmental task of older people is to establish a sense of integrity—a sense that one's life as a whole has been meaningful and satisfying. Those who have experienced a great deal of frustration and suffering may have more misgivings than satisfactions, experiencing despair and depression. Actually, people ordinarily experience both ego integrity and despair, but the healthier the person, the more self-acceptance and personal satisfaction will prevail.

Older people also obtain a sense of their lives as a whole by engaging in the **life review,** *a naturally occurring process of self-review prompted by the realization that life is approaching an end*. Although such a process can lead to wisdom and serenity, it may also evoke some negative feelings, such as regret, anger, guilt, or depression, or obsessional rumination about negative past events such as illness (Kraaij, Pruymboom, & Garnefski, 2002). The process consists of **reminiscence**—*thinking about oneself and reconsideration of past events and their meanings*. Some older people prefer to reminisce in private, whereas others may enjoy doing it more publicly, such as by making a family tree or telling their children and grandchildren about the significant aspects of their lives and family history. Such reminiscing serves to give them a final perspective of their lives while leaving a record of the past to their family and friends.

Summary

Adult Development

Human development is a lifelong process that includes psychological growth as well as biological changes, so that individuals tend to acquire greater coping skills and individuality with age and experience. Although adult development can be described in terms of three broad stages—early, middle, and late adulthood—the age boundaries are often fuzzy, and individual patterns of development vary considerably within each stage.

Decisions, Decisions, Decisions—Early Adulthood

The transition to adulthood from adolescence is more complex and prolonged than is ordinarily understood. Leaving home involves achieving emotional and psychological independence as well as moving out of the family home; going away to college is a natural transition for many people at this age. Close relationships are an important consideration for men and women at this age, and couples in which both partners put their relationship first seem happiest. Couples are giving more thought to whether they want children and, if so, when to have them.

SAME OLD, SAME OLD?—MIDDLE ADULTHOOD

Sometime in between the late 30s and the mid-40s, people experience the midlife transition, a time of personal evaluation that comes with the realization that life is half over. This does not necessarily mean a midlife crisis. The most obvious signs of middle age are certain physical changes such as graying hair and perhaps slower mental reactions. Midlife sometimes brings changes in careers for both sexes, with both women and men changing jobs or careers to fulfill their aspirations and many traditional women taking a job outside the home or returning to school. The biological and psychological changes that accompany the loss of reproductive abilities pose both new anxieties and new opportunities for both sexes, and men and women may experience a new stability in their marriages as they enter their 50s.

AGING GRACEFULLY—LATE ADULTHOOD

The literature on aging recognizes the young elderly and the old elderly, with the old elderly being more ill and less active. As people grow older, their physical functions progressively slow down. Although cognitive functions that depend mostly on one's knowledge base and problem solving may improve with age, memory for information related to time tends to decline. However, people's basic adaptive abilities tend to remain remarkably stable throughout adulthood. Satisfaction in retirement depends on a variety of factors, such as one's attitude toward retirement, health, income, and involvement in meaningful activities such as volunteer work. There is no single best way to age successfully, however, and each individual adapts to old age in his or her own way. Aging is an individualized process. Successful aging depends on one's social network, maintaining a sense of control, and positive reminiscing.

ANSWERS TO AGING QUIZ

1. True. Various aspects of hearing, vision, and touch decline in old age. In many cases, taste and smell also become less sensitive.

2. False. People lose very few of their neurons. The loss starts at about the age of 30 rather than in later adulthood.

3. True. Aged drivers have fewer accidents than those under 30 but more accidents than middle-aged people.

4. False. There are at least as many, if not more, differences among older individuals as among people at other age levels.

5. True. Because of the accumulation of antigens, older people suffer less from short-term ailments such as the common cold. However, the weakening of the immune system makes them more susceptible to life-threatening ailments, such as cancer and pneumonia.

6. False. Recognition memory shows little or no decline with age, in contrast to the marked decline in recall memory.

7. True. Slower reaction time is one of the best-documented facts about older people.

8. False. Less than 5 percent of the population over 65 lives in a nursing home during a given year.

9. False. Although older people become more aware of death, they tend to have less fear of it than other age groups.

10. True. There are more widows than widowers.

SELF-TEST

1. Which of the following is typically an age-related change?
   a. A career change
   b. Having one's first child
   c. Leaving home
   d. Menopause

2. Which of the following is a developmental task of young adulthood?
   a. Leaving home
   b. Choosing a career
   c. Finding a romantic partner
   d. All of the above

3. Compared to couples in the past, married couples are
   a. starting their families later.
   b. having more children.
   c. more likely to include a working husband and a stay-at-home wife.
   d. more desirous of girl than boy babies.

4. The period of personal evaluation that corresponds to the realization that one's life is half over is called
   a. the midlife transition.
   b. reminiscence.
   c. the climacteric.
   d. aging.

5. The most obvious signs of middle age are
   a. more colds and allergies.
   b. significant memory losses.
   c. fewer chronic illnesses.
   d. changes in physical appearance.

6. The correct term for the reduction in fertile sperm and lessened sexual vigor among middle-aged men is
   a. the climacteric.
   b. impotence.
   c. male menopause.
   d. sexual senility.

7. Stereotyping of the elderly is known as
   a. infantilization.
   b. ageism.
   c. climacterosis.
   d. generationism.

8. Older adults that have memory problems but are otherwise healthy and functional are often said to be suffering from
   a. Alzheimer's disease.
   b. "senior" moments.
   c. mild cognitive impairment.
   d. menopause.

9. What factor(s) is (are) most important in determining how people will adjust to retirement?
   a. Health status
   b. Whether retirement was voluntary
   c. Income status
   d. All of these are important

10. What has happened to the number of age-discrimination cases?
   a. They have decreased over time.
   b. They have increased, but only for men.
   c. Overall, they have increased.
   d. There has been no change.

EXERCISES

1. *How have you grown as an adult?* Write a brief paragraph describing your personal development since adolescence. In what ways has your personality changed or remained the same? Comment on the factors that have contributed to your personal growth, such as success at school, disappointment in love, or new responsibilities at work.

2. *Leaving home.* Describe your experience with leaving home. If you're already living on your own, how peaceful or stormy was your departure? If you're still living at home or are away at college part of the year, how well are you coming to terms with this developmental task? How helpful are your parents in this matter?

3. *The midlife transition.* If you're going through the midlife transition or have completed this stage, write a page or so describing your experience. If you are not middle-aged, write about what you think the experience will be like. To what extent has this been, or do you think this will be, a stressful time or crisis for you?

4. *Widows and widowers.* Select an older person you know well who has outlived his or her spouse, including yourself if this applies to you, and comment on how well this person has adjusted to living alone. What has been the most difficult adjustment? Has the experience of loss also brought about personal growth?

5. *Successful aging.* Select someone in your family who has reached late adulthood, such as an aunt, uncle, or grandparent. Or perhaps this applies to you. Then comment on how successfully the person has aged. To what extent has the person kept active or become disengaged from his or her environment? Has this person also grown old in his or her own distinctive way? How has your relationship with this person affected your understanding of aging?

QUESTIONS FOR SELF-REFLECTION

1. In what ways have you mellowed with age and experience?

2. Would you agree that leaving home involves more than moving out of the family home?

3. What were your parents like at your age?

4. At what stage of adulthood are you now? Does this differ from your perceived favorite age?

5. Are you aware that the midlife transition doesn't have to be a crisis? What characteristics of middle age make others assume that the transition is really a crisis?

6. Why do older people report feeling younger than they really are?

7. What kind of older people were you familiar with as a child? Did these experiences fashion your stereotypes of the elderly? If not, what did fashion your anticipated trajectory into old age?

8. What would you like to do when you retire? Why?

9. Do you think that our personal traits become more pronounced with age?

10. What do you think it would be like to live in a nursing home?

FOR FURTHER INFORMATION

RECOMMENDED READINGS

FOGG, N. P., HARRINGTON, P., & HARRINGTON, T. (2004). *College majors handbook with real career paths and payoffs: The actual jobs, earnings, and trends for graduates of 60 college majors.* Indianapolis, IN: Jist Publishing. The title of this book says it all; it is a compendium of useful information about how to match yourself with majors and careers.

FREEMAN, C. (2005). *Creating magic at midlife: 101 questions and answers to reinvent your work, relationships and life!* Santa Barbara, CA: Philogenesis. Written by a clinical social worker, this book helps any middle-aged individual understand that only half of life has been lived. The second half can be just as wonderful and productive as the first half.

HARVEY, J. H., & WEBER, A. L. (2002). *Odyssey of the heart: Close relationships in the 21st century.* Mahwah, NJ: Lawrence Erlbaum. This book provides research on how, why, and when close relationships develop. The book also examines issues such as the conflict between work and family, whether to have children, why divorce occurs, whether cohabitation is a good idea, etc.

NOVAK, M. (2005). *Issues in aging.* Boston: Allyn & Bacon. This book of readings is written for those who are aging as well as those who work with or care for them. The book also discusses what the burgeoning aging population means for U.S. society.

WEBSITES AND THE INTERNET

http://www.employmentguide.com A rich source of information on careers, internships, networking, resume development, and other useful information for job seekers.

http://www.alzheimers.org This is the website for information on Alzheimer's disease with good information for patients and families about this disabling disease.

http://www.caregiving.com The site for finding out about elder care. A good place to find information for those caring for a frail elderly family member.

http://www.aarp.org The website for the largest advocacy group for the elderly, the American Association for Retired Persons. Contains information on the association's advocacy programs, information on retirement and aging, and government lobbying on behalf of our aging population.

http://www.ncoa.org This is the website of the National Council on Aging, a site replete with information about growing older and advocacy for the elderly.

Seeking Selfhood

Shandra was shopping with a friend. She stopped to admire the clothes in a shop window. "Let's go in," suggested her friend. They entered the store and browsed for a few minutes. Then Shandra tried on a pair of jeans. Looking at herself in the mirror, she noticed her hair was in disarray. She instinctively straightened it so that it appeared more the way she wanted it to look. She then noticed that she must have gained 10 or 15 pounds and that her usual size was too tight. Shandra knew she couldn't lose that much weight in a few minutes, so she tried various ways of reconciling her appearance in the mirror with her self-image. She first asked her friend how she looked in the jeans, and her friend replied, "Not bad, but they may be a little tight around your rear end." She then tried on a larger size, but the very idea bothered her. Shandra decided to put off buying new clothes to avoid looking at herself in the mirror. She was also inspired to resume her weight-loss program. One thing is clear from Shandra's shopping spree—the discrepancy between self-concept and the image in the mirror has a powerful influence on behavior.

WHAT IS SELF-CONCEPT?

Essentially, the **self-concept** is *the overall image or awareness we have of ourselves. It includes all those perceptions of "I" and "me," together with the feelings, beliefs, and values associated with them.* As such, the self-concept is actually a complex concept made up of a multiplicity of selves, even though we habitually refer to it in the singular. Ordinarily, we take our self-concept for granted, as when we are engaged in an activity at work or play. At other times, we are very much aware of ourselves, as when we're making an important decision, taking on a heavy responsibility, or are feeling embarrassed. We also may become acutely self-conscious whenever we experience a discrepancy between our self-image and the way we appear to others. In all of these instances, the self-concept exerts a powerful influence, affecting the way we perceive, judge, and behave.

The self-concept provides you, Shandra, and others with a personal identity or sense of who we are. Even though situations and people around us change, our self-concept reassures us that we are basically the same person we were yesterday. In other words, there is coherence or consistency to our thoughts and actions (Nail, Misak, & Davis, 2004). Not only does our self-image sometimes appear more real to us than our bodies, but it also governs the way in which we view our bodies. Our sense of self is so important that we typically resist anyone or anything that threatens it (Mezulis, Abramson, Hyde, & Hankin, 2004). Even the fear of death itself may not be a fear of suffering or of the unknown, so much as it is the deep fear that our personal identity will be dissolved (Pyszczynski & Cox, 2004)—which, for many, is inconceivable.

Research on how we incorporate information about ourselves into our self-concept suggests just this, that we actively manage our self-concept such that we try to maintain a positive view of ourselves (Mezulis et al., 2004). We typically seek positive information about ourselves from our friends and families and from our performance at work or in school or elsewhere. When confronted with information that could have a number of meanings, we generally choose to interpret it in the most positive way we can (Sedikides & Koole, 2004). In other words, most people adopt a **self-serving attributional bias,** defined as *beliefs that glorify the self or conceive of the self as causing the good outcomes that come our way.* For example, we often take personal credit for our successes but blame external causes for our failures.

How many selves we choose to distinguish within our overall self-concept varies by the individual and with age (Bybee & Wells, 2003). At a general level, however, it is common to identify four types of self:

- **Body image,** *the awareness of my body*
- The **self-image,** *the self I see myself to be*
- The **ideal self,** *the self I'd like to be*
- The **social self,** *the ways I feel others see me*

Because body image is discussed in great detail in Chapter 5, let's begin here by looking at the self-image and the ideal self. We'll examine the importance of our social selves in a later section of this chapter.

Self-Image

As noted above, self-image is *the way you see yourself.* It is primarily made up of the many self-perceptions we have acquired growing up and by the way we are currently seen and treated by significant others, especially by our romantic partners. Across the formative years, youth tend to internalize what others think of them—their judgments and expectations—and regard the self accordingly. For example, during middle childhood, teasing by family members can lead to a negative self-image, as indicated by low self-esteem and depression (Keery, Boutelle, van den Berg, & Thompson, 2005). Now, imagine *the long-term* impact of having a parent constantly direct very negative statements (e.g.,"Don't do that, Stupid!" and "What's wrong with you?") on a child's self image. Nevertheless, childhood experiences can be overcome, as we tend to revise our self-images through more recent experience with others, especially with our friends, lovers, teachers, and spouses. However, even a stranger's opinion can influence us now and then (Murray, 2005).

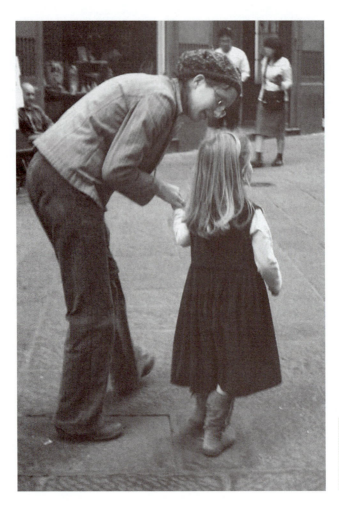

The long-term impact of a parent's constantly criticizing a child can be the loss of the child's self-esteem.

Ideal Self

Another aspect of self is the **ideal self**, that is, *the self you would like to be, including your aspirations, moral ideals, and values.* The ideal self can be a reflection of who we currently are or a portrait of whom we would like to become. However, if the ideal self is quite different from the real self, **social anxiety** (*extreme shyness that can interfere with daily life*) and other psychological problems may result. For example, adolescent girls suffering from bulimia nervosa (a psychological disorder characterized by binge eating and purging) tend to have an ideal self that is vastly different (and thinner) than the real self (Granberg, 2006).

With experience and maturity, our aspirations should increasingly represent self-chosen goals and values (i.e., self-directedness) that express in a healthy, adult way what we've come to expect of *ourselves.* Consequently, our ideal self may serve as an incentive for us to do our best. If we fail to live up to our ideal self, as can be the case, it is healthy to feel we have a choice either to redouble our efforts to achieve our aspirations or to modify them in the direction of more fruitful goals. Ordinarily, we think of having to change our self-image and behavior to better match our ideals. In those instances when our aspirations prove to be excessive or unrealistic, it may be more appropriate for us to modify our ideal self as a way of furthering our growth and self-esteem.

How would you characterize your own ideal self? Do you tend to be idealistic and rather hard on yourself when you fall short of your aims? Or are you more down-to-earth and practical-minded, shrugging off disappointments with yourself and giving it another try? To check on your perceptions, you might do the exercise on self-image and ideal self in Activity 4–1 (page 78).

Multiple Selves

As mentioned above, the overall self-concept is an organized cluster of selves, so it would be more accurate to speak of our multiple selves or **self-complexity** (McConnell et al., 2005). Self-complexity is *the extent to which one's self-concept is comprised of many differentiated self-aspects.* Some self-images arise from the experience of our own bodies. Others reflect needs, interests, traits, and habits acquired through experience, and these self-images may be integrated within our overall self-concept in varying degrees. As such, the self-concept includes hundreds, perhaps thousands, of self-perceptions with varying degrees of clarity and intensity that we have acquired over a lifetime. For example, Shandra's self-concept included her gender role, her body image, her racial identity, her concept of herself as a student, her attitudes and values and whether they were respected by society, and many other components. Interestingly, some individuals have more complex and differentiated selves than do others (Bigler, Neimeyer, & Brown, 2001).

Psychologists now possess evidence that these multiple aspects of self vary greatly from culture to culture (Markus & Kitayama, 2003). For example, self-concepts of the Japanese often include a familial (family-oriented) self as well as a spiritual self, neither of which may play a prominent part in the self-concepts of White Americans (Miller, 1999). Additional research shows that Koreans tend to tolerate inconsistencies in the self-concept better than Americans (Choi & Choi, 2002). Much of the diversity of the self reflects our social and cultural roles, so that even the normally happy person wears "many masks." Much recent research, however, has demonstrated that there is one fairly universal aspect of self, the tendency to evaluate oneself favorably, known as *self-enhancement,* which will be discussed shortly (Sedikides, Gaertner, & Vevea, 2005).

Our various selves usually do exhibit a certain consistency or organizing pattern as a whole (Nail et al., 2004); we refer to them collectively as the self-concept. Think of the self-concept as the "glue" that holds our various experiences, behaviors, and feelings together. People with a fragmented, incoherent view of themselves—such as the severely emotionally disordered—are often unsure of who they are and may behave in a highly inconsistent manner. In contrast, those of us who have achieved a more desirable integration of our various selves may feel a clearer sense of personal identity and behave in a somewhat more consistent manner—"somewhat" because, as we've just described, even the healthiest person's psychic makeup includes a considerable degree of inconsistency. Indeed, self-clarity is related to well-being and adjustment (Bigler et al., 2001).

ACTIVITY 4–1

SELF-IMAGE AND IDEAL SELF

This is an exercise to measure the correspondence between your self-image and ideal self. Reproduce the box containing items A through P. Then cut out the 16 cards or rectangles as indicated by the lines and put them on a table or desk in random order.

First, you're to get a profile of your self-image, or the self you see yourself to be. To do so, arrange the cards in a line, either from top to bottom or left to right. At one end, place the statement that you think describes you best. Then arrange the remaining cards in order, ranging from the next most true and so forth to the least true at the end. Then record the rank number of each item in the column labeled "self." For instance, if you placed card A in the eighth position write "8" next to card A.

Next, repeat this procedure in regard to your ideal self. That is, arrange the cards in the order that describes the self you'd like to be, ranging from the card that you wish were most true of you at one end to that which is least true of your ideal self at the other end. When you've completed your rankings, record the order of the items or cards in the column labeled "ideal."

When you finish ranking the cards and recording the numbers, consult the scoring key at the end of the chapter.

I'm a likable person A	I have sex appeal I
I'm rather self-centered at times B	I'm an anxious person J
I'm physically attractive C	I have above-average intelligence K
I have a strong need for approval D	I'm shy in groups L
I'm usually a hard worker E	I have a good sense of humor M
I daydream too much F	I'm sometimes dishonest N
I can be assertive when necessary G	I have a good disposition O
I often feel discouraged H	I gossip a lot P

Item	Self	Ideal	Differences
A			
B			
C			
D			
E			
F			
G			
H			
I			
J			
K			
L			
M			
N			
O			
P			
		Sum of differences	

CORE CHARACTERISTICS OF SELF-CONCEPT

Critics of the notion of self-concept complain that traditional psychology regards the self-concept as a straitjacket that once acquired during our formative years resists further efforts at change. A more appropriate approach, they contend, would be to view the self-concept as a loosely fitting garment that is continually being altered with experience. Actually, there is some truth to both views.

Once established, the core of the self-concept (i.e., *those aspects of ourselves we regard as very important to us*) generally exhibits a high degree of stability, as seen in the consistent ways we perceive ourselves over time. For example, Shandra was very proud of a core concept dear to her heart—her African American heritage—and little could shake her pride in her racial identity. In contrast, rather peripheral aspects of the self (e.g., musical tastes, food preferences, clothing style) can, and often do, change rather quickly. Essentially, the self-concept functions as a filter through which everything we see or hear passes (Christensen, Wood, & Barrett, 2003). It thereby exerts a selective influence on our experience, so that we typically tend to perceive, judge, and act in ways that are consistent with our self-concept.

Self-Consistency

This characteristic tendency toward self-clarity (Bigler et al., 2001) is known as **self-consistency** (*our tendency to perceive our experiences in a manner consistent with our self-concept*). Experiences that are consistent with our self-concept tend to be perceived accurately and admitted fully into our conscious awareness. These self-perceptions tend to make up the core of our self-concept. Experiences that are *not* consistent with our self-concept are perceived more selectively and sometimes inaccurately. Such experiences are either distorted or kept from awareness. For instance, people will *trivialize threatening information* (e.g., failing a test) *by making the behavior seem less important* (e.g., saying "I don't need this class for my major), a process referred to as **self-immunization** (Greve & Wentura, 2003). Similarly, **mnemonic neglect,** involves *poor recall (or forgetting) of negative feedback that is inconsistent with core aspects of the self-concept.* For example, individuals have difficulty recalling adjectives that are inconsistent with their self-perceptions. In fact, one study found that, during assessments of memory, words were often transformed to similar-sounding words with the opposite meaning (e.g., hopeful becomes hopeless; satisfied becomes dissatisfied), thus creating consistency between self-perceptions and words describing the self (Cartwright, 1956).

Self-Esteem

One of the most important aspects of the self-concept is our **self-esteem**—*the personal evaluation of ourselves and the resulting feelings of worth associated with our self-concept*. Self-esteem is affected by a variety of influences, ranging from significant childhood experiences to our own standards or ideal self and beyond to our general culture (Markus & Kitayama, 2003). Individuals with high self-esteem appear to have been raised by parents who were supportive, expressed a lot of affection, and established firm but reasonable rules. Individuals with low self-esteem usually were brought up by parents who relied on parenting styles that were overly strict, overly permissive, or inconsistent (Park, Crocker, & Mickelson, 2004).

Our self-esteem is also influenced by success and failure, although there is often a low correspondence between people's self-views and their actual performance (Dunning, Heath, & Suls, 2004). Psychologists once thought that a backlog of stored success enhanced self-esteem and repeated failure undermined it. For example, it was once thought that praising children for their successes or achievements would make children think they were intelligent and, thus, give them more confidence. However, recent and important research has demonstrated this is not quite true. Praising children for their *efforts,* rather than for their intelligence, results in children's desire for more challenges. Children obsessed with their own intelligence are afraid to take risks, which may trigger maladaptive achievement patterns (Dweck, 1999).

At the same time, the impact of a particular achievement often depends on the process of comparison with a reference group (Leary, 1999) or on fear of social rejection by one's own group (Sommer & Baumeister, 2002). *The process of using others to compare ourselves to in order to understand who we are relative to them* is known as **social comparison.** Thus, individuals with similar talents and success may vary in their self-esteem, depending on to whom they compare themselves. Interestingly, we often prefer to compare ourselves with friends or others engaged in the same task (Seta, Seta, & McElroy, 2006). Table 4–1 will help you identify some of the signs of high and low self-esteem in yourself.

Although people customarily speak of self-esteem as a single entity—global esteem—our self-esteem also includes many compartmentalized or situation-specific aspects, which vary according to circumstances. For instance, another of Shandra's friends, Mark, enjoyed a great deal of self-confidence while playing tennis but lacked confidence in his writing skills in English composition. Such experiences tend to cluster our self-esteem into four main areas: physical attractiveness, physical abilities, cognitive abilities, and social relationships (Harter, 2006). Thus, our overall self-esteem is more complex than ordinarily portrayed and fluctuates somewhat depending on our experiences (Crocker & Wolfe, 2001).

Self-esteem exerts a powerful influence on people's expectations and their judgments about themselves and others as well as on their behavior (Dunning et al., 2004). Consider the following findings as evidence of this: individuals with high self-esteem do better in school, are more likely to persist in the face of failure, more frequently exit bad interpersonal relationships, and perform better on their jobs than individuals with low self-esteem. The strongest positive finding about self-esteem, though, is that people with high self-esteem are happier (or less depressed) than those with low self-esteem (Baumeister, Campbell, Krueger, & Vohs, 2005). However, positive consequences are *not* always associated with high self-esteem, for it can also be related to antisocial behaviors, such as cheating on tests and annoying or interrupting others. Bullies, for example, often possess overly inflated self-esteem. Another downside is that there is little evidence to show that high self-esteem creates better health for the individual. For example, high

TABLE 4–1	
HIGH AND LOW SELF-ESTEEM	
Signs of High Self-Esteem **Do you . . .**	**Signs of Low Self-Esteem** **Do you . . .**
like your appearance when you see yourself in the mirror?	avoid viewing yourself in the mirror?
feel comfortable with yourself most of the time?	feel discontented with yourself most of the time?
savor your accomplishments?	brag excessively or apologize about your achievements?
regard your failures as opportunities to learn?	make excuses for your failures?
express your opinions readily?	withhold your views, especially if asked?
listen to what others say, even if you disagree?	try to convince others of your views?
accept compliments graciously?	reject compliments or qualify them?
give credit to others when it's due?	envy others and put them down by sarcasm or gossip?
make realistic demands on yourself?	expect too much or too little of yourself?
give and receive affection generously?	withhold your affection out of fear of being hurt?

esteem does not prevent or inhibit cigarette smoking, alcohol or drug abuse, or premarital sexual behavior (Baumeister, Campbell, Krueger, & Vohs, 2003).

In addition, *how* people strive for self-esteem may be just as important, if not more important, for personal growth and adjustment than *whether* their level of self-esteem is either high or low (Crocker & Park, 2004). Here's why:

- Pursuing self-esteem results in mistakes, failures, threats, and other negative consequences that cause anxiety.

- Anxiety inhibits learning, especially from feedback designed to help the esteem-seeker.

- Autonomy or choice is influenced negatively, too. When people in hot pursuit of self-esteem feel they have no choice but to persist, they experience pressure and tension.

- Pursuing self-esteem also negatively impacts relationships because it focuses the pursuer on the self rather than on others who also want attention.

In the end, seeking self-esteem may cause distress in many areas and consequently affect one's physical and mental health in harmful ways. Interestingly, one "cure" for questing for self-esteem is to turn from self-directedness to other-directedness: seeking goals that are beneficial to others as much as or more than to the self (Crocker & Knight, 2005). Another solution may be to seek a self-directed or self-determined life (Pyszczynski & Cox, 2004), as urged in Chapter 1. Seeking self-created standards rather than pursuing self-esteem reduces defensiveness and other negative consequences associated with striving for self-esteem. Shandra, for example, admired the Civil Rights leader Dr. Martin Luther King, because he based his pursuit of racial equality not on what he wanted for himself, but on principles he wished for everyone in our society. In the end, such self-determined standards of value become thoroughly integrated with one's core sense of self (Pyszczynski & Cox, 2004).

Self-Enhancement and Self-Verification

We receive a great deal of information about how people see us through our interactions with them. As a matter of fact, we often make deliberate attempts to elicit such information, whether through actions or direct questioning, and in the modern era, through the Internet as well. Social networking sites, such as Facebook and MySpace, allow individuals to "blog" their lives, post pictures, videos, self-descriptors, etc. and *invite* people to comment. As it turns out, more than 75 percent of the time posted comments are positive (Valkenburg, Peter, & Schouten, 2006). Scientists have proposed different theories concerning the actual kind of reaction or feedback we solicit from others. According to **self-enhancement theory,** *people will try to get positive feedback that affirms their own ideas about their positive qualities.* Most people prefer and seek out positive feedback about themselves, especially for those attributes that they themselves view as positive (primarily because positive self-views are generally adaptive, Taylor & Brown, 1994). Along the same line of thinking, people's autobiographical memory induces them to perceive themselves as better and better over time (e.g., Ross & Wilson, 2003).

In contrast, in accordance with **self-verification theory,** *people want to preserve their own images (both positive and negative) of themselves and therefore elicit feedback that verifies or confirms their own self-perceptions.* Thus, self-verification is important to us, in that it gives us a sense of stability or consistency in an unpredictable world. Also, such confirmation is vital to social interaction because if others see us as we see ourselves, they will have a better idea of how to treat us, what to expect of us, and so forth. In sum, people generally prefer to hear opinions that are positive but also supportive of their own views of themselves.

However, basing self-worth on external sources (such as social standards) is more related to negative psychological outcomes than basing self-worth on more internal aspects of self, such as being a virtuous person. For instance, investment in gender ideals (e.g., men should be independent, decisive, and emotional stable; women should be caring, supportive, emotionally expressive) negatively affects self-esteem for both men and women (Sanchez & Crocker, 2005). Nevertheless, there are some documented sex differences related to the self. Women report engaging more in self-reflection than men do (Rudman & Goodwin, 2004). Similarly, women, especially Western women, possess greater **self-clarity,** *which is the extent to which one's individual self-beliefs are clearly and confidently defined, internally consistent, and stable* (Csank & Conway, 2004). Overall, though, the bulk of the research shows that men's and women's self-esteem levels are not necessarily different (Pierson & Glaeser, 2002).

Can the same be said for racial and ethnic minorities? By definition, **minority groups** *are relatively small in number and/or have less power as compared to majority groups.* Some have suggested that being in a minority group, and noticing differences between the self and members of the majority group, places the individual at a disadvantage for self-esteem. However, research does not support this contention. For instance, in the United States, the self-esteem of racial minorities is just as high as or higher than that of the racial majority, Whites (Twenge & Crocker, 2000). To accomplish this, minorities use some self-protective mechanisms for maintaining self-esteem. For example, members of minority groups often compare themselves to each other rather than to the White majority. In addition, many minority-group members attribute negative feedback and failure to prejudice and discrimination against their group rather than to personal failure (Major, Kaiser, & McCoy, 2003).

However, other recent research has suggested that people repeatedly perceiving themselves to be or actually being the victims of discrimination and prejudice cannot avoid having their psychological adjustment or self-concept negatively impacted. Likewise, the relationship between prejudice and self-concept may be more complex than thought. For example, the relationship between perceived discrimination and self-esteem may well vary across ethnic groups, with individuals from some groups more negatively affected by prejudice than are other groups (Cassidy, O'Connor, Howe, & Warden, 2004).

THE SELF-CONCEPT AND PERSONAL GROWTH

As mentioned earlier, your self-concept continues to change as you mature and develop. Indeed, there is growing recognition that the cluster of selves comprising the self-concept can and does change to a greater extent than previously realized. Self-esteem, for example, is relatively high in childhood, drops during adolescence (particularly for girls), rises gradually throughout adulthood, and then declines in old age (Robins & Trzesniewski, 2005). These developmental trends appear to hold regardless of ethnicity.

Much of the change in our self-concept occurs with experience, but a great deal of change in our self-image comes from adapting to different people and situations (Sanchez & Crocker, 2005). Job changes, new friends, and modifications in responsibilities, like marriage and parenting, all affect the way we see ourselves. Although we retain a stable core of self, the many self-perceptions that make up our overall self-concept are in a state of flux or change and are more readily influenced by current experience than previously thought.

The Self You'd Like to Be

Americans spend millions of dollars every year in the hope of improving themselves. They buy self-help books and CDs, and they attend workshops designed to make you "a better you." One promising approach to self-improvement, and one that will not cost you a dime, consists of visualizing the person you'd like to become—the thin self, the confident self, or the rich self. **Visualization,** also known as **guided imagery,** is *a procedure that helps a person shut off the outside world and bypass the censor we call the brain, enabling the person to see, experience, and learn from an intuitive, feeling, unconscious nature* (Leviton & Leviton, 2004). Visualization has successfully been used to improve performance during sporting activities, reduce perceived levels of stress, improve the immune system, and enhance the comfort of people undergoing medical procedures, such as chemotherapy and wound debridement (Grocke, 2005; Roffe, Schmidt, & Ernst, 2005; Short, Ross-Stewart, & Monsma, 2006; Trakhtenberg, 2008). Visualization works, in part, because it creates a state of **psychological absorption,** during which *emotions, cognitions, and experiences related to the real world are not consciously processed in the typical manner.* The individual not only becomes less aware of their current emotional state (including those related to anxiety), but also of the passage of time (Funk, Chan, Brouwer, & Curtiss, 2006).

Visualizing your "possible selves," including the desired as well as the feared selves, helps you not only to attain goals but also to cope more effectively with the present. A major implication is that we can create new images of ourselves, and this ability, in turn, may help us to handle our present lives more effectively. To help realize your aim of self-improvement, you might elaborate the self or selves you'd like to be. Imagine as vividly as possible how you'll look, how you'll feel, and how you'll act. It also helps to create an image of any feared self, that is, the self that would result if you don't succeed. Think of the failed attempts to lose weight, the mediocre performances in school and at work, and the disappointments in love. Then visualize a better you; a you created from using different strategies to overcome failure. Self-change is difficult but not impossible (Polivy & Herman, 2000). In each instance, vivid mental images of our possible selves may help us to become the person we'd like to be, especially when accompanied by the appropriate efforts. Activity 4–2 (page 84) will help you think more about the person you would like to be.

Our Social Selves

As stated repeatedly above, one of the most common ways our self-concept changes is through our interactions with people, including their perceptions of and reactions toward us. The term **social selves** refers to *the impressions we think others have of us.* It is the way we *think* they view us, which may not necessarily be an accurate representation of their actual views. Nevertheless, our *perception* of how others view us, in turn, greatly influences the way we see ourselves.

We have as many different social selves because we see ourselves somewhat differently with each person we meet. With a stranger, we may be guarded and unsure of ourselves, at least until we get to know what kind of person we're dealing with. A bossy, critical employer may make us feel anxious and inferior, but a close friend who admires and compliments us makes us feel confident and affectionate. It's not that we're being two-faced or untrue to ourselves. Rather, each of these people brings out a different aspect of self. Realizing this fact, we might make a greater effort to seek out people who bring out the best in us.

ACTIVITY 4–2

VISUALIZE THE PERSON YOU'D LIKE TO BE

Select a quiet place where you can relax and have a few minutes to yourself. Then close your eyes and imagine, as vividly as possible, the kind of person you'd like to become.

How would you look?
What would you be wearing?
How would you feel?
Would you be happy, serious, or relaxed?
What would you be doing?
Where would you be?

You might repeat this exercise every night before you go to sleep—say, for a week. Do you notice any difference in yourself?

We can make errors, though, when we assess feedback about ourselves from others. For example, frequently *we overestimate how prominent our own behaviors, appearance, and emotions are to others;* a phenomenon known as the **spotlight effect** (Libby, Eibach, & Gilovich, 2005). In other words, we think the spotlight shines more brightly on us than it really does. Additionally, because we tend to critique ourselves harshly, most individuals expect others to judge them *more harshly* than they really do (Gilovich & Savitsky, 1999).

The way we see ourselves is also vitally affected by the way we behave in different roles and situations. Often, the way we see ourselves leads us to act in a given manner. Equally often, we act in a certain way, and that action, in turn, changes the way we perceive ourselves and the way others see us. As a result, countless qualities—obedience, assertiveness, competitiveness, compassion, ambition, self-worth, and happiness—change remarkably with a change in our circumstances. For instance, our jobs affect us more than we affect our jobs. Many aspects of work, such as routinization, the complexity of tasks, advancement, fringe benefits, and peers, significantly change our self-image, self-worth, job commitment, and moral standards. Thus, many qualities attributed to the self-concept are keyed to what we *do* rather than to our inner notions of what we are.

The realization that our sense of self is affected by social and cultural influences heightens the importance of our social roles and social relationships (Srivastava & Beer, 2005). Once we have chosen to associate with certain friends, select a lover or marriage partner, or attend a given school or job, the people involved help to shape the way we see ourselves. Because of this we need to ask, "Are there overly critical people who devalue us?" We probably should avoid them. "Are there others who see the best in us?" Perhaps we should seek them out more often. In both instances, we can change the way we see ourselves by modifying the social influences on our lives. It would be foolish to think we can change everything about ourselves in this way or that we can always avoid negative people. But the notion of fluid, changing social selves reminds us that we have more possibilities for change and personal growth than we may be using.

Learning from Criticism

How do you feel when you are criticized? Do you feel angry and rejected? Do you feel resentful, even when you're in the wrong? For most people, the answer to these questions is yes. When people have been asked to finish the statement "When I am criticized . . . ," typical responses include "I get upset," "I resent it," "I feel she doesn't love me anymore," and "I wonder when the ax will fall." Sound familiar? All too often, as these comments suggest, people feel that criticism is a personal attack that they must defend themselves against at all costs. As a result, they waste a lot of energy worrying about criticism, justifying themselves, and going to great lengths to avoid it.

Accepting criticism can become a valuable means of personal growth. For example, when asked to complete the statement cited earlier, some people make more positive responses. For example, Shandra said to her friend, "Criticism tells me where the other person is coming from, how that person sees me, and what he or she expects of me." Another example involves an experienced executive who said, "Your critics can tell you where you're going wrong before your friends can." Thus, it is possible to learn the valuable art of taking criticism constructively.

You should perhaps view criticism as a valuable source of new information to be evaluated objectively. Each time you're criticized, you don't necessarily have to rush out and change something about yourself. Instead, criticism should be taken as a cue that *may* require action. Consider also how many times a specific criticism is offered. If several people offer the same criticism for the same behavior, there's a good chance that the criticism is valid and should be acted on. Ask yourself too, "How important is this criticism?" The more important the information is to you, the more likely you'll need to do something about it. Also consider the source of the criticism. Often, people feel they're being criticized unfairly, especially if the other person is under a lot of stress. The more qualified the person is to judge you, the more you should take his or her criticism to heart. Even criticism spoken in frustration or anger may need to be heeded, but take into account the exaggerated emotion of the messenger.

Weigh the pros and cons of acting on a criticism. You should decide whether the benefits that come from acting on the criticism balance or outweigh the effort involved. For example, students who do poorly on tests may wonder whether it's worthwhile to follow the teacher's suggestion to get help in reading comprehension and note-taking skills. On the other hand, if they continue to get low grades, their career goals may be in jeopardy. Put the emotional energy aroused by criticism to work for you, not against you. In addition to interfering with a person's ability to perform well, emotional arousal may also negatively influence self-confidence. Instead, when criticized, try to stay calm. Relax physically. Remind yourself that nobody is trying to hurt you. What this person is saying may be helpful. Then use your emotions as a source of energy to make the necessary changes.

Finally, take positive steps to put the needed changes into action. Don't waste energy defending yourself. Instead, listen carefully to what is being said. Ask for more information. Ask the person for suggested solutions to the criticism. You might ask for this information indirectly, such as, "If you were in my place, what would you do?" Or you might ask, more directly, "What would you like me to do?" People usually criticize something we're doing. But it often comes across as a personal attack because many people do not know how to give criticism constructively. So if someone says, "You're rude and inconsiderate," ask, "In what ways have I been inconsiderate? How would you suggest I

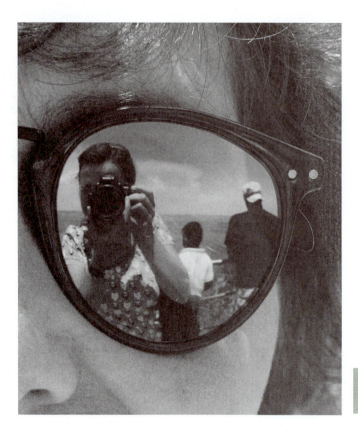

Feedback from others can serve as a useful mirror to the self.

behave?" In this way, you'll focus on something tangible that you can do, which in due time may lead to the desired changes in your self-image and reputation.

Greater Self-Direction

Learning how to listen to others so that we'll grow and benefit from their criticism is difficult enough. Learning to listen to ourselves and be true to our own deepest desires and goals can be even more challenging, especially in a world full of people—parents, peers, politicians, and advertisers, among countless others—intent on making us into somebody else. Carl Rogers (1961) once observed that beneath the bewildering complexity of problems people face—the trouble with grades or an employer or indecision about an unsatisfying marriage—lies one central search. Underneath it all, each person, knowingly or unknowingly, is asking, "Who am I, really? How can I get in touch with this real self, underlying all my surface behavior? How can I become myself?" (p. 108).

Rogers (1980) found that in the process of becoming a new person the individual's experience of growth follows a general pattern. The early stages of self-revision are usually characterized by a movement away from accepting the criticisms of others and the distorted perceptions of the self that followed. This stage also accounts for the prevalence of complaints and self-disparagement so often seen when making significant changes to the self. For example, Pam, a woman in her early 30s, felt that she was being a good wife by giving in to the constant demands of her husband. Although she had tried to meet his demands, each time he would make yet another, until it became an endless series of demands. In the process Pam had become overly submissive and resentful toward her husband. She had also built up a great deal of self-hatred. "I don't like myself this way," Pam said. "How can you have any self-respect when you're always giving in to someone? Yet I've always felt this is the way you have to be if you want to be loved. But I just can't live this way any longer." The disdain in her voice made it clear that Pam had already begun moving away from a self-image designed to please other people.

The later stages of changes to the self are characterized by greater self-direction and self-acceptance. Individuals become more open to and trusting of their own experience. As people come to accept themselves more fully, they may be more accepting of others. Most important, as individuals strive to discover themselves, they become more willing to accept the fact that they are engaged in *a process of becoming.* More specifically, individuals become *more open* to their own experiences. They become *more aware of and comfortable with* the complexity of their feelings. For example, they can experience love and disdain toward the same person. Or they may feel excited and fearful about their new job. In both instances, they become more trusting of their own experience and find it a suitable source for discovering the most satisfying behavior in each immediate situation. A young woman like Shandra considering marriage may ask herself about her boyfriend, "Is this the man I want as my partner in love?" As long as she feels she must justify the decision of marriage, she may see only the good qualities in her prospective mate. Greater openness to her experience would indicate that he has faults as well. The more open the young woman is to the full range of her feelings, the more she can weigh all the pros and cons of such a choice. A mistaken choice might be made, but because there is greater openness to her experience, a quicker correction can also be made. The important point is that she is choosing out of the richness of her own experience rather than out of a sense of obligation or from seeking the approval of others. Activity 4–3 (page 88) provides some activities that you can complete to help you appreciate your own openness to experience and complexities.

Second, as individuals accept themselves more fully, they often become more accepting of others. This is a reversal of **self-alienation,** which occurs *when we fail to acknowledge or accept certain aspects of ourselves. We then feel these qualities are foreign to us and we project them onto others, whom we then dislike.* Thus, the man who, while denying his own dependency needs, appears to be strong and self-sufficient may feel contempt for men who allow themselves to be taken care of when weak or ill. In contrast, a man who recognizes within himself the existence of dependency needs alongside those of adequacy and self-confidence may be more accepting of men who exhibit their need for others. Affirming the complexity of feelings and needs within himself, he can appreciate a wider variety of people as well as the inconsistency they display in different situations. Finally, there is a greater willingness to affirm oneself as *being in a process of becoming.* People engage in the process of self-change hoping to achieve some fixed state in which their problems will be resolved such that they will be more successful in their careers or their marriages will be more satisfying. It is usually a sign of progress when individuals drop such fixed goals and accept a more satisfying realization that they are not a fixed entity but in a process of becoming. They come to appreciate that change is the one true constant in life. People who are experiencing self-growth learn to live more in the present moment. They enjoy the richness and complexity, even the inconsistency, of life as it is, using their aspirations more as guideposts than as fixed points.

ACTIVITY 4–3

SELF-AFFIRMING ACTIVITIES

INSTRUCTIONS: *Do one or more of the following activities. When you have a low point in your self-image, pull out the activity and your answers and reread them.*

- Name five of your strengths.
- List five things you admire about yourself.
- What are your five greatest achievements in life so far?
- Describe five ways you can reward yourself for accomplishments.
- Explain five ways you can make yourself laugh.
- What are five things you can do for someone else to make them feel good?
- List five things you do to treat yourself well.
- What five activities have you recently engaged in that gave you joy?

SOURCE: Adapted from The Center for Mental Health Services/United States Department of Health and Human Services—Substance Abuse and Mental Health Services Administration. (2003). *Building self-esteem: A self-help guide.* Found at www.mentalhealth.org/publications/alloubs/SMA-3715/.

As you can see, personal growth may be unsettling at times. It involves moving away from some of the familiar self-images acquired during our formative years. And it involves seeing yourself in new ways, especially as a more self-directed person. Because each of us has different values and goals, there is no detailed guide to assure us that we are doing the right thing. Nevertheless, understanding the general pattern of growth, as suggested in the preceding pages, may be helpful. Feedback from others may serve as a useful mirror. Increased self-awareness also may be helpful up to a point. *It is optimal rather than constant or excessive awareness that is desirable.* Most important of all, learn to trust yourself. Be open to your own experience. And remember, "The good life is a process, not a state of being. It is a direction, not a destination" (Rogers, 1961, p. 186).

SUMMARY

WHAT IS THE SELF-CONCEPT?

Essentially, the self-concept is the overall image or awareness we have of ourselves. It includes all those perceptions of "I" and "me," together with the feelings, beliefs, and values associated with them. Although the self-concept itself does not do anything, it exerts a tremendous influence on the way we think and act as a whole. Actually, the overall self-concept is an organized cluster of many selves (self-complexity), helping to explain why we do not always act consistently. Commonly, we identify our body image (how we perceive and feel about our body), the self-image (the self we see ourselves to be), the ideal self (the self we'd like to be), and our social selves (the way we feel others see us).

CORE CHARACTERISTICS OF SELF-CONCEPT

One of the core characteristics of the self-concept is its stability over time. Once developed, the self-concept tends to maintain and perpetuate itself as it is. It serves as a filter through which we view our experiences, so that experiences that are not consistent with the self-concept are apt to be distorted or kept out of awareness. The tendency to think and act in a self-consistent manner is also strengthened by our self-esteem—the personal evaluation of ourselves and the resulting feelings of worth associated with the self-concept. Largely because of the self's influence, people generally prefer to hear opinions that support their own views of themselves. Today's psychologists, however, are busy debating whether individuals indeed should pursue high self-esteem, with many psychologists suggesting that this practice is detrimental to the individual.

THE SELF-CONCEPT AND PERSONAL GROWTH

Although we retain a stable core of self, the many selves that make up our overall self-concept (self-complexity) are in a state of flux and are more readily influenced by current experience than previously thought; that is, our self-concept tends to change with personal growth.

We described how visualizing our future possible selves not only helps us to attain them but also aids in our present life adjustment. Also, our social selves—the impressions we think others have of us—may be improved by changing our social roles, circumstances, and the people with whom we associate. Furthermore, we may use personal criticism for growth by putting the energy it arouses to work for us rather than against us, thus using it as an opportunity to learn about ourselves and put the needed changes into action. Ultimately, personal growth involves moving away from negative reflected appraisals from others that distort self-perceptions acquired while growing up and moving toward greater self-acceptance and self-direction. Then we become more open to our own experiences and willing to affirm ourselves in a process of becoming.

SCORING KEY FOR THE SELF-IMAGE AND IDEAL-SELF EXERCISE

To find the correspondence between your self-image and your ideal self, note the difference in the rank for each card. For example, on card A if you ranked your self-image as 8 and your ideal self as 2, the difference would be 6. For each card, record the *absolute* difference between numbers without regard to pluses or minuses. Then total the numbers in the column of differences. A score in the range of 50 would be about average. A difference lower than 30 indicates a high correspondence between your self-image and your ideal self. A score of more than 80 indicates a rather low correspondence between your self-image and ideal self. A high score doesn't necessarily mean that you have problems, however. Remember, this is a self-activity, not a valid test, so use your results to do some self-reflection and personal growth.

1. Which of the following includes all those perceptions of "I" and "me," together with the feelings, beliefs, and values associated with them?
   a. Superego
   b. Self-concept
   c. Ideal self
   d. Body image

2. The self-image is the
   a. self I'd like to be.
   b. self as I think others see me.
   c. self I see myself to be.
   d. image I have of my body.

3. Our ideal self should be
   a. modified when unduly high.
   b. unattainable in principle.
   c. the same as our self-image.
   d. rarely if ever compromised or changed.

4. Forgetting negative feedback that is inconsistent with core aspects of the self-concept is called
   a. self-complexity.
   b. conditions of worth.
   c. self-verification.
   d. mnemonic neglect.

5. Leading psychologists now believe that the pursuit of high self-esteem
   a. is a good idea.
   b. may be detrimental to the individual.
   c. enhances our self-esteem.
   d. does little to alter self-esteem.

6. According to self-enhancement theory, we welcome positive feedback about
   a. all our qualities.
   b. our positive qualities.
   c. our negative qualities.
   d. anything.

7. Who typically has low self-esteem?
   a. Men compared to women
   b. Self-actualized individuals
   c. Children with parents who consistently criticize
   d. Individuals with many different perceptions of the self

8. The social self refers to
   a. how we perceive other people.
   b. the way we think others see us.
   c. how well we get along with others.
   d. the way others see us.

9. The most helpful way of handling personal criticism is to regard it as something that
   a. needs immediate action.
   b. reflects others' faults.
   c. necessitates self-defense.
   d. may require action.

10. During the later stages of personal growth, people have a heightened sense of
    a. self-direction.
    b. fixed personal goals.
    c. self-criticalness.
    d. future orientation.

EXERCISES

1. *Self-image.* This is the self you perceive yourself to be. Using a full 8 ½- by 11-inch page, draw two concentric circles (a circle within a circle)—the inner circle representing the core of your self-concept and the outer circle the more flexible, changeable selves. Within the inner circle list six to eight of your most enduring aspects (traits). In the outer circle list a similar number of aspects of yourself that are more dependent on changing roles and circumstances. How would you describe your overall self-image?

2. *The self you'd like to be.* Among the various possible selves you'd like to be, including any feared self, select one specific image. Visualize it in specific terms as vividly as possible. Write down how you'd look, how you'd feel, and how you'd act. If possible, you might spend several minutes a day for a week daydreaming about your possible self. How did this affect your present self-image and adjustment?

3. *Self-esteem.* Our sense of personal worth fluctuates somewhat from one situation to another. Think of several situations or occasions in which you usually feel good about yourself and exhibit a lot of self-confidence. Then think of several situations in which you feel unsure of yourself and inferior. Can you identify the people or demands that make you feel good or bad about yourself? What are some practical steps you can take to improve your self-esteem?

4. *Identifying your social selves.* We have many social selves, William James observed, because there are many people whose opinions we value. Select five or six people you associate with regularly. Then identify which aspects of yourself are most readily expressed when you're with these people. Jot down some of the shared interests, typical activities, and your feelings and attitudes toward each person. Would you agree that you feel and behave somewhat differently with different people?

5. *How well do you take criticism?* Select an instance when someone criticized you and describe your experience in a page or so. Did you interpret the person's remarks as a personal attack? Or did you try to look beyond the surface of the criticism to what the person was trying to tell you? Looking back, to what extent was this a positive learning experience for you? Jot down some suggestions that will help you to benefit from personal criticism in the future.

QUESTIONS FOR SELF-REFLECTION

1. How would you describe your self-image?

2. Which aspects of your self-concept would you like to change?

3. Do you basically like yourself?

4. Are you more self-confident in some situations than in others?

5. Are you aware of how others see you?

6. When you've accepted something within yourself, are you more accepting of it in others?

7. How well do you take personal criticism?

8. What do you say when complimented by others?

9. Are you aware that self-actualization is a direction rather than a destination?

10. Do you tend to trust your own experiences?

FOR FURTHER INFORMATION

RECOMMENDED READINGS

MCGRAW, P. (2003). *Self matters: Creating your life from the inside out.* New York: Simon & Schuster/Free Press. Popular media psychologist Phil McGraw discusses how you created your own life via defining moments and critical choices. Using this and other information, he helps you define a "new" you.

MYSS, C. (2002). *Self-esteem: Your fundamental power.* Burton, MI: Sun Angel/Sounds True, Inc. Myss helps the reader discover how self-esteem developed in childhood and why it is important to build a sense of esteem for oneself.

SCHIRALDI, G., FANNING, P., & MCKAY, M. (2001). *The self-esteem workbook.* Oakland, CA: New Harbinger Publications. Surprisingly, even though much is known about self-esteem, little is done to actually help an individual raise it. This is a workbook for those folks hoping to feel better about themselves.

TESSER, A., FELSON, R. B., & SULS, J. M. (Eds.). (2000). *Psychological perspectives on self and identity.* Washington, DC: American Psychological Association. A scientific book about self-concept and related concepts.

WEBSITES AND THE INTERNET

http://www.selfgrowth.com/topics.html   Interested in higher self-esteem, in fact, higher everything? This site provides much information about self-improvement and personal growth.

http://www.mentalhelp.net   A site where you can find all kinds of information on the self, such as changing our self-attitudes, the relationship of low self-esteem to depression, and so forth. Search on the word *self.*

http://www.oxygen.com   A site that sells itself as a woman's view of the world; when women realize that their views are shared, they experience more power and esteem. The site has articles on coping, family, health, and other topics.

http://www.myshoes.com   My Shoes is a support group in cyberspace hosted by a clinical psychologist for multiracial children, adolescents, and adults who grapple with the racial identity issue.

http://www.pridelinks.com   A website for gays and lesbians or those interested in the issue of homosexuality, with multiple links and multiple topics, for example, links on health and social supports.

Toward Better Health

Learning Objectives

After completing this chapter, you should be able to

1. Discuss the relationship between body image and psychological well-being.
2. Discuss the major health hazards: obesity, smoking, and alcohol and drug abuse.
3. Describe the three stages of decision making in seeking medical care.
4. Understand why patients do not always comply with medical advice.
5. List several factors related to taking charge of your health.
6. Describe the food pyramid.
7. Explain what makes a personal fitness program effective.
8. Discuss the role of social support in wellness.

Amanda, in her mid-30s, works at a large department store as an artist and designer. She creates some of the art for the store's newspaper and catalog advertising. Amanda also decorates the windows and creates many of the in-store displays. When she is at her desk at work, Amanda drinks one cup of coffee after another. It seems she is always behind deadline, so for lunch she grabs a candy bar and soda pop on the run. When she finally goes home to her apartment, Amanda is too tired to fix herself a decent meal. Instead, she sits with a glass of wine, a bag of chips, and some nacho dip. Typically, Amanda empties the glass of wine she is drinking several times over the course of an evening. Complaining she doesn't have time to do so, Amanda rarely exercises. As a result of her eating and drinking choices, as well as her general lack of exercise, Amanda is overweight. She wears baggy clothes to disguise her plump and expanding figure, an interesting situation given that she works in the fashion industry. Amanda also smokes about a pack of cigarettes a day, a habit she developed in college while sitting in the art student lounge.

Amanda is not now sick and, in fact, feels healthy enough so that she rarely complains of her health to others. But how healthy is she really? Chances are she could be much healthier. The problem basically lies in Amanda's lifestyle—fast, frenzied, and unhealthy. Because Amanda is overweight from her faulty eating and exercise habits, she has a poor body image. It doesn't help that she sometimes has to interact with rail-thin runway models. Also, she lacks awareness of what her sedentary and stressful lifestyle is doing to her. She subscribes as well to the mistaken notion, more subconscious than conscious, that "not being sick" means she is "well."

Clearly, Amanda never completed a health psychology class; otherwise, she might lead a healthier life. **Health psychology**, *a subfield of psychology that is concerned with how psychological and social factors affect health, wellness, and illness,* pertains to much of what follows.

BODY IMAGE

Not unlike Amanda, many people lack a clear image of their bodies and do not take very good care of themselves. You'd think we would have a fairly accurate picture of our own bodies. After all, who is more familiar with your body than you? Each day, we spend an unaccountable amount of time bathing, touching, and grooming ourselves. Naturally, we acquire a great deal of information about our bodies in numerous ways, for example, feedback from others such as our doctors and families. But we have blind spots, just as Amanda does, so our body image approximates rather than coincides with reality. To commence our discussion of body image, compare your actual weight with your ideal weight by using the chart in Figure 5–1 (page 96). The chart also includes information on **Body Mass Index** (BMI), a topic addressed later in the section on obesity. Assess whether you are underweight, overweight, or at ideal weight. Now think about how you feel about any discrepancy between your actual and your ideal weight.

How We Feel About Our Bodies

Traditionally, **body image** refers to *the mental image we form of our own bodies.* As discussed in the previous chapter, body image is a part of our self-concept. Recently, however, the term *body image* has been expanded to include how we *feel* about our bodies as well as how *satisfied* we are with them. Because our society—especially the media—puts so much emphasis on physical appearance, we might expect that many people would be dissatisfied with their bodies. Magazine covers, TV ads, and films do, in fact, bombard us with images that reflect the standard, but often unattainable ideal, of a beautiful body for each sex. Even dolls present to the world body types that are beyond the reach of many. Consider the following as examples of this: For nearly four decades, Mattel's Barbie (if she were real) was estimated to weigh 110 lbs, with measurements of 39-18-33. Like many celebrities of the 1990s, Barbie's body was reshaped and she now sports measurements of 33-17-30. If alive, GI Joe's 5' 10" hyper-muscular body would have an 85-inch chest, 34-inch neck, and 65-inch waist. These numbers nearly double those of the average male physique. Over the last 25 years, action figures, in general, have become leaner and more muscular with the arms, chests, necks, forearms, thighs, and calves increasing in size by 50 to 60 percent (Baghurst, Carlston, Wood, & Wyatt, 2007).

It is also worth noting that overweight individuals are often stigmatized by the media as being selfish, lazy, stupid, ugly, sloppy, and unlikable (Puhl & Latner, 2007). Teasing by others and parental attitudes are also powerful, and negative, influences on body image (Abramovitz, 2002). It is not surprising then, that individuals who don't fit the ideal body tend to have negative feelings about themselves, making it difficult for them to accept themselves as they are and perhaps, in combination with other factors, develop an eating disorder (Neumark-Sztainer et al., 2007).

Are you a healthy weight?

Locate your height in the left-most column and read across the row for that height to your weight. Follow the column of the weight up to the top row that lists the BMI. BMI of 18.5–24.9 is the healthy weight range, BMI of 25–29.9 is the overweight range, and BMI of 30 and above is in the obese range.

BMI	19	20	21	22	23	24	25	26	27	28	29	30	31	32	33	34	35
Height							Weight in Pounds										
4'10"	97	96	100	105	110	115	119	124	129	134	138	143	148	153	158	162	167
4'11"	94	99	104	109	114	119	124	128	133	138	143	148	153	158	163	168	173
5'	97	102	107	112	118	123	128	133	138	143	148	153	158	163	168	174	179
5'1"	100	106	111	116	122	127	132	137	143	148	153	158	164	169	174	180	185
5'2"	104	100	115	120	126	131	136	142	147	153	158	164	169	175	180	186	191
5'3"	107	113	118	124	130	135	141	146	152	158	163	169	175	180	186	194	197
5'4"	110	116	122	128	134	140	145	150	157	163	168	174	180	186	192	197	204
5'5"	114	120	126	132	138	144	150	156	162	168	174	180	186	192	198	204	210
5'6"	118	124	130	136	142	148	155	161	167	173	179	186	192	198	204	210	216
5'7"	121	127	134	140	146	153	159	166	172	178	185	191	198	204	211	217	223
5'8"	125	131	138	144	151	158	164	171	177	184	190	197	203	210	216	223	230
5'9"	128	135	142	149	155	162	169	176	182	189	196	203	209	216	223	230	236
5'10"	132	139	146	153	160	167	174	181	188	195	202	209	216	222	229	226	243
5'11"	136	143	150	157	165	172	179	186	193	200	208	215	222	229	236	243	250
6'	140	147	154	162	169	177	184	191	199	206	213	221	228	235	242	250	258
6'1"	144	151	159	166	174	182	189	197	204	212	219	227	235	242	250	257	265
6'2"	148	155	163	171	179	186	194	202	210	218	225	233	241	249	256	264	272
6'3"	152	160	168	176	184	192	200	208	216	232	232	240	248	256	264	272	279
	Healthy Weight						Overweight					Obese					

FIGURE 5–1

Are you a healthy weight?

SOURCE: Dietary Guidelines for Americans 2005, Washington, DC: Department of Health and Human Services and Department of Agriculture. www.healthierus.gov/dietaryguidelines.

Research indeed bears this out, as multiple studies indicate girls of all ages worry about their weight, and that beauty and fashion magazines, television shows, and movies directly influence the desire to be thin (Bell, Lawton, & Dittmar, 2007; Tiggemann, 2005). However, when women of color watch television shows with primarily minority casts, *greater* body satisfaction is actually seen (Schooler, 2008). Why is this so? The answer lies in the body types of the actors being watched. Shows with predominantly African American casts tend to present a wider range of female body types than shows with primarily White characters (Tirodkar & Jain, 2003). Taken together, these findings suggest that media has the potential to both help and hurt body image, depending on the body types being viewed. What type of bodies are portrayed in the media you consume?

Men are affected by media portrayals, too, although the idealized body for men is muscular; V-shaped with large torso and smaller hips (Tiggemann, 2005). Thus, rather than instilling a desire to be thin, media appears to increase in men a desire to be muscular. For instance, research has shown that images of muscular male models in *Sports Illustrated* negatively influenced how adolescent boys perceived their bodies (Farquhar & Wasylkiw, 2007). However, most studies indicate that dissatisfaction is not as strong in men as it is in women (Tiggemann, 2004). Perhaps the reason is that the media have less impact on men (Green & Pritchard, 2003). Research has found that other factors, such as age and family pressure, best predict body dissatisfaction in men.

Although body dissatisfaction becomes less important over time, it nonetheless remains relatively stable across the lifespan (Tiggemann, 2004). This finding is somewhat surprising given that the bodily changes that occur with age (e.g., weight gain, wrinkles, graying of hair) are thought to increase body dissatisfaction. It may be that, as we age, our expectations for what makes an "age-appropriate body" changes. Thus, it is the perceived shape of our bodies, relative to same-aged individuals, that influences body satisfaction across development. For example, when thinking about the beauty of one's body, 50-year-olds will most likely compare their bodies against the bodies of other 50-year-olds and not against the bodies of 20-year-olds.

Our Ideal Body

The satisfaction with our bodies is greatly influenced by our image of the *ideal* body, an integral part of our overall body image. Specifically, our **ideal body** is *the body we would like to have.* Overall, the closer to the ideal body we are, the less pressure we feel to change. On the other hand, those who are obviously different may feel more pressure to change or hide the disliked parts of their bodies, just as Amanda did in her baggy clothes. Moreover, our ideal body is greatly influenced by the particular body ideals prevalent in our culture. For example, in Jamaican society, plumpness is desirable, so although foreign media are available, the desire for plumpness is strong enough to counteract foreign preoccupation with thinness (Smith & Cogswell, 1994). Nevertheless, a constant bombardment of thin images in the media can take its toll on one's body image. In one of the most intriguing studies conducted on body image to date, researchers investigated the influence of the *introduction* of television in Fiji on adolescent girls' body image. The result indicated that, in comparison to girls who had less than one month of exposure to television, teenage girls with three years of television exposure showed dramatic increases in dieting (70 percent of the sample) and self-induced vomiting (11 percent of the sample). Of note, prior to the introduction of television, these behaviors were virtually unheard of among Fijian girls (Becker, Burwell, Herzog, Hamburg, & Gilman, 2002).

Every society throughout history has had somewhat different ideals of beauty (Brody, 2002). During the seventeenth through nineteenth centuries, artists such as Rubens, Renoir, and Raphael painted women as being plump and curvy. Marilyn Monroe's size 14 physique represented bodily perfection during the 1950s, and a decade later, the model Twiggy and her ultra thin appearance were considered ideal (Derenne & Beresin, 2006). However, at no time in the past has there been such an intense barrage of media attention telling Americans how we should look. As mentioned, for Whites, the ideal man is tall, large, muscular, energetic, and V-shaped. The ideal White woman is slim as well as shapely, smooth-skinned, young, glamorous, and often blonde. These images do not hold true for all people, however. Hispanics, for example, are even more likely than African Americans or Whites to consider themselves overweight (Centers for Disease Control and Prevention, 2001).

More than men, women have issues with their body image, in part due to media representations of the ideal woman.

If you are female, close your eyes and imagine the perfect female body as a *man* would see it. If you are male, what type of male body do you think your *female* counterparts prefer? Compare your answers with those of two friends, one female and one male. Did the answers vary by gender? According to research, they should. Perceptions of what the opposite sex finds ideal or attractive differ substantially from what the opposite sex *actually* finds attractive. This is especially true for women's perceptions of what men want. Women believe that men prefer thin or bony women while men actually do *not* prefer such women (Bergstrom, Neighbors, & Lewis, 2004). Men are more in tune with what women actually find attractive in a man's physique.

HEALTH AND THE MIND–BODY RELATIONSHIP

Today, physicians and mental health professionals pay greater attention to the mutual interactions of the mind and body than they did in the past. Thus, to understand health and illness we must consider how biological, psychological, and social factors interact.

The Immune System

The **immune system** is *a complex surveillance system, including the brain and various blood cells, that defends our bodies by identifying and destroying various foreign invaders.* Because Amanda had a serious case of mononucleosis in college, her immune system was damaged. She likened herself to the proverbial canary in the coal mine. If there was a stomach flu or a cold going around, she was always first to catch it; then and only then would her friends become aware of the latest illness. Although Amanda's immune system was impaired, other individuals possess more robust immune systems. In emphasizing the link between psychological factors (e.g., stress) and physical illness, it is important to note that psychological factors do not appear to *cause* illness directly. Rather, such factors seem to weaken the immune system, thereby making us more *vulnerable* to illness. How does this happen?

First, in times of distress, psychological processes such as depression can prevent us from taking positive health-related measures such as eating well. Moreover, in an attempt to cope with life's difficulties, many people make lifestyle choices that can negatively impact the immune system, such as excessive use of alcohol and drugs. Finally, research has demonstrated that in stressful situations, the body's immune system functions less well (Glaser, 2005). For instance, stress lowers the body's resistance to a variety of physical ailments ranging from herpes viruses to upper respiratory infections.

Personality

There is increasing evidence suggesting that we can bolster our resistance to stress and illness by harnessing the powers of the mind—our thoughts, attitudes, and emotions. Psychologists recognize the importance of five personality traits in their descriptions of individuals' personalities; the traits are *openness to experience* (being open-minded about novelty), *conscientiousness* (diligence), *agreeableness* (being good-natured), *extroversion* (being friendly), and *emotional stability* (anxiety and reactivity). Researchers have demonstrated associations between openness to experience, extroversion, and conscientiousness with perceptions of being in good health and emotional instability with perceptions of having poor health (Goodwin & Engstron, 2002).

Another personality factor that pertains to our ability to resist illness is self-efficacy. **Self-efficacy** is *the belief in one's capabilities to organize and execute actions required to produce given attainments.* With regard to health, self-efficacy enables us to adopt healthy behaviors (such as physical exercise) or to adhere to programs designed to eliminate unhealthy habits (such as smoking) (Bebestos, Chroni, & Theodorakis, 2002; Lippke & Ziegelmann, 2006). People see little point in trying to change if they do not believe they can succeed. How can individuals develop or promote high self-efficacy? According to Albert Bandura (1997), individuals must learn to monitor their own behaviors, especially the ones they wish to change. They must set short-range, attainable goals to motivate and direct their own efforts and enlist positive social support from others to help them sustain the efforts needed to succeed. Modeling after successful others also benefits those embarking on healthier lifestyles. For instance, many people report being inspired to lose weight after watching the hit TV series, *The Biggest Loser,* during which some contestants lose well over 100 lbs. Interestingly, self-efficacy appears to function similarly across cultures with regard to promoting healthy behaviors (Luszczynska, Scholz, & Schwarzer, 2005).

We must guard against emphasizing personality as responsible for our health to such an extent that people are made to feel guilty when they become sick or fail to get well. As mentioned earlier, a multitude of other factors contribute to our physical and mental well-being. Another important factor is lifestyle, which we will discuss next.

Lifestyle Choices

Lifestyle kills more Americans than any other single factor. This cannot be said about citizens of other countries where environmental hazards, disease, war, and starvation account for more deaths. Lifestyle change, then, can be extremely effective in maintaining good health (Wing & Raynor, 2006). Three major health hazards that are directly associated with lifestyle and that can be controlled (though many people have difficulty doing so) are obesity, smoking, and alcohol and drug abuse.

Obesity is *an excessive amount of body fat, usually defined as exceeding the desirable weight for one's height, build, and age.* Recall our earlier discussion of body image and American media. Nowhere is thinness more desirable than in mainstream U.S. society, yet paradoxically, nowhere is obesity more prevalent, probably because food is so available here compared to other countries. Likewise, Americans live a pretty fast-paced life, so they often turn to snacks and fast foods, which are unusually laden with empty calories (Horgen, 2005).

Earlier in the chapter you were introduced to the height and weight table to help you identify whether you are overweight. Another measure introduced earlier is BMI, which is *a measure of total body fat calculated from knowing an individual's height and weight.* You can estimate your BMI by multiplying your total weight times 703 and dividing by your height in inches squared (National Institutes of Health, 2000). BMI combined with waist circumference can be a good indicator of who is gaining or carrying too much weight. Men with a circumference greater than 40 inches and women with a circumference greater than 35 inches are considered at risk for health problems related to obesity. In fact, less than 30 percent of all Americans have a healthy BMI; whereas nearly 70 percent of Americans are overweight or outright obese (Lavie, Milani, & Ventura, 2009). Being overweight or obese is not just a problem for adults either; these health problems in children and adolescents have recently increased threefold, with 14 percent of 2- to 5-year olds, 19 percent of 6- to 11-year-olds and 17 percent of 12- to 19-year-olds considered obese (Ogden et al., 2006). Worldwide, there are over 155 million obese children and adolescents (or 1 in 10) (WorldHeartFederation.org, 2007). High blood pressure, diabetes, stroke, sleep disorders, cancer, and liver and gall bladder diseases are but a few of the complications of weighing too much, and each year, more than 300,000 deaths are linked to obesity in the United States. The more overweight people are, the greater their risk. In general, obese individuals have a 50 to 100 percent increased risk of death from all causes, compared with normal-weight individuals (Mayo Clinic, 2005).

Obesity probably results from an interaction of physiological and psychological factors. We all know overweight people who eat moderately but remain fat and thin people who eat heartily but remain slender. Although apparently some people are born to carry more fat, a lot of obesity results from overeating and insufficient exercise. There is also a variety of psychological and social factors associated with obesity. For instance, obese people tend to be more responsive to external cues, such as the visibility, availability, and smell of food, rather than to the internal cues of hunger. Some individuals also eat more food when with others, especially others who are fast eaters.

People who want to lose weight must somehow help their bodies to use up more calories than they consume. The two basic ways to do so are to (1) change your diet so that you eat less, especially fewer foods high in fat, and (2) exercise more. The benefits of crash diets are generally short-lived. To make matters worse, strict dieting tends to lower the rate of metabolism, so even though you count calories carefully, you will still not lose weight. It's preferable to follow a reasonable diet aimed at a more modest weight loss—say, 1 pound a week—over a longer period of time, combined with regular exercise.

Perhaps you've heard the myth that exercise is self-defeating because it makes you want to eat more. Actually, exercise not only burns up calories but also increases your metabolic rate, so that even when active people are not exercising, their bodies are burning up calories faster. Exercise during and after dieting is an important predictor of successful long-term weight loss (Wing & Raynor, 2006). And small lifestyle changes, such as watching less television, are also related to maintaining weight loss (Raynor, Phelan, Hill, & Wing, 2006). Unfortunately, only 22 percent of U.S. adults get the recommended regular physical activity. The recommendation is five times a week for at least 30 minutes

Obesity has become a national epidemic, which in most cases is preventable.

of vigorous activity such as brisk walking (National Institute of Diabetes and Digestive and Kidney Diseases, 2000).

Self-efficacy also plays an important role, such that individuals who acquire a greater sense of self-control over their eating and exercise habits can successfully manage their weight long after the completion of dieting and treatment programs. Finally, weight-loss programs are a big business in the United States and will probably continue to grow as Americans' girths grow. If you are thinking of joining such a program, make sure that the program meets the guidelines established by the federal government in Box 5–1 (page 102).

Tobacco abuse continues to be a major health hazard (Ostbye & Taylor, 2004). **Tobacco abuse** is *the abuse of tobacco to such an extent that heart, respiratory, and other health-related problems develop.* An estimated 44.5 million adults in the United States smoke cigarettes even though this single behavior will result in death or disability for half of the regular smokers (National Center for Chronic Disease Prevention and Health Promotion, 2005). Tobacco use remains the leading *preventable* cause of death in the United States as well as one of the most expensive habits, increasing health-care costs manifold. Notably, 1 in 6 deaths in the United States are thought to be attributable to smoking. That is more than number of deaths caused by alcohol, homicide, car accidents, illicit drugs, suicide, and AIDS *combined* (Glantz, 2003). There is compelling evidence that cigarette smoking is a major factor in heart disease, lung cancer, emphysema, and other fatal illnesses. In addition, smoking contributes to many forms of cancer, including

Box 5–1

SELECTING A WEIGHT-LOSS PROGRAM

A responsible and safe weight-loss program should be able to document for you the following five features:

1. *The diet should be safe.* It should include all of the Recommended Daily Allowances (RDAs) for vitamins, minerals, and protein.

2. *The weight-loss program should be directed toward a slow, steady weight loss* unless your doctor feels your health condition would benefit from more rapid weight loss.

3. *Check for health problems before starting.* If you plan to lose more than 15 to 20 pounds, suspect or know you have any health problems, or take medication on a regular basis, you should be evaluated by your doctor before beginning your weight-loss program.

4. *The program should include plans for weight maintenance after the weight-loss phase is over.* It is of little benefit to lose a large amount of weight only to regain it. Weight maintenance is the most difficult part of controlling weight and is not consistently implemented in weight-loss programs. The program you select should include help in permanently changing your dietary habits and level of physical activity to alter a lifestyle that may have contributed to weight gain in the past.

5. *Know how much it might cost.* A commercial weight-loss program should provide a detailed statement of fees and costs of additional items such as dietary supplements.

SOURCE: Adapted from "Choosing a safe and successful weight loss program." National Institute of Diabetes & Digestive & Kidney Diseases, 1998. www.niddk.nih.gov/nutrit/pubs/choose.

cancers of the mouth, larynx, bladder, and pancreas. Smokers who also drink alcohol magnify their risks of cancer even more because it enhances the carcinogenic effect of tobacco at certain sites of the body, such as the esophagus, mouth, and larynx (Centers for Disease Control and Prevention, 2002d; Ostbyte & Taylor, 2004).

Greater awareness of the health hazards of smoking and chewing tobacco has prompted some people to give up the habit. Today, 21.6 percent of U.S. adults—over 45 million people—are current smokers. That's down from 22.5 percent in 2002 and 22.8 percent in 2001 (National Center for Chronic Disease Prevention and Health Promotion, 2005). At the same time, these gains should not blind us to the fact that a large number of children and adolescents smoke (23.6 percent), and a large number of young adults smoke (23.8 percent). In fact, 61 percent of cigarette smokers start before the age of 18 (Substance Abuse and Mental Health Services Administration, 2006). That means that a large portion of children living today will die prematurely because of the decision they made to smoke (Centers for Disease Control and Prevention, 2002d). Not surprisingly, tobacco companies are under fire from the public and health officials for this increase. On a second front, many authorities are disturbed that smoking rates are even higher in other countries, many of which have citizens who cannot afford to smoke and who have inadequate health care as it is.

Smoking is a difficult habit to break, but the benefits of smoking cessation are substantial (Ostbyte & Taylor, 2004). However, even conservative estimates imply that half or more of those who quit smoking eventually resume the habit. In addition to the psychological dependence on the smoking habit, nicotine is considered to be physically addictive. Consequently, smokers build a tolerance to nicotine and need to smoke a larger number of cigarettes or ones with higher nicotine content to get the same effect. The average smoker smokes 20 to 30 cigarettes a day—one cigarette about every 30 to 40 minutes. And because the biological half-life of nicotine in humans is about 20 to 30 minutes, habitual smokers keep their systems primed with nicotine during most of their waking hours. Withdrawal from habitual smoking and nicotine produces a variety of symptoms, including nervousness, headaches, dizziness, fatigue, insomnia, sweating, cramps, tremors, and heart palpitations.

Box 5–2 highlights some of the many approaches to reducing **nicotine addiction** or to reducing *the difficulty of quitting smoking when smoking has become habitual.* In recent years, many people have begun using the "patch," which, when attached to one's arm,

---

Box 5–2
TIPS FOR QUITTING

FIVE KEYS FOR QUITTING

Studies have shown that these five steps will help you quit and quit for good. You have the best chances of quitting if you use them together.

1. *Get Ready*

   • Set a quit date.

   • Change your environment.

     1. Get rid of ALL cigarettes and ashtrays in your home, car, and place of work.

     2. Don't let people smoke in your home.

   • Review your past attempts to quit. Think about what worked and what did not.

   • Once you quit, don't smoke—NOT EVEN A PUFF!

2. *Get Support and Encouragement.* Studies have shown that you have a better chance of being successful if you have help. You can get support in many ways:

   • Tell your family, friends, and coworkers that you are going to quit and want their support. Ask them not to smoke around you or leave cigarettes out.

   • Talk to your health care provider (for example, doctor, dentist, nurse, pharmacist, psychologist, or smoking counselor).

3. *Learn New Skills and Behaviors*

   • Try to distract yourself from urges to smoke. Talk to someone, go for a walk, or get busy with a task.

   • When you first try to quit, change your routine. Use a different route to work. Drink tea instead of coffee. Eat breakfast in a different place.

   • Do something to reduce your stress. Take a hot bath, exercise, or read a book.

   • Plan something enjoyable to do every day.

   • Drink a lot of water and other fluids.

4. *Get Medication and Use It Correctly.* Medications can help you stop smoking and lessen the urge to smoke. These double your chance of quitting. The U.S. Food and Drug Administration (FDA) has approved five medications to help you quit smoking:

   • Ask your health care provider for advice and carefully read the information on the package.

   • If you are pregnant or trying to become pregnant, nursing, under age 18, smoking fewer than 10 cigarettes per day, or have a medical condition, talk to your doctor or other health care provider before taking medications.

5. *Be Prepared for Relapse or Difficult Situations.* Most relapses occur within the first three months after quitting. Don't be discouraged if you start smoking again. Remember, most people try several times before they finally quit. Here are some difficult situations to watch for:

   • *Alcohol.* Avoid drinking alcohol. Drinking lowers your chances of success.

   • *Other Smokers.* Being around smoking can make you want to smoke.

   • *Weight Gain.* Many smokers will gain weight when they quit, usually less than 10 pounds. Eat a healthy diet and stay active.

   • *Bad Mood or Depression.* There are a lot of ways to improve your mood other than smoking.

If you are having problems with any of these situations, talk to your doctor or other health care provider.

SOURCE: Adapted from the Centers for Disease Control and Prevention's "You can quit smoking consumer guide" (www.cdc.gov/tobacco/quit_smoking/how_to_quit/you_can_quit/five_keys/).

releases nicotine into the body, thereby reducing the physical craving for a smoke. In addition, a variety of psychological and behavioral methods are available. One approach is monitoring stimulus control, in which smokers become aware of the stimuli and the situations that trigger their smoking. Then they develop alternative behaviors. For instance, Amanda usually lit a cigarette whenever she talked on the telephone or ate spicy food. A friend suggested that she begin holding a glass of water in her right hand while engaging in these activities, thereby breaking the associations between the telephone and smoking and spicy food and cigarettes. Generally, when trying to convince yourself or someone else to quit, it's better to emphasize the *positive* aspects of not smoking, such as the desire to take charge of one's life and to maintain physical fitness, rather than the fear of illness. Although most smokers who give up smoking resume the habit within three months to a year, former smokers may increase their chance of success through the support of friends, spouses, or support groups (Thomas et al., 2005). Also, vigorous exercise helps smokers quit and stay smoke free (Marcus, 1999). Then too, with sufficient motivation, many smokers may give up the habit without any formal program.

Alcohol and drug abuse continues to be a major health hazard for many people. Such abuse may be defined as *the misuse or dependence on a psychoactive substance like alcohol.* Three-fourths of U.S. men and almost two-thirds of women drink alcoholic beverages. Each day, close to 11,000 adolescents drink alcohol for the first time and 3,800 adolescents will smoke their first "joint" (SAMHSA, 2006). However, not all individuals who drink and use drugs develop an addiction. For instance, alcoholism appears to be hereditary, so it is often found recurring in family trees (McGue, 1999). Approximately one-third of both sexes are light drinkers, but at least 1 out of 10 adults is a heavy drinker; the proportion being higher among men, especially those 18 to 25 years old. Activity 5–1 can help you assess whether you are a heavy drinker.

ACTIVITY 5–1

ARE YOU DRINKING TOO MUCH?

INSTRUCTIONS: *Indicate the strength of your agreement on a scale of 1 to 7 for the following statements by circling the appropriate number under the statement.*

1. I drink alcohol heavily after a confrontation or argument or because of emotional pain.

   Strongly disagree   1   2   3   4   5   6   7   Strongly agree

2. I need more and more alcohol to get the same effect.

   Strongly disagree   1   2   3   4   5   6   7   Strongly agree

3. I often remember starting out, beginning to drink, and then drinking more, but that's all I remember.

   Strongly disagree   1   2   3   4   5   6   7   Strongly agree

4. I often black out or don't remember what happened when I was drinking.

   Strongly disagree   1   2   3   4   5   6   7   Strongly agree

5. Not remembering what I was doing when I was drinking causes me alarm to the point of switching drinks, switching jobs, and switching promises to myself.

   Strongly disagree   1   2   3   4   5   6   7   Strongly agree

6. My friends have told me that I lose control when I drink too much alcohol.

   Strongly disagree   1   2   3   4   5   6   7   Strongly agree

7. I realize that others are talking about my drinking too much.

   Strongly disagree   1   2   3   4   5   6   7   Strongly agree

8. My hands shake in the morning and/or I feel hung over after I have been drinking.

   Strongly disagree   1   2   3   4   5   6   7   Strongly agree

9. People seem extremely irritated with me because of my drinking.

   Strongly disagree   1   2   3   4   5   6   7   Strongly agree

10. I often drink more than I eat.

    Strongly disagree   1   2   3   4   5   6   7   Strongly agree

SCORING: Add up all your points for each statement. The higher the total score, the more likely it is that you have an alcohol abuse problem. If you believe that you do have a problem, find professional help as soon as possible.

SOURCE: Adapted from "Moving forward with your life! Leaving alcohol and other drugs behind." U.S. Department of Health and Human Services, National Clearinghouse for Alcohol and Drug Information. http://www.health.org/govpubs/PHD626/.

Alcohol use constitutes a major health hazard in many ways. Nearly two-thirds of the drivers in fatal traffic accidents have been drinking. Automobile accidents involving alcohol are a leading cause of death among youths. Furthermore, people with alcohol-related ailments fill half of all hospital beds in the United States. In addition, chronic heavy drinking is often accompanied by poor nutrition and results in serious damage to many parts of the body, with at least one of every five chronic heavy drinkers developing cirrhosis of the liver. People who develop problems with alcohol and drugs frequently exhibit a familiar sequential pattern. Box 5–3 (page 106) reveals more about this pattern.

Although many programs are available for treating drug abuse, some have a relatively high failure rate. Individuals may not be ready for the complete change in lifestyle demanded by the program, often because of denial on their part, or they may become bored and frustrated with the program or the lifestyle changes demanded by it. A large proportion of people who enter drug treatment drop out in the first few weeks only to reenter the program at a later date, although relapse remains the rule rather than the exception. **Relapse** means *a return to a previous behavior or state*—in this case, a return to drinking alcohol or using drugs. The prevalence of relapse has led some therapists to develop relapse-prevention training, which generally is incorporated into the treatment program. Substance abusers are taught how to cope with high-risk situations—for example, coming into contact with acquaintances who are still addicted—and to prevent small lapses from becoming full-blown relapses. Individuals are encouraged to view lapses as temporary setbacks that they can learn from and avoid in the future. Amanda, for example, went to a smoking cessation program and learned that she should avoid going to dinner with her friends who smoked. She was also taught to think, "Okay, I had a slip. But that doesn't mean I'm all through. I can get back on track."

The best programs prevent substance abuse altogether by teaching parents to take a proactive role in their child's development and understanding of substance abuse (Haggerty, Kosterman, Catalano, & Hawkins, 1999). Additionally, for college students, a group at high risk for alcoholism and use of illicit substances, simple web-based assessments over time can help to prevent such abuse (American Psychological Society, 1999). Similarly, making students aware that the average college student does not get drunk every weekend (e.g., sharing social norms) may also reduce the level of alcohol consumption on college campuses (Haines, Barker, & Rice, 2003).

Box 5–3

DRUG USE: WHEN DOES DRUG USE START? HOW DOES IT PROCEED?

WHAT ARE THE HIGHEST RISK PERIODS FOR DRUG ABUSE AMONG YOUTH?

Research has shown that the key risk periods for drug abuse are during major transitions in children's lives. The first big transition for children is when they leave the security of the family and enter school. Later, when they advance from elementary school to middle school, they often experience new academic and social situations, such as learning to get along with a wider group of peers. It is at this stage—early adolescence—that children are likely to encounter drugs for the first time. When they enter high school, adolescents face additional social, emotional, and educational challenges. At the same time, they may be exposed to greater availability of drugs, drug abusers, and social activities involving drugs. These challenges can increase the risk that they will abuse alcohol, tobacco, and other substances. When young adults leave home for college or work and are on their own for the first time, their risk for drug and alcohol abuse is very high. Consequently, young adult interventions are needed as well. *Because risks appear at every life transition, prevention planners need to choose programs that strengthen protective factors at each stage of development.*

WHEN AND HOW DOES DRUG ABUSE START AND PROGRESS?

Studies, such as the National Survey on Drug Use and Health, indicate that some children are already abusing drugs at age 12 or 13, which likely means that some begin even earlier. Early abuse often includes such substances as tobacco, alcohol, inhalants, marijuana, and prescription drugs such as sleeping pills and anti-anxiety medicines. If drug abuse persists into later adolescence, abusers typically become more heavily involved with marijuana and then advance to other drugs, while continuing their abuse of tobacco and alcohol. Studies have also shown that abuse of drugs in late childhood and early adolescence is associated with greater drug involvement. It is important to note that most youth, however, do not progress to abusing other drugs.

Scientists have proposed various explanations of why some individuals become involved with drugs and then escalate to abuse. One explanation points to a biological cause, such as having a family history of drug or alcohol abuse. Another explanation is that abusing drugs can lead to affiliation with drug-abusing peers, which, in turn, exposes the individual to other drugs. Preventive interventions can provide skills and support to high-risk youth to help decrease escalation to drug abuse.

SOURCE: National Institute on Drug Abuse. (2006). *Preventing drug abuse among children and adolescents.* http://www.nida.nih.gov/Prevention/prevopen.html.

Environmental Issues

Various environments in which we find ourselves are more or less conducive to health problems. You may well be thinking that environmental pollutants or contaminants are one of the major sources for health-related problems. You are correct. About 25 percent of Americans live where the standards for air quality are not met (National Center for Health Statistics, 2002). It has long been known that living near polluting industries can affect one's *physical* health, but living near polluting industries can also affect *mental* health (Downey & Van Willigen, 2005).

Social and psychological environments can be just as toxic. Messages about the popularity of drugs have become a common part of children's lives. Thompson (2005) found that 95 percent of all films depict the use of some unhealthy substance (e.g., cigarettes, alcohol, or drugs), but most do not depict the negative consequences of use. Moreover, around 50 percent of G- and PG-rated films and greater than 80 percent of films rated PG-13 tend to depict characters smoking and/or drinking (Polansky & Glantz, 2004; Roberts, Henriksen, & Christenson, 1999; Thompson & Yokota, 2004). Importantly, viewing such images has been linked with both smoking behavior and early onset teen drinking (Sargent, Willis, Stoolmiller, Gibson, & Gibbons, 2006; Wills et al., 2007). In addition to traditional screen media, the Internet has become a hotbed of information for alcohol and drug use. For instance, there are many websites devoted to the use of illicit drugs. Although providing warnings about the hazards of using drugs, such sites may in fact become "how-to" guides for drug users, with sections devoted to Q & A (in a blog format) and "past experiences." Of note, some of these sites (Erowid.com, Ravesafe.org) state that they promote "safe" and "responsible" drug use. However, rather than promoting cigarette, alcohol, and drug use, mass media could play a role in protecting children from drugs by portraying them as unacceptable, unglamorous, and dangerous (Weiner, Panton, & Weber, 1999).

COPING WITH ILLNESS

Every so often each of us has a minor health problem, such as a stress cold, which we usually treat with a variety of over-the-counter remedies like aspirin, antihistamines, and stomach medicine. However, if the problem persists, especially when it interferes with our everyday lives, we begin to consider seeing a doctor. Whether we are aware of it or not, such experiences set in motion a decision-making process that includes three stages:

(1) *Noticing and interpreting* the seriousness of our symptoms.
(2) *Seeking professional help* when needed.
(3) *Adhering to the prescribed treatment.*

In this section, we'll look at how people react to symptoms and illnesses at each of these three stages.

Noticing and Interpreting Symptoms

Even healthy young adults like Amanda may experience a variety of symptoms, including nasal congestion, sore muscles, stiff joints, headaches, racing heart, dizziness, and constipation or diarrhea. Each of us differs somewhat in the tendency to label our body aches and pains as symptoms of an illness. *People who habitually complain of unfounded ailments or exhibit an undue fear of illness* are often called **hypochondriacs.** On the other hand, some people tend to underreport their physical symptoms. These people are often **extroverts,** *people who tend to be warm, outgoing, and involved in life,* so much so that they don't have time to complain of or notice their ailments. Each person's sense of well-being is a function of both of these traits, the relative strength of each tendency determining how we perceive and interpret our inner state. Individuals high in hypochondriasis report two or three times as many symptoms as the better-adjusted people. Conversely, those high in extroversion generally report fewer ailments.

Psychologists have also identified other coping strategies related to health concerns. One strategy is **avoidance.** In this pattern, *the individual minimizes or denies that there are any symptoms to notice.* Such individuals are believed to cope well with short-term stressors. On the other hand, some individuals actively confront stressors. These individuals use **confrontation** to *note symptoms of an illness are present.* One other means for coping with bad health news is through **downward comparison.** Individuals who choose to do this *compare their own situation to others who are worse off.* For example, Amanda smoked about a pack of cigarettes a day but found herself comparing this habit to that of Virginia, a coworker who smoked almost two packs a day.

There are other personal characteristics that determine typical coping styles related to health behaviors, such as culture. For instance, pain signifies different things in different societies. In the United States, many visits to doctors are prompted by the experience of pain (Turk, 1994). In some cultures, individuals attend to the intensity of pain, whereas in other cultures individuals respond to what they think the pain signifies. Thus, in the latter cultures, minor pain could still signal something serious.

Seeking Help

About the only time it's easy to decide whether to see a doctor is when our symptoms become extreme. At the same time, the decision to seek professional help also depends on many other factors. For instance, if people believe their symptoms have a psychological rather than a physical cause, they are more reluctant to go for help. Also, if their complaints—such as hemorrhoids—are embarrassing to talk about, they may resist treatment. Individuals are also less likely to visit a physician if the ailment seems virus-related or involves the upper half of the body. If people believe the benefits of going to the doctor are not worth the time, trouble, and cost of a visit, especially if the visit is not covered by medical insurance, they may hold back. Furthermore, the dread of a devastating or fateful diagnosis might delay seeking help.

Men and women differ in their readiness to see a doctor. Men seek help less often; on average, they go two or more years without seeing a doctor, a situation that may put them at risk for more fatalities than women (Mansfield, Addis, & Courtenay, 2005). Women generally are more sensitive to changes in their bodies and to pain and, thus, visit physicians more often than men (Barsky, Peekna, & Borus, 2001). Yet men have higher rates of hypertension, ulcers, heart attacks, and cancer and significantly shorter life expectancies. One possible explanation is that men are more preoccupied with the external world and are less attentive to their bodies. Or perhaps men are more reluctant to seek professional help because it implies a "weakness" on their part.

Some of the most glaring differences in help-seeking occur between racial or ethnic minorities and Whites. One of the problems of these minority groups, which are more prone to certain health problems, is lack of health insurance. Large percentages of

African Americans, Asians, Latinos, Pacific Islanders, and Native Americans lack health insurance or other means to pay for health care (Administration on Aging, 2006). Perceived prejudice may also keep these individuals from finding care, but prejudice and discrimination may also be the culprits creating increased stress and thus causing some of the health-related problems in the first place (Carlson & Chamberlain, 2004).

Let's look also at general cultural differences in seeking health care. In the United States, citizens expect to visit a doctor in a professional-looking office or in a pristine and large hospital. Not so in rural India. Individuals there are more likely to seek medical help if the medical center resembles an Indian village, with separate huts housing the lab, surgical suite, pharmacy, and wards (Perry, 2005). In Nepal, where adequate health care is lacking, people are more likely to use health care services if they are endorsed by some of the most important people in their society—grandmothers (Kluger, 2005). In Somalia, the roads are so terrible due to droughts, wars, and lack of care that patients cannot traverse them. Therefore, the nonprofit Save the Children Fund has bought small motorcycles so that health care workers can go to the patients (Kluger, Brunton, & Robinson, 2005).

People in poor health report the greatest amount of dissatisfaction with their health care system. One reason may be that their physicians curtail social conversations with them and cut right to the medical dialogues (Hall, Roter, & Milburn, 1999) and ask more questions than patients (Ohtaki, Ohtaki, & Fetters, 2003). It should come as no surprise, then, that patients' and physicians' perceptions of how well physicians explain medical information differ (Hagihara, Odamaki, Nobutomo, & Tarumi, 2006) and that such encounters are often unproductive (*Harvard Health Letter,* July 2004). However, female doctors spend more time with their patients, allow their patients to talk more so that more communication is exchanged, and explain medical terminology better than male doctors (*Harvard Health Letter,* May 2001). Other research has uncovered that some individuals possess negative stereotypes of modern doctors and that such individuals are less likely to seek treatment and less likely to adhere to treatments (Bogart, Bird, Walt, Delahanty, & Figler, 2004).

Adhering to Treatment

Adherence to treatment regimens is *the degree to which a person's behavior (e.g., taking medications, attending treatment sessions, etc.) coincides with medical or health advice* (Raynor, Wing, & Phelan, 2007). Surprisingly, as many as one-half of all adult patients do not follow or complete the treatment prescribed by their doctor (Osterberg & Blaschke, 2005). For example, Amanda had a sore throat, and before she had finished her medication, the soreness was gone. Thus, Amanda discontinued her medication early and to her dismay, the soreness and hoarseness returned. Interestingly, the patient's personality, gender, and socioeconomic status do not seem to predict accurately who will and will not adhere to treatment plans. Patient characteristics do interact with several other factors to influence compliance. These other factors include, but are not limited to, the nature of the illness (e.g., HIV versus diabetes), patient depression, and the treatment regimen (e.g., medication versus exercise) (Christensen & Johnson, 2002; Raynor et al., 2007).

People may fail to adhere to the prescribed treatment for many other reasons. A common reason for failure to adhere is dissatisfaction with the physician. Patients who have a warm relationship with their doctor and are involved in planning the treatment are more apt to comply with the doctor's orders. Another reason patients do not follow the treatment plan is that many of them do not sufficiently understand the nature of their illness or the doctor's instructions. By contrast, when the desired treatment is explained in everyday language with easy-to-follow written instructions, patients are much more likely to comply. Patients' beliefs about a medication also influence adherence, with individuals who worry about drug dependence or long-term side effects least likely to take the medication as prescribed. Overall, patients' reluctance to take medicine appears most related to their fear of medication and their preference to take as little medicine as possible (Pound et al., 2005; Vermeire, Hearnshaw, Van Royen, & Denekens, 2001).

The way the information is presented is important, too. Information can be presented or framed in *negative* (about potential losses or costs) or *positive* ways (about potential gains). A negatively framed message would be something like this: "If you don't stop smoking, you are likely to die at a young age." A positively framed message is "If you stop smoking, you'll feel better and live longer." Some scientists believe that positively framed messages from medical practitioners are best for promoting *preventive* behaviors such as sticking to a healthy diet, whereas negatively framed messages are best for facilitating *detection* behaviors such as noticing pain (van Assema, Martens, Ruiter, & Brug, 2001). Recent research on the framing of health messages indicates that the situation is more complicated than the mere type of frame—negative or positive. Factors such as involvement of the patient in a particular medical issue are also important (Donovan & Jalleh, 2000). An example would be pregnant women being more involved than nonpregnant women when listening to a message about the importance of infant immunizations.

PROMOTING WELLNESS

Until recently, people in the health care field made little distinction between people who were "not sick" and those who were "healthy" (Friedman, 2005). For all practical purposes, wellness was the absence of sickness. Amanda was one of these believers. She considered herself healthy despite her unhealthy lifestyle. However, in recent years there has been a growing realization that health is considerably more than the absence of a minor or major illness. Today, individuals believe that **wellness** means *the positive ideal of health in which one strives to maintain and improve one's health*. To be healthy is to have the full use of one's body and mind and, despite an occasional bout of illness, to be alert, energetic, and happy to be alive even in old age. As a result, health practitioners and the public alike are beginning to think more in terms of optimum health and wellness.

Optimum health is not something you can get from your doctor, guru, health food store, or wonder supplement. Positive health is something that comes mostly through your *own* efforts, aided by good genes and regular medical care. By viewing your everyday well-being in terms of the positive ideal of health, instead of merely the absence of illness, you may function better and live more enthusiastically than you would have otherwise. Activity 5–2 will help you rate your current health habits.

Taking Charge of Your Own Health

As Americans become better educated and enjoy greater freedom of choice, generally we want to exercise greater personal control over our own health and health care. When seeing the doctor, we don't want to be told to do this or that. Instead, we want to know the evidence and reasoning involved so we can make an informed choice. We also want

ACTIVITY 5–2

HOW DO YOUR HEALTH HABITS RATE?

INSTRUCTIONS: *Circle the appropriate number after each of the following statements and add up the numbers to get a total score for each section. Then check the norms at the end to determine what your score means.*

Eating habits: Almost always   Sometimes   Almost never

1. I eat a variety of foods each day, such as fruits and vegetables, whole-grain breads and cereals, lean meats, dairy products, dry peas and beans, and nuts and seeds.

    4   1   0

2. I limit the amount of fat, saturated fat, and cholesterol I eat (including fat in meats, eggs, butter, cream, shortenings, and organ meats such as liver).

    2   1   0

3. I limit the amount of salt I eat by cooking with only small amounts, not adding salt at the table, and avoiding salty snacks.

    2   1   0

4. I avoid eating too much sugar (especially frequent snacks of sticky candy or soft drinks).

    2   1   0

Eating habits score: _____

Exercise/fitness: Almost always   Sometimes   Almost never

1. I maintain a desired weight, avoiding overweight and underweight.

    3   1   0

2. I do vigorous exercises for 15 to 30 minutes at least three times a week (examples include running, swimming, and brisk walking).

    3   1   0

3. I do exercises that enhance my muscle tone for 15 to 30 minutes at least three times a week (examples include yoga and calisthenics).

    2   1   0

4. I use part of my leisure time participating in individual, family, or team activities that increase my level of fitness (such as gardening, bowling, golf, and baseball).

    2   1   0

Exercise/fitness score: _____

Alcohol and drugs: Almost always   Sometimes   Almost never

1.   I avoid drinking alcoholic beverages or I drink no more than one or two drinks a day.

                        4   1   0

2.   I avoid using alcohol or other drugs (especially illegal drugs) as a way of handling stressful situations or the problems in my life.

                        2   1   0

3.   I am careful not to drink alcohol when taking certain medicines (for example, medicine for sleeping, pain, colds, and allergies).

                        2   1   0

4.   I read and follow the label directions when using prescribed and over-the-counter drugs.

                        2   1   0

Alcohol and drugs score: _____

What your scores mean:

9–10 Excellent   6–8 Good   3–5 Mediocre   0–2 Poor

SOURCE: Adapted from U.S. Department of Health and Human Services, Public Health Service. (1981). *Health style: A self-test* (PHS 81-50155). Washington, DC: Author.

solid information, without getting bogged down in a lot of technical details. As would you and Amanda, most Americans would like to live a longer life but want to enjoy it along the way. Taking the best possible care of ourselves shouldn't have to mean putting everything we enjoy on the "forbidden list." When we are ill, we want to be able to ask the right questions and evaluate the answers. When a medical decision needs to be made, we expect to be a partner in making it; thus, physician behavior can have an impact on a patient's health (*Harvard Health Letter,* October 2006).

Key factors in assuming greater personal responsibility for your own health include the following:

- Understanding how your body works
- Knowing how the body and mind interact
- Managing stress effectively
- Developing healthy eating and exercise habits
- Monitoring your health
- Getting periodic medical checkups
- Keeping your own medical records

- Knowing the health risks related to your family history
- Being aware of health hazards in your lifestyle, workplace, and environment
- Being an active participant in your own health care

Each individual or family should have one or more appropriate resources to be used as a guide to self-care and medical matters. Such books contain a great deal of valuable information about the body's functioning, eating and exercise habits for staying well, home health care for minor problems, and how to asses if medical help is needed. The use of the self-diagnosis symptom charts in the American Medical Association's *Family Medical Guide* is especially helpful in determining when to seek medical assistance.

Taking charge of your own health generally involves basic changes in how you relate to the medical establishment. In traditional practice, individuals are expected to assume the "good" patient role—being cooperative, undemanding, and unquestioning. Such docile behavior often has a detrimental side effect. Patients are anxious and depressed when they have little control over their treatment. In fact, patients are more likely to adhere to treatment plans when they feel they have control or decision-making power over what happens to them medically (McDonald-Miszczak, Maki, & Gould, 2000). Furthermore, because most patients are often cooperative, doctors underestimate patients' desire for information. On the other hand, people who go to the opposite extreme and adopt a "bad" patient role—complaining and demanding a lot from their doctors—may not fare much better because their aggressive behavior usually alienates medical personnel.

Instead, individuals should become *active* participants in their health care in a *collaborative* way, by cooperating with doctors but not surrendering their own rights (*Harvard Health Letter,* January 2006). The aim is to establish a working alliance between doctor and patient, with both working together for the good of the patient. Patients need to know that most doctors are willing to inform them of their medical condition and their options for treatment but that they are expected to take the initiative in asking questions. And doctors need to realize that patients who are informed of their medical problems and given an active role in deciding their course of treatment are more likely to monitor their progress and adhere to the prescribed treatment.

Eating Sensibly

An integral part of a health-producing routine is practicing good health habits such as sensible patterns of eating and drinking, keeping physically fit, getting adequate rest, and visiting a physician regularly. Because more people "kill themselves" with a knife and fork than by any other means, one of the best ways to promote good health is to eat sensibly. Unfortunately, Amanda is not a very good role model. Eating sensibly involves eating a *reasonable* amount of *healthy* food. The amount of food is often measured in **calories**—*a measurement of energy produced by food when oxidized, or "burned," in the body.* The number of calories needed each day depends on such factors as age, sex, size, and rate of metabolism. A woman in her early 20s with a desk job needs about 2,000 calories a day; a woman with a more active life needs about 2,200 calories. A man with a desk job uses about 2,500 calories; one with a fairly active job, such as a carpenter, needs about 2,800 calories. Men and women who are in strenuous jobs or in athletic training may need anywhere from 3,000 to 4,000 calories a day. Sticking to calorie counts is not easy given that high-calorie, fast-food restaurants are everywhere and portion sizes on U.S. tables and in restaurants are increasing. Although results are mixed on studies of

Eating lots of fruits and vegetables is part of any healthy diet.

aging and calorie consumption in humans, some studies demonstrate that calorie restriction postpones age-related declines and delays the onset of late-life diseases such as cancer and heart disease (Lofshult, 2006; Spindler, 2001).

A well-balanced diet includes adequate amounts of various groups of substances: proteins, carbohydrates, certain fats, vitamins, minerals, and fibers. Individuals vary in their nutritional needs because of factors such as their size, age, sex, and level of physical activity. A handy guide to eating a balanced diet is the new food guide pyramid (see www.MyPyramid.gov) issued by the United States Department of Agriculture. The pyramid puts greater emphasis on grains as found in cereal and bread, vegetables, and fruits and less emphasis on foods containing fats and sugar (see Figure 5–2).

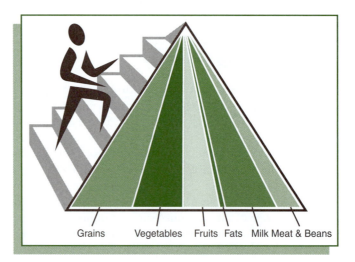

Grains   Vegetables   Fruits   Fats   Milk   Meat & Beans

FIGURE 5–2

My pyramid

Go to mypyramid.gov to create a personally customized pyramid for you.
SOURCE: www.mypyramid.gov

The new pyramid, as depicted here, is just a general representation of good nutrition. By **nutrition**, experts generally mean *a proper, balanced diet that promotes health*. The strength of the new pyramid is that you can *customize* it for your age, sex, and lifestyle by going to the website and indicating your personal characteristics (U.S. Department of Agriculture, 2005). The results will reveal exactly how many servings of or how much of each food group you should consume. Most overweight people have poor nutrition in that they consume too many carbohydrates in the form of high-sugar foods such as donuts and high-fat food such as fast-food French fries. A more desirable diet includes generous amounts of vegetables and fruits, which provide nutrition and energy as well as fiber. Dairy products and meat, along with other protein-laden foods, are needed in fewer servings per day and are used for energy and the growth and repair of body tissue.

Getting Enough Sleep

Have you ever stayed up all night? Perhaps, like Amanda, you've missed several consecutive nights of sleep. The effects of sleep deprivation vary from one person to another. Deprived of sleep, most people make greater errors on routine tasks and experience increased drowsiness, a stronger desire to sleep, and a tendency to fall asleep easily. When they finally fall asleep, chances are they'll sleep a few hours longer than usual, but extra hours of sleep won't make up the total sleep time lost.

Our sleep/wake cycles typically follow a biochemical clock designed to help us conserve energy. Reestablishing our natural sleep cycle is more important than trying to make up all the hours of lost sleep. Although we can accommodate ourselves to a variety of changes such as shift work, jet lag, and all-night study sessions, these adjustments take a toll on our bodies as well as our sense of well-being. How much sleep do you need? Does it vary from other individuals' needs? The average person sleeps about seven hours each night, but the need for sleep again varies from one person to another. You're probably getting enough sleep if you

(1) wake up spontaneously.

(2) feel well rested.

(3) don't have to struggle through periods of sleepiness during the day.

Perhaps you have difficulty sleeping. Box 5–4 (page 116) provides tips for falling asleep faster and better.

Keeping Physically Fit

What comes to mind when you think of fitness? **Physical fitness** is *our ability to function efficiently and effectively, including both health-related and skill-related fitness components.* Do you imagine some muscular person lifting weights? Or do you think of people jogging or running along the road? Whatever you imagine, chances are that it represents only part of what is necessary for overall physical fitness. Actually, physical fitness is the *entire* human organism's ability to function efficiently and effectively and therefore to increase life expectancy. Despite common knowledge that exercise is healthful, 30 percent of the adult population is not active at all (Centers for Disease Control and Prevention, 2005). Moreover, although many people have enthusiastically embarked on vigorous exercise programs at one time or another, most do not sustain their participation.

Box 5–4

CAN'T GET TO SLEEP?

Most of us have trouble falling asleep occasionally. For some, especially older adults, it's a recurring problem. Although there is no magical solution to this age-old complaint, following are some suggestions:

- Go to bed and get up at about the same time each day. Make sure you're allowing enough time for sleep.

- Relax before bedtime. Listen to music or practice yoga. But avoid strenuous exercise.

- Keep your bedroom conducive to sleep. Make sure it's quiet and dark and at a suitable temperature.

- Avoid alcohol and sleeping pills. Although these may put you to sleep sooner, they interfere with your normal sleep cycle.

- Take a lukewarm bath before bed. Hot or cold showers tend to be too stimulating. Sleep is induced when the body's core temperature falls, so you can artificially induce this by taking a warm bath.

- When you're having trouble falling asleep, count sheep or think of something pleasant that will distract you from worrying.

- Take some honey, which releases serotonin, the biochemical that induces sleep and relaxation.

- Don't stay awake fretting that sleeplessness will harm your health.

- If your home remedies don't work, seek professional help at a sleep center.

The body responds to physical activity in ways that have important positive effects on the muscular, skeletal, cardiovascular, respiratory, and endocrine systems. These changes are consistent with a number of health benefits, including a reduced risk of premature mortality and reduced risks of coronary heart disease, hypertension, colon cancer, and diabetes mellitus. Regular participation in physical activity also appears to reduce depression and anxiety, improve mood, and enhance ability to perform daily tasks throughout the life span (Centers for Disease Control and Prevention, 2005; Crone, Smith, & Gough, 2005). Physical fitness also provides us with a sense of mastery, helps us overcome sad moods, and can even help fend off some forms of cancer (Fischer, 1999). Fitness also reduces feelings of depression and anxiety (Centers for Disease Control and Prevention, 2004).

The risks associated with physical activity must also be considered. The most common health problems that have been associated with physical activity are injuries, which can occur with excessive amounts of activity or with suddenly beginning an activity for which the body is not conditioned. Much more serious associated health problems (e.g., heart attack) are rarer, occurring primarily among sedentary people with advanced coronary disease who engage in strenuous activity to which they are unaccustomed. Sedentary people, especially those with preexisting health conditions, who wish to increase their physical activity should check with their physician first and gradually build up to the desired level of activity (National Center for Chronic Disease Prevention and Health Promotion, 1999). Table 5–1 shows some of the calories you can burn doing everyday activities, many of which you may enjoy doing. There are few reasons to be completely inactive!

In selecting your personal exercise program, you may find it helpful to observe the following points:

1. Identify your personal physical fitness needs.   A good way to do so is to consult someone in the physical education department of your college or a specialist in one of the physical fitness centers in your community.

TABLE 5–1	
EXAMPLES OF MODERATE AMOUNTS OF ACTIVITY THAT WILL HELP YOU STAY FIT	
Common Chores	**Sporting Activities**
Washing and waxing a car for 45–60 minutes	Playing volleyball for 45–60 minutes
Washing windows or floors for 45–60 minutes	Playing touch football for 45 minutes
Gardening for 30–45 minutes	Walking 1 3/4 miles in 35 minutes (20 min/mile)
Wheeling self in wheelchair 30–40 minutes	Basketball (shooting baskets) 30 minutes
Pushing a stroller 1 1/2 miles in 30 minutes	Bicycling 5 miles in 30 minutes
Raking leaves for 30 minutes	Dancing fast (social) for 30 minutes
Walking 2 miles in 30 minutes (15 min/mile)	Water aerobics for 30 minutes
Shoveling snow for 15 minutes	Swimming laps for 20 minutes
Stairwalking for 15 minutes	Basketball (playing game) for 15–20 minutes
	Bicycling 4 miles in 15 minutes
	Jumping rope for 15 minutes
	Running 1 1/2 miles in 15 minutes (10 min/mile)

SOURCE: Department of Health and Human Services. (2006). *Guide to physical activity.* http://www.nhlbi.nih.gov/health/public/heart/obesity/lose_wt/phy_act.htm.

2. Select personalized physical exercises to make exercise more enjoyable.   Choose physical activities that are related to your interests, needs, and personality. Choose an activity that feels good to you, regardless of what others do.

3. Vary your activities.   By varying your activities you can include ones that will develop different aspects of physical fitness. This variation also helps to keep exercise interesting and enjoyable. Usually, changes in the weather and the seasons along with availability of facilities suggest some variation in your exercise program.

4. Exercise regularly.   It's best to set aside a time and place for your exercise activities, making exercise part of your daily routine. It's also important to perform your exercises to a level that will promote optimal fitness, usually a minimum of 20 to 30 minutes three times a week. For people who are unable to set aside 30 minutes for physical activity, shorter episodes are clearly better than none (National Center for Chronic Disease Prevention and Health Promotion, 1999).

5. Periodically evaluate and modify your routine.   As time passes, your needs and interests change. Shifts in your work schedule and family responsibilities may also dictate a change in your exercise program. Then, too, your age and overall level of stress should be kept in mind. Listen to your body. Assess how you feel.

Physical fitness is a vital part of the sense of wholeness mentioned earlier, but from all that you have read, it should also be clear that your overall well-being includes other considerations, such as eating habits, work schedules, lifestyles, awareness of health hazards and stress, personal attitudes, and morale.

Finding Social Support

One other means by which we can remain healthy is to *affiliate with others such as friends and family to find comfort and advice,* in other words to seek **social support.** Individuals like Amanda who are sociable are generally healthier than those who are not. Said another way, individuals who have sturdy social support networks are healthier (Jorm,

2005). For example, elderly people with good social support networks report better health (Krause, 2006), and persons suffering from severe brain trauma rehabilitate better with good social support (Tomberg, Toomela, Pulver, & Tikk, 2005). On the contrary, individuals who are socially isolated are at greater risk for health problems than those who are socially engaged. Some caution is needed here, though, because socializing and seeking social support is not for everyone. In other works, in order to truly benefit from a social support network, one must be *ready* to accept the support of others.

SUMMARY

BODY IMAGE

Although Americans may be healthy and fit, they are not necessarily satisfied with their looks. Weight is a major factor, and about one-half of men and women are dissatisfied with their weight. Many Americans are dissatisfied with their bodies because their weight is at odds with the prevailing ideal of slimness in our society as promoted by our media. A somewhat higher proportion of women than men are dissatisfied with their looks, largely because our society encourages women to hold themselves to a stricter standard of thinness than men.

HEALTH AND THE MIND–BODY RELATIONSHIP

The growing acceptance of mind-body unity suggests that psychological factors may play a significant role in almost any physical ailment, not just in the traditional psychosomatic illnesses. The detrimental effects of stress tend to weaken our immune system, thereby making us more susceptible to illness. At the same time, there is increasing evidence that we may bolster our resistance to stress and illness by harnessing the powers of the mind—our thoughts, attitudes, emotions, and sense of control.

Other major health hazards are related to lifestyle and include obesity, cigarette smoking, and alcohol and drug abuse. Obesity and being overweight, affecting over half of all Americans, are associated with an increased risk of illness and death from a variety of causes, including diabetes, high blood pressure, and coronary heart disease.

Many Americans smoke cigarettes. Cigarette smoking is a major factor in heart disease, lung cancer, and emphysema and may be one entry point to illicit drug use. Three-fourths of U.S. adult men and two-thirds of women drink alcoholic beverages. Automobile accidents involving alcohol are still a leading cause of death among youths, and people with alcohol-related ailments fill half of the occupied beds in U.S. hospitals.

COPING WITH ILLNESS

In evaluating the seriousness of our body complaints, we tend to rely on a decision-making process with three stages: (1) noticing and interpreting symptoms, (2) seeking professional help when needed, and (3) adhering to the prescribed treatment. Depending on culture, ethnicity, race, and gender, individuals differ in their tendency to label body aches and pains as symptoms of serious illness and subsequently seek help. Although men are generally more reluctant than women to do so, people are more likely to see a doctor when they have severe, disabling symptoms rather than minor ones, especially in the lower half of the body. As many as half of those who get professional help do not complete the prescribed treatment.

PROMOTING WELLNESS

There is an increased emphasis on optimal health and wellness rather than simply the absence of illness. To be healthy is to have the full use of one's body and mind, despite an occasional bout of illness—and to be alert, energetic, and happy to be alive even in old age. An important factor in the pursuit of positive health is the willingness to take charge of our own health, including greater personal responsibility and more collaboration with health care professionals in all matters pertaining to health.

An integral part of producing a healthy lifestyle is practicing good health habits. Eating sensibly involves both the amount and the kind of food we eat, including a balanced diet that provides the necessary nutrition and calories for someone of our age, size, and lifestyle. Keeping physically fit usually involves following a personalized exercise program especially suited to our interests and needs. Social contact and support is also healthy for most people. The pursuit of wellness, although it is rarely fully achieved, may enable each of us to function better than we would have otherwise.

SELF-TEST

1. _____ help(s) enable us to adopt healthy lifestyles.
   a. Confrontation
   b. Self-efficacy
   c. Downward comparisons
   d. Avoidance

2. A positive body image is strongly associated with
   a. higher self-esteem.
   b. height.
   c. higher intelligence.
   d. sexual interest in the opposite sex.

3. Which of the following kills the most number of people each year?
   a. Alcohol use
   b. AIDS
   c. Tobacco use
   d. Illicit drug use

4. At least one of every five chronic heavy drinkers of alcohol develops
   a. diabetes.
   b. heart attack.
   c. throat cancer.
   d. cirrhosis of the liver.

5. People most likely to label their physical symptoms as an illness are high in
   a. hypochondriasis.
   b. self-esteem.
   c. extroversion.
   d. sensation seeking.

6. About half of the people who discover they have an illness
   a. die within three months.
   b. seek professional help for it.
   c. become depressed over their condition.
   d. complete the prescribed treatment for it.

7. Assuming greater responsibility for your health involves
   a. getting periodic checkups.
   b. using only name-brand drugs.
   c. being a good patient by not asking doctors too many questions.
   d. All of these are responsible behaviors.

8. People with high blood cholesterol tend to eat a lot of food with
   a. carbohydrates.   c. fats.
   b. proteins.   d. fiber.

9. The recommended amount of exercise for a healthy adult is
   a. 10 minutes a day.
   b. 1 hour every day.
   c. 30 minutes three to five times a week.
   d. Healthy adults do not need to exercise.

10. Finding social support
    a. has no effect on health.
    b. has little effect on health.
    c. has negative effects on health.
    d. usually has positive effects on health.

EXERCISES

1. *Do you practice good eating habits?* Describe your eating habits in terms of the calories consumed each day and a balanced diet. If you're not sure how many calories you consume, keep a daily count for at least three days and take an average. How does your calorie count compare to the average for someone like yourself as indicated in the text? Do you also choose foods from each of the major food areas as described in the chapter?

2. *Describe your personal exercise habits.* How much exercise do you get in the course of your daily activities? Would you agree that everyone needs to be physically active on a regular basis? If you have a personalized exercise program, describe it in a paragraph or two.

3. *Identify your biggest health hazard.* Are you guilty of one of the common health hazards, such as overeating, poor nutrition, smoking, drinking, or drug abuse? If so, what are you doing about it? Try eliminating this hazard for five consecutive days and see if you feel better about yourself and your health. Better yet, try to eliminate it over the long term.

4. *Do you suffer from a chronic ailment?* Do you have to cope with some type of chronic or recurring condition, such as an allergy, asthma, arthritis, hypertension, diabetes, migraine headaches, or ulcers? How well are you managing such ailments? Are you aware of the psychosocial factors that may influence your ailments, such as environmental stress and your emotions? What are you doing to improve your condition? Does this ailment affect your self-esteem?

5. *How much control do you exercise over your health?* Do you believe you can minimize your chances of getting sick by practicing good nutrition, regular exercise, positive attitudes, and stress management? Or do you feel that coming down with a cold or the flu is mostly a matter of luck?

QUESTIONS FOR SELF-REFLECTION

1. Which part of your body or face has been the most difficult for you to accept?

2. Do you take care of your body?

3. What aspect of your eating habits would you most like to change?

4. Do you enjoy regular, vigorous physical exercise? If not, why not? How could you alter the latter situation?

5. What is your worst health hazard?

6. If you're a smoker, how many times have you tried to quit? What is it that keeps you from quitting permanently?

7. Are you aware that the use of alcohol easily becomes a health hazard? Be honest; do you have a drug or alcohol problem?

8. Do you often find that a cold or flu was preceded by a period of intense emotional stress?

9. Would you agree that a healthy body and a sound mind go together?

10. Were you securely attached as a child? Do you find that you prefer social support or would you rather cope with your problems alone?

FOR FURTHER INFORMATION

RECOMMENDED READINGS

AMERICAN MEDICAL ASSOCIATION. (2004). *Family medical guide.* Hoboken, NJ: Wiley. A book with up-to-date health care advice from the top association for American physicians.

GREGSON, D., & EFRAN, J. S. (2002). *The Tao of sobriety: Helping you to recover from alcohol and drug addiction.* New York: Thomas Dunne. A classic that helps individuals recognize when they suffer from addiction and abuse as well as how they can tackle these issues.

HIRKOWITZ, M., SMITH, P. B., & DEMENT, W. C. (2004). *Sleep disorders for dummies.* Hoboken, NJ: Wiley. The average person's guide to recognizing and overcoming sleep disorders.

HOEGER, W. W. K., & HOEGER, S. A. (2007). *Fitness and wellness.* Belmont, CA: Wadsworth. A comprehensive fitness and wellness book that also comes with ancillaries such as a log book and a personalized health profile.

SARAFINO, E. P. (2005). *Health psychology: Biopsychosocial perspectives.* Hoboken, NJ: Wiley. A textbook in the zeitgeist field of health psychology, which forms the basis for much of this chapter.

WEBSITES AND THE INTERNET

http://www.nlm.nih.gov/medlineplus/wellnessandlifestyle.html   A government website for links to wellness and health-related information on a plethora of topics, which are listed alphabetically.

http://www.firstpath.com   The site provides valuable diet and fitness tips. It claims to help balance body, mind, and soul.

http://www.healthfinder.gov   A site provided by the government that you can utilize to find information prepared by health agencies under various health topics.

http://www.cdc.gov   The official site for the Centers for Disease Control and Prevention. There is a wealth of information on all types of health concerns as well as links to other sites related to health and wellness.

http://www.seekwellness.com   This site provides lots of tips on all types of health and wellness issues such as fitness, weight control, sexuality, and nutrition.

CHAPTER 6

Taking Charge

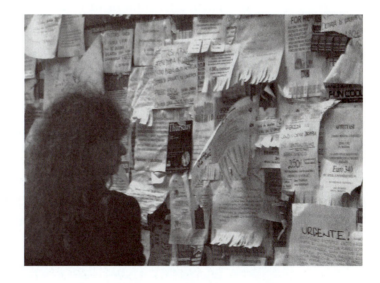

Learning Objectives

After completing this chapter, you should be able to

1. Discuss the importance of perceived control.
2. Describe the explanatory style associated with learned optimism.
3. Identify the stages of decision making.
4. List several suggestions for improving decision-making skills.
5. Describe suggestions for applying sound principles of decision making to your life.
6. Provide an example of someone who has grown because of a decision he or she has made.

Stan, a 46-year-old married student, was facing an important choice. It seems he had lost his job as a foreman in a steel plant during the past year. Then, after months of unsuccessful job hunting and agonizing over his future, Stan had decided to enroll in college to become an engineer. He worked as a handyman part-time to pay the family bills. Recently and unexpectedly, Stan's former employer called and offered him a chance to return to work. "It's a tempting offer," Stan said to himself. "But I'm not sure I want to go back." Stan acknowledged that by taking back his old job he would be able to support his wife and two small children more adequately. "But then I'd always worry about when the next layoff was coming," he thought. At the same time, Stan was under great stress attending school full-time; he was having a difficult time paying bills, and he was constantly tired. Nor was there any assurance he would get a good job as an engineer once he got his degree.

MASTERY AND PERSONAL CONTROL

As you can see, Stan is caught in a major life dilemma. His case illustrates two important concepts in this chapter—personal control and decision making. Like Stan, if we perceive that a goal is attainable, we usually take charge (seek control) and surge into action. In other words, we feel some sense of control or personal mastery over our lives. When we are doubtful that a goal is attainable, we are less likely to feel we have control and less likely to undertake the actions necessary to achieve the goal (Jackson, Weiss, Lundquist, & Soderlind, 2002). Thus, we have to make both large and small decisions in our lives, based in part on whether we perceive we have mastery and control over various events.

Stan, like many of us, is striving to attain a greater degree of self-mastery, or, as psychologists have labeled it, personal control, over his life. **Personal control** means *the achieved amount of control we have over our lives;* this term is often used synonymously with perceived control. Stan resents being at the mercy of a large corporation and having a job that is so vulnerable to the ups and downs of the economy. He realizes that acquiring greater mastery over his life means facing up to important life choices. It's not simply a matter of whether to accept his old job or to remain in school, as hard a choice as this is. It goes deeper than that. Such decisions also involve important value choices in regard to what he wants out of life, what he's willing to settle for, what he is willing to sacrifice, and how hard he's willing to work to get what he wants. It's no surprise that this has been a trying time in Stan's life, with many sleepless nights and numerous heart-to-heart talks with his wife, who supports his decision to attend college. Interestingly, Stan refused the offer of his old job and continued his education.

Stan's experience reminds us of the importance of personal control and of the crucial role of decision making in our lives. We'll begin the chapter by exploring the topic of personal control and its implications for personal adjustment and growth. Then we'll devote the rest of the chapter to the process of decision making, including how we can improve our decision-making skills to facilitate our personal growth.

Personal control has become a very important issue today for many reasons. First, our lives, just as is Stan's, are increasingly shaped by large, impersonal bureaucracies, such as the government and business corporations; they often have more impact on the economy than we do and thus on our personal lives. Then, too, there is greater awareness that our lives are at the mercy of events or conditions beyond our immediate control, such as economic recessions, terrorism, or even hurricanes. On the other hand, the civil rights movement and the other movements that have followed in its wake have taught us that individuals *can* gain greater mastery over their lives by active participation in the democratic process, like participating in demonstrations and boycotts or promoting certain pieces of legislation. In democratic societies that nourish independence and freedom of choice, it is well to remember that each of us has considerable power to shape our destinies through personal decisions, such as the choosing of a career, deciding where to live, and finding a partner, as well as through changing our lifestyles, for example, from eating fast food to starting a healthy diet.

Perceived Control

The aspect of personal control that has received the most attention from psychologists, primarily because it is the most accessible to empirical investigation (Double, 1996), is **perceived control**—*the belief that we can influence the occurrence of events in our environment that affect our lives.* In other words, we sometimes feel or like to feel that we have control over fate, even if we really do not. Perceived control is very important because it appears to be the one type of control that accounts for our motivation to behave in a certain fashion (Jewell & Kidwell, 2005). To return to our opening case, Stan *perceived* that a better education would give him more control over his destiny. Likewise, Stupinsky and associates (2007) found that perceived control positively predicts students' grade point averages. In other words, the more students perceive they can control their grades (e.g., by studying hard, seeking extra help from professors, and so forth), the higher their grades.

An important concept related to perceived control is **locus of control,** which means *the source from which an individual believes control over life events originates—either within the person or outside of the person.* Perceived control is similar to a concept introduced elsewhere in this book (Ajzen, 2002; Judge, Erez, Bono, & Thoreson, 2002; Luszczynska, Benight, & Cieslak, 2009), **self-efficacy,** *belief in one's capabilities to organize and execute the courses of action required to produce given attainments* (Bandura, 1997). Both of these concepts may sound vaguely like what lay people simply call will power (Wargo, 2009).

Psychologists have identified two sources of perceived control (Zuckerman, Knee, Kieffer, & Gagne, 2004). One is an **internal locus of control,** *in which the individual believes he or she has control over life events.* Stan exemplifies a person with a healthy sense of internal sense of control. He believed that if he studied hard and obtained his degree, he and his family would have a better future. The other source of control is **external locus of control,** *in which the individual believes that something outside of him- or herself— such as other individuals, fate, or various external situations—controls life events.* One of Stan's engineering classmates exemplifies this type of control, especially after she did not do well in her first pre-engineering course. She believed that no matter how hard she studied, she would never end up with an engineering degree because of the stigma held by certain professors against women in the engineering field.

A large body of research indicates that perception of control is related to various beneficial outcomes, such as improved well-being, better performance on various tasks, and better coping with adversity (Zuckerman et al., 2004). For example, individuals with an internalized locus of causality or control are more likely to maintain physical fitness routines (Chatzisarantis, Hagger, Biddle, & Karageorghis, 2002), earn better grades (Stupinsky et al., 2007) and better cope with trauma (Frazier, Steward, & Mortensen, 2004). Similarly, individuals with an internal locus of control cope better with pain (Vallerand, Hasenau, Templin, & Collins-Bohler, 2005) and with bereavement (Ong, Bergeman, & Bisconti, 2005). On the other hand, there exists much research that shows individuals who believe in external or low personal control are more prone to diagnosable disorders such as depression and anxiety (Chapman, Kertz, & Woodruff-Borden, 2009; Griffin, Fuhrer, Stansfeld, & Marmot, 2002; Grobani, Krauss, Watson, & Le Briton, 2008) and eating disorders (Sassaroli, Galucci, & Ruggiero, 2008).

Internalized control, however, is very "American" (O'Connor & Shimizu, 2002; Yamaguchi, Gelfand, Ohashi, & Zemba, 2005). We might expect that in Eastern or Asian cultures, which are more collective and interdependent rather than individualistic, an internal locus of control is not as appreciated or expected (Grobani et al., 2008). For instance, Liu and Yussen (2005) found that Chinese students were far more likely than American students to attribute school success to luck, probably because of differences in religion, school feedback, and life philosophy. Likewise, Yamaguchi et al. found that Japanese individuals have an exaggerated sense of collective (group) control as compared to Americans, who possess an exaggerated sense of individual or personal control.

Other differences in locus of control exist. Men have a greater sense of internal control than women, especially when older men and women are compared (Ross & Mirowsky, 2002). Husbands report feeling more mastery (control) than do wives (Cassidy & Davies, 2003). People in developing countries perceive more externalized control than members of industrialized societies (Matsumoto, 2000). Individuals from Western cultures may prefer and have more experience with primary control, whereas individuals reared in Asian cultures may prefer and experience secondary control. **Primary control** *refers to actions directed at attempting to change the world to fit one's needs and desires;* **secondary control** *involves the individual utilizing processes directed at making him- or herself fit into the world better* (Ashman, Shiomura, & Levy, 2006). Some research also indicates age differences in primary and secondary control, with older individuals more likely to use secondary control strategies (Ashman et al.). Given such differences, research reveals that for most people, optimal adjustment is achieved *when the amount of actual control matches the desired need for control* (Conway, Vickers, & French, 1992).

We should add here the newest findings (from neuroscience) that show that the prefrontal cortex plays a major role in our ability to restrain our behavior and impulses (Wargo, 2009). This research, for example, demonstrates that because the prefrontal cortex matures later than other brain systems, adults should be better than children at controlling themselves. Likewise, similar research shows that when our self-control is depleted (and our brain becomes fatigued by too much restraint), we may, in fact, experience even less control than we ordinarily would (Ackerman, Goldstein, Shapiro, & Bargh, 2009; Wargo, 2009). So beware—sticking to a diet may actually cause you to make even more impulsive purchases at the mall or, worse for a dieter, want to eat more sugar.

Protests often provide a sense of control, although those from collective societies, such as Asians, may feel uncomfortable expressing such strong individualism.

Research also demonstrates that individuals high in external control can learn to develop a sense of internal locus of control or self-control (Wargo, 2009). Cone and Owens (1991) enrolled freshmen at risk for failing or dropping out of college in a study skills and adjustment course. At the end of the semester, these students' grade point averages were compared to students who were also at risk but who were not enrolled in the special course. Compared to students not in the class, the students who were registered had higher grades and had shifted to more internalized loci of control. Manger, Eikeland, and Asbjornsen (2002) dipped lower into the age pool and retrained children with an external locus of control to develop more perceived internal control.

Given that a sense of self-control is important to so many facets of life, how much control would you say you have over your personal life? To check on your perception, complete the personal control survey in Activity 6–1 (page 128).

ACTIVITY 6–1

HOW MUCH SELF-CONTROL DO YOU HAVE?

INSTRUCTIONS: *This survey is designed to inspire you to think about how much perceived control you have. For each statement below, circle T for* true *or F for* false *as the statement applies to you.*

T F   **1.** I like to put off decisions as long as I can because situations affecting the decision might change without warning.

T F   **2.** The amount of time I study is unrelated to my grades and whether I leave a favorable impression on my professors.

T F   **3.** Some people are just born lucky; others are not so lucky and in fact seem to be jinxed.

T F   **4.** If people like you, they like you. If they don't, they don't, so there is little point in trying to woo them as friends.

T F   **5.** My health is a matter of how many sick people I am around or whether there is a surge of illness in the community.

T F   **6.** Whether I take care of it or not, something is bound to go wrong at my home once in a while.

T F   **7.** People are born good or bad and rarely change over their life span.

T F   **8.** Even if I am in good shape, factors outside of me, such as the weather and others' competitiveness, keep me from performing well in competitive events.

T F   **9.** I am rather superstitious; I believe in bad omens (such as black cats) and good-luck charms (such as four-leaf clovers).

T F   **10.** There are so many bad drivers on the road that I am bound to be involved in a car accident sooner or later.

T F   **11.** If I carefully consider my options for major decisions, I know I can make the correct decision.

T F   **12.** When my friends and I disagree, I know that we will still be friends because I can argue my points in a reasonable manner.

T F   **13.** If people just keep trying, eventually good things will happen for them.

T F   **14.** When I am shopping for a hard-to-find item, my persistence typically pays off and I find what I need.

T F   **15.** I believe I have good judgment and that in hard times my common sense will prevail.

T F   **16.** I am a firm believer in American resilience; we can overcome negative events such as terrorist attacks.

T   F   **17.** There are times when I feel really angry when things go wrong, but I know I can control my temper and make things better.

T   F   **18.** When I meet a stranger, I feel that I can befriend this person if I so desire.

T   F   **19.** If a crisis occurred, I would be fine because I have the wherewithal to overcome it.

T   F   **20.** If I found myself at a job that was stressful or unappealing, I would take measures to find another and perhaps better job.

SCORING: This scale was designed for this book to encourage you to examine your level of perceived control over your life. Items 1–10 were phrased in the negative, indicating low perceived control. Items 11–20 were phrased in the affirmative, indicating higher levels of perceived control. Fill in the blanks below to determine your perceived level of control.

Total "Fs" or falses for items 1–10 _____

Total "Ts" or trues for items 11–20 _____

Grand Total = _____

INTERPRETATION: The higher your grand total, the more you feel you take charge of your own life. With the highest possible score being 20, a score of 1–5 suggests that you perceive little or no control over your life; a score of 6–10 indicates that you have some doubts that you possess control; a score of 11–15 signifies you believe you have reasonable control; and a score of 16–20 may demonstrate that you perceive high levels of control over your life. Remember that this scale is designed solely to stimulate some thought about your own life. If you scored on the low end (i.e., low perceived control), you might think about how you can increase actual or perceived control over your life by using some of the ideas in this chapter. If you scored at the very high end, consider whether you suffer from the illusion of control.

Other Consequences of Perceived Control

Research has shown that the presence or absence of perceived control or perceived self-mastery has further consequences in our lives, over and above the actual control available to us in a given situation. When we believe we can affect actual outcomes in our lives, choose among them, cope with the consequences, and understand them, we behave in a significantly different way than when we don't hold this belief (Jackson, Weiss, et al., 2002; Jewell & Kidwell, 2005). One such difference is in level of persistence on a task. Stan, for example, sincerely believed that *if he studied hard* he *would* earn a college degree that would eventually garner his family and him a better standard of living. Thus, Stan studied hard in college and persisted at his studies even though now and then he was discouraged by a below-average grade.

People who possess a high degree of perceived control tend to exhibit certain characteristics (Zuckerman et al., 2004). First and foremost, they are likely to seek knowledge and information about the events that affect their lives (Wang & Wu, 2008). Feeling they are in control of their lives, they make greater efforts to acquire information about themselves and their environment. For instance, when facing surgery or a serious illness, patients with a high degree of perceived control are especially likely to seek information about their condition, to ask questions of the doctors and nurses, and to make use of the resources available to them. This is one of the most consistent findings in studies of perceived control. Second, people high in perceived control are likely to attribute responsibility to themselves and to their abilities and efforts rather than to luck or the environment, at least in regard to desirable outcomes. When Stan received high grades in college, he readily attributed them to his hard work and intelligence. Third, people high in perceived control are resistant to social influence and are more likely to take part in social action that helps others. Stan, for example, ignored his brother's chuckles when teased about returning to college only to "ogle the young coeds." Stan instead found time to volunteer at the Special Olympics held each year on the college campus. And finally, individuals high in perceived control such as Stan are strongly achievement-oriented. They appear to work harder at intellectual and performance tasks, and their efforts are rewarded with better grades than those with less perceived control.

As you might expect, there is a strong positive relationship between perceived mastery or self-control and personal adjustment (Jackson, Weiss, et al., 2002; Zuckerman et al., 2004). In American society, individuals high in perceived control tend to be less anxious, better adjusted, and less likely to be classified with psychiatric labels than those with less perceived control. Perhaps the active, self-reliant qualities of those high in mastery lead to the kinds of successes that promote adjustment and growth. Or it may be that believing that one is in charge of one's destiny results in less anxiety and better adjustment.

People high in perceived control also use more effective strategies for coping with stress (Zuckerman et al., 2004). For example, individuals high in perceived mastery tend to use positive coping strategies, such as making a plan of action and sticking to it, taking one step at a time, or getting professional help and doing what is recommended (e.g., Cooper, Okamura, & McNeil, 1995). In contrast, people low in perceived control are more apt to use maladaptive strategies, such as wishing the problem would go away; blaming themselves; and seeking relief through overreacting, drinking, or abusing drugs (Blum, 1998). In the long run, the use of more effective coping strategies promotes better adjustment and growth (e.g., Aspinwall & Taylor, 1992; Zuckerman et al., 2004).

People high in perceived control also are more likely to take steps that will maximize their health and well-being and minimize the risk of illness (Zuckerman et al., 2004). Heth and Somer (2002) report that people with high mastery awareness perceive they have less stress and better health; such individuals also think in ways that enable them to manage environmental demands in more effective ways. These individuals are especially apt to seek information about health maintenance, engage in preventive health practices, adopt more positive attitudes about physical exercise, and participate in physical exercise more regularly. Stan, for example, realized that his college studies and his part-time job were creating stress, so he often went for what he called "stress management walks" when he came home from his day's classes.

People who believe they are in charge of their lives are likely to refrain from or give up the habit of smoking, to successfully complete weight-reduction programs, and to cooperate with prescribed treatment for medical problems. In regard to substance abuse, perceived self-control is a reliable predictor of who will complete the program and who will drop out. High perceived control also helps to predict who will succeed in overcoming eating disorders and successfully recover from heart attacks, and trauma (Luszczynska et al., 2009). Finally, people who feel empowered in their personal lives also demonstrate a relatively high level of happiness or subjective well-being (Klonowicz, 2001; Mellor, Hayashi, Firth, Stokes, Chambers, & Cummins, 2008).

Misperception and Maladjustment

Unfortunately, the misperception of personal control usually tends to have negative consequences. For instance, some individuals habitually believe they have even less control over their lives than they really do (Gilbert, Brown, Pinel, & Wilson, 2000), and thus they prematurely surrender potential self-mastery available to them. Others, even in the same situation, may go to the opposite extreme: Believing they exercise greater control than they actually do, they set themselves up for frustration and eventual disappointment (Seligman, 1994). In both cases, as you will see, such mistaken beliefs about personal control lead to maladaptive behavior (Zuckerman et al., 2004).

When people repeatedly encounter bad outcomes regardless of what they do, such as losing a job because of layoffs (Bjornstad, 2006), they tend to experience a diminished sense of personal control, thereby attributing too little control to themselves. Suppose that no matter how hard Stan studied when he first entered college, he failed every test. Stan might come to think that he could not succeed in college no matter what he did.

Martin Seligman (1981), who has studied this problem extensively, refers to this phenomenon as **learned helplessness**—*a maladaptive passivity that frequently follows an individual's experience with uncontrollable events.* Studies have shown that a host of psychological and physical difficulties follow a series of negative events outside a person's control, like unemployment, accidents, illnesses, death of a spouse, terrorism, and victimization (e.g., Bargal, Ben-Shakhar, & Shalev, 2007). However, uncontrollable events in themselves do not necessarily produce learned helplessness. The crucial matter consists of *how* people explain these events. To the extent they offer a permanent ("It's going to last forever"), universal ("This screws up everything"), and internal ("It's me") explanation for bad events, people tend to surrender control over their lives prematurely and respond poorly to such events when they occur. Accordingly, learned helplessness is associated with a variety of ills, including depression, academic failure, bureaucratic apathy, and premature death.

At the other extreme are people who believe they exercise more control over their lives than they actually do. In some cases, people exaggerate the degree of control they possess when outcomes are positive. Such overestimates of personal control tend to be fairly commonplace (Thompson, 1999; Yamaguchi et al., 2005). People often take more credit for good outcomes than they probably deserve, perhaps as a way of enhancing their self-regard. In other cases, people subscribe to the **illusion of control,** *believing they exert control over what is really a chance-determined event*—such as winning a lottery. From where does this overestimation come? Situational factors such as the familiarity of the situation and past successes influence overestimation. Likewise, personal factors such as a depressed mood or, as mentioned, living in a collective society also affect the illusion of control.

It is probably wise to recognize what we can and cannot effectively change or control (Seligman, 1994). When we want to change or break our bad habits, such as cigarette smoking, experts suggest that we focus on long-term negative consequences and minimize short-term rewards. In other words, we should take a rather futuristic orientation (Chapman, 1999).

Learned Optimism

A helpful way of achieving optimal but realistic perceived control can be seen in what Martin Seligman (1992) calls **learned optimism,** defined as *a learned way of explaining both good and bad life events that in turn enhances our perceived control and adaptive responses to* *them.* Optimism relates to control in that the greater control people perceive over future events, the greater their optimism (Klein & Helwig-Larson, 2002; Ratelle, Vallerand, Chantal, & Provencher, 2004). Optimism is another personal dimension that has been linked to good adjustment (Hirsch, Wolford, LaLonde, Brunk, & Parker-Morris, 2009; Jackson, Weiss, et al., 2002; Ratelle et al.). Optimism is related to better problem solving under stress (Amirkhan, Risinger, & Swickert, 1995), ego resiliency (Klohnen, 1996), better physical health (Cerrato, 2001; Chang, 1996; Jones, DeMore, Cohen, O'Connell, & Jones, 2008; Matthews, Raikkonen, Sutton-Tyrell, & Kuller, 2004), active coping and seeking of social support when appropriate (Aspinwall & Taylor, 1992), and overall psychological well-being (Bood, Archer, & Norlander, 2004; Scheier & Carver, 1993; Ratelle et al.).

As mentioned earlier, Seligman, along with other cognitive theorists, holds that it is not life events in themselves that overwhelm us. Rather, it is our beliefs and interpretations of them and, in turn, our subsequent responses that most affect our lives. Consequently, in learned optimism, the emphasis is on *interpreting life events in a reasonably accurate way* to enhance our perceived control and, thus, our adaptive responses. This goal is accomplished primarily by modifying our explanatory style, that is, the way we explain life events to ourselves (Jackson, Weiss, et al., 2002). The term *learned* precedes the word *optimism* because optimism can be learned. Parents can teach their children optimism by instructing them in problem-solving skills and adaptive coping skills and by modeling optimistic thinking for their children (Jackson, Pratt, Hunsberger, & Pancer, 2005; Scheier & Carver, 1993).

Although there are clear benefits to learned optimism, there is also a danger, namely, whether changing beliefs about failure from internal to external ("It wasn't my fault . . . it was bad luck") will undermine personal responsibility. As a result, Seligman (1992) does not advocate changing beliefs from internal to external in a wholesale manner, although there is one condition under which it is best to do so, namely, depression. When people become depressed, they tend to assume more responsibility—or more accurately, self-blame—for bad events than is warranted (Peterson & Vaidya, 2001).

Furthermore, Seligman (1992) emphasizes that learned optimism is not an absolute; unconditional optimism should not be blindly applied to all situations. Instead, it is a flexible optimism that is more appropriate in some situations than in others. An optimistic explanatory style tends to be appropriate in the following situations:

- If you're in a situation that involves achievement, such as writing a paper, getting a promotion, or winning a game, it helps to be optimistic. If you're concerned about how you will feel, that is, about keeping up your morale or fighting off discouragement and depression, emphasize the positive.

- If you're under chronic stress and your physical health is an issue, an optimistic outlook becomes crucial.

- If you want to lead, inspire others, or gain people's confidence, it's better to use optimism. However, there are also times when optimism is *not* appropriate.

- If your goal involves planning for a risky and uncertain future, do not use optimism.

- If your goal is to counsel others whose future is dim, do not use optimism initially.

- If you want to appear sympathetic to people's troubles, do not start with optimism, although, once confidence and empathy are established, optimism may help.

The basic guideline for choosing optimism or not is to ask what *the cost of failure* is in the particular situation. When the cost of failure is high, optimism is probably the wrong strategy, for example, the partygoer deciding to drive home after drinking too much. When the cost of failure is low, optimism is more appropriate, for example, the sales agent who decides to make one more call at the risk of only losing a little bit of personal time.

PERSONAL RESOLVE AND DECISION MAKING

As you just learned, a major means of exercising personal control or self-mastery is through the decisions we make—our basic life choices as well as everyday decisions. From the moment we awake until we go to sleep at night, we must make decisions or choices between various options (Luce, 2005). Modern life is awash in choices that force us to make decisions (Rosenthal, 2005; Schwartz, 2004). Fortunately, many of our day-to-day decisions, such as when to get up and what to eat for breakfast, are made with little effort, mostly because of our habits and daily routines. It is mainly when we encounter a new and serious problem or face an important life choice, as did Stan when he had to decide between his old job and college, that we become acutely aware of the need to make a decision (Schwartz). Then we may become so overwhelmed by the alternatives or so caught up in the mental anguish of considering the consequences of our choice that we put off making the decision (Anderson, 2003). Worse still, we may make a hasty decision to "get it over with," thereby increasing the risk of a poor decision. In both instances, we lose sight of the overall process of making decisions we can live with.

In this section you will learn about the process of decision making along with valuable aids for making sound decisions and acting on them. **Decision making** is *the process of gathering information about relevant alternatives and making an appropriate choice.*

The Process of Decision Making

Psychologists have formulated a system for making *wise* decisions—the kind of decisions we can live with. They recommend that we proceed systematically through several stages:

1. Rise to the challenge.   This stage involves your recognizing a problem or challenge for what it is, guarding against such hazards as oversimplifying a complex problem. Key question: "What are the risks of doing nothing, not changing, or not deciding?"

2. Search for alternatives.   This stage requires you to have an attitude of openness and flexibility, with a concern for information about all possible alternatives, obvious or not. Key question: "Have I considered all the alternatives?"

3. Evaluate the alternatives.   You should next evaluate all the options with regard to their practicality and consequences. Here you weigh various risks, costs, and possible gains. Key question: "Which is the best alternative?"

4. Make a commitment.   Ordinarily, it's best for you to choose the alternative that gives you maximum benefits at minimum costs. Yet there's the danger of acting impulsively to "get it over with." Key question: "When do I implement the best alternative and let others know my decision?" After due consideration, you should be able to *act on your decision* at this stage.

5. Assess your decision.   After you have acted on your decision, you can learn about your decision-making ability by assessing the quality, results, and consequences of your decision. Because every decision involves some risk, it is important that you do not overreact with disappointment, criticism, and self-blame. The danger here can be changing your mind prematurely or justifying your choice defensively, thus shutting out valuable feedback.

Critical elements in your decision-making process, especially in the earliest stages, are vigorous information seeking and processing. Finding and analyzing information is crucial to deliberate decision making (Hogarth, 2005). In doing so, you should seek out sources of information, take time to know and understand them, and talk to people who are in a position to help. Gathering information takes time and energy, disrupting routines and building tension and conflict, all of which can be unpleasant (Luce, 2005; Schwartz, 2004). Consequently, most of us do not seek sufficient information, although we are more willing to look for new information when we expect the benefits of a decision to outweigh the costs. In our fast-paced society, Americans sometimes expect snap judgments and quick action and chide those who are slow or deliberate when making decisions. Interestingly, research shows that individuals who appear to procrastinate in decision making actually are more systematic and seek more information before they make a decision (Ferrari & Dovidio, 2000). Procrastination in the form of thoughtfulness is not so bad.

It is also easy to use shortcuts in your decision making, especially when you are in a hurry, busy, or tired. Some people, for example, turn to the media (World Wide Web, television, or newspapers) to gather information. The Internet, indeed, has become the number-one source for health information for consumers (Morahan-Martin, 2004) with about 80 percent of Internet users searching (Fox, 2008) and women outnumbering men in such searches (Burst Media, 2009). The danger of this seemingly efficient method is that the media may offer an unrepresentative view of the world (Anastasio, Rose, & Chapman, 1999; Hajjar, Gable, Jenkinson, Kane, & Riley, 2005). The media, particularly the Internet, present a double-edged sword; they may both help and harm people, especially those searching for health information. Information may be readily available but it might also be inaccurate (Gray, 2008). A better idea is to turn to a *variety of sources* that offer a mixture of professional information (Anastasio et al., 1999), thus resulting in your making more realistic and informed decisions.

Unfortunately, in making important life choices, such as that of a career, many of us tend to underestimate the benefits of information gathering and therefore pay a high price for not doing it well or at all. There's nothing more agonizing than discovering a better choice after you've already committed to a less desirable course of action—right? Fortunately for Stan, before he paid his first semester of tuition, a major expense for him, he visited the college's career development center to examine his career projections over the next decade. These projections estimated the number of jobs in various fields and forecasted future salaries. Equipped with this information, Stan was firmly convinced he had made the right decision to enroll in college and study engineering.

Another element in decision making of which to be mindful is **postdecision regret,** *the regret that can be experienced shortly after we have finally made a particularly difficult choice or decision.* It is quite normal after you have made a decision to feel that you may have made an incorrect or poor decision and to experience regret (Connolly & Zeelenberg, 2002; Roese & Summerville, 2005; van Harreveld, van der Pligt, & Nordgren, 2008). We all tend to suffer from the "grass is greener on the other side of the fence" phenomenon, but mostly *after* we make a decision. You're not alone if you experience regret after an important decision. Some of the top life-choice decisions about which Americans experience regret are education, careers, romance, and parenting (Roese & Summerville).

Regret about decision making may have at least three contributory components:

(1) That the outcome is poorer than expected (perhaps because the unchosen alternative really was better) (van Harreveld, van der Pligt, & Nordgren, 2008).

(2) Self-blame for having made a bad decision (Connolly & Zeelenberg, 2002; Gilbert, Morewedge, Risen, & Wilson, 2004; Roese & Summerville, 2005)

(3) Missed opportunities, especially when the missed opportunity was a *near* miss (Roese & Summerville)

We sometimes anticipate regret or other negative emotions *before* the decision (Luce, 2005), but we are all quite familiar with postdecisional regret from our past mistakes (Crawford, McConnell, Lewis, & Sherman, 2002; van Dijk & Zeelenberg, 2005). Moreover, our *actions* tend to generate more regret in the short term while our *inaction* produces more regret in the long run (Gilovich & Medvec, 1995). Similarly, people usually feel more regret because of inaction than from action (Feldman, Miyamoto, & Loftus, 1999). Knowing these parameters may help you avoid or cope better with postdecisional regret when it happens to you.

Psychologists alternatively call *this uncomfortable feeling of regret* **cognitive dissonance.** Most people can live with dissonance and regret, especially if they have carefully planned the decision or are well adjusted. Eventually, the dissonance goes away as we discover that we really did make a good decision or that the unselected alternatives really are less desirable. For Stan, the support of his wife confirmed for him that staying in college rather than returning to his old job was wise. Postdecisional dissonance or regret did not last a long time for Stan. Some individuals cannot live easily with dissonance or postdecisional regret so find ways to make themselves feel better.

One method they use is social comparison (van Harreveld, van der Pligt, & Nordgren, 2008). You will learn more about **social comparison** in other chapters, but for now know that it involves *the process of using others to compare ourselves to in order to understand who we are relative to them.* Especially in instances of a *bad* decision (or bad

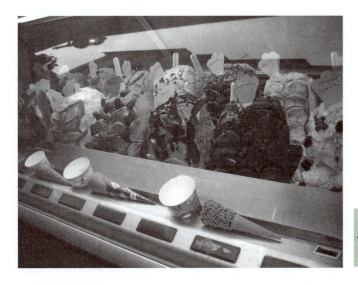

This ice cream might taste good as you eat it but can become "bitter" as post-decisional regret sets in.

performance), individuals prefer to compare themselves to others who have made *worse* decisions (or performed more poorly) (van Harreveld, van der Pligt, & Nordgren, 2008) thus lessening their feelings of regret.

Another common but not always good strategy for reducing regret is **hindsight bias,** *a biased representation of events or information once they have happened or after the fact* (Blank, Musch, & Pohl, 2007; van Harreveld, van der Pligt, & Nordgren, 2008). This is a sort of being-wise-after-the-event, sense-making process that is triggered by surprising or negative events as well as events that inspire "why" questions (as in "Why did that happen?" or "Why did that go wrong?") (Blank, Musch, & Pohl). When we make a poor decision, we are likely to suffer from biased memory such that we begin to explain what happened in terms of inevitability rather than in terms of the facts. For example, if Stan failed his first semester at college, he might say, "Well, of course I made the wrong decision to return to college. I should have known there would be a bias at this college against nontraditional students. That's why I failed. There's no way an older student gets a break around here." Research on hindsight bias (Blank, Musch, & Pohl) shows that it is ubiquitous (everyone experiences it), hard to avoid, and is potentially detrimental because it causes actual memory distortions or worse yet poorer decisions in the future.

There are processes that essentially take decision making out of our hands. When this happens, we again feel uncomfortable, because, as mentioned earlier, we like to have control over our own decisions and our own actions. One manipulative strategy that others use to influence our decision making is known as reactance by social psychologists. **Reactance** *is an oppositional response that occurs when our personal freedom is restricted.* Reactance occurs when others limit our personal freedom by getting us to do what they want us to do rather than what we want. Said another way, reactance is our response to attempts to constrain our freely chosen behaviors (Donnell, Thomas, & Buboltz, 2001). In other words, we lose some control over our decision making. For example, Stan's classmate offered to buy him lunch; only after lunch did the classmate ask to borrow Stan's notes two days before an important exam. Stan didn't loan his notes to the other student because Stan needed them himself, and he was furious that his classmate used the purchased lunch as a pretext for making the request. Perhaps if the classmate hadn't bought lunch, Stan would not have reacted so negatively and loaned the notes anyway. Stan was experiencing reactance.

Making Better Decisions

Keep in mind that your purpose in making a decision is to bring about desired results and avoid undesirable ones. In this sense, only you can define what constitutes a "good" or "bad" decision. At the same time, your personal traits, such as your attitudes, values, and tolerance for ambiguity, can complicate decision making. With such factors in mind, you can improve your decision-making skills by following these suggestions:

- *Use sounder judgment.* Judgment, the raw material of decision making, involves drawing inferences from data. Many decisions are doomed from the start because of poor judgment, often involving the human tendency to simplify complex matters. You probably should replace simplistic, intuitive strategies with the more "investigational" orientation that guides scientists, asking yourself such questions as these: What are the facts? How representative are they? What do the alternatives look like? How much of what is true is due to situational or chance factors? Sounder judgments may lead to better decisions. Recall that Stan did just this when he turned to employment projections before he decided to go to college.

- *Draw up a balance sheet.* This step consists of listing the various advantages and disadvantages of each course of action. A sample balance sheet in Table 6–1 represents Stan's situation before he made his decision. Students like Stan as well as adults of all ages have found that the balance sheet procedure helps them to make a comprehensive appraisal of a situation requiring a decision and promotes contingency planning, that is, figuring out what to do if something in the minus column materializes. People who use this procedure are more likely to stick to their decisions and express fewer regrets about the options not taken.

- *Clarify your values and objectives.* Many conflicts arise from confusion over the values that guided the decision rather than rejection of any alternative decisions. Because values are neither "good" nor "bad" in themselves, this step requires personal examination. Once you have clarified your values, they can be translated into tangible objectives that guide your decisions. For example, often vacillating in their decisions, students are sometimes torn between the need to study, work, socialize, and play. Those who have made a clear choice about what they hope to gain from college will be more likely to resolve their daily decisions effectively.

- *Accept reasonable results.* Nothing is as devastating to decision making as the wish for an "ideal" solution. People with perfectionist tendencies are especially susceptible, because constant striving for perfection guarantees failure. It is usually wiser for you to accept the most reasonable results under the circumstances. Among the methods of combating perfectionism—should it be characteristic of you—are recognizing the advantages and disadvantages of perfectionism and comparing how perfectly you did something with how much you enjoyed it. For example, you may feel that you didn't play tennis very well, but you enjoyed the game nevertheless because of the exercise and companionship, so you decide to continue with the sport.

- *Make the best of faulty decisions.* Despite your best efforts, not every decision will turn out to be a wise one. Some common reasons are limitations in circumstances, unforeseen events, and the difficulty of anticipating how differently you'll view things five, 10, even 20 years down the road. Many people waste time berating themselves or trying to justify their poor decisions. It may be wiser to realize that more often than not people made the best decision possible under the circum-stances. It's better to learn from your mistakes and, whenever possible, to modify your decisions to achieve a more desirable result than beat yourself up. If all else fails, take heart in the fact that no one makes perfect decisions. Box 6–1 (page 138) provides some interesting facts about successful as well as failed decision making.

TABLE 6–1

STAN'S BALANCE SHEET: ATTENDING COLLEGE

Projected Consequences	Positive Anticipations	Negative Anticipations
Tangible gains and losses for me	1. Better job prospects 2. Better income 3. More challenging career	1. Hard courses 2. Financial difficulties 3. Need to start over in new job and career
Positive and negative effects on family	1. Family proud of me 2. Substantial emotional support from family 3. Positive role model for my children	1. Fewer toys and clothes for children 2. Wife will need to work and care for children—more stress for her
Self-approval or disapproval	1. Confidence in mastering challenges 2. Pride in new opportunities	1. Lingering doubts about my academic abilities
Social approval or disapproval	1. Admiration from others for making a midlife change	1. Will be unemployed and perhaps stigmatized due to this

- Half the people who make New Year's resolutions give up within three months? Nearly one-quarter give up the first week?

- Those who put their resolutions in writing or reveal them openly are more likely to achieve them?

- It's easier to choose between two desirable outcomes, such as attaining better health or more money, than between two undesirable ones, such as being ill or poor?

- Our decisions are affected by whether the outcome is presented positively or negatively; for example, more people elect to have surgery when told they have a 90 percent chance of living than when told they have a 10 percent chance of dying?

DECISIONS AND PERSONAL GROWTH

Decisions are especially crucial with regard to personal growth. All too often, people become stuck in self-defeating behaviors because they've never made a decision to change their ways. Change may be resisted because of the inertia of past habits (Anderson, 2003; Blum, 1998), psychological laziness, or simply fear. When confronted with the need for change, people sometimes become defensive and resist, although they may promise to change if threatened with the loss of their jobs or their family's love. However, many of those who enter psychotherapy or a treatment program drop out prematurely, mostly because they haven't made a firm decision to change. For instance, while talking with a classmate who works with alcoholics and people who are drug dependent, Stan asked at what point in the program clients began making significant progress. "It's hard to say," the classmate responded, "because so much depends on when a person makes up his or her mind to change. In fact, we won't even admit people into our program until they have made some sort of commitment to change."

Identifying the Basic Decisions in Your Life

A good beginning point is to examine the basic decisions underlying your everyday behavior, especially problem behaviors such as habitual procrastination or drinking too much alcohol. Although you may be aware that your behavior is a reaction to people and situations, on closer examination you may find that you have subconsciously chosen to act in a certain way. Once a decision is made, you might organize your perceptions and even your life around it. A concrete example might prove useful. Take Stan's wife Susan, for example. Sue had gone to secretarial school and was a secretary before she met Stan. She and Stan married and had a baby. Sue then talked about returning to school—to college—to obtain a better education after their child went to kindergarten, but that is all Sue did. She talked about it.

Have you ever wondered why people procrastinate or fail to put forth their best efforts on important matters? Often such behavior is the outgrowth of a basic life choice to protect oneself from failure or hurt, although the individual may not be aware of it. Perhaps Susan was afraid that she would not succeed in college, but once Stan decided to return to college and give up his job, she had no choice. She had to return to secretarial work to help supplement the family income. College, for now, was out of the question for her. Reactance theory detailed above would help us predict that now, more than ever,

Susan wanted to return to school. Another example was the young man who waited until the end of August to apply for admission to the same college attended by Stan.

In both instances, these individuals have a face-saving excuse if they fail—"I was too late." Somewhere in the dim past, each has made a basic decision to play it safe because of a fear of failure or of getting hurt. Only when they change that decision will they put forth their best efforts and have a greater chance of success. Much negative behavior, such as rebelliousness and defiance, is also the result of a basic life decision, although again not necessarily in the person's awareness. To return to Stan's circumstances, his neighbor's son, Bobby, left home in his late teens because of constant fights with his father, whom he considered overly strict. Nevertheless, even after leaving home, Bobby was still known to be "touchy" and "hard to get along with," by his friends. He was always doing the opposite of what people expected of him, often with disappointing results. Bobby had made a choice in direct opposition to what he deemed as coercive parental authority: On almost everything, he had decided "No!" Until this rebellion, he was an appendage of his parents. But after rebelling, he felt more in charge of his life. This should not surprise us, because the defiance of the young child or adolescent is often the initial step toward autonomy. However, as long as Bobby remained stuck in this initial but negative stage of independence, his life was destined to be controlled more by what he was *against* than what he was *for*.

Making New Decisions

It is only when a *wish* to change leads to a *decision to change* that we can *really change and grow.* For example, many smokers know about the negative health effects of their smoking habit. They say things such as "I'd like to stop smoking" and "I hope to give it up soon" and "I plan to cut down on my smoking" or "I know it's bad for my family and me." Until they *really decide* to stop smoking and learn how to implement that decision, nothing happens or they try and fail.

So far we have assumed that people will automatically decide to change for the better, but this is not always the case. In some instances, people may become so overwhelmed with the anxiety and risks of change or fear postdecisional regret so much that they decide to remain the way they are, however unsatisfying or painful that may be (Anderson, 2003). Nor can someone be forced into growth, especially by therapists who may be adamant about people living up to their human potential. However well intentioned such therapists may be, they can make the same mistakes that parents and spouses are prone to make—namely, trying to tell someone else what he or she *ought* to decide. Rather, the therapist's task should be to help the client discover first what he or she wants to do and then help the client make a personal decision to do it. As most of us have discovered, once you know what you want to do and really decide to do it, you're well on your way. You can use Figure 6–1 to help you make your next few important decisions so that you can learn from them. In fact, copy it and carry it in your wallet if you like! Bring it out and use it when making important decisions.

FIGURE 6–1
Steps in making effective decisions.

Some Practical Applications

One of the most common examples of decision making is decision by default—taking the path of least resistance, taking the most familiar path, or taking no action at all (Anderson, 2003; Chapman, 1999). Putting things off, whether temporarily or indefinitely, while itself a decision (Anderson, 2003), nonetheless is a poor decision. A young man whom Stan knew as his teaching assistant in one of his classes was just such an example. This young man was having considerable difficulty completing his doctoral dissertation, partly because of writer's block and partly because of conflicts with his adviser. The young man became so frustrated that he simply turned his efforts elsewhere. He took the part-time teaching assistant job at the university ("while I finish my degree") and spent more time jogging ("to take my mind off my problems"). Several years later, when asked how his degree program was progressing, he said he had finally "decided" to give it up. Actually, he had made that decision earlier on, hadn't he? The failure to make a positive decision often is itself a decision with fateful consequences.

Overcoming negative, self-defeating behavior usually involves making a positive decision at a basic level of motivation. For example, Stan's sister, Janet, at midlife was bothered by depression and a poor relationship with her work supervisor. She disclosed to Stan that she had spent much time at work complaining and had been especially critical of her boss, often without any apparent reason. During some subsequent counseling, Janet discovered that earlier in her life she had learned to suppress her anger for fear of parental disapproval. She had become a passive "good little girl" but resented those on whom she remained dependent. Gradually, she learned to take more initiative, to show her anger more directly as an expression of her feelings rather than as judgmental remarks that would otherwise put others on the defensive. As Janet became more assertive, she felt less depressed and enjoyed a more satisfying relationship with those in authority.

Sometimes it is wise to make a decision that counters or reverses an earlier commitment that has led to undesirable consequences. For example, Stan's brother-in-law was a 45-year-old lawyer who married the daughter of the senior partner in his firm. He admitted to having married out of "mixed motives." That is, although he had been genuinely attracted to his wife, he had also hoped that her "connections" would enhance his career. He soon discovered that conflicts with his father-in-law complicated his life both at work *and* at home. Consultation with a specialist about his asthma attacks, which seemed worse during joint vacations at his in-laws' summer cottage, suggested that the attacks were brought on by emotional conflicts concerning his in-laws. Gradually, Stan's brother-in-law realized that it had not been a good idea to marry the boss's daughter, so eventually he decided to start his own firm rather than divorce his wife. Although he went through a few lean years, he soon had a flourishing law practice and was much happier in his marriage as well. Failure to make such a courageous decision often results in feelings such as being trapped in one's career, developing drinking problems, or engaging in extramarital affairs and other self-defeating behaviors.

SUMMARY

MASTERY AND PERSONAL CONTROL

We began by discussing the importance of personal control in our lives. Two forms of control are particularly important—internal (person-centered) locus of control and external (situation-centered) locus of control. Emphasis in the literature has been placed on attaining greater perceived control—the belief that we can influence the occurrence of events in our environment that determine our lives. People who underestimate the control they have over their lives sometimes exhibit learned helplessness; those who exaggerate their personal control often exhibit the illusion of control. In both cases, the misperception of control leads to maladaptive behavior. In contrast, people who are high in realistically perceived control tend to be less anxious and better adjusted. A way to achieve optimal perceived control is through what Martin Seligman calls learned optimism—interpreting life events in a reasonably accurate way that enhances our perceived control and, thus, our adaptive response to events.

PERSONAL RESOLVE AND DECISION MAKING

Frequent ways of exercising personal control are through our life choices and everyday decisions. Guidelines for making sound decisions include five stages: Accept the challenge, search for alternatives, evaluate the alternatives, make a commitment, and follow through with the decision. We may improve our decision-making skills by better judgment, the balance sheet procedure, clarifying our objectives, accepting reasonable results, and making the best of a poor decision. Also, we must repeatedly reaffirm our choice to change by abandoning perfectionism, accepting an occasional failure, picking ourselves up, and continuing our commitment to personal growth.

DECISIONS AND PERSONAL GROWTH

We can promote personal growth by seeing our problems in terms of past decisions, examining the consequences of such decisions, and then choosing a more satisfying alternative. In this way, we learn to view our problems and unfulfilled potential more in terms of our decisions than as the result of events and circumstances that simply happen or are beyond our control. However, it's only when a wish to change leads to a personal decision to change that our personal lives begin to improve.

SELF-TEST

1. The belief that you can influence events in your environment that affect your life is known as
   a. perceived control.
   b. external control.
   c. the illusion of control.
   d. a psychological delusion.

2. The maladaptive passivity that frequently follows people's experience with uncontrollable events is called
   a. reactance.
   b. learned helplessness.
   c. the illusion of control.
   d. hindsight bias.

3. People who exhibit high perceived control tend to
   a. exhibit high anxiety.
   b. make only average grades in school.
   c. attribute their successes to good luck.
   d. use effective strategies for coping with stress.

4. The first stage of decision making is to
   a. evaluate the alternatives.   c. accept the challenge.
   b. make a commitment.   d. search for alternatives.

5. The final stage of the decision-making process consists of
   a. following through with your decision.
   b. making a commitment.
   c. evaluating your decision.
   d. accepting the challenge.

6. Saying, "I knew that would happen" after a failed decision, even though you researched solutions carefully before the decision, is an example of
   a. hindsight bias   c. social comparison
   b. reactance   d. none of the above

7. When we feel our personal freedom has been restricted, we experience
   a. reactance.   c. neurosis.
   b. resilience.   d. learned pessimism.

8. A common phenomenon after a decision has been made is the experience of a feeling of
   a. external control.   c. pessimism.
   b. elation.   d. regret.

9. Therapists who are helping clients change should
   a. tell the client what to do.
   b. provide lots of structure to assist client's decision making.
   c. help clients discover what they want to do.
   d. tell clients what they want to hear.

10. Which statement about resolutions and decision making is true?
   a. Ninety percent of us keep our New Year's resolutions.
   b. It is easier to choose between two desirable than two undesirable outcomes.
   c. Putting resolutions in writing doesn't work any better than making them silently.
   d. All of these statements are true.

EXERCISES

1. *Personal control.* To what extent do you believe you can influence the occurrence of events in your environment that affect your life? In a page or so, discuss the degree of personal control you have over your life, emphasizing *perceived* control or the belief that you can control your life. How does your belief affect specific aspects of your life, such as your goals, work, intimate relationships, fitness, and health?

2. *Stages in decision making.* Review the five stages of decision making discussed in the chapter. Select an important decision you're about to make or one you've already made. Then analyze it in terms of the five stages of the decision-making process. How well did you follow these five stages? What do you find to be the most difficult part of making decisions?

3. *Aids in making decisions.* Reread the section on aids (such as the balance sheet method) to making sounder decisions. Then select one of the poorer decisions you've made and review this decision in light of these aids. What do you think you need to do to make better decisions in the future?

4. *Decision making and personal growth.* Select some aspect of your life, such as a habit or problem behavior, that you would like to change. Do you consider the problem behavior to be partly the result of some other decisions you've made? Have you made a deliberate decision to change your behavior, or do you merely wish to change? What do you need to do to really make the change?

QUESTIONS FOR SELF-REFLECTION

1. How much control do you believe you have over your life?

2. Are you inclined to underestimate or overestimate your level of personal control?

3. Do you suffer from the illusion of control when you have little actual control?

4. When there appears to be no choice in a situation, what do you do?

5. How do you go about making important decisions?

6. Do you often "decide" things by not deciding?

7. Are you willing to take calculated risks?

8. What was the best decision you ever made? Why was your decision successful?

9. What was your worst decision? What would you do differently now?

10. Is the grass always greener on the other side of the fence for you? Why do you think this is so?

11. How much truth is there in the saying that "life is what happens to us while we're making other plans"?

12. Is your life too full of choices? Do your choices frequently inspire regret in you?

FOR FURTHER INFORMATION

RECOMMENDED READINGS

DAWES, R. M., & HASTIE, R. (2001). *Rational choice in an uncertain world: The psychology of judgment and decision-making.* Thousand Oaks, CA: Sage. This research-based psychology book discusses what scientists say about the steps in higher-quality decisions and how to make them.

GLADWELL, M. (2007). *Blink: The power of thinking without thinking.* Boston: Little, Brown, & Company. Best-selling science writer, Malcolm Gladwell, using research from cognitive science, discusses making better decisions.

HENDERSON, D. R., & HOOPER, C. L. (2005). *Making great decisions in business and in life.* Chicago, IL: Chicago Park Press. A well-received book on how to make better decisions no matter what the venue.

HUBER, C. (2007). *Making a change for good: A guide to compassionate self-discipline.* Boston: Shambhala Publications. Zen teacher, Cheri Huber, helps the reader understand that our wish to be better because of some deficiency isn't the best path toward self-change. Instead, she suggests that to solve life's problems, we need to look within and find our own intelligence, generosity, and compassion. Only then will we be happier.

RACHLIN, H. (2004). *The science of self-control.* Cambridge, MA: Harvard University Press. A behaviorist writes about how difficult self-control is and why and then offers advice on how to improve it.

WEBSITES AND THE INTERNET

http://www.mapnp.org/library/prsn_prd/decision.htm   A site designed by an expert who guides you through step-by-step decision making.

http://www.scu.edu/ethics/practicing/decision/framework.html   This thoughtful site is dedicated to making *ethical* decisions; we make decisions day in and day out, but not all of them are ethical. Information is provided about what ethics is and is not. Guidelines are provided to help individuals make difficult but ethical decisions.

http://www.macses.ucsf.edu/Research/Psychosocial/notebook/control.html   A source for lots of information about personal control: what it is, how it is measured, and its relationship to our health, socioeconomic status, beliefs, as well as an extensive bibliography.

http://mentalhelp.net/psyhelp/chap4   A subdivision of a well-known site on psychological information, this site helps you understand why you behave as you do by examining such aspects of behavior as procrastination, self-control, and managing difficult behaviors such as loss of control or relapse.

http://www.successconsciousness.com/index_000006.htm   This is a website about conscientiousness and self-discipline. For example, it suggests that will power is not something that exerts us but rather something that is easy. After a discussion of these topics, the reader is provided with exercises to reinforce and improve one's self-discipline.

CHAPTER 7

Managing Motives and Emotions

Du is one of those students never to be forgotten. A pleasant young man, he sat in the rear of the classroom next to the door. He was cheery, articulate, and eager to learn. He spoke up in class whenever possible. He was well liked by his peers and professors alike. Everyone who knew him realized that golf was Du's "reason for being," as he often declared. Du hoped to make it as a professional golfer one day, but "just in case," he said, "I'm attending a community college to obtain an education if my golf career never pays off." Du's parents, who were immigrants, were none too happy about his plans to play sports. Instead, they wanted Du to become a doctor—a dream they held for him from the day they left their homeland. While Du's Asian culture taught him to respect his parents, he could not help but be disappointed that they did not share his enthusiasm for golf.

UNDERSTANDING MOTIVATION

Most of us can sympathize with Du. Sometimes we do the task at hand, especially when it will bring us closer to some desired goal, such as becoming a professional golfer. At other times, we may feel little or no motivation for what we're supposed to do. We procrastinate, we make excuses, and we waste precious time. Not surprisingly, many people, such as parents, teachers, and managers in the workplace, are interested in learning how to motivate people. Essentially, **motivation** has to do with *energizing and directing our efforts toward a meaningful goal.* Our motivation is affected by many influences, some of them rather obvious but others less so.

Many psychologists agree that emotions and motivation are closely linked (Roseman, 2008). When we feel happy, we are eager to continue to feel happy. When we are sad, we are motivated to end the pain as quickly as possible. In the last few parts of the chapter, we will turn our attention to emotions—what they are and how they are expressed verbally and nonverbally. Here is an interesting example, regarding the September 11, 2001, terror attacks on New York and Washington, of the grip emotions have and their relationship to motivation. Dr. Tedd Mitchell (2003) said:

> Conflicting emotions set in: the fear of travel—the defiant need to travel; resignation that another attack was inevitable—and a resolve to prevent an attack no matter what: emotional exhaustion from reliving the event over and over in the media—and an inability to turn off the TV. . . . fortunately the negative emotions brought on by the tragedy were counter-balanced by a flood of positive energy [p. 4].

At the end of this chapter, we will concentrate on specific emotions that are problematic to adjustment, such as anxiety, anger, and jealousy. To end the chapter on an upbeat note, however, we will finish with information on happiness.

Understanding Your Needs

Your understanding of motivation may be enhanced by study of Maslow's **hierarchy of needs,** a growth model of motivation, where **needs** are *tension states that arouse us to seek gratification.* Maslow suggests that our *needs and motives function in a hierarchical manner from the bottom up according to how crucial the need is for survival.* The higher needs are experienced only to the degree that the more basic ones have been relatively satisfied. He describes five levels of needs, from most basic to higher level needs, as follows:

(1) **Physiological needs** *include the need for food, sleep, and sex.*

(2) **Safety needs** *include the need for protection from bodily harm and security from threat, as well as the need for order and stability.*

(3) **Love and belongingness needs** *include the need for acceptance, affection, and approval.*

(4) **Esteem needs** *are the need for self-respect and the sense of achievement.*

(5) **Self-actualizing needs** *include a variety of needs, such as the need for autonomy, uniqueness, aliveness, beauty, and justice in our lives.*

Maslow suggested that fewer individuals have the top needs (e.g., esteem and self-actualizing needs) satisfied compared to basic physiological needs (e.g., fresh water and food). Du's parents, for example, worried about his meeting basic needs: "Du, become a doctor, earn lots of money, then you can feed yourself and care for us in our old age." Du, on the other hand, was more concerned with self-esteem needs; his primary goal was to improve his golf game until he felt satisfied that he was the best player he could be.

Maslow theorized that the lowest level of unmet needs remains the most urgent, thus commanding our attention and efforts. Once a given level of need is satisfied, we become more motivated by the unmet needs at the next-higher level. To that end, as we satisfy our needs for food and shelter we become more concerned about things like job security. Maslow also pointed out that our needs typically remain only relatively satisfied. He once estimated that the average person is only 85 percent satisfied in terms of physiological needs, 70 percent in safety needs, 50 percent in love needs, 40 percent in esteem needs, and only 10 percent in self-growth needs. Therefore, he stated there is constant motivation to meet needs, and recent research has borne him out. The need for self-determination, competence, and autonomy (e.g., self-actualizing needs) may well be universal (Deci & Moller, 2005) as is the basic need for survival (Grouzet et al., 2005). Such striving is part and parcel of personal growth.

An important implication of Maslow's growth model of motivation is that we aren't content to achieve a stable, harmonious state. Instead, once we've reached a relative level of satisfaction, biologically and psychologically, we're increasingly motivated by growth needs. This theory helps to explain why successful people are rarely satisfied to rest on their previous accomplishments. They're constantly striving to attain something better. For example, Du won a junior golf championship when he was just 14 years old. While happy with the win, he was not completely satisfied; he wanted to play in the "big leagues" as he said. Similarly, people who are happily retired seldom sit around doing nothing; they're forever developing new interests and deepening their relationships with others. It seems we're happiest when we're growing and actualizing ourselves.

Differences Between You and Others

Although each of us desires the creature comforts of food and sleep, as well as higher goals such as success in education or sports, the relative strengths of such motives differ from one person to another (Hinsz & Jundt, 2005). Accordingly, we need to think in terms of the individual's personal hierarchy of motives as well as Maslow's generalized pattern. Which motives have top priority for a given person will depend on factors such as inborn dispositions, culture, personal values, gender roles, and past experiences. For example, individuals who have been deprived of love and affection as children may be more motivated by the desire for approval than achievement. Our **motives** (*goal-directed activities that energize and direct behavior*) also change over time depending on the **motive targets** around us—*the people toward whom our attention or motives are directed.* At work you may have a strong motive to compete with your associates. In your leisure hours you may be more concerned about being accepted by your friends. Then again, at home you may feel inclined toward intimacy and involvement with your lover or spouse.

People searching for success favor positive role models who highlight strategies for success. Du's role model was Jack Nicklaus and his uncanny ability to concentrate on his game despite intense stress (O'Connor, 2008). People focusing on failure avoidance are inspired by role models who avoid negative outcomes (Lockwood, Jordan, & Kunda, 2002). As a result, our motives are constantly changing throughout the day, as we move from one situation to another and as we encounter various people. Furthermore, an individual's motives tend to vary across the entire life span and by culture, mostly because of one's experiences and personal growth. As a result, we often invest more or less of ourselves in the same career or same relationship (i.e., marriage) as we grow older.

Everyone's Basic Needs

Like all other beings, you and Du must eat, drink, and avoid extreme pain and injury if you are to survive. Although sex is not essential to our personal survival, it is necessary for the *survival* of the species. Such needs, though shaped by learning in varying degrees, have a clearer *physiological basis*. As a result, they are variously labeled *basic needs*, primary drives, or survival motives.

Basic needs are influenced by both biological and environmental influences. For example, eating and drinking behaviors are affected both by a part of the brain known as the **hypothalamus** (*a small but important structure at the core of the brain that governs many aspects of behavior, such as eating and hormonal activity*) as well as by a variety of learned influences (Nieuwenhuizen & Rutters, 2008). As an illustration, some of the more common learned cues for eating are the smell, sight, and taste of food. Additionally, some individuals learn to use food as a means of relieving emotional stress. Culture also plays a large role in learning various eating habits. Most Americans, for example, prefer white eggs to brown ones; the brown ones appear dirty. On the other hand, Russians do not mind eating brown eggs; in fact, most of the eggs they eat have brown shells.

Psychosocial Motives

The psychosocial motives have less to do with physical survival and more to do with our sense of well-being and psychological competence in dealing with our environment. The notion of *competence* brings us to two important distinctions related to human goals, especially pursuits of a psychosocial nature: intrinsic and extrinsic motivation. **Intrinsic motivation** concerns *active engagement with tasks that people find interesting and that, in turn, promote growth and are freely engaged in out of interest.* In other words, the aim of intrinsically motivated behavior is not to succeed or to reach some other outcome but rather to engage in an activity naturally and spontaneously. Such behaviors are inherently satisfying to pursue in and of themselves. Alternatively, **extrinsic motivation** is *the desire to engage in an activity because it is a means to an end and not because an individual is following his or her inner interests.* Extrinsically motivated behaviors are not based on an individual's need to feel competent and autonomous but on some external reward or outcome (Deci & Ryan, 2008).

Du's life situation offers a good example of each type of motivation. Du loved golf. He liked the game's demands for concentration, the challenge of bettering his game each time, and communing with nature in a beautiful setting. Du was less concerned about earning "big bucks" as a professional golfer than he was with enjoying and improving his game. Du's desire to play golf was intrinsically motivated. On the other hand, Du's attending college was mostly his parents' idea. They deeply desired him to be a successful and rich doctor so that they could all become more "American." Thus, Du's college career was rather extrinsically motivated, although he, himself, did recognize the value of a good education.

Interestingly, external rewards, surveillance, deadlines, and threats undermine intrinsic motivation (Deci & Ryan, 2008). These results are reminiscent of the concept of *locus of control* as reviewed in the previous chapter. Persons with an external locus of control see their fates controlled by forces outside of themselves. Individuals with an internal locus of control feel they control their own fates. Not only do such external influences or controls undermine autonomy and thus intrinsic motivation, they also weaken creativity and problem solving. Then again, internal control or intrinsic motivation has generally been demonstrated to result in increased satisfaction and enhanced well-being. This need for self-determination and need for autonomy appears to be universal, as it has been demonstrated in 15 other cultures (Grouzet et al., 2005).

Some psychosocial motives—such as the motives for stimulation, curiosity, and exploration—seem to be largely inborn and are sometimes labeled *stimulus* needs. Others, like *achievement motivation,* are shaped more extensively by psychological, cultural, and social influences. Because of the complexity of human behavior, there is no one authoritative list of our psychological and social motives. Some of these motives are addressed in other chapters, such as our sexual motives, friendship needs, and the need for personal freedom and control. Here, we'll focus on two of the psychosocial motives not covered elsewhere, namely, the need for stimulation and for achievement.

Stimulation.   We need both sensory and social stimulation. People deprived of both, for instance, prisoners in solitary confinement and subjects in sensory deprivation experiments, display symptoms of stress, including distorted perceptions. They see and hear strange things; they hallucinate, have delusions, and fear losing their sanity. Military personnel in lonely outposts have shown similar reactions, though to a lesser degree. Most of us are rarely placed in a situation in which we suffer from extreme sensory or social isolation. But even after several hours of studying alone, you may feel a need to listen to the radio, call someone on the phone, or talk to a friend, mostly for variation in stimulation.

Perhaps you've noticed how some people have a greater need for trying novel experiences and meeting new people. Others prefer more peaceful activities, such as reading or stamp collecting. Such differences in human behavior are due to the relative strength of the **sensation-seeking motive,** defined as *our tendency to seek out stimulating and novel experiences.* Sensation-seeking motive may be partly dependent on biological factors, like brain stimulation and biochemical secretions (especially dopamine), so that each of us has an optimal arousal level (Zuckerman, 2005). Whenever we find ourselves in situations that arouse us to a significantly lesser or greater extent than our optimal arousal, we become uncomfortable. If not sufficiently aroused, we seek greater stimulation; if we're overly aroused, we try to reduce the stimulation. Partly because of its biological basis, sensation seeking is at a peak during the college years and tends to diminish with age.

Generally speaking, individuals high in sensation seeking seek out stimulating experiences (e.g., watching violent movies; Xie & Lee, 2008) and take more risks—both positive (e.g., kayaking) and negative (e.g., shoplifting). For instance, higher levels of sensation seeking has been linked with unprotected sex, risky driving, and an increased use of alcohol and illicit drugs (Arnold, Fletcher, & Farrow, 2002; Hatfield & Ralston, 2009; Norris et al., 2009; Simons, Gaher, Correia, & Bush, 2005). There are, however, individual differences in sensation-seeking and risk-taking behavior. Although both men and women can be

Thousands of people ride the roily, dangerous waters of Niagara Falls to get a closer view. Is such sensation-seeking normal?

sensation seekers, studies have demonstrated that men often score higher than women on sensation seeking (Arnold et al., 2002) and that men are more prone to boredom (or lack of novelty, which is part of sensation seeking) than women (Vodanovich & Kass, 1990).

Differences in sensation seeking may also influence the way we relate to one another. Low-sensation seekers may feel that high-sensation seekers are foolhardy and hungry for attention. In contrast, high-sensation seekers may feel that low-sensation seekers are timid and boring. A scale for you to assess your level of sensation seeking is provided in Activity 7–1.

ACTIVITY 7–1

HOW MUCH STIMULATION DO YOU NEED?

The need for stimulation is related to sensation seeking. Circle which of the two choices for each statement best describes you.

1.	I prefer to	A. read a book.	B. do something physically exciting.
2.	When driving a car, I generally drive	A. at about the speed limit.	B. over the speed limit.
3.	I would like to	A. return to a place I have already visited.	B. visit a foreign country.
4.	I would describe myself as	A. an introvert.	B. an extrovert.
5.	I like to listen to	A. the same music over and over again.	B. recently released or new music.
6.	As a general theme in my life, I favor	A. risk taking.	B. security.
7.	I would describe my best friends as	A. quirky.	B. conventional.
8.	I often watch	A. adventure movies.	B. romantic movies.
9.	When I know water is cold, I	A. jump right in.	B. submerge myself slowly.
10.	I think I would	A. like hang-gliding.	B. stay anchored on the ground.

SCORING: First, realize that this scale was specially designed for this book. A high score does not necessarily indicate that you are a sensation seeker or an avid escapee from boredom. Similarly, a low score does not necessarily mean that you don't take risks or seek adventure. This scale should be used to help you think about yourself and as a stimulus to class discussion.

For Items 1–5: Answer "A" indicates low need for stimulation or sensation seeking. Answer "B" indicates a high need for thrill seeking and/or avoidance of boredom. Total number of "Bs" _____

For Items 6–10: Answer "A" indicates a need for thrill seeking or avoidance of boredom. Answer "B" indicates low need for stimulation or for sensation seeking. Total number of "As" _____

Now add your scores from both lines here. _____

A total composite score of 1–3 indicates a low need for sensation; a score of 4–7 indicates a moderate need for sensation seeking, and a score of 8–10 indicates a high need for sensation seeking. Using your score, think about whether you are prone to taking unnecessary risks, whether your life needs a little more spark, or have you found just the right balance between serenity and thrill seeking?

Achievement.   Perhaps you've noticed how your friends differ in achievement motivation. Some relish taking on a challenge. No matter what the task, they strive to do their best. Others seem to be happy just getting the job over and done with. In our opening case, Du had a strong motive to succeed, but his desire to succeed at golf eclipsed his need to achieve in his class work.

Achievement motivation is *the desire to accomplish or master something difficult or challenging as independently and successfully as possible.* Actually, achievement motivation is a complex combination of several factors (Corpus, McClintic-Gilbert, & Hayenga, 2009). Two such elements are the **desire for success** or *the urge to succeed* and the counteracting **fear of failure** (*the fear that we will be humiliated by shortcoming*). Each of us has a different mixture of these tendencies, mostly because of our personal makeup and past experiences (Komarraju & Karau, 2005). As a result, the difficulties of the tasks people choose differ. For example, someone who has a strong desire for success and a low fear of failure is more apt to choose moderately difficult but realistic tasks, thus maximizing the chances of success. Another person with an intense desire for success yet coupled with a high fear of failure will set a much lower goal and perhaps be more anxious about achieving these goals. It is worth noting that achievement motivation remains fairly stable over time (Senko & Harackiewicz, 2005). Achievement motivation affects our cognitions, our health, athletic and career functioning, and other activities and behaviors. For example, athletes like Du must learn the required skills, survive a highly competitive selection process, and then execute their skills perfectly in each game. Any and all of these processes can be affected by a sense of achievement motivation.

In collective (as compared to individualistic) societies where individual gain is shunned in favor of the collective good, achievement motivation occurs in a different form. Achievement motivation and satisfaction are not derived from personal accomplishment. Instead, positive feelings about the self come from fulfilling tasks associated with being *inter*dependent with others (Markus & Kitayama, 1991; Matsumoto, 2000). For example, a study of Japanese youngsters demonstrated that self-promotion in the collective society of Japan is viewed quite negatively even by young children. One peer was presented as modest whereas another was presented as a self-promoter. The more modest peer was actually perceived as more athletically competent than the self-promoter was.

Personal Motivation

A secret of being an active, motivated person is setting personal goals and then striving hard to reach them. In one sense, goal setting comes naturally in that we tend to be future-oriented. Most of us are more concerned about today and tomorrow than yesterday. However, it takes some thought and soul-searching to set personal goals or objectives, which is why a lot of people don't bother to do it. Nevertheless, the risk of not doing it can be costly in terms of wasted time and energy.

There are several types of personal goals:

- *Long-range goals* are concerned with the kind of life you want to live with regard to your career, marriage, and lifestyle. It's wise to keep these goals broad and flexible, especially during your college years.
- *Medium-range goals* cover the next five years or so and include the type of education you're seeking or the next step in your career or family life. You have more control over these goals, so you can tell how well you're progressing toward them and modify them accordingly.
- *Short-range goals* apply from the next month or so up to one year from now. You can set these goals quite realistically and should try hard to achieve them.
- *Mini-goals* cover anything from one day to a month. You have a lot of control over these goals and should make them specific.
- *Micro-goals* cover the next 15 minutes to a few hours. Realistically, these are the only goals over which you have direct control.

As you can guess, the shorter the time span covered, the more control you have over your goals. It is only through achieving the modest, short-range goals that you'll ever attain your medium- and long-range goals. Du, for example, wanted to succeed in college so that he could please his parents. He knew that no matter how often his fantasies turned to his golfing dreams, he needed to concentrate on each exam and each semester as short-term goals. Then and only then, he reasoned, would he be able to graduate and please his parents. Maybe then, he reasoned, his parents would let him pursue his golf career (a long-range goal) if only for a few years.

Too often, people make the mistake of setting grandiose or idealized goals (Kayes, 2005) and then quickly become disillusioned because they're making so little progress toward achieving them. It's far better to set *realistic* but desirable goals and then concentrate on achieving your day-to-day goals, which will make it possible to reach your "dream" goals. Remember also that once you've achieved a goal, it's important to set new ones. Keep in mind also that some individuals set large goals even though they would experience less distress day by day if they set smaller goals.

UNDERSTANDING EMOTIONS

We can only imagine the disappointment Du felt when one of his final exams was scheduled at the same time as an important amateur golf tournament in which he hoped to play. Compounding Du's problem was his anxiety about approaching the professor to see if the exam could be rescheduled to accommodate Du. Once again, Du was torn between following his golf dreams and obtaining the education his parents so fervently desired for him. With this example, we turn next to the study of emotions.

What Are Emotions?

Emotions involve *complex patterns of change that include physiological arousal, subjective feelings, cognitive processes, and behavioral reactions*—all in response to situations we perceive to be personally significant. Accordingly, emotions have four components:

1. Physiological arousal. Emotions involve the brain, nervous system, and hormones, so that when you're emotionally aroused your body is aroused.

2. Subjective feelings. Emotions also include subjective awareness, or "feeling," that involves elements of pleasure or displeasure, liking or disliking.

3. Cognitive processes. Emotions also involve cognitive processes such as memories, perceptions, expectations, and interpretations.

4. Behavioral reactions. Emotions also involve behavioral reactions. Facial expressions, as well as gestures and tones of voice, serve to communicate our feelings to others (i.e., expressive reactions). Cries of distress and running for our lives are also adaptive responses that may enhance our chances for survival (i.e., instrumental reactions).

Although some theories of emotion emphasize physiological factors such as the central nervous system and the endocrine system (Howlett, 1999), many contemporary theories of emotion now emphasize the role of cognitive factors (Beitel, Ferrer, & Cecero, 2005; Bonanno, Papa, Lalande, Westphal, & Coifman, 2004). An experience arouses our emotions mostly when the individual *appraises the stimuli as having personal significance.* In this view, an emotional experience cannot be understood as something that happens solely in the person or in the brain but more in our relationship to the environment. The particular emotion that is felt depends largely on how we label a given situation, that is, on how we interpret the personal meaning it has for us (Schachter & Singer, 1962). Here is another example. While Du viewed the conflict between his exam schedule and the golf tournament schedule as anxiety producing, another student might view prepping for both as a challenge and approaching the professor as a welcome opportunity to interact one-on-one with the well-liked professor.

A major implication of the cognitive view of emotions is that each of us has more potential control over our feelings than what was once popularly believed. Whenever we feel angry, jealous, or depressed, we are not simply at the mercy of our momentary feelings (Richards, 2004). Nor should we take our "gut" reactions as infallible, as important as these may be. Instead, it's better to realize that our momentary feelings are partly the result of the way we perceive and respond to an event. Particularly for negative events, it is also important to know that most people fail to understand just how well and how quickly they can cope with them (Wilson & Gilbert, 2005).

Another implication of the cognitive perspective is that interpretation of personal emotions may well underpin psychological adjustment (Bonanno et al., 2004). Perhaps anxiety over emotional expression creates problems for us, or perhaps we consistently misinterpret our own and others' emotional reactions. As Plutchik states, "Most of us often censor our own thoughts and feelings, and we have learned to be cautious about accepting other people's comments about their feelings" (2001, p. 344). Alternatively, perhaps the ability to use a large repertoire of emotions and ability to call on each where *appropriate* may be the key to healthy adjustment (Bonanno et al., 2004).

Experiencing Emotions

Emotions are a kind of barometer of our inner world, giving us an intuitive knowledge about ourselves and our involvement with others at the moment. Intense emotions tell us our lives are strongly affected by some person or event and prompt us to act accordingly. On the other hand, when we feel little or no emotion in a given situation, chances are our needs, goals, or values are not affected; that is, we're not "emotionally involved." Perhaps that's why we're constantly asking each other, "How do you feel about this?" or "What's your reaction to that?" Unfortunately, it's not always easy to say, is it? A major reason is that we often have trouble identifying our feelings at the moment, and even more finding the right words to express them (Solomon, 2005). Then, too, our emotions are in a state of constant flux or change so that we may feel pleased one moment and annoyed the next.

Psychologists have identified two general categories of emotions: primary and secondary. **Primary (basic) emotions** *refer to the initial and direct emotional response to an experience,* such as being frightened at the sound of thunder or the joy of seeing a loved one. Although psychologists do not yet agree on how many primary emotions exist, Plutchik's model (2001) is often cited as a good starting point. He identifies eight primary emotions: joy, acceptance, fear, surprise, sadness, disgust, anger, and anticipation. These emotions can be experienced more or less intensely to *create* other emotions. Think about disgust and its complexities (Marzillier & Davey, 2004). For instance, when you are intensely disgusted with someone, you may experience loathing; when you are moderately disgusted, you may feel dislike; and when only mildly disgusted, you may experience mild disapproval. Thus, many of our feelings may represent a mixture of various primary emotions and thus defy easy labels. Du, for example, was anxious about both his golf and his exams, but he found the golf anxiety mostly to be exhilarating and the exam anxiety to be stressful.

In contrast, **secondary (complex) emotions** are *emotional experiences that are reflective, involve evaluation of the self, and typically follow primary emotions.* For example, after getting angry (a primary emotion) at your sister, you feel shame (a secondary emotion) because of the amount of anger that you expressed. Common secondary emotions include guilt, pride, shame, and embarrassment. Moreover, unlike basic emotions, which appear before a child's first birthday, secondary emotions are not present until the second year of life, accompanying the development of the sense of self (Sroufe, 1996).

Other models of emotions also exist (Trierweiler, Eld, & Lischetzke, 2002). For example, when people from various cultures are asked to report their experience of different emotions, they seem to place emotions along two dimensions—*pleasant versus unpleasant* and *intensely versus weakly aroused* (Tsai, Knutson, & Fung, 2006). Thus, the emotions of contentment, joy, and love would fall into the category of pleasant or positive emotions, whereas anger, disgust, and sadness fall into the category of unpleasant emotions. On the intensity (arousal) scale, rage is more intense than anger, which in turn is more intense than annoyance. On the other hand, love is more intense than liking.

Surprise is a primary emotion, according to psychologists.

Expressing Emotions

Emotions not only motivate us to do certain things and to approach or avoid particular situations, they offer a primary means of communicating with others. However, we often assume it is not always safe to share our intimate feelings, even when casually greeting a good friend. How often has someone asked, "Hey, how ya doin'?" and you answered "Great" when you really were feeling glum or overwhelmed by too much to do? Sharing our feelings is risky and makes us vulnerable to the judgments of others. Some people are so afraid of their inner feelings that they're unable to experience, much less express, their deeper emotions, such as in times of great joy or profound sorrow. Others more in touch with their emotions disclose their feelings freely, whether the emotion be anger or love. Whichever way you're inclined, the most important thing is to find that balance of expression and control of feelings with which you and those around you are most comfortable.

Emotional balance is all the more difficult because of some of the individual differences in emotional expressiveness. Women, for example, report sadder responses to negative personal events than do men (Hess et al., 2000). However, women also smile more than men (LaFrance, Hecht, & Paluck, 2003). Interestingly, across a wide variety of cultures, men more frequently report power*ful* emotions (e.g., anger, contempt, disgust) while women are more likely to report power*less* feelings (e.g., sadness, fear) (Safdar et al., 2009). Scientists have yet to tease out whether such differences are learned or biological. What do you think?

In terms of understanding and recognizing our *own* emotional states, researchers have found that men more than women ruminate about upsetting events and report more inhibition of hostile feelings (McConatha, Lightner, & Deaner, 1994). Across adulthood, whereas older persons think more about upsetting events then their younger counterparts, they express emotions less frequently than younger individuals. Moreover, contrary to stereotypes, the elderly are still highly capable of experiencing profoundly positive emotions (Carstensen & Charles, 1998).

Individual differences also exist in our ability to recognize and interpret others' emotions. For instance, researchers have consistently found that women are better decoders of others' emotions than men (Brody & Hall, 1993). Likewise, everyone is a better decoder of emotions expressed by members of their *own* culture rather than of another culture (Beaupré & Hess, 2005). Perhaps such differences occur because same-race faces and other-race faces activate different parts of the brain (Iidaka, Nogawa, Kansaku, & Sadato, 2008). Moreover, some studies indicate that culture influences the expressions of emotion. For instance, Asians tend to express positive emotions (e.g., happiness) and powerful emotions to a lesser extent than Whites from the United States and Canada (Safdar et al., 2009; Scollon, Diener, Oishi, & Biswas-Diener, 2004).

Nevertheless, facial expressions accompanying many emotions, especially primary ones, are interpreted the same way across cultures. In fact, six different primary emotions are expressed on the human face from a very early age: anger, fear, happiness, sadness, surprise, and disgust (Ekman, 1993; Matsumoto, 2004). Based on cross-cultural research, Matsumoto (2000) claims that there exists a seventh universal emotion—contempt; others claim that jealousy and (primarily parental) love should also be considered universal emotions (Sabini & Silver, 2005). Moreover, race appears to influence emotion recognition in others. For example, Whites tend to recognize happy faces faster than angry faces, but only if the expressions were made by Whites. In contrast, when the same expressions were displayed by Blacks, angry faces were recognized faster than happy expressions (Hugenberg, 2005). Additionally, Whites high in prejudice are more likely to categorize racially ambiguous (i.e., biracial) faces as Black when angry facial expressions are being posed (but not happy ones) (Hugenberg & Bodenhausen, 2003).

For years, psychologists have regarded faces as the key to emotional expression (Bower, 2001; Coulson, 2004). There is little doubt that the face is important, but body postures, vocal changes (e.g., pitch modulation and speed of speech), and hand gestures also signal us as to what others are actually feeling (Azar, 2000; Pell, 2005). Research indicates that deciphering these and other nonverbal information is complicated. For instance, body posture greatly helps us decode anger and sadness but helps little in gauging others' level of disgust (Coulson, 2004).

Another factor that makes recognition and interpretation of expressed emotions slippery is that some individuals purposely try to deceive us by manipulatively using many of these same nonverbal devices (e.g., posture). For example, if Du mustered the courage to approach his professor to change the exam date, thus enabling Du to play in the tournament, Du might appear deferentially apologetic and remorseful in front of the professor but privately feel elation about the prospect of delaying the exam to play his much-loved game. Du, like anyone else, will probably monitor his self-presentation so that the elation does not show.

Identifying deception in others is a difficult task, with the ability to judge whether someone is lying hovering around 50 percent (Bond & DePaulo, 2008). Yet, if others do attempt to deceive us, how can we detect their dishonesty? One helpful aid is **microexpressions,** or *fleeting facial expressions that last only a fraction of a second* (Ekman, 1985b). Microexpressions may be momentary, but they are still detectable by the astute observer (Dimberg, Thunberg, & Elmehed, 2000). Many people try hard to control their outward facial expressions because they believe we think the face is the primary clue to their secrets. Deceivers, however, may blink more or smile more broadly in an effort to deceive (Baron & Byrne, 1997; Porter & ten Brink, 2008) and thus can be exposed. In addition, yet another individual hoping to deceive you may express one emotion followed quickly by another, which can indicate that the person is lying. Some individuals are so good at monitoring and controlling their faces that their true feelings are difficult to detect. Watching for **body leakage,** *where body postures rather than the face leak the truth,* can be just as revealing of emotional deceit. While individuals are concentrating on monitoring their words and their facial expressions, they attend less to their bodies, which consequently betray their true feelings.

Managing Emotions

Because emotions are related to psychological adjustment, it is desirable to manage our feelings well. Learning to express feelings effectively involves a suitable balance between spontaneous expression and deliberate, rational emotional self-regulation. **Emotional self-regulation** refers to *the process by which one inhibits or moderates one's emotional responses in order to remain engaged in thoughtful interaction.* Areas of emotional management needing improvement vary somewhat from one person to another. Some people who are overly emotional and impulsive may blurt out their feelings without much thought; they need to develop better self-control. On the other hand, those who keep their emotions under tight control may need to loosen up, to become more aware of their feelings and more comfortable expressing them appropriately to others.

We can become more adept and practiced at expressing our emotions by sharing our everyday feelings more readily with family and friends we *trust* and those who can provide *productive* feedback. As you become accustomed to sharing your emotions, you'll get more in touch with your feelings. Then, when you experience an intense emotion, like rage or extreme disgust, you should find it easier to recognize your feelings and be more willing to express them *in appropriate and modulated ways.* That is, engage in emotional self-regulation. When you express your feelings openly *and* in a constructive manner, it helps to clear the air and facilitate communication. Sharing your feelings with a willing person may also help you shed light on your emotions, especially when several come flooding forward at the same time.

A technique that is particularly useful for expressing intense emotions, especially negative ones, is the use of an **"I" message** (Gordon & Sands, 1984). Essentially, this message *consists of saying what you honestly feel in a way that encourages others to listen and cooperate. "I" messages are especially helpful in expressing your feelings about someone whose behavior has become a problem for you.* An "I" message consists of four components.

- First, *describe the other person's objectionable behavior* in specific but nonjudgmental terms. For instance, you might use the phrase "when you fail to return my book on time" instead of "you're irresponsible." Avoid using fuzzy and accusatory responses or guessing the person's motives. Such communication only intensifies the person's resistance to changing the behavior.

- Second, *point out the specific ways in which that person's behavior affects you.* In most instances, people are not deliberately trying to make life miserable for you; they simply aren't aware of the consequences of their actions. Once a person becomes more aware of how the behavior has become a problem for you, the person is usually willing to modify it.

- Third, *tell the person how you feel about the behavior in a way that "owns" your emotions.* To do this, you should generally start your sentences with the pronoun *I.* Say "I feel hurt" instead of "you hurt me." Avoid projecting your emotions onto the other person.

- Finally, *tell the person what you want done to correct the situation.* For example, if you object to the casual way telephone messages are left for you, you might say something like this: "I don't have the information I need and I feel frustrated when you don't write down my telephone messages. I'd appreciate your writing down my telephone messages."

Initially, "I" messages may seem a bit contrived or stiff. But as you become more experienced in using them you'll feel more comfortable expressing your feelings in this way. Table 7–1 provides more tips on "I" messages.

Let's next look at specific emotions in more detail. Although we will concentrate on troubling emotions such as anxiety and anger, we will end on an upbeat note—happiness.

Special Emotions

Anxiety.   Du probably felt as much anxiety about his examinations as he did his somewhat unrealistic prospects as a golf professional. **Anxiety** is *a vague, unpleasant feeling that serves as an emotional alarm signal, warning us of an impending threat or danger.* In ancient times, anxiety may have been evoked by natural disasters, predators, or inter-clan hostilities; its arousing nature may have been adaptive in that it helped humans survive. Today, our worries tend to be related less to survival and more to everyday frustrations, bureaucracies, personal achievements, and other non-life-threatening issues (Zeidner & Matthews, 2005). Unfortunately, we sometimes feel quite anxious when there is little actual danger, for example, when making a speech or going to the dentist. As a professor once said, "There is little point to test anxiety; I have yet to see a midterm leap off a desk and viciously attack someone."

When a threat is real (not imagined) and can be pinpointed, such as the fear of failing an examination or visiting a prominent professor's office to request a favor, moderate

TABLE 7–1			
EXAMPLES OF "I" MESSAGES			
Nonjudgmental Description of Person's Behavior	**Concrete Effects on Me**	**My Feelings About It**	**What I'd Prefer the Person to Do**
1. If you don't complete what you promised to do	then I have to do it in addition to my other tasks	and I feel annoyed	I wish you would do what you've promised
2. Each time you criticize my work without telling me what I'm doing wrong	I don't know how to improve it	and I feel frustrated and resentful	Tell me what I'm doing wrong so I can correct what I'm doing wrong
3. When you change your mind at the last minute	it's too late to make other plans	and I feel angry and disappointed	Give me more advance notice when you think things may not work out

levels of anxiety may motivate us to take the necessary steps to avoid a gaffe. On the other hand, people who are prone to unusually high, chronic, "free-floating" anxiety tend to overreact to stressful situations, frequently making the situations worse. Furthermore, high levels of anxiety can distort our perception and thinking so much that our performance is impaired. Finally, anxiety siphons off energy by keeping us mobilized for action when none is needed. It makes us tense and tired, thereby robbing us of much of the enjoyment of life (Starcevic, 2005). Anxiety in modern life does not seem to serve to protect us and improve our survival; it is the bane of modern existence for many.

You are not alone if you suffer from anxiety, as it is quite common. For instance, somewhere between 20 and 50 percent of adults have math- and computer-related anxieties. Many more adults, 60 percent, suffer from social anxiety or general timidity about social situations. And evaluation apprehension (the fear of others' appraisals of us) is nearly universal across people of different ages, genders, and cultures (Zeidner & Matthews, 2005). One specific form of evaluation apprehension is test anxiety, which also appears to be widespread. Test anxiety is a familiar problem for most students like you and Du. Does test anxiety help you to learn better or does it interfere with your performance? A lot depends on you *and* on your situation.

Generally, the relationship between anxiety and test performance takes the form of an inverted-U curve, as depicted in Figure 7–1. That is, at low levels of anxiety, we remain unmotivated and perform well only on easy, not difficult, tasks. Moderate levels of worry tend to enhance performance (Perkins & Corr, 2005), at least up to a point. But at high levels of anxiety, many people become distracted and overwhelmed, thereby performing more poorly on tests. Recognize, too, that people differ widely on their optimal level of anxiety—the degree of anxiety at which they do their best (Zeidner & Matthews, 2005). People with relatively low levels of anxiety often do their best only when challenged, as in a highly competitive situation. Those with characteristically high levels of anxiety tend to do better, at least on difficult tasks, under conditions of less pressure. Which of these two patterns do you most resemble? Do you find it depends somewhat on the situation as well as on your own mastery of required skills and motivation?

So, how do you cope with test anxiety? First, adaptive coping in exam situations involves a flexible use of multiple coping strategies. In other words, when one strategy

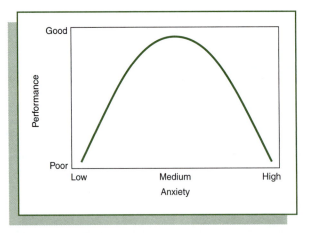

FIGURE 7–1
The relationship between anxiety and performance.

does not work, the individual needs to be able to turn to another. Here are a few anxiety-reducing strategies from which to choose. When you find yourself getting anxious during a test, you can employ anxiety-reducing statements ("I know I can do it" and "I'll take one question at a time and do my best on each question"), as they can ease tensions. Additionally, try to avoid negative and self-defeating thoughts (e.g., "I'm going to fail this test" or "All of these questions are too hard"), as they distract you from the primary task of exam taking (Hopko, Crittendon, Grant, & Wilson, 2005). Another effective method for coping with test anxiety is to study hard and learn well (Beilock, Kulp, Holt, & Carr, 2004), a strategy that increases confidence and thus decreases test anxiety. Good study techniques were reviewed in the "How to Study" section (PQ4R) at the beginning of this book.

Second, effective coping strategies should match both the context and the individual. This means that the individual needs to be comfortable with the strategy and also that the strategy should be appropriate to the level of challenge of the examination. Happily, most students cope effectively because they utilize active coping, in which they plan study time and techniques, suppress competing activities (such as socializing with friends), and reframe the stressful event positively (e.g., "A good grade means a higher GPA and perhaps a better job when I graduate") (Zeidner, 1995).

Anger.   Du's roommate often teases him that he is as bad a golfer as he is a student and that he is going "nowhere fast." Du loses his temper because he feels humiliated and is tired of the teasing, no matter how good-natured. Du is not alone in his angry moments. A basketball coach yells profanities at the referee after a controversial call. A teenage girl screams "I hate you" at her mother who won't let her stay out as late as her friends' parents allow. A red-faced worker slams his fist on the table to make his point during a dispute with his boss. All these people are venting **anger**—*feelings of displeasure or resentment over (perceived) mistreatment.*

For decades, psychologists have been investigating whether holding anger in or *venting anger out* (i.e., **catharsis**) is the best way to deal with this type of negative emotion. Many of you have grown up with the idea that when you're angry, it's healthy to "get it off your chest" or "let it all hang out." Holding anger in, goes the popular notion, leads to all kinds of problems—high blood pressure, increased risk of heart attacks, depression, and suicide. On the other hand, we have all seen people blowing off steam and who afterward seemed pleased or relieved. So where does the truth lie?

Deciding whether venting anger is healthful or hurtful actually depends on *how* you vent your anger. Many studies find that venting anger behaviorally (e.g., hitting a pillow; playing a violent video game) or verbally (yelling and screaming) only results in more anger and aggression (Anderson & Bushman, 2002). On the other hand, a recent study found that expressive writing (designed to express emotions, especially negative ones like anger) actually helped lower blood pressure in participants in the research (McGuire, Greenberg, & Gevirtz, 2005). Sometimes doing nothing or displacing anger onto a more productive project (e.g., drawing) may be an effective way to manage anger. There is some truth to the notion that people who unduly suppress or hold in their high levels of anger are more prone to high blood pressure and heart attacks. Whether held in or exploded, hostility and anger are not beneficial to us. We therefore need to learn to address them better.

There is lots of evidence that we can learn to effectively manage our anger (Potter-Efron, 2005). First, certain child-rearing practices can go a long way toward preventing inappropriate forms of anger expression (Roelofs, Meesters, Ter Huurne, Bamelis, & Muris, 2006). Developmentally appropriate strategies for encouraging children to responsibly manage anger include modeling by parents of appropriate anger management, avoiding shaming a child's anger, and increasing the child's understanding of anger as well as the sense of control over anger-arousing events (Landy, 2009).

Eliminating exposure to aggressive models also helps (Kirsh, 2006). Parents might want to monitor their child's consumption of media violence. There is much evidence that watching televised violence, playing violent video games, and the like, increases aggressive feelings, aggressive thoughts, aggressive behaviors, and it desensitizes (i.e., violence bothers us less and less) us to its effects (Huesmann, 2007). Parents also need to be cautious about physically punishing their children, especially when the child has a temper tantrum or has acted aggressively toward another. Such parents are modeling the very behavior they are trying to eliminate in their children. Children and adults who are isolated also have difficulty managing anger. Perhaps it is the individual's failure to properly manage anger or some other negative traits that has turned friends away. Box 7–1 further suggests that school bullies are often depressed and angry and, thus, turn their anger on their victims. On the other hand, increasing social supports so that the angry person can discuss anger with others often improves anger management (Dahlen & Martin, 2005).

Training in social skills that teach us to get along with others is another option. If we don't know how to respond appropriately to others, we sometimes lose our tempers or they lose theirs. Social skills training helps individuals find alternative solutions to provocations. Such training can be effective, even after a few hours (Martsch, 2005). For other individuals, therapy might be the only answer. Therapy should convey the sense that anger is destructive and that better communication and problem-solving skills and increased empathy for the target of the anger all reduce anger. Such therapy has been shown to be effective for adolescents and adults who show strong levels of anger and little control (DiGuiseppe & Tafrate, 2003).

Jealousy.   Essentially, **jealousy** is *a complex emotion that occurs when we fear losing a close relationship with another person or have lost it already.* Jealousy can be contrasted with **envy,** *which is distinguished by feelings of inferiority, longing, resentment, and disapproval.* Jealousy is characterized by fear of loss, distrust, anxiety, and anger (Parrott & Smith, 1993). Jealousy is especially apt to occur in romantic and sexual relationships, so that it is popularly known as romantic jealousy. Romantic jealousy can be normal or pathological (obsessional); today, many Americans view jealousy as an embarrassing emotion at best (Marazziti et al., 2003).

It is commonly thought that jealousy is a measure of devotion and that the lack of jealousy means the absence of love. Admittedly, jealousy may contribute positively, however indirectly, to close relationships like marriage. Laypeople may believe that high jealousy is linked to "strong love," "establishing ground rules," and an "increased commitment" in the marriage. However, many psychologists regard jealousy as an unnecessary and destructive emotion in close relationships (Wigman, Graham-Kevan, & Archer, 2008). In fact, recently Tallis (2005) has raised the issue that passionate love with its dark side of jealousy, dependence on another, and consequential anxiety is related to mental illness. What do you think about the possibility that love and/or jealousy may be forms of psychopathology?

The occurrence of jealousy depends largely on the interaction between jealousy-evoking situations and the personalities of the people involved as well as their relationship. Some situations are especially apt to trigger jealousy, such as the following:

- The person you like goes out with someone else.
- Someone gets closer to a person to whom you are attracted.
- Your lover or spouse tells you how sexy a former boyfriend/girlfriend was.

Box 7–1

Bullying—A National Epidemic

Just what is bullying? A good definition comes to us from the childhood education literature. **Bullying** is *repeated, unprovoked, harmful actions by one child or children against another.* The bullying acts can be physical (e.g., punching or kicking) or psychological (e.g., name-calling or taunting) and can occur in person or via the Internet, more commonly referred to as "cyber-bullying" (Stassen Berger, 2007).

Bullying may be rampant in U.S. schools (Flynt & Morton, 2004). One out of every five children reports being a bully while 25 to 50 percent of the children report being the victim of bullying (Flynt & Morton, 2004). Moreover, 10 percent of children and adolescents have been cyber-bullied (Kowalski & Limber, 2007). Interestingly, boys are stereotyped as bullies because aggression, which is linked to anger, is one of the only acceptable emotions for males (Elias, 1999b). Girls tend to bully as much as boys (Hoffman, 2002), but the type of bullying may vary. Girls are more likely to use gossiping, taunting, glaring, and bad-mouthing (i.e., relational bullying), whereas boys are more likely to use physical forms of aggression (i.e., direct bullying) (James & Owens, 2005; Woods & White, 2005). Interestingly, both males and females tend to be crueler in their bullying to those of the same sex than they are to those of the opposite sex (Ladd, 2005).

Bullies have different motives for picking on other children. Some children may bully because they have too high or too low self-esteem (Bullock, 2002). Other children have learned from their parents to hit back or become more aggressive when their self-esteem is threatened. Other bullies taunt and bully because they, themselves, have been bullied. And some studies show that bullies may be depressed. For these children, especially for boys, the most acceptable way to express their misery is to act macho rather than sad (Elias, 1999b).

Victims of bullying may go largely unnoticed by teachers and parents, in part because teasing in childhood is sometimes considered "normal" (Bullock, 2002). However, bullying has serious psychological

and social consequences for those who bully and are bullied (Nishina, Juvoven, & Witkow, 2005). Depression, low self-esteem, social isolation, and behavior problems are some of the effects (Pace, 2001; Stassen Berger, 2007). Victims of bullies tend to be children who are different from the typical student in the school (Flynt & Morton, 2004). Because schools, themselves, may inspire a "culture of sameness," children who are different and do not fit in are bullied. Such children are ethnically or racially different, dress differently, are weaker or smaller, disabled, or more passive (Bullock, 2002).

There are steps that parents and teachers can take to help victims of bullying (Smith, Pepler, & Rigby, 2004). The first is to recognize signs of victimization. If a child is experiencing the following, suspect bullying:

- Behavioral changes (e.g., more aggressive or more withdrawn)
- Frequent crying or depression
- Lower self-esteem
- Unexplained injuries
- Academic difficulties not manifested earlier
- Unexplained health problems such as stomach pains or fatigue
- Fear of school or desire to avoid school

After both teachers and parents observe the symptoms, they should talk in private to the children whom they suspect are bullies or victims. Second, many schools have instituted bullying prevention programs, although many programs have not been assessed at present. Some of these programs include using a peer mediator (someone empowered to intervene in the bullying) or a mentor who can help protect the victim (such as an adult or an older student). Finally, children can be taught not to tolerate bullying but rather to report it to parents, teachers, or other adults.

- Your lover or spouse visits a person he or she used to go out with.
- You find that your partner is having an affair.
- You are the second spouse of your mate and he or she has to pay support to the first spouse.

The response to jealousy also depends on the exact situation and the personalities of the individuals involved. Some people are especially prone to jealousy; such individuals are characterized by low self-esteem, high levels of anxiety, a negative view toward the world, low levels of life satisfaction, little control over their lives, low threshold of emotional arousal, and a greater sensitivity to threatening stimuli in social environments (Guerrero & Andersen, 1998). Beyond these characteristics, those with pathological (obsessional) jealousy possess unfounded suspicion of a partner's fidelity. These suspicions modify thoughts, feelings, and behaviors. For example, a pathologically jealous person obsessively checks the whereabouts of the object of affection and argues often with that person about jealousy or makes groundless accusations against that person (Marazziti et al., 2005).

Although the potential for jealousy may be inherent in our biological makeup (Easton, Shackelford, & Schipper, 2007) cultural influences carry as much or more weight in determining which situations provoke jealousy and how it is manifested. For instance, when jealous, the French get mad, whereas the Dutch become sad. The Germans prefer not to fight about it but rather to talk it out, while the Italians don't even want to talk about it. It appears that Americans are mostly concerned about what their friends will think (Zummuner & Fischer, 1995).

Yoshimura (2004) conducted an extensive study of coping with jealousy and communication between romantic partners. To list but a few strategies, coping and communication methods can vary among the following:

- Face-to-face interactions with the partner to avoidance of the partner or the rival.
- Jealous violence to more positive solutions such as initiating an open discussion.
- Problem-focused coping such as repairing the relationship to emotion-focused coping such as soothing the other person.

Some methods of coping are productive, such as using apologies, increasing affection, and using reassurances; others are less productive, such as making up excuses, being manipulative or vengeful, and arguing. What perhaps is most important about Yoshimura's research is that the *initial* expression of jealousy strongly influenced the trajectory of the rest of the cycle. In other words, positive communications at the onset, such as "I'm sorry I made you feel jealous; I want to reassure you that I love you very much" resulted in the most positive response from the partner. As expected, initial negative communications such as "You're just insecure" disintegrated into further negative interactions.

How people *appraise* and then *cope* with jealousy-evoking situations is especially important. For instance, men and women have jealousy mechanisms that are activated by different types of infidelity. Men appear more upset over sexual infidelity while women seem more upset over emotional infidelity (Fernandez, Vera-Villarroel, Sierra, & Zubeidat, 2007; Schützwohl, 2006). Additional research has focused on how, for men, romantic jealousy can devolve into domestic violence. Men have several different strategies for dealing with jealousy. One is *direct guarding,* where, for example a man drops in unexpectedly to see what his girlfriend is doing. Another is what the researchers call *negative inducement,* as in threatening a romantic partner who has shown attention to another man. A third method men use to guard against rivals is through *public signals of possession,* such as holding a wife's hand when other men are around. Yet another approach is *positive inducement,* where the man helps a woman when she really needs help or brings flowers to cheer her up. Not surprisingly, the first three tactics are much better predictors of the use of violence toward romantic partners to "keep them in line" than was the last, more positive approach. However, the strongest predictor of all for violence was emotional manipulation that included pleading that the man cannot live without his female partner or that he would die if she ever left. Excessive direct guarding and monopolization of time also predicted violence toward the female partner as well (Shackelford, Goetz, Buss, Euler, & Hoier, 2005).

Happiness.   Imagine Du's happiness and surprise when his professor readily agreed to delay Du's exam. In fact, Du was amazed at the professor's warmth and approachability. Du's only other experience with the professor was attending his lectures in a large auditorium. The professor revealed to Du that he, too, loved golf and had hoped to pursue golf professionally only to have his efforts thwarted by his parents who wanted him to obtain an advanced, prestigious degree. The professor continued that a Ph.D. in chemistry with weekend golf outings and well-timed golfing vacations was the compromise that met both his personal needs and his parents' lofty wishes.

Happiness, or as psychologists refer to it, **subjective well-being (SWB),** *includes a preponderance of positive thoughts and feelings about one's life.* People high in SWB have a global sense that work, marriage, and other life domains are satisfactory. They experience and report pleasant rather than anxious, angry, or depressive emotions. Happy people are less self-focused, less hostile, and less vulnerable to disease. They are more loving, forgiving, trusting, energetic, decisive, creative, helpful, and sociable than unhappy people (Lyubomirsky, Sheldon, & Schkade, 2005; Myers, 1993). Study after study shows that happy people have high self-esteem, a sense of personal control, optimism, and extroversion (Cohn, Fredrickson, Brown, Mikels, & Conway, 2009; Diener & Seligman, 2002); happy people often lose a sense of time and self because they find a task challenging and absorbing (Myers & Diener, 1995).

Additionally, Myers and Diener dismiss many myths about happiness. For example, happiness does not discriminate between genders; in cross-cultural research both men and women have equal opportunities to find happiness (Michalos, 1991). The sources of men's and women's happiness, however, may differ. Cross-cultural studies suggest that men's well-being is better predicted by self-esteem, whereas women's well-being or happiness was predicted somewhat by self-esteem but also by relationship harmony (Reid, 2004). Aging does not necessarily involve a decline in happiness either (Shmotkin, 2005; Westerhof & Barrett, 2005). Although there is also only a modest correlation between wealth and happiness (Fischer, 2008), as Myers and Diener (1995) persuasively state, "[wealth's] absence can breed misery, yet its presence is no guarantee of happiness" (p. 13). Race, culture, and ethnicity are also not predictors of happiness.

Several studies point out that happy people outnumber unhappy people in many cultures (Shmotkin, 2005; Suhail & Chaudhry, 2004), perhaps because one of the overarching principles of happiness is a sense of "owning" one's goals, that is, pursuing one's life goals because of an authentic desire to do so. Research has demonstrated that members of both individualistic and collective cultures experience well-being when they pursue self-chosen goals. True, in an individualistic culture a self-selected goal may be "a better life for myself" while in a collective society a self-selected goal may be "to fit in better." Nonetheless, when individuals' goals are self-concordant, the individual reports higher levels of happiness and well-being than when goals are not self-selected (Sheldon et al., 2004). Everyone, then, has the possibility for happiness. Motivation and emotion indeed are related. If by now you have not set life goals for yourself, isn't it time to think about doing so in order to promote your own subjective well-being?

SUMMARY

UNDERSTANDING MOTIVATION

Maslow's hierarchy of needs is a popular theory of motivation. At the bottom of the hierarchy are basic needs such as the need for food and the need for safety or security. The middle but narrower level involves the need for belonging or the need to fit in and be accepted. At the top levels are self-esteem needs and self-actualizing tendencies, respectively. Self-esteem needs involve the need to feel a sense of self-worth and achievement, whereas self-actualization includes a sense of autonomy and uniqueness. These higher-level needs cannot be met if the lower-level needs are unfulfilled.

Hunger is an example of a basic need. Most basic needs are biological but can be shaped by learning. Psychosocial needs are related to our sense of competence, include the need for stimulation and novelty, of which one form is sensation seeking, and achievement or the need for success. Such motives vary by individual. Culture, gender, and other factors that influence learning shape our individual methods for responding to and meeting these needs.

UNDERSTANDING EMOTIONS

Emotions are complex changes that include physical arousal and cognitive interpretations of a situation. Emotions are very important to psychological adjustment. The cognitive view of emotions is that our interpretation of them is actually more important in influencing our reaction than the actual arousal or the provoking stimulus. Although psychologists have not yet agreed on the primary emotions, there is general agreement that several emotions are universally expressed: anger, fear, happiness, sadness, and surprise. Culture can greatly influence the intensity of emotional expression, though. Another tricky part of emotions is that people attempt to deceive us about their emotions by altering their nonverbal communications (the face and the body). We can learn healthy methods for managing our emotions so that we express them at socially appropriate times and in acceptable intensities and ways.

Anxiety is a common unpleasant emotion, but it can serve as a useful alarm that warns us of threat. Most causes for anxiety in modern life are less related to survival and more related to dealing with everyday frustrations. One example is test anxiety, which is especially detrimental to unprepared students, as it can diminish performance. Being well prepared for an examination helps overcome test anxiety.

Anger is yet another problematic emotion. Research with perpetually hostile individuals has shown that hostility can lead to coronary disease. Learning to respond in nonhostile ways is therefore important to mental and physical health. One good method for avoiding anger and aggression is to raise children to recognize their anger and to manage it when they are young. Angry, depressed children often bully their peers. Parents can and should act as positive role models for their children.

Jealousy is a third negative emotion with which individuals have to cope. Jealousy often occurs in a romantic context. Many individuals need to learn to cope with jealousy in active and constructive ways where they express their intention of improving the relationships. Extreme forms of jealousy and manipulative strategies can sometimes result in violence against romantic partners.

Happiness is a positive emotion associated with subjective well-being. According to research, happiness is available to everyone regardless of sex, race, or income level. Happy people are less hostile, less vulnerable to disease, and more forgiving, trusting, and energetic than unhappy people.

SELF-TEST

1. In Maslow's concept of the hierarchy of needs, the most urgent need commanding our attention is
   a. self-actualization.
   b. security.
   c. belongingness.
   d. the lowest unmet need.

2. The part of the brain that is especially responsive to the changes in blood chemistry associated with hunger is the
   a. hypothalamus.
   b. medulla.
   c. cerebellum.
   d. frontal lobe.

3. Research demonstrates that differences in our sensation-seeking motives are thought to be partly dependent on
   a. biological factors.
   b. educational levels.
   c. intelligence.
   d. age.

4. Individuals with a strong need for achievement tend to choose tasks with
   a. low risks.
   b. minimum rewards.
   c. maximum rewards.
   d. medium risks.

5. Which of the following best expresses self-efficacy?
   a. "I can do it."
   b. "Maybe tomorrow."
   c. "Some things are better left unsaid."
   d. "I hope I get a better grade than my classmate."

6. The cognitive appraisal view of emotions holds that our emotions depend primarily on
   a. how people treat us.
   b. hormonal arousal.
   c. how we interpret situations.
   d. activity on the left side of the brain.

7. Fleeting facial changes that last only a second that tip us off to a person's true emotions are known as
   a. body leakage.
   b. microexpressions.
   c. unconscious denial.
   d. "I" messages.

8. Responding to someone's objectionable behavior with an "I" message normally includes our
   a. perception of the other person's feelings.
   b. positive rather than negative emotions.
   c. opinion of the person's behavior.
   d. nonjudgmental description of the person's behavior.

9. People who are the most successful in interpreting nonverbal messages are
   a. likely female, not male.
   b. living in individualistic societies.
   c. low in expressiveness themselves.
   d. high in creativity.

10. Jealousy is a blend of emotions, predominated by
    a. anticipation.   c. love.
    b. disgust.   d. fear of loss.

EXERCISES

1. *Seeking new experiences.* Sometimes the stimulation from new experiences helps to revitalize your motivation and zest for life. You might try several of the following suggestions: Taste a food you've never tried. Take up a new sport or hobby. Invite someone out socially you would like to know better. Attend a workshop or a special course you're interested in. Perhaps you can add other ideas. Try several of these suggestions, and write about your reactions in a page or so. Would you agree that variety is the spice of life?

2. *Assess your achievement motivation.* Look at your achievement motivation in a specific area of your life—a class you're taking, your motivation in school as a whole, your job, or progress toward your career goals. Then answer the following questions:

   • How strongly do you want to succeed?

   • Do you believe your ability is crucial, or is success mostly a matter of luck?

   • How much do you enjoy what you're doing?

   • Do you have the skills needed to succeed? If not, what are you doing about this problem?

   Honest responses to such questions may help you to understand the strength of your achievement motivation and what's needed to increase it.

3. *Share your everyday feelings.* Do you share your feelings as readily as you'd like? If not, you might try this exercise. A good way to begin sharing your feelings is to share some of the safe, everyday feelings. For example, whenever you're especially pleased by something another person has done for you, tell this person how you feel about it. The practice of sharing these safe feelings may help you to become more aware of and comfortable in sharing your deeper feelings.

4. *Practice sending "I" messages.* Think of several situations in which someone else's behavior has become a problem for you. Then write out the appropriate "I" messages under the respective four headings, as explained and illustrated in this chapter. If you feel comfortable doing so, you might try expressing some of these "I" messages in person.

5. *Happiness.* Are you generally a happy person? Why did you come to the answer you did? If yes, what can you do to maintain your current level of well-being? If not, can you think of ways you can improve your general level of happiness?

QUESTIONS FOR SELF-REFLECTION

1. What are some of the dominant motives in your life?
2. Has overeating or snacking between meals become a problem for you?
3. How strong is your sensation-seeking motive?
4. How strong is your achievement motive in school? In your career?
5. When asked, can you readily say "how you feel"?
6. Would you characterize yourself as an emotionally expressive person?
7. Did you grow up in a home in which people expressed their feelings freely?
8. Which emotions are the hardest for you to express?
9. How do you usually cope with anxiety?
10. What makes you happy?

FOR FURTHER INFORMATION

RECOMMENDED READINGS

BLAIR, G. R. (2005). *The ten commandments of goal-setting.* Syracuse, NY: The GoalsGuy. This book provides a blueprint for achieving goals you set.

EKMAN, P. (2004). *Emotions revealed: Recognizing faces and feelings to improve communication and emotional life.* New York: Owl Books. This book discloses how to read faces; the information is based on scientific research.

HIRSCH, G. (2001). *Helping college students succeed: A model for effective intervention.* New York: Brunner-Routledge. If you are having trouble making your way through college, this is the book for you.

MCKAY, G., & DINKMEYER, D. (2002). *How you feel is up to you: The power of emotional choice* (2nd ed.). Atascadero, CA: Impact Publishers. A book that discusses the power of emotions and emotional regulation.

POTTER-EFRON, R. (2001). *Stop the anger now: A workbook for the prevention, containment, and resolution of anger.* Oakland, CA: New Harbinger Publications. A book about anger management.

Websites and the Internet

http://www.helpself.com/iq-test.htm   Test your emotional IQ at this site. A self-help site with other useful information besides emotional intelligence.

http://www.mtn.org/EA   The site of Emotions Anonymous. The site offers to use social support to assist individuals over the Internet to deal with a variety of troubling emotions.

http://elvers.stjoe.udayton.edu/history/history.asp   A site to research Abraham Maslow and his motivational theory. In fact, link to the psychology part of the site and you can find biographical information on many well-known psychologists.

http://www.mindtools.com/page6.html   A site designed to help you improve your goal-setting strategies. The site also contains information on time management, decision making, interpersonal communication, and other necessary life skills.

http://www.authentichappiness.sas.upenn.edu   Dr. Martin Seligman's website for positive psychology. The site contains questionnaires, newsletter articles, and more.

Making and Keeping Friends

Learning Objectives

After completing this chapter, you should be able to

1. Discuss several factors affecting our impressions of others.
2. Explicate reasons people form mistaken impressions.
3. Know how shyness shapes relationships.
4. Explain the influence of physical attractiveness on interpersonal relations.
5. Discuss how mutual self-disclosure shapes friendships.
6. Know the similarities and differences between same-sex and opposite-sex friendships.
7. List several major reasons friendships break up.
8. Learn what the causes and consequences of loneliness are.
9. Provide suggestions for someone who is lonely and wants to overcome the loneliness.

Anita and Gale were best friends. They probably never would have met were it not for their positions at Ramona Community College. Gale grew up in a middle-class family in Minnesota, where her father was a journalist and her mother an engineer. Anita grew up in Texas. Her life trajectory was not as easy as Gale's. Anita's father left home was she very young. Anita's mother worked at various low-paying jobs, such as a housekeeper at a motel. Her mother always said that she wanted her daughter to have a better life. Her daughter did. Anita's mother ensured that Anita had the opportunity to attend first a community college and then a good four-year college. Anita was encouraged by her professors to continue her education. She pursued a master's degree and soon found herself in the position of being a new professor at Ramona. When Anita arrived, Gale was already a professor there. Gale was in her 40s, Anita in her late 20s. Gale was White and middle class; Anita was Latina and, before acquiring her education, working-class.

The two women seemingly had nothing in common, but Gale was immediately taken by this intelligent and personable young woman. Because they were the only two women in the department, Gale decided to informally mentor Anita through her early years as a fledgling professor. That is how their friendship began. Both women soon learned that they really did have common interests. Each enjoyed rhythm and blues, foreign films, and Tex-Mex cuisine. Their attitudes about politics and religion were very different, though. Gale was strongly Republican, rather conservative, and hardly religious. Anita was devoutly religious and a solid Democrat. Is the story of their friendship typical? How do people form friendships? Why do friendships dissolve? These and other issues are the focus of this chapter.

MEETING PEOPLE

Like Anita and Gale, do you have at least one good friend with whom to share secrets, troubles, and joy? Each of us needs intimate as well as more superficial social relationships. On the one hand, we need a network of people to fulfill a variety of needs, such as the exchange of services and the alleviation of stress through friendly activities. On the other hand, each of us also needs a deep, caring relationship with one or more special persons, such as a close friend, lover, or spouse. Sharing our deepest thoughts and feelings with an understanding companion who accepts us—despite our faults—is one of life's most satisfying experiences (Steiner, 2002). It makes us feel at home in the world despite the usual ups and downs that occur during our lives. Those who lack close relationships often experience emotional isolation and loneliness, regardless of their network of other acquaintances. As you can see, friendships are crucial components to successful adjustment, but how do we go about making friends in the first place?

Are First Impressions Most Important?

When Gale first met Anita, Anita seemed very bright and engaging. Anita, on the other hand, wondered if a woman so senior to her would ever be friendly. From the beginning, they were busy forming **first impressions** of each other. *These are the initial impressions we form of others in which we tend to judge them on the basis of very little information.* Forming such impressions seems to be a very natural and inescapable process. Moreover, first impressions (which are formed quickly) can endure for weeks (Sunnafrank, Ramirez, & Metts, 2004).

In impression formation, we do not treat all information equally. Upon meeting a new person, incoming negative and positive information is used differently. Negative information is given more weight and is viewed as being more stable. But why? As it turns out, positive behavior is the *expected* social norm. We simply anticipate, and expect, positive behavior from all people. When someone behaves badly, we assume the behavior was done *intentionally,* thus the person is evaluated as being bad. Because we are unlikely to voluntarily interact further with this type of person, our initial negative impression maintains itself (Denrell, 2005).

All of us do this—form indelible first impressions of other people. Again, why? One reason has to do with the need for understanding people around us, especially if we think we may have to interact with them in the future. We think forming impressions of others helps us better predict their behavior. Another reason may be **social comparison,** *which involves using others as a source of comparison to understand who we are relative to them* (e.g., comparing ourselves to classmates on intelligence). Whatever the reasons, the basic principle of person perception remains the same: We frequently tend to form extensive impressions of others on the basis of very little information.

In terms of making friends, first impressions are of the upmost importance (Ybarra, 2001). That is, subsequent impressions or interactions with others alter our first impressions of them very little. But how are these first impressions formed? At first, when people such as Anita and Gale meet, they have *surface contact* or *zero acquaintanceship*. They see each other and perhaps only exchange greetings at most. After this stage, though, people need to decide whether to continue the interaction. Psychologists have explored the factors that determine whether we indeed will continue the interaction. While luck plays a role, there are other factors that predictably attract us to others (Foster, 2005). Let's explore them.

Physical Attractiveness.   Another person's physical appearance is important in determining our impressions of them, whether they be potential friends or prospective romantic partners. Being pretty or handsome makes a strong first impression on others. Height, weight, sex, facial features, and dress all affect our senses and feelings. In fact, much research has concluded that physical appearance may be one of the most powerful determinants of our impressions of others. The more physically attractive someone is, the more positively we judge that person. Attractive people are judged to be more interesting, intelligent, compassionate, sociable, and better adjusted than less attractive people (Langlois et al., 2000; Olson & Marshuetz, 2005). They are regarded as more successful in their careers and happier in their personal lives. Physical attractiveness is also associated with such diverse accomplishments as earning higher grades, landing better jobs, obtaining faster promotions, and having less serious psychological disorders (Jackson, Hunter, & Hodge, 1995; Judge, Hurst, & Simon, 2009).

People in our society are considered attractive if they have symmetrical faces (Rhodes, Yoshikawa, Clark, Lee, McKay, & Akamatsu, 2001), a waist circumference that is about 70 percent or 80 percent of their hip circumference (George, Swami, Cornelissen, & Tovee, 2008), and are fairly thin (Derenne & Beresin, 2006). As it turns out, having attractive *friends* might also influence your own level of perceived attractiveness. Recent research indicates that on Facebook, profile owners with pictures of attractive friends posted on their "walls" are rated as more attractive than profile owners with less attractive friends (Walther, Van Der Heide, Kim, Westerman, & Tong, 2008). In contrast, people we regard as physically *un*attractive are typically judged unfavorably. Like beauty, ugliness is mostly in the eye of the beholder. For some, obesity or homely facial features appear to be ugly, as are irregular features such as large noses, discolored skin, or physical handicaps (Crandall, 1994). Whatever the case, unattractive people may be discriminated against for no good reason (Puhl & Latner, 2007).

Most of the aforementioned findings have been demonstrated in a variety of cultures. In fact, there are so many cultural similarities in the parameters of attractiveness that some researchers believe they are biologically determined (Langlois et al., 2000). For instance, Americans, Brazilians, and Russians prefer large eyes, small noses, and full lips (Jones, 1995). These generalities are true up to a point. Individuals within various ethnic and racial groups tend to show some degree of ethnocentrism when judging the attractiveness of others. That is, they find members of their own group more attractive than members of other groups (Schooler, Ward, Merriwether, & Caruthers, 2004).

As you look around, it is obvious that few people of either sex have an ideal face or figure. Most of us have some attractive features as well as others we'd like to change. At the same time, each of us manages to modify the cultural expectations regarding physical attractiveness to fit our partners and ourselves (Fudge, Knapp, & Theune, 2002). For example, the better we like someone, the more we modify our subjective evaluation of that person's physical attractiveness. Beauty undeniably is in the eye of the beholder. Hence, there are any number of people in the world who would consider each one of us attractive—a good thing for you to keep in mind.

Each of us may fantasize about having a highly attractive romantic partner. In reality, when it comes to choosing a date or romantic partner, *we usually settle for someone like ourselves, at least in regard to physical attractiveness.* This tendency has been labeled the **matching hypothesis.** For example, Little, Burt, and Perrett (2006) asked independent raters to rate faces on attractiveness and other factors; the rated individuals were married (unbeknownst to the raters). Results showed that raters perceived similar levels of attractiveness for pairs of married partners.

If you're in a stable romantic relationship, to what degree does the matching hypothesis apply to your relationship? Can you think of couples that are exceptions to this rule? All things considered, how important do you think physical attractiveness is in love, marriage, and friendship?

Reputations.   Reputation also affects our first impressions of others. Suppose Gale is your friend and says, "I can't wait for you to meet Anita." Even before you meet Anita, you'll probably find yourself forming a positive image of her based on what Gale tells you. Should you later discover Anita has some unfavorable qualities Gale didn't tell you about, chances are you'll give her the benefit of the doubt. Of course, it works the other way, too. If someone says, "I hear that professor named Gale is a terrible teacher," you may find yourself forming a negative impression of her, rightly or wrongly. Such is the power of reputation (Sleebos, Ellemers, & de Gilder, 2006).

Similarity.   One other reason that we initially notice and decide to like others is that they seem similar to us; some scientists have even posited genetic and evolutionary reasons for this notion (Rushton & Bons, 2005). Even if people are not really similar to us, we often assume that they are. Research has shown there is a strong correlation between liking and similarity (Morry & Gaines, 2005). In particular, people with the same attitudes are attracted to one another. "Birds of a feather [really] do flock together." How does this happen? When people interact, they cannot help noticing each other's age, sex, height, and other physical features. Shortly after, they begin to disclose attitudes and values to each other. However, the *proportion* of similar attitudes, not the raw number of similar attitudes, is most important. Figure 8–1 depicts how attitude similarity and liking are related.

There is less agreement about the importance of similarity based on needs and personal traits. According to one view, people with similar needs and personalities are

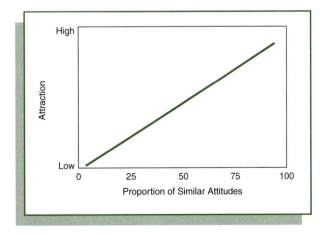

FIGURE 8–1
Attitude similarity and friendship.
The higher the proportion of similar attitudes between two people, the more they like each other.

attracted to each other; the other view is that people who are complementary (opposite but compatible) in their needs and traits are attracted. Actually, the *theory of complementarity* tends to apply mostly to *specific* traits rather than to the meshing of two personalities as a whole. A talkative person may therefore become attracted to someone who is quiet; a dominant individual might seek out a more dependent partner. Also, complementarity probably isn't important in the early stages of attraction, although it may become more important in a long-term relationship like marriage. Nevertheless, even among married couples, the weight of evidence seems to favor similarity as most influencing liking (Myers, 1998).

Propinquity.   Chances are that at some point in time your friends lived nearby, attended the same school, or worked at the same place, just as Gale and Anita did. Geographic nearness is especially important in the early stages of attraction, although the Internet is quickly changing this. First, the more you come into contact with people, the more opportunities you have for getting to know them better. This factor is called proximity or **propinquity,** meaning *physical closeness.* Many studies have demonstrated that the farther away a person lives or sits (in class, for example), the less likely that person is to become a friend (Smith & Weber, 2005). Being in close proximity also exposes us more to that individual so that we apparently come to know him of her better. It is also true that "the better I know you, the better I know you." In other words, as we become more familiar with someone, we become better judges of that person's facial expressions and other nonverbal cues (Sternglanz & DePaulo, 2004).

There's also a strong association between interaction and liking. That is, "the more I see you, the more I like you." And it works the other way, too: The more you like someone, the more you *want* to socialize with him or her (Vittengl & Holt, 2000). We also tend to emphasize the positive qualities and minimize the negative qualities of people we like to associate with (Denrell, 2005). Otherwise, we would probably feel that we're stuck with an unpleasant friend, coworker, or roommate, resulting in the build-up of resentment. Because our mainstream American social norms imply *cooperative* relationships with others, we make special efforts to get along with people we live or work with, or else life might just be too miserable.

If it's true that the more you associate with someone, the more you like that person, then the longer couples are married the happier they should be—right? Because this is obviously not the case for many couples, other factors, such as compatibility, are involved. As a result, when there are serious differences or basic incompatibilities between two individuals, close contact may lead to overt conflict, resentment, and alienation. In such cases, "familiarity breeds contempt." It is well known among those who work in the justice system that in assault and murder cases, the leading suspects are likely to be lovers, spouses, or ex-spouses.

Nonverbal Signals.   Our impressions of others are also shaped by a variety of nonverbal signals (Aronoff, 2006). In general, if a new acquaintance's face or gestures remind us of someone else that we know and like, we transfer our positive feelings about the old acquaintance to the new one. On the other hand, we also tend to transfer our negative feelings about a disliked person onto a new acquaintance who reminds us of the disliked person (Anderson & Berk, 1998). Additionally, a person's posture and gestures also affect our impressions. Those who stand erect or walk youthfully make a more favorable impression than those who slouch. Also, people who point, glare, and interrupt a lot make a more negative impression than those who are attentive to what we say.

As you might guess, the face plays an especially vital role in our perception of others. Gaze, or looking into someone else's eyes, is very important. We are favorably impressed with people who smile and look us in the eye. People who make eye contact with us are apt to be seen as more trustworthy and likable unless they gaze into our eyes for an uncomfortably long time. Those who avoid our gaze, whether from shyness or deceit, may strike us less favorably. In addition, those whose faces appear angular seem to us to be threatening or angry while those whose faces appear rounded are perceived as happy and likable (Aronoff, 2006; Bar & Neta, 2006). Look at the faces in Figure 8–2 to see how they affect you.

As mentioned in the previous chapter, some facial expressions are universal (Matsumoto, 2002). In other words, a smiling face in Nigeria communicates joy in much the same way a smiling face communicates joy in Germany. However, there is one culturally based caveat that needs to be taken into consideration: Just as languages and voices contain accents, so, too, do facial expressions of emotion. Such nonverbal "accents" can even identify the expresser's nationality or culture (Beaupré & Hess, 2005).

Verbal Signals.   There are also dimensions of other people's verbal communication patterns that shape our perceptions of them—not the words and their meanings, but other features of verbal communication, such as the rate of speech, pauses, and pitch. *These unspoken but important features of spoken communications* are called **paralinguistics.** Certain paralinguistic cues—such as gestures—when used without speech, can actually take on the full burden of communication to another person (Goldin-Meadow, 2006). As I'm sure many of you have experienced, paralinguistic cues are *absent* when writing emails, engaging in online chat, and texting others. As a result, the accuracy and comprehension of electronic messages may be negatively affected (Kruger, Epley, Parker, & Ng, 2005). Thus, when you communicate via the Internet or cellular service, it is important to make sure that your word choice clearly relays your intended meaning.

Recently, paralinguistic cues have been used to detect deception and lying. For instance, word repeats, speech speed, and nonverbal animation level differ between true and false statements (Davis, Markus, Walters, Vorus, & Connors, 2005). There also are nonverbal as well as verbal communication differences between men and women. You can read more about the relationships of gender to paralinguistics and spoken communications in Box 8–1, "When Men and Women Communicate" (page 178).

FIGURE 8–2
We perceive rounded faces as happier and more likable than angular faces.

Box 8–1

WHEN MEN AND WOMEN COMMUNICATE

When a man and a woman converse with each other . . .

- Men interpret "backchannels" (e.g., "uh-huh") differently from women as if they were raised in two different cultures (Mulak et al., 1998).

- Women and men respond similarly to comforting messages that are person-centered (Jones & Burleson, 2003).

- Men have more difficulty interpreting what women are saying than women have interpreting what men are saying (Edwards, 1998).

- In terms of nonverbal communication, women more directly orient their bodies to the speaker and use gaze, while men lean forward and show more postural congruence with the speaker (Guerrero, 1997).

- Women underestimate men's commitment, and men overperceive women's sexual intent (Haselton, 2003).

- Men increase their responsiveness when women use a facilitative style; on the other hand, women maintain a similar rate of response regardless of the gender of the facilitative speaker (Hannah & Murachver, 1999).

- Men do most of the talking, more of the interrupting, and raise fewer topics than women (Atwater, 1992).

Some of these gender differences may be meaningless, because it is not "men" versus "women" per se, but rather masculinity and femininity (traits available to both men and women) that create the aforementioned differences (Basow & Rubenfield, 2003)

Mistaken Impressions

Mistaken impressions are *false or erroneous perceptions of others, often based on insufficient evidence.* Anita initially assumed that Gale would not be interested in being friends with her because of their age difference. Anita was mistaken. The biggest single reason we misjudge others is the lack of sufficient information about them, as first happened when Anita met Gale. Nor should this be surprising, given our tendency to "size up" people so hastily. When we quickly assess someone, we generally use **heuristics** or *mental shortcuts* for making complex decisions. One such shortcut or heuristic is the **false consensus effect,** *in which we assume others feel as we do* (Wojcieszak & Price, 2009). We might guess, then, that if Gale initially liked Anita, she also falsely assumed that Anita liked her in return. Additionally, we also form mistaken impressions of others because of false cues, such as underestimating the importance of the situation the other people are in and stereotypes.

Stereotypes are *widespread generalizations that have little, if any, basis in fact and are typically held about groups of people.* Whenever people begin statements with phrases such as "*all* teachers" or "*those people* are all the same," they're slipping into stereotypical thinking. Stereotypes are learned in one of three main ways—by actual contact with an individual from the stereotyped group, by discussing the stereotyped group with others, and by encountering stereotypes in the media (Kirsh, 2010; Ruscher, Cralley, & O'Farrell, 2005). In fact, children frequently encounter both racial (e.g., minorities are perpetrators of crime) and gender stereotypes (e.g., women are emotional; men are independent and aggressive) in the media (e.g., Baker & Raney, 2007; Jansz & Martis, 2007; Li-Vollmer, 2002). For instance, one recent study found that children's picture books depict males as more independent and creative than females. Moreover, males were rarely shown doing household chores or caring for children (Hamilton, Anderson, Broaddus, & Young, 2006). Another study found that commercial advertisements tend to show females, more so than males, engaging in either passive activities (e.g., sitting and talking) or domestic chores (Davis, 2003). Finally, there are over 7,000 extremist websites, newsgroups, blogs, chat rooms, and clubs on the Internet that promote a whole host of stereotypes and prejudices. (The Simon Wiesenthal Center, 2007).

Research shows that the tendency to stereotype is quite natural and occurs automatically (Lepore & Brown, 2002). Moreover, stereotyping might be our *dominant* response, in both private and public settings (Lambert et al., 2003). Unfortunately, if the stereotype is negative, the biased holder of the stereotype is unlikely to associate further with the target of the bias, thus maintaining the negative stereotype (Sherman, Stroessner, Conrey, & Azam, 2005). Do you use stereotypes? Why? Do you, yourself, sometimes feel misunderstood because of stereotypes? If so, which ones? How do you respond to others when they aim a stereotype or prejudice against you? Is your response productive?

We also tend to label people good or bad because we know they possess (at least) a few good or a few bad characteristics. This is called the halo effect or devil effect. In the former case, it's as if the people we like wear a halo over their heads like an angel, and can do no wrong. In other words, the **halo effect** *is inferring uniformly positive traits from the appearance of a few positive traits.* For example, when we regard people as warm and outgoing, we also attribute all sorts of other positive qualities to them, such as intelligence and industriousness. Conversely, if we see others as cold and withdrawn, we tend to attribute additional negative qualities to them. Hence, the **devil (horns) effect** means *inferring uniformly negative traits from an appearance of a few negative traits.* In reality, of course, few individuals are all good or all bad. Instead, you should bear in mind that each of us is a complex mixture of traits, some desirable and others not so desirable (Palmer & Loveland, 2008).

We often form impressions of others based on very little information, for example whether the individual wears eyeglasses.

Another source of error is that we frequently misjudge people by not taking sufficient account of *situational* influences on their behavior. That is, we make erroneous **attributions** *in which we search for the causes for our own or someone else's behavior.* We assume that people are *always* acting in character (i.e., the behavior is trait induced). For example, if Anita dropped her coffee, Gale might think of her as clumsy rather than attribute the spill to the fact that the coffee was hot. The truth is that people are often constrained by their immediate situations. *The tendency to overattribute people's behavior to their personalities rather than to their circumstances* is so pervasive and of such importance to social perception that it has been called the **fundamental attribution error** (Tal-Or & Papirman, 2007). To avoid misjudging people, we must take account of the powerful and changing influences of their situations. Thus, it is wise to observe someone in a *variety* of different situations *across time* in order to know what that person is really like.

Shyness

"Everyone but me was having such a good time laughing and talking," said Anita after the fall opening-day faculty reception. "Gale was moving around the room greeting friends. There I was trying to think of something to say to this woman I hardly knew. She must have felt sorry for me. I couldn't wait until the party was over."

Does this sound familiar? **Shyness**—*the tendency to avoid contact or familiarity with others*—afflicts people of all ages, but especially the young. A large number of Americans identify themselves as shy (Saunders & Chester, 2008), and almost half of all Americans report a chronic problem with shyness (Marano, 2005). Similarly, about 80 percent of American college students report they have been shy at some point in their lives (Carducci & Zimbardo, 1995). It is now thought that more women suffer from shyness than men (Walsh, 2002). Shyness is typically consistent across situations and over time; in other words, shyness seems to be an enduring personality trait (Crozier, 2005). Shyness means different things for different people and covers a wide range of feelings and behaviors, but overall the experience of shyness (e.g., fear of social rejection and of social incompetence) is essentially the same in most cultures (Jackson, Flaherty, & Kosuth, 2000).

At one end of the shyness spectrum are those people who are not especially apprehensive about meeting people. When they are alone, it is because they prefer being in nature or working with ideas or things rather than with people. In the middle range are those who are sometimes embarrassed or occasionally lack self-confidence and prefer their own company (Crozier, 2005). Such individuals hesitate to ask for a date or a favor from others. At the other extreme are individuals whose shyness has become a sad form of self-imprisonment. *In its extreme form, shyness is called* **social anxiety** *or* **social phobia** *and may severely interfere with a person's life* (Heiser, Turner, Beidel, & Roberson-Nay, 2009). For example, some individuals with social phobia turn to alcohol to lubricate their social interactions, that is, they drink to inhibit their shyness (Santesso, Schmidt, & Fox, 2004). For this extreme form of shyness, antidepressants or anti-anxiety medication can be used for treatment (Robinson & Hood, 2007). Other psychological interventions, such as social skills training, may work equally well (Albano & Hayward, 2004).

People who are habitually shy are different: They see shyness as something within themselves, that is, as a personal trait (Bruch & Belkin, 2001). However, most dislike being shy, because shyness creates many problems for them: feeling lonely, being overly self-conscious and unassertive, having difficulty making friends, being unable to think clearly in the presence of others, or freezing up in the middle of a conversation (Bruch, Hamer, & Heimberg, 1995; Carducci & Zimbardo, 1995; Jackson, Fritch, Nagasaka, & Gunderson, 2002). Moreover, it is not uncommon for shy people to be depressed and misunderstood by others (Jackson et al., 2002). They are apt to be regarded as aloof, condescending, emotionally "cold," and egocentric rather than shy. Almost all of us tend to be shy in some situations, such as meeting strangers, dealing with people of the opposite sex, and being in large groups. To learn more about your own shyness level, answer the quiz on shyness found in Activity 8–1, "How Shy Are You?"

ACTIVITY 8–1

HOW SHY ARE YOU?

INSTRUCTIONS: *For each of the following statements, indicate your level of agreement on a scale of one (1) = "strongly disagree" to seven (7) "strongly agree."*

1. I like to go on blind dates or to go out with someone I hardly know.

    Strongly disagree   1   2   3   4   5   6   7   Strongly agree

2. When I have to give a speech or participate in a debate, I approach the task with confidence.

    Strongly disagree   1   2   3   4   5   6   7   Strongly agree

3. I am assertive enough to stop a stranger on the street and ask what time it is.

    Strongly disagree   1   2   3   4   5   6   7   Strongly agree

4. When there are lots of strangers at a social gathering, I enjoy meeting them.

    Strongly disagree   1   2   3   4   5   6   7   Strongly agree

5. I am not bashful about meeting other people I do not already know.

    Strongly disagree   1   2   3   4   5   6   7   Strongly agree

6. When a small group of people is talking, I am one of the individuals who participates most.

    Strongly disagree   1   2   3   4   5   6   7   Strongly agree

7. I do not mind riding in crowded elevators even if all of us strangers should become trapped together.

    Strongly disagree   1   2   3   4   5   6   7   Strongly agree

8. If I think that my grade is incorrect, I am not timid about approaching the professor.

    Strongly disagree   1   2   3   4   5   6   7   Strongly agree

9. I feel I can readily ask my neighbors or friends for favors.

    Strongly disagree   1   2   3   4   5   6   7   Strongly agree

10. I generally feel comfortable the first day of class regardless of whether I know anyone else in the room.

    Strongly disagree   1   2   3   4   5   6   7   Strongly agree

SCORING: Add up your scores and record the total here: _____

The highest possible score is 70. If you scored at the high end of the scale (i.e., 50–70), you likely have confidence in your social skills and enjoy the company of other people, whether they are friends or strangers. If you scored at the low end of the scale (0–20), you might want to think about how shy you really are and what you can do to overcome shyness if it is a detriment to you. Remember, though, that the scale was developed for this book and is not scientific. The scale is intended to start you thinking about your own level of comfort around other people.

In American culture, we value freedom, cherish our independence, and celebrate bravado, so shy people do not fit our mainstream culture. However, this is not true in all cultures. In many Asian cultures, for example, reticent individuals are often thought to be more socially sensitive than extroverted individuals and therefore are more accepted by their peers (Sakuragi, 2004). Cross-cultural research shows that Israelis tend to be the least shy (Carducci & Zimbardo, 1995).

Where does shyness originate? Although some shyness can be traced to biology, most psychologists assume it is the result of *both* biological and environmental influences (Aron, Aron, & Davies, 2005). If you or someone you know suffers from shyness, rest assured that shyness can be reduced by learning to modify shyness when it creates problems (Albano & Hayward, 2004). Here's how:

- Strive to reduce the inner monitoring of your own thoughts, feelings, and actions, especially the concern for how people see you and whether they will reject you. Instead, focus on your participation in the activity.
- Identify those aspects of situations that elicit shyness, such as meeting new people, as well as the social skills you may be lacking.
- Develop your social skills, such as how to initiate and carry on a conversation and how to assert yourself. In other words, allow yourself some successes on the interpersonal front.
- Keep in mind that shyness subsides when you step out of your usual identity, as in when you become totally absorbed in something or when you are helping others.
- Try to stop being so self-critical and perfectionistic. If shyness has become too disabling, seek counseling or therapy.

Interestingly, shyness is on the rise in America. The advent of technology in the form of email and voice mail has reduced the need for us to meet face-to-face (Yuen & Lavin, 2004). Some experts claim that these electronic means of communication have the potential to isolate us from others, reduce our social well-being, and increase our isolation (Scealy, Phillips, & Stevenson, 2002). By using the Internet and other less personal means of communication, the opportunities for shy people to practice their face-to-face interpersonal skills are decreased. On the other hand, if face-to-face interaction is so feared that individuals are lonely and isolated from others, technology may afford some opportunities for meeting others (Brunet & Schmidt, 2008). Probably a balance of electronic and interpersonal communication is best.

KEEPING FRIENDS

While we treasure our solitude, most of us cherish time with our friends and family. The desire for human connectedness and attachment is a fundamental human motive. Perhaps it was Gale and Anita's desire to have a good friend inside the psychology department that brought them together in the first place. Think about how you've met your good friends. Can you recall what attracted you to one another? Did you become friends instantly or did the relationship grow slowly? Did you actively have to cultivate the friendship?

Frequently, we're attracted to people with whom we have a lot in common, as mentioned earlier. We may be interested in the same career goals or taking the same classes. In some instances, we're attracted to people who are different from us; they complement us in some way. Then, too, a lot depends on the "chemistry," or subjective factors, when people meet. And, surely, you have noticed how we seem to get along with some people better than others almost from the start.

Friendships Are Precious

After we have formed our first impressions and decided whether we want to continue the interaction, the more we get to know someone the more likely our relationship will ripen into friendship as did Gale and Anita's. **Friendship** can be defined as *the affectionate attachment between two or more people.* We usually think of a friend as someone we've known a long time, which is often true. Yet friendship has more to do with *the quality of the relationship* rather than with the frequency of association. A high-quality friendship is characterized by helping one another, intimacy or the disclosing of secrets, mutual praise for successes, loyalty, and other positive features (Berndt, 2002). Friendships provide warmth and closeness that are often missing in other daily transactions. Close friendships can save us from depression and loneliness and thus enhance our mental and social well-being (Zea, Reisen, Poppen, Bianchi, & Echeverry, 2005). Friendships in childhood are especially crucial and have been demonstrated to be related to whether a child is victimized or accepted by peers (Asher & Paquette, 2003).

When Friends Get Together

Not surprisingly, one of the most common activities among friends is having an intimate talk. This is one of the activities most frequently mentioned by men, women, and children (Berndt, 2002). Just as Anita and Gale might, you may call a friend to tell her about an embarrassing incident that happened to you in class. Or your friend may want to talk about the trouble he's having with his girlfriend. In both instances, sharing your feelings and getting someone else's reaction on the subject may be extremely helpful. Another frequently mentioned activity, especially for men, is doing a favor for a friend. Perhaps you ask to borrow a friend's car. Or your friend may want you to pick her up after work. Asking or doing a favor for someone else presupposes a great deal of trust as well as give-and-take in a relationship, both important qualities of friendship.

As mentioned in the chapter on stress, one of the greatest favors friends can do for each other is to lend a listening ear. This form of social assistance is called **social support** and is defined elsewhere in the book as *a process whereby one individual or group offers comfort and advice to others who can use it as a means of coping.* Although people who report good general well-being have only a few close friends, they often report high levels of sharing of intimate and personal information with those friends (Reynolds & Repetti,

Friends often disclose intimate information to each other, especially those high in self-esteem.

2006). Sometimes a casual friend becomes a close friend *because* that person listens sympathetically to some personal problem. Faced with crises, many people will turn to a friend before talking about it with their families, because a friend may serve as a sounding board and provide needed support without the conflict of kinship loyalties.

Do you have friends you could turn to in a personal crisis? If so, who are they? Remember, though, that people who frequently ask their friends to share serious problems that are more properly discussed with a professional may be asking too much. In these instances, it's often best to refer a friend to the appropriate help, while you remain supportive. Box 8–2 further elaborates upon this theme.

Box 8–2

TO WHOM CAN YOU TURN?

There's an old saying—"A friend in need is a friend indeed." With this in mind, think of all the people you call your friends. Now list the names of those

who would really listen to you when you need to talk;

with whom you can share your innermost feelings;

to whom can you turn when you're very upset;

with whom you can be totally yourself;

whom you can count on to help during a personal crisis.

If you can name only two or three people, your personal support system may be too narrow. Perhaps your name isn't on enough other people's lists, too. After all, friendship is a two-way affair.

Young adults are more apt to turn to their peers than their families when in need. People who are middle-aged or older are more inclined to seek out members of their families (Steiner, 2001), perhaps because the current generation of older people has been socialized this way. With a growing population of elderly and the development of adult communities, perhaps future generations of older people will be more peer-oriented (Buys, 2001).

Self-Disclosure—Those Little Secrets

As the relationship between two people progresses from strangers to acquaintances to close friends, individuals disclose a greater breadth and depth of information about themselves. Disclosure is a way to bring us closer to others (Gibbs et al., 2006). **Self-disclosure** is *the sharing of intimate or personal information with others.* For example, Anita and Gale shared an apartment for a month when Anita's new apartment was being refurbished, so Anita met Gale's husband, Rick. At first Rick and Anita talked about common, benign topics such as their favorite movies, baseball teams, and foods. By the end of Anita's stay, all three felt more comfortable talking about a greater variety of subjects, such as their career goals, leisure activities, and more intimate matters like health concerns, families, religious beliefs, and political preferences. As Rick and Anita became good friends, they developed greater trust in each other and shared matters that might have threatened a weaker relationship.

As it turns out, self-disclosure, especially of personal secrets, has health benefits (Patterson & Singer, 2007). For instance, recent research has demonstrated that writing about positive or traumatic experiences, for as little as two minutes a day, can lead to a dramatic reduction in health-related complaints (Burton & King, 2008). What is it about disclosure that promotes well-being? One notion is that the teller of the secret gains new insights into the secret, and as such, no longer has to expend effort hiding it. Still, increasingly higher levels of self-disclosure do not always lead to greater intimacy between two people and can sometimes backfire. Ordinarily, the more you disclose about yourself, the more your friend will reciprocate (Morry, 2005). If your friend does not feel sufficiently comfortable or trustful in the relationship, however, he or she may not reciprocate such intimate self-disclosure. Knowing intimate details about you would help your friend hold a power advantage over you. Eventually, you'd back off and restrict your communication to more superficial matters to balance the power. In other instances, someone may share information that presents a conflict in the relationship, so that both partners may retreat to more superficial levels of sharing.

Gale and Anita were fortunate in that they each shared intimate information with the other, trusted the other to maintain confidentiality, and forgave one another for angry outbursts. Other individuals, however, differ in their willingness to share personal information for several reasons. Those who enjoy high self-esteem feel not only more comfortable sharing personal information about themselves but also greater security that comes with close relationships. Those with low self-esteem are more apt to withhold personal information and thereby fail to learn about themselves through closeness with others.

Men and women also differ in their willingness to share personal matters face-to-face or even electronically (Fehr, 2004). Pairs of women characteristically engage in more intimate disclosure than do pairs of men (Dolgin, Meyer, & Schwartz, 1991). In fact, female–female friendship pairs seem particularly close (Dolgin & Kim, 1994). Disclosure by men is less reciprocal. That means men disclose less than is disclosed to them (Parker & deVries, 1993), and their disclosures are apt to cover less personal topics such as politics or school (Oxley, Dzindolet, & Miller, 2002). Some psychologists suspect that women use disclosure to enhance interpersonal connectedness, whereas men use disclosure to strive for mastery and power (Suh, Moskowitz, Fournier, & Zuroff, 2004). However, with the diminishment of gender-role stereotypes, we can expect men to engage in more self-disclosure than has been the case in the past.

There are also significant cultural differences in how acceptable self-disclosure is. Several studies have found that the Asians are less likely to explore their inner reactions as frequently and thoroughly as do Americans. The result is less self-disclosure in Japan and Taiwan than in the United States. On the other hand, Americans typically disclose more information, especially on superficial topics, such as interests, work, and finances, than do Taiwanese (Chen, 1995; Kito, 2005). Thus, there are general cultural differences between Eastern and Western societies in self-disclosure. Finally, differences in self-disclosure have been found in two seemingly similar cultures, the former Soviet-bloc countries of Hungary and Russia. Self-disclosure was far more common in Hungary than in Russia (Goodwin, Nizharadze, Luu, Kosa, & Emelyanova, 1999). The latter finding suggests that even among apparently similar cultures there exist differences in self-disclosure.

Same-Sex Friends, Opposite-Sex Friends

Friendship is not necessarily more important to one sex than to the other, but it does tend to have different meanings for men and women. More specifically, intimacy plays a more central role among women friends (Fehr, 2004), so the case of Anita and Gale in this chapter fits our subject well. Women generally are more physically and emotionally expressive in their friendships than men. Also, as we've already seen, women are more apt to share intimate details about their lives, such as their worries, joys, and secrets. At the same time, women experience greater anxiety over close relationships. Tensions, jealousies, and rejections are more common in friendships between women, whereas men are apt to engage in outright disputes over money, property, and dominance. Usually, men are not as emotionally close in their friendships with other men (Oxley et al., 2002). Instead, they are more likely than women to seek out a male friend to share in a particular activity, like tennis or hunting, or to ask a favor. Yet, when in the throes of a serious personal problem, men are just as inclined to seek out a close friend.

In addition, with changing gender roles, neither the "activity friend" nor the "all-purpose friend" friendship style is distinctively male or female. Women, whose active lives now include everything from working lunches to health-club workouts, are discovering the pleasure of activity friends. And men, realizing the importance of a personal support system, are discovering the value of an all-purpose friend with whom they share their deeper feelings and concerns. Neither friendship style gives an advantage in mental health, achievement, or the enjoyment of life. Most of us are better off with a mixture of both types of friends of both sexes. Each type of friend brings out and sharpens different aspects of ourselves.

Can you be a close friend with someone of the opposite sex without being romantically or sexually involved with this person? Some people remain skeptical; but now that men and women are working side by side just about everywhere, more people of both sexes are choosing friends of the opposite sex. Most people feel that opposite-sex friendships are different, in that they may easily turn into romantic relationships that are clearly more intense and dynamic than friendships (Collins & van Dulmen, 2006). In fact, opposite-sex and same-sex friendships are different from each other. Men tend to perceive sex with their women friends as more beneficial than did women friends with their men friends. On the other hand, women report more benefit from receiving protection from their men friends than men report about their women friends. There is one similarity, however, between the two sexes: When learning how to best attract a mate, both males and females turn more to opposite-sex friends than to same-sex friends (Benenson & Alavi, 2004). Because an opposite-sex friend is a potential mate, do men and women friends have to work to keep their friendships platonic? The answer seems to be yes. Messman, Canary, and Hause (2000) studied motives for remaining in a platonic state with someone of the opposite sex. In their study, the reported motives for maintaining the relationship as friends only were, in order from most to least important,

- wanting to safeguard the friendship as a friendship.
- not being physically attracted to the other person.
- fearing disapproval from a network of mutual friends.
- already being committed to a third party.
- avoiding risk (i.e., experiencing hurt) related to the relationship.
- not being ready to be in a romantic relationship with the friend.

The researchers also found that the main maintenance strategy for friendship was to play a supportive role (giving comfort, advice, and encouragement) to the opposite-sex friend. In fact, this supportive role, as well as taking part in shared activities, was related to positive friendships where no one in the pair benefited from the relationship more than the other person. When there was imbalance (or inequity) in the friendship, negative maintenance strategies (to avoid a romantic involvement) were likely to be employed, such as fearing disapproval of mutual friends. Opposite-sex friendships indeed are different from same-sex friendships.

Staying Friends

"There's no friend like an old friend," goes the time-honored saying. With old friends we can relax and be ourselves without much fear of rejection. We're familiar with each other's mannerisms and make allowances for each other's weaknesses. Staying friends depends more on the special qualities of the relationship (Bagwell et al., 2005) and less on the frequency of contact between two people. Most of us have some friends we don't see very often, but we still consider them friends. We may keep in touch by calling occasionally or exchanging cards, letters, or emails. Class reunions and vacations also afford opportunities for renewing old ties, as do social networking sites such as Facebook. At the same time, physical separation often exacts a toll on friendship, as when high school best friends attending separate colleges (Oswald & Clark, 2003). When people are asked why friendships cool off, the most frequently cited reason is that one person has moved away. In fact, the most common reason people cite for the breakup of friendships is simply life transitions (Davis, 1996). Specific life changes that affect friendships include marriage, childbirth, new jobs, and different schedules. Not surprisingly, breakups in friendships are more likely to happen if one person's life situation changes and the other person's does not.

Apart from life transitions, the most common reason friendships end is feeling betrayed by a friend; in other words, trust is broken (Sheets & Lugar, 2005). **Trust** can be defined as *people's abstract, positive expectations that they can count on friends and partners to care for them and be responsive to their needs, now and in the future.* The importance of trust and the ability to keep a confidence in friendship cannot be overestimated. For example, research has found that the demise of friendships typically occurs as a result of a basic expectation of friendship being broken. In some instances, there were minor infringements, such as using a personal item without asking permission. Other cases involved more serious offenses, such as "repeating things I said in confidence" or "trying to seduce my wife." Sadly, trust in others has declined steadily in the United States. In fact, if trust continues to decline at its present rate, our society may well become pervaded by mistrust rather than trust (Robinson & Jackson, 2001).

There are yet other reasons friendships cool. Friendships may also break off because the individuals discover they have very different views on matters that are important to them. Not surprisingly, this is the third most frequently cited reason for ending a friendship. Curiously, in some cases, increasing intimacy between friends, such as may be occasioned by taking a vacation together, may make them more aware of their differences than their similarities, or they find they have less in common than originally believed. But friendship is such a deeply satisfying experience that each of us will continue making new friends throughout life, while cherishing the special closeness that comes with a long-lasting friendship.

Loneliness

Anita was fortunate to have someone like Gale meet her, mentor her, and befriend her. On the other hand, some people have trouble forming or keeping close friendships, and they experience loneliness. Essentially, **loneliness** is *a subjective state reflecting the fact that the quality and quantity of relationships wanted is lower than the quality and quantity of relationships available.* Do not confuse loneliness with solitude, which is a more objective and, often, a desired state denoting the absence of people. You can feel lonely despite being surrounded by others if you don't feel close to those people (Hawkley, Thisted, & Cacioppo, 2009). On the other hand, in terms of solitude, you have many friends but deliberately seek brief periods away from them without feeling lonely. It thus appears that loneliness is largely a state of mind that results from the gap between our desire for closeness and the failure to find it (Rokach & Neto, 2005). Loneliness can be associated with depression, anxiety, unhappiness, and shyness (Asher & Paquette, 2003). It is also associated with other health factors. Lonely people, for instance, tend to smoke more, have a more sedentary lifestyle, and be more obese than those who are socially connected (Cacioppo, Hawkley, & Berntson, 2003). Interestingly, the *duration* of loneliness rather than the intensity of it may be related to reported psychological and somatic stress symptoms (DeBerard & Kleinknecht, 1995).

Ironically, traditional college students who are surrounded by hundreds, even thousands, of peers suffer more loneliness than any other age group (Wiseman, Mayseless, & Sharabany, 2006). Having loosened ties with their parents, people this age are actively seeking intimacy with their peers, especially those of the opposite sex. The idealism of youth, plus the desire for intimacy and a happy marriage, makes them especially sensitive to the discrepancy between their expectations of intimacy and their actual relationships. Moreover, college may be the first time some adolescents are away from their parents. Loneliness tends to decline over the years, leveling off throughout middle age, though less so among women than men. Although older adults spend much of their time alone, most of them are less prone to loneliness than popularly depicted, probably because they have learned to put their need for companionship in better perspective. However, loneliness appears to increase again among those in their 80s, reflecting, in part, the greater sense of disengagement from life among those at an advanced age (Perlman, 1991). General loneliness in our society may increase in the future due to changes in our population. In the past decade, the number of people living alone has increased by 20 percent and the number of single-parent households has increased by 21 percent (Cacioppo et al., 2003).

Think about how often you feel lonely—rarely, sometimes, or often? Which areas of your life are most affected—your social life or your love life? Then read the next few paragraphs and see if any of the information describes you.

Many factors contribute to loneliness. People who have grown up with warm and helpful parents (i.e., securely attached to their parents) are less likely to report loneliness

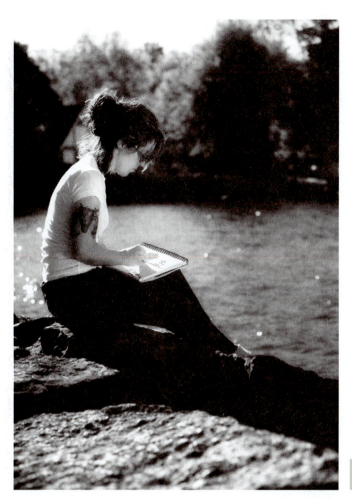

Loneliness and solitude are quite different.

in adulthood than those who describe their parents as disagreeable and unhelpful. Some of the loneliest people are those whose parents divorced when they were younger than 6 years old, partly because young children misperceive parental divorce as abandonment. In contrast, people who have lost a parent through death experience no corresponding increase in loneliness, probably because they realize that the loss was not intentional or their fault. People with low self-esteem tend to experience loneliness more than people who have high esteem. Individuals with low esteem are often lonely because their beliefs in their own unworthiness limit their recognition of positive feedback from others. This keeps them from taking steps to reduce their loneliness.

Another reason for loneliness is that some individuals are rejected by others because they have poor social skills (Efrati-Virtzer & Margalit, 2009). Children who lack appropriate social skills are sometimes rejected by their friends because they are aggressive, withdrawn, or fail to show appropriate responses to others' needs. These people are low in **emotional intelligence** or **EI:** *Emotional intelligence is the ability to regulate one's own emotions and to be empathic for others' emotions.* Specifically, emotional intelligence is comprised of four abilities (Salovey & Grewal, 2005), the ability

- to detect and decipher emotions in the self or others.
- to harness emotions to facilitate various cognitive activities such as problem solving.

- to comprehend emotion language such as slight variations between emotions (e.g., happy versus ecstatic).
- to regulate one's own and others' emotions.

Studies show that people with high EI engage in better-quality interactions with their friends and possess better impression management skills (Lopes et al., 2004). Other research indicates that those high in EI advance their careers even faster than people with high levels of general intelligence (Schutte et al., 2001), and they show better levels of performance under stress than those low in EI (Lyons & Schneider, 2005).

Culture affects loneliness, too (Rokach & Neto, 2005). The emphasis on personal fulfillment, often at the expense of stable relationships and commitment to others, is thought to make Americans especially prone to loneliness. Immigrants and long-term visitors to the United States are likely to report feeling very lonely, too, but for other reasons (Ditommaso, Brannen, & Burgess, 2005). In one study of international students, cultural distance predicted mood disturbance or maladjustment (Ward & Searle, 1991). In other words, the further the student's culture was sociologically from U.S. culture, the more lonely and depressed was the student. Canadian students are less apt to be lonely than students from Nigeria. Befriending international students and helping them adjust by assisting them with understanding our culture would be a very kind and considerate thing to do. At the same time, you would have the interesting opportunity to learn more about their culture.

How well we cope with loneliness depends largely on how we interpret its causes. People who suffer the most from loneliness tend to exaggerate its internal aspects and minimize its external ones. Thus, people who blame their loneliness on their personal inadequacies ("I'm lonely because I'm unlovable" or "My lover and I have split up because I gained too much weight and have no will power") make themselves even more lonely and depressed. Eliminating such negative thoughts can help reduce loneliness. Additionally, people are more likely to overcome loneliness when they focus on the *external, situational* factors that contribute to it: "It's hard to meet people in large classes" or "I'll stop working so much and get out and meet more people." Similarly, people who react to loneliness in passive ways—watching television, crying, and sleeping—feel even lonelier. Those who adopt more active or behavioral strategies—writing a letter or calling up an acquaintance—are more likely to alleviate their loneliness. Social skills training can help change behaviors, too (Cook et al., 2008). The best course is to continue developing your interpersonal skills so that you always have access to a broad network of social ties as well as a circle of close friends.

SUMMARY

MEETING PEOPLE

We began the chapter by pointing out that each of us tends to have both a network of social ties with which to fulfill a variety of needs *and* a smaller circle of close friends with whom we can be more intimate. We begin acquaintances with surface contacts, then, based upon first impressions, we decide whether to continue the interaction.

We're attracted to people for a variety of reasons, including such factors as familiarity, physical attractiveness, and similarity to us, especially similarity to our attitudes. The more we interact with someone, the more we tend to like that person, unless we discover serious differences or basic incompatibilities. Also, we tend to judge physically attractive people more favorably than others, even on matters that have little or nothing to do with physical appearance. In long-term relationships, however, we're often attracted to someone on the basis of a mixture of similar and complementary needs.

When meeting people, we tend to form erroneous impressions of others on the basis of limited information, usually judging by such factors as a person's physical appearance (especially attractiveness), stereotypes, and nonverbal cues such as gaze. Not surprisingly, the most common reason for misjudging people is the lack of sufficient information, causing reliance instead on false cues and stereotypes, and the failure to account for the situational influences on people's behavior. Shy people, in particular, tend to be misperceived as aloof and disinterested, largely because of their silence and lack of eye contact. Shyness can be overcome.

KEEPING FRIENDS

As society becomes more complex and impersonal, we value close friends even more. At the same time, we're choosing friends from a wider diversity of people than in the past, including more opposite-sex friends. Close friends frequently get together for good talk and companionship, in addition to sharing a variety of other activities. There's a close link between friendship and mutual self-disclosure, so that emotional sharing often strengthens the bond of friendship. Generally, opposite-sex friends tend to supplement rather than displace our same-sex friends and may or may not be part of a sexual relationship; certain reasons are cited by same-sex friends for not turning the friendship into a romantic alliance. Staying friends with someone depends more on the special quality of the relationship than on the frequency of contact. The two most common reasons friendships break up are that one person moves away or one feels betrayed by the other.

Essentially, loneliness is a state of mind that results from the gap between our desire for closeness and the failure to find it. People who suffer the most from loneliness tend to blame themselves for their plight or resort to passive strategies, such as watching television or sleeping. In contrast, those who cope best with loneliness tend to recognize the situational factors involved and take more active steps to alleviate them, such as calling up a friend. Immigrants or international visitors often have problems adjusting to their new culture and therefore feel lonely.

SELF-TEST

1. Our initial impressions of people are generally based on
    a. their family backgrounds.   c. very little information.
    b. negative stereotypes.   d. their body language.

2. We often misjudge people when we fail to consider how their behavior is affected by
    a. situational influences.   c. moral principles.
    b. social status.   d. unconscious motives.

3. Shy people are especially apt to be misjudged by others as
    a. intelligent.   c. aggressive.
    b. cold.   d. undersexed.

4. The more familiar we become with a person, the more we tend to
   a. envy that person.   c. criticize that person.
   b. dislike that person.   d. like that person.

5. Research suggests we're attracted to people according to the proportion of shared
   a. attitudes.   c. motives.
   b. interests.   d. traits.

6. According to the fundamental attribution error, we often blame _____ rather than _____ for others' behaviors.
   a. traits/situations   c. strangers/friends
   b. friends/family   d. situations/traits

7. One of the most important activities among same-sex and opposite-sex friends is
   a. taking a vacation together.   c. sharing a beer.
   b. having an intimate talk.   d. All of these are equally important.

8. The process of revealing intimate information about ourselves is called
   a. self-disclosure.   c. attribution.
   b. bragging.   d. all of these.

9. Almost half of Americans report that they feel
   a. renewed nationalism and pride.
   b. chronic shyness.
   c. in love with another person.
   d. closer to opposite- than same-sex friends.

10. The most frequently cited reason for friendships breaking up is that one person has
    a. moved away.   c. been promoted at work.
    b. borrowed money.   d. inherited lots of money.

EXERCISES

1. *First impressions.* Look around in your classes and select someone you haven't met. Jot down your impressions of this person. Then make it a point to introduce yourself and become better acquainted. To what extent was your initial impression accurate or inaccurate? What steps can you take to improve your accuracy next time you meet a stranger?

2. *Write a personal ad about yourself.* Suppose you were writing a personal ad for the classified section devoted to introducing singles. How would you describe yourself? How would you describe the type of person you're looking for? Write a paragraph about why you gave those particular descriptions.

3. *Self-disclosure.* Write a paragraph or two including your thoughts on the following matters: How comfortable do you feel sharing personal information with friends? With whom do you share the most? Which topics do you share? If married, do you share more with your spouse or with your friends? Are the friends to whom you disclose same-sex or opposite-sex? Would you agree that the rewards of mutual self-disclosure outweigh the risks?

4. *Social support.* To whom can you turn? If you were experiencing a personal crisis, to whom would you turn for help—your family or friends? Which person would you seek out first? Explain the reasons for your answers. If you do not have good social support, how can you cultivate some friends to whom to disclose?

5. *Intimacy and growth.* Think of a close friendship or love relationship. Then describe your relationship in a page or so, including your thoughts on the following points: Do you both maintain other friendships? If lovers, are you also friends? Can each of you experience closeness without giving up your individuality? To what extent does this relationship encourage each of you to grow as a person?

QUESTIONS FOR SELF-REFLECTION

1. How much do you judge by first impressions? Are they accurate?

2. Do you make a good first impression on others? If not, how can you correct this?

3. Are you ever bothered by shyness? Loneliness? How can you overcome each?

4. Do you usually find that the more you know someone, the better you like the person?

5. How important are good looks to you in being attracted to someone of the opposite sex?

6. Do some of your friends have interests and personalities quite different from yours?

7. Who is your best friend? With which people do you feel most comfortable sharing secrets?

8. Do you have a close friend of the opposite sex? Do you have a close friend of the same sex? If you have both, how are these two friends similar? How are they different?

9. Have you ever been betrayed by a close friend? How did you react?

10. Have you ever befriended another person from a different country? How was that person's culture similar to yours? How was it different?

FOR FURTHER INFORMATION

RECOMMENDED READINGS

COPELAND, M. E. (2002). *The loneliness workbook: A guide to developing and maintaining lasting connections.* Oakland, CA: New Harbinger Press. A practical handbook for those who are lonely.

GOLEMAN, D. (2005). *Emotional intelligence: 10th anniversary edition.* New York: Bantam Books. Learn all about EQ and why it is just as or more important than IQ. An updated version of Goleman's incisive book on emotional intelligence.

HILLIARD, E. B. (2005). *Living fully with shyness and social anxiety: A comprehensive guide to gaining social confidence.* New York: Marlowe & Company. A therapist-written book that provides practical but small incremental steps toward overcoming shyness and social anxiety.

PAUL, M. (2005). *The friendship crisis: Finding, making, and keeping friends when you're not a kid anymore.* Emmaus, PA: Rodale. Emphasizing women's close relationships, Paul reveals how friendships can make or break our lives. There is something to be learned for men in this book also.

YAGER, J. (2002). *When friendship hurts: How to cope with friends who betray, abandon, or wound you.* New York: Simon & Schuster. Our friends can hurt us in a number of ways such as betrayal. This book helps heal the pain of a betrayed friendship.

WEBSITES AND THE INTERNET

http://www.cyberparent.com/friendship　A site with click-on links to information about friendship, for example, how to make friends, maintain friends, and why friendships end.

http://www.adaa.org　Anxiety Disorders Association of America. A site where you can find much information about social phobias.

http://www.shyness.com　If you are shy or want to research shyness and social anxiety, this is the page for you. There are resources and links to other sites, a shyness questionnaire, and social support for shy people offered on the site.

http://www.bbbsa.org　This is the website of a truly amazing organization—Big Brothers/ Big Sisters. This organization provides older mentors or friends, usually college students, for children who need good role models. Research demonstrates that this program is highly successful in that the "bigs" steer the "littles" toward better lives.

http://www.WeboOfLoneliness.com　A site that explains what loneliness is, what causes it, and how others have coped. Essays and poems about loneliness are also available.

Leader or Follower?

Learning Objectives

After completing this chapter, you should be able to

1. Name and describe various types of groups.
2. Discuss how groups form and re-form.
3. Provide reasons why people join groups.
4. Describe how groups communicate.
5. Explain how the shape and size of a group affect communication.
6. Understand various types of social influence such as conformity and compliance.
7. Describe how individuals become leaders.
8. Explain various types of leader styles and traits.
9. Know how and when groups go wrong.
10. Recognize the symptoms of group dysfunction.
11. Discuss some of the "cures" for groups when they go wrong.

Roy grew up in the cornfields of Iowa. His father, Harry, inherited the family farm and soon married Sara, Roy's mother. Sara and Harry were excited and proud the day their baby boy, Roy, was born. Sara and Harry developed great plans for their child from the moment of his arrival. Sara and Harry hoped that Roy would attend college and become an engineer or a lawyer so that he would not have to lead the hard farming life they had.

Sara and Harry pushed hard for Roy to achieve in school. High grades, they thought, were Roy's ticket out of the cornfields. Although Roy was resistant at first, much like any child who enjoyed playing rather than studying, he soon settled into his studies and was near the top of his class. Upon graduation, Roy was accepted to a large university in the East and even landed a good scholarship, thus relieving his parents of a huge financial burden.

September 5, 2003, was a day his parents were never to forget. Roy left for college and rarely returned to the cornfields. What happened to Roy? While at college, Roy became fascinated with a local group called the Akaries, a group that worshiped the sun, moon, and stars and believed that soon the world would end. Once Roy became fully initiated into this group, a well-known cult in the same city as the university, Sara and Harry never heard from him again.

How do groups such as the Akaries form? Why do some individuals such as Roy become followers, whereas others become revered leaders? Do all groups function the same? Do all groups have leaders? Is there such a thing as a dysfunctional group? These and other questions are the focus of this chapter on being part of a group.

KINDS OF GROUPS

Groups are all around us. Everywhere we look we see people in groups. People congregate in their places of worship, families can be seen in restaurants around the United States, and college classrooms are filled to the brim with eager students. Football fans collectively cheer for their favorite teams, and sororities and fraternities hold their deliberations on new members in the privacy of their houses. Everywhere—groups.

What kinds of groups are there and how do they differ? There are many different kinds of groups, each with its own characteristics, but we have space to review only a few of them here.

Favored Groups—Primary Groups

Perhaps the most immediately important group in your life is your **primary group.** *This group is important because it is small, intimate, and interacts face-to-face.* For these and other reasons primary groups have much influence on us. Of course, in turn, we can have great impact on them. Primary groups typically function through face-to-face interaction, as do families or suitemates in residence halls. A nuclear family, for example, has immense effects on its members. Parents instill in their children the same values, dreams, and culture as their own. Children often adopt their parents' religion, political views, and other likes and dislikes. College roommates sometimes become more like each other the more they live together. Happy husbands and wives often influence each other; they share the same friends, the same preferences for politicians, music, and television programs. Sometimes wives and husbands even laugh, walk, and talk the same way. The Akaries, although somewhat large with 22 members, could be classified as a primary group because the members were so close-knit and interdependent on one another.

Bigger Than Both of Us—Secondary Groups

Another type of group is a **secondary group.** *These groups are usually larger than primary groups, have a formal or contractual reason for coming together, often disband when the reason for their existence evaporates, and are less likely to engage in regular face-to-face interaction.* An example of this type of group would be the class for which you are reading this book. The class has a formal reason for coming together (to learn about adjustment and personal growth) and may not engage in much face-to-face (student-to-student) interaction. Other examples would be a church congregation or a social club such as the psychology club. Secondary groups, then, often configure in an audience rather than in a face-to-face, interaction pattern.

What Goes Wrong at Rock Concerts?—Collectives

You may have read about stampedes of people and riots in the streets. The cheering football spectators mentioned earlier can number in the tens of thousands if the stadium is large enough. Fans at a rock concert offer another example. These groups, called **collectives,** *tend to be very large and are less likely to have a true leader or clear rules* compared with primary and secondary groups. Collectives often form and disband for no readily apparent reasons.

Because collectives are large and without clear-cut rules, they can often be disorderly. We have witnessed this tragedy of disorderliness, especially at sporting events where crowds distressed over a major loss to another team begin pushing and shoving, with fans often trampled to death in the ensuing stampede.

"Us" Versus "Them"—In-Groups and Out-Groups

There are two other very important groups that influence you (Halevy, Bornstein, & Sagiv, 2008; Hewstone, Rubin, & Willis, 2002). One is *the group with which you identify*—the **in-group.** The in-group can be contrasted with the **out-group,** *the group that we perceive as being different from (outside of) your own group.* In-group/out-group perceptions can develop based on ethnicity, gender, age, religion, occupation, attitudes, athletic prowess, academic ability, and income level, among other factors. To the locals around Roy's campus, the Akaries in their strange wardrobes and weird haircuts were clearly the out-group; to the Akaries, the rest of the world was the out-group. Their own respective group was the in-group.

> [O]ne of the most pervasive forms of categorization among humans is the distinction between *us* and *them*. People generally view ingroup members, i.e., "us," more positively than outgroup members, i.e., "them," and also allocate more rewards to the ingroup, compared to the outgroup. . . . This occurs when participants are divided into groups arbitrarily in the laboratory . . . as well as when group membership is based on longstanding cultural or social relations (Brown, Bradley, & Lang, 2006, p. 303).

What is most important about the distinctions we make between our own group and the out-group is that these differentiations often result in prejudiced attitudes and negative behavior against the out-group (Brown et al., 2006; Carnaghi & Maass, 2007; Fiske, 2002; Mackie, Devos, & Smith, 2000). The distinction can be based on barely visible differences such as skin tone shades, with individuals having darker skin experiencing more prejudice than individuals of the same race with lighter skin (Brown, 2004). **Prejudice** is *an unfair, often negative attitude toward another person or group based solely on group membership* (Dovidio & Gaertner, 1999; Dovidio, Glick, & Rudman, 2005). Prejudice is sometimes accompanied by behaviors whereby the group against which the prejudice is held is discriminated against or treated worse than our own group. *When we apply unfair or negative treatment to groups on the basis of such features as age, sex, or race,* this is called **discrimination.** Although the two usually occur together, prejudice can occur without discrimination and discrimination can occur without prejudice. For example, a restaurant owner could harbor negative attitudes toward Native Americans but still serve them in his restaurant because of the laws against discrimination. Prejudice can also prompt **stereotypes,** or *widespread generalizations about people (based solely on their group membership) that have little if any basis in fact.*

Psychologists are concerned about prejudice, discrimination, and stereotypes because they invariably lead to negative and unfair evaluations of individuals in the out-group (Bodenhausen, 1990; Carnaghi & Maass, 2007; Ensari & Miller, 2005).

Prejudice and its correlates produce stress in the out-group (Contrada et al., 2000) and may cause damage to the self-esteem of the targets of prejudice (e.g., Platow, Byrne, & Ryan, 2005). Interestingly, one reason biased individuals hold prejudices is that they seek to enhance their own self-esteem by viewing their group as superior to the out-group (Major & Eccleston 2005). Similarly, in-groups can be hard on their own members when a member deviates from or disagrees with the group (Conway & Schaller, 2005; Marques, Abrams, & Serodio, 2001). The overarching message you should take away from this information is that group dynamics can be harsh and unpleasant, but they need not be. For example, while *intergroup* contact is not always successful at breaking down stereotypes, prejudice, and in-group–out-group barriers (Antonio, 2004; Neili, 2008), some research shows that it does work (Pettigrew & Tropp, 2008; Quillian & Campbell, 2003).

Another significant point about in-groups and out-groups is that their importance varies by culture (Hornsey & Jetten, 2005; Matsumoto, 2000). We have already made the distinction elsewhere in this book between collectivistic and individualistic cultures. To review, **individualistic cultures** *value the individual's gains* (*needs, wants, and autonomy*) *over those of the group.* In an individualistic culture, people have more in-groups; that is, they belong to more organizations such as music clubs, Girl Scouts, and so forth (Matsumoto). Therefore, people in individualistic cultures are not as attached to any particular in-group as are people in **collectivistic cultures,** in which *collective or societal gain is cherished over individual advancement.* Perhaps because of their multiple memberships, individuals in individualistic cultures make fewer distinctions between in-groups and out-groups (Matsumoto). In collective societies, people have fewer in-groups, so they are more attached to the groups of which they are members (Matsumoto). Survival of the group is more dependent on the effective functioning of the group as a whole rather than that of individuals. Similarly, members of individualistic cultures self-enhance on independence (from the group) dimensions, whereas members of collective societies self-enhance based on loyalty to the group (Hornsey & Jetten). Finally, Johnson, Kulesa, Cho, and Shavitt (2005) believe that in individualistic cultures, people are far more expressive of their own independent views, whereas in collectivistic cultures, individuals, seeking harmony, are more likely to take a middling approach to volatile issues.

HOW DO GROUPS FORM?

Think about a fairly new group that you recently joined. How and why did the group form? Why did you join? Did the group evolve or change from its original form or purpose?

The initial stage in group development is **forming** (McGrew, Bilotta, & Deeney, 1999; Tuckman, 1965), *where individuals come together to form the group.* When Roy became entranced by the Akaries, the group was already well formed. In other groups, in the forming stage, members sometimes do not know each other as well as they will later in the developmental process; they are simply coming together as a group. Even in a new marriage, where the couple has dated for months, the new wife may not know that her new husband prefers to watch game shows rather than the political debates she favors. If enough differences exist, friction can build and squabbles might begin in a group. Initially, though, most group members step forward with their best and most cooperative foot as the group forms and people (sometimes secretly) jockey for positions.

When group members learn more about each other's attitudes and predilections, differences among individuals lead to *the second stage,* **storming** (Tuckman, 1965). In this stage, which can follow quickly on the heels of the first, *individuals disagree or often openly conflict when they learn each other's opinions.* In the first year of marriage, for example, a new couple may have several arguments.

This stage is a troublesome one. Members may decide too much friction exists and leave the group. For example, some individuals initially attracted to the Akaries did not remain long when they realized how extreme the Akaries were. Other members may decide that it is best to remain passive rather than be pulled into the fray, and others are so vociferous and aggressive about promoting their agendas that the remaining members intensely dislike them. At this point it may seem that the group will never start functioning. If group members recognize that this is a normal group stage, however, they can move beyond their differences to the next, more productive stage. As with personal growth, group growth can happen in stages and develop via adversity.

When roles become more sharply defined, when groups finally come to terms with how they will function, when rules by which they will function become clearer, the group is said to be **norming** (Tuckman, 1965). That is, through discourse and debate *the group eventually comes to consensus about the rules under which it will operate.* As just mentioned, roles start to emerge in groups in the storming and norming stages. A **role** *is a set of rules that defines how an individual in a particular post in a group will behave.* Also as mentioned previously, each group develops its own idiosyncratic **norms,** *standards or unwritten rules by which it will function and by which it will exert pressure on nonconforming members.* For example, the married couple with one television may agree that the husband will squeeze the toothpaste from the end because it creates less waste. The wife may agree that every other night they will watch what her husband prefers and on off nights the couple will watch what she likes. The Akari group had very strange norms to outsiders. In his posh bedroom, the leader, Otu, was allowed to have sex with any woman in the group, except married women and young girls. Other single men had to remain celibate and live in their collective bunkroom.

Once a group has formed, has worked through its initial disagreements, and has developed norms, the group is ready to function well. **Performing** (Tuckman, 1965) *is the final stage of group development. It is during this stage that the group functions better and actually performs its business,* whether it is the rearing of children in a marriage or developing a strategic plan for a work team. Once this developmental pattern has been played out by a group, new issues can arise or new members can be added. The group then cycles through these stages again (see Figure 9–1). Be aware, though, that some theorists have suggested that other processes exist, such as de-norming, de-storming, and de-forming (McGrew et al., 1999).

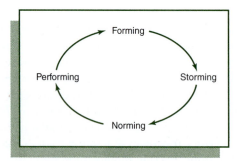

FIGURE 9–1
The cycle of group formation.

WHY JOIN A GROUP?

Why would individuals follow a cult leader such as Otu? What would draw intelligent men and women to the Akaries? What makes you join some clubs, teams, or committees but resist pressure to join others?

Social psychologists have identified a multitude of reasons for people's joining groups. People sometimes connect with groups because groups offer possibilities not available to us as individuals. One possibility that groups offer is the chance to **affiliate,** *to be with others who are similar to us or whom we like.* The Akaries afforded the opportunity to individuals with the same spiritual and political attitudes to be with similar others and test out their novel, but bizarre, ideas. Sororities and fraternities fill this need by attracting new members who generally are very similar to existing members. Synagogues, churches, and mosques offer more than religious support; they also offer the chance to socialize with members of the same faith. In fact, our awareness of others and our social interactions are now believed to have biological underpinnings in specialized neurons in the brain (Chen, 2009).

Groups also offer us information we might not otherwise possess. Although most people in America have access to the media, some do not avail themselves of television and Internet news because they do not have the time, do not speak English, or cannot afford electronic media. Groups to which we belong can keep us informed about important as well as mundane issues. Groups, however, offer us more than mere facts. Groups help us *understand* whether we harbor attitudes that represent a minority or majority position in a group. Groups also help us understand our position in the social order. An example is this: When you receive examinations back in a college class, you may think that a score of 37 is terrible until you see that the classmates around you received 25, 19, and 32. Now the 37 feels better, doesn't it? *Groups, then, allow us to compare ourselves to others and understand who we are relative to them.* This is the process of **social comparison.** We generally select another person with whom to compare ourselves based on that person's expertise, similarity to us, and previous level of agreement (Schwinghammer, Stapel, & Blanton, 2006; Stapel & Johnson, 2007; Suls, Martin, & Wheeler, 2002).

The concept of social support (Moritsugu, Wong, & Duffy, 2010), introduced elsewhere in the book, is also important to groups. You may recall that **social support** is *a process whereby one individual or group offers psychological and sometimes physical aid to another individual or group.* Primary groups, especially of friends and family, can offer us much-needed social support. When something goes wrong in our lives, when we have difficult decisions to make, and even when something wonderful has happened (for instance, receiving a promotion), groups can give us a needed boost. Friends can give us affection and sympathy when we suffer the loss of a loved one. Our families can enhance our joy when we have succeeded. Groups, then, offer social support that research has repeatedly demonstrated is important to our mental health (e.g., Helgeson & Cohen, 1996; Moritsugu, Wong, & Duffy).

Groups also give us more collective power. There may be needs we have that we simply cannot meet alone. For example, the Akaries may have been composed of individuals who for one reason or another were failures elsewhere. By joining, members realized their collective power and ability to influence others. One individual who was influenced by the Akaries was John, Roy's roommate, who was educated in journalism but who joined the Akaries shortly after applying to and being rejected by journalism graduate schools. He found work at the Akaries' home-base and was able to support himself.

WHAT GOES ON IN GROUPS?

You have already been introduced to two group processes, development of roles and development of norms. There are other processes that are unique to groups and would rarely be discussed with regard to an individual. These processes include communication, social influence, social loafing, and group polarization, which are all important to decision making and performance in groups.

What Did You Say?—Communication Patterns

One of the most important group processes is communication. Intragroup communication is important to all the other processes discussed next. *Intragroup* means *within* a group; communication within a group allows group members to coordinate their actions, share information, and express emotions and ideas—all of which are important to decision making and performance.

Networks.   Some of the earliest research on group communication concerned communication networks within groups (Davis & Newstrom, 1985). There are **centralized communication networks** *in which one or two individuals control the flow of information.* One such network is the wheel, in which a centralized individual or node with spokes or channels extends outward to other individuals or nodes. The wheel is similar to a university, where all department chairs go to a dean or vice president who makes final funding, personnel, and other decisions. Certainly, Otu was the important focal point or the center of the group known as the Akaries. The wheel and other networks are depicted in Figure 9–2.

Centralized networks can be contrasted to *decentralized* communication networks. In **decentralized communication networks,** *individuals can communicate relatively freely with one another.* An example of a decentralized network is the circle, also shown in Figure 9–2. Rumors that pass from one person to another, then to yet another, and back to the original source offer an example of the circle. Of course, there are other centralized and decentralized systems. Can you think of other concrete examples for all of the networks represented in Figure 9–2?

Centralized and decentralized networks result in different types of performance in groups. In research on groups, performance (how many widgets were made, how

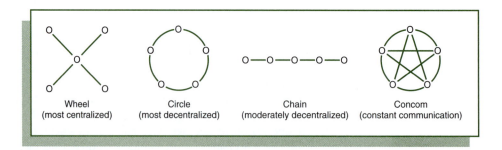

| Wheel (most centralized) | Circle (most decentralized) | Chain (moderately decentralized) | Concom (constant communication) |

FIGURE 9–2
Examples of various communication networks
"O" represents an individual, and the lines represent the communication links between individuals.

long the group met, how good was the group's decision, for example) is usually measured. Centralized networks are much more efficient and thus work capably and effectively, but mostly on simple tasks or simple decisions. When tasks are complicated or decisions require complex input and deliberation, decentralized networks are generally best.

Group Size.   As you might well imagine, one other group factor that affects quality of communication and therefore quality of the group's work and members' satisfaction is the *size* of the group. Groups vary in their size depending on the situation. Juries are usually composed of 12 individuals, university academic departments can be as small as two people or as large as 60, and families typically average between three and five members in the United States. Wheelan (2009) found that group size is a crucial factor influencing group development and group productivity. Very large groups were not as successful as smaller groups of three to eight members.

Other factors related to group size are how the communications are perceived. In small groups, group discussions actually appear to be interactive dialogues or conversations. In larger groups, the discourse resembles a monologue in which a few individuals dominate or speak sequentially (Fay, Garrod, & Carletta, 2000).

Electronic Communication.   As our world turns more and more to electronic forms of communication, it will be interesting to verify whether the principles just described still hold true. You should realize that it is not just you and your friends or family who communicate electronically but also transnational work teams and governmental officials. In electronic communication the opportunity for miscommunication is likely increased compared to face-to-face communication where nonverbal cues enhance interpersonal understanding (Sivunen, 2006; Wilson, Straus, & McEvily, 2006; Workman, 2007). Moreoever, research shows that email users are largely unaware of these limitations; they know what they intend to communicate, so they assume that their audience does as well (Kruger et al., 2005). Text messaging may prove even more troublesome because texters send truncated or abbreviated messages.

There are other problems with electronic communication. Wilson, Straus, and McEvily (2006) found that trust is greater in face-to-face rather than electronic meetings. Other researchers have found that electronic communication, especially at workplaces, is more task-oriented and more efficient than face-to-face meetings (e.g., Lantz, 2001). This effect may be all right, but *only if* group members do not miss the socializing aspects of work.

Electronic communication also enables its users to expand their group's size and influence and to heighten the number of social contacts. Drentea and Moren-Cross (2005) found that cyberspace fosters social support. More specifically, they found that the use of the Internet helps build community spirit as well as provides both emotional and instrumental support to its users. On the other hand, the Internet can also be used to promote racism, terrorism, and other harmful movements (Adams & Roscigno, 2005). Finally, several studies (e.g., Adrianson, 2001; Lind, 2001; Sánchez-Franco, 2006) have found gender differences in the way men and women use and respond to technology. Sánchez-Franco noted that males tend to be more focused and intentional in their Internet use (e.g., newsrooms), whereas females utilize the Internet for social engagement (e.g., chat rooms). Additionally, females report lower computer self-efficacy than do males.

Compared to face-to-face communication, electronic communication may result in more miscommunication because it lacks subtle cues such as facial expressions.

You Want Me to Do What?—Social Influence

Certainly, many people have tried to use social influence on you—family members, friends, teachers, and advertisers to mention but a few. Just what is social influence? **Social influence** involves *efforts on the part of one person to alter the behavior or attitudes of one or more others.* Otu and other cult leaders have immense social influence over their followers. Other groups and leaders have such influence, too, although often not to the extremes of cults. Social influence can occur at three different levels. We can publicly go along with others but refuse to change our private beliefs. An example of this would be that you are seated in the snack bar between classes and three friends all declare that they are voting for a political candidate whom you detest. In a hurry to make your next class, you do not want to debate with them so nod your head in agreement. Another level of social influence is when you behave like others or are influenced by others because you are attracted to them. Very often when you begin to steadily date someone, you adopt the new date's tastes for food and music. If you and your date then part company, you return to your own tastes in cuisine and melody. The third level is one where someone has truly influenced you so much that you change forever. At this level, an individual or group convinces you that you should adopt their ideas, behaviors, and tastes. This third and most important type of influence is the kind Otu exerted over his followers, Roy, and the rest of the Akaries.

How and why do people gain influence over others? Three processes—conformity, compliance, and obedience—shed light on the mechanisms (Mason, Conrey, & Smith, 2007).

Conformity.   You may already have a nodding acquaintance with conformity, but let's define it anyway. **Conformity** is a *change in behavior due to the real or imagined influence (pressure) of other people.* When U.S. youths started wearing baseball caps backwards, they were conforming to agemate pressure to conform, to be like others their age. No one issued official orders or laws proclaiming that youths needed to wear their caps backward. There was subtle peer pressure to conform.

Conformity has been well examined since the seminal research of Solomon Asch. Asch (1951) requested subjects to come to an experimental room one at a time. When the subject entered the room, the subject was confronted by what appeared to be other subjects. These other subjects actually were **confederates** or *friends of the experimenter who were told by the experimenter how to behave.* The subject and confederates were asked to judge lines as to which two were closest in length.

At first, confederates gave correct answers; then confederates gave wrong answers. Asch reasoned that the real subjects would stand their ground and give the correct answer, thus refusing to conform. Asch, to his surprise, found that many subjects conformed to the apparently wrong answer. Asch concluded that the tendency to conform in our society is strong, even on obviously easy tasks and even when no one forces conformity Since Asch's initial research, scientists have discovered factors that enhance or reduce conformity. We are most likely to conform to the wrong answer when our responses are public and face-to-face (Bond, 2005) and when the proportion of other conformists is high (Coultas, 2004).

It is also important to comment on individual and cultural differences in conformity. Despite Asch's results, many Americans espouse independence and autonomy, so shun conformity. Cultures that emphasize **interdependence** (*mutual dependence among individuals in a given group or society*) also exist. Many of these are collectivist societies. Conformity and harmony is an integral part of the social fabric of these cultures (Johnson et al., 2005). Some examples of more interdependent cultures (where conformity to group norms is *expected*) are the Zimbabwean and Lebanese cultures (Smith & Bond, 1993). On the other hand, research is now pointing out the fact that some collective cultures are not as conformist as we expected (Takano & Sogon, 2008). Perhaps as cultures have come into contact with each other, distinctions between collective and individualistic societies are disappearing. With regard to gender, Schwartz and Rubel (2005) found no sex differences in the value of conformity across 70 different cultures; in each culture, men and women conformed equally frequently.

Compliance.   Another process of social influence is compliance. **Compliance** may be defined as a *change in behavior in response to a direct request from another person to do so.* Compliance, like conformity, is an everyday phenomenon. When your professor requests that you take your seats so that she can begin lecturing, you sit down, thus complying with her entreaty. When your sister calls you to the dinner table, you usually come in response to her request. Note that we sometimes comply publicly but disagree with the request privately, just as is true for conformity.

There are conditions under which we are more or less likely to comply. In mainstream U.S. society, a **norm of reciprocity** (Park & Antonioni, 2007) is common. *This unwritten rule guides reciprocal behavior related to the granting of favors.* If someone does you a favor, you feel compelled to return (reciprocate) the favor. For example, when you borrow your roommate's umbrella, you are obligated (tit for tat) to let her borrow something of yours. When food companies give away free samples, there is some feeling of obligation on the consumer's part to buy the product.

Another method to induce compliance is **ingratiation,** which involves *managing the impressions you leave on others so that they will like you more and comply with your requests. Flattery* is a form of ingratiation by which the flatterer hopes that the flattered individual will give in to a certain request. Another form of ingratiation is *opinion conformity,* in which one individual publicly agrees with another so that the other person will like the ingratiator. The ingratiator who uses opinion conformity can later ask the other individual for a favor.

Sometimes a two-step approach to compliance increases its likelihood. There are several two-step processes, one of which will suffice as an example here. In the **door-in-the-face effect** (Cialdini & Goldstein, 2004), *the requester first issues a large, unreasonable request. When the respondent answers "no," the requester makes the truly desired but smaller and more reasonable demand.* Not wanting to appear difficult or stubborn, the respondent often answers "yes" to the second, smaller request. For example, a rather calculating friend may ask to borrow your new, expensive car to impress his new date. Not having driven the car much yourself, you quickly answer "no." The friend then asks to borrow $15 for the same date, to which you more readily agree.

As you can see, both ingratiation and the door-in-the-face technique are manipulative ways to bring about compliance. These methods are *not* presented here so that you can hone your skills using them. Rather, it is good for you to recognize when others are manipulating you with these techniques.

Obedience.   **Obedience** involves *following a direct order or command.* The command typically comes from someone who has the capacity to enforce the order if it is not followed. You probably think of an army officer issuing an order that soldiers follow. Otu's followers were surely obedient to him, but are other individuals so servile? Surprisingly, many Americans are obedient to different authority figures. A classic series of studies on obedience demonstrates our propensity to obey.

In 1974, Stanley Milgram published his dramatic *Obedience to Authority.* He detailed a series of studies on obedience to authority figures that rattled the psychological world. Imagine that you are in the following prototype of Milgram's experiment. You are led to a room and introduced to Mr. Wallace, a kindly older man who is to be the learner in the study. You are going to be the teacher. Mr. Wallace is to learn a list of words. Each time he errs, you are to give him an electric shock that you are both told will be painful but will cause no permanent tissue damage. For each error, you are to proceed up the shock generator one step. The first step is 15 volts and labeled "slight shock." The other end is 450 volts and labeled only with "XXX"—to designate its dangerous nature. As the teacher you are not aware that the experiment is fixed such that you are not really administering shocks and that Mr. Wallace is really a confederate (the experimenter's assistant) and has been told how to act.

As you proceed up the shock generator, you hear Mr. Wallace's groans. Eventually, Mr. Wallace refuses to continue and states that he has a heart problem. Finally, Mr. Wallace becomes silent. Each time you query the experimenter (the authority figure) about Mr. Wallace's condition, the experimenter urges you to continue. The experimenter reminds you that although the shocks may be painful, they cause no permanent damage. The experimenter requests that you continue.

The most dramatic and disconcerting part of these studies was that 65 percent of the U.S. subjects went all the way up the shock generator at the urging of the experimenter. It would be easy to explain away these results by suggesting that the subjects were disturbed or that they were all aggressive men. Milgram assured us that all subjects were mentally healthy and that even women shocked the learner at about the same rate. If for

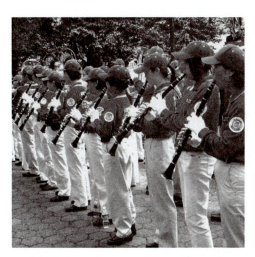

Some cultures emphasize compliance and conformity while others condone individualism and self-expression.

some reason obedience is not desirable, there are techniques for reducing it. Placing the "victim" closer to the obedient person or putting the authority figure farther away are two such methods.

Let the Other Guy Do It—Social Loafing

Have you ever "goofed off" in a group? If you haven't, have you observed others "not holding up their end of the deal"? Another process that occurs in groups is loafing. **Social loafing** *means that individuals contribute less to a group effort than they would contribute to an individual effort* (Smith, Kerr, Markus, & Stasson, 2001). For example, if individuals are asked one at a time to paint a mural or to clap for an athlete, they put more effort into the performance than they would if asked to perform as a group (Kayes, Kayes, & Kolb, 2005). In fact, the larger the group, the less individual effort everyone puts into his or her performance (i.e., the more the social loafing). Relatively new research also indicates that social loafing may be a particular problem of online communities (Blanchard & Henle, 2008; Chidambaram & Tung, 2005; Ling et al., 2005), perhaps because they are so large and so anonymous.

Groups can reduce social loafing in a number of ways (Karau & Williams, 1993). When people believe their performance will be evaluated, when the task is important or meaningful, when failure is possible if loafing occurs, or when individual members value the group, loafing is minimized. People who enjoy the challenge of cognitive tasks are also less likely to loaf whether alone or in a large group (Smith et al., 2001).

There are also cultural differences in amounts of social loafing. As mentioned elsewhere, many Western societies are individualistic; individuals are expected to be independent and autonomous, so they contribute less to group efforts. In more collective societies in which group effort is valued, social loafing is less likely to occur (Hong, Wyer, & Fong, 2008; Triandis, 1999).

All in Favor Say "Aye"—Group Polarization

Surely you have worked in groups that make decisions requiring consensus or unanimity. This is how most committees function. Indeed, consensus is the foundation for democracy.

FIGURE 9–3
The group polarization effect.
Groups often make more extreme decisions (conservative or risky) than individuals.

In 1964, Kogan and Wallach compared how individuals versus groups make decisions. In their study, participants were given a series of social dilemmas and asked to select a solution for the dilemma. For example, participants were asked to decide whether a risky experimental drug should be administered to a dying patient. The solutions varied on amount of risk. Kogan and Wallach determined that *groups coming to consensus make riskier decisions than individuals.* They labeled this phenomenon **risky shift.** The researchers explained that *individuals in groups feel less responsible for the risk so are willing to make riskier decisions in groups,* in a process known as **responsibility diffusion.**

Subsequent research (Myers & Arenson, 1972), however, demonstrated that some groups tend to make more conservative decisions than individuals. That is, if individuals in the group made fairly conservative decisions before joining the group, they tend to make even more conservative decisions in a group. In other words, *groups are likely to shift to either a more conservative or a riskier decision than individuals alone make.* This newer phenomenon is the **group polarization effect** (Palmer & Loveland, 2008; Prislin & Wood, 2005), as depicted in Figure 9–3. One factor that predicts whether individuals in a group will press for caution or for risk is—you guessed it—culture. In African cultures, for example, caution is valued over risk. In U.S. culture, risk and bravado are valued over caution (Gologor, 1977). Given that you, too, spend so much time in groups, you need to be aware of these effects so that you can override their consequences and make the best possible decisions.

ARE LEADERS MADE OR BORN?

Have you ever led a group? Do you think you have leadership qualities? Or would you rather sit back silently and let someone else have the limelight? By reading the next passages, you should understand yourself better as well as the challenges facing all leaders of groups.

In almost all groups, someone rises as leader. Committees elect their leaders; corporations retain presidents appointed by the board of directors; some countries are governed by a self-appointed dictator while others have hereditary rulers or elected officials. Leaders are vitally important because research has confirmed that groups with leaders outperform groups without leaders (De-Souza & Klein, 1995). How do leaders emerge and what qualities make for good leadership? The answers to these questions are difficult because each situation is so different from the next. A summary of some of the literature is all that space allows here. Let us first examine theories about the origins of leaders.

The Great Man Theory

Did Otu possess certain traits at birth that set him on the path to leadership? The earliest theory of leadership was the **great man theory** (Mayseless & Popper, 2007). The theory predated feminism so the term "man" was used. This theory suggests that *great leaders are born with a certain common set of traits.* If an individual possesses these traits, such as good public speaking skills or high intelligence, then that person will become a leader and can lead in a variety of situations. If not, the individual is out of luck. Researchers thus assumed that they ought to be able to assess great leaders and find common characteristics or traits (Zaccaro, 2007). Simonton (1987) did just that. Simonton gathered information from a variety of sources about the presidents of the United States. Information collected included personality attributes as well as demographic and educational factors. Out of 100 characteristics, only three correlated with how effective (e.g., great) each president was in office. One factor was family size, another was height, and the third was number of books published. Presidents are more likely to have been born into small families and to be tall. There were no personality factors that consistently correlated with performance in office. The great man theory was essentially abandoned in favor of other notions of leadership, but other trait approaches to leadership are again becoming popular (Zaccaro). For example, see the information on transformational leaders below.

Situational Explanations of Leadership

Other explanations for the emergence of leaders involve the situation people find themselves in (Vroom & Jago, 2007). In other words, perhaps being in the right place at the right time means that you are likely to become a leader. For example, if you sit at the head of the table with everyone else seated at the sides, you might be appointed leader of the group (Jackson, Engstrom, & Hassenzahl, 2005). If someone else sat in the same seat, that person instead might emerge as leader. Another example is this: A tour group is visiting France. Only one person in the group speaks French. This person interprets and translates for everyone else in the group, thus becomes the leader. It would be a different story if the same person were in Tibet and could speak only French. The French speaker would probably not be the leader. In other words, according to this notion of leadership, the situation creates the leader. Perhaps Otu found some dejected social outcasts who needed a leader or a spiritual "center" (as Otu called it) at that moment in their lives, and he deftly slipped in as leader of these needy people.

Contingency Theory

Some of the most popular theories of leadership are those that combine personal factors with situational factors (Somech, 2006). In other words, these theories suggest that you have to have the right leadership qualities for *that particular* situation (Zaccaro, 2007). Then and only then will you be an effective leader. One such theory is Fiedler's (1978; Zaccaro) **contingency theory of leadership.** *The theory identifies two attributes or styles of leaders known as people-oriented or task-oriented, which are effective at leading in different situations.* **People- or relationship-oriented leaders** *concern themselves with members' feelings and relationships* (van Emmerick, Hetty, Euwema, & Wendt, 2008). In contrast, **task-oriented leaders** *are primarily concerned with getting the job done well and in a timely fashion.* That is, they initiate structures that allow tasks to get done (van Emmerick, Euwema, & Wendt). Fiedler measured these two styles by asking leaders to rate their least-preferred coworker.

ACTIVITY 9–1

WHAT TYPE OF LEADER ARE YOU?

INSTRUCTIONS: *Rate your* least favorite classmate *on the following dimensions by placing an "X" in the appropriate space. First impressions are best.*

Friendly	_____ _____ _____ _____ _____ _____ _____	Unfriendly
Cold	_____ _____ _____ _____ _____ _____ _____	Warm
Strong	_____ _____ _____ _____ _____ _____ _____	Weak
Honest	_____ _____ _____ _____ _____ _____ _____	Dishonest
Active	_____ _____ _____ _____ _____ _____ _____	Passive
Bad	_____ _____ _____ _____ _____ _____ _____	Good
Intelligent	_____ _____ _____ _____ _____ _____ _____	Unintelligent
Closed-minded	_____ _____ _____ _____ _____ _____ _____	Open-minded

Now rate your most favorite classmate *on the following scale by placing an X in the appropriate space. First impressions are best. Try not to let your ratings of the least favorite classmate influence these ratings (i.e., don't use comparisons).*

Friendly	_____ _____ _____ _____ _____ _____ _____	Unfriendly
Cold	_____ _____ _____ _____ _____ _____ _____	Warm
Strong	_____ _____ _____ _____ _____ _____ _____	Weak
Honest	_____ _____ _____ _____ _____ _____ _____	Dishonest
Active	_____ _____ _____ _____ _____ _____ _____	Passive
Bad	_____ _____ _____ _____ _____ _____ _____	Good
Intelligent	_____ _____ _____ _____ _____ _____ _____	Unintelligent
Closed-minded	_____ _____ _____ _____ _____ _____ _____	Open-minded

Look at how close the Xs are for each designated classmate. Were your ratings for least favorite classmate similar to the ratings for your most favorite classmate? In other words, were the Xs located in about the same position on the scales? If yes, then you possess a person-oriented leadership style. If they are farther apart (at opposite ends of each scale), then you may possess a task-oriented leadership style. This scale is designed to assist you in thinking about your own personal style of leadership. Remember that both styles have their advantages. Good leaders learn to adopt each style when the situation dictates.

Interestingly and not unpredictably, the people-oriented leader sees the good in this coworker even though the worker is not well liked. The task leader, interested more in performance than people, has stronger negative feelings toward those coworkers who do not do their jobs well (Kaplan & Kaiser, 2003). Activity 9–1 presents a scale similar to that of Fiedler.

The situations differ under which each of these leaders is effective (DeYoung, 2005; Judge, Piccolo, & Ilies, 2004; Morris, Brotheridge, & Urbanski, 2005). Without a doubt, you know situations in which the task to be done is clear and members of the group have good relationships. This is what Fiedler calls a *high control situation* as compared to *low or medium control situations*. Results of research demonstrate that task-oriented leaders are most effective in high or low control situations. On the other hand, people-oriented leaders are most effective in medium control situations. Fiedler strongly suggests that leader style should match the situation. One style alone does not produce an effective leader across all situations as suggested by the Great Man theory or trait theories in general. A better theory might be one that emphasizes the balance between task- and people-oriented styles matched to appropriate situations and that then results in maximal effectiveness of leaders for their groups (Kaplan & Kaiser, 2003).

Contemporary Theories

As mentioned earlier, trait theories of leadership are again emerging as important (Zacarro, 2007). One such trait is emotional intelligence, or EI. Briefly, **emotional intelligence** is *the ability to regulate one's own emotions and to be empathic for others' emotions.* Leaders high in EI are self-aware, have exceptionally good interpersonal skills, evince self-control and social awareness, and know how to manage interpersonal relationships (e.g., possess good conflict management skills) (Dearborn, 2002). Leaders with EI are also confident without being arrogant. These traits make the person with EI very popular with others. Daniel Goleman (2005), who has written much about this concept, empirically examined whether people with EI are also good leaders. The answer is yes. Goleman found that EI is twice as important as any other personal characteristic (e.g., possession of technical skills) for predicting who will achieve the highest roles in organizations. Moreover, EI accounted for 90 percent of the difference in the profiles of high- versus low-ranking individuals in organizations, with high-ranking individuals having much EI. Researchers have also found that high EI distinguishes outstanding leaders from mediocre leaders as well as predicts which leader will have high organizational performance with high-EI leaders performing better than their low-EI counterparts (Goleman, 1998, 2005; Koman & Wolff, 2008).

Emotionally intelligent leaders may share some traits with another type of leader—**the charismatic leader**—(Brown & Moshavi, 2005), especially in the realm of self-awareness (Sosik, 2001). *This type of leader inspires social change, is visionary, and appeals to followers' self-concepts and values* (Bedell-Avers, Hunter, & Mumford, 2008). The charismatic leader often guides followers to solutions that alleviate the problems they face. Some experts on leadership have also linked charismatic leaders to transformational leaders (Jacobsen & House, 2001). Leaders high in emotional intelligence may also resemble **transformational leaders** (Barbuto & Burbach, 2006; Bass & Riggio, 2006; Mandell & Pherwani, 2003). Transformational leaders *stimulate interest among colleagues and followers to view their work from a new perspective. The leader does this by generating awareness of the mission or vision of the organization and helps members to look beyond their own interests* (Mandell & Pherwani). Such leaders raise their followers to a higher level of morality and motivation by moving followers to work toward the greater good or shared goals (Alimo-Metcalfe & Alban-Metcalfe, 2001; Bass & Riggio; Nielsen, Randall, Yarker, & Brenner, 2008). No matter what label we apply to these types of leaders, they usually have a positive impact on their followers (e.g., Nielsen, Randall, Yarker, & Brenner; Stewart, 2006; Xirasagar, Samuels, & Stoskopf, 2005). On the other hand, these same leaders can be detrimental to their followers, for example, when they foster dependency on the leader, as Otu did (Kark, Shamir, & Chen, 2003; Mayseless & Popper, 2007). As much as they may appeal to you, such leaders can be unpopular in times of threat when task-oriented leaders may be preferred (Cohen, Solomon, Maxfield, Pyszczynski, & Greenberg, 2004), although Mayseless and Popper disagree with this last conclusion.

Gender and Leadership

As you can tell from the dated name of the Great Man theory, interest in women as leaders has developed only recently, in part because of the feminist movement and in part because there are now more women involved in leadership roles, such as Katie Couric and Hillary Clinton. In 1976, 21 percent of all managers were women; by 1999 the percentage had increased to 46 (Powell, Butterfield, & Parent, 2002). Today, about half of all managers are women (U.S. Department of Labor, 2007). Researchers examining acceptance of women as leaders have found that while people today place less emphasis on masculine traits for leaders (Eagly, 2007; Hogue & Lord, 2007), a good leader is still perceived more often as masculine than feminine (Powell et al.; Sczesny, Bosnak, Neff, & Schyns, 2004). Perhaps because of this, women are not as likely as men to become leaders (Ritter & Yoder, 2004), and when they do lead, they are still not as well received as men (Ayman, Korabik, & Morris, 2009; Hogue & Lord, 2007; Eagly; Koch, 2005).

Several studies examine the styles with which men and women lead. Sczesny et al. (2004) found that the scientific literature supports that women are more people-oriented and men more task-oriented. Regarding the characteristic of transformational leadership, some studies have found no sex differences (e.g., van Engen, van der Leeden, & Willemsen, 2001) while others have found that women are more likely to be trans-formational leaders than men (Eagly, 2007; van Engen & Willemsen, 2004), perhaps because women have higher emotional intelligence (Mandell & Pherwani, 2003).

Women also tend to consult more with subordinates, that is, to be more democratic, utilize larger social networks, and share more information and power with colleagues than do men (Helgeson, 1990). Eagly and Johnson (1990) as well as Wheelan and Verdi (1992) contend that women are every bit as task-oriented as men, especially because this is a criterion by which organizations select and train leaders. Eagly (Eagly, 2007; Eagly, Karau, & Makhijani 1995) found that men and women are equally effective as leaders, but women are more effective when their roles are defined in feminine terms; men are more effective when their roles are defined in masculine terms. One set of authors concluded that for women to be perceived as effective leaders they need to demonstrate sensitivity *and* strength, although men need only demonstrate strength (Johnson, Murphy, Zewdie, & Reichard, 2008).

If women are equally as effective as men (but perhaps retain different styles) (Eagly & Johannesen-Schmidt, 2001), why are there so few women leaders? Several factors help explain this societal phenomenon. As you read this passage, see if you can think of other reasons. Eagly, Makhijani, and Klonsky (1992) in a literature review found that women leaders tend to be slightly less positively evaluated than men while Koch (2005) found that women leaders have more negative affect directed at them than do men. Butler and Geis (1990) found that this is especially true when men are doing the evaluating. Another reason fewer women achieve top leadership positions may be that because of societal pressure they are more conflicted about mixing career and family (Crosby, 1991). For example, although most women work outside the home, it is still relatively common to see television portray women as homemakers (Jewell, 1993) and not in leadership roles (Lauzen & Dozier, 2005). A final reason suggested by the psychological literature is that *women are more likely than men to be placed in precarious leadership positions,* known as the **glass cliff** (Ryan, Haslam, & Postmes, 2007). This means women may be set up for failure as leaders more often than are men.

Culture and Leadership

The literature on culture and leadership is ever increasing, first, because the U.S. workforce is diversifying, and second, because different leadership expectations and styles are firmly ensconced in other cultures. Just as important is the fact that many U.S., Canadian, and other companies have "gone global" with offices or factories scattered around the world (Chrobot-Mason, Ruderman, Weber, Ohlott, & Dalton, 2007).

One extremely important dimension of leader or managerial style that differs across cultures is **power distance,** which is *the idea that people in groups accept the concept that people in an organization rightfully have different levels of power and authority* (Hofstede, 2001; Johnson et al., 2005; MacNab & Associates, 2007). In a high-power-distance culture, the leader makes decisions because he or she has the authority to do so. That is, the subordinates accept large distances in the distribution of power and expect leaders to behave autocratically, be somewhat paternalistic, be subject to different rules than subordinates, and enjoy privileges not available to subordinates. In other words, the managers or leaders are not psychologically close to their subordinates. Examples of high-power-distance cultures are Mexico and India.

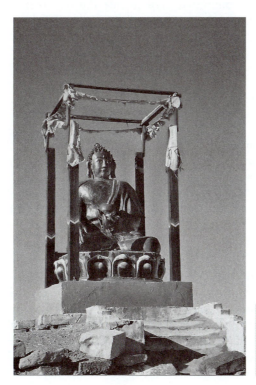

Many Asian societies are high-power-distance cultures where followers accept that leaders have more authority than they do.

In medium-power-distance cultures such as the United States, Canada, and Italy, subordinates expect to be consulted but will sometimes accept autocratic behavior. Subordinates also expect rules and policies to apply to all; however, they will accept some status differences between superiors and subordinates. In low-power-distance cultures, subordinates expect to be consulted on most issues, prefer a participatory and democratic style of leadership, and often rebel if superiors appear to be stepping outside their authority or possess status symbols. Rules are seen as applicable to all. Examples of such cultures are those of Denmark and Israel.

Research has begun on the effects of various levels of power differences on groups and performance (Johnson et al., 2005). Erez, Kleinbeck, and Thierry (2001) report that, in high-power-distance societies, motivational strategies designed to get groups to work harder are more effective if they are initiated and implemented by superiors with high status. Furthermore, negative supervisory reactions toward subordinates—such as criticism—are more demoralizing and trigger stronger defensive reactions in high-power-distance societies. Cho and Cheon (2005) found that in terms of Internet communications, members of high-power-distance societies (e.g., Japan and Korea) are more likely to interact with one another rather than superiors as compared to members of low-power-distance societies (e.g., the United States and Britain), who are likely to interact with (and have greater access to) authority figures.

WHEN GROUPS GO WRONG

On May 24, 2005, Sara and Harry received the sad news that their son Roy was dead. The Akaries had committed mass suicide the day after their predicted doomsday when the world did not end. You will likely agree that the Akaries functioned in a peculiar and dysfunctional manner, as can any group. In this last section, we will look at dysfunction in groups.

The Fiasco of Groupthink

There are several important concepts related to dysfunction in groups. One such concept is groupthink, introduced extensively to the psychological literature by Irving Janis (1982). **Groupthink** is *the tendency for groups to reach a consensus prematurely because the desire for harmony overrides the process of critical thinking and the search for the best decision.* Groupthink occurs when a group becomes more concerned with maintaining consensus and cohesion than with developing good ideas. Let us look at how groupthink develops and how it can be prevented. When groupthink is not present, well-functioning groups make sound decisions.

Antecedents of Groupthink.   Groupthink begins when a group is close-knit and the members view the group as attractive, just as Roy strived to become a member of his beloved Akaries. In fact, cohesiveness or how close group members are to one another is posited to underlie much of the groupthink phenomenon (Henningsen, Henningsen, Eden, & Cruz, 2006). The group becomes somewhat isolated. The leader usually is directive, that is, controls the discussion or promotes his or her own preference (Ahlfinger & Esser, 2001). As with many cults, the Akaries kept outside influences to a minimum; Otu himself was also very directive, especially about the planned suicide the day after the failed doomsday prediction.

Symptoms of Groupthink.   Janis as well as Henningsen et al. (2006) have detailed symptoms of groupthink for us. Knowing these symptoms, you should be able to sense groupthink commencing and stop it before poor decisions are made.

One symptom of this phenomenon is the **illusion of invulnerability.** The group is so close-knit and in agreement that *the members believe they are invincible; they can do no wrong.* This occurs because no one in the group wants to dissent and break the cohesiveness. In fact, dissenters are quickly dismissed or pressured to conform to the group's sentiments. In the Akaries, individuals were physically punished with spanking or were dumped in a pit of raw sewage when they disagreed with Otu. *The individuals who take it upon themselves to censor dissenters* Janis labeled **mindguards.** When Sara and Harry investigated this strange cult to which their son had belonged, the authorities told them that the Akaries had had special lieutenants who saw to the punishment of errant group members. Because dissension then ceases, the group comes to think that it is unanimous and morally correct. What makes the process of unanimity and self-righteousness likely is that the group also stereotypes the out-group (the opposition). Members may denigrate the out-group as lazy, stupid, or incapable.

Consequences of Groupthink.   You are aware by now that groupthink results in defective decision making and in most cases disastrous decisions. These decisions are a consequence of several other processes. The group

- generally discusses only one or two ideas.
- fails to survey all possible alternative solutions.
- commits the blunder of not looking at all possible risks.
- avoids discussing the downside of its chosen alternative.
- and never develops any contingency plans in case something goes wrong.

Groupthink is a sinister and destructive process that is best avoided by groups.

Preventing Groupthink.   Fortunately, groupthink can be averted. One means to prevent it is to promote open inquiry and skepticism, something Otu did not allow. Perhaps the group can appoint an official devil's advocate, or the group leader can invite criticism and open debate about each alternative. To ensure that a number of alternatives are generated, subgroups can be formed. Each group should produce its own solutions; consequently, several alternatives result. Once an alternative has been selected, a second-chance meeting should occur. In this way the group has the opportunity to rethink its position and to express any remaining doubts. The leader also should refrain from expressing his or her opinion at the outset so as to foster the generation of options. One last recommendation is to call on outside experts so that the group does not remain isolated and decisions can be made by better-informed group members. You should fill out the information requested in Activity 9–2 (page 216), to see whether you recently have been subjected to groupthink.

ACTIVITY 9–2

GROUPTHINK—HAS IT HAPPENED TO YOU?

INSTRUCTIONS: *Think about a group situation you were in where the group made an important decision. Using the following true (T) or false (F) scale, indicate whether the following statements describe the situation.*

1. Early in our deliberations, the group leader announced his or her preferences.   T   F

2. Our group was particularly friendly and close-knit.   T   F

3. The group was not very tolerant of dissent or disagreement.   T   F

4. Once we understood the issue, we developed our ideas quickly.   T   F

5. I don't think the group ever recognized the ramifications of its final decision.   T   F

6. The group did not generate ideas in case things went wrong after our decision was implemented.   T   F

7. Our group was a bit self-righteous during our deliberations.   T   F

8. People outside the group were ignored or even made fun of.   T   F

9. Once we decided what we wanted to do, we quickly went off topic and chatted about personal issues.   T   F

10. The group looked unanimous, but I think some people privately disagreed.   T   F

- Count up the number of Ts. The higher the number, the more likely your group suffered from groupthink.
- Now examine how good your decision was. Did it work?
- Were others outside of the group pleased with the decision?
- Did anything go wrong during implementation or afterward?

If your group was fraught with groupthink as indicated by your score (a high number of "trues"), then your answers should indicate the final decision was rather poor. Was it? If yes, what will you do differently next time?

A Little Shove Goes a Long Way— Group Conflict

When you enthusiastically join a group, you hope that the group is free of conflict; however, all of us probably can recall instances of intragroup (within-group) and intergroup (between-group) conflict. When Roy called his parents to tell them that he had joined the Akaries, his parents were shocked. They threatened to cut off any financial support to him and to disinherit him so that he would not inherit the family farm. This open conflict between Roy and his parents offers a poignant example of the first type of conflict—intragroup conflict. As for intergroup conflict, the taunting of the Akaries that some of the university students carried out offers another moving example.

The Good Side of Conflict.   Conflict need not always be deleterious (Bippus, 2005; De Dreu, 2005). In fact, some experts in the field of conflict resolution think conflict can be pleasurable (Harper, 2004). Conflict can be useful in terms of testing and assessing ourselves, others, and the issues facing us. Conflict challenges us to develop creative responses and solutions. Conflict can also result in much positive social change. Witness, for example, how the civil unrest of the 1950s resulted in advances for African Americans and other people of color. Moreover, conflict with a second group can sometimes increase cohesiveness within a group. Conflict, then, is not always bad.

The Downside of Conflict.   Conflicts typically are the result of complex mixed motives where a number of divergent motives fuel the conflict. For instance, individuals and groups generally want more than just to win the conflict. Sometimes they also hope to inflict revenge, humiliation, or punishment on the other side or to make the other side suffer a greater loss than they themselves have. Another major problem with conflict is that it sometimes seems to escalate out of control (Chrobot-Mason et al., 2007; Kennedy & Pronin, 2008). In other words, a little shove really does go a long way (De Dreu, 2005). Besides being unpleasant, then, conflicts are complex and often difficult.

Many factors contribute to conflict escalation (Heifetz & Segev, 2005; Rubin, Pruitt, & Kim, 1994). Threats are one such factor. When one group or party threatens another, the other side often responds with a like threat. For example, in international conflict, if one country threatens invasion, the threatened country often responds with a counterattack or at least a threat of retaliation (Huntington, 1999). As you can imagine, threat and retaliation are not productive responses to conflict. Heterogeneity of a larger group, say a business organization, can also spawn conflict and escalation among various groups (Chrobot-Mason et al., 2007).

Our biases toward others, such as stereotypes and prejudice, also fuel conflict escalation (Bargal, 2004; Ledgerwood & Chaiken, 2007). Such perceptions divide conflicting groups into "us" versus "them," or in-group and out-group, quite easily. The **fundamental attribution error** in part accounts for this division. When you fall prey to the fundamental attribution error, you *overattribute other people's behaviors to personality (traits) rather than to situations.* If a divorcing spouse does something negative such as threaten the other spouse with stopping child support, the threatened spouse asserts that the threatener is inherently bad. It does not occur to the threatened partner that something in the situation (such as a bad day at work or fatigue) accounts for the threat. Once this negative image is established, the self-fulfilling prophecy sustains it. The **self-fulfilling prophecy** *occurs when people's expectations become a reality by virtue of their own behavior.* Once the spouse threatens to stop payments, the other spouse becomes embittered and counterthreatens. The counterthreat induces further threats and negative behaviors from the first spouse and so on.

Culture and Conflict.   International conflict was mentioned earlier. However, much conflict also occurs within a culture. Psychologists, sociologists, and anthropologists have noted that different cultures manage conflict differently (e.g., Cushner, 2005). Specifically, the distinction between collectivistic cultures and individualistic cultures again becomes important (Hofstede, 2001; Johnson et al., 2005; Oetzel & Ting-Toomey, 2003). Recall that collectivist societies value group efforts over individual efforts, but the converse is true for *individualistic cultures.* Many Asian cultures are far more collectivistic than U.S., Canadian, and Western European cultures (Johnson et al.; Matsumoto, 2000). In collectivistic cultures, face-saving is important so that the self-respect and image of the disputants is maintained (Ulijn, Rutkowski, Kumar, & Zhu, 2005). In many collectivistic cultures, opponents would purposely try to avoid humiliating or conflicting with others. In individualistic societies, individuals are more concerned with saving their *own* images, so might well debase or denigrate their opponent.

Oetzel and Ting-Toomey (2003) examined face-saving in conflict situations between these two types of cultures. **Face-saving** *relates to saving one's own or someone else's image.* The researchers thought that the strategies individuals in these two cultures adopted for managing conflict might differ due to face-saving strategies. In collective or interdependent cultures, results revealed that negotiators in conflicts appear to help the *other* party save face, while in individualistic cultures, *self-*face-saving was more predominant. Furthermore, participants from individualistic cultures used dominance as a style of negotiating, whereas individuals from collective cultures were more likely to utilize avoidant or integrative solutions. You will read about integrative solutions momentarily.

Conflict Management.   Luckily, experts in conflictology have developed several strategies for dealing with conflict. When conflict is completely settled, the experts say that conflict *resolution* has occurred. At other times, conflict can at best be *managed;* that is, conflict cannot be settled but only contained or kept from escalating. Groups are more likely to be fiercely competitive with each other than are two individuals in conflict (Insko, Schopler, Hoyle, Dardis, & Graetz, 1990).

Because most conflicts are mixed-motive conflicts (e.g., "Even if I lose, I want to keep my opponent from gaining much"), it is not always true that when one side loses, the other must win. Groups and individuals in conflict can look for integrative solutions. **Integrative solutions** are *those that take into account the needs of both sides such that both sides can win something.* At first, it may sound as if integrative solutions involve compromise. In compromise, though, each side must also lose a little to win a little. Integrative solutions go *beyond* compromise.

Charles Osgood (1962) introduced a negotiating technique designed to end or lower the level of conflict. The technique is known as **GRIT,** or **graduated and reciprocated initiatives in tension reduction.** With this technique *each side gradually concedes something to the other side.* For example, in international conflict, one side might concede a small piece of disputed territory. Because of the norm of reciprocity (mentioned earlier), pressure exists on the other side to concede something as well (Park & Antonioni, 2007), perhaps a partial troop retreat in international war. Often these concessions are made *public* so as to keep pressure to reciprocate on both sides. The key here, then, is *communication with the public* as well as with the other side. There is always a danger with GRIT that one side will not reciprocate and in fact take advantage of the other, conceding side. Should this happen, the side that made the concession needs to respond with a like competitive action so that the other side knows the first will not be taken advantage of.

There are other possibilities for conflict management and resolution. One final method to be addressed here is the intervention of a third party (Arnold, 2007; Wilburn, 2006). Third parties are usually mediators or arbitrators. **Mediators** are *neutral third parties who intervene in conflict and who help the two disputing parties come to common agreements via communication, creative problem solving, and other techniques.* **Arbitrators** are similar to mediators in that they are *neutral third parties who, using the same techniques, assist the parties with the conflict, hope that the parties can resolve their differences, but if they cannot, render a binding decision upon the parties* (Duffy, Grosch, & Olczak, 1991; Moritsugu, Wong, & Duffy, 2010).

Every state in the United States houses mediation or neighborhood justice centers as alternatives to the courts (McGillis, 1997). The typical case is a two-party dispute over property, but some centers handle felonies such as rape where the rapist and victim meet face-to-face. Mediators and arbitrators are used in many different arenas to facilitate the resolution of conflict. Mediators, in particular, have been assigned to international, environmental, business, family, neighborhood, and other conflicts with a high degree of success (Beardsley, Quinn, Biswas, & Wilkenfeld, 2006; Duffy et al., 1991; Moritsugu, Wong, & Duffy, 2010). Empirical research has also demonstrated that mediation involves a humanistic growth process. Individuals who successfully mediate their conflicts function at a higher level on Maslow's needs hierarchy (see Chapter 7) after mediation (Duffy & Thomson, 1992).

As you can determine we rarely operate in isolation. Most humans are social beings; for that reason, groups affect us daily in myriad ways. Understanding how groups form and function, comprehending why people join groups, recognizing detrimental group processes when they first develop, and knowing how to correct dysfunctional group behaviors are valuable coping skills and are necessary to personal growth and interpersonal relationships.

SUMMARY

KINDS OF GROUPS

There are several different types of groups to which we can belong. The most important group is our primary group, the small, close-knit, face-to-face groups formed by family or friends. Secondary groups are larger and less intimate, whereas collectives are very large. We usually also distinguish our own group, or in-group, from other outside groups, or out-groups. In-groups are our reference points for our feelings about ourselves.

HOW DO GROUPS FORM?

Groups go through a developmental process just as do humans. Groups come together in the forming stage and then usually move quickly to the storming stage when friction exists. Once the storming is over, the group agrees on norms or rules by which it functions and then moves to the performing or productive stage. Groups sometimes slide back to one of these stages and the process recycles.

WHY JOIN A GROUP?

Individuals join groups for a variety of reasons. One reason is that groups furnish us with the opportunity to affiliate or to be with similar others; groups also provide us with social support or psychological aid. Groups, too, often possess more information and more collective power than a single individual would.

WHAT GOES ON IN GROUPS?

Several processes operate no matter what the type of group. Various centralized or decentralized communication systems typically develop. Individuals in groups also try to influence one another through pressures to conform, comply, or obey. Some individuals feel they do not have to work as hard in a group, in which their individual efforts are less likely to be noticed, a phenomenon known as social loafing. Groups often become polarized in their decision making, whereby groups make more extreme decisions than individuals. This is known as the group polarization effect.

ARE LEADERS MADE OR BORN?

Psychologists are unsure exactly why someone in a group emerges as leader. Traits, the situation (i.e., someone being in the right place at the right time), or some combination of the two may account for leader evolution. Several theories have attempted to explain why people emerge or are effective as leaders, but no one theory to date has successfully explained this phenomenon. Contingency theory combines both traits and situations. The theory posits that there are two leadership styles—person-centered, in which the leader attends to group members' feelings and relationships, and task-centered, in which the leader is concerned about success and about meeting goals. The effectiveness of the group is dependent or contingent on leader style and the quality of the situation in which the group finds itself. There are several other styles or traits related to leadership, including self-awareness (high emotional intelligence), charisma, and ability to transform groups with perceptive vision.

Research has also examined gender issues related to leadership. Women are just as effective as men in leadership positions, although the stereotype of the typical effective leader is masculine. Women, however, often are not found in such positions for reasons including the perception that they should not act in masculine ways.

WHEN GROUPS GO WRONG

There are several negative group processes. One is groupthink, where groups value cohesiveness or "sticking together" over sound decision making. Groupthink often ends in disastrous decisions. Another is conflict. Although conflict is not always bad, conflict can sometimes keep a group from performing well. There are known techniques for overcoming both of these phenomena. For example, appointing a devil's advocate who criticizes the group's decisions is helpful in preventing groupthink. For conflict, integrative solutions or third-party intervention provide the opportunity for the parties in conflict to come to some mutual understanding.

SELF-TEST

1. A family represents which type of group?
   a. Primary
   b. Secondary
   c. A collective
   d. Out-group

2. The group with which we identify most is known as our
   a. in-group.
   b. aggregate group.
   c. norming group.
   d. secondary group.

3. The second stage of group formation is the _____ stage.
    a. forming.
    b. storming.
    c. norming.
    d. performing.

4. For what reasons do members usually join groups?
    a. Affiliation
    b. Collective power
    c. Social comparison
    d. All of these

5. An example of a centralized group communication network is
    a. circle.
    b. chain.
    c. wheel.
    d. hierarchy.

6. When people issue an *appeal* for us to do something, they are actually requesting that we
    a. obey.
    b. conform.
    c. comply.
    d. collectivize.

7. Tony realizes that his psychology class is large, so he need not contribute often. This is an example of
    a. social loafing.
    b. authoritarianism.
    c. the norm of reciprocity.
    d. group polarization.

8. People-oriented leaders are most effective in
    a. all situations.
    b. bad situations.
    c. moderately good situations.
    d. good situations.

9. The phenomenon by which groups value cohesiveness over sound decision making is known as
    a. groupthink.
    b. conformity.
    c. norming.
    d. responsibility diffusion.

10. An outside, neutral person who has the power to make *binding* decisions in a conflict is a
    a. mediator.
    b. arbitrator.
    c. expediter.
    d. GRIT.

EXERCISES

1. *Kinds of groups.* Think about the primary and secondary groups to which you belong. Do the characteristics of your groups fit the descriptions in the book? If not, why not?

2. *New groups.* Watch a newly forming committee or some other group. Did the group go through the stages of group development as outlined in this chapter?

3. *Why join groups?* Ask a number of people why they join the groups they choose. Do the reasons conform to those cited in the book? Are they different from your reasons?

4. *Social support.* Make a list of occasions on which someone offered you social support in the last two months. Do the occasions have anything in common? What kinds of support were offered?

5. *Electronic communication.* Have you ever used electronic communication in a group of which you are a member? Write a few paragraphs about how these communications differed from face-to-face communications.

6. *Group consensus.* Observe a group coming to consensus about some issue. Do you see any signs of groupthink? How could or did the group have avoided this phenomenon?

7. *Leadership.* For the groups of which you are a member, think about how the leader was selected. Can you add anything to the literature on leader emergence based on your experience? How well does your experience fit any of the theories presented?

QUESTIONS FOR SELF-REFLECTION

1. Why did you join the groups you did? Why did you leave any of the groups?

2. Who are the members of your in-group? Do you think that your in-group will remain the same over a lifetime? Why or why not?

3. Be honest—are there out-groups in your life? Who are the members? Would it be better for you and for them if they weren't in your out-group? How can you overcome stereotyping this group or conflicting with its members?

4. When groups are storming, have you contributed to the storming or tried to move the group toward norming and performing? What were your motives for doing what you did? Did others resist you? Why?

5. Are you as likely to offer social support to someone in need as others are to offer you support?

6. What do you enjoy more—face-to-face communication with others or electronic (phone, email, etc.) communication? Why?

7. Are you a conformist or a nonconformist? Is one better than the other for you given your life circumstances? Could you change strategy if you wanted to?

8. Do you do your fair share of work in the groups of which you are a member? Why or why not? Do you think you need to change your contribution level?

9. Are you a leader of any groups? If you are a leader, why? If you do not lead any groups, why not? Are you more comfortable being a leader or a follower? Why?

10. Reflect on your life; have you experienced groupthink? What were the results of the groupthink process? Can you reverse any of the poor decisions?

FOR FURTHER INFORMATION

RECOMMENDED READINGS

BOYATZIS, R. E., & MCKEE, A. (2005). *Resonant leadership: Renewing yourself and connecting with others through mindfulness, hope, and compassion.* Cambridge, MA: Harvard Business School Press. The authors propose that leaders with emotional intelligence need to move beyond using solely this quality to lead; otherwise, they burn out. Boyatzis and McKee provide useful suggestions for executives who want to motivate their employees and improve the bottom line.

HARPER, G. (2004). *The joy of conflict: Transforming victims, villains, and heroes in the workplace and at home.* British Columbia, CA: New Society Publishers. Written by a real mediator and conflict management expert, the book provides practical, humorous, and well-received methods for managing conflict.

LUSTIG, M. W., & KOESTER, J. (2009). *Intercultural competence: Interpersonal communication across cultures.* Boston: Allyn & Bacon. Theory and practice are combined in this readable book about how to home in accurately on both verbal and nonverbal cues of people from a variety of cultures—a valuable skill for leaders, members of groups, and anyone in international businesses.

PERLOW, L. A. (2003). *When you say yes, but mean no: How silencing conflict wrecks relationships and companies . . . and what you can do about it.* New York: Random House. We are fond of silencing conflict and taking an easier way out. Sometimes ignoring conflict can be as destructive as surfacing it. Why this is so and what to do about it are the topic of this practical book.

WHEELEN, S. (2004). *Group processes: A developmental perspective.* Boston: Allyn & Bacon. This book provides a standard social psychological viewpoint of group processes. The author provides both theory and research to address issues specific to group dynamics.

WEBSITES AND THE INTERNET

http://www.managementhelp.org/grp_skll/theory/theory.htm   A website on group dynamics that includes information on how groups form, how to conduct team building, etc. There are also links to library and other resources.

http://www.alleydog.com/links-sp/social.asp   This site offers links to other sites that are concerned with social psychology, including topics on group behavior.

http://www.richmond.edu/~dforsyth/gd   A site that contains much information on the history of study of groups, how research on groups is performed, how groups structure themselves, the nature of group influence, and more. It reinforces many of the concepts in the chapter.

http://www.mindtools.com/pages/article/newLDR_84.htm   A large site devoted to leadership and managerial skills, including but not limited to leadership styles as well as group decision making, communication, and problem solving.

http://www.uiowa.edu/~grpproc/index.html   A site sponsored by the Center for the Study of Group Processes. It includes free access to the electronic journal *Current Research in Social Psychology.*

At Work and Play

Learning Objectives

After completing this chapter, you should be able to

1. Explain the importance of self-assessment in career choice.
2. Discuss the process of identifying a compatible career.
3. Understand why education is important to your career and life success.
4. Describe the changing demographic picture of the labor force.
5. Identify several major issues facing women and minorities in the workplace.
6. List several of the fastest growing careers requiring a college degree.
7. Understand what leisure is and why it is important to personal growth.
8. Discuss work and leisure patterns for various groups.

Kristin was thrilled. She had just marched down the aisle of the stadium at her university to celebrate her graduation. In the days that followed, Kristin lazed her time away watching TV, surfing the Internet, and texting her friends. In the third week after her graduation, her father asked, "Krissy, do you have a résumé?" "Sure, Dad," she answered. "The university career center helped me assemble it." "Good, tomorrow we are getting in the car and we are going to drop off your résumé in downtown Manhattan." During the next week, Krissy gave her résumé and cover letter to over 45 different businesses. Unfortunately, nothing happened: The phone never rang; no one asked for an interview. Kristin was disheartened. Her parents kept insisting that she get out of the house and find a job. She finally landed a job waiting on tables at the local country club. However, Kristin was a psychology major with a business minor and had hoped to work in a big company recruiting new employees. So, Kristin kept sending her résumé and cover letters. She was determined that waitressing was only a means to pay off her student loans until something better came along.

One day a large department store in New York City requested an interview. The store was interested in Kristin because she had completed an internship in a human resources department for a smaller store near her university. Kristin landed the job of her dreams. She was indeed to be a recruiter—but not just any recruiter. Her job was to hire celebrities for big publicity functions at the flagship store.

CHOOSING YOUR CAREER

Kristin's experience illustrates some of the perils and promises of finding your own niche in the **workplace,** or *place of paid employment outside the home.* On the minus side, you can see that no matter how well educated you are, you can still end up without a **job.** A major reason for unemployment is often the lack of a good system for matching people with careers and jobs. As a result, in addition to millions of unemployed people, it has been estimated that many people in the United States are **underemployed**— *working in a job beneath their abilities or education.*

On the plus side, Kristin's success story shows what you can do when you take the initiative and make the most of your opportunities. Notice that in reassessing her **career**—*one's purposeful life pattern of work, as seen in the sequence of jobs held throughout one's life*—Kristin needed to take stock of what she had to offer and what she really wanted. One of the keys to Kristin's success was her eventual emphasis on a positive, take-charge attitude. All of these points are relevant for our own lives because we, too, face the challenges of choosing a compatible career and finding a job that uses our talents.

Taking Stock of Yourself

When choosing a career goal, it's best to begin by taking stock of yourself. Such self-assessment should include a consideration of your interests, abilities, personality, and personal values. What are your interests? Which school subjects do you like the most? Which hobbies do you enjoy? Which recreational and sports activities do you play or follow? In each case, try to determine what it is that most interests you; whether it's the activity itself or the people you're doing it with. Generally, the intrinsic or internal enjoyment of the activity is one of your best guides to the choice of a career.

What are you good at? People often balk at this question. They say, "I haven't done anything but go to school" or "I've been busy raising three kids." The implication of such remarks is that these people don't have any marketable skills. But when they are confronted with a checklist of things they can do, the picture brightens. For example, a woman who has organized a mothers' cooperative day care, planned field trips for children, and managed the family budget has had considerable experience with management skills, a very important ability for a variety of jobs. *A* **skill** *is the ability to perform a task well. It is usually developed over time through training or experience.* A skill can be used to do work in many jobs or it can be used in learning. Occupations are classified based on how frequently different types of skills (e.g., artistic, communication, interpersonal, managerial, mathematical, mechanical, and scientific) are used and by what level of skill is usually needed.

One way to find out what you're good at is to reflect upon your achievements, including those in school or elsewhere. Perhaps you won a spelling bee or were the all-around athlete-scholar. You may have been elected to an office of a large student organization. Select several achievements in each of the five-year periods of your life. What do these achievements have in common? What characteristics do they *not* share? What can you learn about yourself and your goals and skills from your achievements?

Your personality also offers valuable clues for choosing a compatible career. Each of us possesses a unique combination of traits, needs, and motives that make some work environments more compatible for us than others. For example, a meticulous homemaker may be good at working on computers, a field that requires the ability to manage details with precision. Many times our experience in part-time and summer jobs helps us see which type of work environments we like the most as well as which we don't like. Kristin, for instance, loved her position in the human resources department at the store, in part because it matched her training, including her business skills and her desire as a psychology major to work with others.

Your values are also an important consideration, especially your **work values**—*what brings you the most enjoyment or satisfaction in a career or job.* All too often, we take our work values for granted, becoming aware of them only when faced with job dissatisfaction, job changes, or decisions about jobs. An example is the choice between a job we enjoy that doesn't pay well and one that we don't especially like that does. However, the sooner we clarify our work values, the easier it will be to make a satisfying decision regarding a career or job.

Identifying Compatible Careers

Once you have a better understanding of your interests and abilities, you're ready to match yourself with a compatible career. With more than 20,000 different careers to choose from, this can be a formidable task. Fortunately, there are many helpful resources such as the *Occupational Outlook Handbook* (OOH) published by the Bureau of Labor Statistics. This handbook contains more than 20 basic career groups, each with dozens of related occupations. An **occupation** is *the activities and responsibilities necessary to perform given work tasks in a particular line of work,* such as nursing or marketing. For example, health-related careers include physicians, physician's assistants, registered nurses, practical nurses, medical technicians, and the like. For each career, the handbook provides information on the type of work involved, places of employment, entrance requirements, working conditions, and employment outlook. The OOH also has an introductory section with helpful information on such topics as how to find a job and employment opportunities. The OOH, revised every two years, is available in most libraries and job counseling centers or can also be found online at http://www.bls.gov. In addition, the book provides job search tips and links to information about the job market in each state.

In identifying compatible careers, it's often advisable to talk over your plans with an interested teacher, school counselor, mentor, or someone in your field of interest. Professionals in university counseling centers and career development centers spend a good part of their time assisting people with their career planning. They also have access to a wide assortment of psychological inventories for this purpose. These inventories may furnish valuable leads to compatible careers for someone with your interests, especially when discussed with a counselor. Don't wait until you are looking for a job to assess your strengths and values; working with these centers while you are a freshman or sophomore can be an invaluable guide to planning your education before you graduate or hit the job market.

The *Strong Interest Inventory* probably dominates the field of career assessment as the most popular instrument and has been demonstrated to be very effective in dealing with the complexities of career interests (Bailey, Larson, Borgen, & Gasser, 2008). It is usually administered by a professional counselor and is widely used for career guidance. Using this inventory, you indicate your preferences (like, dislike, or indifferent) for various careers, school subjects, activities, amusements, and types of people as well as indicate something about your own personal characteristics. Computer-scored printouts organize the results around six basic categories, which are briefly described here:

- *Realistic*—practical, stable, persistent (example: engineer)
- *Investigative*—task-oriented, introspective, and independent (example: biologist)

- *Artistic*—creative, impulsive, and expressive (example: musician)
- *Social*—sociable, responsible, and humanistic (example: social worker)
- *Enterprising*—aggressive, confident, and energetic (example: stockbroker)
- *Conventional*—predictable, conforming, conscientious, and obedient (example: accountant)

The results of the *Strong Interest Inventory* include information on general career themes, basic interests, and specific careers with which you are most compatible. Discussion of the results with a counselor usually provides valuable leads to the most compatible careers for you. To help you prepare to see a career counselor, think about which of these descriptors best fits you. Which others come close to describing you, and which do not describe you at all?

Several other inventories exist (Smith & Campbell, 2009), so an important question is "How helpful are these inventories?" A lot depends on how they are used. If you take them in hopes that they'll tell you which career you should choose—a common misunderstanding—you'll probably be disappointed. Nor will the results predict how successful or happy you'll be in a given career, in as much as these factors depend on your abilities, personal motivation, and so on. Instead, these inventories are best used as an aid in making an *informed career choice*. For instance, those who choose careers very similar to their career profiles tend to remain in their careers, whereas those who enter careers highly dissimilar to their profiles eventually tend to drop out of them (Hansen & Dik, 2005). When you consider all the time and money invested in preparing for a career, this information can be extremely helpful to you.

Arriving at Your Career Decision

If you're like most people, you'll end up with not just one but a number of potentially compatible careers. Ultimately, you must make a decision about which is the best career for you. In the process of deciding on a career, you should guard against certain pitfalls. One is the accidental choice, which consists of choosing a career mostly because of attraction to one's first job. People who fall into this trap may discover later, to their regret, that they would have been happier or more successful in another line of work. Another pitfall is the choice of a career or job because of its external trappings, like money, prestige, power, or security. In the long run, it's better to choose a work activity that is enjoyable in itself, as long as the financial rewards are adequate. A major mistake is not exploring your career options sufficiently. Kristin, for example, knew she did not want to be a waitress all of her life. On the other hand, she was not sure about what she did want to do. Just as with Kristin, you must take the initiative and engage in an *active* process of finding a compatible career, as already discussed. Still another pitfall has to do with the timing of your decision, with the risk of making a premature decision or of waiting too long to decide. People who make strong career commitments in their early 20s, *before* they are fully informed about careers, often regret their choices later. On the other hand, those who delay making a career commitment until their mid-30s (e.g., stay-at-home mothers) usually deprive themselves of the necessary work experience to make a wise choice. Thus, you need to choose a career goal but be willing to modify that choice in light of your subsequent experiences and personal growth.

Preparing for Your Career

Once you've determined your career goal, you'll need to know how to prepare for it. Kristin was only partly prepared in that she had held a single internship and at the last minute developed her résumé. She had no further strategies for finding her first professional-level job until her father told her to drop off her résumé at various businesses. As you might expect, there are many ways to prepare for a career. Some careers are entered through an apprenticeship, vocational-technical school, internships, or on-the-job training programs. Others require a two- or four-year college degree. In addition, careers such as teaching, accounting, and nursing also require a state license or some type of certification. Professions such as clinical psychology, medicine, and law also require an advanced degree, supervised training, and a state license. Because you are already enrolled in some sort of post–high school education, you may have begun the appropriate education for your career. On the other hand, others of you, especially those in a liberal arts program, may not have arrived at a firm career goal. But in either case, an integral part of career planning is finding out the appropriate educational requirements for your chosen career.

College is supposed to make you a better-informed person and provide access to higher status and better-paying careers. Naturally, college graduates continue to have higher lifetime earnings and lower unemployment rates than high school graduates, as shown in Table 10–1. For instance, people with a four-year college degree earn substantially more than high school graduates the same age. Those with graduate or professional degrees enjoy an even greater advantage. Of course, people's salaries vary considerably depending on many factors, such as the field of study, actual position held, and geographic location. Given the rapid changes in the job market, and the fact that one in nine persons changes careers every year, some of the most valuable but often overlooked advantages of a college education are the abilities for critical thinking, appreciation of lifelong learning, and enhanced adaptation to continuing change.

There are several important aspects pertaining to landing your first full-time professional position. One important aspect, as Kristin found out, is the résumé. Another important step is the job interview. It is never too early to start preparing yourself for both. Activity 10–1 (page 230) introduces you to some of the complexities of the job interview and preparing for it.

TABLE 10–1

EDUCATION AND PAY: THE BETTER THE EDUCATION, THE BETTER THE PAY

Average earnings in 2007, based on education level, for people 18 or older

Education Level	Average Salary
No high school diploma	$24,881
High school diploma	33,609
Some college, no degree	39,106
Associate degree	41,447
Bachelor's degree	59,365
Master's degree	70,559
Doctoral degree	95,785
Professional degree	121,340

Source: U.S. Census Bureau (2008). http://www.census.gov/hhes/www/macro/032008/perinc/new03_001.htm

ACTIVITY 10–1

THE JOB INTERVIEW

Securing a job usually involves one or more formal interviews. Your major goal is to convince the employer that you are the person for the job, that is, that you have the necessary qualifications and personal qualities and would fit into the organization. It's best to create a favorable impression. Be confident and ambitious, emphasizing your strengths. If asked about your weaknesses, admit a minor one such as "At times I'm too conscientious." Also, it's generally best not to furnish more information than requested by the employer. Finally, a crucial part of a successful job interview is preparing for the interview. Consider the following job interview tips.

Preparation:
- Learn about the organization.
- Have a specific job or jobs in mind.
- Review your qualifications for the job.
- Prepare answers to broad questions about yourself.
- Review your résumé.
- Practice an interview with a friend or relative.
- Arrive before the scheduled time of your interview.

Personal appearance:
- Be well groomed.
- Dress appropriately.
- Do not chew gum or smoke.

The interview:
- Relax and answer each question concisely.
- Respond promptly.
- Use good manners.
- Learn the name of your interviewer and greet him or her with a firm handshake.
- Use proper English—avoid slang.
- Be cooperative and enthusiastic.
- Use body language to show interest.
- Ask questions about the position and the organization, but avoid questions whose answers can easily be found on the company website. Also avoid asking questions about salary and benefits unless a job offer is made.
- Thank the interviewer when you leave and, as a follow-up, in writing.

Test (if employer gives one):
- Listen closely to instructions.
- Read each question carefully.
- Write legibly and clearly.
- Budget your time wisely and don't dwell on one question.

Information to bring to an interview:
- Social Security card.
- Government-issued identification (driver's license).
- Résumé. Although not all employers require applicants to bring a résumé, you should be able to furnish the interviewer information about your education, training, and previous employment.
- References. Employers typically require three references. Get permission before using anyone as a reference. Make sure that this person will give you a good reference. Try to avoid using relatives as references.
- Transcripts. Employers may require an official copy of transcripts to verify grades, coursework, dates of attendance, and highest grade completed or degree awarded.

SOURCE: Adapted from U.S. Department of Labor, Bureau of Labor Statistics (2008). *Occupational Outlook Handbook.* http://www.bls.gov/OCO/

Perhaps you believe as Kristin did that she merely had to look at the newspaper classified advertisements to find a position. She did this dutifully each day shortly after she graduated. Her parents, however, knew that 80 percent of available jobs are never advertised and that over half of all employees obtain their jobs through people they know (U. S. Department of Labor, 2004). Although not exhaustive, here is a list of possible places to search for a position:

- Apply in person or walk in the door with your résumé as did Kristin.
- Search Internet job sites such as Monster.com.
- Use an employment agency or recruiter that hires individuals for companies.
- Find a position through the university or college career service center.
- Use your and your parents' networks of personal contacts to find job openings.
- Look in professional journals and newsletters or attend professional conferences.
- Visit job fairs or other venues where jobs are posted.

Do you know which of these is most fruitful and, on the other hand, which search strategy results in few good matches, if any, between job seekers and employers? With the proliferation of job search engines on the World Wide Web, you might think that this is the most productive method. Wrong! Knowing now what Kristen's parents know about the value of personal contacts in job searches, you should be cultivating contacts with knowledgeable others—perhaps alumni from your campus, neighbors, volunteer or internship supervisors, or other mentors you know—who can point you to job openings upon your graduation. This strategy is called **networking,** or *using personal contacts to establish career opportunities.* You might think that this provides you with an unfair advantage over any other candidates—which it might. This is, however, a perfectly acceptable and ethical technique, especially given that up to half of all position openings are unadvertised.

YOUR CAREER OUTLOOK

How promising your job is often depends on the outlook for your field. Do you know the outlook for your chosen career? Are the job openings in your field expected to remain stable? Or is rapid growth of jobs projected? Kristin based her career choice of wanting to work in human resource management on her love of psychology and the results of the *Strong Interest Inventory,* which indicated she was also attracted to business environments. Although it's difficult to answer all possible questions about specific jobs, the Bureau of Labor Statistics periodically makes informed projections of jobs in the various careers. Because employment projections, by their nature, are somewhat imprecise, you should not use them as the sole basis for a career decision. But such projections can help you assess future opportunities in the careers that interest you.

Forecasting Your Career's Growth

The number and types of jobs available in the years ahead depend on the interaction of many factors, especially economic, demographic, and technological factors. By analyzing changes in the economy and the factors involved, the Bureau of Labor Statistics develops projections of future demands for many careers. To make these projections, authorities must make some assumptions about the growth of the labor force,

The service sector (such as food service) is expected to grow while manufacturing (such as the cut-and-sew sector) is expected to decline.

economic inflation, and unemployment. You can find the Bureau of Labor Statistics website at www.bls.gov.

Since the beginning of the recession in December 2007, the unemployment rate in the United States has increased to over 9 percent. However, higher levels of education are associated with lower rates of unemployment. For instance, the employment rate of individuals without a high school diploma is more than three times that of those holding a bachelor's, master's, or doctoral degree and more than two times the rate of unemployment for those holding an associate degree (U.S. Department of Labor, 2009). Nevertheless, there are jobs out there. As projected through 2016 by the U.S. Department of Labor, total employment is expected to increase by about 1.2 percent per year; adding nearly 13 million jobs total. The service sector (finance, real estate, health care, communication, data processing, etc.) is expected to dominate employment growth. In contrast, manufacturing services are expected to decline the most. Table 10–2 provides you more detail on the changing employment sector.

Changing Jobs or Careers

Looking over the job projections and alternative career patterns may start you thinking about your own career goal. Perhaps you already have a firm career direction and are busily preparing for it. Someone else may have doubts or reservations. Either way, remember that it's perfectly natural to modify your career goal with experience and with greater knowledge of career opportunities. People are often reluctant to change their career goals for many reasons. Sometimes they would rather keep to their original goal than risk disappointing their parents, spouses, or peers. They forget they are choosing for *themselves*—not for anyone else. People also fear that switching career goals may be regarded as an admission of failure, but to continue in a direction you have misgivings about will only make matters worse. Then, too, individuals may overestimate the price of changing career goals. After gathering all the facts, you may find that the penalties are not

TABLE 10–2	
INDUSTRIES WITH THE LARGEST WAGE AND SALARY EMPLOYMENT GROWTH AND DECLINE	
	Annual Rate of Change (%)
Employment Growth	
Management, Scientific, and Technical Consulting Services	+5.9
Individual and Family Services	5.7
Home Health Care Services	4.5
Financial Investments and Related Activities	3.9
Computer Systems Design and Related Services	3.3
Residential Care Facilities	3.3
Employment Decline	
Cut and Sew Apparel Manufacturing	−8.4
Computer and Peripheral Equipment Manufacturing	4.0
Iron and Steel Mills and Ferroalloy Manufacturing	3.9
Fabric Mills	3.8
Pulp, Paper, and Paperboard Mills	3.6
Rubber Product Manufacturing	3.3

SOURCES: Bureau of Labor Statistics. http://www.bls.gov/emp/emplargestind.htm

as great as expected. The longer you delay changing career goals or careers, the more difficult it is. More often than not, the positive gains outweigh the costs.

People are changing jobs more frequently than in the past. The time a worker keeps a job has steadily declined, and the typical U.S. worker has more jobs (or employers) in his or her lifetime than workers during the 1950s. The typical pattern is that an individual tends to hold several brief jobs in the first few years after graduation, then settles into a position that lasts several years. Workers in their 30s who stay with the same employer for five years or more are likely to remain in that job for a long time. As men and women get older, they make fewer job changes. By the age of 40, workers will make about two more job changes; at 50, only one more. Few people change jobs in their 60s, and most of them are probably moving into second careers because of retirement. At the same time, there are exceptions to this pattern. A small number of workers exhibit extremely stable job patterns throughout their careers. Others change jobs every few years until they reach retirement.

There are many reasons individuals change careers, jobs, or employers. One important and often overlooked reason is burnout. Burnout in our fast-paced work-a-day life is a problem more and more psychologists are researching and trying to understand. Box 10–1 explicates some of the issues surrounding burnout. Some of the other reasons for changing jobs or careers, such as low job satisfaction, are reviewed next.

Box 10–1

Job Burnout—Don't Let It Happen to You

There are many factors that can make a job unsatisfying. Some work is dangerous—for example, working on a construction crew or a deep sea fishing boat. Other jobs are boring and monotonous, like assembly-line work. In other instances, employees may not be well matched to or well trained for their jobs. Some positions provide solitary work, where employees cannot socialize or talk to one another during the course of the day. Other occupations allow little room for advancement or new skills acquisition. Some posts provide for little responsibility or underutilize the individual's education or capabilities. Other jobs might require individuals to work too hard and, thus, to experience overload. One other very important aspect of job satisfaction and performance is job burnout.

Burnout is *a psychological syndrome of emotional exhaustion, depersonalization, and reduced personal accomplishment that occurs among individuals, especially those who do "people work"* (Peisah, Latif, Wilhelm, & Williams, 2009). Let's look in greater detail at this definition. Emotional exhaustion is the primary symptom or characteristic of burnout. Emotional exhaustion typically means that the person feels exhausted or drained from the stress of the job. Stress can come from a steady stream of problematic clients, long work hours, too much responsibility, and a myriad of other factors. Depersonalization means that clients, customers, or others with whom the burned-out individual comes in contact are not seen as particularly human anymore; they are numbers or faceless souls. The burned-out employee interacts with them in a detached, impersonal, and cynical manner. Finally, the sufferer's performance may decline or the individual may feel that he or she no longer makes a difference—no matter how well or how many hours the individual works. Human service workers are probably most affected by burnout, although those in other occupations certainly are eligible as well. Teachers, nurses, police, and social workers are good examples of people prone to burnout (Adams, Boscarino, & Figley, 2006).

Men and women are equally likely to burn out, although women's health may suffer more from job
(continued)

Box 10–1 (*continued*)

stress and those who are unmarried are more prone to it (Toker, Shirom, Shapira, Berliner, & Melamed, 2005). Some researchers suggest that low levels of hardiness, poor self-esteem, an external locus of control (e.g., being controlled by forces beyond the individual), and an avoidant coping style typically constitute the profile of a stress-prone or burned-out individual (Maslach, Schaufeli, & Leiter, 2001). Other researchers suggest that different personality dimensions result in burnout, for example, emotional instability, conscientiousness, and even high self-efficacy (Burke, Matthiesen, & Pallesen, 2006; Wierda-Boer, Gerris, & Vermulst, 2009). We should not forget, however, that certain job characteristics can also contribute to burnout and job fatigue, namely time pressures, role ambiguity, long working hours, low control over the work, and so forth (Sonnentag & Zijlstra, 2006).

The best way to avoid burnout is to prevent it in the first place. Before you take a job, consider whether you and the job are a good fit. If the job requires you to report early to work, are you an early riser? If you like being creative on the job, is there room for creativity in the day-to-day routine of the job? If you are a social butterfly, does the position provide you possibilities for interacting with customers and coworkers? Does the job require public speaking; are you frightened to get up in front of a large audience? Consider all aspects of the position as well as your personality and preferred work environment. Don't take the job if it isn't a good match.

If you find yourself victimized by burnout, you can still escape some of its consequences. One of the most important ways to reduce the effects of burnout is to have a good social support system. Perhaps coworkers feel the same way you do but cope better; talk to them and see what helps them. Family members who know about your work may also offer a sympathetic ear and some good advice for how to deal with burnout. A good sense of humor and the ability to have fun can also help you better manage this type of job stress (Talbot & Lumden, 2000). Perhaps you can put up some funny pictures or cartoons in the break room or ask coworkers to bring in the joke of the day. Be sure that you allow for leisure time, covered elsewhere in this chapter, off the job, too. Try not to come home from work so exhausted that you can't do a few fun things after work.

You might also think about how you do your job. Are there positive aspects you could focus on more? Why did you take the position in the first place? Perhaps you can realign your work values with the initial aspects of the job that interested or excited you. Perhaps you or your supervisor can think of ways to expand your job to include elements that make the job more exciting or more rewarding. Maybe there are new skills you can learn or utilize, too. If you are a good employee, your boss will want to keep you and keep you happy.

Finally, as can any other type of stress, burnout can cause physical and mental health problems, so it is best to confront it when it happens (Eriksson, Starrin, & Janson, 2008). If burnout becomes too intense and too much for you to handle, perhaps it is time to do another self-assessment and find a new job in a different company or even a new occupation. Don't let burnout get the best of you.

CONTEMPORARY ISSUES IN THE WORLD OF WORK

During our teens and 20s, most of us gain considerable work experience through a variety of part-time and summer jobs and, in many cases, full-time jobs. Although these jobs may not have been especially interesting or related to our career goals, they do provide practical knowledge. Experience in the workplace teaches us how to budget our time; take responsibility for a job; and, most important, get along with other people. Finding and holding our first satisfying full-time job in our chosen career is much more involved and important, however. Following are some issues important to any job.

Job Satisfaction

Job satisfaction is *people's feelings about different aspects of their jobs; how well one likes a given job, depending on such factors as pay and coworkers.* People who are satisfied with their jobs not only are less susceptible to stress-related illnesses but also visit the doctor less frequently and live longer than those who are dissatisfied in their jobs—all important considerations.

Despite all the griping you hear (and perhaps your own choice comments) on the job, a substantial majority of Americans are satisfied with their jobs (U.S. Merit Systems Protections Board, 2005). Many of these same individuals say they would continue to work even if they didn't need the money (AARP, 2002). This does not mean, though, that these same individuals are happy with all aspects of their jobs. College-educated workers, especially those in the professions and executive positions, are generally more satisfied with their jobs than those with less education. Workers in unskilled and service jobs tend to be less satisfied. Sales personnel tend to fall below the norm in job satisfaction, despite being fairly well compensated.

Satisfaction on the job depends heavily on the work activity itself. People generally prefer work that involves contact with others, is interesting, offers the opportunity to learn new skills, and allows them some independence (Mohr & Zoghi, 2006). Interestingly, how well you feel you perform on the job is only somewhat related to your level of job satisfaction. That is, only a moderately positive relationship exists between performance and job satisfaction (Joner, 2005). Some people who love their jobs perform well while others who love their jobs do not. Some people who do not acquire satisfaction from their jobs perform well anyway; others who do not like their jobs do not perform well at all. Thus, there are other reasons that explain our job performance outside of job satisfaction (Edwards, Bell, Arthur, & Decuir, 2008).

Job satisfaction also depends to a great extent on the working conditions of the job. In addition to a rewarding job, workers generally prefer having a job that provides for advancement, job security, and good working hours. They also want friendly, cooperative coworkers and considerate supervisors. Workers also experience less stress at work when they are allowed some control or can make decisions on their own (Spector, 2002). Pay for work is not only a means of recognizing job performance or success; it also may be used to purchase other items we want. One study demonstrated, however, that going after the highest paying job does not necessarily result in high job satisfaction (Iyengar, Wells, & Schwartz, 2006). In particular, workers are frequently concerned with their pay *relative* to those around them, with greater job satisfaction associated with a higher pay ranking (Brown, Gardner, Oswald, & Qian, 2008). For the majority of people in the middle and working classes who are caught between materialistic aspirations and economic pressures, pay has become an increasingly important part of job satisfaction.

Many other variables affect satisfaction on the job. Age and years on the job continue to be important considerations. Recent graduates initially enjoy high job satisfaction, as did Kristin. As soon as the novelty of the work wears off and reality sets in, job satisfaction can drop sharply. The drop occurred for Kristin when she realized that another employee doing much the same job but with a little less experience was earning almost 15 percent more than she was. After five years on the job, satisfaction tends to rise steadily with age and years on the job. Major reasons include greater job security and better pay as well as more realistic expectations. The rising level of education among younger workers helps account for the relative dissatisfaction among younger, better-educated workers. The major exception is for workers with professional and graduate degrees, such as doctors and lawyers, who generally are happy in their work. However, unlike blue-collar workers, who reach a plateau in earnings relatively early, college-educated workers generally reap the rewards of greater education in the later years of their careers.

Workers who are not promoted often complain of favoritism, suggesting that getting ahead on the job depends more on "whom you know" rather than on what you know. Surveys of larger samples of workers provide a more balanced view; when asked about ways to get ahead in the job, most workers emphasize the importance of performing the job well, working extra hours, and being willing to accept responsibility. At the same time, almost half of them realize the importance of knowing the "right people" and having highly visible work assignments.

These issues suggest the importance of knowing how promotions are made in the organization you work for. Many companies make their policies on promotion clear in the employment interview or at the time of hiring. If not, you should inquire about them. You should know to what extent promotions are based on such factors as education, work experience, job performance, and seniority. For example, Kristin was hired by the department store to bolster sagging sales, which she did in record time. She initiated an innovative advertising campaign based on celebrity appearances and never hesitated to take work home during evening hours or over weekends. As a result, Kristin believed she was responsible for the increase in sales. When her supervisor was promoted, Kristin hoped to be considered for the job, but someone from the outside was brought in to become the new manager. When Kristin asked why, she was told that coworkers and a few celebrities had complained of her aggressive, high-handed style. Kristin had expected to be promoted primarily because of the sales results, but her superiors had judged her by a broader standard, including how well she related to people. Such misunderstanding could have been avoided if either Kristin or her boss had clarified the standards for promotion at the outset.

Technology and Work

The addition of technology into American work sites is affecting how people work and whether they are satisfied with their jobs. Computers, electronic organizers, smartphones, voice mail, and teleconferencing are but a few of the innovations. In addition, **telecommuting,** which is defined as *either periodic or regular work for one's employer performed at home or another remote location,* is becoming increasingly commonplace. Currently there are close to 35 million full- and part-time telecommuters working in the United States, up 43 percent since 2003 (WorldatWork, 2009).

Whether technology actually *increases* job satisfaction is unknown, as the studies investigating this issue have produced contradictory results. Although several studies indicate that workers immersed in technology are more satisfied with their jobs than traditional employees (Akkirman & Harris, 2005), others studies have failed to show the benefits of technological access (Meyer, 2006). Thus, current research indicates that there are both positive and negative aspects of a technological "workplace." For example, instant messaging can both enhance collaboration among employees spread out geographically as well as causing workers to miss the richness of face-to-face communication. Moreover, even though instant messaging can increase feelings of privacy at work, employees tend to find them distracting, and a hindrance to job production (Cameron & Webster, 2004). Some employees are even being fired because they spend *too much* time playing with technology, such as the World Wide Web.

Cyberslacking is *the overuse of the Internet in the workplace for purposes other than work.* Because of cyberslacking, some employers monitor their employees' online behavior; this raises interesting and difficult ethical issues (Armour, 1999). Cyber harassment, chain e-mails, joke e-mails, and other objectionable forms of communication are proliferating in the workplace, too, with women more likely to be the recipients of these than men (Whitty & Carr, 2006).

Another way technology is changing our working life is by **e-recruiting,** in which *job candidates are screened by phone, video, or computer* (Russell, 2007) rather than in a face-to-face interview. If this happens to you, you might want to practice with a friend who can give you feedback before the actual interview, because there is much less nonverbal feedback from an interviewer using an electronic method of interviewing.

Diversity in the Workplace

One of the major shifts in the workplace between now and 2050 will be the changing demographic picture of the labor force. Although Whites will continue to account for the vast majority of workers, as they did in 1990, their share will decline from 73 percent to 52.8 percent (see Figure 10–1). In contrast, both the number and the

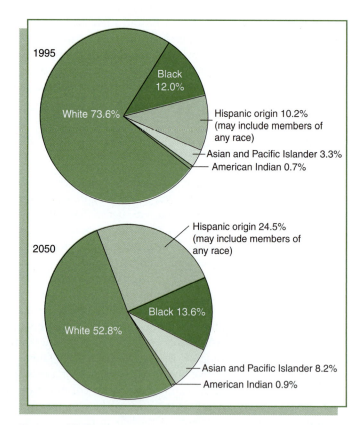

FIGURE 10–1

The U.S. workforce is more diverse.

SOURCE: Bureau of Labor Statistics. http://www.dol.gov/asp/programs/history/human/reports/futurework/ report/chapter1/chart1.

proportion of minority workers will increase. Hispanics, non-Hispanic Blacks, and Asian and other ethnic groups are projected to account for an increasing share of the labor force. By 2050, Hispanics will constitute a greater share of the labor force than will Blacks. Asians and others continue to have the fastest growth rates but still are expected to remain the smallest of the four labor force groups (U.S. Department of Labor, 2007).

A significant percentage of new jobs will require some form of postsecondary or college education. For example, employment in occupations requiring a bachelor's degree is expected to grow 17 percent by 2016, and jobs requiring an associate's degree are projected to grow 19 percent. The gap between the limited educational level of some immigrants and minorities coupled with the rising demand for educated workers will make it difficult for some to find a job or, once hired, to find job satisfaction and advancement.

A key factor will be improving the educational level of minority students. Although high school graduation rates have improved among minority groups in the past 20 years, especially among African Americans, they still lag compared to that of Whites (Brown & Rodriguez, 2009). With the exception of Asians, minority groups earn an even smaller proportion of post-secondary degrees (U.S. Census Bureau, 2009). Consequently, unless colleges attract more minority students, minority group members will lack the necessary skills to succeed in the workplace.

Research on job satisfaction in multicultural organizations has just begun and is admittedly rather scant. In some studies, African Americans report lower job satisfaction than Whites (Mau & Kopischke, 2001). One study also revealed that Hispanic Americans are particularly likely to experience more job stress than non-Hispanics (Rodriguez-Calcagno & Brewer, 2005). Other studies show few to no race or ethnic differences (Greenhaus, Parasuraman, & Wormley, 1990) or even demonstrate high job satisfaction for minorities (e.g., Tangri, Thomas, Mednick, & Lee, 2003). One reason for these findings may be differences in the kinds of jobs and organizations analyzed in the various studies. Another factor might be whether the researched organizations were fairly diverse (heterogeneous) (Wharton, Rotolo, & Bird, 2000). In any event, White U.S. residents and Canadians will face the same problems as minorities because North American corporations are internationalizing and sending their employees to other countries or bringing people from other countries to work in the home organization (Matsumoto, 2000).

Internationalization of North American business means that we will need to understand cultural similarities and differences better if we are to work together. This means it will be wise for you to understand others' work habits and work values. Throughout this book, we have made the distinction between two general types of cultures—*collectivistic* and *individualistic*—so we will use this distinction again to elucidate differences in work behaviors. In individualized cultures like the mainstream U.S. one, people have an easier time distinguishing between work time and personal time and also between work activities and social activities. In such cultures, initiative, challenge, and freedom on the job are valued and encouraged. On the other hand, in collectivistic societies, people view their work groups and work organizations as fundamental parts of themselves (like families), so the bonds between individuals and organizations are stronger. Work is also seen as the fulfillment of an obligation to a larger group (e.g., to family or to society) rather than as a means to accumulate money. Organizations in collectivistic societies are considered morally responsible for the welfare of their employees and are expected to care for them across their life spans (Matsumoto, 2003).

Women are making the workplace more diverse, too. Currently, women comprise 47 percent of the workforce. However, the most notable inequity between men and women in the workplace is the earnings gap. In 2007, women's pay was 80 percent of men's (U.S. Department of Labor, 2007). A major reason for the earnings gap is that many women enter lower-paying service jobs such as secretarial positions. Until recently, most women have been crowded into less than 10 percent of the Labor Department's job categories. Women are overrepresented in careers such as secretaries, nurses, and librarians; they are underrepresented in careers such as engineers, dentists, and physicians. Another reason for the discrepancy in pay between the sexes is that women workers have had less education and work experience, but this factor, too, is changing. Entering college classes now contain slightly more women than men—a relatively recent phenomenon (Mather & Adams, 2007). Although the proportion of women in the traditional male careers remains small, the rate of increase has been dramatic. For instance, in the past 40 years the percentage of college professors who are women has increased. Compared to the past, there are now more women physicians, more women in the life and physical sciences, and more women engineers, lawyers, and judges.

Among the other issues that concern women in the workplace are role conflicts between home and work, opportunities for advancement, sexual harassment, and childcare. For example, in comparison to working men, working women report spending more time completing various chores at home (Braun, Lewin-Epstein, Stier, & Baumgärtner, 2008). Although few studies report sex differences in job satisfaction, women are less happy about opportunities for advancement. Admittedly, some companies offer better opportunities for women than others.

Additionally, ambitious women often feel that their careers are hindered by a glass ceiling (Ortiz & Roscigno, 2009). Although they can see through it, they can't pass beyond this invisible barrier, mostly because of stereotyped attitudes and expectations in the workplace. For example, a smaller percentage of the top management jobs are held by women than men. Similarly, women who are promoted into better managerial positions are likely to have salaries that lag behind those of their male colleagues.

Sexual harassment is a problem faced more often by women than by men. **Sexual harassment**—*any unwanted attention of a sexual nature occurring in the workplace that interferes with a person's ability to work*—is now illegal. Sexual harassment includes but is not limited to unwelcome sexual advances, physical contact, offensive language, and threats of punishment for rejection of these acts. Instances of sexual harassment still abound in many places and create double jeopardy (prejudice and harassment) for minority women (Berdahl & Moore, 2006; Buchanan & Fitzgerald, 2008). In order to reduce such instances, the Equal Employment Opportunity Commission (EEOC) has issued guidelines for preventing sexual harassment. These guidelines suggest that employers should raise the consciousness of employees about the subject of sexual harassment, express strong disapproval of such behavior, inform all workers of their right to raise the specter of sexual harassment, explain the appropriate procedures for making a complaint, and sensitize everyone concerned. Box 10–2 further discusses how you can better cope with sexual harassment.

Still another issue for women and also men is balancing family and work responsibilities (Day & Chamberlain, 2006). A good example is finding adequate childcare such that both the mother and father can work. Today, most married women—the traditional childcare providers—in the workplace have children; over half have preschool-age children. High-quality day care is hard to find, difficult to afford, and still not fully tax deductible in most cases. Presently, only a small proportion of

Box 10–2

Coping with Sexual Harassment on the Job

At a workshop on this topic, when women were asked to share their experiences, a recently hired college graduate said, "My boss hinted I'd get a raise faster if I went out with him." A young married woman complained, "One man makes these suggestive remarks like 'You look happy today—it was that kind of night, eh?' "A middle-aged woman said, "A male colleague can't keep his hands off me."

Sexual harassment in the workplace takes many forms. A familiar practice is directing catcalls, whistles, and demeaning words like "doll" at women. Another one is recurring, offensive flirtation. Although most sexual harassment is verbal, physical patting, pawing, or sexual advances are not uncommon. Soliciting sexual favors for promotion at work is often cited in lawsuits against large companies.

Although each situation is different, some suggested strategies are usually helpful in dealing with sexual harassment on the job.

1. Make it clear when you disapprove. Say directly but tactfully something such as, "I find that remark offensive."

2. Jot down the time, place, and manner of such incidents. Who are the biggest offenders? Under what circumstances?

3. Talk about the incident to other workers. Find out how many other women (or in some instances, men) have been harassed.

4. Take positive steps in raising the awareness of male workers. Report offensive incidents to supervisors. Discuss problems of sexual harassment at staff meetings. Encourage workshops on the subject.

If necessary, make an official complaint to your employer, either orally or in writing, depending on the situation. As a last resort, contact federal agencies, like the Equal Employment Opportunity Commission.

employers provide childcare facilities for their workers. As an increasing proportion of women enter the workplace, issues such as maternity leaves and subsidized day care may become valued fringe benefits (Moritsugu, Wong, & Duffy, 2010). There are other issues where work matters spill over to home and vice versa. For example, studies indicate that emotional transmission, that is, carrying anger or anxiety from one place to another, occurs from work to home for both men and women (Matjasko & Feldman, 2006). Today, many Americans are still searching for a good balance between home and work activities.

LEISURE TIME

No matter how much you like your job, it's important to have sufficient time off to do many of the other things you enjoy in life. In other words, **leisure** (*time free from work or duty that may be spent in recreational activities of one's choice*) is as important as work. Most Americans feel that they are working more and playing less—a perception now being confirmed. Harris (1987) pointed out that in little more than a decade, the number of hours Americans work would increase from about 40 hours per week to 48 hours. That time has passed, and Harris has been proven right; the amount of leisure time available to the average person has dropped (Lagerfeld, 1999). Interestingly, Americans, unlike their other Western counterparts, are likely *not* to use all the vacation time they have earned (Guinto, 2005).

This dramatic change can be accounted for in several ways. A major factor is the growing practice of businesses and other organizations to employ fewer workers, often assigning additional responsibilities rather than hiring more full-time workers. The stated aim is to increase productivity, but the average worker often feels overworked. As Kristin remarked after several years on the job, "I find that I'm working harder just to stay even." Working more than 60 hours a week, administrators and managers are most apt to put in the longest workweek (Brett & Stroh, 2003). Many baby boomers, perhaps your parents or grandparents, work over 50 hours a week. Small-business people also work over 50 hours a week. Although women in dual-income families work almost the same number of hours as men do, they have less leisure time, mostly because they do many more chores at home, as mentioned earlier. Ironically, the most affluent sectors of society—college graduates, professionals, and those with incomes of $50,000 or more—work the longest hours and have the least time for leisure.

This trend runs counter to predictions 25 years ago, when it was assumed that automation and technology would shorten the workweek and give us more leisure time (Whitty & Carr, 2006). Actually, the opposite has occurred, perhaps because computer owners are determined to perfect and re-perfect their work. Another factor that accounts for less leisure time is that our work often *spills over* into our leisure time (Hilbrecht, Shaw, Johnson, & Andrey, 2008). For example, some people go on vacation but take work or at least their computer or Blackberry with them. Another factor that contributes to the seeming compression of leisure time is that more and more people are working from home; they use computers or other electronic methods for connecting to their workplace, so the distinction between work and home is blurring (Kirk & Belovics, 2006).

The growing commitment to work has heightened the nation's productivity, helping the United States to compete in the global market. But by the same token, the precarious balance of work and play (Greaves, 2005) has become even more threatened. Many people are becoming so absorbed with work that they aren't giving the loving attention needed to make their marriages work or providing growing children with enough attention or taking part in community endeavors. Meanwhile, time is at

The precarious balance of work and leisure is becoming threatened. Many people are too absorbed in work — so much so that they don't use all of their vacation days.

a premium in our society such that leisure time is an even more precious commodity. People must now think carefully about the most desirable way to spend their leisure hours (Fagan & Press, 2008).

What Is Leisure?

There are many things we do outside of work that are anything but leisure, for example, cleaning up after meals, dusting our homes, studying, and visiting the dentist. Such activities are usually labeled **maintenance activities,** *nonleisure and nonwork time spent in activities necessary for the maintenance of life.* In contrast, leisure has to do with the way we use our free time, our motivation for doing it, the meaning it has for us, and how it affects our lives. From an adjustment perspective, the purpose of leisure is the cultivation of the self and the pursuit of the higher things of life. Playing a musical instrument primarily for the enjoyment of it or bicycling for pleasure are examples of **unconditional leisure;** these are *activities freely chosen, excluding work and maintenance activities.* People who have a satisfying leisure life, such as Kristin, who played tennis with her friends in her spare time, often find they must acquire certain skills and play often enough to keep up their game. At the same time, individuals who are highly competitive or perfectionistic may become so concerned about their performance that the pleasure in their leisure activities is lost. True leisure, then, is considered something we do primarily for the enjoyment we get out of it.

Work and Leisure

Most Americans regard their work and leisure activities as separate—and perhaps unrelated—parts of their lives. When Kristin was disappointed that she did not receive her promotion after her supervisor was promoted, she nonetheless enjoyed her friends and recreational life, especially tennis. Another person may have a very satisfying career, with little or no time for play. In each instance, a person's involvement and satisfaction in work and leisure are related to personal characteristics, needs, and values.

Researchers have studied leisure activities based on sex, race, and age. For example, Talbot, Fleg, and Metter (2003) examined women's and men's leisure activity levels over several decades. Their results indicate that especially for men, national recommendations to become more physically active appear to have had a modest effect. Several studies have found that African Americans have lower levels of leisure-time activity than Whites and that this difference might be accounted for by discriminatory behavior (Stodolska, 2005) or differences in preferences for leisure activities (Shinew, Floyd, & Parry, 2004).

Not everyone in these particular demographic classifications fits neatly into these patterns. What pattern describes your involvement and satisfaction in work and play? Are you more work-oriented or more leisure-oriented? In what ways would you like to change your pattern? The answers to these questions are just as important to your mental health as are notions about what career you think is best for you. Multiple studies have shown that leisure activities help us cope better with negative life events, assist us in our overall adjustment (Spiers & Walker, 2009), and improve our sleep and overall physical well-being (Tucker, Dahlgren, Akerstedt, & Waterhouse, 2008).

Using Leisure Positively

By the time people have arrived home after a hard day's work and eaten dinner, they're often too tired to do anything else. When asked their favorite way to spend an evening, the majority, including Kristin, says watching television. Adults now watch television an average of four to six hours a day, most of it in the evening. Although people watch television primarily for entertainment and to a lesser extent for the news, watching television is also a time to relax and unwind, or to recuperate, which is mostly a maintenance activity, as described earlier. The ease with which someone may push a button and be entertained for hours on end remains a great temptation. At the same time, individuals who have curtailed their TV habits are usually amazed at how many other interesting things there are to do in life.

In contrast, the *positive* use of leisure requires a certain degree of choice. Ideally, you should select activities that are compatible with your interests and lifestyle rather than simply doing whatever is convenient at the time or what your friends want to do. Kristin was fortunate to have friends who also enjoyed tennis. They typically played every other Saturday morning. Kristin knew, however, that there were Saturdays when she would be too tired to play and preferred to sleep late. She would call her friends on Friday night to inform them of her decision.

To enjoy an activity to the fullest, you usually have to acquire the necessary skills. You must also budget your time and money to keep up the activity. For example, people who take pride in their tennis game tend to play regularly and probably derive greater satisfaction than those, like Kristin, who play only occasionally. If learning the skills and budgeting time and money are too stressful for you, perhaps you should switch to another form of leisure activity. Leisure activities can become stressful (Hébert, 2005) but needn't be.

A favorite American form of leisure is taking a vacation. About half the population takes some type of vacation each year, typically a one- or two-week vacation. Most people feel little or no guilt taking time off for a vacation. When asked the main reasons for taking a vacation, their responses reflect a variety of motives. The most common motive is to relax. Other motives are intellectual stimulation, family togetherness, adventure, self-discovery, and escape. After the vacation, most people are glad to be back home and look forward to returning to work. Only a few feel depressed at facing the familiar routine. Many Americans feel that work is more important than leisure, and they seek not so much a leisure-filled life as a better balance of the two. Now that more women are working outside the home, leisure has become even more important for families. Furthermore, the advent of more flexible work schedules enables people to take long weekends, which promise to make short vacations a regular event rather than a once-a-year affair.

Leisure becomes increasingly important from midlife on because of all the changes in people's lives. By this time, people are reassessing their needs and values and what they want out of life. Also, people this age tend to have more job security, more discretionary income, more free time, and more paid vacation time than younger adults. For many, this may be the first time they've been able to follow their own inclinations without having to worry about the productivity of their efforts. Now they can take up interests and express abilities not previously used in career and family responsibilities. In short, leisure becomes a means of personal growth (Chen & Fu, 2008).

Constructive leisure activities are also an important way to prepare for retirement. People who have developed rewarding leisure activities as well as a network of social and family relationships are more able to make the crucial shift from full-time work to a satisfying retirement. A common and very constructive leisure activity is performing volunteer work. You can read more about volunteering in Box 10–3.

Box 10–3

VOLUNTEERING IN AMERICA

You don't have to wait to retire or be elderly to jump on the volunteer wagon. You can join over 65 million U.S. volunteers (almost one-third of our population) now. In fact, nonprofit organizations appear to be flourishing because of their volunteer base. In the 1970s, there were only 5,000 nonprofits registered with the federal government. Today, the number has soared to nearly 45,000 (Russo, 2005). Those individuals who do not volunteer report that they often lack time, have health or medical problems, or family responsibilities that interfere.

All types of people volunteer, although middle-aged persons and teens have the highest volunteer rates, as do married and employed persons. Both men and women spend an average of about 50 hours a year volunteering at various organizations, including educational, religious, and community service organizations (U.S. Department of Labor, 2009). Volunteers complete a wide variety of tasks for their organizations, such as fund-raising, food service, general labor, transportation, and teaching (from highest to lowest in frequency). These individuals either step forward of their own initiative or are asked by the organization to volunteer.

Volunteering not only gives back to your community or organization for everything it has done for you but also provides free on-the-job training, helps you explore possible careers, builds your résumé, and establishes networking connections (and perhaps letters of recommendation) for use after your graduation. And a recent survey of volunteers also found that volunteer work was directly linked to career advancement because volunteers learned leadership skills, developed confidence, practiced interpersonal cooperation, and enhanced communication skills while they volunteered (Women's Way, 2006). A wonderful website exists to get you started searching for a volunteer opportunity if you have not already found one: www.volunteermatch.org. At this site, you can search by zip code and interest area (such as emergency services, animal care, arts and culture, religion, etc.). Your campus might also house a volunteer office or you can ask the local Chamber of Commerce for a list of nonprofits (or even for-profits) that take volunteers.

One final thing, volunteering may be good for you! Research has shown that volunteering among the elderly is associated with reduced mortality, fewer health problems, and less depression (Ayalon, 2008; Harris & Thoreson, 2005).

SUMMARY

CHOOSING YOUR CAREER

We began the chapter by discussing the process of choosing a career, one's overall or life pattern of work. In choosing a career goal, it's best to begin by taking stock of yourself, including your interests, abilities, personality, and work values. Then you're ready to explore the career options available to you, realizing that there are a variety of career inventories that may help to identify the most compatible careers for someone like yourself. A commonly utilized scale is the *Strong Interest Inventory,* but others exist. You should also be aware of certain pitfalls in decision making, such as arriving at a career goal prematurely or unduly delaying the choice of a career. It's best to keep your career goal somewhat flexible and to be willing to modify it in light of subsequent experience, especially while you are in college.

YOUR CAREER OUTLOOK

Career outlook depends on the interaction of many factors, especially the makeup of the labor force and the growth of the various careers as well as one's own career choice. Major changes in the labor force include the increase of minority and women workers. Because jobs for college-educated workers will grow faster than average, college graduates will continue to have higher rates of employment and lifetime earnings. In contrast, people with less than a high school education will find it difficult to get good jobs with good pay and chances for advancement. There is also more mobility in the workplace today, with the typical American worker now having more jobs in his or her lifetime.

CONTEMPORARY ISSUES IN THE WORLD OF WORK

Satisfaction on the job depends heavily on how interesting and meaningful the work activity itself is, as well as the conditions on the job itself. One major change in our working lives is the increase in technology. Technology on the job affects different employees in different ways—sometimes increasing or decreasing job satisfaction. Another major shift now taking place in the workplace is the increase in the number and proportion of minority and international workers. Our workplaces are indeed becoming multicultural. However, because of the gap between the limited educational level of many of these individuals, such as recent immigrants, and the rising demand for educated workers, it will be difficult for some individuals to find a suitable job, much less achieve job satisfaction and advancement. Also, more women now work outside the home; among the many issues that concern modern employees are the earnings gap between the sexes, opportunities for advancement, sexual harassment, role conflicts between home and work, and availability of childcare.

LEISURE TIME

No matter how much you like your job, it's important to have time off for other things you enjoy. Most Americans are working more hours per week and having fewer hours for leisure than they did in the past. Consequently, leisure—time free from work that may be spent in meaningful activities—becomes more and more of an issue in our society. The value of leisure and whether we engage in leisure activities varies with gender and race. A favorite form of leisure is taking a vacation, and half the population takes some type of vacation each year. The positive use of leisure becomes increasingly important from midlife on as we reassess what we want out of life. Volunteer work is a valuable and common form of leisure activity.

SELF-TEST

1. In choosing a career goal, it's best to begin by
   a. taking a test.
   b. seeking counseling.
   c. taking stock of yourself.
   d. getting parental advice.

2. Inventories such as the *Strong Interest Inventory* help to predict which careers you
   a. are most compatible with.
   b. will succeed in.
   c. are best trained for.
   d. will be happy in.

3. Which of the following is widely regarded as the major advantage of a college education?
   a. greater social skills.
   b. better job opportunities.
   c. advanced cognitive abilities.
   d. more factual knowledge.

4. Above all, most people are looking for a job that provides
   a. interesting work.
   b. contact with other people.
   c. a feeling of accomplishment.
   d. all of the above.

5. Which of the following groups will have a smaller proportion of people in the workplace by the year 2050?
   a. Whites
   b. Asian Americans
   c. Hispanics
   d. African Americans

6. The greatest inequity between men and women in the workplace is the gap between their
   a. earnings.
   b. job productivity.
   c. education.
   d. job qualifications.

7. In the future, which jobs are expected to have the biggest numerical decrease in workers?
   a. Health care
   b. Mining
   c. Manufacturing
   d. Agriculture

8. Which statement is true about American workers changing their careers?
   a. Americans seek jobs and then keep them a long time.
   b. Job changes are more common in late career rather than early career.
   c. Americans are fairly prone to changing jobs.
   d. In the 1950s Americans changed jobs frequently.

9. Compared with people in the 1970s, the average American now
   a. works more hours a week.
   b. has more leisure time.
   c. works fewer days a week.
   d. takes longer vacations.

10. The most common reason for taking a vacation is
   a. self-discovery.
   b. relaxation.
   c. family togetherness.
   d. escape.

EXERCISES

1. *Explore your career interests.* Make an extensive list of all the activities you've enjoyed, including school courses, extracurricular activities, full- and part-time jobs, hobbies, and sports. Then select a dozen of the most satisfying activities and rank them from the most enjoyable down. Ask yourself what made each activity satisfying. Was it the activity itself? Or was it mostly the people you did it with or the recognition or money involved? Activities that are intrinsically enjoyable are usually the best indications of the types of careers you'll enjoy.

2. *Identify compatible careers.* Go to your campus career development center or career guidance center and take some type of career inventory like *Holland's Self-Directed Search* or one that requires professional supervision, like the *Strong Interest Inventory*. Then review the results with a trained counselor.

3. *Become better informed about your career goal.* How much do you know about your chosen career? You might find it helpful to look up some basic information about it in a resource like the *Occupational Outlook Handbook*. Look up your chosen career or one you're interested in. Then write down information on the following: (1) description of the work, (2) typical places of employment, (3) educational and entry requirements, and (4) employment outlook. This exercise should give you a more realistic view of your career goal and how to prepare for it.

4. *Favorite leisure activities.* What do you like to do in your leisure time? Do you have enough time for play and leisure? Do you like solitary or social leisure activities? What can you learn about yourself given your analysis of leisure time?

5. *Think about your work and leisure cycles.* In what ways would you like to change your patterns of work and play? How would you keep your patterns the same? Why?

QUESTIONS FOR SELF-REFLECTION

1. Do you have a specific career goal?

2. If not, are you actively engaged in choosing a career—or are you "waiting for things to just happen"?

3. Do you believe that hard work eventually pays off?

4. What are the three most important things you look for in a job?

5. If you won a million dollars in the state lottery, would you continue to work? Why or why not?

6. What is the projected outlook for your chosen career?

7. If you were to change careers, what would your alternate career choice be?

8. Have you ever been unemployed? What did it feel like? How did you overcome these feelings?

9. What is the most important thing you've learned from part-time jobs?

10. What is your favorite leisure activity?

FOR FURTHER INFORMATION

RECOMMENDED READINGS

BOLLES, R. N. (2010). *What color is your parachute? 2010: A practical manual for job-hunters and career-changers.* Berkeley, CA: Ten Speed Press. A classic on matching your personal needs and desires to various jobs.

IBARRA, H. (2003). *Working identity: Unconventional strategies for reinventing your career.* Cambridge, MA: Harvard Business School Publishing. Many Americans change jobs; Ibarra examines this trend and how to successfully and creatively switch careers.

LEITER, M. P., & MASLACH, C. (2005). *Banishing burnout: Six strategies for improving your relationship with work.* San Francisco, CA: Jossey-Bass. A very readable book on an important subject by some of the leading experts on the topic.

POLLAN, S. M., & LEVINE, M. (2002). *Second acts: Creating the life you really want, building the career you truly desire.* New York: HarperCollins. The authors take the reader on a journey through self-assessment to help the individual find the most compatible career.

SCHEIN, E. H. (2006). *Career anchors: Self-assessment.* Hoboken, NJ: Pfeiffer. Besides providing a self-survey to discover your own strengths and talents, this book includes basic career descriptions so that readers can find the jobs with which they are most compatible.

WEBSITES AND THE INTERNET

http://www.monster.com A site for anyone who wants work, is working, or has retired from work. Something for everyone.

http://www.employmentguide.com/site/index.html Here you can search for a job by type of job, by specific employers, or by geographic location.

http://www.careers.org Another site that can help you find jobs and information about work, including information about working in other countries.

http://www.collegegrad.com A job site designed specially for recent college graduates.

http://www.dol.gov The website of the U.S. Department of Labor with an abundance of information on job search strategies, data on career outlook, the *Occupational Outlook Handbook,* affirmative action, and other important issues.

CHAPTER 11

Sexuality

Learning Objectives

After completing this chapter, you should be able to

1. Discuss changing views of sexuality in our society.
2. Recognize the importance of sexual communication for a mutually satisfying sex life.
3. Describe the human sexual response cycle for men and women.
4. Identify various sexual dysfunctions in both sexes.
5. Distinguish the most effective contraceptive methods from one another.
6. List ways to reduce your risk of getting AIDS.
7. Understand various aspects of sexual abuse of children.
8. Describe the effects of rape on victims.
9. Know how to reduce the distress caused by sexual victimization.

After taking a test during their evening class, Carol and Kim stood in the hallway discussing some of the questions. Both felt tense, and both agreed they needed some time to unwind. They decided to visit a café near the campus. Because the café was crowded, they had to share a table with two male students whom they didn't know. Striking up a conversation, they soon discovered several areas of mutual interest. Carol found that Jeff was also a psychology major and shared her career aspirations with him. Kim soon discovered that she and Bob, Jeff's friend, liked the same musical groups. Initially, the four of them enjoyed talking and interacting. However, as the evening wore on, the men began drinking too much beer and telling sordid jokes. The women felt very uncomfortable. Furthermore, Carol and Kim became aware that what the women intended as friendliness was being perceived by the men as a sexual invitation. Sensing that an awkward situation was imminent, the women excused themselves and left.

MEN AND WOMEN

Changing Views of Sexuality

Today, men and women are discovering that they cannot achieve true sexual satisfaction until they realize that sex is not something a man *does to* or *for* a woman, or vice versa. Instead, men and women are learning that sex is something a man and a woman *do together as equal participants.* If one partner is critical, unresponsive, or at best passive, the emotional vitality of the couple's sex life steadily weakens and eventually withers away. In contrast, when both partners are actively involved and when each person spontaneously communicates feelings, the other person's excitement and responsiveness is heightened. Thus, the quality of a couple's sex life, along with their overall relationship, is greatly enriched by a fully shared partnership (Greene & Faulkner, 2005).

However, the experience of Kim and Carol and Jeff and Bob demonstrates how an individual's approach to sexual satisfaction can be hampered by **gender stereotypes**— *widespread generalities about the characteristics and behaviors of men and women that exaggerate the differences between the sexes,* thereby setting the stage for misunderstanding and frustration. For example, there's a long-standing belief that men enjoy sex more than women do. Although this stereotype is beginning to diminish as younger generations are socialized differently, there is ample evidence that men and women still subscribe to it in varying degrees (Regan & Atkins, 2006). Another commonly held stereotype is that, whereas women fantasize about having sex with familiar partners, men fantasize about having sex with strangers. In general, men's attitudes are stereotyped to be more permissive and promiscuous than women's when it comes to sex. Thus, because of these stereotypes men may regard women as sexual challenges or objects to be obtained. In contrast, having been taught that men are lustful creatures with "sex on the brain," a woman might feel she must assume the role of "controller," regulating the pace of sexual encounters, at the expenses of her own personal satisfaction. As you can see, gender stereotypes make it difficult to achieve a fully shared partnership because partners are not viewed, nor subsequently treated, as equals.

Nevertheless, there are some real differences between men and women when it comes to sex. For example, women (more than men) tend to "romanticize" or feel that love ought to play an important role in sexuality (Regan, Durvasula, Howell, Ureño, & Rea, 2004). Women are also more likely to endorse sexuality in a *committed* relationship, whereas men are more likely to engage in *casual* sex (McCabe, 2005). Moreover, men do report greater sexual desire than women and, on a more negative note, men tend to be more sexually aggressive than women as well (Chung, 2005). And as Carol and Kim found out, men are more likely than women to misinterpret friendly behaviors as sexual overtures (Lindgren, Parkhill, George, & Hendershot, 2008).

In addition to gender stereotypes, sexuality is also influenced by the sexual content of magazines, television/movies, music, video games, and other forms of media. Exposure to sexual media is of special concern during the teen years, when adolescents' sexuality is beginning to blossom (Eggermont, 2005). In fact, many adolescents consume media to help them understand the new sexual landscape before them (Kim et al., 2006). Here

Marketers often depict women as sex objects, sometimes to such an extreme that body parts are missing or disjointed as shown in this window display.

are just a few examples of the sexual media that youth *under the age of 18* are exposed to: (1) sex and romance are the most frequently written about topic in magazines read by teenage girls; with nearly one-fifth of headlines focused on issues of sexuality (Davalos, Davalos, & Layton, 2007); (2) men's magazines and magazines directed at teens present women as sex objects more so than any other type of non-pornographic magazine (Stankiewicz & Rosselli, 2008); (3) between 44 and 81 percent of music videos show men and women in revealing clothing, depict scences involving sexual innuendo, and provide indications that sexual behavior has or is about to take place (Zurbriggen et al., 2007); (4) 70 percent of the top 20 shows popular with adolescents average nearly seven scenes of sexual content per hour (Eyal, Kunkel, Biely, & Finnerty 2007); and (5) 38 percent of 16- to 17-year-olds reported successfully seeking out online sexually explicit content (Wolak, Mitchell, & Finkelhor, 2007).

So, just what are teens learning from these sources of sexual information? Although frequently mentioning the importance of "safe sex," the media tend to characterize sex as a casual, fun, natural, and an overall positive activity (Epstein & Ward, 2008). However, conflicting messages are also given. Whereas for women, sexuality is shown to be controlled, discrete, restricted, and responsible, for men, an active sex life is viewed as acceptable and even encouraged (Ward, 2003). As you can see, the media frequently portrays sexuality in a manner consistent with the gender stereotypes mentioned above.

Here's a sobering finding: Across adolescence, youth report learning more about sexuality from media than from their parents (Somers & Surmann, 2004). Moreover, recent data suggests that for many teens, the sexual messages provided by the media may be having an effect, as 34 percent of ninth graders, 43 percent of tenth graders, 51 percent of eleventh graders, and 63 percent of twelfth graders report having sexual intercourse at least once. Surprising to many is the fact that more than 50 percent of adolescents have engaged in oral sex by the time they graduate high school. In addition, youth with a heavy sexual media diet are more likely to engage in sexual intercourse and partake in noncoital sexual activity (e.g., genital touching) than light viewers (Collins et al., 2004). Thus, the media's portrayal of sex appears to be an important determinant of teens' decision making regarding sexual activity (L'Engle, Brown, & Kenneavy, 2006).

Sexual Communication

One of the most astounding things about sexual behavior, at any age, is the reluctance of most people to talk about sex with their lovers or spouses. It's as if talking about sex would spoil the spontaneity—which might be only partly true. A lot depends on how you talk about your sex life. Frequently, people don't have the foggiest notion of their partner's sexual likes or dislikes. Consequently, well-intentioned caresses are not fully appreciated because they're either too heavy-handed, too quick, or too far off the mark—all matters that could be easily corrected by a few words murmured at the right time. However, it's best to avoid discussing sex in a calculating or clinical way. Likewise, it might be best if couples avoid talking about sex immediately before or after, lest it put their partner on the defensive (McCarthy & McCarthy, 2009).

The most important part of sexual communication is the attitude you and your partner have toward each other. Especially crucial is the sense of trust and mutual empathy—the sense that each cares for the other and knows this feeling is reciprocated (Holmberg & Blair, 2009). A lot depends on the spirit and tone of voice in which you say something and your partner's willingness to discuss it in good faith. For instance, in making a request, you might say something like "I'd prefer doing something together before we have sex, such as taking a walk." You may also want to ask a yes-or-no question, such as "Did you enjoy that?" Or you could ask an open-ended question, such as "What part of our sexual relationship would you most like to improve?" Some individuals prefer either-or questions such as "Do you want to talk about this now or at a later time?" Open-ended and either-or questions encourage more participation from your partner than simple yes-or-no questions. It's also important to use questions selectively and, of course, *really* listen to what your partner is saying to you. To assess your own level of communication in intimate relationships, you and your partner could complete Activity 11–1 and then discuss the results.

ACTIVITY 11–1

HOW WELL DO YOU AND YOUR PARTNER COMMUNICATE SEXUAL FEELINGS?

This exercise is designed to give you some indication of your level of communication in close relationships. This survey was designed specifically for your own self-understanding. It is not a scientifically derived survey.

With your partner or significant other in mind, respond to each of the following questions by answering true (T) or false (F) in the blank.

_____ **1.** I readily tell my partner my wishes and needs.

_____ **2.** My significant other knows my favorite foods, television shows, and hobbies.

_____ **3.** My partner and I calmly discuss financial problems.

_____ **4.** My partner and I are able to give each other criticism without becoming angry.

_____ **5.** My companion and I are able to understand each other even without speaking.

_____ **6.** We discuss with sensitivity and sympathy one another's problems at work.

_____ **7.** If my partner does something I do not like, I can straightforwardly tell him or her.

_____ **8.** When we fight, our fights are problem-focused and of short duration.

_____ **9.** My significant other enjoys my sense of humor, even if he or she is the target of it.

_____ **10.** My partner and I know each other's sexual desires and preferences.

_____ **11.** When my companion tells me a secret, it remains a secret with me.

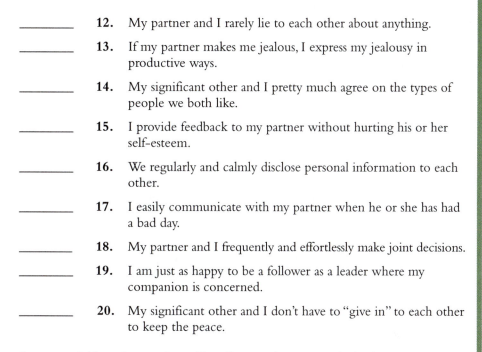

_____ **12.** My partner and I rarely lie to each other about anything.

_____ **13.** If my partner makes me jealous, I express my jealousy in productive ways.

_____ **14.** My significant other and I pretty much agree on the types of people we both like.

_____ **15.** I provide feedback to my partner without hurting his or her self-esteem.

_____ **16.** We regularly and calmly disclose personal information to each other.

_____ **17.** I easily communicate with my partner when he or she has had a bad day.

_____ **18.** My partner and I frequently and effortlessly make joint decisions.

_____ **19.** I am just as happy to be a follower as a leader where my companion is concerned.

_____ **20.** My significant other and I don't have to "give in" to each other to keep the peace.

SCORING: Add up the number of "true" or Ts; chances are, the higher your score, the better your communication skills with your intimate companion, with 20 being the highest score. If you had a low score (for example, below 7), you don't necessarily have poor communication skills. You might, however, want to sit down with your partner and discuss whether there are better ways to communicate with each other.

Giving and receiving criticism regarding sexuality is a touchy but important matter. In fact, some highly destructive patterns have been identified (Gottman & Carrere, 2000). One pattern is **criticism** *that entails attacking the partner's character,* for example, calling the partner "selfish." Another pattern is **contempt,** *in which insults are used to denigrate the partner's sexuality.* A third damaging type of communication is **defensiveness,** *in which we make excuses or refuse to take responsibility for our sexuality or use some other self-protective defense.* Finally, withdrawal is lethal to sexual relationships. In **withdrawal** *we ignore our partners by watching TV or turning our backs on them.*

When you feel the urge to criticize, ask yourself, "What's the reason for my saying this?" If there's no good reason, perhaps it's better *not* to say it. When you feel you must criticize, express your remarks in a nonjudgmental way—using "I" messages, as discussed in the chapter on emotions and motivation (Chapter 7). Whenever possible, demonstrate what you mean. If one person feels a partner has been too frenetic during foreplay, he or she might place one hand on the partner's and demonstrate a slower method, saying, "This is what I prefer." When receiving criticism, try not to overreact. Look beyond the words to what your partner is trying to tell you. Remember, often, the goal of sexual criticism is to enhance both partners' sexual satisfaction, with the end result being a fully shared partnership.

Initiating and Refusing Sex

Nowhere is sexual communication put to the test more than in initiating and refusing sex (Bevan, 2003). Some people don't communicate very well in this area and expect their partners to be mind readers. Others have developed nonverbal cues or elaborate rituals to signal their interest in sex. For example, one of Carol's friends once said to her, "When John gets out the good wine and suggests we cuddle up and watch a movie, I know what he's *really* thinking."

Men have traditionally taken the initiative in sexual intercourse, but nowadays men and women are moving away from such restricted notions of what "men must do" or what "women must not do" (Greene & Faulkner, 2005; Wilde & Diekman, 2005). The more couples can initiate and refuse sex on an equal basis, however, the more satisfied they are with their sex lives. Not surprisingly, they also engage in sex more frequently than other couples. Among married, cohabiting, and committed couples alike, most couples who share the initiator and refuser roles equally are more satisfied with the quality of their sex life, compared to couples for whom sexual initiation is not equal.

Finally, it is not just our sexual desires that we need to communicate to our partners; we also need to discuss with our partners their and our sexual histories. Few people are comfortable asking partners, both romantic partners and relative strangers, if they have been exposed to sexually transmitted diseases or whether they use contraception (Ryan, Franzetta, Manlove, & Holcombe, 2007). But these are *very important* aspects of human sexuality, so broaching the subject with our partners is a must. It is worth noting that individuals who raise this topic with their prospective sexual partners also tend to use contraception, are less likely to use drugs and alcohol, and are more likely to believe in committed relationships (Moore & Davidson, 2000).

SEXUAL RESPONSIVENESS

A week or so after their initial meeting Carol ran into Jeff in the Student Union. Jeff apologized for his previous drunken behavior and started talking to Carol about college life. They soon found out that they went to high schools in the same city and that they both enjoy basketball and trying new foods. After dining at a Thai restaurant and spending the night talking, Jeff and Carol agreed to go out on an "official" date. Eventually, their dating led to a sexual relationship.

The Sexual Response Cycle

Despite people's reluctance to discuss their sex lives, researchers have been able to better understand human sexuality due to the pioneering work of William Masters and Virginia Johnson (1966, 1979). Through an extensive series of interviews and controlled observations of volunteers masturbating and engaging in **sexual intercourse** (here defined as *penetration of the vagina by the penis*), Masters and Johnson identified *the basic sexual response patterns of men and women*. These patterns consist of certain common physiological changes that occur in a predictable sequence and are collectively labeled the **sexual response cycle**. What follows is a modified version of the cycle, incorporating some of the recent changes suggested by other authorities in the field. We'll describe five phases of the sexual response cycle: (1) transition, (2) excitement, (3) plateau, (4) orgasm, and (5) resolution.

Transition (or Desire).   In the sexual response cycle, **transition** is *the gradual shift from a nonsexual to a sexual state of being and includes the awakening of sexual desire and a readiness for sexual arousal*. We're all familiar with the importance of "getting ready" for a special evening out. The same is true with sex. Although individuals vary widely in regard to what puts them in the mood for sex, certain activities commonly facilitate the transition. Some people enjoy a relaxed, candle-lit meal; others may prefer dancing, listening to certain music, or watching a romantic or erotic movie. Touching, massage, and relaxing in hot water are also favorite ways to get into the mood for sex. However, men, more so than women, tend to be impatient and less in tuned or interested in the need for transition. Many women prefer a more gradual transition, accompanied by emotional sharing and tender caressing and kissing. Some partners like to use erotic materials to stimulate each other. Interestingly, most of the erotica produced in the United States is designed to stimulate sexual interest in men, not women (Attwood, 2005). This may be because men find visual images more sexually arousing than do women (Canli & Gabrieli, 2004).

Excitement.   *Sexual arousal,* or excitement, involves a combination of mental and sensory stimulation. **Excitement** means that *sexual arousal causes increased muscle tension, engorgement of the genitals with blood, and increased heart rate*. Each partner's anticipation of sex is an important part of getting in the mood. Sexual desire is also heightened through the stimulation of the senses: Sights, sounds, the sense of smell, and even taste combine to heighten excitement. Mutual caressing of various parts of the body, especially the erogenous zones, almost always intensifies sexual arousal, even when sexual desire is initially low in one partner. As Carol once said, "Sometimes in the beginning I'm not much in the mood for sex, but I rarely end up feeling that way." It is during this stage that the man's penis becomes erect and the woman also experiences arousal (or engorgement with blood) of her sex organs. The length of this stage varies greatly among individuals and couples.

Sexual arousal also depends greatly on psychological changes in the central nervous system, such as thoughts and feelings about a specific partner or the sexual act (Toates, 2009). Many people become aroused more readily through erotic fantasies. For some, fantasy provides an initial boost to sexual arousal, whereas for others, an orgasm can't be experienced without it. Erotic fantasy serves a variety of functions, ranging from the reduction of anxiety to the focusing of our thoughts and feelings (Kahr, 2008; Meana & Nunnink, 2006). Sexual fantasies are especially helpful in counteracting boredom, a common obstacle in long-term relationships like marriage. Common fantasies include reliving a past sexual experience with another attractive person or even having sex with a famous partner.

There are some gender differences in fantasies (Canli & Gabrieli, 2004). Men fantasize about women's bodies, physical appearance, and sexual activity, whereas women fantasize about their own attractiveness to men. Men are likely to fantasize about being dominant and women fantasize about the emotional or romantic context of the sexual activity. Men and women, though, seem equally likely to fantasize (Zurbriggen & Yost, 2004). Interestingly, research on the fantasies of gay men and lesbians has found similar gender effects except that the fantasized partner is usually of the same sex (Chivers, Rieger, Latty, & Bailey, 2004). As revealed, men and women are often aroused by different stimuli, thereby setting the stage for misunderstanding between the sexes. At the same time, *individual* differences tend to outweigh *gender* differences, so that each person needs to be appreciated in terms of his or her own preferences.

Plateau.   The **plateau** phase *occurs just before orgasm; in this phase, sexual arousal becomes more pronounced*. It is usually quite brief, lasting anywhere from a few seconds to several minutes. It's difficult to define the onset of this phase because there is no clear outward sign, such as erection of the man's penis or lubrication of the woman's vagina. Actually, the usual signs of sexual arousal become more pronounced as the individuals approach orgasm. The heart beats faster and breathing grows more rapid. Increasing muscle tension and blood pressure lead to engorgement of the sex organs, promoting the partner's readiness for orgasm. Men rarely lose their erection at this phase. Women also experience a marked increase in the swelling of the outer third of the vagina, making stimulation even more pleasurable. At this point, the partner who is moving faster toward orgasm, often the man, may need to slow down or vary the stimulation from time to time so that both partners can reach orgasm at the same time if they so desire.

Orgasm.   **Orgasm** is *the climax of sexual excitement that is pleasurable and releases tension.* As this climax of sexual excitement approaches, the partners may sense that orgasm is inevitable. Men usually realize orgasm accompanied by tingling muscle spasms throughout the body and perhaps uncontrollable cries and moans. However, women may arrive at the heightened sexual tension of the plateau phase without necessarily experiencing orgasm. This is sometimes the case during penile-vaginal intercourse when the man reaches orgasm first or when he replaces manual or oral stimulation with penetration as the female approaches orgasm.

During orgasm, muscles in and around the man's penis contract rhythmically, causing the forcible ejaculation of semen. Similarly, the outer third of the woman's vagina contracts rhythmically along with the pulsation of her uterus. For both sexes, the first few contractions are the most intense and pleasurable, followed by weaker and slower contractions. Individuals of both sexes vary considerably in their subjective reports of orgasm.

Resolution.   When no further stimulation occurs, orgasm is immediately followed by the **resolution phase**, where *the body returns to its normal, nonexcited phase.* Heart rate, blood pressure, and breathing quickly subside. Muscle tension usually dissipates within 5 minutes after orgasm. Men lose about 50 percent of their erection within a minute or so after orgasm, and the remainder in the next several minutes. Men also enter into a **refractory period**—*a time when added stimulation will not result in orgasm.* The length of time varies widely, from a few minutes to several days, depending on such factors as the man's age, health, and frequency of previous sexual activity as well as his sexual desire for his partner. Women experience no equivalent refractory period. Most women are physically capable of another orgasm, though they may not desire it or experience it. Women who have not experienced orgasm after high levels of arousal usually experience a slow resolution. However, when both partners have attained orgasm, they generally find this a pleasant and relaxed time.

Individual Differences

In addition to the refractory period in males, there are some important variations between men's and women's experience of sex. First, there are marked differences in sexual arousal in men and women. Some of the differences have already been noted. One major difference is that brain imaging studies of men and women have revealed that even when men and women view identical sexually arousing material, the male amygdala and hypothalamus are more strongly activated *even when women report greater arousal* (Canli & Gabrieli, 2004). Moreover, when viewing sexual material, men respond to the sexual attractiveness of the female participants and to watching as an observer or imagining oneself as a participant. Women, on the other hand, tend to respond more exclusively to imaging themselves as a participant (Meana & Nunnik, 2006).

Much of the difference in sexual activity between the sexes may be due to cultural factors, especially those that restrict women's sexuality more than men's. One of the clearest examples is the double standard in sex, which implies that the same sexual behavior is evaluated differently, depending on whether a man or a woman engages in it. At the same time, there are other factors not easily classified as biological or cultural that may contribute to the differences in sexual arousal between men and women. For instance, when asked, "What has prevented you from freely expressing your sexuality?" women are more likely than men to report being affected by fear of pregnancy, guilt, lack of desire, and social disapproval. The fact that women can become pregnant and men do not remains a factor even in this era of more effective contraceptives.

Also, the differences between male and female sexuality tend to change across the life span (Sex Information and Education Council of the United States [SIECUS], 2002). The teenage male's sexuality is very intense and almost exclusively genitally focused. But as he ages, his refractory period becomes longer, he becomes satisfied with fewer orgasms a week, and his focus of sexuality is not so completely genital. Sex becomes a more sensuously diffuse experience, including a greater emotional component in relation to his partner. In women, the process is often quite different, as their sexual awakening tends to occur much later. While they are in their teens and 20s, their arousal and orgasmic response may be slow and inconsistent. However, by the time they reach their 30s, women's sexual responsivity has become quicker and more intense, especially among sexually experienced women. In sum, men seem to begin with an intense, genitally focused sexuality and only later develop an appreciation for the sensuous and emotional aspects of sex. In contrast, women have an earlier awareness of the sensuous and emotional aspects of sex and tend to develop the capacity for intense genital response later (Hyde & DeLameter, 1997).

Another major difference between the sexes is the greater orgasmic variation among women compared to men, both in the physiology of orgasm and in the individual's subjective awareness of sexual climax. Masters, Johnson, and Kolodny (1988b) identified three basic patterns of the sexual response cycle in women, though only one for men.

- One pattern resembles the male pattern and differs mainly in the woman's capacity for additional orgasms.

- A second shows a prolonged, fluctuating plateau phase, with small surges toward orgasm, followed by a gradual resolution. This is sometimes referred to as "skimming" because of the lack of a single, intense climax and is most often reported by young or sexually inexperienced women.

- Another pattern shows a rapid rise in sexual excitement leading to a single, intense orgasm and quick resolution.

Masters and colleagues suggest that after many experiences of intercourse, some women gradually change their sexual response from one to the other of the patterns.

Although men exhibit fewer variations, it would be a mistake to assume that all men experience the sexual response cycle in the same way. Some men have reported extended periods of intense sexual stimulation before reaching orgasm. Others have experienced several mild sexual climaxes, finally leading to an expulsion of semen. Still others have prolonged pelvic contractions after ejaculation. A marked difference between the sexes is **multiple orgasms**—*two or more sexual climaxes within a short period of time*—with women more likely to have multiple orgasms. Although it is not uncommon for women to have several orgasms in quick succession, multiple orgasms are the exception rather than the rule for men. Multiple orgasm, though, is best seen as a potential area to be explored by some rather than an ultimate goal for all.

Sexual orientation is *a component of sexuality and is characterized by enduring emotional, romantic, or sexual attraction to a particular gender.* The three main sexual orientations include **homosexuality**, *which involves attraction to someone of the same sex;* **heterosexuality**, *which involves attraction to someone of the opposite sex;* and **bisexuality**, *which involves attraction to members of either sex* (Kinsey, Pomeroy, & Martin, 1948). There are additional, but less common, patterns related to sexuality, as explored in Box 11–1. Interestingly, researchers have also discovered that some people's sexual orientation is fluid; that is, they go from bisexuality to homosexuality or heterosexuality to homosexuality as they develop (Rosario, Schrimshaw, Hunter, & Braun, 2006).

No one knows how many heterosexuals, homosexuals, and bisexuals live in the United States (Savin-Williams, 2006). These numbers are extremely difficult to ascertain. Homosexuality in particular carries a social stigma and thus is a difficult and complex developmental process for some individuals and keeps some homosexuals "closeted" or secretive about their sexual orientation (Kurdek, 2005; Rosario et al., 2006). In fact, homosexuality was so stigmatized in the past that the American Psychiatric Association in its *early* history considered homosexuality to be a mental disorder. *This is not true today.*

Furthermore, there are heterosexual individuals who are **homophobic** and, thus, stigmatize variations on sexual orientation; that is, they are *afraid of homosexuals or hold negative attitudes toward homosexuals* for various reasons, causing the targets of their negative attitudes to keep their orientation to themselves. Herek (2000b) suggests that better terminology might be **sexual prejudice**—*all the negative attitudes based on sexual orientation, whether the target is homosexual, bisexual, or heterosexual.* Sexual prejudice has declined somewhat over the last two decades. In the 1970s and 1980s, two-thirds of surveyed Americans said that homosexuality was "always wrong." That figure dropped to 56 percent by the 1990s. Many Americans now also believe that a gay person should not be denied employment and that same-sex domestic partners should have some rights, such as employee health benefits (Herek, 2000b). Sexual prejudice is more likely to be manifested in individuals who do not personally know or think they know any homosexuals and in very religious individuals or those who possess anxiety about gender roles (Green, 2005; Herek, 2000a).

There is a question in the adjustment literature about whether homosexuals cope well in the face of the strong stigma against their sexual orientation (Safren & Pantalone, 2006). D'Augelli, Hershberger, and Pilkingston (1998) suggest that disclosure of homosexual orientation to friends and family is the second most significant life stressor for homosexuals, with the most significant being initial discovery of their own homoerotic attractions. One reason disclosure is difficult is because unlike other marginalized groups (e.g., racial minorities), most young homosexuals are not raised in a community of similar others (Rosario et al., 2006). Edwards (1996a, 1996b), however, found in two different studies that homosexual youth cope as well as and are as well adjusted as heterosexual youths. This seems especially true when homosexual individuals accept their sexual orientation (Dupras, 1994). The same can be said for the gay individual whose family or friends are supportive when disclosure about homosexuality is made (Elizur & Ziv, 2001; Kurdek, 2005). On the other hand, several studies suggest that homosexual individuals report more suicidal ideation, suicide attempts, self-injurious behavior, drug use, and use of therapeutic interventions than heterosexuals do (Balsam, Beauchaine, Mickey, & Rothblum, 2005; Rosario, Schrimshaw, & Hunter, 2009). Moreover, the stigma attached to homosexuality may contribute to depression and other mental disorders.

Box 11–1

WHAT YOU SHOULD KNOW ABOUT SEXUAL ORIENTATION

The American Psychological Association (2004a) states that it is important for society to be better educated about sexual orientation:

> Educating all people about sexual orientation and homosexuality is likely to diminish anti-gay prejudice. Accurate information about homosexuality is especially important to young people struggling with their own sexual identity. Fears that access to such information will affect one's [own] sexual orientation are not valid.

In addition to heterosexuality, homosexuality, and bisexuality, there are additional variations in sexual orientation. They include but are not limited to:

- **Crossdressers:** These are individuals who *occasionally wear clothing of the opposite gender.* Most crossdressers are heterosexual.

- **Transvestites:** Transvestites are people who *dress to look like the opposite gender.* Some transvestites wear other-gender clothing full-time and successfully pass as the opposite sex.

- **Transsexuals:** Transgendered people who *believe that they were born into the body of the wrong sex* are called transsexuals. They sometimes want to change this situation through hormone therapy and gender reassignment surgery.

- **Intersexed persons:** Some people *are born with chromosomal or hormonal birth defects so that they do not readily fit into "male" or "female" categories.*

Discovering that one's sexual orientation is not heterosexual—the predominant orientation in our society—can be distressing because of societal stigmas and prejudices against homosexuality. *When an individual accepts his or her sexual orientation as homosexual (or bisexual) and then tells others,* this is called **coming out**. Research has found that coming out involves many processes for the homosexual individual (as well as for others who are told), including but not limited to challenging one's own beliefs and self-concept, developing new methods of communication, managing conflicts differently, changing established relationships with other people, and asking questions of the self and others (Oswald, 2000).

When the gay person's family and friends are supportive, the individual copes much better with this revelation (Willoughby, Malik, & Lindahl, 2006). Gay men, however, seem to be more estranged from their families, especially their fathers, than heterosexual men and lesbians (Bobrow & Bailey, 2001). Surprisingly, gay men and lesbians report that their intimate relationships with their partners are not very affected by parental disapproval (LaSala, 2002). In fact, in relationships where the homosexual partner is fairly visible, families (siblings and parents) are more likely to include the partner in family rituals (e.g., birthday celebrations) (Oswald, 2002). When families do not accept or support their homosexual family member, involvement in the gay and lesbian community and support at school can help diminish psychological distress (Lasser, Tharinger, & Cloth, 2006).

Because there is often sexual prejudice against individuals who differ from the majority, the federal government believes that sexual orientation merits special attention. It prohibits federal employees from discriminating against job applicants and fellow employees on the basis of sexual orientation as well as on the basis of race, color, sex, religion, national origin, age, disability, marital status, or political affiliation. SIECUS also notes that many public schools are now trying to reduce sexual prejudice and discrimination by offering education to students about sexual orientation. Nearly half of a random sample of high school health teachers said they formally taught about homosexuality in their classes. Apparently, there is a need for such information in the schools. Compared to heterosexual students, gay, lesbian, and bisexual youths are four times as likely to be threatened with a weapon on school property, and over 86 percent of them report hearing homophobic remarks from classmates or school staff (SIECUS, 2001).

Love and Sex

So far we've been emphasizing the physical aspects of sex. What about the attitudes and relationships between the partners? For example, if Carol and Kim had become sexually involved with Jeff and Bob on the first night, would they have experienced guilt and shame? Would they find themselves more attracted to the men? Healthy, guilt-free people can function well sexually and derive pleasure from sex without being in love. Masters and Johnson observed that there is nothing inherently "bad" about sex without love, especially if both parties consent. Under certain circumstances, for some people, sex without love may be enjoyable in its own right (Masters, Johnson, & Kolodny, 1995). However, in reality a great deal depends on the individuals involved, especially their value systems. For example, Carol did not want to have sex with Jeff the first few nights she dated him. Another woman might have reacted quite differently and have seen the opportunity for sex on the first date to be an exciting adventure or a way to feel closer to her date, but Carol wanted to get to know Jeff better and feel that he acknowledged some commitment toward her before even thinking of having sex with him.

It is worth emphasizing that *love can enrich sex,* especially in a long-term relationship like marriage. The affection and commitment two people enjoy in their relationship can enhance their overall pleasure, compensating somewhat for the loss of sensual excitement that can occur after years in a committed relationship. In contrast, couples that have sex mechanically, especially when one or both partners have little or no affection for the other, soon discover that sex itself is no longer satisfying.

Romantic love, *which consists of intimacy or closeness and passion,* may lead to satisfying sex, at least for a while, although the satisfaction may soon diminish as romantic ardor cools. In contrast, for couples in a long-term relationship, romantic love often matures into **companionate love,** *a kind of loving but practical relationship based primarily on emotional closeness and commitment rather than physical, sexual intimacy.* Indeed, many

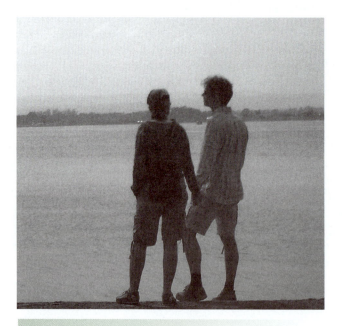

Love and commitment enrich sexuality.

therapists have worked with hundreds of couples with a loving, committed relationship (companionate love) whose sex life is disappointing. In the United States at least, the ideal type of love remains that of **consummate love,** *a complete and balanced love characterized by emotional closeness, sexual intimacy, and commitment between the partners.* Of note, marital happiness and a satisfying sex life are positively correlated, although it is almost impossible to distinguish between cause and effect. Thus, for most couples, but not necessarily all, a good sex life and happy relationship go together. Love not only strengthens the closeness and commitment between a man and woman but also engenders better sex. It is no coincidence that most couples refer to sexual intercourse by the phrase "making love"; sex and love seem to go together in mainstream America.

PRACTICAL ISSUES

The emphasis on sexual fulfillment in recent years has had some beneficial effects. Today, there appears to be more objective information about sex, increased sexual communication between partners, and less anxiety and guilt over harmless sexual practices like masturbation. At the same time, such changes have been accompanied by new anxieties. Many sexually normal men worry about their sexual performance. A woman who is not orgasmic may suffer the same loss of self-esteem as the man who has a fairly flaccid erection. Then, too, the increasing sexual activity outside of marriage today has accentuated the perennial problems of birth control, unwanted pregnancies, and sexually transmitted diseases. Most disturbing of all is the occurrence of sexual victimization in our society, as seen in rape.

Sexual Dysfunctions

Even sexually experienced couples discover that each time they engage in sex, it is different. Sometimes sex is highly pleasurable for both partners; at other times it is less satisfying for one or both of them. Such occasional problems are usually not serious; they often are caused by fatigue or stress. For instance, alcohol consumption and certain antidepressants can interfere with sexual activity (Haberfellner, 2007; Johnson, Phelps, & Cottler, 2004). When sexual disorders persist or become distressful to individuals such that they cannot enjoy sex, the disorders typically are classified as sexual dysfunctions.

    Sexual dysfunctions include *persistent problems that prevent an individual from engaging in or enjoying sexual intercourse.* Sexual dysfunctions may be grouped according to the phase of the sexual response cycle in which they occur. They include difficulties of desire, arousal, and orgasm. **Hypoactive sexual desire,** sometimes called **inhibited sexual desire,** refers to a *lack of interest in sex.* There is a higher incidence of this disorder in women than in men (Heimen, 2008). In some instances, the lack of desire may be a realistic response, such as with a partner who practices poor hygiene or is verbally abusive. In many cases, it reflects the individual's preoccupation with a life problem such as a death in the family or a problem at work. Emotional factors are often involved, and boredom is a frequent cause of inhibited sexual desire; so is anger, especially buried anger. Other factors are anxiety, guilt, low self-esteem, depression, and the fear of intimacy. Prolonged frustration from the lack of arousal or orgasm may result in low sexual desire. And a person who feels pressured into sex or feels guilty about saying "no" may become less and less interested in sex. Some people may be so fearful of sexual pleasure or closeness that they unconsciously prevent themselves from feeling sexual desire by developing a "turn-off" mechanism. By becoming angry, fearful, or distracted, they draw on the natural inhibiting mechanisms that suppress sexual desire, and the lack of desire appears to emerge automatically.

Emphasis should not necessarily be placed solely on the psychological causes of this disorder because the cause can also be physiological. For example, in women who have experienced menopause, low estrogen levels, or lack of vaginal lubrication can reduce sexual feelings or make sex painful. In fact, the literature seems to be moving away from the emphasis mainly on psychological causes, as promoted by Masters and Johnson, toward biomedical and organic causes of sexual disorders (Dennerstein & Hayes, 2005). Similarly, the issue of low sexual desire often stems from the fact that one partner simply has a higher level of desire than the other, and as a result, defines the partner with lower desire as having a disorder.

Aversion to sex refers to *anxiety, disgust, repulsion, and other negative emotions toward sex.* Although both men and women experience sexual aversion, it is more common among women. Individuals who are repelled by sex often have a history of childhood sexual abuse, such as incest, or have been victims of sexual assault. In some instances, such individuals have been subject to constant pressuring or bargaining for sex in a relationship. Repeated but unsuccessful attempts to please a sexual partner may eventually lead to the avoidance of sex. Finally, anxiety about conflicts in one's sexual identity or orientation may also create fear of sex (Masters et al., 1995).

Another type of sexual dysfunction is **inhibited sexual arousal,** which is *insufficient sexual arousal.* This disorder occurs most as **erectile inhibition** (*impotency*) and **inhibited vaginal lubrication** (*when insufficient vasocongestion and insufficient lubrication occur in women*). Men who suffer from inhibited sexual arousal usually have **secondary erectile inhibition**—that is, *they've previously experienced erections but are consistently unable to have an erection of sufficient firmness to penetrate the woman's vagina.* Most men have occasional difficulties with erections, usually because of fatigue or stress. It's only when this difficulty continues to occur or becomes distressing to the man or his partner that it should come to the attention of a professional. Many factors may contribute to erectile inhibition.

Physiological factors related to erectile inhibition include severe diabetes and the effect of certain drugs, especially alcohol, narcotics, amphetamines, and some prescribed medications. Worry and criticism from a partner may also lead to erectile inhibition. In most instances, erectile inhibition is only a passing problem, but sometimes these experiences may generate such concern and anxiety that they develop into a chronic pattern. The man's anxiety assumes the form of a "spectator's role." That is, instead of relaxing and letting his erection occur spontaneously, he watches and judges his own performance. Thus, his self-critical attitude and tenseness contribute to the erectile problem. Treatment consists of helping the man learn how to relax and let things happen. It's especially important not to overreact to the temporary loss of erection.

Inhibited vaginal lubrication in the woman is similar to the man's lack of erection because in both cases *insufficient vasocongestion occurs.* Normally, during sexual stimulation the congestion of blood vessels causes the vaginal walls to secrete droplets of fluid, which eventually form a shiny film on the walls of the vagina. Lack of lubrication doesn't always mean something is wrong. Frequently, the woman is not sufficiently stimulated. Also, during prolonged intercourse with lengthy plateau periods the woman may have a decrease in vaginal lubrication. In such instances, increased stimulation of the woman's clitoris or other parts of her body may help to increase vaginal lubrication. Older women who have passed the age of menopause sometimes supplement their vaginal lubrication by adding small amounts of vaginal jelly or use a cream containing estradiol (by prescription from a physician) to enhance the thickness of their thinning vaginal walls.

The most common difficulty of the orgasmic phase in the sexual response cycle is **premature** (*early orgasm in a man*) or **retarded ejaculation** (*the delay or absence of orgasm in a man*) and *delay or absence of orgasm (for the woman),* known as **female orgasmic disorder.** Premature ejaculation consists of experiencing orgasm so quickly that the man's enjoyment of sex is significantly lessened or his partner is not contented. It is a common problem for men; as many as half of the cases of erectile disorder may be due to organic factors (Richardson, 1991). Another common reason is that men have become accustomed to experiencing orgasm quickly so as to demonstrate their sexual prowess or avoid discovery of the couple having sex. Fortunately, this condition is readily treatable through such measures as the stop-start technique in which the man, usually with the aid of his partner, practices recognizing the sensations of impending orgasm and momentarily stops stimulation until he gradually learns to delay ejaculation.

The most common problems for women are slowness or inability to experience orgasm. Because orgasm is a reflex, an involuntary reaction, and differs considerably from one individual to another, it may help to see this problem in the context of women's overall sexual response. On one extreme are the women who have never climaxed at all. Next are the women who require intense clitoral stimulation for orgasm. Third are women who need direct clitoral stimulation but are able to climax with their partners. Also near the middle are women who can climax during sex but only after lengthy and vigorous stimulation. Near the upper range are women who require only brief penetration to climax, and at the very extreme are the women who can experience orgasm via fantasy or breast stimulation alone.

Women who have never experienced orgasm sometimes lack knowledge of their own sexual response cycle, something that is often learned by other women through masturbation. These women may become orgasmic by minimizing their inhibitions and by maximizing their sexual stimulation through masturbation. A more common issue is slowness or failure to climax through intercourse with a partner. This problem is not surprising, considering that orgasm is usually triggered through sensory stimulation of the clitoral area, which is accomplished only indirectly during intercourse. Consequently, only about one-half of women experience orgasm regularly through intercourse (Masters et al., 1995). Those who prefer vaginal orgasm and are unable to experience it may need more intense thrusting on the man's part.

There are many more women who need direct clitoral stimulation, either by manual or oral stimulation from the man or who prefer self-stimulation, in addition to the penile-vaginal thrusting during intercourse to reach climax. Women frequently complain that men don't know how to provide clitoral stimulation. Men tend to be impatient, rubbing the clitoris directly or too long, thereby irritating it. Women usually prefer a more indirect, playful approach, which may include caressing one side of the clitoral shaft or use of an indirect, circular motion of the whole clitoral area. Keep in mind that even healthy, sexually experienced women do not always reach orgasm, either because of fatigue or temporary, situational factors. Also bear in mind that this need not necessarily be a problem. As you recall from the chapter on aging (Chapter 3), Viagra and other medications are designed to help alleviate some of these sexual dysfunctions.

Contraception

The availability and use of reliable birth control and contraceptive methods has become increasingly important in recent years for several reasons, especially because half of all pregnancies are unplanned (Guttmacher Institute, 2004) and because of the deadly AIDS epidemic. Although Carol liked Jeff very much, she knew she was not ready to have his children or to marry him. Even among married couples, there's a tendency to have planned and wanted children.

U.S. women are not particularly happy with the contraceptive choices available to them. They also are not happy that the burden of birth control typically falls on them, with fewer methods available to men. As their relationship progressed, Carol and Jeff had several discussions about birth control. Jeff wanted Carol to start using birth-control pills; she replied that she did not want to do so and that he should just buy condoms. Unlike Carol, most women have tried several contraceptive methods in the search for one that suits them best, but they feel that every method requires tradeoffs among safety, convenience, and effectiveness. What most women and men want are birth-control methods that do not require them to make tradeoffs. The effectiveness of the various contraceptives, along with their general type and a brief description, are shown in Table 11–1. Typically, condoms and

TABLE 11–1
COMPARATIVE EFFECTIVENESS OF BIRTH-CONTROL METHODS

Contraceptive Type	Definition	Type	Failure Rate
Birth-Control Pill (Oral Contraceptive)	A hormonal pill taken daily to prevent ovulation or fertilization.	Hormonal	8%
Implants	Small capsules inserted into the arm that release hormones to prevent ovulation.	Hormonal	<1%
Injection	An injection of a hormone that prevents ovulation.	Hormonal	3%
Emergency Contraception	An emergency, high dose of birth-control pills taken within 72 hours (three days) of unprotected sex.	Hormonal	25%
IUD	A T-shaped, plastic device placed inside the uterus that contains copper or hormones.	Hormonal	<1%
Male Condom	A thin, latex or polyurethane sheath that covers the penis.	Barrier	15%
Female Condom	A polyurethane sheath or pouch that lines the vagina.	Barrier	21%
Cervical Cap	A small rubber or plastic cup that fits over the cervix	Barrier	16–32%
Diaphragm	A round rubber dome inserted inside the vagina to cover the cervix.	Barrier	16%
Contraceptive Sponge	A foam sponge containing spermicide placed inside the vagina.	Barrier	16–32%
Spermicide	A cream, foam, jelly, or insert that kills sperm.	Barrier	29%
Natural Family Planning	Avoiding sexual intercourse near the time of ovulation, when pregnancy is most likely to occur.	Other	25%
Sterilization	A permanent, surgical procedure that blocks the pathways of egg or sperm.	Other	<2%

SOURCE: U.S. Department of Health and Human Services. *Sexual development and health: Issues.* http://www.4parents.gov/topics/contraception.htm.

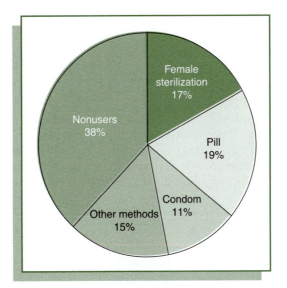

FIGURE 11–1

Current contraceptive status of Americans.

SOURCE: Mosher, W. D., Martinez, G. M., Chandra, A., Abma, J. C. and Willson, S. J. (2004). Use of contraception and use of family planning services in the United States: 1982–2002. Advance Data: From Health and Vital Statistics, 1–46.

birth-control pills are most popular among people in their teens and 20s. It is important for couples to choose the method of protection that suits them best.

Shared responsibility for contraception can enhance a relationship. When one partner takes an active interest in contraception, the other is less likely to feel resentment over assuming all the responsibility. Men and women can share responsibility for contraception in several ways. An important step is discussing the matter of protection or prevention before first engaging in intercourse. Unfortunately, this initial step is rarely taken, mostly because of the fear of spoiling the spontaneity of sex. Figure 11–1 depicts the most popular methods of birth control that Americans have settled on for now. Note that nonusers included women hoping to become pregnant, women not currently engaging in intercourse, and women already sterile due to surgery. In the large "other methods" category, male sterilization was a common method. For more in-depth information on birth control, go to Guttmacher.org.

Sexually Transmitted Diseases

When Jeff and Carol first started having sex, they did not discuss whether each of them was sexually healthy. Carol, in particular, did not know that Jeff had had a variety of other sex partners, each of whom could have been a risk to Carol as well as Jeff. As one sex educator was fond of stating, "You are having sex with everyone your sex partner has had sex with," the gist of which is that you need to know your sex partner's or partners' histories. Many **sexually transmitted diseases (STDs),** a broader and less value-laden term than *venereal disease, may be transmitted primarily through sexual interaction.* Although many of these diseases can be treated successfully, many are on the rise because of increased sexual activity and a tendency to have more than one sexual partner, especially during one's youth. The incidence of STDs is highest among those in the 20- to 24-year-old group, with the next highest incidence among those in the 15- to 19-year-old group and then among the 25- to 29-year-olds. Those age groups represent many traditional college students or recent college graduates.

Gonorrhea is a *common sexually transmitted bacterial infection that sometimes produces a cloudy, smelly discharge and a burning sensation upon urination.* Gonorrhea increased dramatically through the 1960s and 1970s, but the trend has slowed (CDC, 2002a). Nonetheless, there are over 700,000 new cases reported each year (CDC, 2009). A condom may help prevent the transmission of gonorrhea during intercourse, but it doesn't guarantee immunity. Early symptoms in men include a bad-smelling, cloudy discharge from the penis and a burning sensation during urination. Many women fail to seek treatment because they have so few early symptoms that they don't realize they are infected. Untreated gonorrhea is the single most common cause of sterility among men. Women with untreated gonorrhea may experience inflammation of the fallopian tubes, infertility, birth malformations, or menstrual disorders. Fortunately, in most cases, when it is discovered, it is easily treated with penicillin.

Chlamydia—*a bacterium that is spread by sexual contact and that affects both males and females*—has rapidly become one of the most common sexually transmitted diseases and continues to be widespread (CDC, 2002a). In 2006, there were over 1 million cases of chlamydia reported to the government, although this number is thought to be grossly underestimated. As many as 2.3 million Americans may be infected each year (CDC, 2009). An estimated 10 percent of all college students are affected by this disease. A condom can help prevent the spread of chlamydia.

Men who contract the infection have symptoms similar to gonorrhea, such as a discharge from the penis and a mild burning sensation during urination. Women with chlamydia infections show little or no symptoms and are often unaware of the disease until they are informed by an infected partner. On the other hand, a woman may have the infection for a long time, during which period she may pass it on to her sexual partners. If left untreated in women, it may result in cervical inflammation or pelvic inflammatory disease and, if a woman is pregnant, it may cause eye damage to infants at birth. In men, it may spread to the prostate. It is important that an infected person get a laboratory diagnosis before receiving treatment because the symptoms are often confused with those of gonorrhea, though the disease is usually treated with a different drug, tetracycline, rather than penicillin as is used in gonorrhea.

Genital herpes is *one of several herpes viral infections (herpes simplex virus) that are primarily transmitted through sexual contact.* It has increased dramatically in recent years, with over 45 million (or 1 out of 5) Americans currently infected (CDC, 2009). Symptoms usually appear within several days after sexual contact with an infected partner: one or more small, red, painful bumps (papules) in the genital area, such as on the man's penis and the woman's labia and inner vaginal walls. These bumps change into blisters, which eventually rupture into painful open sores. The person continues to be contagious throughout this time. In addition to the periodic discomfort, genital herpes can have serious complications. Pregnant women may require a cesarean section if active herpes is in the birth canal at the time of delivery. Cervical cancer is associated with HPV. CDC website indicates that genital herpes is associated with a higher likelihood of contracting HIV. To date, there is no real cure for genital herpes, but medical researchers are pursuing effective treatments. Current treatment consists of the drugs that reduce discomfort and assists healing during an outbreak.

Syphilis, though less common now than herpes and gonorrhea (CDC, 2002a), is a far more serious disease. *Syphilis is caused by a spiral-shaped bacterium, or spirochete.* Although fewer than 36,000 new cases of syphilis are recorded each year, the actual incidence is thought to be much higher. Syphilis is caused when the spiral-shaped bacteria are transmitted through sexual contact. It is not transmitted exclusively by vaginal sex; other organs of the body can be the sites of entry. The early signs of syphilis are painless sores at the place of sexual contact, usually the man's penis and the inner walls of the woman's vagina or cervix in heterosexual couples. Although the sores usually disappear within a month or two, in later stages, a skin rash and other sores may appear, along with sores on other parts of the body. These symptoms eventually disappear, but if the disease is left untreated, it may progress to an advanced stage, causing brain damage, heart failure, blindness, or paralysis. Fortunately, syphilis is readily detected through a blood test, and there is a highly effective treatment when it is detected in its *early* stages.

Compared to other STDs, **AIDS** (*acquired immune deficiency syndrome, which is caused by a virus known as HIV and transmitted primarily through body fluids*) is a fairly new disease by historic standards that has achieved national and worldwide prominence in recent years because of its growing threat. Also in comparison to other STDs, AIDS is far more deadly. Recent statistics indicate that more than 1 million persons in the United States had been diagnosed with the AIDS virus and more than 500,000 of them had died (CDC, 2009). Public health officials believe that the numbers are even greater than this; a large number of people have AIDS but do not yet know it. Knowing about AIDS, then, might literally save your life. To test your knowledge, take the AIDS Quiz in Activity 11–2 (page 270).

People who are initially infected generally show no symptoms and have no antibodies to the disease, so blood tests may come back negative. Individuals can carry this disease and be asymptomatic for long periods of time, years in fact. Because the AIDS virus destroys the T-helper cells in the body's immune system, infections that would ordinarily be less harmful to a person with a normal immune system can produce devastating, ultimately lethal diseases in the person with AIDS—for example, a common cold. This is often when it becomes apparent that the individual has AIDS. By this time it may be too late for the infected individual's sex partners; they may have already contracted the illness.

Although AIDS or HIV is classified as a sexually transmitted disease, it is communicated through blood or blood products containing the virus. As such, AIDS can be transmitted in ways other than sexual activity, such as sharing needles. Of note, the risk of catching AIDS through blood transfusions has diminished considerably because of more careful screening of blood donors and programs for intravenous drug users. Infection with other STDs increases the transmission probability for HIV. By all indications, HIV does not readily penetrate intact body surfaces, so there is little danger of getting it through a kiss, a sneeze, a handshake, or a toilet seat. Instead, HIV is acquired by direct exposure of one's bloodstream to the virus, which is carried by body fluids—notably blood and semen. The stereotype in the United States is that HIV or AIDS is a gay man's disease. However, HIV can also be transmitted through vaginal intercourse, from men to women or, less commonly, from women to men. Gay men represent the largest group living with AIDS (50 percent of all AIDS patients) followed by heterosexuals (33 percent), and intravenous drug users (16 percent). Of all adults in the United States, African Americans (49 percent of cases) and Whites (30 percent of all cases) have been hardest hit by this epidemic (CDC, 2009).

No single pattern of symptoms fits all cases of AIDS. Some common symptoms include a progressive, unexplained weight loss; persistent fever (often accompanied by night sweats); swollen lymph nodes in the neck, armpits, and groin; reddish purple spots on the skin; chronic fatigue; and unexplained diarrhea or bloody stools. Symptoms may

ACTIVITY 11–2

AIDS QUIZ

Which of the following statements are true?

1. You can tell by looking that someone has the AIDS virus.

2. People cannot become infected with the HIV virus by donating blood.

3. The AIDS virus can enter the body through the vagina, penis, rectum, or mouth.

4. It's possible to get the AIDS virus from hugging, kissing, or a toilet seat.

5. Condoms are an effective but not a foolproof way to prevent the spread of the AIDS virus.

6. The AIDS virus may live in the human body for years before symptoms actually appear.

7. The AIDS virus may be spread through sneezing and coughing.

8. Any unprotected person can become infected with the AIDS virus through sexual intercourse.

9. If you think you've been exposed to the AIDS virus, you should get an AIDS test.

10. Presently, there is no cure for AIDS.

Answers: Numbers 1, 4, and 7 are false. The others are true.

SOURCE: *Understanding AIDS* (1988). (HHS Publication No. 88-8404). Washington, DC: U.S. Government Printing Office.

remain unchanged for months or may be quickly followed by additional infections. There are psychological symptoms as well because HIV has a direct effect on the central nervous system (Matlin, 1999). These symptoms include altering the neurotransmitter dopamine, as well as cognitive problems such as difficulty remembering and paying attention. People afflicted with AIDS tend to have one overwhelming infection after another until their immune system gives out. AIDS in the past was usually fatal, though with today's modern cocktails of medication some individuals are surviving much longer.

People can reduce their risk for AIDS by following some practical guidelines, such as those shown in Box 11–2. Using latex condoms is a good start. Research has demonstrated that although college students and others seem to possess knowledge about the transmission of AIDS, their behaviors, such as engaging in casual sex, leave them at risk (Roberts & Kennedy, 2006). As psychologists know, behaviors do not always follow from attitudes. Ultimately, of course, the surest way to prevent the infection will be the development of a vaccine. Although research efforts are being intensified, there are no guarantees, and a vaccine may very well take a long time. Meanwhile, the threat of AIDS will and should be a major influence on people's sexual habits and lifestyles for the foreseeable future.

Box 11–2

HOW TO REDUCE YOUR RISK OF GETTING AIDS

You can reduce your risk of getting AIDS by following these guidelines:

- Avoid sexual contact with people known to have AIDS or suspected of having AIDS.

- Do not use intravenous or other illicit drugs. If you use intravenous drugs, do not share needles or syringes (boiling does not guarantee sterility).

- Do not have sex with people who use intravenous drugs.

- Avoid anal intercourse, with or without the use of condoms.

- Avoid oral contact with semen.

- Do not have sex with prostitutes.

- Have sex only with someone you know well, preferably a person who has not had multiple sex partners. *Always* ask your partners about their sex histories.

- Use *latex* condoms during sexual intercourse. Condoms are an effective, though by no means foolproof, way of preventing the spread of AIDS.

Sexual Victimization

Another issue that attracts public concern is **sexual victimization,** which *occurs when a person is coerced to engage in sexual acts under duress or force.* To go back to our opening vignette, Carol was fortunate that she found Jeff, who turned out to be a loving, sensitive man. Other people are not so fortunate; they become victims of sexual exploitation when they are forced to comply with sexual acts under duress. Sexual victimization may take many forms, ranging from the sexual abuse of a child by a parent, relative, or family friend to an adult who feels coerced to engage in offensive sexual acts by his or her partner. In this section, we'll focus on two particularly exploitative forms of sexual victimization: sexual abuse of children and rape.

Sexual Abuse of Children.   Approximately 90,000 children are victims of sexual abuse every year (Finkelhor & Jones, 2004). Most often the abuser is a family member, close relative, or friend—usually a man. Women can also sexually abuse children, and their abuse can be just as severe (Orange & Brodwin, 2005). Not uncommonly, the abuser has been a victim of sexual abuse as a child (Prentky, Knight, & Lee, 2006). In many instances, sexual abuse is not limited to a single episode and may not involve physical force. Sexual interactions generally consist of touching and fondling the genitals of the child, though some child molesters may engage in intercourse. Sexual abuse is most likely to involve prepubescent children between 9 and 12 years of age.

The immediate effects of child sexual abuse include increased anxiety, anger, eating or sleep disturbances, guilt, withdrawal, and other psychological problems of adjustment (Jumper, 1995). Abused children are sometimes preoccupied with sex, as seen in an unusual interest in the sex organs, sex play, and nudity. They're also likely to exhibit a host of physical complaints, such as rashes, headaches, and vomiting, all without medical explanation. The child's emotional trauma can be magnified when parents overreact to the discovery of sexual abuse. It is important, however, that parents show sufficient concern, such as making certain the child is not left alone with the suspected abuser as well as reporting incidents of sexual abuse to the police. Above all, the child needs to know that the parents will protect the child from other abuse and that the parents still love the child.

In adulthood, even when there are no serious psychological problems, victims of sexual abuse often have other problems, such as difficulty engaging in sex or compulsively engaging in sex. Also, abused women may feel isolated and distrustful of men. They're likely to feel anxious, depressed, and guilt-ridden. One of the most disturbing findings is the effect childhood sexual abuse has on the next generation. Boys who are abused are at increased risk of becoming child molesters themselves, and girls are more likely to produce children who are abused. Fortunately, most victims of childhood sexual abuse—and molesters—can benefit from psychotherapy.

Child Pornography.   Child pornography—in fact, all pornography—has been around for centuries. However, the Internet has greatly increased the possibility that more and more people have access to it despite the fact that *all* states have laws against it. **Child pornography** is *a visual depiction of a minor engaging in sexually explicit conduct, especially one lacking serious literary, artistic, political, or scientific value.* Most children depicted in pornography are girls between the ages of 6 and 12. The main exploiters or consumers of child pornography are White, unmarried men older than 25 years of age, although individuals attracted to child pornography come from all economic and educational levels and all types of communities. Some, but not all, consumers have criminal histories and are socially isolated (National Center for Missing and Exploited Children, 2006).

Children engaged in these activities are altered forever, not just by the exploitation but by the fact that the pornographer, using modern technology, can keep reproducing the images of the child over and over again. The pornographer can also use these images to blackmail the child into silence. These children not only suffer physical trauma such as bruising and STDs but also experience depression, withdrawal, anger, and mental disorders (National Center for Missing and Exploited Children, 2006). These effects can linger into adulthood if left untreated.

Rape.   **Rape**—*sexual intercourse under conditions of actual or threatened force that overcome the victim's resistance*—has long been a problem in American society. Although the rape of males has increased in recent years, the overwhelming majority of rapes involve male rapists and female victims. One of the most disturbing findings is that almost half of all rape victims are younger than 18 at the time of the attack (Rape, Abuse, and Incest National Network [RAINN], 2006b). Equally unsettling is the fact that only a few rapes are ever reported to the police. Contrary to popular myth that strangers hiding in bushes commit rape, most rapes are committed by *someone known to the victim* (RAINN).

Date rape—*coercive sexual activity that occurs during a date*—has become a widespread problem on many college campuses and elsewhere. However, victims (women) of date rape are often reluctant to label such assaults rape, mostly because of the common misconception that rape must be committed by a stranger under conditions of extreme force. "Force," however, means something different to each sex. Women tend to say they were physically coerced to have sex, whereas men are more apt to feel they were responding to psychological pressures. (Box 11–3 discusses other misconceptions or myths about rape.) Such gender differences are also reflected in the long-term effects of rape. The majority of women feel that the date rape had a long-term impact on them, whereas most men disbelieve such effects.

Studies of rape victims show that rape usually has a devastating effect on the victim's mental health (RAINN, 2006a). Almost one-third of all rape victims develop rape-related posttraumatic stress disorder (RR-PTSD) sometime during their lives. In turn, RR-PTSD dramatically increases the victim's risk for major alcohol and drug abuse problems. Rape survivors may experience a variety of emotional repercussions in two phases. The acute phase begins immediately after the assault and may continue for hours, days, or weeks. During the first few hours after being assaulted, the woman may react in an expressive manner—crying and being very upset. Or in some instances, a woman may maintain a controlled, subdued manner and only later become aware of her feelings. Victims commonly report anxiety, shame, anger, guilt, self-blame, and a sense of powerlessness. Physical symptoms include headaches, nausea, premenstrual disturbance, and pain syndromes.

Box 11–3

MYTHS ABOUT SEXUAL ASSAULT

Myth 1: *Victims provoke sexual assaults when they dress provocatively or act in a promiscuous manner.*

Fact: Rape and sexual assault are crimes of violence and control that stem from a person's determination to exercise power over another. Neither provocative dress nor promiscuous behavior is an invitation for unwanted sexual activity.

Myth 2: *If a person goes to someone's room or house or goes to a bar, she assumes the risk of sexual assault. If something happens later, she can't claim that she was raped or sexually assaulted because she should have known not to go to those places.*

Fact: This "assumption of risk" wrongfully places the responsibility of the offender's actions on the victim. Even if a person went voluntarily to someone's residence or room and consented to engage in some sexual activity, it does not serve as a blanket consent for *all* sexual activity. When someone says "No" or "Stop," that means STOP. Sexual activity forced upon another without consent is sexual assault.

Myth 3: *It's not sexual assault if it happens after drinking or taking drugs.*

Fact: Being under the influence of alcohol or drugs is not an invitation for nonconsensual sexual activity. A person under the influence of drugs or alcohol *does not cause* others to assault her; *others choose* to take advantage of the situation and sexually assault her because she is in a vulnerable position. Many state laws hold that a person who is cognitively impaired due to the influence of drugs or alcohol is *not able to consent* to sexual activity.

Myth 4: *Rape can be avoided if women avoid dark alleys or other "dangerous" places where strangers might be hiding or lurking.*

Fact: Rape and sexual assault can occur at any time, in many places, to anyone. According to a report based on FBI data, almost 70 percent of sexual assaults reported to law enforcement occurred in the residence of the victim, the offender, or another individual.

Myth 5: *A person who has really been sexually assaulted will be hysterical.*

Fact: Victims of sexual violence exhibit a spectrum of responses to the assault, which can include calm, hysteria, withdrawal, anger, apathy, denial, and shock. Being sexually assaulted is a very traumatic experience. Reactions to the assault and the length of time needed to process through the experience vary with each person.

Myth 6: *All sexual assault victims will report the crime immediately to the police. If they do not report it or delay in reporting it, then they must have changed their minds after it happened, wanted revenge, or didn't want to look like they were sexually active.*

Fact: There are many reasons why a sexual assault victim may not report the assault to the police. It is not easy to talk about being sexually assaulted. The experience of retelling what happened may cause the person to relive the trauma. Other reasons for not immediately reporting the assault or not reporting it at all include fear of retaliation by the offender, fear of not being believed, fear of being blamed for the assault, fear of being "revictimized" if the case goes through the criminal justice system, belief that the offender will not be held accountable, wanting to forget the assault ever happened, not recognizing that what happened was sexual assault, shame, and/or shock. In fact, reporting a sexual assault incident to the police is

(continued)

Box 11–3 *(continued)*

the exception and not the norm. Victims can report a sexual assault to criminal justice authorities at any time so long as the incident is reported within the jurisdiction's statute of limitations.

Myth 7:　*Only young, pretty women are assaulted.*

Fact:　The belief that only young, pretty women are sexually assaulted stems from the myth that sexual assault is based on sex and physical attraction. Sexual assault is *a crime of power and control* and offenders often choose people whom they perceive as most vulnerable to attack or over whom they believe they can assert power. Sexual assault victims come from all walks of life.

Myth 8:　*It's only rape if the victim puts up a fight and resists.*

Fact:　Many states do not require a victim to resist in order to charge the offender with rape or sexual assault. In addition, there are many reasons why a victim of sexual assault would not fight or resist her attacker. She may feel that fighting or resisting will make her attacker angry, resulting in more severe injury. She may not fight or resist as a coping mechanism for dealing with the trauma of being sexually assaulted.

Myth 9:　*Someone can only be sexually assaulted if a weapon was involved.*

Fact:　In many cases of sexual assault, a weapon is not involved. The offender often uses physical strength, physical violence, intimidation, threats, or a combination of these tactics to overpower the victim. As pointed out above, most sexual assaults are perpetrated by someone known to the victim. An offender often uses the victim's trust developed through their relationship to create an opportunity to commit the sexual assault.

Myth 10:　*Rape is mostly an interracial crime.*

Fact:　The vast majority of violent crimes, which include sexual assaults and rapes, are intraracial, meaning the victim and the offender are of the same race. This is not true, however, for rapes and sexual assaults committed against Native American women. American Indian victims reported that approximately 8 in 10 rapes or sexual assaults were perpetrated by Whites. Native American women also experience a higher rate of sexual assault victimization than any other race.

SOURCE: U.S. Department of Justice, Office of Violence Against Women (2006). *Myths and facts about sexual violence.* http://www.usdoj.gov/ovw/MythsFactSexualViolence.htm

Nervousness and fear may continue into the second, reorganization phase, which may last for years. Women often fear retaliation by the rapist. They might also harbor negative feelings about sex. Some date rape victims greatly reduce the frequency of their sexual activity or discover that they have sexual disorders. Rape, therefore, is usually a very traumatic experience that interferes more with the psychological aspects of sexual activity than the physiological response. Fortunately, the passage of time, combined with gentle support from others and psychotherapy, can help to alleviate the effects of rape for many victims. Furthermore, improvements in the police and court system, which make them more sensitive to and supportive of rape victims, along with the establishment of rape victim advocate programs, not only increase the likelihood that victims will report the crime but also help them in making an effective recovery.

SUMMARY

MEN AND WOMEN

At the outset, the chapter helped you to understand that our attitudes about sex are often distorted by gender stereotypes. At the same time, the ongoing changes in gender roles in our society are giving rise to a healthier sexuality; for example, sexual intercourse is understood as something partners do together as equal participants. Personal communication about sexual matters tends to be more effective when partners express themselves clearly and listen to each other. Nowhere is sexual communication put to the test more than in initiating and refusing sex. Although the more emotionally expressive partner tends to initiate sex most of the time, couples whose partners share the initiator and refuser roles equally tend to have more satisfactory sex lives than other couples.

SEXUAL RESPONSIVENESS

There are five phases of the sexual response cycle: transition, excitement, plateau, orgasm, and resolution. A major difference between the sexes is the greater variation among women in the physiology and subjective awareness of orgasm, especially in the woman's ability to have several orgasms in quick succession. At the same time, individual differences tend to outweigh gender differences, so that each person needs to be understood and appreciated in terms of personal preferences. Some people now feel it is necessary to be in love to enjoy sex. Love, rather, can enrich sex, especially in long-term relationships.

PRACTICAL ISSUES

Common sexual dysfunctions include the lack of sexual desire, erectile inhibition and premature ejaculation in men, and inhibited vaginal lubrication and female orgasmic disorder in women. Each method of birth control has its advantages and disadvantages, with the final choice often involving a tradeoff among safety, convenience, and effectiveness. Sexually transmitted diseases, such as chlamydia, gonorrhea, genital herpes, and syphilis, continue to present a health hazard, although they can be effectively treated. In contrast, AIDS is a deadly disease that poses a growing threat. Although the majority of AIDS victims in the United States have been homosexuals and intravenous drug users, the risk of AIDS from heterosexual intercourse is increasing. Another problem attracting public concern is sexual victimization, including sexual abuse of children and rape. One of the most disturbing findings is that most rape victims are younger than 18, and the rapist is known by the victim. Although coercive sex continues to be a problem, improvements in the justice system, along with the establishment of sex victim advocate programs, increase the likelihood that victims will report the crime and be helped in making an effective recovery.

SELF-TEST

1. Which of the following is a destructive pattern of sexual communication?
   a. Contempt
   b. Withdrawal
   c. Criticism
   d. All of the above

2. The most important part of sexual communication is the partners'
   a. persuasive skills.
   b. use of questions.
   c. factual knowledge of sex.
   d. attitudes toward each other.

3. Married and unmarried couples alike tend to be more satisfied with their sex lives when the initiative for sexual intercourse is
   a. taken mostly by the man.
   b. shared equally by both partners.
   c. taken mostly by the woman.
   d. always taken by the man.

4. The sex fantasies of men and women
  a. are identical to one another.
  b. are different from one another.
  c. occur in the excitement phase.
  d. occur in the resolution phase.

5. Multiple orgasms are
  a. more common in women.
  b. experienced by most men.
  c. more common in men.
  d. equally common for men and women.

6. Is love necessary to a sexual relationship? Love
  a. is necessary to enjoy sex.
  b. must be experienced before orgasm is possible.
  c. enriches sex.
  d. interferes with the enjoyment of sex.

7. The most common sexual dysfunction among men during the orgasm phase of the sexual response cycle is
  a. premature or retarded ejaculation.
  b. inhibited sexual desire.
  c. difficulty maintaining an erection.
  d. inhibited sexual arousal.

8. Which of the following birth-control techniques has the best effectiveness rating?
  a. Cervical cap
  b. Condom
  c. Birth-control pills
  d. Diaphragm

9. The most common sexually transmitted disease in the United States is
  a. gonorrhea.
  b. genital herpes.
  c. AIDS.
  d. chlamydia.

10. Victims of childhood sexual abuse are most likely to be
  a. boys 13 to 15.
  b. children between 9 to 12.
  c. girls 3 to 7.
  d. children under 7.

EXERCISES

1. *Sexual communication.* What has been the most difficult part of sexual communication for you? Have you discovered your partner's sexual likes and dislikes? Do you have difficulty initiating sex? How well can you refuse an unwanted sexual invitation or accept rejection?

2. *How important is love for sex?* Do you feel two people can enjoy sex without being in love? Or do you feel people must be in love to have good sex? Write a short paragraph explaining your views about sex and love.

3. *Sharing sexual fantasies.* If you're married or sexually active in a secure relationship, share some of your sexual fantasies with your partner. Such sharing is usually more helpful when it is mutual. It may be wise to begin with mild fantasies that can help desensitize fears and embarrassment and enable you to judge the impact of such sharing on your partner as well as yourself. It's also best to avoid sharing fantasies that would shock your partner or threaten the relationship.

4. *Shared responsibility for contraception.* How do you feel about men sharing the responsibility for birth control? What are some of the pros and cons? Does it present any special problems for the woman?

5. *Sexual victimization.* Suppose you were asked to suggest ways to decrease the incidence of sexual victimization, for example, childhood sexual abuse and rape, in our society. Write a page or more describing the changes you would propose.

QUESTIONS FOR SELF-REFLECTION

1. When was the last time you read a book about sex by a recognized authority in the field?

2. How well do you and your partner communicate about sex? How can you improve your communications?

3. Do you and your partner share the initiative for sex? Or does one of you usually initiate sex?

4. Must physical hugging and touching always lead to sexual intercourse?

5. Are you aware of what is sexually arousing for your partner?

6. Do you and your partner agree about the relationship between sex and love?

7. Are you aware that an occasional sexual dysfunction may be due to emotional stress that particular day?

8. How safe is your method of contraception? Does your partner share your concerns about contraception?

9. Can you recognize the symptoms of prevalent STDs?

10. Are you familiar with the practical guidelines for avoiding AIDS?

FOR FURTHER INFORMATION

RECOMMENDED READINGS

COMFORT, A. (2002). *The joy of sex.* Victoria, BC, Canada: Crown Publishing. Fully revised and completely updated for the twenty-first century. This is a classic that swept in on the heels of the sexual revolution.

CROOKS, R. L., & BAUER, K. (2004). *Our sexuality.* Belmont, CA: Wadsworth. One of the leading books on all aspects of human sexuality.

DOMITRZ, M. (2005). *Voices of courage: Inspiration from survivors of sexual assault.* Greenfield, WI: Awareness Publications. You will read the stories of survivors of sexual assault. Their experiences and their recovery are made very real by means of their own essays, poems, and memoirs.

KAMINSKY, N. (2003). *Affirmative gay relationship.* Binghamton, NY: Haworth Press. The author takes gays and lesbians through the steps of finding a life partner.

WOODS, S. G. (2002). *Everything you need to know about STDs.* New York: Rosen. Important and timely information on sexually transmitted diseases.

WEBSITES AND THE INTERNET

http://www.ngltf.org   A good place to find information on gay and lesbian issues.

http://www.siecus.org   The site of the Sexuality Information and Education Council of the United States (SIECUS), a national, nonprofit organization that affirms sexuality as a natural and healthy part of living.

http://www.4parents.gov   A government website that guides parents through helpful information on a variety of topics, especially teen sexuality. The site provides helpful tips for parents who find discussing such topics with their children difficult.

http://www.arhp.org   A site maintained by the Association of Reproductive Health Professionals with much information about reproductive health.

http://www.sexuality.org/safesex.html#C2   A place to find quality information about safe sex. There is some fairly explicit information here, but it is presented in a no-nonsense style.

CHAPTER 12

Love and Commitment

Learning Objectives

After completing this chapter, you should be able to

1. Describe several theories about the nature of love.
2. Discuss the influence of cohabitation on marriage and divorce.
3. Discuss the factors that make for a happy and lasting committed relationship.
4. Distinguish between better and worse communication patterns couples use.
5. Identify several different ways couples attempt to manage conflict.
6. Describe the typical changes that occur in marriages and other committed relationships over time.
7. Understand what sexual orientation is and how it influences our partner choices.
8. Describe various aspects of the divorce experience.
9. Know what domestic violence or partner abuse is as well as its causes and consequences.
10. Discuss the challenges faced by single-parent and blended families.

David and Diane, both in their early 20s, have been going together for three years. They met in their college biology class. They're in love with each other and have discussed the possibility of living together as well as of marriage. Both left home and first took apartments with their high school friends who are attending the same college. Dave and Diane soon realized, however, that they could share an apartment, spend more time with each other, and save more money.

Having worked through many of the differences in their interests, they enjoy spending as much time together as their busy schedules permit. Because they attend some of the same classes, they also study together. Both want a close, rewarding relationship, in which they're best friends as well as lovers, but they're having some difficulty achieving it. Diane complains that David is preoccupied with his part-time automobile parts sales job. She also complains that when they are together, all he wants to do is watch sports on television. David argues that he is too tired to go to a movie or to dinner after attending classes, studying, and working. Even when they're together, Diane says David doesn't share his feelings with her. This trait has become especially troublesome when he's moody and won't explain why. In David's view, Diane doesn't understand that this is a critical stage in his plans to become a car dealership manager and that Diane is more concerned about getting married than about him and their careers. Also, David feels Diane is too possessive at times, for example, her recent jealousy over his casual friendship with a woman at the district sales office. David readily admits that talk of marriage at this point in his life makes him feel "trapped." Diane believes that David's feelings have been shaped, at least in part, by his parents' recent, messy divorce. Consequently, she worries about how committed David is to their relationship and about their future together.

LOVE AND INTIMACY

Like so many other couples in young adulthood, David and Diane want a great deal of closeness in their relationship. At the same time, they're having difficulty developing it partly because they've both grown up in families lacking the very warmth and intimacy they seek. Consequently, David feels uneasy when people get too close to him, and Diane worries about loved ones leaving her. Some couples grow in love and understanding and eventually achieve a satisfying relationship despite their different backgrounds and shortcomings. Other couples are not so fortunate. Faced with frustration and disillusionment, many of them simply split up. Countless others continue in conflict-laden relationships or empty marriages. Let's see what happens to David and Diane.

The Ingredients of Love

Psychologists recognize that **intimate relationships** (or *close relationships*) and friendships overlap to a considerable extent. Both lovers and friends initially seek out others who are similar to them (Lucas et al., 2004). Both types of couples enjoy each other's company, despite occasional disappointments. Individuals in both types of relationships generally accept each other as they are, without trying to make their partner over into a different person. We apparently want friends and lovers who can validate our self-concept (Murray, Holmes, & Griffin, 2000). Both friends and lovers know they can count on each other in times of need. Also, they can confide in each other without fear of betrayal. Friends and lovers understand each other and make allowances when the other person occasionally acts in an unexpected or annoying manner. Finally, research demonstrates that we want the same personal characteristics in friends and lovers—warmth, kindness, openness, acceptance, respect, trust, and understanding—but we prefer *higher* levels of these attributes in our lovers than in our friends (Beste, Bergner, & Nauta, 2003).

At the same time, love relationships are distinctively different from friendships. **Love** can be defined as *deep and tender feelings of affection for or attachment to one or more persons.* Essentially, it appears that love heightens the potential for both positive and negative aspects of close relationships, making love relationships not only more rewarding but also more frustrating. Typically, love relationships, but not friendships, are characterized by a fascination and preoccupation with their partners in an exclusive sexual relationship (Lucas et al., 2004). There is also intense caring for each other in love relationships, even more so than in friendships, for example, being an advocate for a lover and giving more of oneself. However, because of the greater exclusiveness and emotional involvement between them, lovers also experience greater conflict, distress, and mutual criticism in their relationships than do friends (Rogge, Bradbury, Hahlweg, Engl, & Thurmaier, 2006).

The Internet has certainly changed the way some individuals search for romantic partners. Box 12–1 discusses this new "marketplace" through the eyes of psychologists. Read it and then ponder whether you think this is a good way to meet potential lovers.

The intensely satisfying but unstable nature of love relationships is often attributed to a special variety of love—**romantic love**—*the strong, emotional attachment to a person of the opposite sex and, on occasion, the same sex*. Researchers have identified two main types of this oft sought after love: passionate and companionate. Passionate love best fits our notion of romantic love. **Passionate love** is *an intense emotional reaction to a*

Box 12–1

ROMANCE ON THE INTERNET

Today, there is a booming business related to meeting people in our mobile, technocratic world. Globally, revenues from Internet dating are approaching a billion dollars annually (Johnson, 2005). Moreover, the number of personal ads on the Internet has tripled, with the leading website, *Match.com,* experiencing 154 percent growth, with over 100 million members since 2000 (Donaldson-Evans, 2003; PR Newswire, 2009). Online personals allow users to market themselves to a very broad audience, to present themselves via a number of different media (e.g., prose, video), and to interact with potential dates fairly anonymously, via email, chat, and instant messaging (Gibbs, Ellison, & Heino, 2006). In fact, the Internet has revolutionized the way in which people search for prospective romantic partners (Whitty, 2008).

Perusing the personal ads provides a good window on interpersonal relationships in different cultures. For example, personal ads in China emphasize family and society whereas ads in America emphasize individualism (Parekh & Beresin, 2001). With regards to gender, both heterosexual men and women tend to emphasize personality, good looks, slimness, and professional careers (Lance, 1998). Homosexual men tend to place a strong emphasis on physical appearance, sexual relations, and health issues (Bartholome, Tewksbury, & Bruzzone, 2000; Phua, Hopper, & Vazquez, 2002).

Not all individuals posting personal ads on the Internet are interested in long-term relationships. The proliferation of "adult" oriented websites geared toward short-term liaisons, such as *AdultFriendFinder.com* and *AshleyMadison.com,* attest to this fact. Nevertheless, those who are seeking a partner to grow old with tend to be more honest, disclose more, and make their disclosures more consciously and intentionally than those not interested in enduring relationships. In terms of effectiveness (e.g., the ad resulted in an acquaintanceship), positive self-disclosure appears to be the most effective. Similarly, those who disclose a lot of personal information in ads are more likely not only to find success, but also to learn more about the recipient of the advertisement, perhaps due to the **norm of reciprocity** (defined as *an unwritten rule that guides reciprocal behavior related to the granting of favors*). For instance, analysis of online communication has revealed that when one participant disclosed more information about the self, the recipient also disclosed more (Gibbs et al., 2006).

However, when it comes to establishing a relationship, complete and total honesty does not always appear to be the best policy. Researchers have found that *greater* honesty actually has a *detrimental* effect on the establishment of long-term relationships, especially when revealing personal flaws. Interestingly, while the vast majority of individuals feel that they are honest about their own disclosures, they feel that others tend to misrepresent themselves (Gibbs et al., 2006). Taken as a whole, the research on Internet personal ads suggests that " . . . the Internet [is] a medium for identity manipulation . . . or at least selective self-presentation" (Gibbs et al., p. 169). Remember, although some online dating services claim that their matches are based on scientific strategies, the research design and sampling techniques of these sites have been shown to be seriously flawed (Houran, Lange, Rentfrow, & Bruckner, 2004). As the old saying goes, "Buyer beware."

potential romantic partner who may not even love you in return. This is the "head-over-heels" reaction some of us experience when we first realize we are in love. This type of love is what David and Diane first experienced. Within days of meeting each other, David had a desperate crush on Diane and, likewise, Diane soon "fell" for David. As is true of passionate love, they were initially blind to each other's foibles and faults (Neff & Karney, 2005).

Hatfield (1988) claims that three conditions must be met in order for individuals to *feel* they have fallen madly in love:

- The individuals must be exposed to romantic images (as in the media) and role models that lead to the expectation that love is possible.
- The individual must come into contact with an appropriate person to love. "Appropriate," of course, is culturally defined.
- Intense arousal must be present. For example, sexual excitement can change our arousal level, and we can confuse it with perceptions that we are in love.

Another type of love identified by Hatfield is **companionate love**, defined as *a loving but practical relationship based primarily on emotional closeness and commitment rather than physical, sexual intimacy.* This is a practical kind of love that involves trust, caring, and tolerance for the partner's flaws. Companionate love is more moderate emotionally than passionate love and it takes longer to develop as well. Companionate love tends to be more characteristic of long-term relationships, including many happy marriages and some friendships. Perhaps this kind of love had not yet developed between Diane and David, for they were becoming more critical of each other as their relationship evolved over time.

Rather than viewing love as dichotomy (romantic and companionate), Sternberg's (2004) **triangular theory of love** suggests that *love has three components, intimacy, passion, and commitment.* **Intimacy** is *the emotional aspect of love and includes closeness, sharing, communication, and support.* Intimacy tends to develop slowly in the beginning and then progress more steadily until it levels off and later declines. An apparent lack of intimacy may mean that the relationship is dying. Or intimacy may be present but taken for granted, requiring some disruption, such as a family crisis or separation, to make people more aware of how close they really are.

Passion, *the emotional or motivational aspect of love, involves physiological arousal and an intense desire to be united with the loved one.* Unlike intimacy, sexual motivation blossoms quickly. But after a while, you get used to it, or "habituated," so that increased exposure to the person no longer brings the arousal and satisfaction it once did. Worse still, when you break up with the person, you may experience withdrawal symptoms—depression, irritability, and loss of desire.

Commitment, *the cognitive aspect of love, includes both the short-term affirmation of your love for the person and the long-term commitment to maintain that love.* This may well be the aspect that was missing long term from Diane and David's relationship. Commitment usually develops in a more straightforward manner than does intimacy or passion. In long-lasting relationships, commitment increases gradually at first and then more rapidly. As the relationship continues, commitment levels off. If the relationship begins to weaken, the level of commitment will decline. And if the relationship falls apart, commitment falls back to zero. In contrast to romantic love, the love of a parent for a child usually is marked by a high and unconditional level of commitment.

Can you think of any other components of love that are missing from either of the theories mentioned above? Does one of these theories better describe your current or past love relationship? Why?

Many social scientists are discovering that love is a universal phenomenon (Hatfield & Rapson, 1993). However, its importance in helping us select appropriate others to whom to commit or to marry varies by culture. Elsewhere in this book we have discussed two main types of cultures: individualistic and collectivistic societies. The United States embraces a decidedly individualistic culture, whereas India, Japan, and other Asian countries promulgate collectivism. Dion and Dion (1993; 2005) propose that romantic love is more likely to be an important basis for marriage in individualistic than in collectivistic societies. Similarly, psychological intimacy in marriage is thought to be more important for marital satisfaction in individualistic than in collectivistic societies. Finally, although intimacy is important in individualistic marriages, intimacy can be more problematic because of individualism in such societies compared to collective societies.

Research supports some of these contentions. In general, individuals from individualistic cultures place more emphasis love as a basis for establishing a marriage, as compared individuals from collectivistic societies. Love is also a stronger reason for establishing a marriage in individualistic cultures than for dissolving a marriage. For example, in selecting marriage partners, individuals from the United States assigned the highest worth to love, whereas those from India emphasized love the least (Levine, Sato, Hashimoto, & Verma, 1995). In such cultures, rather than marrying the loved person or romantic partner, couples *learn* to love each other after they marry (Matsumoto, 2000). Interestingly, countries that do not emphasize romance in mate selection have lower divorce rates. Does this finding surprising you?

Love and Close Relationships

Diane sometimes accused David of being "just like his father," whom she judged to be lazy—a couch potato who would rather watch sports on TV than attend community events or help with housework. The way people approach close relationships as adults, as well as their view of love in general, can be a reflection of early childhood experiences. More specifically, childhood attachment to parents appears to influence adult attachment style to romantic partners (Kanemasa & Daibo, 2003). **Attachment style,** which means *our typical style of becoming involved with others,* can be divided into three main types—secure, avoidant, and anxious-ambivalent (Hazan & Shaver, 1994).

Securely attached people *believe it's easy to get close to others, and they report happy and trusting love relationships.* As adults, individuals these individuals demonstrate relatively positive images of romantic love and value the importance of relationships. Their romances last the longest and end in divorce least often. Many of them feel that romantic love never fades. People in this group see their parents as especially loving, responsive, and warm. Neither David nor Diane apparently was securely attached to his or her parents in childhood, but neither was willing to discuss this with the other.

Those who form **avoidant attachments** *feel uneasy when people get too close to them.* Because they fear intimacy, they have trouble trusting and depending on others and are prone to jealousy. They hold a cynical picture of love, believing that the head-over-heels romantic love depicted in movies and novels does not exist in real life. Instead, they feel

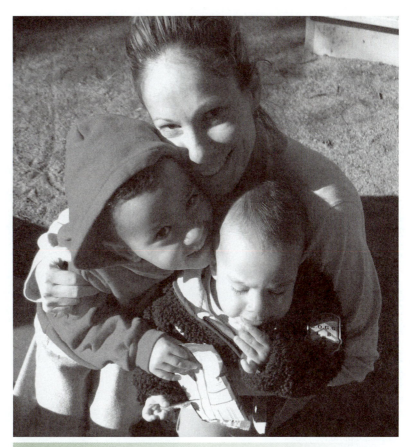

Individuals who as children were securely attached to their caregiver have longer lasting romantic relationships and are less likely to divorce.

it is rare to find someone to fall in love with, and even then romantic love seldom lasts. They also tend to regard romantic relationships as unimportant. Avoidant adults generally rate their parents rather harshly, seeing their mothers as not very likable, if not rejecting, and their fathers as uncaring.

The third group, called **anxious–ambivalent,** *includes people who desire a high level of closeness* that many partners don't seem willing to give. They also worry a lot about loved ones leaving them. Accordingly, these people experience emotional extremes as well as jealousy in their relationships. They find it easy to "fall in love" but difficult to find "true love." They generally give more mixed reports about their parents, relaying both extremely positive and extremely negative characteristics. Box 12–2 (page 286) discusses another important but more troubling type of relationship, partner abuse.

Some researchers have questioned whether factors in intimate relationships that are important to women are as important to men. Emotional intimacy is of almost equal importance for the happiness of both sexes. However, men and women often differ in how they experience intimacy. For women, emotional intimacy generally leads to greater happiness in their relationships as wives and mothers. Women also value respect from, open communication with, and fidelity by, their partners more than men do (Hall & Mosemak, 1999).

Box 12–2

PARTNER ABUSE

Despite better education and more laws, one in four U.S. women is estimated to experience domestic violence in her lifetime. Although men can be victims of domestic violence, women comprise 85 percent of all victims (National Coalition Against Domestic Violence [NCADV], 2005). Intimate partner violence makes up about 20 percent of all nonfatal violent crimes experienced by women (Rennison, 2003). Over half of all women and one-third of all men murdered are killed by their significant others (Kessler, Molnar, Feurer, & Applebaum, 2001).

Just what is partner abuse or domestic violence? NCADV (2005) provides this definition: **Battering** is *a pattern of behavior used to establish power and control over another person through fear and intimidation, often including the threat or use of violence. Battering happens when one person believes he or she is entitled to control another.*

Domestic violence against intimate partners can involve married or unmarried heterosexual women and men as well as lesbian and gay couples. Across cultures, the most common abusive situation involves a man and a woman, with the woman as the victim (Kim, Park, & Emery, 2009). This situation, in which a man is abusive toward a woman, results in the most negative consequences of all, such as serious physical injury and death (Russo, 2008). Trends in partner abuse and violence fortunately indicate that this type of violence may be declining (Rennison, 2003). Figure 12–1 depicts these trends in more detail.

Many theories have been developed to explain why some men use violence against their partners. These theories include family dysfunction, inadequate communication skills, provocation by women, stress, chemical dependency, lack of spirituality, and economic hardship. While such issues may be associated

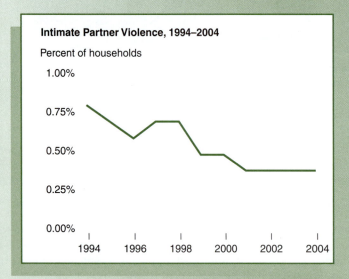

FIGURE 12–1
Intimate partner violence.

SOURCE: Bureau of Justice Statistics (April 2006). Crime and the Nation's Households, 2004. U.S. Department of Justice: Washington, DC.

(*continued*)

Box 12–2 (*continued*)

with battering of women, they are not the *true* causes. Why? Removing these associated factors will not end men's violence against women. The batterer begins and continues his behavior because violence is an effective method for gaining and keeping control over another person, and he unfortunately does not usually suffer adverse consequences as a result of his behavior. Risk factors that predict violence against a partner include unemployment, drug use, having witnessed similar violence as a child, low income, and low educational levels, especially for male abusers. Very few of these men are truly antisocial, but most lack good communication skills and have a high need to control and overpower their partners (Ehrensaft, 2009; Ingrassia & Beck, 1994). Cohabiting men are most likely to kill their partners, with the risk for abusive murder going down with the women's age (Shackelford & Mouzos, 2005).

Batterers come from all groups and backgrounds and from all personality profiles. However, some characteristics fit a general profile of a batterer:

- A batterer objectifies women. Overall, he sees women as property or sexual objects.

- A batterer has low self-esteem and feels powerless and ineffective in the world. He may appear successful, but inside he feels inadequate.

- A batterer externalizes the causes of his behavior. He blames his violence on circumstances such as stress, his partner's behavior, a "bad day," alcohol, or other factors.

- A batterer may be pleasant and charming between periods of violence and is often seen as a "nice guy" to outsiders.

- A batter provides behavioral warning signs, including extreme jealousy, possessiveness, a bad temper, unpredictability, cruelty to animals, and verbal abusiveness (NCADV, 2005).

Abusive partners frequently minimize or deny what they have done and frequently blame the victim. Much of the violence occurs in a predictable cycle or pattern, too. First is *the stage of escalation or tension building,* which many victims learn to recognize and thus try to avoid with such techniques as sidestepping certain topics or avoiding various conversations. The second stage in the cycle of violence is *the actual violence,* which is often explosive. The third stage, strangely enough, *involves the abuser begging for forgiveness,* offering love and promises never to batter again and even engaging in sex with the victim.

The victims of such abuse find extricating themselves from such relationships difficult, especially if they are financially dependent on the abuser (Fleury-Steiner, Bybee, Sullivan, Belknap, & Melton, 2006). Besides the horror of the physical bruises, victims often suffer loss of self-esteem, repeated threats of violence, debilitating depression, and stalking if an escape to safety is attempted. Given these, many victims find leaving the abuser to be impossible. Historically, violence against women has not been treated as a "real" crime. Thankfully, today assault, battering, and domestic violence are generally considered crimes. In recognition of this cycle and that victims are unable to escape, some states have passed laws mandating the arrest of batterers. Police, however, sometimes have little training in such matters or find domestic disputes unglamorous or downright dangerous (Moritsugu, Wong, & Duffy, 2010). There is increasing evidence, though, that battering or domestic violence is being taken more seriously by the justice system, with increased rates of police notification, arrest, and judicial involvement (Cho & Wilke, 2005). Sadly, when the police do intervene, they often arrest both parties—even the victim—rather than the primary aggressor (Finn, Blackwell, Stalans, Studdard, & Dugan, 2004).

Psychologists have tried to intervene in this cycle and typically work with the batterer. Some counselors offer group therapy for abusers in which the abusers confront each other. Other therapists offer anger management classes for abusers. Other therapists suggest treatment with medication.

In the meantime, the cycle of violence continues. If you are a victim or know a victim of partner violence, you can receive referral and support information by calling the National Victim Center (800-FYI-Call); there is also a website for more information: www.ncvc.org. Other resources include the National Coalition Against Domestic Violence (NCADV) at www.ncadv.org and The National Domestic Violence Hotline: 1-800-799-7233.

COMMITMENT

Once a couple has formed, the individuals often indicate their commitment to each other by living together (cohabitation) or becoming engaged and later married. In both cases, they often are committed to each other exclusively; that is, they do not date or feel romantic attraction to others. Let's look at each of these states in more detail.

Cohabitation

Couples who begin living together, as did Diane and David, often experience greater intimacy than other dating couples their age, at least in the short run. Although people of varying ages and prior marital statuses engage in **cohabitation** or *the practice of unmarried persons living together, sharing bed and board,* the largest proportion is in their 20s to 40s. Some drift into this type of arrangement, often keeping a place of their own (Peterson, 2002). Others deliberately set up a joint household from the outset, as did Diane and David. The number of cohabitating couples in the United States has grown sixfold from the 1970s (Smith, 2003). The last national census found that 5.5 million couples were living together, up from 3.2 million in 1990, with economics driving this increase (i.e., it is cheaper for two people to live together than apart) (Smock, Manning, & Porter, 2005). Some investigators state that cohabitation in the United States is now the most common path to marriage (Smock et al., 2005). Others note that cohabitation is far more common elsewhere, for example, Sweden (Kiernan, 2004).

Some people who cohabit have a different set of values, believing that relationships are breakable if they're not personally satisfying. In fact, early researchers identified the **cohabitation effect** (Guzzo, 2009), *where couples that cohabit first have greater marital instability than couples that do not cohabit.* Cohabitation often does not result in marriage, and, when it does, it is more likely to result in divorce (Rhoades, Stanley, & Markman, 2009). However, other factors, such as length of the cohabitation, reasons for cohabiting (e.g., a test of compatibility before marriage), and problem-solving ability appear to be stronger predictors of marital instability (Cohan & Kleinbaum, 2002). Many cohabiting couples can and do go on to successful marriages (Phillips & Sweeney, 2005).

About one-half of cohabiting couples eventually marry. Some researchers claim that it is men, in particular, who are less committed to the institution of marriage (Peterson, 2002) or even to cohabitation. As a result, they are more likely to stay single and simply cohabit or divorce once married rather than stay in a less-than-satisfying relationship. Some of these individuals tend to be independent-minded and believe that their right to personal happiness takes precedence over a marital relationship, or they do not have strong respect for marriage as a social tradition. At the same time, much of this research evidence reflects the increasing economic status of women, who may have less financial need to marry than in the past. Also, today there is a greater acceptance of sex outside of marriage and a greater emphasis on personal satisfaction in close relationships. Perhaps this was David and Diane's problem, even after they married.

Marriage and Other Committed Relationships

Although marriage as an institution is being challenged by alternative arrangements such as cohabitation, it is not going out of style. **Marriage** is *the state of being married, usually the legal union of two people.* Most people in the United States still want to marry, though they usually don't condemn someone who isn't married. There are other forms of commitment, too, such as common-law marriages (recognized in some states) and committed gay relationships. Some states as well as Canada allow marriage between same-sex couples. We may value marriage for heterosexual couples, but attitudes toward homosexual or gay marriages tend to vary immensely. While the issue of gay marriage is "emotionally charged and highly politicized" (Leiblum, 2004), the issue is advancing through U.S. society faster than other, similar issues, such as interracial marriage, did (Wilkinson & Kitzinger, 2005).

Although many Americans report that same-sex marriage undermines the traditional American family and/or their own religious beliefs, a majority of Americans do support some rights for same-sex civil unions, such as inheritance and access to the partner's health insurance (Brewer & Wilcox, 2005). About this societal division, Andrew Sullivan (2003) says, "Every day, if you're a gay person, you see amazing advances and terrifying setbacks. . . . Wal-Mart set rules . . . to protect its gay employees from discrimination [but] the Vatican comes out and announces that granting legal recognition to gay spouses will destroy the family and society" (p. 35). Most Americans also think children should be reared within a marriage. Marriage is seen as promoting the welfare of children and the stability of society. Ironically, this pits against each other the issues of the value of marriage to children and of gay parents raising children (Naples, 2004). The matters of gay marriage and gay parenting will likely continue to be debated in courtrooms, in legislative chambers, and at kitchen tables for years to come (Rosato, 2006).

All couples today in nearly all regions of the world tend to wait a bit longer to marry, with the median age of first marriages rising slightly each year. Consequently, many people marry during their 20s and 30s. Perhaps this is a positive trend, because the older people are when they marry, the longer the marriage lasts (CDC, 2001). The reasons for this are varied, but a rise in education and economic modernization are thought to explain this trend (Saardchom & Lemaire, 2005).

For the most part, heterosexuals and gays tend to marry or commit to partners of similar age, education, ethnic or social background, race, and religion. Much of this tendency reflects the ways we have been socialized as well as the opportunities for meeting people, with physical proximity increasing the chances for attraction. As our society becomes more mobile and diverse, however, people are marrying or committing to others who cross many of these familiar boundaries, because factors such as similar values rather than similar demographics play a more important role in today's world. According to Matsumoto (2000), these diverse marriages (e.g., intercultural marriages) are especially prone to conflicts about love and intimacy. Surprisingly, however, such marriages are *not* more divorce prone.

Many people tend to marry or make commitments to significant others out of mixed (multiple negative and positive) motives, many of them unclear even to themselves. The tradition of marriage, along with the social, legal, and especially economic advantages of marriage, plays a larger role than is commonly realized (Smock et al., 2005). When asked, though, most Americans characteristically say they marry because they are in love. Now that marriage is no longer necessary for economic survival, the satisfaction of sexual desire, or, for that matter, the rearing of children, love has become the major rationale for getting and staying married. Even upper-class couples and royalty, who have traditionally married for social reasons, now prefer marriages based on love.

Most American couples believe in voluntary marriage. **Voluntary marriages** are *ones based on the assumption that two people will remain married only as long as they are in love.* When they are no longer in love, it's mutually understood they will separate. This seemed

Although cultural and religious backgrounds can influence wedding ceremony and dress, love is still the primary reason for getting married in America.

to be David and Diane's mode of operating as well. As they came to understand that they no longer loved each other, divorce became a stronger option. When people marry or commit to a significant other on the basis of romantic love—with its emphasis on emotional and physical intimacy—it's no surprise so many relationships and marriages fail; that is, if the love diminishes, the marriage fails. On the other hand, the longer a couple lives together, especially in a satisfying, committed relationship, the more both partners come to value companionate love, with a greater emphasis on personal intimacy and commitment than physical attraction.

The alarming marital divorce rate, hovering at about 50 percent for some groups (Maher, 2003), has prompted social scientists to turn their attention to successful marriages and what makes them work. Until recently, marital "success" meant longevity, that is, how long the marriage lasted. Divorce was universally regarded as a failure on the part of both partners. However, the changes in values in recent years have shifted the emphasis to the *quality* of the marital relationship rather than its duration. Success in marriage is interpreted more in terms of marital satisfaction, especially in the relationship aspects of marriage, such as mature love, intimacy, and companionship. **Marital satisfaction** is *the sense of gratification and contentment in a marriage.* David and Diane's marital satisfaction was often quite low because they argued a great deal. Divorce is often taken to be the price one pays to end a dead or destructive relationship, often to seek a more satisfying one. Such changes pose some nagging questions. Must marital happiness exact such a high price? Can't people live in long-lasting relationships without becoming bored or having a devitalized relationship? In other words, is it possible to have marriages that are both happy *and* enduring? To test your attitudes about marriage, take the Marital Myths Quiz provided in Activity 12–1.

Let's first look at *new* marriages. What are they like? How can we predict whether a new marriage will survive? John Gottman and Sybil Carrere (2000) have longitudinally studied marriages. When a newly married couple argues—and most do—Gottman claims

---

ACTIVITY 12–1

MARITAL MYTHS

INSTRUCTIONS: *Some truisms about marriage follow. Indicate which of them you think are true (T) and which are false (F). Then check your responses by consulting the correct answers at the end of the chapter.*

1.	More than 9 out of 10 Americans eventually marry.	T	F
2.	Partners who live together before marriage are less apt to get divorced than those who did not do so.	T	F
3.	Marriage should be a 50–50 partnership.	T	F
4.	Husbands and wives should be best friends.	T	F
5.	Differences and incompatibilities between partners are the major causes of marital dissatisfaction.	T	F
6.	Married people are happier and healthier than single individuals.	T	F
7.	Most divorces are initiated by women.	T	F
8.	Extramarital affairs will destroy a marriage.	T	F
9.	Children are damaged more by a legal divorce than by remaining in an intact but unhappy home.	T	F
10.	Married people tend to live longer than unmarried people.	T	F

he can tell within 3 minutes whether the marriage will flourish or fail. Newlyweds heading for divorce start an argument by sending out hostile vibes through their tone of voice, facial gestures, and what they say. The biggest problems occur when the woman brings up an issue "harshly" and critically, and the man responds with great negativity. Other research has shown that women initiate discussion about relationship problems about 80 percent of the time (Peterson, 1999a).

Happy couples argue, but when they do, they use five times more positive than negative behaviors (Fincham, 2003). For example, when the wife is angry, the husband might inject humor into one of his responses. Such playfulness helps to reduce emotional tension caused by the conflict. Happy couples also accept the fact that they will have differences with which they will always have to cope. For instance, one partner might not be very talkative while the other partner prefers to engage in extensive conversations. Thus, the ability to tolerate these types of inevitable differences leads to happier marriages.

Other research exists on what keeps love alive. Becoming more attitudinally similar is one factor (Kalmijn, 2005). When a couple's attitudes are measured early in their relationships, the partners' attitudes may differ. However, with the passage of time there is attitude alignment, wherein their attitudes become more similar and, thus, less likely to cause arguments. An example of this is where the couple initially disagrees about methods of birth control (e.g., he wants her to use birth-control pills; she fears side effects and wants him to use condoms, which he hates). Later in the relationship, there may be more attitudinal similarity, with partners settling on a third type of birth control.

Because it is thought to serve as a strategy to keep the relationship alive, self-disclosure is also important. **Self-disclosure** is *the sharing of intimate or personal information with another.* Sprecher and Hendrick (2004) found that men and women indicate similar high levels of self-disclosure in close relationships. When high disclosure is present, the researchers established that there are high relationship esteem (i.e., confidence in the partner), good relationship quality, and high responsiveness between the partners. Couples who eventually marry typically maintain the same high levels of disclosure. Self-disclosure, then, is a good quality, so even though raising the issue about a partner's sexual history is sticky, it is often the safest route to safe sex and may even bolster the relationship.

On the other hand, self-disclosure carries the risks of rejection due to a particular disclosure and of ensuing insecurity. In order to feel secure in a relationship, people need to believe that their partners see qualities in them that merit attention, nurturance, and care (Murray, 2005). When one partner of a couple feels threatened and rejected, his or her self-esteem may diminish, which subsequently diminishes closeness. Murray suggests that only when people are able to quell their concerns about self-protection are they free to think and behave in ways that create the kinds of bonds that will satisfy their need for connectedness.

Gottman also claims there are certain emotions and styles that prove toxic for new marriages. Criticism, contempt, defensiveness, and withdrawal tend to be particularly destructive. Not being good friends is one other factor that destroys marriages—one partner does not give the other partner the benefit of the doubt in difficult times or remains emotionally disengaged in the relationship (Gottman & Carrere, 2000). Similarly, negative emotions can also end relationships or cause discord, especially men's negative emotions (Rauer & Volling, 2005).

The flip side of the question, then, is what characterizes long-term, satisfactory marriages. First, a major factor identified in almost every longitudinal study of marriage is "joint problem-solving ability." This factor is mentioned by over two-thirds of the highly satisfied couples but by one-third of the unsatisfied couples. Second, when asked specifically to cite the factors they believe contribute to the longevity of their relationship, almost half of the satisfied couples say they "have fun" together and cherish such experiences, yet fun, humor, and playfulness are not even mentioned by the mildly satisfied and unsatisfied couples.

Third, one of the best predictors of marital success is the quality of the couple's communication—even before marriage—presumably because it is more *how* differences and problems are handled than how frequently they occur. David and Diane thought they were good communicators before they were married, but perhaps they were not, because rather than discuss negative events, they both suppressed their anger and withdrew from one another until the pent-up anger made them explode in rage. Fourth, one of the strongest predictors of marital success is "affective affirmation"—the communication of loving, accepting attitudes or the unconditional approval of one's mate. Diane's sometimes sharp criticism of David's couch potato behavior certainly was not approving or affirming of him. Nor was David's taunting of Diane when she went into one of her "moods." We would predict that Diane and David need to improve their communications if they are to have a long and happy relationship.

Other factors found to contribute to long and happy relationships include empathic ability for understanding a partner's feelings, a good balance of time spent together and separately, a satisfying sexual relationship, and mutual willingness to make adjustments to each other (Schwartz, 2002). Of note, marital stability is good in the sense that research finds that marriage provides a protective factor to partners; that is, marriage, but not necessarily cohabitation, enhances one's psychological well-being (Kim & McKenry, 2002).

Such findings support the importance of companionate love in long-term happy marriages and other committed relationships. That is, happy couples are more apt to place importance on interpersonal intimacy and commitment to a lasting relationship than on physical satisfaction. Couples who are fortunate enough to sustain a vital sex life, more often because of the quality of their sex life than the frequency of intercourse, may experience **consummate love**—*the balanced combination of intimacy, commitment, and passion.*

ADJUSTING TO INTIMATE RELATIONSHIPS

Whether couples achieve a lasting, happy relationship depends to a large extent on what happens *after* they marry or commit to one another in some other way—over and above how well matched they are in such matters as compatibility. **Couple adjustment** means *the changes and adjustments in a couple's relationship during the course of their committed or married life.* Of great importance to couple adjustment is each partner's flexibility and willingness to transform, especially in our rapidly changing society. A major difference between today's couples and those of the past is the lack of clearly defined roles for each partner. The changing nature of gender roles creates problems for all types of couples as they settle down to live together. **Gender roles** refers *to the social and cultural expectations about what is appropriate for males and females.* Even the most mundane tasks may become a problem, as with David and Diane. Who cooks? Who takes out the trash? Who pays the bills? Getting along in a committed relationship, though, involves the larger questions of authority, fairness, power sharing, and fulfillment of needs.

Sharing Responsibilities

Partners, especially marriage partners, are sharing responsibilities to a greater degree today than in the past. As a result, the respective role expectations between partners, especially married couples, are becoming more flexible and functional. More women, for example, are sharing the provider role by working outside the home. Interestingly, women are better than men at preventing stress spillover between work and home (Martin, 1999). Men are expected to provide greater emotional support in the relationship, including help with child rearing. Decision making has also become more democratic, especially among dual-income couples.

A major area of adjustment for many couples concerns employment outside the home. Today, most women like the option of working outside the home and feel it helps their relationship and family. Realize, however, that household tasks and the amount of time needed to complete them are constant whether both individuals in a relationship work outside the home or not. In U.S. families, women overall perform 65 to 75 percent of the household chores. Diane often complained to David that after they started living together, she did 150 percent of the daily chores! David retorted that this was fair. He was going to school *and* working; she, on the other hand, was only attending school.

If women do work outside of the home, does this mean that they will do fewer chores or that their mates will assist with housework? Several studies demonstrate that women still do more housework than men even when the women work outside of the home (Sayer, 2005). Consequently, when the woman serves in other multiple roles such as child or parent care provider and is also employed, she might well feel exhausted (Streich, Casper, & Salvaggio, 2008). Besides her anger with David, this feeling will likely be one Diane experiences if and when she obtains a job.

Although egalitarian relationships seem to be the ideal, one difficulty that comes with the increased sharing of responsibilities is the issue of fairness. More specifically, there is a tendency for each partner to want greater rewards at no additional costs. Indeed, perceived inequity is one of the great instigators to conflict (Fincham, 2003). One person may want the partner to work to help pay the bills but still expect the partner to continue doing all the same chores as before. In turn, the other partner may want to keep most of his or her earnings but expect the other partner to help out more around the house. Research has shown that when husbands increase their share of the housework, marital quality improves for women but not for men (Amato, Johnson, Booth, & Rogers, 2003).

More couples need to learn means to resolve these issues so that domestic work is equitably distributed. Three interactive factors that boost men's housework performance are whether in their childhoods their mother worked, a father was present in the home, and the man currently is married (Gupta, 2006). Married men who live in divorce-friendly societies are also more likely to help with housework (Yodanis, 2005). Interestingly, relative to heterosexual couples, gay partners tended to assign household labor more fairly, resolve conflicts more constructively, and experience a more equal level of satisfaction with the relationship (Dunne, 2000; Kurdek, 2005). Overall, then, scientific research paints a more positive picture of gay and lesbian couples than popularly believed and indicates that they tend to be more similar to, than different from, heterosexual couples.

Communication and Conflict

These ongoing historic and marital changes in responsibilities make communication and conflict management even more important in committed relationships. Few committed couples never argue. Although many couples argue, the priorities of particular problems vary from couple to couple. For instance, some couples feel conflicts over money are one of their leading problems. Some regard sexual incompatibilities as the major problem. Other couples complain of unrealistic expectations, lack of affection, and power struggles. Other problems include issues related to child rearing, such as disciplinary style and basic childcare. Moreover, with the birth of a child comes a decline in passionate love and an increase in marital dissatisfaction (Puterbaugh, 2005). Other issues that create conflict are in-laws, romantic or sexual affairs, drug use, problematic drinking, money spending, and jealousy (Fincham, 2003; Yarab & Allgeier, 1997). However, the most common problem (appearing at the top or next to the top of almost every list) is difficulty in communication. Again and again, husbands and wives like David and Diane complain, "We just can't talk to each other." For example, adult children often find themselves sandwiched between caring for their aging parents and their own children as well as holding jobs (Lawrence, Goodnow, Woods, & Karantzas, 2002). Such multiple roles are often, but not always, stressful (Stephens & Franks, 1999). The stress might be miscommunicated or not communicated at all until it explodes in a fight. If members of a couple would discuss what is bothering them at the onset rather than waiting for the issue to escalate, there likely would be fewer fights in intimate relationships.

Why can't couples communicate? They usually communicate very well with their friends and siblings. Partners do talk to each other all the time. They say such things as "What are we having for dinner?" and "I'll be home later than usual tonight." This type of communication is easy enough. The failure in communication tends to occur at a deeper level of sharing feelings, expectations, intentions, and personal needs. It's in these areas that partners have trouble getting through to each other. In most instances both partners long for intimacy and tenderness. The price of being open, however, may be vulnerability. Settling into a kind of guarded communication, each partner may tend to hold back. These difficulties in communication are further compounded as couples try to mesh their lives more closely. As they become involved with each other, some areas of disagreement are inevitable, much as was true for Diane and David. As couples struggle to resolve their disagreements, the sparks can fly. Interestingly, anger is not always the most destructive emotion in marriage, since both happy and unhappy couples fight.

Making the Relationship Better

Some marital conflict prevention programs are available that couples can utilize *before* they marry (Halford, O'Donnell, Lizzio, & Wilson, 2006). Research has demonstrated that premarital education results in higher levels of satisfaction, better commitment to marriage, lower levels of conflict, and also reduced chances of divorce (Stanley, Amato, Johnson, & Markman, 2006). For those couples that marry and cannot alter their own relationship, after-the-fact couples therapy might be a viable solution (Wood, Crane, Schaalje, & Law, 2005). The assumption here is that conflict is not all bad. Indeed, conflict is an inevitable part of vital, close relationships; it may help individuals learn more about themselves and each other and may deepen their relationship. Stated a different way, marital discord can be a growth experience.

One approach advocated by counselors is emotion-focused therapy, which has been demonstrated to be the most effective of all therapies for relationship problems (Wood et al., 2005). **Emotion focused therapy** or **EFT** is *a cognitive therapy that provides a technique for changing basic thought and emotional patterns.* Specifically, the goal of EFT is to help partners feel securely connected by fostering feelings of safety, accessibility, and responsiveness. Couples are usually taught active listening, where one partner can paraphrase what the other has said, in order to encourage a better relational environment between them. Once the feelings of security and receptiveness develop, couples can better process and send clear messages to each other, see each other's perspective, and do collaborative problem solving (Johnson & Patz, 2003). The success rate for this form of therapy is claimed to be high, purportedly as high as 70 to 75 percent (Underwood, 2002a).

Although couples therapy cannot redeem all marriages, couples of younger ages, lower levels of depression, flexibility regarding gender roles, and egalitarian attitudes leave therapy the most satisfied. Likewise, couples in therapy who are similar in their coping strategies are more satisfied with their marriages than those whose coping strategies differ. Similarly, couples that use "repair attempts" (such as humor in mid-fight) have happier marriages in the end (Bray & Jouriles, 1995; Fincham, 2003; Gray-Little, Baucom, & Hamby, 1996).

David and Diane, rather than engage a family therapist, used another option—a family mediation service. **Mediation** is *intervention in a conflict by a neutral third party who assists the conflicting parties in managing or resolving their disputes.* Mediators, the neutral individuals, can manage more than family disputes, whether the conflicts are between married individuals or couples seeking to dissolve their marriages. For example, mediators are often used to intercede in neighborhood, school, consumer, and other disputes. Here the focus is on committed relationships, such as marriage. In family mediation, the mediator listens as both sides tell their stories and then tries to help them find concrete and mutually agreed-upon solutions to their problems. For example, Diane complained that David did little housework, and David defended himself by saying that he was tired from work. The mediator worked out an agreement that Diane would cook dinner and David would do the dishes each night. On evenings when they were too tired to prepare dinner and do the dishes, they would go out to an inexpensive restaurant and split the bill. Unfortunately, the process did not work well for David and Diane, but for other couples, family mediation has a remarkable success rate (varying from 80 percent to 90 percent), with most couples being satisfied with the process and complying with mediated agreements (Duffy, 1991). There are family mediators and mediation centers in every state in the United States; most large cities have their own centers. Mediation as an alternative to courts, especially when children are involved, has grown enormously in the last few years (Underwood, 2002b).

Sexuality

Partners such as newlyweds bring greater sexual knowledge and experience to their marriages today than in the past, but they're also more likely to judge their sex lives by higher standards. Couples today are engaging in sexual intercourse more frequently than couples did in the past (Smith, 2003), with an average of two to three times a week for couples in their 20s and 30s. They're also open to a wider array of sexual practices, use a greater variety of sexual positions, and engage in sex for a longer time.

The longer couples—unmarried and married alike—live together, the less frequently they have sexual intercourse (Brewis & Meyer, 2005; Smith, 2003). Reasons usually cited include the lack of time or physical energy. Perhaps a more important factor is the decline of sexual ardor because the partners have become "accustomed to each other." The decrease in physical vigor associated with aging is also a related factor, especially among couples in middle and late adulthood. Couples with children also complain about the lack of privacy. Actually, the longer couples are married, the more attention they pay to the *quality* of sex rather than to its frequency. Do couples have sex more frequently because they are happy in their marriage? Or does the frequency of sex serve to strengthen a couple's love? It's hard to tell. One point is clear: For most couples, though not necessarily all, a good sex life and a happy relationship go together.

Most couples aspire to the ideal of sexual monogamy, regardless of whether they adhere to it. But when asked if they've ever had sex outside of marriage, it's a different story. Today, researchers estimate that between 20 to 50 percent of U.S. women and 30 to 60 percent of U.S. men have engaged in extramarital sex (Vangelisti & Gerstenberger, 2004). Infidelity is both a cause and consequence of poor marital quality (Previti & Amato, 2004). Having had a high number of prior sex partners, being male, and thinking about sex several times a day are also predictors of marital affairs (Treas & Giesen, 2000).

Changes Over Time

Around the same time that David and Diane married, two of their friends from the same college, Reshia and Erwin, also married each other. After only two years of marital bliss, Diane and David's marriage goes steadily downhill. One squabble leads to another; within a few years they are headed to divorce court. On the other hand, their friends who married one another the same summer report that their marriage has become happier with each passing year. They are saddened to learn that their friends David and Diane are on the brink of divorce.

How do these patterns develop? What makes them persist? Is there any hope that unhappy marriages can be saved? Let's look at the communication and thought patterns in which happy and unhappy couples find themselves. Couples who are happy tend to make relationship-enhancing attributions for the partner's behaviors. Couples who are unhappy tend to make distress-enhancing attributions (Gordon, Friedman, Miller, & Gaertner, 2005). We can attribute the cause to the person, such as blaming traits, or to something external, such as to fate or to the situation. If a husband, for example, does something negative such as forget his wife's birthday, the wife can attribute the forgetfulness to the fact that her husband is unreliable and uncaring *or* so busy at work that he simply and unintentionally forgot. In happy couples, the wife makes the attribution that the husband is just plain busy and unintentionally forgot. In unhappy couples, the wife makes the attribution that the husband is unreliable and uncaring.

On the other hand, if a wife does something positive for her husband, such as surprise him at work with a birthday party, the attributions are the reverse. In the happy couple, the husband attributes the surprise to his wife's kind heart. In the unhappy couple, the husband assumes his wife merely wants to impress his coworkers or check up on him because she doesn't trust him. Research has shown that intentional negative trait attributions distance partners and hurt feelings (Vangelisti & Young, 2000). Thus, although attributions play a large role in causing and maintaining relationship distress, they can also play a role in relationship happiness.

The lesson here is that couples need to monitor the attributions they make toward each other early in their relationships. If they find themselves in the distress-maintaining attributional mode, they should talk about why they are making these attributions, decide what they can do to reverse the types of attributions they are making, and take other appropriate measures. Table 12–1 (page 298) provides another example of these attributional styles. Early in their marriage, Diane and David had unfortunately developed this negative attributional style.

TABLE 12–1

AN EXAMPLE OF ATTRIBUTIONS OF HAPPY AND UNHAPPY COUPLES

	In *Happy* Couples the Wife Says:	In *Unhappy* Couples the Wife Says:
Positive event: The husband remembers his wife's birthday with a present.	"He's so sweet; he never forgets my birthday."	"Hah, he's up to something; he never gives me gifts unless he wants something from me, like forgiveness."
Negative event: The husband forgets his wife's birthday.	"He hardly ever forgets: he must be having a hard week at work."	"That's just like him to forget; he never remembers events important to me."

DIVORCE AND ITS CONSEQUENCES

Diane and David eventually concluded that their marriage could not be salvaged. Unfortunately, like Diane and David's marriage, many marriages now end in **divorce,** *the legal dissolution of marriage.* The divorce rate among Americans has more than doubled in the past 40 years, with approximately one out of every two marriages now ending in divorce. Each year over 1 million couples get divorced, most of them within the first seven years of marriage (CDC, 2002b). Twenty percent of first marriages end within five years and 33 percent of first marriages end within 10 years (Maher, 2003). These data mean that by age 18, 40 percent of U.S. children will have experienced parental divorce (Greene, Anderson, Doyle, & Riedelbach, 2006).

Why the dramatic rise in the divorce rate in the United States? Many different reasons, ranging from the lack of preparation for marriage to fading religious values, have been put forth. A major factor has been the gradual shift away from the traditional notion that marriage is forever to the idea that the primary goal of marriage is happiness and fulfillment. This shift in values has also been accompanied by changes in the laws that make it easier for couples to get divorced.

The Divorce Experience

The decision to divorce usually comes after a long period of mutual alienation, often accompanied by a separation, in which both partners suffer from damaged self-esteem, hurt, and loneliness. This sounds like Diane and David, doesn't it? In some instances, the estranged couple may have sought help from professionals such as couples counselors, family therapists, or family mediators. Studies by psychologists and sociologists indicate that the wife is the key player in divorce and adjusting to it (Amato & Previti, 2003). As is true for dating relationships, in heterosexual relationships women are more likely to initiate the breakup than men (Helgeson, 1994). In fact, women make more specific plans and are more likely to implement their plans for divorce. Women also think more about divorce and talk to their friends during the decision making (Crane, Soderquist, & Gardner, 1995).

No matter how good or bad the relationship has been, the process of getting divorced is almost always painful (Hendrick, 2006), especially for those that did not initiate the legal dissolution of the marriage (Baum, 2007). Divorce and the end of a committed relationship, as in cohabitation, is a complex experience because so many things are happening at once. The partners tend to withdraw emotionally from each other or coexist with a great deal of mutual antagonism (Perilloux & Buss, 2008). The legal aspects of the breakup are not only expensive but emotionally draining as well, including the settlement of property, money, and child custody/visitation issues. Disapproval and rejection by friends, family members, and coworkers can also be distressing. Separating oneself from the influence of a former partner and becoming an autonomous social being again can be difficult. By way of example, David and Diane divorced after seven years of marriage. They both found it hard to reenter the world of dating and to set up and support independent households. These changes may be quite intimidating and draining at first, but some are potentially the most constructive aspects of divorce in that the individual may experience considerable personal growth (Barber, 2006). Nevertheless, it takes most people two or three years to recover fully from the distress of a divorce, and many do not recover completely (Lucas, 2005). Men typically come out of a breakup with only moderate financial declines while for women the consequences frequently prove more precipitous (Avellar & Smock, 2005). The increasing number of support groups available for divorced people helps to alleviate much of the loneliness and emotional pain that inevitably accompany divorce. Recognize also that for gay couples, the breakup of a long-term, committed relationship can be equally traumatic and distressing (Harkless & Fowers, 2005).

A divorce involving parents can be particularly painful for the parents *and* for the children (Wallerstein & Lewis, 2005). The courts tend to follow the principle of "the best interests of the child," which traditionally meant that custody was given to the primary nurturer, the wife. Today, there is a tendency to award **joint or shared custody** (*which usually means joint decision making about the child's care*) and in some cases to award custody solely to the father. The partner who is not granted residential custody of the children (i.e., the parent with whom the child does not reside) is usually granted certain visitation rights (Rohrbaugh, 2008).

Single-Parent Families

How children are affected by their parents' breakup varies considerably, depending on such factors as the intensity of the parental conflict, the child's personality, the age and sex of the child, whether the child is uprooted from familiar friends in the process, and the custodial parent–child relationship. Some psychologists argue that divorce makes children vulnerable to depression and other psychological disorders (Wallerstein & Lewis, 2005). On the other hand, studies show that parental discord before and after a divorce influences children's adjustment more powerfully than does the actual divorce (Bing, Nelson, & Wesolowski, 2009). Grandparents also suffer when their adult children divorce, because they may not be able to see their grandchildren as frequently as before or at all (Drew & Silverstein, 2007).

Divorce typically provides children with a double dose of stress. Immediately after their parents' divorce, many children feel resentful and depressed (Maher, 2003). Older children and adolescents are especially apt to exhibit heightened aggression. However, within a few years, most children do adjust to the new living arrangements. Then, about three to five years after the divorce, there may be a second dose of stress associated with either parent's remarriage (Dunn, O'Connor, & Cheng, 2005). Because most divorced mothers and fathers remarry (CDC, 2002b), many children of divorce gain a stepparent. The stepparent's intrusion into the home may initially be an unwelcome event, disrupting the single parent's relationship with his or her children. All of this turmoil necessitates another period of readjustment.

Children and adolescents today are more likely to grow up in single-parent families, in part due to higher divorce rates and to fewer marriages by pregnant women (Rubin, 1999). The high rate of out-of-wedlock births combined with the greater proportion of women who never marry and those who remain single after divorce all contribute to the increase in female-headed homes and subsequent problems, such as poverty. Children living with a single mother are *six times* more likely to live in poverty than are children with married parents (Maher, 2003). However, this problem is an integral part of a larger, more complex pattern attributable to a combination of social, economic, and cultural factors. Other major factors include the high rates of unemployment, poverty, and housing instability of single mothers (Sleek, 1998). Many single mothers either hold dead-end jobs, require public assistance, or do not receive their child support. This means a large number of children and teenagers are growing up in father-absent, economically deprived homes, thereby setting the stage for problem behaviors such as dropping out of school, delinquency, alcohol and drug abuse, and unwed pregnancy (Maher, 2003). Given these discouraging statistics about the effects of divorce on children, couples need to think carefully about developing a committed relationship that may result in children, especially if the relationship is not a solid one at the onset. There are successful programs designed to assist children of divorce cope better with the myriad stressors associated with family dissolution. One such program is Pedro-Carroll's (2005) *Children of Divorce Intervention Program*.

Remarriage

Despite the painful experience of divorce, most divorced people remarry—one-fourth within one year of their divorce (CDC, 2002c; Maher, 2003). Diane did eventually remarry, but David never did. In most instances, a divorced person marries another divorced person, probably because they share similar experiences or are the same age. Then, too, participation in various support groups that have been recently formed, such as Parents Without Partners, increases the likelihood of meeting and marrying someone like themselves.

You might ask, "How successful are these second marriages?" To be frank, it's difficult to answer because the record is mixed. Statistically, second marriages are even more likely to end in divorce (CDC, 2002c). You should be aware, however, that there are a small number of "repeaters," who marry and divorce several times, thus inflating the overall divorce figures for remarriages. Many second marriages are successful both in terms of marital happiness and longevity. When the divorce repeaters are removed from consideration, the outlook for second marriages may be better than previously thought. At least six out of 10 remarriages last, which is higher than first marriages. Partners in a second marriage often benefit from their mistakes in an earlier marriage. They know full well the value of give-and-take in a close relationship like marriage. Age and maturity also help. Most of all, remarried people usually realize the value of commitment and thus work harder at their second marriage.

An increasing number of remarriages now involve stepchildren (Pacey, 2005), as mentioned. About half of these children have stepparents, mostly stepfathers because of the tendency for children to live with their mothers. Other children are born after the remarriage of the partners. The majority of remarried couples, however, have children only from the previous marriage, with no children from the remarriage. Only a very small number of *remarried couples have children of their own in addition to children from previous marriages of both partners. Such families are called* **blended families.**

Remarriages involving children pose special demands on the adults as well as the children. The man Diane married after her divorce had two preteen daughters. Diane found coping with the new marriage and her ready-made family trying, especially because she and her husband had little child-free time to build mutual understanding and acceptance of each other (Pacey, 2005). As with Diane, when partners perceive that stepchildren cause family problems, they report more marital unhappiness and more thoughts about divorce in their remarriages (Knox & Zusman, 2001). When the children are young, the stepparent has more opportunity to develop rapport and trust with the children, but when adolescents are involved, it's more difficult for everyone. If the new partner too quickly assumes parental authority, especially in matters of discipline, the children may be resentful. Both parents must make allowances for the children's initial suspicion and resistance.

Part of the problem is that the role of stepparent is not well defined. This problem is often compounded by the child's continued interaction with the remaining biological parent. When both parents in the home develop a good working relationship, talking things out and cooperating on parental issues, stepparent families can do at least as well as intact families, if not better, in many cases (Bjornsen, 2005).

SUMMARY

LOVE AND INTIMACY

We began the chapter by discussing the intensely satisfying but often unstable nature of love relationships. Although most people retain a stubborn faith in romantic love, they regard it as only the first stage of love, from which a more mature love should grow. Individuals from most Western (individualistic) societies have been exposed to romantic images in the media, have come in contact with someone to love, and have experienced the strong emotional arousal they label as love. Thus, they report the experience of passionate or romantic love. A second type of love, companionate love, in which the company and friendship of the lover is enjoyed, can develop later. Sternberg's view is that ideal love includes equal and generous amounts of the three essential components of love—intimacy, passion, and commitment.

COMMITMENT

Couples who live together before marriage may enjoy greater intimacy than other dating couples; this type of union is known as cohabitation. Cohabitation, however, does not always result in marriage, and marriages after cohabitation are not as likely to last. Most Americans will eventually marry, most of them in their 20s and 30s. People who marry, especially those from individualistic societies, believe in voluntary marriage—the assumption that they will remain married only as long as they are in love. When they are no longer in love, it's mutually understood they will divorce. In contrast, one of the keys to lasting, happy marriages is the couple's commitment to marriage as a long-term relationship and their willingness to communicate and work through their conflicts.

ADJUSTING TO INTIMATE RELATIONSHIPS

A major change in marriage is today's lack of fixed roles for husbands and wives and other committed couples, with a greater sharing of responsibilities between partners than in the past. Difficulty in personal communication continues to be a major problem for many couples. In contrast, good communication is necessary for resolving the inevitable differences and conflicts that surface in any close relationship.

A satisfying sex life is also an important part of a committed relationship like marriage, with a strong association between a satisfying sex life and satisfaction with the relationship itself. Although the average committed relationship tends to devitalize over time, partners who remain open to each other and continue growing in their relationship report increasing happiness.

DIVORCE AND ITS CONSEQUENCES

The divorce rate has more than doubled in the past few decades, with about one out of every two marriages now ending in divorce. Getting a divorce or breaking up a long-term committed relationship involves overlapping and painful experiences, including the emotional, legal, economic, parental, and community aspects. How children are affected by divorce depends on a variety of factors, such as the age and sex of the child and custody arrangements.

Most divorced people eventually remarry, some of them achieving happy marriages. Remarriages involving children from a previous marriage pose special demands on the adults as well as the children. Such families are called blended families. For families troubled by conflict, family mediation and emotion focused therapy offer effective solutions.

SCORING KEY FOR THE MARITAL MYTHS QUIZ

1. True. More than 9 out of 10 Americans eventually marry, most of them in their 20s and 30s.

2. False. As discussed in the text, couples that live together before marriage may be more apt to divorce than other couples, mostly because of the attitudes and values they bring to the marriage. Newer studies, however, are indicating that these findings may be changing.

3. False. Changing circumstances often trigger differing ratios of input between partners. For instance, a 30–70 ratio of husband to wife might be characteristic of a newly married couple in which the man is busy starting a new business, though the ratio might well be reversed (70–30) later in the marriage if the wife works and assumes more responsibilities at home because her husband has a life-threatening illness.

4. True. This factor is mostly true in that love and friendship are overlapping relationships. Sexuality adds a special dimension to marriage and love relationships that is not found in friendships.

5. False. It is the lack of high-quality communication in discussing their differences rather than the differences themselves that is a major cause of marital dissatisfaction.

6. True. Studies show that married individuals report being healthier and happier than single individuals.

7. True. In contrast to the past, most divorces are now initiated by women. One reason may be women's greater concern with the quality of the marriage relationship, with divorcing women reporting more dissatisfaction with their marriages than divorcing men.

8. False. This factor varies. Extramarital affairs may rejuvenate some marriages, make no difference to others, and prove downright destructive to still others. A lot depends on how both partners deal with an extramarital affair.

9. False. Although studies vary, there is mounting evidence that children are damaged more by the conflict-ridden atmosphere of an intact home, especially when it is long-standing, than by the legal divorce itself.

10. True. On the average, married people, not simply happily married couples, live longer than unmarried people. One reason may be the need to look after someone else; another may be the emotional support people receive from their partners.

SELF-TEST

1. Compared to close friendships, romantic relationships are characterized by greater
   a. stability.
   b. trust.
   c. volatility.
   d. acceptance.

2. Couples in long-term relationships characterized by intimacy and commitment but little or no passion exhibit
   a. romantic love.
   b. companionate love.
   c. consummate love.
   d. empty love.

3. A common and destructive emotion in an unhappy marriage is
   a. all of the following.
   b. rejection.
   c. anger.
   d. contempt.

4. Couples with happy and enduring marriages attribute their success to _____ attachments in childhood.
   a. secure
   b. avoidant
   c. ambivalent
   d. intense

5. Sexual orientation is generally distinguished by
   a. mental illness and extreme emotionality.
   b. attraction to individuals of a particular gender.
   c. transsexuality and bisexuality but not heterosexuality.
   d. confused gender role and hermaphroditism.

6. The most common conflict among married couples is
   a. sharing household chores.
   b. sexual incompatibility.
   c. problems with in-laws.
   d. who earns the most money.

7. Partners in unhappy marriages make _____ attributions about each other.
   a. positive and negative
   b. distress-enhancing
   c. neutral but emphatic
   d. humorous and playful

8. A blended family
   a. is racially mixed.
   b. is like a business partnership.
   c. involves stepparents and their children.
   d. all of the above.

9. Twenty-five percent of divorced people tend to
   a. never marry again.
   b. remarry the same partner.
   c. remarry someone who has never been married.
   d. remarry within one year of their divorce.

10. What process attempts to bring together divorcing couples with a neutral person to come to agreements about how they will reduce conflict?
    a. Family mediation
    b. Cohabitation
    c. Blending
    d. Family therapy

EXERCISES

1. *Qualities desired in a significant other.* Make a list of some personal qualities you would like in a significant other. You might list a dozen such qualities; then go back and check the three most important ones. Write a short paragraph telling why these three qualities are the most important. You might do the same for personal qualities you would *not* like in a partner. Again, list a dozen such qualities and check the three most important ones. Why do you think these qualities are undesirable?

2. *Qualities you offer to a prospective significant other.* Make a list of the major personal strengths and weaknesses you would bring to a committed relationship. What are the three most desirable qualities you have to offer? What are some of your less desirable qualities that might affect the marriage? If you are already committed to someone or if you are married, you might ask your partner to add to your list. Try to list more desirable qualities than undesirable ones.

3. *The marriage relationship.* If you are going steady, engaged, living with someone, or married, describe the type of relationship you have with your partner. Are you also friends? Do you and your partner return each other's love? Or is one of you more emotionally involved in the relationship than the other? To what extent are both of you relationship-oriented?

4. *Adjustment.* If you're living with someone or married, what has been your major adjustment in learning to live together? Has it involved learning how to communicate and handle conflict? Or has it had to do with specific problems involving money, house chores, or sex? Select one or two of the most difficult adjustments you've had in your current relationship, and write a page or so about it. Is there anything you learned in this chapter that can help you better adjust?

5. *Your attitudes toward homosexuality.* Have you closely examined your attitudes toward homosexuality? Think about your past reactions when you have found

out that someone is gay or have been introduced to a gay person. Have you been open-minded? Have you behaved the same way you did toward other people? If you answer "no" to these questions, why do you think you hold the attitudes you do? Do you think you can or should change your attitudes with regard to the issue of homosexuality?

QUESTIONS FOR SELF-REFLECTION

1. Can you be in love with more than one person at a time?

2. How can you tell whether your partner loves you?

3. Are you and your partner equally emotionally involved in your relationship?

4. Do you believe that living together before marriage ensures a happier marriage?

5. If you are living with someone or are married, to what extent are the household chores shared? Is your arrangement fair? Would your partner agree?

6. Do you and your partner "fight fair" so that you can disagree without undermining your relationship?

7. To what extent do you feel that sexual satisfaction and relationship satisfaction go together?

8. If you or your parents have gone through a divorce, what was the hardest part for you?

9. As a single person or single parent, which characteristics do you most desire in a mate?

10. If your current situation—married, cohabiting, single, or otherwise—involves children, how does the presence of children influence your prospects for love and commitment in the future?

FOR FURTHER INFORMATION

RECOMMENDED READINGS

FRIEL, J. C., & FRIEL, L. D. (2002). *The seven happy things couples do . . . plus one.* Deerfield Beach, FL: Health Communications. Drawing on private practice and research, psychologists reveal what makes couples happy.

GOTTMAN, J., GOTTMAN, J. S., & DECLAIRE, J. (2006). *Ten lessons to transform your marriage.* New York: Crown. Leading relationship experts, cited in the text, present their views and research on making marriage work.

LOVE, P. (2001). *The truth about love: The highs, the lows, and how you can make it last forever.* New York: Simon & Schuster. A therapist discusses the psychological and physiological components of love and the predictable patterns of highs and lows related to it.

MERCER, D., & PRUETT, M. (2001). *Your divorce advisor: A lawyer and a psychologist guide you through the legal and emotional landscape of divorce.* New York: Simon & Schuster. This book shows divorcing persons how to negotiate, keep a healthy perspective, and protect assets.

ROSENBLUM, K. E., & TRAVIS, T. C. (2005). *The meaning of difference: American constructions of race, sex and gender, social class, and sexual orientation.* New York: McGraw-Hill. The authors examine the concept of "difference" in America, with sexual orientation being one difference. They acknowledge that the same social processes may underlie how all differences are construed.

WEBSITES AND THE INTERNET

http://www.smartmarriages.com   The site for the Coalition for Marriage, Families, and Couples Education.

http://www.aamft.org   This site is supported by the American Association of Marriage and Family Therapists. It is a general information source on families; also contains referral information for family therapy.

http://www.qrd.org   This site presents the "Queer Resources Directory." It contains lots of information on homosexuality concerning families, religion, health, gay culture, and so forth.

http://www.divorcecentral.com   This site is for individuals contemplating or experiencing divorce. Laws are available by state as well as chat lines and other supports.

http://www.gettingremarried.com   A website for those considering remarriage with helpful advice on blended families, second weddings, prenuptial agreements, financial planning, etc.

Stress!

Steve arrives at the office late, after a harrowing 30-minute delay on the expressway. He is told the boss wants to see him right away. "I wonder what that's about?" Steve muses to himself, as he takes off his coat and heads upstairs. He's ushered inside the boss's office, only to find the boss pacing back and forth. The boss is furious. The big deal they were counting on with a major corporation has just fallen through. The boss makes it clear that if Steve values his job, he'd better have a good explanation. Steve gropes for words. "Frankly, I'm stunned. I can't imagine what happened," he says. "Let me call and talk to the people over there and find out the story." Steve's boss continues making accusations about Steve's incompetence and his uncertain future with the company. Eventually, Steve feels enraged at being treated this way. He is tempted to yell back at his boss but knows this is neither a mature nor productive response. Instead, he returns to his office to cool off. His stomach churning, his neck muscles tense, and his blood pressure rising, he sits down at his desk. He reaches for a Maalox and an aspirin.

OH NO!—UNDERSTANDING STRESS

Steve is discovering that the modern world is no less perilous than the jungle. He feels that extra burst of adrenaline that primes his muscles and steadies his nerves for a fight. Steve knows that the primitive "fight-or-flight" response used by his Stone Age ancestors is no longer appropriate; in fact, it's dangerous. When people like Steve lash out aggressively with their fists or weapons, they jeopardize the very welfare of society itself. Should they try to escape through alcohol or drugs, they only succeed in making their problems worse (American Psychological Association [APA], 2006a, b). Instead, they must learn how better to manage stress and the intense emotions it arouses in a manner more appropriate for our times.

TABLE 13–1
STATISTICS ON STRESS

- Over half of Americans view job stress as a major problem in their lives.
- One-fourth of American workers say their stress is so severe that they feel a "nervous breakdown" is imminent.
- More than three out of every five doctor's office visits are for stress-related problems.
- Up to 90 percent of reported illnesses and disease may be stress-related.
- More women than men report feeling superstressed, including 23 percent of female (as opposed to 19 percent of male) executives and professionals. In college, about 38 percent of women as compared to 20 percent of men report high stress levels.
- Young people are more affected by stress; 75 percent of 18- to 24-year-olds have suffered from stress at work.

Stress takes a heavy toll on our nation's well-being (Stambor, 2006). Leaders of industry are alarmed about stress causing absenteeism, decreasing productivity, and increasing medical expenses, all of which are estimated to cost businesses over $350 a year. Stress has also become a major contributor, either directly or indirectly, to coronary heart disease, cancer, lung ailments, accidental injuries, cirrhosis of the liver, and suicide (Monroe, 2008)—six of the leading causes of death in the United States. Many of the deleterious effects of stress are due to its effect on the immune system (Segerstrom & Miller, 2004). In short, it seems as if our modern way of life has become a major source of stress. Table 13–1 presents other important statistics on stress so that you can judge for yourself how large a problem stress is for modern life.

Just like Steve, a majority of adult Americans experience "high stress" at one time or another. Many report that they feel "great stress" at least once or twice a week or live with high stress every day. Stress has become the price paid for being affluent and successful. Twice as many high-income as low-income people suffer from the tension of stress. Also, the more educated people are, the more likely they are to suffer extreme stress. Executives, managers, and professionals suffer more heavily from stress than those in other occupations. Interestingly, most executives do not use all the vacation time they are entitled to (Daniels, 2002; Guinto, 2005).

Conceptualizing Stress

Stress is difficult to define, partly because it means different things to different people. The overall experience of stress can include instigating causes or stimuli followed by various stress responses, as well as our perception of what is stressful to us as individuals (Monroe, 2008). Most definitions tend to emphasize one of these aspects of stress more than the other. Those that emphasize the *stimuli or instigating factors* describe stress in terms of **stressors**—*the variety of external and internal stimuli that evoke stress,* such as a highly competitive work environment, college roommate conflicts, or worries about appearance.

Other specialists believe **stress** can be defined as *the pattern of responses individuals make to events that disturb their equilibrium or exceed coping abilities.* When events disrupt our usual level of functioning and require us to make an *extra effort* to reestablish our equilibrium, we experience stress. Accordingly, besides *behavioral reactions,* stress also involves *physiological reactions* that occur in response to stressful events, such as the increased flow of adrenaline that mobilizes us for an extra effort.

Some experts emphasize the importance of our *perception* of such events (Monroe, 2008). One person, for example, may perceive a car's not starting and being late for a test as a normal part of life. Another person, who responds quite differently, might feel extremely distressed at being late for the exam as well as worried that the stress will affect the exam outcome.

We should be careful not to equate stress solely with distress. Instead, stress is a multifaceted phenomenon that may even have beneficial effects in some cases (Reynolds & Turner, 2008), such as when an athlete needs a little stress to become motivated for a big game. Hans Selye (1991) (see also Goldstein & Kopin, 2007; McEwen, 2005; Pfaff, Martin, & Ribeiro, 2007), a noted stress researcher, has described four basic variations of stress, each with its own label. *When events have a harmful effect,* stress is correctly labeled **distress.** Unfortunately, much of the stress in modern society is distressing. As noted, stress may also have a beneficial effect (Almeida, 2005; Daniels, 2002; Linley & Joseph, 2004; Reynolds & Turner, 2008). Beginning a new job, getting married, or taking up an exciting sport like skydiving may have a stimulating effect that results in personal growth. Selye suggests we call this **eustress,** or *good stress.* He has also described two more variations of stress. **Hyperstress,** or *excessive stress,* usually occurs when events, including positive ones, pile up and stretch the limits of our adaptability. For example, individuals who are already under stress at work and home may experience hyperstress when a terrorist attack occurs. **Hypostress,** or *insufficient stress,* is apt to occur when we lack stimulation. Monotonous jobs typically inspire hypostress. Bored people may resort to sensation-seeking behaviors mentioned elsewhere in the book, such as experimenting with drugs or taking up a risky sport such as hang gliding.

There are other ways of categorizing or conceptualizing stress. The study of major life events as obvious stressors comes to mind (Monroe, 2008; Reynolds & Turner, 2008). Holmes and Rahe (1967; Almeida, 2005; Cassidy et al., 2004) realized that negative life events, such as the loss of a job or the death of a loved one, are usually quite stressful. At the same time, they acknowledged that positive events such as beginning college or getting married can be stressful, too. Consequently, the most important factor in this approach is *the total impact of various life changes,* both positive and negative, in combination with *the amount of readjustment* these events require. Many studies have found that changes in life intensity as measured by Holmes and Rahe's scale are closely linked with the onset of various illnesses. Accordingly, the combined stress of life events has been related to sudden cardiac death, stroke, diabetes and other chronic illnesses, depression, complications of pregnancy and birth, everyday colds, flare-up of multiple sclerosis, and many other physical problems (Cropley & Steptoe, 2005; Tosevski & Milovancevic, 2006).

Despite its usefulness, the life-events approach to stress has several limitations (e.g., Bennett & Miller, 2006; Monroe, 2008). In fact, there are many criticisms, but we will mention only a few here. First, the particular events selected may not be equally relevant for all groups of people, such as blue- versus white-collar workers or *young adults versus the elderly.* Second, the life-events approach does not take into account how individuals perceive a given change, much less how well they adapt to it. Third, because the life-events approach is built around change, it fails to include a great deal of stress that comes with chronic or repeated conditions, such as a boring job or a long-lasting unsatisfying marriage. Finally, it leaves out the "little things" in everyday life that often get to us, such as losing your car keys or snapping a shoelace when you're in a rush in the morning.

To date, scientists do not know which theory about the causes of stress is correct: the theory about major life stressors (such as natural disasters) or the theory about daily hassles (such as being late for work).

More recently, attention has turned to stress associated with everyday difficulties, such as concerns about owing money or about being stuck in traffic (Bennett & Miller, 2006; Monroe, 2008). Steve, the individual in our opening case, was facing several hassles the day his boss confronted him. He was not only dismayed that his boss was angry and accusatory, but he was also confused about why the big deal did not go through. In addition, Steve was having renewed difficulties with his former wife about his visitation with their children. His ex-wife also wanted to increase the amount of child support he paid her, which would financially strap him. Finally, Steve thought he had better buy a new car soon, because his old car had broken down three times in the previous two weeks.

Lazarus (1993; Almeida, 2005) has found that daily hassles sometimes have a greater effect on our moods and health than do the major misfortunes of life. However, people vary considerably in terms of what bothers them (Almeida). Among traditional college students, the most commonly reported hassles are anxiety over tests and grades (Kieffer, Cronin, & Gawet, 2006; MacGeorge, Samter, & Gillihan, 2005). Box 13–1 (page 312) presents supplementary information on college students and stress. Middle-aged people are bothered more by worries over health and money. Professional people feel they have too much to do and not enough time to do it and have difficulty relaxing. Daily hassles common to all groups are misplacing or losing things, worrying over physical appearance, and having too many things to do. Lazarus has found a strong link between daily hassles and psychological and physical health, with people who suffer frequent, intense hassles having the poorest health.

Box 13–1

COLLEGE STUDENTS AND STRESS

College students experience lots of stress, and the causes of stress are often different from those for other groups in our general population. College students, especially in their first year (Singh & Upadhyay, 2008), are exposed to new social norms and customs, different peer groups, work overload, a change in lifestyle, as well as more demands on their time and their self-control than in high school.

The transition to college is particularly difficult, with a large number of freshmen reporting overwhelming stress (Pritchard & Wilson, 2006; Reisberg, 2000), but college alone, no matter what year a student is in, stimulates additional stress. For example, one in four students expects to have to work full-time while attending college (*Techniques*, 2000). Curiously, the data on college students also mimic the data on the population at large in that college women report more stress than college men (Darling, McWey, Howard, & Olmstead, 2007; Hudd et al., 2000; Reisberg) and rely more on emotion-focused coping than do men (MacGeorge et al., 2005).

Stress in college students has been associated with a variety of negative outcomes. Increases in smoking, drinking (especially beer), consuming junk food, and committing suicide among distressed college students have all been documented by researchers (Economos, Hildebrandt, & Hyatt, 2008; Hudd et al., 2000; Kieffer et al., 2006). A concomitant decline in healthy eating habits, fitness, and other positive health behaviors, such as vitamin taking, are also well documented. Additionally, stressed students are significantly less pleased with their grade-point averages and their health (Hudd et al.). It is unclear whether high levels of stress produce lower grades and poor health or whether poor levels of academic performance and fitness result in added stress (Hudd et al.).

Faculty who often are requested to mentor students have a difficult time gauging how much stress the students are under (Misra, McKean, West, & Russo, 2000). Thus, faculty might not be the best first line of defense for recognizing and reducing college student stress. On the other hand, many campuses offer counseling services for their students as well as workshops on stress reduction, study habits, and career counseling. Many campuses house support groups for common disorders that accompany stress, such as eating disorders or depression.

Do you know what services your campus has available? Perhaps you need to explore them for yourself or someone close to you?

A final approach to conceptualizing stress is *the self-perception of "global" (or generalized and pervasive) stress* in our lives. Some psychologists call this **chronic stress** (Pfaff et al., 2007) as opposed to **acute stress,** which is *stress that is a momentary response to imminent danger and is relieved when the danger is over* (Dinan, 2005; Sagy, 2005). Most medical professionals consider *chronic* stress the most harmful. Steve's boss's surprisingly angry outburst at Steve might be considered an acute stressor, while Steve's long-running feud with his ex-wife is more typical of chronic stress.

Stress and You

How you perceive a given stressor may make it more or less stressful (Monroe, 2008). Some people take criticism of their work as a personal attack, become highly distressed as Steve did, and waste a lot of energy defending themselves. Other people may take similar criticism as a challenge to improve their work, thereby experiencing less stress. Age and gender were mentioned earlier as individualized factors that contribute to the perception of stress, with women and young individuals more likely to report higher stress. Other factors, such as personality traits like neuroticism (Zautra, Affleck, Tennen, Reich, & Davis, 2005), can be a factor in the experience of stress. One well-known personality syndrome is the Type A personality. Type As are more likely to develop stress-related illnesses because of personal traits. (**Stress-related illnesses** are *those illnesses affected by our emotions, lifestyles, or environment,* such as a stress-related heart attack). People with **Type A personality** syndrome tend to be *competitive, argumentative, time-urgent, ambitious, and impatient as well as hostile* (Jamal, 2005). They judge themselves and others by rigorous standards. When others fail to maintain the high standards set by the Type A individual, the Type A person can be nasty. As a result, Type As keep themselves (and others) under constant stress and are more likely to develop heart disease (Mohan, 2006) than other, more *relaxed* individuals known as **Type Bs.** More recently, psychologists have begun researching another personality factor, persistence, which may also contribute to heart disease and other stress-related illnesses (Miller & Wrosch, 2007). Persistence, while essential in modicum to happiness and success, may become detrimental when we cannot disengage from unattainable goals. We need to know when to give up a losing battle.

Another factor that can add to distress is other people's reactions to us. Prejudice against us because of the groups to which we belong is but one example (Harrell, 2000; Thompson, 2002). Cassidy and colleagues (2004) sampled young, ethnic minority people (Chinese, Pakistani, and Indian) to examine the relationship between perceived ethnic discrimination and psychological distress. The researchers found that anxiety (distress) significantly predicted levels of perceived discrimination; that is, higher anxiety was related to higher perceived discrimination. The authors caution that cause and effect are not yet known, but this and other research clearly demonstrate a link between stress and discrimination.

Many other *situational factors* (factors outside of the individual) can contribute to our experience of stress. Here are some additional situational factors that contribute alone or in combination to add to our experience of distress:

- *Physical stressors* such as too much to do or too many demands on our time and attention
- *Lack of control* over decisions and demands in our personal life or our work life
- *Unpredictability* of events that therefore find us unprepared to cope with them
- *Lack of social support* from friends and family
- *Poor interpersonal relations* with family members, friends, or coworkers
- *Role conflict* in which one role (for example, a job) conflicts with another role (for example, being a readily available parent)
- *Career concerns* including finding a job, receiving a promotion, and being unemployed
- *Unpleasant or dangerous physical conditions* such as a noisy work environment

With the possibility of affecting thousands of people at a time, terrorism is now a major threat and stimulant for stress in the United States. Terrorism's unpredictability and uncontrollability render it a topic for special treatment and is pursued further in Box 13–2 (page 314). The list of situational factors certainly is not exhaustive. This unit is long enough, however, to convince you that there are multiple factors, both personal and situational, that contribute to our rising level of stress.

Box 13–2

TERRORISM, MASS TRAGEDIES, AND THEIR EFFECTS

Americans need ways to cope with the anxiety produced by senseless tragedies such as the terrorist attacks in New York and Washington, not to mention the continued threat of future attacks. Recent natural disasters such as hurricanes and the possibility of pandemics also distress many. No one who sees or hears about a tragedy of this kind is untouched by it—and in an era of instant mass communications, the number of people exposed to such violence in one way or another is significant. Most of us will experience occasional anxiety and stress that will fade over time. For some, however, such feelings may not go away on their own.

WHAT ARE COMMON REACTIONS?

Mass tragedies can affect us in many ways: physically, emotionally, and mentally. They can make people feel angry, enraged, confused, sad, anxious, tired, or even guilty. When those feelings don't go away over a few weeks, or when they seem to get worse, it may be appropriate to seek help for yourself or the person in your life who is experiencing these difficulties.

WAYS TO EASE THE STRESS

There are many proactive ways to manage the distress: Talk with someone about your feelings—anger, sorrow, and other emotions—even though it may be difficult.

Take steps to promote your own physical and emotional healing by staying active in your daily life patterns or by adjusting them. Maintain a normal household and daily routine, and be sure to spend time with family and friends, especially as forms of support.

As the anniversary of a disaster or traumatic event approaches, many survivors report a return of restlessness and fear. The psychological literature calls it the **anniversary reaction** and defines it as *an individual's response to unresolved grief resulting from significant losses.* The anniversary reaction can involve several days or even weeks of anxiety, anger, nightmares, flashbacks, depression, or fear. Not all survivors of a disaster or traumatic events experience an anniversary reaction.

On a more positive note, the anniversary of a disaster or traumatic event also can provide an opportunity for emotional healing. Individuals can make significant progress in working through the natural grieving process by acknowledging the feelings and issues that surface during their anniversary reaction. These feelings and issues can help individuals develop perspective on the event and figure out where it fits in their hearts, minds, and lives.

SOURCE: Adapted from the website of the U. S. Department of Health and Human Services—Substance Abuse and Mental Health Services Administration, Mentalhealth.org (February 2003).

YIKES!—REACTIONS TO STRESS

Stress manifests itself in a variety of ways. The most common sign of stress is increased nervousness, anxiety, and tension. Many people experience tension headaches, and others say their stress shows up as anger and irritability with others. Some Americans report that stress also takes its toll in fatigue or depression (Monroe & Reid, 2009). Other symptoms of stress include muscle aches, stomachaches, an overall feeling of being upset, insomnia, loss of sleep, compulsive eating or loss of appetite, a feeling of frustration, crying, yelling, and screaming. Research demonstrates that people under stress have more heart attacks and strokes, catch more colds, and respond less well to flu vaccines (Adler, 1999).

Many of these symptoms are part of the body's physiological stress response—automatic, built-in reactions over which we have little control. As previously mentioned, the familiar symptoms of stress can result from our psychological reactions to events that are more dependent on the way we *perceive* the world and our capacity for dealing with it rather than to the actual stressor. In this section, we'll examine both physiological and psychological reactions. We'll also look at how individuals differ in their characteristic responses to stress.

Physiological Stress Reactions

Hans Selye (1991), a pioneer in the study of how stress affects the body, maintains that in addition to the body's specific responses to a particular stressor (e.g., sweating in response to heat), there *also is a characteristic pattern of nonspecific physiological mechanisms that are activated in response to almost any stressor.* Selye called this pattern the **general adaptation syndrome.** It *consists of three progressive stages: the alarm reaction, the stage of resistance, and the stage of exhaustion.*

Alarm Reaction.   In *the initial emergency response to stress-provoking agents, the body attempts to restore its normal functioning; this is known as the* **alarm reaction.** The alarm reaction consists of complicated body and biochemical changes that produce similar symptoms regardless of the type of stressor. For this reason people in the beginning stages of different illnesses often complain of common symptoms such as fever, headache, aching muscles and joints, loss of appetite, and a generally tired feeling.

Stage of Resistance.   If our exposure to stressful situations continues, the alarm reaction is followed by the **stage of resistance,** in which *the human organism develops an increased resistance to the stressor.* The symptoms of the alarm stage disappear, and body resistance rises above its normal level to cope with the continued stress. The price of this resistance includes increased secretions from various glands, lowered resistance to infections, and the "diseases of adaptation." Stress-induced peptic ulcers and high blood pressure are common examples, though not all cases of these disorders are induced by stress.

In an important literature review, Segerstrom and Miller (2004) examined the relationship between stress and immune system functioning. They found that many studies emphasize the causal link between exposure to chronic stressors and suppression of the immune system. Furthermore, Glaser (2005) in another review of studies on stress and health confirms that stress makes us more susceptible to viruses—not just colds but HIV, which causes AIDS—and diminishes wound healing as well as lowers immunity.

Stage of Exhaustion.   If chronic stress continues too long, the **stage of exhaustion** is reached. *The body is unable to continue secreting its hormones at the increased rate, so the organism can no longer adapt to chronic stress. Body defenses break down, adaptation energy runs out, and the physical symptoms of the alarm reaction reappear.* The symptoms of this stage are similar to aging in many respects, except that the symptoms of exhaustion, depending on the severity of one's condition, are more or less reversible.

Selye (1980) originally held that the stress response occurs in reaction to various stressors, including illness. However, his theory also relates how a chronic stress reaction can itself lead to illness and accentuate aging. Continued stress responses use up the body's store of adaptive energy. Although the person who is successfully coping with specific stressors may lead an active, healthy life, each experience of stress uses up some adaptive energy. It might be better to use our energy more wisely rather than wasting it on so many false alarms, which are better ignored. Continual stress can eventually damage the various organs of the body, but different parts of our bodies do not suffer stress at an even rate. Each person's "weakest link" is determined partly by genetic vulnerability and partly by the type and severity of the stress experienced. In any event, reducing our level of stress may help us lead longer and healthier lives.

There exist today explanations other than Selye's about the effects of stress on us. Psychologists often speak of the **fight-or-flight response** with regard to stress (Korte, Koolhaas, Wingfield, & McEwen, 2005). **Fight,** of course, means *confronting the stressor,* and **flight** means *fleeing from the stressor.* When the stressor is insurmountable, we flee; when it is capable of being vanquished, we often fight it. Specifically, a stress response starts in the brain when the brain detects or perceives a stressor; Steve's brain was indeed on high alert after his boss confronted him. Certain parts of the brain, such as the **amygdala** (*which directs signal traffic in the brain and triggers an all-systems alarm*) and the **pituitary gland** (*the master gland of the endocrine or hormonal system*), signal the rest of the body to prepare to fight or to flee. The body responds by increasing the flow of various hormones such as adrenaline and cortisol (*Harvard Women's Health Watch,* 2003). Similarly, nerve cells release and respond to various neurotransmitters. These changes cause the rest of the body to change. For example, nonessential processes slow down while the heart races, the senses sharpen, the lungs work harder, and the muscles tense (Johnson, 2003; Lemonick, 2003; National Institute of Mental Health [NIMH], 2001a).

When the stressor disappears or subsides, so, too, do many of the physiological responses, and the body relaxes. Fight or flight is no longer necessary. On the other hand, if the stress response is activated too often or turned on for too long, these emergency responses to stress can actually turn against the body, causing damage. One of the reasons that protracted stress is so detrimental is that certain hormones can stay elevated. Most hormones return to their base rate or to normal after the stressor is gone, but glucocorticoids (e.g., epinephrine) can stay elevated indefinitely, especially if the stress is chronic. Chronic elevation can actually reduce the effectiveness of the immune system some studies show (Lemonick, 2003). Prolonged physiological response to stress consequently can cause or worsen many of the health problems described earlier (*Harvard Women's Health Watch,* 2003; Shafirkin, 2003).

Other scientists have found the fight-or-flight explanation of stress responses too simplistic and at the same time have criticized Selye's model for not being more inclusive regarding the physiological mechanisms involved in stress responses (Monroe, 2008). McEwen (2005) suggests the concepts of allostasis and allostatic load. **Allostasis** means *achieving stability through changes via a process that maintains balance among the physiological factors essential for life,* such as body temperature, blood pressure, heart rate, and oxygen level. **Allostatic load** refers to *cumulative changes that reflect the cost to the body of adapting repeatedly to demands (i.e., stresses) placed upon it.* This view takes into account a time frame. Over the short run, bodily functions associated with allostasis provide *protective effects against stress,* but over the long run, stressors can have *damaging effects* and adversely affect our life by resulting in poorer health (McEwen; Almeida, 2005). Put another way, allostasis helps us physiologically manage stress, but chronic allostatic overload means we eventually become too distressed. It is, as McEwen suggests, the difference between "stressed" and "stressed out."

Psychological Stress Reactions

Unlike the body's stress reactions, our psychological reactions typically are shaped by learning and are heavily dependent on the way we perceive our world. Included here are a wide variety of cognitive, emotional, and behavioral responses to stress.

Because most stressors evoke **anxiety**—*the vague, unpleasant feeling that something bad is about to happen*—common psychological reactions to stress are defense mechanisms, according to some psychologists. They are called **defense mechanisms,** or sometimes "ego defense" mechanisms, because they are used to protect oneself from perceived threat (Cramer, 2003, 2006; Thobaben, 2005). Although defense mechanisms are influenced to some extent by learning, many psychologists believe they are *automatic unconscious mechanisms that protect us from the awareness of anxiety, thereby helping us to maintain a sense of self-worth in the face of threat* (see Table 13–2 for examples). Although the notion of defense mechanisms was dismissed by academic psychology some years ago, more recently, social and cognitive psychologists have found evidence for such processes (Baumeister, Dale, & Sommer, 1998; Thobaben).

Each of us relies on such mechanisms at one time or another, especially when we feel threatened, and regardless of whether the objective situation warrants it. As emergency reactions, they diminish our awareness of anxiety and help to maintain our sense of adequacy and self-worth in the face of threat. Because defense mechanisms also involve self-deception and a distortion of social reality, habitual reliance on defense mechanisms can prove maladaptive and can stifle personal growth.

How people behave under stress depends partly on the level of stress experienced. Mild stress can energize us to become more alert, active, and resourceful. Medium stress tends to have a disruptive effect on our lives, especially on complex behaviors such as writing a term paper. Very high levels of stress can be extremely troublesome. Under such stress, people become less sensitive to their surroundings, easily irritated, and more apt to resort to unhealthy coping devices such as consuming too much alcohol or not getting enough sleep. Stress also evokes a wide range of emotions, ranging from a sense of exhilaration in the face of minor, challenging stressors to the more familiar negative emotions of anxiety, anger, fear, jealousy, and discouragement. Stressful life experiences involving separation or loss of friends and loved ones are frequently associated with depression.

Fortunately, Steve, the man in the opening vignette, did not suffer from severe stress. Steve was lucky, because at its highest level, stress can be debilitating. Severe stress tends to inhibit behavior and may lead to apathy and immobility, as in clinically depressed individuals who feel helpless in the face of overwhelming frustration or deprivation

TABLE 13–2	
A FEW RECOGNIZED DEFENSE MECHANISMS	
Defense Mechanism	**Definition**
Repression	Excluding unacceptable ideas or feelings from consciousness
Denial	Misperceiving threatening objects or events as harmless
Regression	Reverting to a form of behavior that was more appropriate at an earlier stage of development
Rationalization	Justifying our unacceptable behavior with "good" reasons
Intellectualization	Reducing anxiety by analyzing threatening issues in an emotionally detached way
Projection	Attributing our unacceptable ideas or feelings to others
Displacement	Redirecting threatening ideas or impulses onto less threatening objects
Sublimation	Channeling socially unacceptable urges into acceptable behaviors
Reaction formation	Developing conscious feelings and behaviors opposite to the unconscious, anxiety-arousing ones

(Monroe & Reid, 2009). In addition, survivors of traumatic events, such as rape victims, terrorists' hostages, and veterans of combat, may cope well at the time of the trauma but months later experience a delayed emotional reaction known as posttraumatic stress disorder (PTSD). **Posttraumatic stress disorder** is *a severe anxiety disorder characterized by symptoms of anxiety and avoidance behavior, resulting from an unusually distressing event such as being assaulted.* Box 13–3 discusses posttraumatic stress disorder in more detail.

How Do You React to Stress?

Each of us reacts to stress, even a repetitive stressor such as college examinations, somewhat differently. There are recognized individual differences in the experience of stress

Box 13–3

POSTTRAUMATIC STRESS DISORDER (PTSD)

Posttraumatic stress disorder (PTSD) is an anxiety disorder that can develop after exposure to a terrifying event or ordeal in which grave physical harm occurred or was threatened (NIMH, 2001a). The types of events that trigger PTSD usually lie outside the realm of ordinary human loss and grief. Examples are plane crashes, earthquakes, floods, assaults, rapes, hostage taking, torture, murders, and military combat. The most frequent cause for Americans is automobile accidents (Blanchard & Hickling, 2003). The war in Iraq is predicted to produce an even higher rate of mental casualties than other wars (Baum, 2004; Zabriskie, 2004). Nearly half of the U.S. adult population is exposed to at least one traumatic event during their lifetimes, yet only 10 percent of women and 5 percent of men develop posttraumatic stress disorder (Ozer & Weiss, 2004). In fact, we now know that many adults do successfully navigate disastrous events (Bonanno, Galea, Bucciarelli, & Vlahov, 2007). These individuals have spawned the growth of studies on resilience, which is discussed in a few pages.

The symptoms of this disorder can begin immediately after the traumatic event or 3 to 6 months afterward (McFarland, 2005). However, it is not unusual for the symptoms to emerge only after a much longer period, which is characteristic of the chronic or delayed forms of the disorder (Marshall et al., 2007; NIMH, 2001a). Victims involuntarily reexperience the past traumatic event in dreams, which include "flashbacks" of the event accompanied by the original emotions of fear, shock, and horror,

especially when they experience reminders of the trauma. They also experience an emotional numbness toward their everyday world. Frequently, they have trouble concentrating at work during the day and difficulty sleeping at night. Feeling alienated from others, they may also lose interest in people. Angry outbursts and irritability are also signs of PTSD. The possibility of PTSD is greatest for those who have suffered past traumas (Ai, Evans-Campbell, Santangelo, & Cascio, 2006). Interestingly, scientists using brain imaging and other sophisticated techniques have found neural changes in victims of PTSD; these physiological changes may account for some of the more chronic symptoms, such as flashbacks and blunted emotions (NIMH).

Scientists today are trying to discover what treatments work best for individuals with PTSD. Possibilities include various medications, group therapy, cognitive-behavioral therapy (discussed elsewhere in the book), and exposure therapy, where the individual repeatedly and gradually relives the trauma under controlled conditions (NIMH, 2001a). Early research also showed that giving individuals the chance to talk about the trauma very soon after the event might reduce the symptoms of PTSD. However, a literature review indicates that crisis intervention or debriefing actually may *not* work and, in fact, might impede natural recovery (McNally, Bryant, & Ehlers, 2003). It may also be that various treatments work best for different types of trauma (NIMH) or victims. We clearly need more research on this issue.

and in coping. Gender, for example, may serve as a valuable "window" that influences not only how individuals appraise stress but also how they cope with stress (Gianakos, 2002). Peter, Hammarström, Hallqvist, Siegrist, and Theorell (2006) suggest that occupational gender segregation and unequal power and control issues exist that may affect how men and women perceive and cope with stress. Vegg, Spielberger, and Wassala (2002) add that women experience multiple and overlapping roles (e.g., occupation versus family) that can create more stress than men experience. Women also react to a wider range of stressors and say they feel stress more often than men (Eaton & Graham, 2008; Matud, 2004). Research has also shown that women are more likely to cope with stress through social support (sharing emotions and stressful experiences with their friends) than are men (APA, 2004b; Darling et al., 2007).

Finally, Matud (2004) and Eaton and Bradley (2008) reported more emotion-focused coping on the part of women and more problem-focused coping on the part of men. In **emotion-focused coping** *the individual tries to alter the emotional reaction to stress,* for example, by expressing rather than suppressing feelings. In **problem-focused coping** *the individual tries to change the environment or find a solution,* for example, by applying lessons learned from earlier experiences. In the past, psychologists have considered emotion-focused coping less adaptive than problem-focused coping (Austenfeld & Stanton, 2004). However, newer studies are demonstrating that emotion-focused coping is just as adaptive (Austenfeld & Stanton). In fact, positive emotions such as gratitude and love can buffer stress during crises such airplane crashes and terror attacks (Fredrickson, Tugade, Waugh, & Larkin, 2003).

Another individual difference is that some individuals seem better able to take stress in stride. Studies of top executives in *Fortune* 500 companies have shown that those who cope with stress most successfully have what the researchers call **psychological hardiness**—*the attitude that allows them to make the most of the situation.* The three trademarks of hardy individuals are feelings of *challenge* (instead of threat), *commitment* (rather than alienation), and *control* (as opposed to powerlessness) (Bonanno, 2004; Maddi, 2005). The executives who do well with stress feel stimulated by change and stress (challenge). They are also intensely involved in what they are doing (commitment), and they are not usually overcome by feelings of powerlessness even in very difficult situations (control). The last issue, control, is especially noteworthy. In probing the relationship among stress, physical illness, and psychological disorders, the importance of personal control recurs again and again. Being able to acknowledge heightened stress, as well as its effects on you, while maintaining reasonable control of yourself and, if possible, the situation at hand is vital to managing stress successfully.

As mentioned above, a related concept is **resilience** (Almedom, 2005), *positive growth or positive adaptation following brief periods of stress after some stressful disruption or extreme adversity* (Campbell-Sills, Cohan, & Stein, 2006). Resilience was once thought to be rare or even pathological; today, however, psychologists understand that it is more common than previously believed (Bonanno, 2004; 2005). Interestingly, it now appears to be the most common trajectory of all after distress and trauma (Bonanno, 2005; Bonanno et al., 2007).

Resilience after trauma is quite different from recovery after trauma. Resilience is characterized by relatively *mild and short-lived disruption* and recovery of a *stable trajectory* of healthy functioning. Mere recovery after trauma is typified by *significant* disruption to normal functioning that *declines only gradually* (Bonanno, 2005). In other words, resilient individuals bounce back from stressful experiences quickly and effectively (Tugade & Fredrickson, 2004). Such people use humor, positive emotions, cognitive flexibility, cognitive reappraisal, social support, and optimism to cope with adversity (Southwick, Vythilingam, & Charney, 2005), Stress and trauma, therefore, need not be negative or stressful. The important message here is that individuals can and do experience personal growth during adverse times.

By taking the self-assessment in Activity 13–1, you can begin to identify your own stress–coping style.

ACTIVITY 13–1

WHAT'S YOUR STRESS STYLE?

INSTRUCTIONS: *For each of the following statements, indicate your level of agreement by circling the appropriate number below the statement.*

1. When I am under stress, I become angry more quickly than usual.

    Strongly disagree   1   2   3   4   5   6   7   Strongly agree

2. During stressful times, my health habits (such as maintaining a good diet) decline.

    Strongly disagree   1   2   3   4   5   6   7   Strongly agree

3. When I am under stress, I have difficulty concentrating.

    Strongly disagree   1   2   3   4   5   6   7   Strongly agree

4. Despite being in sticky situations, I find I can resort to humor or positive thinking to help myself get through it.

    Strongly disagree   1   2   3   4   5   6   7   Strongly agree

5. When I am under stress, I react with more anxiety than do other people.

    Strongly disagree   1   2   3   4   5   6   7   Strongly agree

6. At times of stress, my nervous habits (such as nail biting or hair twisting) become more prevalent.

    Strongly disagree   1   2   3   4   5   6   7   Strongly agree

7. Stress makes my memory worse.

    Strongly disagree   1   2   3   4   5   6   7   Strongly agree

8. When I am under stress, I become easily frustrated and tense.

    Strongly disagree   1   2   3   4   5   6   7   Strongly agree

9. Stress makes me cry more easily than at other times.

    Strongly disagree   1   2   3   4   5   6   7   Strongly agree

10. I have a harder time learning as well as studying for exams when under stress.

Strongly disagree   1   2   3   4   5   6   7   Strongly agree

11. I find stress challenging at times and sometimes even exhilarating.

Strongly disagree   1   2   3   4   5   6   7   Strongly agree

12. After a distressing event, I take a few quiet moments to learn about myself and my reaction.

Strongly disagree   1   2   3   4   5   6   7   Strongly agree

SCORING: This self-assessor was designed specially for this book. Your findings, therefore, should be used only as a tool to stimulate critical thinking about how you cope with stress.

Emotional reactions to stress are measured in questions 1, 5, and 8.

Behavioral reactions to stress are measured in questions 2, 6, and 9.

Cognitive reactions to stress are measured in questions 3, 7, and 10.

Resilient reactions to stress are measured in questions 4, 11, 12.

Add up your points for each reaction cluster and write your total for that cluster in the space provided below:

Emotional reactions _____

Behavioral reactions _____

Cognitive reactions _____

Resilient reactions _____

Total for all reactions _____

Now decide if the scale did an accurate job measuring your typical reaction. For example, would your family or best friend concur with your scores? If you scored highest for emotional reactions, would they agree that you are emotional in stressful situations? Also, consider your total score. In some ways it indicates whether your reactions to stress are too strong or perhaps whether you are under high levels of stress. Now think about ways that you can better react or cope with stress and how you can reduce the total amount of stress that you have.

PHEW!—MANAGING STRESS

Managing stress successfully involves more than relying on the automatic, symptom-reducing reactions to stress, as helpful as these may be. Managing stress means taking charge, directing and controlling our responses to stressors, thereby modifying the overall stress. Steve, for example, realized that punching his boss was not a productive response to the distress and, in fact, could cause him much trouble. Instead, he returned to his office to process thoughtfully what had happened. While there are many other ways to cope with stress, most of them fall under two major headings: modifying your environment and altering yourself or your response.

Modifying Your Environment

Soon after his boss berated Steve, a camera he had on special order finally arrived. He quickly discovered it was not exactly what he wanted. What should he do? What would you do? You could return to the store and tell the clerk a mistake had been made and then proceed to order the correct model of camera. Or you could simply accept the camera on hand and leave, making sure never to buy anything in that store again. There's yet another option: You could refuse to accept the order and, instead, choose another camera more to your liking from among those already in stock.

These responses illustrate some of the basic ways to modify your environment: assertiveness, withdrawal, or compromise. They are considered *environmental* rather than personal responses to stress because they either change your environment or change the responses of others who are creating stress for you. Let's look at each of these strategies.

1. Assertiveness is the preferred way to manage stress whenever there is a reasonable possibility of success. Assertiveness is *the expression of one's rights and feelings in a direct way without violating the rights of others.* Such an approach consists of direct attempts at modifying the stressful situation itself. Common examples are returning a defective product to a store or speaking up in response to an unreasonable request.

For example, if Steve were an unassertive person, he could have let his boss take advantage of him on various occasions, which would only build up Steve's resentment. Then in the moment of anger when his boss confronted him about the deal falling through, he might have lashed out aggressively, making the situation even more stressful. In contrast, assertiveness has to do with expressing rights and desires without infringing on those of others. Assertiveness is a rational and constructive way of handling stress, which in turn tends to alleviate the stress involved. Steve could have assertively told his boss how frustrated he became when he was given conflicting orders, as when the boss wanted him to close two important deals at the same time. As often happens, his boss might be unaware of the inconsistencies in his requests and change his ways, alleviating much of Steve's stress.

2. Withdrawal means *removing oneself physically or emotionally from an activity, organization, or person.* Withdrawal may be an appropriate response to stress, especially when a stressful situation cannot be successfully modified through assertiveness or compromise (discussed next). By returning to his office the day his boss yelled at him, Steve practiced withdrawal. Another example of withdrawal would be the consumer who actively shops at a different store after getting no satisfaction from the first store's customer service center. Withdrawal is neither good nor bad in itself. Much depends on how it is used. On the one hand, if someone habitually withdraws from stressful situations, that person may drift into a constricted lifestyle that prevents adequate adjustment or personal growth. On the other hand, the use of withdrawal as a temporary strategy may be a valuable means of coping with stress that has become overwhelming or detrimental to one's health. Some examples of temporary withdrawal are destitute students dropping out of school until they can earn more money or marital partners agreeing to a separation while they seek counseling. When no suitable solution is forthcoming, despite the best efforts of the people involved, a permanent withdrawal may be more appropriate.

3. Compromise is still another adaptive response to stress and *occurs when an adjustment is made by modifying opposing ideas or behaviors.* In contrast to withdrawal, compromise allows us to remain in the stressful situation but in a less active way than does the assertive approach. Compromise is most likely to be used when someone holds a higher rank or authority than another or when both participants are at a standstill. The three most common types of compromise are conformity, negotiation, and substitution.

Conformity *as a response to stressful situations involves a change in our behavior due to another's direct influence.* Let's say Steve worked as a buyer for a large corporation that has just established a more elaborate procedure for purchasing, including much more paperwork and more signatures for approval. At the outset, he detests the change. He may comply outwardly by adopting the new procedure even though he dislikes it. Or he could conform to the new demands because he likes his superiors and coworkers enough to accommodate the added stress. Inasmuch as jobs are not easy to get or hold, Steve may take the new procedures in stride and decide that changing his attitude is the most realistic approach, because endless strife and resentment may be more stressful than accommodation or outright assertion. The key question in any type of conformity response, however, is whether the price of the compromise is worth it.

Negotiation is a more active and promising way to achieve compromise in many stressful situations. Negotiation means that *we make mutual concessions with another person.* Steve, for example, might have calmly negotiated more time to explore what went wrong with the big deal, with his boss agreeing that he would give Steve only three days to explore the deal and navigate it again before their next meeting. Often used in the public area of labor management and political disputes, negotiation has now become more widely used at the interpersonal level among coworkers, marriage partners, and friends. Negotiation is preferable to conformity wherever possible because it involves mutual accommodation among the participants.

Substitution means that *we seek alternative goals with another person.* Substitution is another way to achieve compromise with another person when negotiation or conformity is not appropriate. If a woman desires to resume her college education but has small children and cannot enroll full-time, she may decide that the best alternative is to attend part-time. In this case, a substitute means was found to achieve the same goal. At other times, it may become necessary to choose a completely different substitute goal. For example, if Steve explores why the deal fell through, finds that indeed it was his fault, and does not want to be on the receiving end of his boss's ire, he might seek a position with a different company.

Compromise itself is neither good nor bad. Much depends on the relation between the satisfaction achieved and the price paid for the reduction of stress. Habitual compromise may bring more frustration and conflict than a more assertive approach. Too many people suffer in stale jobs or conflict-ridden marriages longer than necessary because compromise has become the easy way out. A life of passive accommodation to undue stress may be more stressful than an assertive or avoidant (withdrawal) approach.

Altering Your Lifestyle

We ultimately have more control over ourselves than over our environment. As a result, we may choose to modify something about ourselves or about our behaviors as a way of better managing stress. There are many possibilities, including developing greater tolerance for stress, altering our everyday habits, learning to control distressing thoughts, acquiring problem-solving skills, and seeking social support.

First, *build up a greater tolerance for stress.* **Stress tolerance** can be defined as *the degree of stress you can handle or how long you can put up with a demanding task without acting in an irrational or disorganized way.* Many of the competent, successful people we admire are probably under a great deal more stress than we realize; they've simply acquired a high tolerance for it. Greater tolerance for pressure—deadlines, competition, criticism from others—usually comes with greater experience and skill. People in high-pressure jobs such as police, surgeons, and firefighters have learned how to stay calm in the face of stress through months and years of experience on the job. Our tolerance for frustration can also be improved by selecting reasonable goals and adjusting our expectations to match the realities of the immediate situation. Likewise, expecting too much of ourselves is a frequent source of frustration. Each of us is disappointed with ourselves from time to time. Rather than wallow in self-pity, it's more helpful to ask what we can do to remedy the situation and then learn from our experience for future reference.

Second, *change your pace of life.* Steve had probably experienced traffic delays before; had he only left earlier on that fateful morning, he would have experienced less stress when his boss was furious over the deal that fell through. You might be bringing a lot of stress on yourself by rushing around and trying to accomplish too much in too little time. A fast pace of life makes you walk, talk, conduct business, and do almost everything faster. Kircaldy, Furnham and Levine (2001) have shown that the pace of life in the United States is already much faster than in other

Slowing our pace of life is a good way to manage stress.

countries. Others echo this notion and blame the increasing pace on our reliance on technology (Wajcman, 2008). Only Japan seems to have a faster pace. Individuals as young as 18 who feel time pressure have blood pressure that is much higher than individuals who don't put themselves under such pressure (Gupta, 2002). Slowing down, then, serves us well. Frequently, we could also lighten the stress by means of better time management.

Third, *learn to control distressful thoughts.* Perhaps you've had the experience of glancing at the first question on a test and muttering to yourself, "If the rest of this test is this hard, I'm going to flunk it." Ironically, such negative self-monitoring interferes with your performance, making you do worse on the test. You can control distressful thoughts by using the following strategy. First, become aware of your negative, catastrophic manner of thinking. You'll probably notice how such thoughts lead you to assume the worst, such as "I'll never make it," "How did I get into this mess?" or "What the heck am I going to do now?" Second, formulate positive thoughts that are incompatible with your distressful thoughts. Some examples are "I can do it; just take it one step at a time," and "I'll keep doing my best and see how things turn out." It also helps to relax and give yourself a mental pat on the back when you've successfully managed distressing thoughts. Take a few minutes to acknowledge to yourself, "I did it; it worked. I'm pleased with the progress I'm making."

Another way to manage distressing thoughts is to replace them with humorous thoughts; humor really works to reduce stress (Cann & Etzel, 2008; Connor & Zhang, 2006; Garrick, 2006; Godfrey, 2004). Do not minimize your stress by making fun of distressing events; rather, take some time to enjoy humor. Read some cartoons, go to lunch with a friend and tell jokes, recall funny events from your life. Humor is a valuable form of coping that can have physiological as well as psychological benefits for distressed individuals. When people laugh, there is a reduction in chemicals associated with stress, and the activity of the immune system frequently is enhanced (Martin, 2001). Humor can also mitigate trauma reactions (Garrick) and reduce anxiety (Szabo, Ainsworth, & Danks, 2005).

Fourth, if needed, *seek help with problem-solving skills.* Most colleges and many community agencies offer a variety of workshops on topics such as assertiveness training, job-hunting skills, and stress management. Some people are wise enough to take such training as a way of bolstering their repertoire of social skills. Others seek it only after encountering problems. Another means for finding help is simply to turn to friends. Numerous studies have shown that we manage stress and trauma more successfully when we have the support of a spouse, close friend, or support group (e.g., Scarpa, Haden, & Hurley, 2006).

Having access to friends and support groups may help to alleviate stress in several ways. Perhaps if Steve had had a trusted office mate with whom he could share his stressful ordeal with the boss, he could have coped better. Why? First, close relationships provide the opportunity to share painful feelings, which if kept to ourselves become more burdensome. Second, friends provide emotional support through their expressions of concern and affection. Third, the understanding and reassurance of our friends may bolster our self-esteem throughout the low periods of our lives. Fourth, concerned friends and support groups may provide information and advice that may help us to reach more effective solutions to our problems, especially support groups that are oriented to a particular problem, such as the death of a spouse. Fifth, friends can enhance positive experiences in our lives (Moritsugu, Wong, & Duffy, 2010). Remember, though, we don't have to turn to friends only in times of trouble; friends can enhance the experience of joy, too.

Using Stress for Personal Growth

How we choose to alter our lifestyle or modify our environment is up to us. Stress management, like stress itself, is a personal matter. Each of us faces a different combination of stressful events at work and at home. The important thing to remember is that we can do something to manage stress more effectively. We don't have to be passive victims to whom things happen. Instead, we can look at ourselves as active agents who take charge of our lives. No matter how stressful the situation, there's always something we can do to reduce the stress.

Keep in mind that stress can be a valuable means of self-understanding. We don't fully know what we can do until we have to do it. Each time we successfully get through a stressful situation, like a difficult course at school or a trying problem in our love life, we gain in self-confidence. Even experiences of disappointment and failure are sometimes blessings in disguise. Perhaps we weren't ready for the task at hand, or we were pursuing the wrong goals. Sometimes a minor failure today can save us from a bigger letdown later on.

Finally, we can make stress work for us. Remember that stress is not synonymous with distress or stressed out. Too little stress and we become bored and lazy. Too much and we become tense, make mistakes, and get sick more easily. To get the most out of life, each of us needs to find our optimal level of stress and the types of stress we handle best. Properly managed, stress gives zest to life. A stressful situation can challenge us to try harder, evoking our best and bringing personal growth.

SUMMARY

OH NO!—UNDERSTANDING STRESS

The great majority of adult Americans experience a high level of stress at one time or another. One in four people lives with high stress daily. Stress is defined as the pattern of specific and nonspecific responses an organism makes to stimulus events that disturb its equilibrium and tax its ability to cope. However, stress may have beneficial as well as harmful effects, depending on the person and the situation. A major source of stress is the combination of various life changes, both positive and negative, including major life events as well as daily hassles. At the same time, our overall experience of stress is affected by a variety of personal and situational factors, such as how we perceive events and the degree of control we believe we have over them.

YIKES!—REACTIONS TO STRESS

Some reactions to stress occur more or less spontaneously, including physiological reactions as well as certain emotional, behavioral reactions. Many of our body's reactions to stress can be understood in relation to Selye's general adaptation syndrome, either in the initial alarm reaction or the successive stages of resistance or exhaustion. Another explanation for the effects of stress on our bodies relates to the notion of fight or flight, which also produces physiological responses to stressors. A third conceptualization is that of allostasis and allostatic overload. Psychological reactions to stress include the familiar defense mechanisms, or emergency responses, such as rationalization as well as other emotional reactions that vary somewhat with the level of stress. At the same time, each of us experiences the same stressful situations somewhat differently, depending on our particular personality and coping strategies.

PHEW!—MANAGING STRESS

Managing stress successfully involves more than automatic, symptom-reducing reactions to stress. Stress management means taking charge, directing and controlling our responses to stress so that we modify the overall stress. The two major ways of doing so are modifying our environment and altering our lifestyle. The three main ways of modifying the situational sources of stress are assertiveness, the preferred response; withdrawal, when appropriate; and compromise, especially negotiation, because it involves mutual accommodation among participants.

Alleviating stress by altering our lifestyle includes building greater stress tolerance, changing our pace of life, controlling distressful thoughts, and acquiring problem-solving skills. Finally, remember that stress is not synonymous with distress. Instead, to get the most out of life, each of us needs to find our optimal level of stress and use it as a method of growth.

SELF-TEST

1. Stress that has a beneficial effect on us is called
   a. eustress.
   b. hypostress.
   c. distress.
   d. hyperstress.

2. When under stress, how do people react? With
   a. cognitive changes.
   b. emotional changes.
   c. behavioral changes.
   d. any of the above.

3. An alternative explanation to Selye's general adaptation syndrome to explain the body's reaction to stress is
   a. the fight-or-flight response.
   b. eustress vs. distress.
   c. the alarm reaction.
   d. social isolation response.

4. The first stage in the general adaptation syndrome is
   a. any of the following can be first.
   b. exhaustion.
   c. alarm.
   d. resistance.

5. Symptoms of stress-related illnesses such as a peptic ulcer are most likely to develop in which stage of the general adaptation syndrome?
   a. Exhaustion
   b. Resistance
   c. Alarm reaction
   d. Flight

6. The exclusion of unacceptable ideas or feelings from consciousness is called
   a. suppression.
   b. rationalization.
   c. repression.
   d. denial.

7. One *environmental* means for managing stress is
   a. using compromise.
   b. self-deprecation.
   c. building stress tolerance.
   d. using problem-focused coping.

8. You're returning a recently purchased, defective coat. An assertive response would be to
   a. apologize, then ask to have the coat repaired.
   b. threaten to sue the store and a specific employee.
   c. complain about the poor quality of the merchandise.
   d. ask for another coat without the defect.

9. A desirable way of handling stress that involves mutual accommodation among all the participants is
   a. denial.
   b. conformity.
   c. negotiation.
   d. withdrawal.

10. New research indicates that most people manage distress and even trauma
    a. with resilience or hardiness.
    b. very poorly at best.
    c. via anxiety and depression.
    d. by withdrawal or compromise.

EXERCISES

1. *Take an inventory of your stress.* List the most common ways you manage stress. When you think back over the past six months, did you handle stress well? If not, why not? Do you think that if you changed how you react to stress, you would manage stress better?

2. *Daily hassles.* Jot down some of the little things in everyday life that annoy or distress you, for example, a friend who is perpetually late or being stuck in traffic. Which hassles bother you the most? Select two or three of them and suggest specific ways you could make them less troublesome.

3. *Defense mechanisms.* Think of a particular situation in which you reacted defensively. Which defense mechanism(s) did you rely on? How well did you cope with this situation? If you face a similar situation in the future, would you handle it differently? How so?

4. *Describe your most stressful experience.* In a page or so, tell what made the incident or experience so stressful and how you coped with it. How well did your coping mechanisms work in this situation?

5. *Managing stress assertively.* Recall a stressful situation that you wished you had handled in a more assertive manner. How did you react in this situation? What happened as a result? If you're faced with a similar situation in the future, how could you handle it more assertively?

QUESTIONS FOR SELF-REFLECTION

1. Can you recall several instances when stress had a beneficial effect?

2. Which situations do you find most distressing?

3. What are some of the "little things" that get you down?

4. Would you agree that having some control over your work activities makes them less stressful?

5. How can you tell when you're under a lot of stress?

6. When you become defensive, how do you behave?

7. Are you inclined to abuse alcohol or drugs when under stress?

8. What are some ways you've modified your environment to decrease stress?

9. Have you tried altering your lifestyle as a way of alleviating stress?

10. Do you believe that you have the traits of hardiness and resilience?

11. All things considered, how well do you manage stress?

FOR FURTHER INFORMATION

RECOMMENDED READINGS

CHARLESWORTH, E. A., & NATHAN, R. G. (2004). *Stress management: A comprehensive guide to wellness.* New York: Ballantine Books. The authors not only discuss stress and how to manage it, they highlight how to move beyond recovery to wellness.

EPSTEIN, R. (2000). *The big book of stress-relief games.* New York: McGraw-Hill. A fun book filled with ways to help relieve stress.

McEWEN, B. S., & LASLEY, E. N. (2002). *The end of stress as we know it.* Washington, DC: Joseph Henry Press. A scientific book that examines how the brain and stress respond to each other with an eye toward understanding how to prevent the physiological damage stress creates.

PRESTON, J. (2002). *Survivors: Stories and strategies to heal the hurt.* Atascadero, CA: Impact Publishers. Using the stories of four different people, the book shows how people cope with difficult experiences.

SCAER, R. C. (2005). *The trauma spectrum: Hidden wounds and human resilience.* New York: W. W. Norton. An exceptionally good book on trauma with new information on resiliency.

WEBSITES AND THE INTERNET

http://www.stressrelease.com Contains lots of information on stress, such as the reasons for it and tips on stress management. Check out the online resources section.

http://www.stress.org The site for the American Institute of Stress, which is committed to developing a better understanding of how to tap into the vast innate potential that resides in each of us for preventing disease and promoting health.

http://www.humorproject.com A site with many humor resources and products and information.

http://www.mentalhealth.org The site of the U.S. Department of Health and Human Services—Division on Substance Abuse and Mental Health Services Administration. Excellent information on trauma and terrorism, especially for parents and teachers.

http://www.psychologymatters.org/trauma.html Part of the American Psychological Association's online public information site. Includes material on trauma, stress, and hardiness.

Understanding Mental Disorders

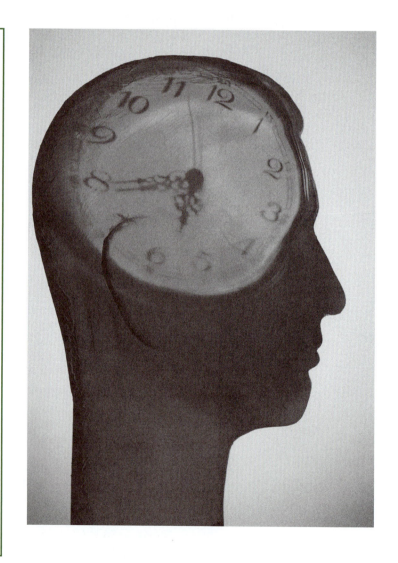

With a good job in the loan department of a bank, Lisa, age 23, was a happy young adult, or so it seemed. She began working for the bank immediately upon her graduation from college and slowly worked her way up through the ranks such that she held a good mid-level management job. She was engaged to Hans, a modest young man who worked in a different department of the bank. Lisa had recently moved back home in the same city to live with her widowed mother, who was having some health problems, one of which was a deep depression due to the recent loss of her husband. Although Lisa was not very happy about this arrangement, as it restricted her freedom after work and the time she could spend with Hans, she nonetheless felt it was her duty as a good daughter—and an only child—to care for her ailing mother. Just when Lisa thought her mother was improving, her mother suddenly died. The surprise of this event deepened Lisa's angst. At the same time, her mother's health care and funeral left Lisa and the estate with some large unpaid bills. Lisa became more depressed as she tried to manage the aftermath of her mother's death, including paying the bills and estate taxes, negotiating with the funeral home, and settling other matters related to her mother's estate. Three months after her mother's death, Lisa was greeted by another unpleasant surprise. Hans announced that he had been given a promotion, was seeing someone else, and wanted to break their engagement. In the time that Lisa had been caring for her mother, Hans had met another woman. Again, Lisa was stunned and dismayed. As if this weren't enough to worry her, there were rumors at the bank that her department would shortly be downsized. With all this bad news, Lisa soon found that she had difficulty getting out of bed each morning. She would then stand in her closet for a long time trying to decide what to wear to work. In fact, Lisa began missing work; she would call in sick even though she really felt she was "just tired." Eventually, Lisa's coworkers began noticing that she appeared somewhat disheveled—not the old meticulous, orderly Lisa. Lisa's formerly short hair went uncut and unkempt. Sometimes she wore the same sweater and wrinkled skirt all week only to have the same garments reappear the following week. Lisa's coworkers also noticed she was losing weight. One day Lisa did not materialize for work and neither did she call in sick. After this happened three more days in a row, one of her closest coworkers went to Lisa's house to find her in bed alternately staring at the ceiling and sighing. Lisa appeared normal, at least she was able to carry on a rather normal conversation, albeit groggily, but she did not want to get out of bed or to eat anything. The coworker also found that the house was a mess. There was garbage overflowing the cans, newspapers piled in front of the door, and clothing strewn everywhere; the mail was unopened, and old cat food containers littered the kitchen. "What was wrong with Lisa?" wondered her friend.

PSYCHOLOGICAL DISORDERS

Among themselves, Lisa's coworkers and friends might call her "neurotic" or "nuts." Others might refer to her as a "weirdo." Upon hearing of her admission to the local hospital, they might say Lisa was having a "nervous breakdown." Psychologists and other mental health professionals generally avoid such terms because not only are they negative, they are stigmatizing. Instead, specialists tend to focus on more relevant matters, such as Lisa's intense personal distress and the degree of impairment in her everyday behavior. In short, mental health professionals would be concerned about the type and severity of Lisa's disorder and, thus, how best to help her. They might also be interested in her family history of similar disorders. As it turned out, Lisa was suffering from a major depressive episode.

The study of psychological disorders is often associated with abnormal behavior because many disorders involve thoughts, feelings, or actions that are not considered "normal." Abnormal behavior and psychological disorders, however, are not synonymous. For instance, some forms of depression are too common to be labeled abnormal or statistically "out of the normal" but are nevertheless classified as psychological disorders. Other behaviors may be considered socially deviant or unusual, such as running nude across the field at a soccer game, without being considered a psychological disorder. Consequently, we'll begin by looking at some of the common standards used in defining psychological disorders and the incidence of such disorders. We will then turn to how disorders are classified, so as to provide you with some general background on this topic.

What Are Psychological Disorders?

You may be surprised to know that there is no precise and universally agreed-on standard that distinguishes between abnormal and normal behavior or, for that matter, between the presence of a psychological disorder and no disorder. Probably the most widely accepted guide in these matters is the *Diagnostic and Statistical Manual of Mental Disorders,* Fourth Edition (text revision), or DSM-IV-TR, published by the American Psychiatric Association. This manual is popularly referred to in shorthand as the DSM (American Psychiatric Association, 2000). The DSM is a controversial manual and is undergoing yet another revision probably available in 2012 (*Clinical Psychiatry News,* 2001; *Harvard Mental Health Letter,* 2002a; Genova, 2003; Hinshaw & Stier, 2008). At the outset, the authors acknowledge the difficulties in defining a psychological disorder, much less specifying precise boundaries for particular disorders. For now, let us define **psychological disorder** as *a clinically significant behavioral or psychological pattern that is associated with* (1) *present personal distress;* (2) *disability or impairment in one or more important areas of functioning, e.g., maladaptive behaviors;* (3) *significantly increased risk of suffering disability, pain, or death; and* (4) *an important loss of freedom or personal control* (American Psychiatric Association).

As noted in the definition, a major factor in diagnosing a disorder is the individual's level of **personal distress,** which is *intense or chronic negative self-awareness that interferes with one's sense of well-being or functioning.* Someone with a chronic fear of heights or a marked change in mood such as Lisa's severe depression might be diagnosed as having a psychological disorder. When Lisa would not get out of bed or take out the trash because it seemed too onerous, we begin to suspect that Lisa had a mental disorder. On the other hand, people who behave in an unusual or eccentric way but are otherwise happy would probably not be so diagnosed. If Lisa were artistic and saved empty cat food cans and other pieces of metal to produce sculptures, we would not assume that she was "ill." As useful as this standard of personal distress is, it isn't sufficiently comprehensive to help us define or diagnose a mental disorder.

Another important feature in defining a disorder is **maladaptive behavior,** *significant impairment in one or more areas of psychological functioning, especially the ability to work and to get along with others.* As implied in the definition, people with psychological disorders usually suffer from a significant impairment in their inability to work, to care for themselves, or to get along with family and friends. This is a *practical* approach because it focuses on behavior that is relevant to daily living. Accordingly, when Lisa manifested intense grief in response to her mother's death, she was not considered to have a disorder because she was able to plan and attend her mother's funeral in appropriate ways. It was her eventual inability to care for herself and her inability to get out of bed and work that led others to believe she was experiencing problems.

A third issue of relevance is the individual's *increased risk for suffering disability, pain, or death.* Individuals who exhibit maladaptive behaviors and impairments in daily living put themselves at risk for harm, for example, people who are addicted to certain substances often fail to take care of themselves. Lisa, too, had stopped taking care of herself; she did not take showers, comb her hair, brush her teeth, nor maintain a healthy diet. Lisa did not keep her apartment clean and so allowed the trash to pile up as she sank deeper and deeper into depression.

Another dimension of mental disorder is *the violation of social norms.* **Social norms** are *generalized expectations regarding appropriate behavior in a given situation or society.* People in every studied society live by certain rules of what is acceptable and unacceptable. When an individual repeatedly violates commonly accepted social norms, that person may be considered to have a psychological disorder if other conditions also prevail. Such rule violations can result in *the loss of freedom and control* for the individual because others fear the individual will hurt them or hurt him- or herself. Lisa's supervisor, for example, was thinking of talking to her about her recent and too casual mode of dress as well as her unkempt hair. It may well be the violation of social norms that intimidates others when they witness the socially inappropriate behavior of someone with a mental disorder. This fear factor can lead to stigmatization of those with mental disorders. In fact, research has shown that despite increased availability of information on mental disorders, stigma against those who suffer it has actually increased (Hinshaw & Stier, 2008). You can read more about stigma in Box 14–1.

You already know that social norms not only vary from culture to culture but sometimes vary within a culture. In most societies, people commonly eat in public but do not urinate in front of others. Each society has social norms about what is appropriate to eat

---

Box 14–1

ANTISTIGMA: DO YOU KNOW THE FACTS?

Stigma is not just a matter of using the wrong word. Stigma is about disrespect. **Stigma** is *the use of negative labels to identify a person living with a mental disorder or with another distinguishing feature and who you believe differs from you.* Stigma is a barrier, because it causes exclusion, rejection, and devaluation of the stigmatized individual (Weiss & Ramakrishna, 2006). Fear of stigma, and the resulting discrimination, discourages individuals and their families from getting the help they need (Gary, 2005; Vaccaro, 2004). An estimated 22 to 23 percent of the U.S. population experiences a mental disorder in any given year, but almost half of these individuals do not seek treatment.

The following information encourages the use of positive images to refer to people with mental disorders and underscores the reality that mental disorders can be successfully treated:

- Do you know that stigma is not a matter of using the wrong word or action?

- Do you know that stigma is about disrespect and using negative labels to identify a person living with a mental disorder?

- Do you know that stigma is a barrier that discourages individuals and their families from seeking help?

- Do you know that many people would rather tell employers they committed a petty crime and served time in jail than admit to having been in a psychiatric hospital?

- Do you know that stigma can result in inadequate insurance coverage for mental health services?

- Do you know that stigma leads to fear, mistrust, and violence against people living with mental disorder and their families?

- Do you know that stigma can cause families and friends to turn their backs on people with mental disorders?

- Do you know that stigma can prevent people from obtaining access to needed mental health services?

DO'S

- Do use respectful language.

- Do emphasize abilities, not limitations.

- Do tell someone if they express a stigmatizing attitude.

DON'TS

- Don't portray successful persons with disabilities as superhuman.

- Don't use generic labels such as *retarded* or *mentally ill.*

- Don't use terms like *crazy, lunatic, manic-depressive,* or *slow-functioning.*

SOURCE: SAMHSA's National Mental Health Information Center (2003). The Center for Mental Health Services. http://www.mentalhealth.org/publications/allpubs/OEL99-0004/default.asp.

(yogurt or pig's intestines) and how to eat (for example, with chopsticks or a spoon). In the United States, it is often acceptable to eat food at a rock concert or sporting event but not at a church or funeral service. It would be unusual, though, to see an American consuming blini (Russian pancakes) and borsch (beet soup) at a basketball game.

If you understand the significance of these cultural differences, you will not be surprised to know that the frequency of mental disorders varies from culture to culture, too (NIMH, 2007c; Osborne, 2001; Xiao-Ping, 2004). For instance, the prevalence of depression is low in China and many parts of Africa—just the opposite of its occurrence in the United States. One explanation is that in Western (or individualistic) societies, individuals are more likely to be held personally responsible for their failures and misfortunes and thus may be more susceptible to depression as they turn their focus inward to their own perceived deficits. Box 14–2 discusses the issue of diversity and mental disorder in more detail.

Box 14–2

DIVERSITY AND MENTAL DISORDER

The United States is home to a boundless array of cultures, races, and ethnicities. Diversity has enriched our nation by bringing global ideas, perspectives, and productive contributions to all areas of contemporary life. The enduring contributions of minorities, like those of all Americans, rest on a foundation of mental health. Mental health is fundamental to overall health and productivity. It is the basis for successful contributions to family, community, and society. Throughout the life span, mental health is the wellspring of thinking and communication skills, learning, resilience, and self-esteem. It is all too easy to dismiss the value of mental health until problems appear.

Major mental disorders like schizophrenia, bipolar disorder, and depression are found worldwide, across all racial and ethnic groups, wherever researchers have surveyed. In the United States, based on the available evidence, the prevalence of mental disorders for racial and ethnic minorities is similar to that for Whites. There are, however, several documented and important disparities affecting mental health care of racial and ethnic minorities compared with that of Whites (Gary, 2005; Nelson, 2006; Schraufhagel, Wagner, Miranda, & Roy-Byrne, 2006; Moritsugu, Wong & Duffy, 2010):

- Minorities have less access to and availability of mental health services.

- Minorities are less likely to receive needed mental health services.

Minorities are less likely to receive needed mental health services.

(continued)

Box 14–2 *(continued)*

- Minorities in treatment often receive a poorer quality of mental health care.

- Minorities are underrepresented in mental health research.

A constellation of barriers deters minorities from reaching treatment. Many of these barriers operate for all Americans: cost, fragmentation of services, lack of availability of services, and societal stigma of mental disorders. But additional barriers deter racial and ethnic minorities: mistrust and fear of treatment, racism and discrimination, and differences in language and communication (Nelson, 2006). For example, the diagnosis and treatment of mental disorders greatly depend on verbal communication and trust between patient and clinician. More broadly, mental health care disparities may also stem from minorities' historical and present-day struggles with racism and discrimination (Nelson) that affect their mental health, contribute to their lower economic, social, and political status, and diminish health professionals' desire to communicate with them.

Ethnic and racial minorities collectively experience a greater disability burden from mental disorders than do Whites. This higher level of burden stems from minorities' receiving less care and poorer quality of care, rather than from their disorders being inherently more severe or prevalent in the community. By receiving effective treatment, they have greater burdens of disability in terms of lost workdays and limitations in daily activities. Most troubling of all, the burden for minorities is growing. Racial and ethnic groups are becoming more populous, all the while experiencing continuing inequality of income and economic opportunity.

Culture also plays a pivotal role in mental health, mental disorder, and mental health services (NIMH, 2007c). Understanding the wide-ranging roles of culture enables the mental health field to design and deliver services that are more responsive to the needs of racial and ethnic minorities. **Culture** is broadly defined as *the ideas, customs, arts, and skills that characterize a group of people during a given period of history*. The term *culture* is as applicable to Whites as it is to racial and ethnic minorities.

With a seemingly endless range of cultural subgroups and individual variations, culture is important because it bears upon what *all* people bring to the clinical setting. It can account for variations in how consumers communicate their symptoms and which ones they report. Some aspects of culture may also underlie **culture-bound syndromes**—*sets of symptoms much more common in some societies than in others*. More often, culture bears upon whether people even seek help in the first place, what types of help they seek, what coping styles and social supports they have, and how much stigma they attach to mental disorder. All cultures also feature strengths, such as resilience and adaptive ways of coping, which buffer some people from developing certain disorders.

Culture is a concept not limited to individuals with mental disorders and their families. It also applies to the professionals who treat them. Every group of professionals embodies a "culture" in the sense that they, too, have a shared set of beliefs, norms, and values. A professional's culture can be gleaned from the jargon used, the orientation and emphasis in their handbooks, and their mindset or way of looking at the world. They may view symptoms, diagnoses, and treatments in ways that sometimes diverge from their clients' views, especially when the cultural backgrounds of the consumer and provider are dissimilar. This divergence of viewpoints can create barriers to effective care.

Source: Adapted from *Mental health: A report of the Surgeon General* (1999). http://www.mentalhealth.org/cre/execsummary.

As you can see, there is no simple way of determining when someone has a psychological disorder. In practice, mental health professionals rely on a combination of standards to determine whether a given behavior is normal. To review, the four factors most likely taken into account when arriving at a diagnosis are (1) personal distress, (2) significant impairment in one or more areas of functioning, (3) the social acceptability (norms) of the individual's behavior, and (4) an important loss of personal control.

How Common Are Psychological Disorders?

Mental disorders are a burden worldwide. Surprisingly, mental disorders rank second after cardiovascular diseases in the **global burden of diseases**, which is *a measure of years of life lost to disability throughout the world*. Donna Shalala, former U.S. Secretary of Health and Human Services, in a major report on the subject said that the burden of mental disorders has long been profoundly underestimated. Shalala said that major depression is equivalent in terms of hardship to blindness or paraplegia (Shalala, 1999). Approximately 14.8 million U.S. adults alone have a depressive disorder in any given year (National Institute of Mental Health [NIMH], 2006a) and each year, major mental disorders cost the United States $193 billion annually in lost earnings (NIMH, 2008a). Worldwide, schizophrenia is listed as the eighth leading cause of disability in terms of adjusted (reduced) life years, not to mention the burden it places on the caregivers (Rössler, Salize, van Os, & Riecher-Rössler, 2005). Thus, it is important for us to understand and to study mental disorders.

Much information about the extent of psychological disorders comes from in-depth surveys of representative samples of the population, along with admission figures to various mental health facilities such as psychiatric hospitals and community mental health clinics. Two frequently used terms are *incidence* and *prevalence*. **Incidence** refers to *the number of new cases of disorders reported during a given period*. This term is usually distinguished from **prevalence**, which refers to *the total number of active cases that can be identified in a given population at a particular time* (Moritsugu, Wong, & Duffy, 2010).

During any one-year period, mental health professionals estimate that one in four adults will suffer from some type of psychological disorder (NIMH, 2006d). Overall, about one out of every three persons will experience at least one significant psychological problem in his or her lifetime. People who have a psychological disorder usually experience their first symptoms by early adulthood (Keller, 2008; NIMH, 2006d); three-fourths of those surveyed reported their first symptoms by age 24. In this case, Lisa is typical. However, symptoms of alcohol abuse, obsessive-compulsive behavior, bipolar disorder, and schizophrenia appear somewhat earlier, at a median age near 20.

There is a popular notion that more women than men are "emotionally disturbed." Is there any truth to this view? Apparently not. When all disorders are taken into account, men and women are equally likely to suffer from psychological disorders. However, the patterns of disorders differ somewhat between the sexes (World Health Organization [WHO], 2006). Women suffer more from phobias (intense and irrational fear) and depression (a sense of hopelessness and lack of pleasure in life much like that experienced by Lisa), and men are more apt to abuse alcohol and drugs and exhibit long-term antisocial behavior (WHO). At the same time, women are twice as likely as men to seek help, which may have given the mistaken impression in the past that women were more troubled by mental disorder than men.

How Are Disorders Classified?

Because there are no sharp boundaries between the various psychological disorders (Office of the Surgeon General, 1999), or between a psychological disorder and no disorder, you can readily appreciate the difficulty of classifying disorders. The coworker who went to Lisa's home was fairly sure there was something amiss with Lisa but was not certain what it was. A psychologist or psychiatrist might also need some time to diagnose the type and extent of Lisa's disorder. However, within the limitations mentioned earlier, the DSM classifies, defines, and describes over 200 psychological disorders, using practical criteria as the basis of classification. To arrive at a **diagnosis**—*in which the problem is classified within a set of recognized categories of abnormal behavior*—the clinician compares the behavior of the "patient" with the description in the manual and then selects the label of the description that best fits the problem. The purpose is to provide an accurate description of the person's overall problem and functioning, along with a prediction for the course of the disorder, which helps during treatment. The diagnosis also helps professionals communicate with and understand one another.

Throughout the DSM, the emphasis is on classifying behavior patterns, *not* people, as is often thought. Thus, the manual refers to "people who exhibit the symptoms of schizophrenia" rather than to "schizophrenics." Also, the terminology refers to "mental health professionals" and "clinicians" instead of "psychiatrists," thereby acknowledging the broader range of professionals who deal with people with psychological disorders. Finally, the emphasis is on describing rather than interpreting psychological disorders, especially when the causal factors are unknown. Thus, the DSM gives clinicians a practical, behavioral approach to dealing with people exhibiting symptoms of psychological disorders.

In the rest of this chapter, we'll describe two different sets of disorders: (1) the more common disorders, such as the anxiety disorders, affective or mood disorders, and personality disorders, as well as (2) the more serious but less common disorders such as schizophrenia. In addition, some of the other disorders as well as some thought-provoking issues will be highlighted in separate boxed items.

ANXIETY DISORDERS: THE MOST COMMON DISORDERS

Most of us experience anxiety or fear some of the time; it is a natural emotional response to stress and is often a normal part of life (*Harvard Women's Health Watch,* 2002; Monroe & Reid, 2009). Being anxious before a big job interview is to be expected. In fact, when Lisa first interviewed for her bank job, which she really wanted when she was fresh out of college, she felt jittery but was able to compose herself.

Sometimes anxiety can be energizing; extremely high levels of anxiety, though, can be immobilizing. High anxiety can prevent people from leaving their homes. It can also make them block out daily news events, avoid other people, refuse to answer the phone, and in general not enjoy everyday life. In individuals with **anxiety disorders,** *a group of disorders characterized by symptoms of excessive or inappropriate anxiety or attempts to escape from such anxiety,* the anxiety is out of all proportion to the stressful situation. In fact, anxiety may occur in the absence of any specific danger. In brief, anxiety disorders may be experienced in several ways:

- **Generalized anxiety disorder** identified as *a chronic state of diffuse or free-floating anxiety.* In this disorder, the anxiety itself becomes the predominant disturbance.
- **Phobic disorder** is *intense anxiety evoked by some specific and irrational object or activity,* such as flying in a plane.
- **Obsessive-compulsive disorder** is marked by *the involuntary dwelling on an unwelcome thought or the involuntary repetition of an unnecessary action.*

Let's review these in detail.

Generalized Anxiety Disorder

The main characteristic of generalized anxiety disorder is a persistent sense of "free-floating" anxiety. The person is anxious most of the time or suffers from periodic panic attacks, as occurs in the closely related panic disorder. People who are chronically anxious can't say what they are afraid of. All they know is that they feel on edge all the time. They generally worry a lot and anticipate the occurrence of something bad. Lisa, for example, felt this way when her mother was ill, but the anxiety did not yet incapacitate her. Anxiety may disrupt the everyday functioning of individuals with generalized anxiety disorder such that they may find it hard to concentrate and make decisions. People with this disorder may also develop headaches, muscular tension, indigestion, a strained face, and fidgeting. Frequently, they become apprehensive about their anxiety and fear their condition will cause ulcers or a heart attack or make them go crazy.

Chronically anxious people can also suffer from **panic attacks,** *characterized by the occurrence of severe panic.* These intense attacks occur in the absence of a feared situation and usually last 15 to 30 minutes (Mentalhelp.net, 2000a). In some instances, the attack occurs in response to a specific phobic situation, such as driving in city traffic or speaking publicly. At other times, the panic does not seem to be produced by a specific instigator. In a panic attack, anxiety increases to an almost intolerable level. The individual breaks out in a cold sweat, feels dizzy, and may have difficulty breathing. Victims almost always have a feeling of inescapable doom, as if they won't make it to safety or will die. Panic attacks usually last only a few minutes but may continue for hours. Because panic attacks are unpredictable, they often create additional anxiety, and the victims avoid certain situations in which they fear losing control, being helpless, or experiencing panic. To determine your own general level of anxiety, try the scale in Activity 14–1.

ACTIVITY 14–1

How Anxious Are You?

The following scale was developed for this book. It is designed for you to think about your characteristic anxiety level or your trait anxiety. This is not a scientific scale. If you have a high score, you might think about whether anxiety interferes with your academic performance or other important behaviors and then consider ways you can lower your anxiety level.

Place a check mark next to each statement that is typical or characteristic of you:

_____   I often have a sense of dread or impending doom but cannot always identify what it is I fear.

_____   I find that I am afraid of things others do not seem to be afraid of.

_____   My friends think I worry more than they do about examinations, meeting deadlines, and so forth.

_____   I seem to have more stomachaches, headaches, and other signs of anxiety than others do.

_____ I frequently feel restless and tense and do not sleep as well as I should.

_____ Many times, I try to avoid situations that cause me anxiety, such as public speaking or meeting strangers.

_____ I probably perspire and have rapid heartbeats when it is inappropriate (e.g., when I have not been exercising).

_____ Decisions, especially important decisions, are usually difficult for me to make.

_____ Compared to others, I feel that I have difficulty concentrating on even the simplest of tasks.

_____ My friends are not as afraid as I am of everyday situations, such as becoming lost in a new part of a city.

SCORING: Add up the number of check marks. The highest score you can receive is 10. If you scored 7 or higher, you might want to consider whether you have high anxiety levels and whether these high levels interfere with your life. If you decide "yes," you should explore ways to reduce your anxiety. Professional help or some of the techniques in the following chapter on psychotherapy may prove useful.

Phobias: Fear of Something That Won't Really Hurt

Phobic disorders are _characterized by a persistent and irrational fear of a specific object or activity, accompanied by a compelling desire to avoid it._ The object or activity typically does not merit such intense fear. Most of us experience an irrational avoidance of selected objects, like spiders or snakes, but it usually has no major impact on our lives. In contrast, when the avoidance becomes a _significant_ source of distress to the individual and interferes with everyday behavior, the diagnosis of a phobic disorder is warranted. There are several major types of phobic disorders: simple phobias, social phobias, and agoraphobia.

Simple phobias are _the most common type of phobia in the general population. Commonly feared objects include animals, particularly dogs, snakes, and insects._ Other simple phobias are **acrophobia,** _the fear of heights,_ and **claustrophobia,** _the fear of closed places._ Most simple phobias originate in childhood and disappear without treatment. However, the more intense fears that persist into adulthood generally don't disappear without treatment.

Social phobia is _an extreme form of shyness that can interfere with an individual's daily life and involves a chronic, irrational fear of and a compelling desire to avoid situations where others may scrutinize the individual._ If confronted with the necessity of entering such a situation, the person experiences marked anxiety and attempts to avoid it. Examples are an intense fear of speaking or performing in public, eating in public, using public lavatories, and writing in the presence of others. Although this type of disorder itself is rarely incapacitating, it does result in considerable inconvenience, such as avoiding a trip that involves the use of a public lavatory. Also, in an effort to relieve their anxiety, individuals with this disorder often abuse alcohol, barbiturates, and other anti-anxiety medications.

Agoraphobia, classically known as "_fear of open spaces,_" is typically the most severe phobic reaction and the one for which people most often seek treatment. Agoraphobia is *a cluster of different fears, all of which evoke intense anxiety about crowds or open spaces,* such as crowded stores, elevators or tunnels, or public transportation. This type of phobia tends to occur in the late teens or early 20s, although it can occur later in life. During outbreaks of this phobia, refusing to go outside, the victims are often housebound. If they go out, they take great care to avoid certain situations, such as being in an elevator. Box 14–3 presents the names and descriptions of other types of phobias. Some people "medicate" themselves with alcohol or other substances so as to curb their fear.

Obsessive-Compulsive Disorder: The Doubting Disease

The essential feature of **obsessive-compulsive disorder** (OCD) involves the *involuntary dwelling on an unwelcome thought or the involuntary repetition of an unnecessary act.* It has sometimes been called the "doubting disease" (Groopman, 2000) because many individuals with OCD develop habitual behaviors to help them avoid anxiety. Anxiety occurs when the individual does not engage in a particular thought or uses avoidance behavior, for example, repeatedly checking a door previously locked or compulsively washing one's hands. Research suggests that a critical feature of OCD is an *overinflated sense of responsibility* (Arntz, Voncken, & Goosen, 2007; Mentalhelp.net, 2000a).

An **obsession** is *a thought or image that keeps recurring in the mind, despite the individual's attempts to ignore or resist it.* Similarly, a **compulsion** is *an act that the individual feels compelled to repeat again and again, usually in a ritualistic fashion or according to certain rules.* The act is performed with a sense of compulsion, coupled with a desire to resist such action, at least initially. The individual usually realizes that the behavior is senseless and does not derive pleasure from carrying it out, though doing so provides a release of tension. OCD is thought to be caused by disruption of the basal ganglia of the brain. The basal ganglia is a region in the brain that filters messages (*Harvard Mental Health Letter,* 1998).

Most of us experience mild obsessions from time to time. Lisa sometimes found herself repeatedly humming a tune she didn't even like. These minor obsessions are temporary and do not interfere with everyday activities. In contrast, pathological obsessions reoccur day after day. They sometimes involve thoughts of lust and violence, partly because of their association with the individual's anxiety and guilt, which makes the thoughts even more

---

Box 14–3

DO YOU RECOGNIZE ANY OF THESE PHOBIAS?

Acrophobia—fear of heights

Autophobia—fear of oneself

Decidophobia—fear of making decisions

Ergophobia—fear of work

Gamophobia—fear of marriage

Hypergiaphobia—fear of responsibility

Monophobia—fear of being alone

Mysophobia—fear of dirt

Nyctophobia—fear of darkness

Ophidiophobia—fear of snakes

Topophobia—fear of performing (stage fright)

Triskaidekaphobia—fear of the number 13

Zoophobia—fear of animals

disruptive. Examples are the fear of being contaminated by germs or the fear that one will kill one's child or spouse. Such compulsions tend to fall into several categories (Mentalhelp.net, 2000a), such as *hoarders,* who collect almost anything and cannot get rid of it; *repeaters,* who feel they must repeat a behavior a set number of times; or *orderers,* who want their possessions in certain places and arranged in certain ways.

Trauma and Disaster

Let's continue our discussion of anxiety disorders. Because terrorist activity has haunted Americans since before September 11, 2001, psychologists have turned concerted attention to victims of trauma and disaster (Marshall et al., 2007).

In the chapter on stress, **posttraumatic stress disorder** (PTSD) is briefly reviewed. In short, *PTSD is a severe anxiety disorder characterized by symptoms of anxiety and avoidance behavior; this disorder results from an unusually stressful event such as being assaulted.* Of course, other events can be traumatic and include but are not limited to the devastation of wars, natural disasters, sniper attacks, rapes, plane crashes, terrorism, horrific car accidents, and murders. As you can see, most of the causes of PTSD involve life-threatening events (*Harvard Women's Health Watch,* 2005). PTSD is commonly typified by intense fear, flashbacks (reliving the event over and over again), and nightmares (Nemeroff et al., 2006). Other signs that a person is suffering from PTSD include mood swings, irritability, depression, crying often, limited attention span, difficulty concentrating, confusion, poor work or school performance, self-medication with drugs or alcohol, headaches, sleep disturbance, and stomach problems among others.

Certain individuals are more prone to PTSD than others (McNally et al., 2003; Nemeroff et al., 2006). These persons include those directly exposed to the trauma, such as crime witnesses, fire or police personnel, victims who narrowly escape death, emergency

Police and other first responders are more likely than those not exposed to trauma to suffer from post-traumatic stress disorder.

rescue and medical workers, and those who have already lost a loved one, especially in a traumatic fashion. Women are more likely than men to be vulnerable to PTSD (NIMH, 2006e); children are also more vulnerable than adults, especially if they have been abused or are suffering from chronic stress such as living in a war zone. People who lack social support or have a preexisting mental disorder are also more susceptible to PTSD (*Harvard Mental Health Letter,* 2002a; McNally et al.).

There is much you can do to help yourself (or someone else) cope better with trauma. One idea is to avoid too much media coverage, which after the September 11 terror attacks seemed to exaggerate and extend fears of Americans as well as of Israelis and the British (Marshall et al., 2007). Here are some other ways to ease the stress (Center for Mental Health Services [CMHS], 2003).

- Be sure to talk to someone about your feelings, no matter how difficult this may be.
- Spend time with family and friends, particularly in enjoyable activities.
- Do not hold yourself responsible for the event or for not responding sooner or better.
- Promote healing by staying active in daily patterns. Continue to work, rest, relax, and exercise.
- Maintain normal routines but limit demanding responsibilities.
- Participate in memorials, rituals, and other symbolic events related to the trauma.
- If self-help strategies are not working, seek professional help.

MOOD DISORDERS

What Is Depression?

Most of us go through periods of time when nothing seems to go right. For example, when Lisa's mother became ill and Lisa decided to move in with her, Lisa's car died. Her old landlord informed her that she would not receive back the security deposit for her apartment. Then Lisa lost her purse and was so worried about identity theft that she spent hour upon hour on the phone to cancel her credit cards and change her bank accounts. Like Lisa, you and other individuals lose their wallets, experience car trouble, and may have problems in their close relationships all at the same time. We may say we're "depressed," but we're usually not suffering from a diagnosable psychological disorder. Our mood is one of mild dejection or dysphoria that generally passes within a matter of days. In contrast, when the disturbance of one's mood is more severe and persistent just as Lisa's eventually became, it may be classified as depression, one of the various mood disorders. **Depression** is *an emotional state characterized by intense and unrealistic sadness that may assume a variety of forms, some more severe and chronic than others.* Depression is one of the most common disorders in our society. Many suicides in the United States are committed by people suffering from depression (Haas et al., 2008; Rochford.org, 2000; Schindehette, Calandra, Podesta, & Williams, 2004; Williams, Crane, Barnhofer, Van der Does, & Segal, 2006).

Depression can assume a variety of forms. In many instances, people experience the symptoms of depression only to a mild or moderate degree, so they may continue their everyday activities. Others may suffer from any number of the common symptoms of depression, including decreased energy, loss of interest in everyday activities such as eating, feelings of inadequacy, periods of crying, and a pessimistic attitude. You may have recognized some of these symptoms in the case of Lisa.

It is estimated that three-quarters of all college students suffer some symptoms of depression during college, one-quarter of them at any one time. In almost half of these students, the depression is serious enough to require professional help. Depression may be triggered by the stress of student life, academic pressures, and the felt need to make a career decision (Haas et al., 2008). Depression is often brought on by cognitive distortions, such as exaggerating the importance of getting good grades or the loss of a love relationship. When students confront their actual problems instead of dwelling on their distorted self-perceptions, they tend to have more success in breaking out of their depression. People who suffer from major depression experience many of the same symptoms, but in a more severe and chronic way. In some cases, major and severe depression may include psychotic features such as delusions and hallucinations. This condition almost always interferes with everyday functioning, and in some instances, periods of hospitalization and medication may be necessary (Hanson et al., 2005). Contrary to popular belief, a major depression can occur at any age. The age of onset is fairly evenly distributed throughout adult life. It is estimated that depression affects over 18 million Americans at any given time, with women *possibly* affected more than men (NIMH, 2006a; Schrof & Schultz, 1999). Box 14–4 discusses in some detail sex differences. More than half of those who experience one episode of major depression will eventually have another within two years.

Some people are more vulnerable to *depression at certain times of the year, especially the winter months.* They suffer from a peculiar mood disorder commonly labeled **SAD— seasonal affective disorder.** The causes remain unclear. Because more than two-thirds of those with this syndrome have a close relative with a mood disorder, genetic factors are suspected. Another theory is that gloomy winter weather disturbs the body's natural clock, affecting the production of serotonin and melatonin. During darkness, the pineal gland in the brain secretes larger amounts of the hormone melatonin, associated with drowsiness and lethargy. Light suppresses the secretion of this chemical. Although the extra melatonin secreted in winter doesn't disturb the body's chemical balance in most people, those with SAD may suffer from an overdose of this hormone. Interestingly, new research reveals that not everyone living in winter darkness suffers from SAD. Icelanders, for example, have lower levels of SAD than Americans, perhaps because of some unique adaptive mechanism (Raymond, 2000). So far, people with SAD are finding relief with light therapy (Mallikarjun, 2005; Sher, 2004). During the winter months, they spend time each day in front of a sun-box, a device fitted with powerful fluorescent lights that emit the full spectrum of natural daylight.

Depression has been attributed to a variety of causes, ranging from biological factors such as genes and biochemical processes to social and cultural influences (*Harvard Mental Health Letter,* 2005; Kelsey, 1999). Cognitive theorists point out that people can make themselves depressed by negative thinking or pessimistic cognitive styles (Alloy, Abramson, & Frances, 1999; NIMH, 2002). In contrast, some types of depression run in families, suggesting that biological vulnerability can be inherited. In some families, major depression also seems to occur generation after generation. Depression, however, can also occur in people who have no family history of depression. Whether inherited or not, major depressive disorder is often associated with changes in brain structures or brain function (NIMH).

Depression is one of the most treatable of all disorders, but only about half of the sufferers will be adequately diagnosed. Perhaps only 15 percent of those diagnosed will

Box 14–4

MEN, WOMEN, AND DEPRESSION

Women are more prone to depression than men; at least that is what is believed by American psychologists and psychiatrists. Women, therefore, are twice as likely as men to be diagnosed with depression (Mentalhelp.net, 2005). Let's look a little closer at this issue.

Why are women more depressed? Or are they? One might readily assume that there are biochemical differences, for example, hormonal differences, between men and women that leave women more vulnerable to depression. In support of this view, the differences in depression between men and women do not emerge until after puberty (Mayo Clinic, 2002; Mentalhelp.net, 2005; NIMH, 2006g). It was also once believed that women were simply more likely to seek professional help for depression compared with men, inflating the figures for women. Studies have demonstrated that this is not true; women really do suffer more from depression (NIMH).

There are other plausible explanations for the higher rates of depression in women than in men. Many of the other explanations pertain to societal and cultural causes (Mayo Clinic, 2002; NIMH, 2006a). Women have unequal power and status compared to men. For example, there is generally more discrimination against

women in the workplace. Minority women face the double whammy of race *and* sex discrimination, with suicide of young Black teens due to depression increasingly of concern (NIMH, 2009a). Discrimination is a difficult burden to bear. Furthermore, women are more likely to live in poverty than men; many are single mothers.

Women also do more housework than men. Few people report liking such chores. In fact, one study demonstrated that there is a relationship between amount of household strain, housework performed, and depressive symptoms (NIMH, 2006g). Working and married women juggle multiple tasks and suffer from work overload (Mayo Clinic, 2002; Mentalhelp.net, 2010).

Newer brain imaging research has also shown that the brain region affected by depression is eight times larger in women than in men (Foote & Seibert, 1999). Women and men also learn to manage stress and emotions in different ways. Women may be less inclined to act on their problems and more inclined to dwell (ruminate) on them (Mayo Clinic, 2002; Mentalhelp.net, 2003). These and other factors, then, are likely to contribute to higher rates of depression in women than in men (Mayo Clinic).

---

get adequate treatment, because some family physicians see depression as a character weakness rather than as a health issue (Kelsey, 1999; Schrof & Schultz, 1999).

Suicide: Who and Why?

Astonishingly, suicide is more common than homicide (murder) in U.S. society (NIMH, 2003). In fact, suicides outnumber homicides five to three. Suicide also outranks AIDS/HIV deaths by two to one (NIMH). As mentioned, people who take their own lives, or attempt to do so are very often depressed (Rochford.org, 2000; Schindehette et al., 2004; Williams et al., 2006); thus, our discussion of suicide is subsumed under the topic of mood disorders. Accurate figures on suicide are even more difficult to obtain than statistics on depression. One reason is that many people who commit suicide prefer to make their deaths look accidental, enabling their survivors to be spared the stigma associated with suicide. If the truth were known, as many as one out of six single-car accidents might actually be a suicide. Despite incomplete statistics, official figures indicate that about 30,000 people commit suicide each year in the United States (Rochford.org). However, most authorities estimate the actual cases of suicide to be two or three times that number. Thus, about every 5 minutes someone takes his or her life. If suicide *attempts* are included, someone somewhere is contemplating self-destruction every minute.

Adolescents (Haas et al., 2008) and the aged are the most likely to commit suicide. White elderly men have the highest suicide rate of any group (NIMH, 2003). Especially alarming is the fact that the suicide rate for young people in the 15- to 24-year-old group has tripled in the last 30 years; suicide is now the third leading cause of death for them (Haas et al.). Suicide rates generally increase with age before decreasing, except for male Caucasians. Men are more likely than women to commit suicide, and Whites are more likely than African Americans. Men are more successful than women, partly because men tend to use swifter and more violent means, such as a gun. In contrast, women are more likely to take pills or turn on gas, which often allows time for intervention.

Why do people commit suicide? Surprisingly, suicide is more prevalent in affluent societies, so much so that it has been described as a disease of civilization. At the level of individual behavior, many possible motives have been suggested: escaping from pain or stress, trying to eliminate unacceptable feelings, turning aggression inward, punishing others by making them feel guilty, and acting impulsively on momentary feelings of desperation. Suicidal people often suffer from "tunnel vision"—the misperception that suicide is the *only* alternative to seemingly unsolvable problems in living. The tragedy is that such problems are often transitory, whereas the solution of suicide is permanent.

A study of adolescents attempting suicide found that compared to nonattempters, attempters were more likely to report a past suicide attempt, to report suicidal ideas in the past, and to be depressed (Rotheram-Borus, Walker, & Ferns, 1996). Curiously, severely depressed people are more likely to take their lives *as their situations improve*. When they are most depressed, they may not have sufficient energy to take their own lives, as was true for Lisa. In addition, autopsies of suicide victims have found abnormally low levels of **serotonin**—*a neurotransmitter that has been linked to depression*—suggesting that biochemical deficiencies may play a role in suicide. Box 14–5 alerts you to some of the other warning signs of an impending suicide.

The prevention of suicide has received great attention in recent years. Environmental approaches include tightening control of prescription sedatives, controlling gun purchases

Box 14–5

WARNING SIGNS OF SUICIDE

- Expression of suicidal thoughts or a preoccupation with death
- Prior suicide attempts
- Death of a close friend or family member
- Giving away prized possessions
- Depression or hopelessness
- Despair over a chronic illness
- Social isolation

- Change in sleeping and eating habits
- Marked personality changes
- Abuse of alcohol or drugs
- Sense of hopelessness
- Neglect of personal welfare
- Self-inflicted injury or other reckless behavior
- Divorce or stress in the family
- Job loss or loss of esteem or sense of security

Many public parks now contain emergency phones as one means to prevent suicide.

through legislation, and increasing protective measures (e.g., putting fencing around the observation platform of the Empire State Building in New York City). Another approach is to increase community awareness and resources for dealing with suicide. Many communities now have suicide and crisis intervention hotlines available 24 hours a day. Volunteers at these crisis services usually have specific goals, such as determining the seriousness of the suicide threat, establishing and conveying empathy, understanding of the caller's problems, describing available resources, and getting some sort of agreement that the caller will seek help.

Contrary to the myth that people who threaten to kill themselves seldom do so, most people who commit suicide express some suicidal intent, directly or indirectly, within several months before their deaths. It helps to recognize the warning signs, as noted in Box 14–5. If you notice the warning signals of suicide in a family member or friend, do your best to see that he or she gets professional help.

What Is Bipolar Disorder?

Unlike Lisa, some people experience *an alternation of elated and depressive moods, popularly known as manic depression* but now termed **bipolar disorder** (Perry, 2005). Usually, this disorder first appears as **mania,** in which *the individual exhibits such symptoms as an expansive mood, increased social activity, talkativeness, sleeplessness, and reckless behavior.* The subsequent episodes can occur in any one of several patterns. For example, one mood may be followed immediately by its opposite, with normal intervals occurring between the manic-depressive pairs.

In addition to the manic episodes, there are other characteristics that distinguish bipolar disorder from major depression. First, bipolar disorder is much less common than major depression, affecting between 0.4 and 1.2 percent of the population. Second, bipolar disorder is equally prevalent among men and women. Third, although married people are less susceptible to major depression, they enjoy no such advantage in regard to bipolar disorder. Fourth, although major depression can occur at any time in life, bipolar disorder usually appears before the age of 30. And bipolar episodes tend to be briefer and more frequent than those in major depression. Finally, bipolar disorder is more likely to run in families. In fact, scientists are hot on the trail of the unique metabolic activity of the brains of bipolar individuals (Perry, 2005).

OTHER COMMON DISORDERS

Many other psychological disorders are described in the DSM, covering almost every conceivable complaint, from compulsive gambling to delusional (paranoid) disorder. We cannot possibly cover all disorders in this chapter; your college may offer an abnormal psychology course that you can take if you wish to learn about other diagnoses. Here, we'll describe three types of disorders that are of special interest because they are commonly misunderstood or are found with some frequency among college students: eating disorders, personality disorders, and schizophrenia, one of the most disabling of all disorders.

Do You Have an Eating Disorder?

Pam is Lisa's second cousin. She was a 17-year-old who was somewhat overweight for her age. She blamed much of her weight gain on her mother, who constantly urged her as a child to eat more. "Think about all the starving kids in (she would name different countries) who'd love this food," admonished her mother. Pam also blames her current boyfriend, who threatens to break off their relationship "if you get any fatter." Her fear of getting fatter coupled with a desire to become socially attractive have led her to experiment with strict diets. Pam has also been inspired by ultrathin models and television stars (Kirsh, 2010). As a result, Pam's weight recently plunged from 153 pounds to 102 pounds in less than a year.

Pam was recently diagnosed as having **anorexia nervosa,** *an eating disorder characterized by a severe loss of appetite and weight. The essential features of this eating disorder are a fear of becoming fat along with a disturbance in body image and a refusal to maintain normal weight.* In other words, the individual relentlessly pursues thinness. Eating disorders are not due to a failure of will or behavior; rather, they are real, treatable medical illnesses in which certain maladaptive patterns of eating take on a life of their own (NIMH, 2006b). Being 85 percent of normal body weight, along with other physical signs such as the suspension of menstrual periods, is usually sufficient for this diagnosis. When Pam stopped menstruating, she feared she was pregnant; how wrong she was! The weight loss is usually accomplished by a reduction in total food intake, especially foods high in carbohydrates and fats, use of laxatives or diuretics, and sometimes strenuous and excessive exercise.

Anorexic disturbance is *the way in which one's body weight or shape is experienced and includes undue influence of body weight or shape on self-evaluation or denial of the seriousness of the current low body weight* (NIMH, 2006b). Those who suffer from this disorder do not realize they are getting dangerously thin, even when they examine themselves in the mirror. "Dangerously thin" is not a misstatement; up to 20 percent of people who have an eating disorder die from it (Anred.com, 2000; NIMH, 2006b). It is also conjectured that the eating habits of these girls may have been so regulated by their parents that they have not learned to interpret the inner signals that they are hungry. Instead, they have an obsessional need to control their lives primarily through their eating habits, often engaging in elaborate rituals to ensure they will not eat too much. For example, Pam was observed to push her food around her plate a number of times before nibbling a tiny bit of it and then licking her empty fork several times. It appeared that she was eating because of all the commotion. In actual fact, she was eating very little.

Cheryl lives in the same large city as Lisa and Pam. Cheryl is 5 feet, 8 inches tall, is 20 years old, and had always been somewhat chubby for her age. For the past several years, however, she has begun to indulge in binge eating followed by purges of the consumed food. For instance, Cheryl will eat a quart of ice cream and a plate of brownies, gobbling the food down quite rapidly, with little chewing. Once she has started to eat, she feels a loss of control. She feels as though she cannot stop eating. Later, in secret, she induces vomiting by sticking her finger down her throat. The vomiting decreases the physical pain of overeating, thereby allowing continued eating. The entire cycle is followed by self-criticism ("Why do I eat so much?") and depression ("I'll never be able to stop myself; I am a failure").

Cheryl's condition is **bulimia nervosa,** *an eating disorder characterized by excessive overeating or uncontrolled binge eating followed by self-induced vomiting.* This disorder is closely related to but different from anorexia, which is more common (NIMH, 2006b). Whereas the aim of the anorexic is to lose weight, the bulimic attempts to eat without gaining weight. The essential features of this disorder are episodic eating sprees, or binges, accompanied by an awareness that this eating pattern is abnormal—a fear of not being able to stop eating voluntarily and a depressed mood and self-disparaging thoughts. "You have no self-control—shame on you!" criticizes the little voice in the bulimic's head. The bulimic is also unhappy with her body image, as is the anorexic (Joiner, Wonderlich, Metalsky, & Schmidt, 1995; NIMH). Individuals who suffer from bulimia sometimes diet excessively between binges, perhaps they, too, have been encouraged to do so by the media or by websites that actually laud disordered eating and weight control practices (Kirsh, 2010).

Like anorexia, bulimia is more common among girls (NIMH, 2007b), especially those in the middle and upper socioeconomic groups. Although the estimated frequency of the disorder varies considerably, about one in four college-age women are involved in bulimic behavior (Anred.com, 2000). Research also indicates that gay men is prone to eating disorders because they, too, hope to please male partners. On the other hand, lesbians and heterosexual men are less prone to eating disorders (Siever, 1994). Similarly, African American women are less critical of their bodies and therefore less likely to develop an eating disorder than White women (Powell & Kahn, 1995).

Certain types of obesity can also be considered eating disorders. Compulsive or binge eating constitutes a distinct disorder and may be the most frequent eating disorder (NIMH, 2007b). **Binge eating** is *characterized by eating an excessive amount of food within a discrete period of time and by a sense of lack of control over eating during the episode* (NIMH, 2006b). Whereas most overweight people generally consume more calories than they expend over the course of each day, compulsive overeaters or binge eaters consume large amounts of food in a very short time without the subsequent use of purges or exercise. Often the binge eater eats alone due to embarrassment about the loss of control. It is estimated that about one-third or more of all individuals in weight-control programs report frequent episodes of compulsive overeating. Compulsive overeaters exhibit a higher-than-average incidence of psychological problems, especially depression. Eating more often in response to positive or negative emotional states (NIMH, 2006b), compulsive overeaters also tend to experience greater mood fluctuations during the course of the day. Binge eating is commonly triggered by tension, hunger, consumption of any food, boredom, craving for specific foods, and solitude or loneliness. Think here about your pattern of eating. Do you overeat? Undereat? Get enough exercise or get too much exercise such that you are too thin?

One of the most useful approaches to compulsive overeating is to set a weight goal that is more consistent with one's weight history than that obtainable from a normative chart or from images in the mass media. Another approach is to prevent eating disorders altogether; research has demonstrated that some prevention programs can reduce these disorders by over fifty percent (Stice, Shaw & Marti, 2007).

What Are Personality Disorders?

Personality traits are *enduring patterns of thinking, feeling, acting, and relating to others that we exhibit in a wide range of situations.* However, *when personality traits are so inflexible and maladaptive that they cause marked impairment in individuals' social and occupational life,* such individuals may have one of the **personality disorders.** A new national survey that tracked the prevalence of such disorders estimates that 9 percent of the U.S. population may meet the criteria according to the DSM (NIMH, 2007a). These disorders are generally longstanding and result in a pattern of deviation from accepted social norms, so obviously this diagnosis did not pertain to Lisa. These disorders are unique in that they tend to cause less distress to the individuals themselves than to others who live and work with them. As a result, these individuals resist getting professional help. Scientists now believe that many of the personality disorders described here are caused by childhood abuse and neglect (Battle et al., 2004). Several personality disorders that rank among the most common will be discussed here.

The **narcissistic personality** is *a disorder characterized by an undue sense of self-importance, often accompanied by a sense of inferiority.* This disorder is thought to be the characteristic personality disorder of our time, mainly because so many otherwise normal individuals in our society exhibit undue self-interest. Whereas a certain degree of self-interest may shield us from the effects of criticism or failure, excessive self-interest can be maladaptive, especially when the cravings for affection and reassurance become insatiable. People with this disorder generally exhibit a grandiose sense of self-importance in behavior or fantasy, often accompanied by a sense of inferiority. They exaggerate their talents and accomplishments and expect to be treated as special without the appropriate achievements. They are, however, hypersensitive to others' evaluation and react to criticism with arrogance and contempt. They believe they are unique and can be understood only by special people. Whatever the cause, narcissism may be fostered by many forces in today's society, such as our preoccupation with self-fulfillment, the "overvaluing" of children, heightened expectations and sense of entitlement among youths, the prominence of celebrities, and our pervasive consumer orientation.

One of the most unsettling personality disorders is the **antisocial personality,** *another personality disorder characterized by long-standing habits of maladaptive thought and behavior that violate the rights of others*—formerly called the psychopathic or sociopathic personality. These people have a history of chronic antisocial behavior, in which they disregard others' rights. They tend to get in trouble with the law because of their predatory attitude toward people and their disregard for others' rights. They may act in an impulsive manner such as stealing a pack of cigarettes or a car—whichever seems easier at the moment. They often are irresponsible, walking out on their jobs or spouses. Antisocial personalities lack a normal conscience and, with little or no guilt, are manipulative toward others.

You well might ask, "How can people get away with such outrageous behavior?" One explanation may be their superficial charm, poise, and intelligence, all of which disarm their victims. Moreover, Western society may encourage antisocial tendencies by

Box 14–6

OTHER PERSONALITY DISORDERS

Paranoid personality: Characterized by a basic distrust of others. Usually such distrust and suspiciousness is without basis.

Schizoid personality: Evidenced by social isolation and shallow emotions. Lacks close friends or confidants.

Histrionic personality: Characterized by attention seeking and excessive emotionality. Uses dramatic behaviors and physical appearance to draw attention to self.

Avoidant personality: Demonstrated by social constriction, low self-esteem, and extreme avoidance of negative self-appraisals.

Obsessive-compulsive personality: Not to be confused with OCD. Marked by the need to maintain control and order. Has a preoccupation with perfection, details, rules, and so forth that interferes with task completion.

glamorizing fame and success, so that superficial charm and lack of concern for others may help antisocial people get ahead. In many cases, they have grown up in a family in which they have been undersocialized, with one or more of their parents exhibiting antisocial behavior.

Another common personality disorder is **borderline personality disorder.** *The individual who suffers from this disorder shows impulsive behaviors and unstable social relationships as well as unstable self-image.* The impulsiveness is often self-damaging, such as substance abuse or reckless driving. This individual may also make suicidal threats or may self-mutilate in a desperate move to capture the attention of those who might abandon him or her. The individual's mood is also unstable, with intense or inappropriate episodes of irritability, anxiety, combativeness, and even euphoria. The individual manifests these symptoms in a variety of settings such as work or home. This personality disorder, in particular, is very disturbing to those close to the borderline individual; it strains interpersonal relationships to the breaking point. Psychotherapists often do not like to work with such individuals because of their manipulativeness and their tendency to want help at all times (Perry, 1997). Box 14–6 delineates other prevalent personality disorders.

Schizophrenia—The Enigmatic Disorder

Most of us can understand what it's like to be panic-stricken or depressed, but the bizarre behavior of a person with schizophrenia remains a mystery to us. Schizophrenia is a chronic and very disabling disorder (NIMH, 2006f); it baffles and frustrates psychologists. Schizophrenia erroneously has been called "split personality" by the public. Here are some facts about schizophrenia (NIMH, 2006f):

- In the United States, approximately 2.4 million adults, or about 1.1 percent of the population age 18 and older in a given year, have schizophrenia.
- Rates of schizophrenia are very similar from country to country—about 1 percent of the population.
- Schizophrenia ranks among the top 10 causes of disability in developed countries worldwide.
- The risk of suicide is serious in people with schizophrenia (Anonymous, *Living with Schizophrenia,* 2009).

Because *schizophrenia* is a label given to a group of related disorders, it's impossible to describe the "typical" person with schizophrenia. We might define **schizophrenia** as *a group of related psychotic disorders characterized by severe disorganization of thoughts, perceptions, and emotions; bizarre behavior; and social withdrawal.* The essential features of these disorders include **psychotic symptoms,** *symptoms that are signs of psychosis and that include hallucinations such as hearing voices, marked impairment in self-care and social relationships, and other signs of severe disturbance.* To diagnose schizophrenia or other disorders where psychotic symptoms are apparent, there must be continuous signs of the disturbance for at least six months, including an active phase of at least one week or less if the symptoms have been successfully treated (American Psychiatric Association, 1994). Here are other symptoms:

1. Disorders of speech.   One of the most striking features of individuals suffering from schizophrenia is their peculiar use of language—in both the form and the content of thought and speech. There is a loosening of associations of thought and rambling, disjointed speech. Words that have no association beyond the fact that they sound alike—such as *clang* and *fang*—may be juxtaposed with each other.

2. Distorted beliefs.   This major disturbance in the content of thought involves **delusions**—*beliefs that have no basis in reality.* For example, individuals may feel they are being spied on or plotted against by their families.

3. Distorted perceptions.   Individuals suffering from schizophrenia seem to perceive the world differently from other people. They have difficulty focusing on certain aspects of their environment while screening out other information. Instead, their inner world is flooded with an undifferentiated mass of sensory data, resulting in odd associations, inner confusion, and bizarre speech. In addition, many schizophrenics experience **hallucinations**—*sensory perceptions that occur in the absence of any appropriate external stimulus.* The most common hallucination is hearing voices that characteristically order these people to commit some forbidden act or that accuse them of having done some terrible misdeed.

4. Blunted or inappropriate emotions.   Schizophrenia is characterized by blunted affect (emotions), or in more severe cases, a lack of emotions. Schizophrenic individuals may stare with a blank expression or speak in a flat, monotonous voice. Or they may display inappropriate emotions, such as giggling when talking about some painful experience.

5. Social withdrawal.   People who eventually have a schizophrenic episode tend to be loners, preferring animals, nature, or inanimate objects to human company. Perhaps they are preoccupied with their inner world, or having learned that they are often misunderstood, they prefer to keep to themselves. When in the presence of others, they avoid eye contact and tend to stand or sit at a greater distance from people than others do. They are also emotionally distant, making it difficult to establish satisfying close relationships with them.

Despite extensive research, the causes of schizophrenia are not fully understood. For a long while, a dysfunctional family environment was regarded as a major cause of this disorder, but in recent years there has been increasing evidence that genetic, neurological, and biochemical factors may play an even greater role (NIMH, 2006f, 2008b). Nevertheless, about half of the identical twins that always share the same genes with a schizophrenic twin do not develop this disorder (NIMH, 2006f). Thus, a predisposition by itself does not appear sufficient for the development of schizophrenia. The **diathesis-stress hypothesis** views *schizophrenia as the interaction of a genetic vulnerability (the diathesis or predisposition) with environmental stressors.* That is, schizophrenic individuals tend to inherit a lower threshold to certain types of stress, which, if exceeded, may precipitate an acute episode of the disorder. If an individual manages to keep the level of environmental stress well below a particular threshold and despite a genetic predisposition, that person may never experience an acute episode of schizophrenia. The initial onset of schizophrenia usually occurs in adolescence or early adulthood. You might think that Lisa, a young adult under stress, would be a candidate for schizophrenia, but without the genetic propensity for schizophrenia, she instead developed depression.

Schizophrenia may appear abruptly, with marked changes in behavior in a matter of days or weeks, or there may be a gradual deterioration in functioning over many years. During this initial phase, individuals with schizophrenia are socially withdrawn. They display blunted or shallow emotions and have trouble communicating with others. They may neglect personal hygiene, schoolwork, or jobs. By this time, such individuals may have begun to exhibit the bizarre behavior and psychotic symptoms signaling the onset of the active phase. The *active phase* of the disorder is often precipitated by intense psychological stress, such as the loss of a job, rejection in love, or the death of a parent. During this period, the psychotic symptoms become prominent. Schizophrenic individuals begin to hallucinate, hold delusions, and exhibit incoherent and illogical thought and bizarre behavior. However, no one person manifests all these symptoms; each individual exhibits a somewhat different pattern.

In the *residual phase,* individuals with schizophrenia may recover from the acute episode in a matter of weeks or months. Some of the psychotic symptoms, such as hallucinations or delusions, may persist, although they are no longer accompanied by

Box 14–7
OUTLOOK FOR RECOVERY

How well an individual recovers from the active phase of schizophrenia depends on a variety of factors, especially the following:

1. *Premorbid adjustment.* The more adequately the person functioned before the disorder, the better the outcome.

2. *Triggering event.* If the disorder is triggered by a specific event, such as the death of a loved one, the possibility of recovery is more favorable.

3. *Sudden onset.* The more quickly the disorder develops, the more favorable the outcome.

4. *Age of onset.* The later in life the initial episode of schizophrenia appears, the better. Men are more at risk before the age of 25; women are more at risk after 25.

5. *Affective behavior.* Symptoms of anxiety and other emotions, including depression, are favorable signs. A state of hopelessness not accompanied by depression is a poor sign.

6. *Content of delusions and hallucinations.* The more delusions involve feelings of guilt and responsibility, the better the outlook. Conversely, the more the delusions and hallucinations blame others and exonerate the individual, the more severe the disorder.

7. *Type of schizophrenia.* Paranoid schizophrenia, the most common type, has a better outlook, mostly because the individual's cognitive functioning remains relatively intact compared with other types of schizophrenia.

8. *Response to the disorder and the treatment.* The more insight individuals have concerning what makes them ill, the more responsive they are to the medication; the more cooperative they are with their therapists, the better their chances of recovery.

9. *Family support.* The more understanding and supportive these individuals' families are, the better their chances of a good recovery.

intense emotion. These individuals may continue to exhibit eccentric behavior and odd thoughts, for example, believing they are able to control events through magical thinking. As a result, many of them are not ready to fully resume everyday responsibilities, such as holding a job or running a household.

There is a considerable difference of opinion about the outlook for individuals who have suffered an acute schizophrenic episode. Traditionally, clinicians adhered to the principle of thirds; that is, about one-third of the people who have experienced a schizophrenic episode make a good recovery, another one-third make a partial recovery with occasional relapses, and still another one-third remain chronically impaired. However, with improved methods of treatment, powerful antipsychotic drugs, more favorable attitudes toward those afflicted with this disorder, and more sophisticated research strategies, a larger proportion of schizophrenic individuals are making at least a partial recovery (NIMH, 2006f). How well an individual recovers from an acute schizophrenic episode depends on many factors. Refer back to Box 14–7 (page 353), which details some of the other factors that predict who possibly will recover from schizophrenia.

APPLYING THIS TO YOURSELF

What does all this mean for you? First, the number of people with mental disorders is small, but we should never dismiss their difficulties nor stigmatize them. Second, the likelihood that you have one of these disorders is low, but if you think you are having adjustment problems, seek help. There is lots of it available, as you will read in the next chapter. If you are attending an educational program in a community unfamiliar to you, your campus counseling center, the dean of students, a dormitory adviser, or a psychology professor can help you find appropriate assistance. If you are a community member, you probably have a community mental health center nearby. Finally, psychologists know that every now and then all of us experience some sort of mental health issue. Psychologists are currently working to enhance our own overall well-being, and not just by reducing the incidence and prevalence of disorders (Huppert, 2009) or by alleviating the distress of those who suffer from them. There is little reason all of us cannot feel more mentally healthy.

SUMMARY

PSYCHOLOGICAL DISORDERS

We began the chapter by noting that there is no simple way to determine whether someone has a psychological disorder. In practice, professionals rely on a combination of standards, such as the presence of personal distress, significant impairment in behavior, the social acceptability of the behavior, and an important loss of personal control. Overall, about one out of every three persons will experience at least one significant psychological problem in his or her lifetime, ranging from the mildly disabling anxiety disorders to severe ones like schizophrenia. In the DSM, an authoritative guide to the various disorders, the emphasis is on describing the characteristic behavior patterns of the various disorders rather than interpreting the possible causes, which are often unknown.

ANXIETY DISORDERS: THE MOST COMMON DISORDERS

In an anxiety disorder, the level of anxiety is out of proportion to the stressful situation or may occur in the absence of any actual danger. Anxiety may be experienced in different ways in the various disorders. In generalized anxiety disorder, a chronic sense of diffuse or free-floating anxiety becomes the predominant disturbance, and the person is anxious most of the time. In contrast, the phobic disorders are characterized by a chronic, irrational fear of a specific object or activity, together with a compelling desire to avoid it, that is, use avoidance behaviors. The essential features of obsessive-compulsive disorder are recurrent obsessions or compulsions or both, as seen in people preoccupied with various checking and cleaning rituals.

MOOD DISORDERS

The mood disorders involve different types of mood disturbances, including extreme elation and depression. Depression may range from mild despondency to a major depressive disorder that is so disabling it requires hospitalization. Seasonal affective disorder is a form of depression that seems to be caused by the short and dark winter days in some parts of the world. Suicide now ranks as one of the leading causes of death among young men and women. Suicide is also more common among the elderly. In contrast, bipolar disorder, popularly known as manic depression, involves depression alternating with extreme elation and usually appears in young adults.

OTHER COMMON DISORDERS

Anorexia is an eating disorder primarily of adolescent girls that is characterized by a disturbance in body image and eating habits and results in a loss of normal body weight. Bulimia, a related eating disorder, involves episodic eating binges accompanied by a fear of not being able to stop eating voluntarily, eventually followed by a depressive mood. Recently, attention has been given to compulsive or binge eaters, those who consume large amounts of food in a very short time without the subsequent use of purgatives or exercise.

People with personality disorders are characterized by maladaptive behavior patterns that impair their social and occupational lives. The disorder may be more noticeable to those around the individual rather than to the individual. Those with a narcissistic personality disorder have an exaggerated sense of self-importance and need constant reassurance to maintain their inflated esteem. In contrast, those with an antisocial personality disorder get into trouble because of their predatory attitude toward people and their disregard for others' rights. The borderline personality is impulsive, has disturbed interpersonal relationships, is manipulative, and can be self-damaging. Other personality disorders exist.

Schizophrenia, one of the most severely disabling of all the psychological disorders, affects about 1 percent of the U.S. population sometime during their lives. Symptoms include disordered thought, imaginary voices, blunted emotions, and social withdrawal. Although the causes of schizophrenia are not fully understood, it is thought that it results from an interaction of a genetic predisposition and environmental stress.

APPLYING THIS TO YOURSELF

It is unlikely you suffer from a mental disorder. You should, however, not stigmatize those who do, and you should seek help if you think you or anyone else needs it. Psychologists are now working on enhancing our well-being, not just focusing on those individuals who have a mental disorder.

SELF-TEST

1. A major factor in determining whether someone has a psychological disorder is the presence of
   a. interpersonal conflicts.
   b. personal distress.
   c. lack of behavior.
   d. anxiety.

2. The most common group of psychological disorders in the United States are the
   a. anxiety disorders.
   b. personality disorders.
   c. schizophrenic disorders.
   d. mood disorders.

3. A chronic state of free-floating anxiety is often the main symptom of which one of the following disorders?
   a. Phobic disorder
   b. Generalized anxiety disorder
   c. Bipolar disorder
   d. Personality disorder

4. The best example of a social phobia is someone with an intense fear of
   a. closed places.
   b. crowded stores.
   c. public speaking.
   d. being in elevators, even if with others.

5. The person who reenters the house several times to make certain the stove has been turned off before leaving for work probably has
   a. a mood disorder.
   b. a simple phobia.
   c. a personality disorder.
   d. obsessive-compulsive disorder.

6. In contrast to major depression, bipolar disorder
   a. commonly appears before age 30.
   b. affects more women than men.
   c. results in suicidal tendencies.
   d. is less likely to run in families.

7. Which statement regarding suicide is correct?
   a. More women succeed in committing suicide than men.
   b. Suicide is more common in the old than in middle-aged adults.
   c. Suicide is less prevalent in affluent than impoverished societies.
   d. Suicide goes hand in hand with phobias.

8. The eating disorder characterized by episodic eating binges and purges is called
   a. Anorexia nervosa
   b. Fasting disorder
   c. Bulimia nervosa
   d. Compulsive overeating

9. People who have a history of chronic "deviant" behavior with little or no regard for the rights of others probably have
   a. a schizophrenic disorder.
   b. antisocial personality disorder.
   c. bipolar disorder.
   d. multiple personality disorder.

10. Which of the following factors generally indicates a *favorable* sign of recovery for someone experiencing an acute schizophrenic episode?
    a. Sudden onset
    b. Resignation to being sick
    c. Lack of emotions
    d. Onset in adolescence

EXERCISES

1. *Have you ever experienced a panic attack?* Even if you've only experienced intense anxiety, write a page or so describing what it was like. Be sure to include what occasioned the anxiety and how it affected you. Also, write about how well you cope with similar situations today.

2. *Are you bothered by an intense fear or phobia?* If you were to list your worst fears, which ones would you include? Do you share some of the more common fears, such as the fear of snakes or spiders? Or are you bothered by other fears? What are you doing to overcome your fears?

3. *Managing the "blues."* Most of us have times when we feel down. The important thing is knowing how to handle ourselves so that we can snap out of such low moments. Write a page or so describing how you cope with discouragement and depression. How effective is your approach?

4. *Feeling better.* When you feel down, do you try to think of happier moments? What makes you happy? What makes you sad? Do the two "triggers" have anything in common (e.g., such as family events), or does each moment have its own trigger?

5. *Have you known someone who committed suicide?* To what extent did this person exhibit the characteristics discussed in the chapter? Also, in retrospect, did the person display any of the warning signs of suicide? At this point, do you think you're better able to recognize individuals with a high risk for suicide? If you suspected someone was suicidal, what would you do?

6. *Psychological disorders in the family.* Do you have relatives who have suffered from a psychological disorder? If so, which ones? Are any of these disorders those that tend to run in families, for example, schizophrenia or major depression? What steps, if any, are you taking to avoid such problems?

7. *Distinguish schizophrenia from the commonly used term "split personality."* People tend to confuse these two. Do you know the difference between them? Can someone have a split personality? To test yourself, you might write a paragraph or so explaining how the two terms differ. Ask your instructor to check your answer to make certain you really understand the differences.

QUESTIONS FOR SELF-REFLECTION

1. Do you believe society tolerates greater deviance than in the past? What are the advantages and disadvantages of greater tolerance?

2. When you become anxious about something, how does this affect you? Does anxiety energize you? When you are relaxed, how do you feel? How is your behavior different in these two situations?

3. How do you cope with occasional feelings of despondency or depression? Do you live in a climate that might induce seasonal affective disorder? Do you suffer from it? What can you do about this disorder?

4. Do you think women are more apt to seek professional help for their mental disorders than men? Why?

5. Would you agree that depression among men is often masked by drinking or drug problems?

6. Do you know someone who has attempted suicide or who succeeded? How did the suicide affect you?

7. How would you account for the high suicide rate among older White men? Do you think the reasons adolescents and the elderly commit suicide are different from White men's reasons?

8. What are some of the chronic self-destructive behaviors people engage in? Why do you think people engage in these behaviors? Can people change voluntarily, or do most people need professional help?

9. Are you aware that some individuals who have experienced acute schizophrenic episodes resume normal lives? What do you think brings on remission from schizophrenia? Can you imagine what it is like to live as an individual with schizophrenia?

FOR FURTHER INFORMATION

RECOMMENDED READINGS

BOURNE, E. J. (2005). *The anxiety and phobia workbook*. Oakland, CA: New Harbinger Publications. This workbook discusses the causes of fears and anxieties, treatments for anxiety, the relationship of self-esteem to anxiety, and lifestyle changes designed to help you overcome anxiety and phobias.

CASTLE, D. G., & BUCKLEY, P. F. (2008). *Schizophrenia*. Oxford, England: Oxford University Press. Two leading professionals on psychosis lead the reader through information on this complex condition—its diagnosis, evaluation and treatment

FAIRBURN, C. G., & BROWNELL, K. D. (2005). *Eating disorders and obesity: A comprehensive handbook*. New York: Guilford Press. The second edition of this well-reviewed book offers a compendium of the latest information on all types of eating disorders, including obesity.

RIPLEY, A. (2008). *Unthinkable: Who survives when disaster strikes—And why*. New York: Random House. Most of us live within striking distance of natural or man-made disasters, whether we want to think about it or not. Ripley helps us understand that we needn't be paralyzed; we can emulate the very behaviors of survivors of real trauma.

WILLIAMS, J. M. G., KABAT-ZINN, J., SEGAL, Z.V., & TEASDALE, J. D. (2007). *The mindful way through depression: Freeing yourself from chronic unhappiness.* New York: Guilford. Experts on cognitive behavioral therapy and mindfulness help those suffering from depression and related disorders out of the mental habits that trap them in the rut of negative thoughts and despair.

WEBSITES AND THE INTERNET

http://www.psycom.net/depression.central.html   A site provided by a psychiatrist about depression in all ages and groups of people with information on genetics and other causes of depression. The site also contains information on other mood disorders and links to other sites.

http://www.save.org/   A valuable site on suicide, its warning signs, misconceptions about suicide, and how a forgotten group, survivors, can better cope with their loss.

http://www.mentalhealth.com/   Contains information about all types of mental disorders with good information on a large variety of personality disorders and phobias. The information includes symptoms, treatments, and relevant research on each.

http://mentalhelp.net/   A good general resource for information on a variety of disorders. Has chat rooms, book lists, possibilities for participating in research projects, and so forth.

http://www.nimh.nih.gov/publicat/schizoph.cfm   A government website with a wealth of information about schizophrenia for individuals with schizophrenia, their family members, and their friends.

If You Go for Help

Learning Objectives

After completing this chapter, you should be able to

1. Know how to use the terms *psychotherapy* and *therapist*.
2. Describe the main features of insight therapy.
3. Explain the methods or various forms of insight therapy.
4. Differentiate one approach to therapy from other approaches.
5. Know about the various forms of multiperson therapy, e.g., family therapy.
6. Describe the major categories of psychoactive drugs used in biomedical therapy.
7. Discuss the importance of community-based services for comprehensive mental health care.
8. Debate whether psychotherapy is effective.

Since moving back home three months ago, Sergei has been at odds with his parents, who emigrated with him from Russia when Sergei was 10. Sergei admits he's going through a difficult time in his life. He recently lost his job—again—and is having trouble making the payments for his car. To make matters worse, he has just asked his father for another small loan to help him through his present financial crisis. Sergei's parents see things differently. They feel that Sergei is floundering and has no sense of direction in his life. His friends think he is depressed, as seen in his constant but vague complaints, fatigue, and boredom. Since the recent breakup with his girlfriend, Sergei has been staying out late and drinking heavily several evenings each week and then refusing to get up in the morning. Sergei's friends are concerned and insist he get therapy. Sergei agrees very reluctantly after they apply much pressure to him. "But I'll see the shrink just once," he says, "mostly to satisfy you I'm not crazy." His parents, however, are Russian immigrants and do not want Sergei sharing their family problems with a stranger. They remember all too well when secrets shared with strangers in Soviet Russia resulted in the informant's disappearance. Sergei's friends insist that he should give the therapist a chance. "Okay, okay, I'll give it a try. But I'm not making any promises."

Why are people like Sergei so reluctant to seek professional help? The answers vary from one person to another, with cost of therapy now leading the list. Some individuals, especially those with little education, resist getting help because of the stigma associated with mental disorders. In the popular mind, psychotherapy is for people who are "crazy." Unfortunately, seeking assistance for a mental disorder remains stigmatized (Gary, 2005; Shalala, 1999; Vaccaro, 2004; Weiss & Ramakrishna, 2006). Among other reasons, some people do not seek treatment because they simply don't know where to turn for help. See Figure 15–1 (page 362) for a more complete list of reasons.

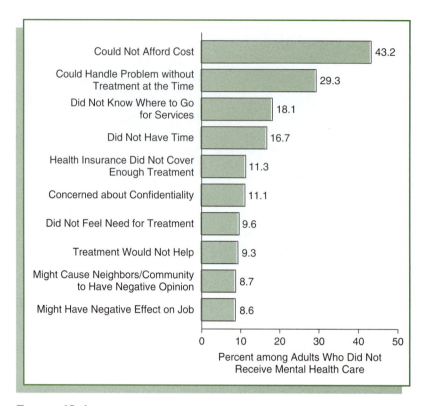

FIGURE 15–1

**Reasons for Not Receiving Mental Health Services
in the Past Year (2007)**

SOURCE: Substance Abuse and Mental Health Services Administration, Office of Applied
Studies (2008). *Results from the 2007 National Survey on Drug Use and Health: National Findings*
(NSDUH Series H-34, DHHS Publication No. SMA 08-4343). Rockville, MD.

Psychotherapy is *the helping process in which a trained, socially sanctioned therapist performs
certain activities that will facilitate a change in the client's attitudes and behaviors.* In practice, psychotherapy is more likely to be used by people with the milder disturbances, who seek it
as a means of personal growth as well as for the relief of symptoms. However, in our society, which places a high value on self-sufficiency, getting help may be seen as an admission
of weakness. This is probably the major reason men are less likely than women to seek professional help for psychological problems. It's more acceptable for women to express their
emotions and admit weakness. Men are expected to cope on their own and, as a result,
often mask their problems with alcohol and drugs, as Sergei is doing. In any event, only
about one in five adults with a serious psychological problem will seek help from a mental health professional such as a psychiatrist or psychologist. Family physicians, clergy, and
other types of counselors such as social workers may see many other individuals.

Would you recognize when to seek help? If you have been in counseling, have you
reassessed yourself lately to see if you could use a mental health tune-up? Do you have
friends like Sergei who would encourage you to seek assistance if they thought you were
depressed or were drinking too much? Or would you do what thousands of Americans
do, avoid therapy because of the stigma, cost, or inconvenience? To assess whether you
might be a candidate for psychotherapy or some other form of assistance for a mental
disorder, complete the assessment found in Activity 15–1.

ACTIVITY 15–1

TAKING A LOOK AT YOURSELF

INSTRUCTIONS: *The following self-assessor was developed by the federal government to help consumers understand if and when they might need assistance with mental health issues. Do any of the following feelings or experiences make you feel miserable or get in the way of doing the things you want to do most or all of the time? Place a check mark in front of those statements that do.*

_____ **1.** Feeling as though your life is hopeless and you are worthless

_____ **2.** Wanting to end your life

_____ **3.** Thinking you are so great that you are world famous, or that you can do supernatural things

_____ **4.** Feeling anxious

_____ **5.** Being afraid of common things like going outdoors or of being seen in certain places

_____ **6.** Feeling as though something bad is going to happen and being afraid of everything

_____ **7.** Being very "shaky," nervous, continually upset and irritable

_____ **8.** Having a hard time controlling your behavior

_____ **9.** Being unable to sit still

_____ **10.** Doing things over and over again—finding it very hard to stop doing things like washing your hands, counting everything, or collecting things you don't need

_____ **11.** Doing strange or risky things—like wearing winter clothes in the summer and summer clothes in the winter, or driving too fast

_____ **12.** Believing unusual things—such as that the television or radio is talking to you, or that the smoke alarms or digital clocks in public buildings are taking pictures of you

_____ **13.** Saying things over and over that don't make any sense

_____ **14.** Hearing voices in your head

_____ **15.** Seeing things you know aren't really there

_____ **16.** Feeling as if everyone is against you or out to get you

_____ **17.** Feeling out of touch with the world

_____ **18.** Having periods of time go by when you don't know what has happened or how the time has passed—you don't remember being there but others say you were

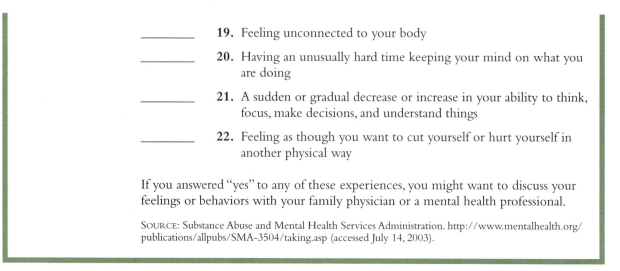

A major problem in choosing a **therapist**—*a person trained to help people with psychological problems*—is sorting through the various approaches to therapy. There are hundreds of different forms of therapy, including various insight therapies as well as many types of behavioral and group therapies. Despite their differences, most therapies share certain common goals. All of them afford clients relief from their symptoms, such as intolerable anxiety or depression. Many of them offer clients better understanding of their thoughts, feelings, motives, and relationships. They also help clients modify their problem behaviors, such as excessive fear (e.g., phobias) or compulsive gambling. In addition, many therapies help clients to improve their interpersonal relationships at home and work.

Different schools of therapy emphasize some of these goals more than others; some may put more emphasis on adjustment, whereas others may concentrate on growth or address emotional responses. Because the talking cure is the best known and appeared first on the psychotherapy landscape, we'll commence with insight therapies. There are three main schools of insight therapy: psychoanalysis, person-centered, cognitive-behavioral (Demorest, 2005). Most forms of psychotherapy involve **insight therapies**—*those that bring change by increasing self understanding.* A controversy exists in the current therapy literature as to whether **insight** or *self-understanding* is necessary for therapeutic change. Some experts claim that self-understanding leads to symptom reduction and improvement in mental health (e.g., Kivlighan, Multon, & Patton, 2000; Patterson & Joseph, 2007), whereas others claim insight is not necessary for meaningful change to occur (Norum, 2000).

INSIGHT THERAPIES—THE TALKING CURE

Psychoanalysis

According to Sigmund Freud (1965), the founder of psychoanalysis, psychological disturbances are due to anxiety about hidden conflicts among the different parts of our unconscious personality. Thus, **psychoanalysis** involves *psychotherapy aimed at helping the person gain insight and mastery over unconscious conflicts.* If not expressed directly, these unconscious impulses and conflicts seek *in*direct release in all kinds of symptoms. The therapist's or analyst's purpose is to help the individual gain insight and conscious awareness of these unconscious desires or conflicts, thereby gaining emotional release and eventual mastery of them (Stern, 2006).

The core of the psychoanalytic approach is the analysis of **transference**— *the unconscious tendency of clients to project onto the therapist their feelings and fantasies, both positive and negative, about significant others in their childhood.* Therapists deliberately foster the development of the transference relationship through their own neutrality and relative passivity. Then, as the therapy proceeds, the therapist analyzes or explains the transference process to help clients achieve insight into the influence of the past on their present behavior (Luborsky & Barrett, 2006; Meissner, 2008; Stern, 2006).

"Working through" the transference relationship involves an exploration of unconscious material and defenses and includes a variety of techniques. One of the historically earliest of these was **free association.** In classic psychoanalysis, the individual is asked to lie down on a couch, relax, clear the mind of everyday thoughts, and then *say whatever comes to mind regardless of how trivial it sounds.* Sometimes clients are encouraged to talk about their dreams. Although these recollections might appear irrelevant, the well-trained analyst may use dream interpretation to shed light on the clients' problems. *When an individual hesitates or is reluctant to talk about some painful experience,* this is seen as a sign of **resistance** (Carrere, 2008; Civitarese, Foresti, & Giovanno, 2008). For example, if Sergei had elected to see a psychoanalyst, he might have been reluctant to discuss his immigrant background. The therapist would have viewed this as important simply because Sergei would not talk about it. The therapist may wait or may use another approach to the area of resistance so eventually this problem can be overcome. By analyzing resistances, the therapist helps the clients see how they handle anxiety-provoking material. Today, some of these psychoanalytic concepts, such as resistance, have been accepted by other practitioners and therapists, although the assumed causes and methods for dealing with them may differ (Beutler, Moleiro, & Talebi, 2002; Grabhorn, Kaufhold, Michal, & Overbeck, 2005). Other Freudian concepts have also stood the test of time and, in fact, may be making a comeback because of recent scientific support (see Gedo, 2002; Gibbons, Crits-Christoph, & Hearson, 2008).

Traditionally, psychoanalysis involved hour-long sessions three to five times a week, often lasting several years. At the level of current fees, this schedule would make psychoanalysis prohibitively expensive for all but a privileged few. As a result, there have been many changes in this approach. Now psychoanalytic therapy may involve only one or two sessions a week and often lasts only 20 or 30 sessions. The therapist sits facing the client and takes a more active role in therapy compared to the impenetrable "mirror" role advocated by Freud. Psychoanalytic therapists are also likely to be more eclectic than in the past, using techniques from other approaches when appropriate. At the same time, the emphasis remains on gaining insight and self-mastery of the unconscious forces affecting one's behavior. There are few definitive studies showing analysis to be effective compared to no treatment or to be better than other therapies, but the results of the bulk of studies are encouraging (American Psychoanalytic Association, 1999). Blatt and Shahar (2004) demonstrated that psychoanalysis is more effective with clients who are ruminative, self-reflective, and introspective than therapy such as the person-centered approach, described next. The prevailing climate at this time toward psychoanalysis is not favorable, however (Salo, 2008).

Before Freud developed the talking cure and pharmaceutical companies manufactured antipsychotic medications, there were few methods for managing mental disorders except for the more inhumane ones such as this bizarre apparatus and the straight jacket in the opening photograph.

The Person-Centered Approach

One of the major alternatives to psychoanalysis is Carl Rogers's humanistic approach to therapy. Toward the end of his career, Rogers (1980; Cornelius-White & Cornelius-White, 2005) changed the name of his approach from *client-centered therapy* to **person-centered therapy**, as a way of indicating that the same principles apply to a variety of fields of human interaction as well as to psychotherapy. According to this view, *the helper's genuineness, acceptance, and empathic understanding of the client are necessary and sufficient conditions for producing therapeutic change.*

Rogers developed his view of therapy out of his own experience as a therapist. Early in his career he was counseling a mother about her son, who was having problems. No matter what strategy he tried, he got nowhere. Finally, he admitted his failure. As the mother walked toward the door, she turned and asked Rogers if he ever saw adult clients. Then the woman returned to her seat and began pouring out her own problems. She spoke of her own sense of confusion and failure and her despair about her marriage, all of which were more pertinent to her son's problems than the sterile case-history approach they had followed before. After many more interviews, the woman felt better about her marriage, after which her son's problem behavior melted away as well. Rogers felt the improvement had come because he had followed her lead, because he had listened and understood rather than imposed his diagnostic understanding on her. This was the first of many experiences that gradually led Rogers to the view that therapeutic progress comes mostly from respecting and responding to the client's own frame of reference and inherent potential for growth.

Therapists using the Rogerian approach believe that all of us have within ourselves vast resources for self-understanding and for altering our behavior and that these resources can be tapped if the proper climate for change can be provided. According to Rogers (1980), *three* conditions must be present for a growth-producing therapeutic climate. All of them pertain to the client-therapist relationship (Elliotti & Freire, 2007; Overholser, 2007).

- *First, the therapist must be genuine, or "congruent."* That is, there should be close matching between what the therapist experiences at the gut level and what is expressed to the clients.

- *The second essential is an attitude of acceptance and caring.* When the therapist is accepting of and caring toward the clients at the moment, therapeutic change is more likely to occur. Therapists accept clients unconditionally, so that they are free to feel what is going on at the moment—whether confusion, resentment, fear, or love (Elliotti & Freire, 2007). This *positive, unconditional acceptance* (and caring for) clients is called **unconditional positive regard** (Gibson, 2005; Greenberg & Watson, 2006).

- *The third aspect of the therapeutic relationship is empathic understanding.* That is, the therapist accurately senses the feelings and personal meanings that the clients are experiencing and communicates this understanding to them (Elliotti & Freire; Macneil, Hasty, Evans, Redlich, & Berk, 2009).

Recent research has borne out that Rogers's brand of therapy promotes client and therapist co-thinking and co-experiencing (Bohart & Byock, 2005) as well as has supported Rogers's emphasis on the therapeutic relationship as a means to change (Kirschenbaum & Jourdan, 2005). Other studies of Rogers's therapeutic techniques have demonstrated support for Rogers's concepts of empathy and unconditional positive regard as critical elements of effective therapy (Kirschenbaum & Jourdan). Finally, neuroscience is offering a new look at Rogers' concepts, indicating a correspondence between his basic concepts such as self-actualization and the vital role of feelings in thought processes (Motschnig-Pitrik & Lux, 2008).

There are new approaches to therapy, not just insight therapy, developing every decade. For a sample at what else is available, see Box 15–1 (page 368).

Box 15–1

What Are Alternative Forms of Therapy?

An alternative approach to mental health care is one that emphasizes the interrelationship between mind, body, and spirit. Although some alternative approaches have a long history, many remain controversial. The National Center for Complementary and Alternative Medicine at the National Institutes of Health was created in 1992 to help evaluate alternative methods of treatment and to integrate those that are effective into mainstream health care. It is crucial, however, to consult with your health care providers about the approaches you are using to achieve mental wellness. Also, before receiving alternative services, check to be sure the provider is properly certified by an appropriate accrediting agency. The following are examples and do not represent all possible alternative forms of therapy.

General Therapies

- Diet and Nutrition
- Pastoral Counseling
- Animal-Assisted Therapies

Expressive Therapies

- Art Therapy
- Dance/Movement Therapy
- Music/Sound Therapy
- Yoga/Meditation

Relaxation and Stress-Reduction Techniques

- Biofeedback
- Guided Imagery or Visualization
- Massage Therapy

Source: Substance Abuse and Mental Health Services Administration. http://www.mentalhealth.org/publications/allpubs/ken98-0044/default.asp (retrieved July 14, 2003).

COGNITIVE-BEHAVIORAL THERAPIES

Just when you thought there couldn't possibly be other ways to address psychological problems, there are! Today, a large and diverse group of therapists characterize their orientation as *either behavioral or cognitive, which, respectively, attempt to modify maladaptive behavior or faulty thinking.* These psychologists practice **cognitive therapy**, **behavioral therapy**, or **cognitive-behavioral therapy**, depending on whether they combine the two approaches. In fact, combining the two has garnered so much support that the national association for behavior therapy has changed its name to include the notion of cognitions (Goldfried, 2007). Having developed from research psychology more than clinical practice, these approaches focus on the problems themselves and how to modify them rather than on what caused them or on the client's emotions. Although you will read the descriptions of the behavioral and cognitive approaches separately here, keep in mind that the trend is toward combining elements of each into a more inclusive alliance labeled *cognitive-behavioral therapies.* Research now strongly supports that this combined approach results in both short- and long-term effectiveness for a variety of disorders (Butler, Chapman, Forman, & Beck, 2006; Gallanter & Kleber, 2008; Northey, 2009; NIMH, 2009b; Rachman, 2008), for example, depression, generalized anxiety disorder, panic disorder, posttraumatic stress disorder, chronic pain, bulimia nervosa, obsessive-compulsive disorder, and even schizophrenia. Cognitive behavior therapy's success has spawned a plethora of related therapies (e.g., dialectical behavior therapy and functional analytic psychotherapy), none of which, according to research, has yet proven quite as effective as the original formulation (Nilsson, 2008).

Behavioral Therapies

Instead of searching for the underlying causes of the client's difficulties, as in many insight therapies, behavioral therapists focus directly on the problem behaviors involved. For example, instead of focusing on Sergei's Russian childhood and his reticence about disclosing personal information to strangers, behavioral therapists would focus on his present problems of drinking too much, being unemployed, and being adversarial toward his well-intentioned parents. Their aim would be to help Sergei replace these maladaptive behaviors with more appropriate and satisfying ones. Typically, **behavioral therapy** involves *discovering the factors that trigger and reinforce the problem behavior, specifying a target behavior to replace it, and then, by manipulating these factors, bringing out the desired behavior.* In the process, behavioral therapists help clients to develop the necessary skills or behaviors to cope more effectively with their life situations.

Behavioral therapists draw on a repertoire of behavioral methods of proven effectiveness, for example, desensitization, aversive counterconditioning, token economies, modeling, and social skills training such as assertiveness training. For instance, many of our fears are acquired through the process of conditioned responses, based on the principles of classical conditioning. One form of therapy for countering such fears is desensitization. **Desensitization** [sometimes now known as exposure-based therapy (NIMH, 2009b)], developed by Joseph Wolpe, is a *method of controlling anxiety by learning to associate an incompatible response, like relaxation, with the fear-provoking stimulus.* By linking (e.g., exposing) the feared object or situation to something pleasant, like relaxation, the client becomes "desensitized" to the fearful situation.

Desensitization is especially effective with fears and phobias. Wolpe (1973) tells of a 24-year-old art student who came for treatment because of her fear of taking examinations, which had resulted in repeated failures. Wolpe began by making up a hierarchy of imagined situations that made her anxious, culminating with the day of the examination. Then he taught her how to relax her body muscles and gradually associate the relaxed state with each of the feared situations. After 10 sessions, the art student felt free from anxiety at the highest level of the hierarchy. Four months later, she took and successfully passed her examinations without any disruptive anxiety.

Cognitive Therapies

Cognitive therapists, drawing on a different set of principles, *focus on faulty cognitive processes as the crucial element in maladaptive behavior.* A major reason for this focus is their belief that cognitive processes—such as attention, perception, thoughts, and beliefs— may affect behavior independently of the stimuli traditionally emphasized by behaviorists. Indeed, cognitive therapists claim that people's actions are often shaped more by their own *interpretation* and *reactions* to external events than to the events themselves. Aaron Beck's **cognitive therapy** (1979; Dozois, Frewen, & Covin, 2006) is a very well-known and successful form of therapy. *Its central assumption is that the emotional and behavioral problems result from the individual's distorted thoughts and reactions to external events rather than from the events themselves.* Stated another way, this therapy proposes that individuals' beliefs affect their interpretation and response to various life circumstances, thereby contributing to emotional adjustment or maladjustment (Dozois et al.).

For example, Melissa, a friend of Sergei's, discovered that she had earned a low grade on her first test in psychology. She felt discouraged and soon engaged in some self-defeating thinking: "How stupid can I be! I'll never make a good grade in this course. I might as well drop it." A cognitive therapist might point out that Melissa is overreacting to her poor performance. The therapist would point out a more realistic evaluation of her situation, for example: "This was just the first test, not the final exam; besides, your grades in other classes are quite good." A cognitive-behavioral therapist would also help alter cognitions as well as help Melissa take positive steps to improve her performance, such as talking to the professor to discover the particular reasons she did poorly on the test, getting suggestions for improving her performance on the next test, and finding out what her chances are for eventually earning a good grade in the course. The therapist might instruct Melissa how to monitor her self-defeating thoughts, correct her thinking, and prepare more effectively for the next test now. Cognitive therapists thus differ from insight therapists in that they do not probe for deep-seated causes of the client's problems.

Status of Psychotherapy Today

There are, as always, many therapists who continue to practice the type of therapy for which they have been trained, modifying their orientation somewhat with experience. An increasing number of therapists, however, would characterize themselves as eclectic, in the sense of having been exposed to more than one theoretical orientation in their training and continuing to add new techniques to their repertoires. Some of them actually drift away from their primary form of therapy, purposefully or mindlessly, making the comparison of various psychotherapies difficult (Waller, 2009). Others seem more intent on being able to use the most appropriate treatment strategy for a given client's problems rather than remaining pigeonholed in a particular form of therapy. As a result, in practice, many therapists incorporate aspects of more than one type of therapy as well as different behavioral techniques. This eclectic approach indeed may be more effective than any single approach by itself (Kensit, 2000). One other pattern that has been documented is that all forms of psychotherapy take place over shorter periods of time; those with severe mental disorders are the only ones who are treated long-term (Olfson, Marcus, Druss, & Pincus, 2002). The probable cause of the decrease in time spent by clients is the limitation set by health insurance companies.

OTHER APPROACHES TO TREATMENT

In addition to the individual therapies discussed so far, there are a wide variety of other types of interventions. For instance, group therapies have mushroomed in number and type in the past several decades. Groups not only offer opportunities for people to interact with others with similar problems but also are more cost-efficient, saving time and money—an important consideration today. We'll specially examine family therapy because the disruption of marriages and families has become a major source of stress in our society. Also, the gains in medicine and technology have produced more powerful drugs and sophisticated biomedical therapies, which have become an integral part of many treatment programs, so we'll examine them, too. Finally, one of the most dramatic changes in regard to treating individuals with mental disorders is the shift away from prolonged stays in large institutions to the use of community-based services, as you will

Box 15–2

MUTUAL-HELP GROUPS

Today, more than 12 million people participate in an estimated 500,000 **self-help** or **mutual-help groups**—*groups whose members share a common problem and meet regularly to discuss their concerns without the guidance of professionals.*

Although these groups frequently have multiple functions, such as fostering self-help and lobbying for reform, most have the same underlying purpose—to provide social support as well as practical help in dealing with a problem common to all members. A major assumption is that no one understands you or can help you better than someone who has the same problem, whether it's obesity, depression, or alcoholism. New members may approach their first meeting with apprehension, wondering what the group can do for them or what it will ask in return. Experienced members, well aware of these mixed emotions, encourage new members to feel relaxed and welcome. In an atmosphere that is friendly and compassionate, new members soon realize that their participation is voluntary, with no strings attached.

There is usually an unwritten code of confidentiality within the group. Even when there is a series of steps to recovery, as in the various "Anonymous" groups, members can proceed at their own pace. Some groups, especially those that deal with addictive behavior or emotional disorders, may use a "buddy" or "sponsor" system so that a new member can count on a familiar person for encouragement and support. All in all, mutual-help groups provide an atmosphere of acceptance and support that encourages their members to communicate more openly, view their problems more objectively, and find more effective coping strategies. Research demonstrates that most mutual-help groups are effective in producing member change (Moritsugu, Wong, & Duffy, 2010).

Numerous agencies and clearinghouses provide information on mutual-help groups. If you fail to find the mutual-help groups of interest in your phone book, visit the American Self-Help Clearing House website at http://selfhelpgroups.org, which houses a directory of self-help groups.

see shortly. Before you read further about professionally led groups, read Box 15–2 about mutual-help or self-help groups in which laypersons assist one another. Sometimes the help of a professional is not necessary; a good friend can be just as healing.

Family, Couples, and Relationship Therapy

Relationship Therapy. Married and unmarried couples alike usually come to relationship therapy because of some crisis—such as infidelity on the part of one partner—or a breakdown in communication. Although each person tends to blame the partner for the predicament, therapists tend to focus more on the partners' interaction and relationship. For instance, if one person has engaged in an extramarital affair, instead of joining in the blame, the therapist may ask each partner what he or she thinks caused this situation. Perhaps the offending partner has a personality problem or wants to "get back at" the other partner. Either way, the therapist helps both of them become more aware of how they treat each other; how they may unwittingly hurt each other; and most important, how they may nurture each other. The therapist often has to help the couple clarify the extent to which they really want to work at the marriage and, if so, how to proceed. Therapy that goes beyond individual intervention is more complex because of the various relationships and alliances involved (Rait, 2000). Despite the complexity, research reveals strong evidence for its effectiveness (Becvar, 2008).

Family Therapy.   **Family therapy,** as the name implies, *involves the larger family unit, including children and adolescents, on the assumption that the disturbance of one family member reflects problems in the overall family patterns.* There are now dozens of different types of family therapy, which vary in their theoretical approaches, range of techniques, and procedures. Some therapists prefer to see the entire family from beginning to end. Others may see the parents for a couple of sessions, then the children for a couple of sessions, and finally bring them all together. Still others, such as contextual therapists, who adhere to an intergenerational approach, may even involve members of the extended family in therapy. In Sergei's case, perhaps his grandparents would participate if they were available, particularly because in Russian culture extended families are considered very important. Implicit in all such therapies is the assumption that families function as systems, so the individual's problems are best understood and treated as an integral part of the family milieu.

Here is an example other than Sergei. Suppose a teenager is having trouble in school or is doing something that indicates a problem. The usual course of events is to make the teenager the client, leaving untouched the larger background of problems at home. However, professionals oriented to family therapy may discover upon further investigation that the teenager is simply the most sensitive and vulnerable person in the family and has become the scapegoat of a troubled family. When this is the case, it may be necessary to see other members of the family to get a better understanding of the family's dynamics.

Biomedical Therapies

In contrast to the various forms of verbal therapy, **biomedical therapies** are *strategies that rely on direct physiological intervention to treat the symptoms of psychological disorders.* In recent years, there has been a rapid accumulation of evidence that many disorders are related to biochemical abnormalities, especially unusually high or low levels of **neurotransmitters**—*chemical substances* (or messengers) *involved in the transmission of neural impulses between neurons.* As a result, psychoactive drugs have especially become an indispensable part of treatment. Many of those with severe disorders like schizophrenia may be treated primarily with drugs. Those with less severe disorders may be treated with medication, but often in conjunction with the other therapies discussed so far. In fact, research demonstrates that this is a good strategy. Cuijpers, van Straten, Warmerdam, and Andersson (2009) analyzed the literature on psychotherapy compared to psychotherapy *combined with* biomedical therapies and found that combined approaches are indeed most effective. In truth, combined therapy is now the most common mode of treatment in psychiatry (Gabbard, 2007) and is currently considered *the* standard of care for many mental disorders (King & Anderson, 2004).

Drug therapies continue to be the most widely used biomedical therapies. In fact, there have been significant increases in the use of psychotropic medications. Three major medication categories are antianxiety, antidepressant, and antipsychotic drugs (NIMH, 2006c). Sergei would be an unlikely candidate for such therapies; these medications do not mix well with alcohol.

Antianxiety drugs are the most commonly prescribed psychoactive drugs in the United States. These are *drugs that are used primarily for alleviating anxiety, including minor tranquilizers.* In most cases, family physicians prescribe a tranquilizer for people going through a difficult time, but these drugs are also used in the treatment of anxiety disorders, stress-related disorders, and withdrawal from alcohol or other drugs

(NIMH, 2006c, 2009c). As useful as these medications are, they do not cure anxiety, and they are not without side effects. Also, when used in combination with alcohol or other central nervous system depressants, these drugs can be dangerous or even fatal. Finally, the most common criticism of antianxiety medications is that they may provide such prompt alleviation of symptoms that people avoid solving their problems in behavioral or social ways.

Antidepressants *are used to treat depression and elevate mood, usually by increasing the level of certain neurotransmitters,* especially norepinephrine and serotonin. These drugs help to relieve many of the typical symptoms of depression, such as sleeplessness or excessive sleepiness, chronic fatigue, loss of appetite, loss of sex drive, sadness, and feelings of worthlessness, but again do not provide a cure. A significant disadvantage of these drugs is that they do not begin to take effect for about two to four weeks—which can be a long time for seriously depressed people waiting for relief. Newer, quicker-acting antidepressants have been introduced, but it remains to be seen whether they will be as effective. Antidepressants are the medication class whose use has most dramatically increased in recent years (Olfson et al., 2002).

Lithium—*a natural mineral salt and mood stabilizer—is used to treat people with bipolar disorder.* Lithium is capable of terminating three-fourths of all manic episodes (unduly elevated moods) and some cases of depression. When taken regularly, in maintenance doses, lithium eliminates or at least diminishes mood swings in bipolar disorder (NIMH, 2006c). However, because the effective dosage is close to a toxic one, it is difficult to prescribe the proper maintenance dosage of lithium. Furthermore, many patients stop taking their medication because lithium takes away the sense of well-being they feel in their manic or excited state. The interruption of lithium treatment usually leaves patients just as vulnerable to the disabling manic episodes as they were before treatment began. New drugs have been developed and are being prescribed now.

Antipsychotic drugs, as the name suggests, are used to treat the symptoms of severe disorders such as schizophrenia (NIMH, 2006c). *These medications primarily relieve the symptoms of psychoses, such as extreme agitation, hyperactivity, hallucinations, and delusions.* As mentioned earlier, the use of antipsychotic drugs is often the primary treatment for patients with schizophrenia, especially those chronically impaired. These drugs are thought to work by blocking the activity of dopamine and other neurotransmitters, thereby reducing hallucinations, delusions, and bizarre behavior. However, they do not cure the apathy, social withdrawal, or interpersonal difficulties found in people with schizophrenia, for which psychotherapy is usually helpful. Antipsychotic drugs also have several side effects. In producing calm, they may produce apathy as well, reducing the patient to a zombielike state. Also, a small proportion of patients develop **tardive dyskinesia,** *characterized by jerking movements around the neck and face and involuntary protrusions of the tongue.* Today, newer medications with fewer side effects are available. These are called *atypical antipsychotics* and appear to be more effective than older medications (NIMH). Despite the disadvantages and the criticisms surrounding the use of such drugs, antipsychotic drugs have been the single biggest factor in reducing the institutionalized patient population in the United States from over half a million in the 1950s to about one-third that number today (Moritsugu, Wong, & Duffy, 2010). Over two-thirds of individuals with schizophrenia who regularly take their medication can remain out of the hospital. Consequently, most professionals who work with them believe the value of the drugs outweighs their potential for adverse side effects.

Electroconvulsive therapy (ECT), for reasons that are not completely understood, helps to relieve severe depression in some patients. ECT *involves the administration* *of an electric current to the patient's brain to produce a convulsion.* Although people often react negatively when it is mentioned, ECT has been refined and is done in a more humane manner than in the past (NIMH, 2006c). For severely depressed individuals for whom medication is ineffective, ECT usually involves six to 10 treatments, spaced over a period of several weeks. An electric current of approximately 70 to 130 volts is administered to the temple area for a fraction of a second, causing convulsions for a minute or so. Within half an hour, the patient awakens and remembers nothing of the treatment. The most common side effect is memory loss, especially the recall of events before the treatment. Despite the controversy over ECT, its effectiveness in treating severe illness is recognized as useful by the American Psychiatric Association and similar organizations in other countries (NIMH, 2009a).

Psychosurgery is an even more drastic procedure (Egan, 2005), so much so that Sergei certainly would not be a candidate for it. This is *surgery designed to destroy or disconnect brain tissue in an attempt to regulate abnormal behavior.* Psychosurgery is aimed at reducing abnormal behavior. In the earlier prefrontal lobotomies, the surgeon severed the nerves connecting the frontal lobes of the brain with the emotion-controlling centers. Although many severely disturbed patients became calm, others emerged from surgery in a vegetative state. As a result, professionals welcomed the introduction of antipsychotic drugs, which produce similar results in a safer, reversible manner. Since then, the surgical procedure has been refined. However, lobotomies are still the treatment of *last resort* and are used only rarely, mostly for severely depressed, suicidal patients who have not responded to other treatments.

After reading these passages on biopsychological approaches to treatment of mental disorders, you may be wondering whether we can use less intrusive physiological methods for improving our mental status. After all, each of the techniques just described can have serious side effects. The answer is yes, as you will see in Box 15–3.

Box 15–3

ALLEVIATING DEPRESSION THROUGH EXERCISE

Dozens of studies link regular physical exercise with lower levels of depression and anxiety (e.g., Tkachuk & Martin, 1999; Barbour & Blumental, 2005). Most studies point to the fact that regular exercise is a cost-effective treatment for mild to moderate depression. Some studies also indicate that exercise may be a viable treatment in conjunction with other treatments for schizophrenia and anxiety disorders (Tkachuk & Martin). In other words, people who exercise regularly are less depressed. Some researchers, however, realize it might work the other way around, namely, that people who are more depressed simply exercise less. Yet other researchers temper their enthusiasm by suggesting that we need more research on the link between exercise and depression (Daley, 2008).

It is not exactly clear how or why exercise affects depression. Some explanations focus on the changes in body and brain chemistry (e.g., Zheng et al., 2006), resulting in rising levels of endorphins in the blood during exercise. Other explanations suggest that the sense of mastery over one's body gained through exercise may contribute to a greater sense of personal control over other aspects of one's life as well, thereby alleviating the passivity and helplessness often found in depressed people. Because the more severe types of depression typically result from a complex interaction of genetic, physiological, and psychological factors, exercise is best seen as only one facet in the overall treatment of depression—but one that should not be overlooked.

Community-Based Services

Is your stereotype of a person with a mental disorder that of a homeless person, sleeping on the streets, carting around possessions in a stolen grocery cart? Does your stereotype include the person begging, urinating on the street, and curling up on apartment house stoops during cold snaps? This is the image we often hold of the mentally ill. This description need not be the case but sometimes is (Moritsugu, Duffy, & Wong, 2010).

The introduction of antipsychotic drugs, along with convincing evidence that custodial care in large mental hospitals is detrimental, led to the release of large numbers of ex-patients into the community over the past 40 years. Even recent studies of institutionalized individuals with mental disorders indicate that much of the time spent in the hospitals is spent in loneliness, without treatment, and without interaction with others (Yawar, 2008). Because most of these individuals require some type of treatment, as do others in the community who wish to avoid hospitalization, mental health professionals have responded by providing more **community-based services** (Moritsugu, Duffy, & Wong, 2010). This is a general term meaning that *mental health services are located in the individual's own community or nearby.* The passage of the Community Mental Health Centers Act in 1963 aimed to create a **community mental health center** for every 50,000 people in the United States. These include *a variety of mental health services located in the patient's own community.* Everyone in the catchment area (an area of geographical coverage) for the center would have access to the needed psychological services at the

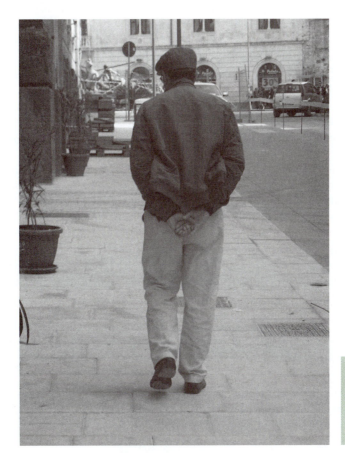

Although they often fail, community-based services are designed in part to prevent those with mental disorders from becoming homeless.

center at affordable fees, without having to leave the community. Although the actual services provided by these centers have fallen far short of the initial vision, they have been a major factor in the nationwide shift away from hospitalization to community-based care (Moritsugu, Duffy, & Wong).

As you might expect, outpatient services are the most heavily used services of local mental health centers. The goal of outpatient services is to provide help for individuals without disrupting their normal routine. Most mental health centers offer short-term therapy for individuals in the community with a variety of problems, ranging from domestic disputes to severe emotional disturbances.

The more comprehensive centers also provide alternatives to hospital care, such as day hospitals, halfway houses, and emergency or crisis services. **Day hospitals** that *provide part-time care in a hospital setting for those with mental disorders* have been established throughout the United States. These treatment centers provide the needed therapeutic care to patients from morning until late afternoon and then allow them to return to their families in the evening. Another type of agency that has proliferated in recent years is the **halfway house**—*a residence in which newly released patients and ex-addicts can live under supervision for a short period of time while they make the crucial transition in their lives from a setting with close supervision and other restrictions.* Halfway houses are also called *group homes* and *board-and-care homes*. The best halfway houses are small residences that are staffed by paraprofessionals who help the residents learn to live together and acquire the appropriate skills for returning to community life (Moritsugu, Duffy, & Wong). **Crisis intervention** has also emerged in response to a widespread need for *immediate treatment for those who are in a state of acute crisis but do not need treatment for many sessions.* Most people who come for short-term crisis counseling do not continue in treatment for more than a few sessions. In addition, a variety of telephone hotlines is now available in many communities. Even police in some cities, who are often the first to come in contact with a mentally disordered person in crisis, receive some crisis intervention training (Moritsugu, Duffy, & Wong).

Community-based services often fall short of what is needed, mostly because of insufficient funding and the resultant inadequacies in facilities, staffing, and carefully thought-out and coordinated programs that address the needs of the community (Moritsugu, Duffy, & Wong, 2010). Because of these inadequacies, the return of former patients to the community has slowed significantly. Even when individuals return to the community, they lack the necessary supervision and support to stay there (NAMI, 2006). In large cities, many of them become "street people" before returning to the hospital—hence, our stereotype. As a result, in many regions, *the number of admissions to mental hospitals has increased rather than decreased, leading to a "revolving-door" syndrome* or **transinstitutionalization** (Moritsugu, Duffy, & Wong). The revolving-door syndrome and the presence of so many former mental patients in jails, on the streets, and in nursing homes remind us that although comprehensive community-based care is an excellent idea, it is far from achieving its original goals (Moritsugu, Duffy, & Wong).

HOW WELL DOES THERAPY WORK?

Have you ever wondered what therapy is like? Have you ever wondered if therapy would work for you? Better yet, have you ever questioned whether psychotherapy works at all? For many years, hardly anyone bothered to ask such a question. Therapists and clients alike held a kind of blind faith that therapy does work. Then after reviewing various studies on the subject, Hans Eysenck (1966) shocked the world of therapy by concluding that over time, clients *not in therapy* improved as much as did clients *in therapy.* Eysenck's claims were hotly contested and challenged by others. Since that time, scientists have typically asked three main questions about the effectiveness of therapy:

(1) Is therapy better than no therapy?

(2) Is one particular type of therapy more effective than others?

(3) Are certain disorders more amenable to certain therapies?

Let's address these questions in order of presentation.

Is psychotherapy effective? Extensive early studies confirmed that therapy tends to have positive effects. For example, the American Psychiatric Association, which developed a commission on psychotherapy, says that based on research, at the end of therapy, the average treated patient is better off than 80 percent of untreated patients (Gabbard & Lazar, 2004). Another organization, the American Psychological Association, whose members are psychologists rather than psychiatrists, says:

> There is convincing evidence that most people who have at least several sessions of psychotherapy are far better off than untreated individuals with emotional difficulties. One major study showed that 50 percent of patients noticeably improved after eight sessions while 75 percent of the individuals in psychotherapy improved by the end of six months (American Psychological Association, 1998).

You might ask yourself if these two organizations have a conflict of interest in making such declarations. In fact, psychologists and psychiatrists have begun taking a closer look at the question of whether psychotherapy is effective. A strenuous and more recent debate about evidence-based therapy is drawing renewed attention to this issue (Goodheart, Kazdin, Sternberg, 2006; Lilienfeld, 2007; Nathan, 2007; NAMI, 2006; Paul, 2007; Staines & Cleland, 2007). **Evidence-based therapy** means *therapy proven effective through rigorous research methodologies.* Some debaters on the issue argue that even though there are few studies that show psychotherapy does more harm than good, there is some evidence to this effect (Lilienfeld, 2007). Others argue that while studies demonstrate some psychotherapy is better than no treatment, most such studies are replete with numerous biases and design problems (Staines & Cleland, 2007). Others chime in that it is no wonder that clinicians are confused on this issue if scientists cannot disentangle their own research findings (Nathan, 2007), while yet others add that even after years of research on the topic, we still have little to no idea what mechanisms produce therapeutic change (Kazdin, 2007). For example, perhaps exploring feelings rather than mere symptom relief is most important in producing change (Ladislav, 2007). The best answer to date on the issue of whether psychotherapy works is, "we need more and better designed studies."

Research has also attempted to provide some idea about what elements make therapy effective, no matter what the theoretical underpinning (Kolden et al., 2006; O'Donohue, Buchanan, & Fisher, 2000). One important aspect found over and over again is *the match or quality of fit between the client and the therapist,* known as the **therapeutic alliance** (Kolden et al.; Meissner, 2008; Overholser, 2007). One way to provide a good match is for *the client to become an active consumer of information,* that is, to ask questions about the therapist's qualifications, for explanations about the diagnosis, and so forth.

For example, a client and therapist characteristic that affects efficacy of therapy is cultural background (Kress, Eriksen, Rayle, & Ford, 2005; NAMI, 2006). Recall that Sergei's Russian parents wanted to keep their family problems to themselves and not share them with a stranger, in this case his therapist. Some research has suggested that Asian and Hispanic Americans tend to underutilize mental health care services (Bui & Takeuchi, 1992; Sue, Fujino, Hu, Takeuchi, & Zane, 1991). Sue et al. argue that even when ethnic minorities seek mental health care, they tend to have higher dropout rates than Whites. What Sue et al. suggest is that the mental health care professional shares the same ethnic background as the client.

Therapy is not exclusively dependent on the therapist's skills, the disorder, and the type of therapy. The client's traits and motives are also important (Vogel, Wester, Wei, & Boysen, 2005). The type of person likely to benefit most from psychotherapy is someone who is articulate (Moyers et al., 2007), motivated, anxious to change, capable of becoming personally involved in therapy, and believes in psychological processes as explanations for behavior (Nietzel, Bernstein, & Milich, 1991).

Another important ingredient is *length of treatment,* with longer treatments yielding better results (Seligman, 1995). In research on the number of sessions required for treatment, 20 or fewer sessions seem to be the norm today for effective treatment, with some researchers arguing that even a single session is effective (Miller, 2008). Assigning "homework," focusing on skills building and problem solving, and repeating assessments also appear to contribute to effective interventions (O'Donohue et al., 2000).

This leads us to our second question: *Is one type of psychotherapy more effective than another?* The answer the scientific literature provides is that *there is little difference among types of interpersonal psychotherapy* (Hunsley & Di Giulio, 2002; Luborsky et al., 2003; Wampold, Minami, Tierney, Baskin, & Bhati, 2005). Some claim that, once again, the studies examining such differences are seriously flawed (e.g., Hunsley & Di Giulio). You have read it before—we need more and better studies on the issue of which therapy is best, if any.

We now arrive at our last question: *Is one type of therapy better or worse for any particular disorder?* Although more research is merited on all of these issues, the answer to this third question at this point seems to be "yes." To date, cognitive-behavior therapies appear to be highly effective for anxiety disorders and depression (Butler et al., 2006; NIMH, 2009b; Rachman, 2008) and substance abuse disorders (Galanter & Kleber, 2008). Psychoactive drugs are most effective for treating schizophrenic disorders (Hollon, Thase, & Markowitz, 2002), while a combination of medication and psychotherapy appears most effective for the treatment of depression (Cuijpers et al., 2009). As more answers become available through research, psychotherapists may increasingly offer specific treatments for particular problems or integrate different approaches that may be more effective than a single approach with certain individuals.

FINDING HELP

Being knowledgeable about psychotherapy is one thing. Knowing how to get professional help for yourself and others is another matter. Should you or someone like Sergei have the occasion to seek professional help, you might consider the following questions:

1. When should you seek professional help?   As you might expect, there is no simple answer to this question, as so much depends on the particular person and the situation. However, a simple rule is this: Whenever your problems begin to interfere with your work and personal life, it's time to seek professional help. Also, when your present methods of coping with your problems no longer work, that's another sign that you may need help, especially when your family or friends are tired of being used as therapists and become openly concerned about you. Most important, whenever you feel overwhelmed and desperate and don't know what to do, it's best to seek help.

2. **Where do you find help?**   Help is available in a wide variety of settings. A large proportion of therapists work in comprehensive mental health centers that are now available in many communities. Staffed by a combination of psychiatrists, psychologists, social workers, and counselors, these centers offer a variety of services, including emergency help, all at a nominal fee that depends on income and ability to pay. See Box 15–4 for a description of the various types of mental health professionals available.

Many therapists work in private practice, either in a group or individual setting. They are usually listed in the yellow pages by their respective professions, for example, psychiatrists, psychologists, social workers, or family therapists. Although some are expensive, you may be reimbursed for part of the fee, depending on the type of insurance you have. Investigate with your health insurance company first. If you don't have insurance, some clinics provide low-cost or free services.

Many private social service or human service agencies provide short-term counseling and support for such matters as family problems, addiction problems, and career counseling. Also, many private and public hospitals offer emergency help for psychological problems. Then, too, most high schools and colleges have counseling

---

Box 15–4

Who Are the Therapists?

Unlike law or medicine, in which there is a single path to professional practice, there are many routes to becoming a psychotherapist. Because few states regulate the practice of psychotherapy as such, the question of who may legitimately conduct psychotherapy is governed by state law or professional boards within the respective professions.

- **Psychiatrists** *are medical doctors who specialize in the treatment of mental illness.* They usually spend three to four years training in a clinical setting following their medical degree and can treat the psychological disorders requiring drugs and hospitalization.

- **Psychoanalysts** *are psychiatrists or other mental health professionals who have received several years of additional training in personality theory and the therapeutic methods of one of the founding analysts,* such as Freud, Jung, Adler, or Sullivan.

- **Psychologists** *receive clinical training in the methods of psychological assessment and treatment as part of a program in clinical, counseling, or school psychology.* They may have a Ph.D., Ed.D., or Psy.D. degree.

- **Psychiatric (or clinical) social workers** *receive supervised clinical training as part of their master's degree program in the field of social work, and some earn a doctorate as well.* They tend to be community-oriented and usually work as part of a clinical team, though many now enter private practice.

- **Counselors** *receive training in personality theory and counseling skills, usually at the master's-degree level. Their counseling emphasis tends to reflect their respective professional affiliations, depending on whether they are doing marriage counseling, career counseling, pastoral counseling (clergy), or some other type.*

- **Paraprofessionals** (*para* meaning "akin to") *have two- or four-year degrees (or sometimes no degree at all) and work in the mental health field.* Sometimes as many as half the staff members of a community mental health center work at the paraprofessional level, assisting in the helping process in a variety of ways.

centers, which provide psychological help as well as academic guidance and career counseling. If all else fails, the American Psychological Association Practice Directorate at 800-374-2723 can aim you toward an appropriate state organization that can make a local referral.

3. What should you look for in a therapist? Among the major considerations for choosing a therapist should be (a) whether the therapist is professionally trained and certified and (b) how comfortable you feel with this person. Ordinarily, people must be properly qualified to list themselves as psychiatrists, psychologists, or social workers in the telephone directory. Also, professionals are encouraged to display their state license and other certificates in a prominent place in their office. But you will also want to feel comfortable talking to the therapist. Does this person really listen to you? Is the person warm and empathic without being condescending? Does this person understand and appreciate your particular point of view? Box 15–5 discusses a rapidly growing trend that will make therapy seemingly available to everyone, no matter how remote a region they live in. This trend involves therapy via computers and the Internet.

4. What can you expect from therapy? Most therapies provide certain common benefits, such as an empathic, caring, and trusting relationship; hope for the demoralized; and a new way of understanding yourself and the world. Beyond this, a lot depends on the goals and progress made in your particular therapy. People seeking relatively short-term therapy usually acquire a better understanding of their problems as well as the necessary skills to cope with a personal or family crisis. Those undergoing

Box 15–5

COMPUTERS AND THERAPY: WAVE OF THE FUTURE?

An increasing number of psychotherapists are offering online help; in fact, technology may become an important part of psychotherapy delivery in the next decade (Newman, 2004). There are now so many online therapists that no one quite knows what to name this new form of therapy: etherapy, ecounseling, cybertherapy, telecounseling (Elleven & Allen, 2004), or remote therapy (Bee et al., 2008).

Many therapists are setting up World Wide Web pages accessible to millions of Americans with credit cards and computers. Cybertherapists claim that Internet clients can avoid stigma, obtain treatment at almost any time or place, and proceed at their own pace (Spek et al., 2006). Others, however, provide the caveat that cybertherapy does not allow for as detailed probing as does face-to-face intervention (Bee et al., 2008). Newman (2004) suggests that research now shows that contrary to many criticisms, technology need not necessarily compromise the all-important therapeutic alliance between client and therapist.

Critics of cybertherapy (Haveren, Habben, & Kuther, 2005) argue that ethical issues are beginning to emerge; for example, confidentiality may be betrayed if the wrong person receives an electronic message either to or from the therapist or client. Critics also argue that the client may know little about the online therapist's qualifications because of the geographic distance between client and therapist and that clients who are not computer savvy may feel uncomfortable with cybertherapy.

Other means for finding help online are rapidly developing. For example, social support is offered in the form of chat lines, bulletin boards, and news groups for individuals with specific disorders. Similarly, some psychological journals have gone online so that mental health consumers can do their own literature searches. One rich website is the one offered by the American Psychological Association; see especially information on the link to "Monitor on Psychology."

relatively long-term therapy, such as psychoanalytic therapy, aspire to more fundamental changes in their personality and may remain in therapy longer.

5. How long must you go?   In the past, the lack of objective guidelines made it difficult for therapists and clients alike to know how long therapy should last. However, the recent trend toward short-term therapies and the increased concern for containing health care costs have made the length of therapy a major issue. At the same time, the rate of improvement varies considerably among different types of clients. Consequently, the appropriate length of treatment often becomes an empirical issue to be decided by clients and their therapists with some interference from insurance carriers.

As a practical guide for deciding when to terminate therapy, consider two key questions: First, is the crisis or problem that brought you to therapy under control? You need not have resolved all of your difficulties, but you should have more understanding and control over your life so that your difficulties do not interfere with your work and personal activities. Second, can you maintain the gains acquired in therapy on your own? It's best to discuss these two issues with your therapist before deciding to terminate therapy. At the same time, bear in mind that in therapy, as in all close relationships, there will be unsettling as well as gratifying occasions.

SUMMARY

INSIGHT THERAPIES—THE TALKING CURE

Many people suffering from a psychological disorder will not get help from a mental health professional, such as a psychologist. Many will be seen by their family physician or a counselor. Traditionally, clients have sought out insight-oriented therapies, which bring about change by increasing self-understanding.

Modern psychoanalytic therapists use a modified version of Freud's ideas and techniques to help clients achieve insight into and self-mastery of the unconscious forces in their lives. In contrast, Rogers's person-centered approach assumes that individuals have within themselves vast resources for self-understanding and growth, which may be actualized within a caring and empathic relationship conducive to change.

COGNITIVE-BEHAVIORAL THERAPIES

Cognitive-behavioral approaches developed out of research and experimental psychology and tend to focus on the maladaptive thoughts and behaviors themselves rather than on their causes or on emotions. Behavioral therapists focus directly on the client's problem behaviors, with the aim of replacing maladaptive behaviors with more appropriate and satisfying ones. For instance, in desensitization, the client learns to substitute a new response, such as relaxation, for an old, maladaptive response, such as anxiety or fear. Cognitive therapies tend to focus on the irrational thoughts and beliefs that contribute to problem behaviors.

Today, there is an increasing alliance between behavioral and cognitive therapies. As a result, more therapists characterize their orientation as cognitive-behavioral, with the goal of modifying faulty assumptions and thought patterns and then relying on established behavioral procedures like relaxation training to help modify the problem behavior.

OTHER APPROACHES TO TREATMENT

The various group therapies, including family and couples therapy, deal with the individual as a function of group dynamics or family structure and utilize the group process to help members achieve mutually satisfying solutions. Biomedical therapies treat the symptoms of psychological problems with direct physical intervention, including drugs—antianxiety, antidepressant, and antipsychotic drugs; electroconvulsive therapy; and psychosurgery.

One of the most dramatic changes in mental health care has been the marked shift from prolonged stays in large institutions to the use of community-based services. Although the latter have expanded to include a variety of services, such as day hospitals and halfway houses, outpatient services continue to be the most widely used.

HOW WELL DOES THERAPY WORK?

Studies, although many are poorly designed, tend to show that psychotherapy generally works better than no therapy, and clients who have had therapy are better off than untreated clients. Much of the current research focuses on specific, measurable factors that make therapy effective, such as client characteristics. Also, some approaches appear to be especially well suited to certain problems, such as the cognitive-behavioral approach for people suffering from anxiety or mild to moderate depression.

FINDING HELP

Individuals who are considering professional help might benefit from asking the following questions: (1) When should I seek professional help? (2) Where can I find it? (3) What should I look for in a therapist? (4) What can I expect from therapy? and (5) How long must I stay in therapy?

SELF-TEST

1. The process of helping clients gain insight into their unconscious conflicts through such techniques as the analysis of transference is called
   a. behavior therapy.
   b. logotherapy.
   c. psychoanalysis.
   d. multimodal therapy.

2. To establish the proper climate for change, a person-centered therapist strives to be accepting, empathic, and
   a. genuine.
   b. interpretive.
   c. objective.
   d. judgmental.

3. Which of the following techniques is especially effective in treating fears and phobias?
   a. transference.
   b. desensitization.
   c. person-centered therapy.
   d. gestalt therapy.

4. The therapeutic approach of modifying clients' behavior by changing their irrational thoughts is called
   a. cognitive therapy.
   c. psychoanalysis.
   b. existential therapy.
   d. actualization therapy.

5. Which of the following approaches assumes that people's problems are best understood and treated as an integral part of the groups to which they belong?
   a. Existential therapy
   c. Family therapy
   b. Logotherapy
   d. Psychoanalysis

6. Which of the following groups of psychoactive drugs are the most widely prescribed in the United States?
   a. Antianxiety drugs
   c. Lithium derivatives
   b. Antidepressants
   d. Antipsychotic drugs

7. The setting in which people with mental disorders receive part-time treatment in a hospital is called a (an)
   a. day hospital.
   c. state hospital.
   b. halfway house.
   d. inpatient service.

8. Has research really shown that psychotherapy is effective?
   a. Yes, quite definitively
   b. Only psychoanalysis is effective
   c. No, we need better studies
   d. No, people get better with the mere passage of time

9. What is one of the problems with computerized therapy compared to face-to-face therapy?
   a. Increased likelihood of loss of confidentiality
   b. Increased stigma
   c. Internet therapy is more expensive
   d. All of these are problems

10. Professionals who are medical doctors but who specialize in treating mental disorders are
    a. psychiatrists.
    c. social workers.
    b. psychologists.
    d. counselors.

EXERCISES

1. *How do you feel about getting help?* Write a paragraph describing your attitude toward getting help for a psychological problem. To what extent do you feel that psychological help is a sign of personal weakness? How severe would the problem have to be before you sought help? Be honest.

2. *To whom would you turn for help?* Suppose you needed psychological help immediately. To whom would you turn? Write down the name, address, and telephone number of the person or agency. If you're unable to do so, you might ask for appropriate referrals from your state psychological association or a local employee assistance program at work. You might also think about why you selected this person or agency.

3. *Distinguishing between psychiatrists and psychologists.* People often confuse these two professionals. Reread Box 15–4. Then write a paragraph or so describing the differences between these two types of professionals. What services are usually reserved for psychiatrists? What types of problems or psychological disorders are most appropriate for psychologists?

4. *First-person account of therapy.* If you've participated in counseling or therapy, write a page or two describing your experience. In what ways was it beneficial? Do you have any misgivings about it? On the basis of your experience, what suggestions would you make to those considering therapy? If you have never been in therapy, imagine that you have been for counseling and write about why you think it might be beneficial or not.

5. *Mutual-help groups.* Perhaps you've participated in a group like Parents Without Partners or Alcoholics Anonymous. If yes, write a page or so describing your experience. If not, which type of mutual-help group would you be most interested in joining and why? You might visit the website for the American Self-Help Clearing House to obtain a list of such groups (http://selfhelpgroups.org).

QUESTIONS FOR SELF-REFLECTION

1. Do you believe that friends can be good medicine?

2. If you were looking for a therapist, either for yourself or someone else, where would you seek advice?

3. What are some personal qualities you would look for in a therapist? Professional qualities?

4. Have you ever considered using desensitization to reduce your own anxieties or fears?

5. Do you think some of your limitations or problems might be related to family patterns, present or past?

6. Have you ever belonged to a mutual-help or self-help group?

7. Would you agree that people have to want to change in order to benefit fully from therapy?

8. Do you think that asking for help when you need it is itself a mark of maturity? Weakness?

9. Are you aware that many people experience personal growth (as well as the relief of symptoms) in psychotherapy? How can therapy help people grow?

10. If you went for help, what kind of therapy (e.g., person-centered) would you seek? Why?

FOR FURTHER INFORMATION

RECOMMENDED READINGS

COREY, G. (2005). *Theory and practice of counseling and psychotherapy.* Belmont, CA: Brooks/Cole. A leading textbook on counseling and psychotherapy covering the principles of counseling as well as the orientation and techniques of various theories of therapy.

HOWARD, S. (2008). *The heart and soul of a therapist: Rage, fear, desire, loss, and love in the psychotherapy relationship.* Lanham, MD: University Press of America. The all-important therapeutic alliance produces change. Howard explores in clear, readable language both therapist and client characteristics and behaviors that enhance or sabotage this relationship.

MILLON, T. (2004). *Masters of the mind: Exploring the story of mental illness from ancient times to the new millennium.* Hoboken, NJ: Wiley. Millon is one of the leading authorities on mental disorders and interventions. Here he reviews the history of mental illness and its treatment.

PRESTON, J., O'NEAL, J. H., & TALAGA, M. (2008). *Consumer's guide to psychiatric drugs: Straight talk for patients and their families.* New York: Simon & Schuster. This accessible, everyday guide written by a psychologist, a psychiatrist, and a pharmacist discusses diagnosis as well as treatment.

YALOM, I. D. (2003). *The gift of therapy: An open letter to a new generation of therapists and their patients.* New York: HarperCollins. Through cases and stories, Yalom examines therapy through the eyes of the therapist and the client.

WEBSITES AND THE INTERNET

http://www.compwellness.com A website devoted to less traditional forms of treatment for mental disorders.

http://www.apa.org The American Psychological Association's website that offers scientific and practical information on a variety of topics related to therapy and related issues.

http://www.nami.org The website for the National Alliance for the Mentally Ill, an advocacy group for the mentally ill and their families.

http://nypsychotherapy.com The site of the New York Psychotherapy Group, which provides information on whether therapy helps, various forms of therapy, what to expect from therapy, the use of medications, and more. Click on "Articles and FAQs."

http://www.mentalhelp.net A website with a wealth of information for lay consumers, including information on all types of treatments for mental disorders.

Good Grief, Death, and Dying

Two people hold sharply contrasting attitudes toward death. Mark, who is in his late 40s, bristles at the mention of the word *death.* Those who know him well say this reaction may have something to do with the tragic loss of his older brother in a car accident when Mark was a young adult. In any event, Mark refuses to attend funerals, even for his closest friends. One can only speculate how Mark would react if his wife or children should die before he does. For years, Mark has boasted that the only way he'll ever go to a cemetery is "feet first" when he's carried there for his own burial.

Joanna, a widow in her early 80s, maintains a very different attitude toward death. She is grieving over the recent loss of her husband, to whom she was happily married for 62 years. She talks openly with her friends about how much she misses him. She regularly tends to the plants at the family plot. Knowing that her husband never liked being alone, she sometimes pauses by his grave to talk to him. "Don't worry," she says, "I'll be with you one day." Then she glances at the unused gravesite adjacent to her husband's, together with the stone containing her name. How does she feel about seeing her own tombstone? "Well, you see," she replies, "we saved a little money by getting both done at the same time." With which of these people's attitudes toward death do you most identify?

DEATH AND DYING

Death is a difficult concept to define, much less to think about and understand. A common definition of **death** is *the cessation of life as measured by the absence of breathing, heartbeat, and electrical activity of the brain.* Some of us would prefer to think we're like Joanna, with her open and matter-of-fact attitude toward death. At other times, we realize that we may be more like Mark, with his characteristic denial of death. Perhaps most of us fall somewhere in between these two extremes.

Actually, some denial of death such as Mark holds is probably necessary *and* normal to function effectively. Death, especially the possibility of our own death, is such a harsh reality that few people can face it directly. Denial helps to keep our anxiety level over the threat of our own demise at a low, manageable level. Denial also helps us to avoid thoughts of being separated from loved ones, whose relationship to us is essential to our self-esteem and well-being. Then, too, there's another reason for not thinking about death—the idea that it's futile to think about the inevitable. Because we aren't certain what comes after death, death typically is a most unpleasant thought. As Ben Franklin said, "In this world nothing can be said to be certain, except death and taxes." Interestingly, both Joanna and Mark, via their individual styles of coping with the prospect of death, agree with Franklin.

An excessive or inappropriate denial of death such as Mark's, however, tends to be counterproductive. For instance, people who constantly reassure themselves that "It can't happen to me" or who insist "I don't want to think about it" may continue to smoke, drink alcohol, eat junk food, and drive too fast, all of which increase their vulnerability to dying. Similarly, the denial of death makes us avoid the aged or the seriously ill, who may remind us of our own mortality but who may need our friendship and care. Joanna, being more comfortable with death than Mark, was able to stay at her dying husband's side and support him through this passage.

We'll begin this chapter by considering some of the realities of death, such as the everyday risks of dying, death anxiety, and the experience of dying. In the middle section, we'll describe the process of grief and the importance of working through emotions associated with personal loss. Then in the final section, we'll examine some of the ethical and practical issues associated with dying, such as the right to die, funerals, and how the awareness of our mortality and experiences of loss can enrich the meaning of life itself.

Risks of Dying

Every day each of us risks dying as a consequence of engaging or not engaging in certain activities. Risk-taking may increase death anxiety; in some people, however, it may not. To become more aware of your level of death anxiety, you can complete the Death Anxiety Scale in Activity 16–1 before reading further. After you know your score, contemplate how your level of anxiety affects your life, if at all. Do you take risks? Are you scared to death of death? Is your death anxiety keeping you from attending funerals of close friends and family or sitting with a loved one who is terminally ill?

People tend to overestimate the risk of death from sensational causes such as accidents and homicides and underestimate the risk of death from nonspectacular causes such as heart attacks, strokes, and diabetes. Such misjudgments arise from our tendency to believe an event is likely to occur if we can easily imagine or recall it, which is further compounded by the media's practice of overreporting dramatic, negative events such as accidents and homicides. Newspapers carry three times as many articles about death from homicide as about death from disease, although disease takes 100 lives to every 1 homicide. Because most of these deaths are noted in the obituary columns rather than the headlines, we underestimate the risk of death from familiar hazards such as smoking, surgery, and diseases. These are, however, the very things over which each of us has a great deal of control.

As you might suspect, the risk of dying varies greatly from one person to another, depending on such factors as lifestyle, heredity, and gender. Health habits and lifestyles, as mentioned elsewhere in this book, are especially important. People who smoke a pack

ACTIVITY 16–1

What's Your Level of Death Anxiety?

INSTRUCTIONS: *For each of the following statements, indicate your degree of agreement by circling the appropriate number below the statement.*

1. As I read this chapter on death and grief, I feel uncomfortable.

    Strongly disagree   1   2   3   4   5   6   7   Strongly agree

2. I am not distressed by the thought of planning my own funeral.

    Strongly disagree   1   2   3   4   5   6   7   Strongly agree

3. When I know someone is terminally ill, I find it difficult to visit.

    Strongly disagree   1   2   3   4   5   6   7   Strongly agree

4. If I knew it would save me money, I would buy a burial plot in advance.

    Strongly disagree   1   2   3   4   5   6   7   Strongly agree

5. I prefer not to attend funerals or other death-related events.

    Strongly disagree   1   2   3   4   5   6   7   Strongly agree

6. Thoughts of my own death do not significantly trouble me.

    Strongly disagree   1   2   3   4   5   6   7   Strongly agree

7. I am careful not to take physical risks other, more adventurous people might take.

    Strongly disagree   1   2   3   4   5   6   7   Strongly agree

8. The sight of cemeteries and funeral homes does not bother me.

    Strongly disagree   1   2   3   4   5   6   7   Strongly agree

9. I worry greatly that after death, there is nothingness.

    Strongly disagree   1   2   3   4   5   6   7   Strongly agree

10. I try to attend the calling hours for friends and family who have recently died.

    Strongly disagree   1   2   3   4   5   6   7   Strongly agree

SCORING: The even-numbered items need to be reverse scored so that disagreement signals higher death anxiety; that means for even-numbered items, a 1 becomes a 7, a 2 becomes a 6 and so on.

Total for odd-numbered items: _____

Total for even-numbered items (after reverse scoring) _____

Grand total _____

Interpretation: This scale was developed for your own personal information and awareness. It has no scientific validity or reliability. A high score does not necessarily mean there is something wrong with you or that you suffer tremendous death anxiety. A low score does not necessarily mean that you manage the idea of death well. Instead, this scale is designed to stimulate you to think about the concept of death as well as about your level of death-related anxiety.

70–55   = You may have high levels of death anxiety.

54–40   = You may have moderately high levels of death anxiety.

39–25   = You probably are neither comfortable nor uncomfortable with the topic of death.

24–10   = You may be only somewhat distressed by the topic of death.

9 and below = You may be at peace with the idea of death, or, on the other hand, uncaring.

or more of cigarettes a day can expect to die five or six years sooner than those who don't smoke. Similarly, those who are overweight by 50 pounds or more die many years sooner than those closer to their ideal weights.

People who have healthy eating and exercise habits not only keep themselves more fit but also tend to live longer than those with less healthy habits. Personality and stress management are also important. Whereas individuals who are intense, hostile, and easily angered tend to die sooner than average, those who are relaxed and easygoing live longer than average (Cohen & Pressman, 2006; White, 2008). Table 16–1 lists some of the leading causes of death in the United States. Notice that the first few reasons are related to unhealthy lifestyles such as smoking.

Heredity also affects our life expectancy. It is well known that people with long-lived parents and grandparents tend to live longer than those whose close relatives die before 50. However, if your relatives are not noted for their longevity, you need not

TABLE 16–1
LEADING CAUSES OF DEATH IN THE UNITED STATES, 2006

Cause	Number of Deaths
Heart disease	631,636
Cancer	559,888
Stroke	137,119
Chronic lower respiratory disease	124,583
Accidents	121,599
Diabetes	72,449
Alzheimer's disease	72,432
Pneumonia/influenza	56,326
Kidney disease	42,453

Source: Centers for Disease Control and Prevention, National Center for Health Statistics.
http://www.cdc.gov/nchs/deaths.htm (accessed June 14, 2009).

become fatalistic. Instead, you might make even greater efforts to adopt healthier eating and exercise habits. For instance, because most of the men in Mark's family died before the age of 50, he continued his "eat, drink, and be merry" outlook. Mark was sure he would be dead by middle age anyway. At the insistence of his doctor and wife, he underwent a coronary bypass operation and began eating healthier foods. He refused to exercise, though.

Awareness of Death

Despite attempts at denial, each of us, like Mark, has some awareness of our own mortality (Bartalos, 2009; Fawcett, 2004). For instance, suppose you were asked, "How often do you think about your own death?" If your reply is "once in a while," you've got a lot of company. About half the people asked this question answer "occasionally." Another fourth say "frequently" or "very frequently," whereas another fourth claim they rarely have thoughts about their own death.

Actually, our personal awareness of death fluctuates somewhat every day. Most of the time, we have very little awareness of death. The personal awareness of death also varies somewhat by age. Interestingly, people in their late 20s are the most fearful of all, perhaps partly because they have most of their lives ahead of them. The terrorist attacks of September 11, 2001, however, served to make them and teens even more sensitive to awareness of death (Halpern-Felshner & Millstein, 2002). In fact, we are all more aware of our own mortality due to the terrorist attacks (Bartalos, 2009). Then, too, the leading causes of death for youths—accidents, homicide, and suicide—imply that death often comes cruelly and tragically to them.

As individuals reach late adulthood, they generally *think* about death more often and talk about it more openly. The increase in chronic illnesses and the death of close friends at this age are all reminders that death is the natural end of life. Older people, however, are usually *less fearful* of death than other age groups. After all, they've already lived a reasonably long life and may feel they have less to look forward to. Also, those with a deep religious faith, including a belief in some kind of afterlife, are thought to be generally less fearful of death (Krause, 2005). Such a belief may provide an important mechanism for dealing with the anxieties of aging and death. When Joanna, a regular churchgoer, was asked if she feared death, she replied, "I'm more worried about ending up in a nursing home, being in pain, or becoming a burden to my children than I am of dying. I've made my peace with death." In fact, many Americans feel the same way; they may be more afraid of *the process* of dying than death itself.

Near-Death Experiences

Suppose you're knocked unconscious in an automobile accident and taken to the hospital. Critically injured, you're put on a life-support system that keeps you alive. After a couple of days, you regain consciousness, only to discover that you almost died. There's a small chance you could have had a **near-death experience**—*the distinctive state of recall associated with being brought back to life from the verge of death.*

Accounts of these experiences show striking similarities. There are even some cross-cultural similarities but with different nuances shaped by language and cultural experiences (Belanti, Perera, & Jagadheesan, 2008). Initially, individuals experience a detachment from their bodies and are pulled through a dark tunnel. Then they find themselves in another kind of "spiritual body," in which physical objects present no barrier and movement from one place to another is almost instantaneous. While in this state, they may have a reunion with long-lost friends and loved ones. One of the most incredible elements is the appearance of a brilliant light, perceived as a warm, loving "being of light," which fosters a kind of life review in a nonjudgmental way. Finally, people report being drawn back through the dark tunnel and undergoing a rapid reentry into their bodies (*Harvard Health Letter*, 2002; van Lommel, van Wees, Meyers, & Elfferich, 2001). For most people, the near-death experience brings a profound change in attitudes. They not only become less fearful of death but are also more concerned with loving and valuing the life they have (Koerner, 1997). There is also an increase in spirituality (Musgrave, 1997) as well as more concern for others and less concern for material possessions (Groth-Marnat & Summers, 1998). No matter what the age, race, sex, or education level, the near-death experience seems transforming.

Although many who have had near-death experiences prefer to view them as spiritual encounters, researchers are taking the mysticism out of such occurrences by claiming that they are physiological events, hallucinations, or other changes in cognition created by the nervous system or anesthesia (Buzzi, Couper, Bardy, & Evans, 2002; Dieguez, 2008; Greyson, 2005; Koerner, 1997). Any of these critics claim that research on near-death experiences is replete with research problems (e.g., when dying individuals know about near-death experiences, they are more likely to report them; Greyson). Others, such as Elisabeth Kübler-Ross (1997b), believe that near-death phenomena are an integral part of the more inclusive experience of dying, including the physical level (loss of consciousness), psychic level (out-of-body awareness), and spiritual level (glimpse of nonjudgmental light or the realm of God).

The Experience of Dying

By **experience of dying,** we mean *the sequence of physiological and psychological changes experienced by individuals who are dying.* Now that people are likely to die in a hospital, often sedated and isolated from all but their immediate family and hospital personnel, the experience of dying has become something of a mystery for the average person. Many people have never been in the presence of someone who is dying. Even people who have sat with a loved one or friend who is dying have only a limited awareness of the dying person's inner world or how to communicate with that person. This statement sadly is true even for professional caregivers, such as physicians and hospice care workers (Fenwick, Loverlace, & Brayne, 2007; Fitzsimons et al., 2007).

One of the best-known pioneers in this field is Elisabeth Kübler-Ross. She and her colleagues interviewed more than 500 terminally ill people at the University of Chicago hospital. Kübler-Ross (1975) found that even when patients were not told of the seriousness of their illnesses, they usually sensed that fact as well as the approximate time of their deaths. Compared to the 1970s, doctors today are more likely to reveal to patients their terminal prognosis (Barnett, 2006; Field & Copp, 1999), because Kübler-Ross's efforts have made medical schools more likely to incorporate such information into their curricula (Block & Billings, 2005). Hence, there is a growing realization that when persons indicate a willingness to know the truth about their impending death, it may be wiser to give the relevant information than to protect them with a conspiracy of concealment (Barnett). This also provides them with some time to get their affairs in order, for example, write a will if they do not have one or say a special goodbye to loved ones.

Kübler-Ross (1993, 1997b) noted that individuals tend to go through several stages in dying, although there is considerable overlap between these stages. The first stage consists of a **denial of death,** *with people characteristically feeling, "No, not me; this cannot happen to me."* Such denial protects them from the deep emotions associated with death and provides time to cope with the disturbing facts (Zimmerman, 2004). Later, individuals tend to show small signs that they are now willing to talk about death. In the second stage, denial eventually gives way to the emotions of anger and **resentment,** *especially toward individuals who are healthy.* "Why me?" people ask. The sight of others enjoying their health evokes envy, jealousy, and anger. The dying often take their feelings out on those closest to them, mostly because of what these people represent—life and health. Consequently, it is important for those nearby not to take these remarks personally, but to help dying individuals express their feelings.

The third stage characteristically consists of attempts to **bargain for time** in *which the dying individual attempts to negotiate with others (e.g., God) who might help him or her live longer.* Individuals at this stage often say, "I know I'm dying but. . . ." Then they indulge in a bit of magical thinking or negotiation: "If I cooperate with the doctor or my family, maybe God will let me live until my daughter graduates or my son gets married." When individuals tend to drop the "but" and admit, "Yes, I'm dying," they enter the fourth stage, **depression,** *characterized by intense and sometimes unrealistic sadness.* In a sense this is a natural response to the threat of losing their life, and it is very important to allow dying people to grieve and express their sadness. One of the worst things a friend can do is deny these feelings and say, "Cheer up." Thus, it is important for family and friends as well as professionals to learn to accept their own feelings about death so that they can help dying people accept their own impending death without dwelling on it unduly.

The final stage is the **acceptance** of death, though not all dying persons reach this stage. By this time, most *people who are dying have pretty much accepted death and have disengaged themselves from others.* They may ask for fewer visitors, but often they don't want to die alone. Although most people prefer to die at home (Administration on Aging, 2005), they are more likely to die in a hospital. In fact, much of the pain of dying comes from mental anguish, especially the fear of being separated from loved ones.

Elisabeth Kübler-Ross (1975, 1993; Meagher, 2007) was the first to point out that the experience of dying is not a fixed, inevitable process and that many people do not follow these stages (Wright, 2002). For some, anger remains the dominant mood throughout, whereas others are depressed until the end, as was Joanna's husband, although he died quickly. Many experts go even further and hold that individual differences are more pronounced in the experience of dying than are differences in stages (e.g., Corr, 1993; Quigley & Schatz, 1999; Wright). Consequently, each person experiences the dying process in a unique way because of such factors as age, sex, and personality differences, as well as cultural backgrounds and the nature of various types of illnesses. While Kübler-Ross' work is not without critics, she did much to raise awareness that dying is an important but much neglected (by professionals) process (Rothaupt & Becker, 2007) and to inspire interest in the hospice, legal and ethical movements related to death and dying (Meagher, 2007).

BEREAVEMENT AND GRIEF

To lose a loved one or friend through death is to lose part of ourselves. It's a very painful experience that is labeled variously as bereavement, grief, or mourning. **Bereavement** ("to be deprived of") is *the process of adjusting to the experience of loss, especially to the death of friends or loved ones.* It involves the overall experience of loss. **Grief** refers to *the intense* *emotional suffering that accompanies our experience of loss,* and **mourning** refers to *the outward expressions of bereavement and grief.*

Because death is one of the universal rites of passage, most societies have mourning customs to facilitate the expression of grief. In the past, in American culture, widows dressed in black and widowers wore black armbands. Such dress explained the show of grief on the part of the bereaved and afforded them an opportunity to talk about their loss and to receive the needed sympathy. However, many of these customs have been modified or given up. Wakes and visiting hours have been replaced by brief funerals and memorial services. Ordinarily, the bereaved today are expected to resume their usual dress and activities as soon as possible.

Grief Work

Sigmund Freud gave us the notion of grief work (Rothaupt & Becker, 2007). **Grief work** consists of *the healthy process of working through the emotions associated with loss, freeing ourselves emotionally from the deceased, readjusting to life without that person, resuming ordinary activities, and forming new relationships.* The grief process can parallel the experience of dying and involves many of the same stages (Kübler-Ross & Kessler, 2005; Maciewjewski, Zhang, Block, & Prigerson, 2007; Rothaupt & Becker; Stroebe, Schut, & Stroebe, 2005). Grief work takes time (thus it is called "work") and may not ever be fully completed. Why? There are individual differences (Boerner, Wortman, & Bonanno, 2005) in how people grieve, but we will describe the typical experience here.

Initially, we may react to a person's death with a sense of shock and disbelief, especially when death occurs unexpectedly, for example, as in suicide (Houck, 2007). When we've been anticipating a person's death, as in the case of a terminally ill friend, our initial response may be subdued and accompanied by a sense of relief. Joanna experienced a sense

After a deadly shooting at their school and despite their own grief, the Amish astonished the world by forgiving the shooter and attending his funeral.

of relief after caring for her failing husband for several months. Her sense of relief, though, only served to make her feel guilty later. Guilt may be as normal to grief as is sadness. Some of our guilt may be "survivor's guilt," that is, feeling guilty simply because we're still alive and the other person is not.

The emotional intensity of grief in these early stages often appears in the disguise of physical symptoms. In fact, although grief is not a disease, it is associated with increased health problems and increased likelihood of the griever's own death (Stroebe, Schut, & Stroebe, 2007). In the early months of bereavement, the most common symptoms of grief are crying, depressed feelings, lack of appetite, and difficulties concentrating at work or at home. Another common symptom is lack of interaction with others (Monk, Houck, & Shear, 2006). Fortunately for Joanna, these symptoms did not last long, because she was a particularly resilient person. Some people rely on sleeping pills and tranquilizers at some point during their bereavement.

In the final stage of grief, we usually come to terms with our loss (acceptance) and resume our everyday activities (Maciewjewski et al., 2007). This stage may occur anytime from a few months to a year or more after the initial loss, depending on how close we were to the person and the circumstances surrounding the death. Research has shown that about one year is the norm for normal grief work (Lindstrom, 1995) and that the most intense and negative emotions have peaked by six months (Maciewjewski et al.), but some professionals in the field of grief and bereavement find that normal grief can extend way beyond the first year (Davis, 2001). Depression and other emotional reactions to the death of a loved one generally decline over the first year (Grad & Zavasnik, 1999). From that time on, we're likely to recall the deceased person with pleasant memories. In some ways, we never fully get over the death of a loved one, such as a parent, child, or spouse.

Know that recent literature is moving away from the notion of grief work (Rothaupt & Becker, 2007) and toward more growth-oriented theories of bereavement in recognition that grief represents only a part of the self, the emotional self. Therefore, grief doesn't just involve mourning, it includes reflecting on the person who died and the meanings as well as anticipated changes for the bereaved. In this new model, the survivor assimilates the reality that the deceased is gone, expresses the emotional pain of the loss, develops new strategies for coping in a world without the loved one, and develops new beliefs and attitudes about life, death, love and compassion. In this model, grief needn't be distressing.

Unresolved Grief

Psychological Reactions.   **Unresolved grief** is *a psychological state in which a person's emotional reaction to loss remains repressed, often being manifested in unexplained physical or psychological symptoms.* Also called **complicated grief,** this prolonged and impairing type of grief may assume a variety of forms, from unexplained physical complaints to psychological symptoms (Boelen & van den Bout, 2007; Bonanno & Kaltman, 2001; Shear, Frank, Houck, & Reynolds, 2005; Warren, 1997). In some instances, the psychological reactions are obviously related to the loss. For example, some people avoid their grief (Bonanno, Papa, Lalande, Zhang, & Noll, 2005); they can't bring themselves to return to the house, hospital, or room where a person has died because of unresolved grief. In other cases, unresolved grief may be more disguised as in unexplained outbursts of anger.

On the other hand, some individuals do just the opposite. Instead of thinking too little about their loved one or the death, they think too much about their grief and the loss of their loved one. Studies have also shown that rumination about the death, that is, preoccupation with the death, can be detrimental (Michael & Snyder, 2005). Individuals who ruminate or constantly rehash details of the death, especially when they have few social supports and many other stressors, experience more depression and pessimism than those who don't ruminate (Nolen-Hoeksema, Parker, & Larson, 1994). Some bereavement experts suggest that this type of prolonged or complex grieving is abnormal or requires special attention by professionals (e.g., Boelen, de Keijser, van den Hout, & van den Bout, 2007; Shear et al., 2005). Others claim that there are really very few cases of delayed grief or abnormal bereavement (Bonanno & Kaltman, 2001).

Physical Reactions.   People who live alone, especially those without close friends, are perhaps the most likely to have difficulty working through their grief. Men are likely to die a few years after the death of their wives, although women's chances of dying are less affected by their husband's death. Widowed men between the ages of 55 and 65 die at a 60 percent higher rate than married men the same age. The most likely explanation is that the quality of life changes more drastically for men than for women, possibly because of their greater reliance on wives for their emotional and daily needs. Women also tend to have a better support system (family and friends) for coping with their grief. However, when widowers remarry, they have an even lower mortality rate than their married counterparts who have never lost a spouse.

Good Grief

So far, we've seen that it is sometimes better to go through the full experience of bereavement, however painful it may be, than to get over it too quickly or to ruminate too intently. In this regard, Joanna was coping better with her loss than was Mark, even years later. There are, however, some positive aspects of grief. Grief may be a learning experience that helps us grow (Bonanno, Moskowitz, Papa, & Folkman, 2005; Gamino & Sewell, 2004). Grief helps us appreciate loved ones and friends more fully despite their shortcomings. Grief also helps us value our relationships with those still living. In short, **good grief** means *that we have learned and grown in our bereavement.* In fact, there now exists research that documents how bereavement indeed contributes to growth (Cadell, Regehr, & Hemsworth, 2003).

There are several ways to make the experience of bereavement more effective: talking it out, feeling it out, and acting it out. Even though it may be very difficult to talk about the death of a loved one for the first several weeks, this may be exactly when talking it out can be most helpful. A friend should attempt to listen and help the bereaved person to talk out feelings rather than cut the mourner off. Although you may be uncomfortable discussing death, the bereaved person may well need someone to talk to. Those who grieve with adequate social support are less likely to be depressed (Stroebe, Zech, Stroebe, & Abakoumkin, 2005) and may recover from their grief faster, too (Caserta & Lund, 1992; Nolen-Hoeksema et al., 1994).

Another way of resolving grief is to express it in other relevant ways. Sometimes just sheer physical activity, such as a brisk walk, helps to alleviate the tension and sadness of bereavement, at least temporarily. Funeral rituals also can afford an outlet for grief. Taking care of the affairs of the deceased may be therapeutic as well as helpful. As the executor of her husband's estate, Joanna found herself faced with a great deal of correspondence and many legal transactions. She initially regarded it as a burden but soon realized it was one of the few tangible things she could do for her deceased husband and their grown children. Finally, some studies indicate that **grief therapy,** which *assists the bereaved to cope with the death of a loved one,* is effective in helping the survivor cope with intense grief (e.g., Allumbaught & Hoyt, 1999; Boelen et al., 2007; Shear et al., 2005).

LIFE AND DEATH IN PERSPECTIVE

In 1900, more than half of all deaths were of children who died early from disease and hunger. By 1955, life expectancy was 48 years of age, and by 1995, it was 65 years of age (Kleespies, 2004). Now that the average life expectancy is over 78 years, more people are apt to suffer from chronic diseases, such as the many forms of cancer, heart disease, and kidney failure.

Because Americans are living longer and are dying from chronic rather than acute illnesses, death comes more slowly and often occurs in hospitals, which tend to be large and impersonal institutions, geared more to the treatment of acute illnesses and the prolonging of life. Consequently, this change in the context of death presents new ethical issues (Haddad, 2003; Kleespies, 2004; Anonymous, 2005), such as the use of lifesaving machines and the right to die in a dignified way. Examining such issues may help us put life and death in better perspective.

The Right to Die

Joanna remembers what her husband was like in the early years of their marriage. He was a fun-loving, hard-working, out-of-doors kind of person. Then, 10 months ago, Joanna's husband was diagnosed with melanoma (a skin cancer), which left him very incapacitated and eventually in a coma. His health disintegrated so quickly that he was unable to tell Joanna what his last wishes were. He was sustained in the end by a feeding tube and intravenous painkillers at the hospital, as there was no hospice or alternative care nearby. At that point, Joanna, together with her grown children, wanted to have the feeding tube removed. All of them believed that her husband would not want to continue existing in this way.

Patients like Joanna's husband pose an ethical dilemma for their families and doctors regarding the right to die. The **right to die** is *the legal and ethical view that competent individuals who are able to understand treatment choices and their consequences have the right to decide their own fate, such as the withholding of treatment that would delay death.* Family members are torn between their desire to be loyal to their loved one and the emotional and financial realities of supporting someone in a permanent vegetative state (Doka, 2005; Kleespies, 2004). Doctors also face the conflict between their duty to sustain life and their obligation to relieve suffering. Doctors often continue treatment because of their moral commitments or the fear of the legal consequences of doing otherwise (Davidson, 2000; Jauhar, 2003). In recent years, the American Medical Association's Council on Ethical and Judicial Affairs has provided some guidelines for doctors in such situations. After struggling with the issue for two years, the seven-member panel affirmed that it is not unethical for doctors to discontinue all life-support systems for patients who are in an irreversible coma, as was Joanna's husband, even if death is not imminent. A more controversial provision is that food and water are on the list of treatments that might be withheld. In each case, the patient's wishes—as far as can be determined—should be respected and the patient's dignity maintained. In fact, research has found that one of a dying person's main concerns is loss of dignity, such as becoming dependent on someone else for care (Chochinov et al., 2002). The council's decision reflects growing public support on such issues. Many Americans, including terminal patients themselves (Wilson et al., 2007), support the idea that terminally ill patients or patients in great pain should be allowed to die. Others support physician-assisted suicide; these supporters are less religious than those who oppose physician-assisted suicide (Westman, Hunt, Cicillini, & Lewandowski, 1999; Wilson et al.).

A president's commission on this subject, including doctors, lawyers, theologians, and others, has concluded that competent patients who are able to understand treatment choices and their consequences have an all but absolute right to decide their fate. When a person is incompetent, a surrogate, usually a family member, should be given the authority to make these decisions. Such thinking has led to the growing use of instruments like a **living will**, in which *a person instructs doctors and family members to stop using life-sustaining procedures in the event of a terminal condition*. To date, only a small percentage of Americans have made out living wills. To encourage more people to do so, a new law requires all federally funded hospitals, nursing homes, and hospices to tell incoming patients of their right to write a living will. Living wills are sometimes known as advance directives or health care proxies.

It is important for health care providers to honor patients' choices (Kleespies, 2004), but some doctors may be unwilling to care for dying patients (Jauhar, 2003). In fact, research suggests that living wills not only do not guarantee patients' wishes but suggests that the patient self-determination movement may be a failure (O'Reilly, 2009). Family members often experience ambivalence and even conflict as they struggle to meet the dying person's wishes. For example, one family member may hold the health care proxy, but other family members disagree with that individual's decisions. Family members may find it difficult to witness the slow deterioration of a loved one and even be repulsed by that person's appearance (Doka, 2005). Because living wills and health care proxies are relatively new to our society, experience, time, and more research are needed to sort out all of the advantages and disadvantages of this new system of dying.

A Natural Death

One of the dangers of the right-to-die movement is that it may unwittingly program people to die quickly. Which is better? A sudden death such as the one experienced by Mark's brother? Or one anticipated because of a terminal illness as in Joanna's husband's case? In sudden death, the dying are supposed to have been spared the suffering of a terminal illness. Also, in the case of sudden death, the survivors have been saved from the burden of taking care of a terminally ill loved one or having to watch someone die slowly. A fast death helps us to avoid our social responsibilities, such as caring for the lingering convalescent and the aged. On the other hand, in the case of a prolonged death, everyone has more time to say goodbye, to put affairs in order, and to plan end-of-life care preferences, but watching a loved one's prolonged death distresses most families. Neither death is really "better" than the other. Interestingly, though, the revolt against needless prolongation of life may incline us toward an equally "unnatural" hastening of death. A quick, induced death, however, does not answer the key questions: How old is too old? How ill is too ill? At what point should a person on a heart-lung apparatus be allowed to die? When does life cease to have meaning? Perhaps the nearest we come to a "natural" death is helping people die at their own pace and style.

The hospice movement for the terminally ill represents a giant step toward the kind of humane and supportive community needed for a dignified death. The hospice is a place or method for taking care of those approaching the end of their lives. Specifically, **hospice** is *a system of care that integrates a physical facility for the terminally ill with the patient's family and home to enable the patient to die with dignity*. As mentioned earlier, much of the

TABLE 16–2	
HOSPICE CARE (INCLUDING IN-HOME CARE) IN THE UNITED STATES, 2007	
• Number of hospice programs	4,700
• Number of hospice patients	1,400,000
• Percent of in-home hospice patients	70.3
• Leading need for hospice care	Terminal cancer
• Median stay in hospice care	20 days

SOURCE: National Hospice and Palliative Care Organization (2004). *NHPCO Fact and figures: Hospice care in America.* NHPCO.org (accessed June 14, 2009).

suffering of the terminally ill consists of the treatments, the impersonal atmosphere, and the sense of isolation experienced in hospitals. In contrast, the hospice is a community that helps people to live, not merely exist, while they are dying (Hospice Foundation of America, 2003). Table 16–2 provides you with some interesting statistics about hospice care in the United States.

In some cases, patients may spend their final days at home being taken care of by loved ones and by trained volunteers. In addition to helping with such practical matters as pain control and preparing meals, hospice personnel also give emotional support and guidance to family members. The aim throughout is to provide a humane and support-ive community in which the patient may die with dignity (Hospice Foundation of America, 2003). Begun in England, the hospice movement has since spread to other countries, including the United States and Canada. The increasing population of elderly people and rising costs of hospitalization are such that the hospice movement is likely to expand in the years ahead.

Research is just now revealing whether the hospice movement is successful. For example, there are many reasons for the dying and their loved ones to be dissatisfied with hospice or palliative care (Shiozaki, Morita, Hirai, Sakaguchi, Tsuneto, & Shima, 2005). Some hospice professionals suggest that hospice stays are too short (Plonk & Arnold, 2005); the recommended hospice stay is three months to allow time to provide patients and their families adequate physical and psychological support (Shockett, Teno, Miller, & Stuart, 2005). As you read in Table 16–2, the typical stay is much shorter. One reason is that exact time of death is never clearly predictable in terminal illnesses. Also, physicians may be reluctant to make timely referrals to hospice because the patient and the family have not fully accepted that the illness is terminal. Another factor is that health care professionals may be reluctant to discuss end-of-life issues with families and patients. Indeed, Parker et al. (2007) found that caregivers and terminally ill patients both expressed high needs for information that were never addressed by professionals. The reality today appears to be that physicians refer patients too late to hospice programs, which causes families to be less satisfied with the experience (Shockett et al.).

There are many individuals who prefer to die at home (with or without hospice ser-vices). One study, for example, found that 63 percent of terminally ill patients preferred to be at home when death occurs (Brazil, Howell, Bedard, Krueger, & Heidebrecht, 2005). Besides health care professionals, the families, friends, and other volunteers in the community provide much care to the dying. Box 16–1 (page 400) discusses who these caregivers are, the immense stress they experience, and the need for caregivers to care for themselves. Self-control afforded to the dying must be balanced with consideration for the well-being of these informal caregivers (Brazil et al.).

Box 16–1

GUARDIAN ANGELS: CAREGIVERS

Older Americans, those dying from AIDS and cancer, the disabled, and others often need assistance from professional and lay caregivers. Some recipients require permanent care; others need assistance during convalescence. Friends and families often become the primary caregivers. They are not professional caregivers like home health aides, yet they are often expected to perform some of the very same duties. Dependent individuals typically cannot do their own shopping, bathing, or cooking, so depend on caregivers. Caregivers also act as chauffeurs, fill out insurance forms, give medications, take care of financial arrangements, and act as physical or emotional therapists, among other duties. Two reasons the number of caregivers has skyrocketed is that more Americans are living longer and more want to die in their own homes, which would not be possible without the assistance of voluntary caregivers. We seem, however, to be reaching a caregiver crisis (Gavzer, 2000) in that so many caregivers are expected to do so much.

Who are these guardian angels stepping in to help? Over 50 million U.S. households report that their homes include someone who cannot care for him- or herself (National Family Caregivers Association, 2005); the care provided by these "angels" would cost $257 billion a year if provided by nonvolunteers (National Family Caregivers Association). Caregivers are frequently family members—typically women or grown daughters (Gavzer, 2000; Lawrence et al., 2002). Many of these caregivers work part- or full-time in a highly mobile society, which means they may not live close to the care recipient. Caregivers might also be neighbors, friends, church members, or anyone else. In fact, there are more nonpaid caregivers in the United States than paid or professional caregivers. The primary recipients of care are often family members, but some caregivers assist neighbors, friends, and, in some cases, individuals who are almost complete strangers, such as homeless or runaway children.

Some informal caregivers are full-time or nearly full-time caregivers. The stress of full-time caregiving can be enormous (Li, 2005; Pinquart & Sörensen, 2005; Waldrop, 2007). Individuals who have been caregivers for extended periods of time report depression and frustration (*Harvard Women's Health Watch,* 2003; Li; *Mental Health Weekly,* 2002; Pinquart & Sörensen). One study even found that heart disease is more prevalent in caregivers than noncaregivers (*Health & Medicine Week,* 2003).

Caregivers often need help themselves. They may need some medical training as well as emotional and social support. Caregivers also need respite from their many duties. Caregiving is both emotionally and physically exhausting. To assist caregivers, local support groups are springing up all around the country (Gavzer, 2000; Savard, Leduc, Lebei, Beland, & Bergman, 2006). These groups offer advice, emotional support, and often respite care in which another member fills in for a few hours a week. If you are a caregiver or expect to be, you can join the National Family Caregivers Association (www.thefamilycaregiver.org). There are also specialized national groups for individuals caring for those with AIDS, Alzheimer's, physical disabilities, the elderly, and others requiring specialized assistance in living. Most of these organizations maintain easily accessible websites. Other programs include community nursing and respite programs for the caregivers (*Hospice Management Advisor,* 2003). In any event, if you become or are a caregiver, don't forget to take care of yourself.

Funerals and Other Services

When death finally comes, it is typically recognized by the family and the community as a rite of passage. In most societies, parting with the dead is recognized by some kind of **funeral**—*the ceremonies and rituals associated with the burial or cremation of the dead.* Such rites may enable survivors to maintain order and experience a form of closure.

Grieving over the loss of a loved one may help us relate more deeply to those who remain. A visit to the cemetery of the deceased is one method for coping with grief.

In earlier eras, when belief in an afterlife was a more dominant influence on human affairs, funerals were held primarily for the benefit of the dead. Death was seen as a passage to heaven or eternal life. In today's more secularized U.S. society, however, the emphasis on death and funerals tends to be more materialistic. Although it is the dead who are remembered at funerals, the ceremony often is more for the benefit of the survivors. Families sometimes get caught in a status game, selecting expensive bronze caskets, ornate headstones, and choice burial sites to maintain their position in society. The funeral industry has been criticized for exploiting people in their time of bereavement, but defenders point out that bereaved family members themselves are partly to blame because they choose on the basis of their emotions rather than common sense. Funerals are typically the fourth-largest consumer purchase, following a house, car, and wedding.

Death and Growth

It may seem strange linking death to growth. Ordinarily, death is seen as the end of growth and existence. In the larger scheme of things, death is an integral part of life that gives meaning to human existence and, in fact, can foster further growth (Bonanno, Moskowitz, et al., 2005; Gamino & Sewell, 2004; Kübler-Ross, 1997a). It sets a limit on our lives, thus reminding us to spend our days on the things that matter most. Individuals who have recovered from intense mourning also develop hope that other adverse events can be overcome (Gamino & Sewell, 2004). Similarly, grieving over the loss of a loved one may help us relate more deeply to those who remain. As Joanna said, "I've begun to take time to smell the roses."

Far from being morbid, thinking about your own death may give you a new perspective on life. For instance, if you were told you had only a limited time to live, how would you spend the time? What unfinished business would you be most concerned about? Which people would you most want to be with? Pondering the answers to such questions may help you to clarify what is really important to you. You should plan to do these things before it's too late. Elisabeth Kübler-Ross (1975) stated that the greatest lesson we may learn from dying is simply "LIVE, so you do not have to look back and say, 'God, how I wasted my life'" (p. xix).

SUMMARY

DEATH AND DYING

The prospect of our own death is sometimes so frightening that a little denial of death is necessary for us to function effectively. However, people tend to underestimate the risk of death from nonspectacular causes, such as heart attacks, stress, and diabetes, and overestimate the risk of death from sensational causes, such as accidents and homicides. Although most people think about their own deaths occasionally, older people think about death more often but appear less fearful of it. Also, near-death experiences tend to make people less fearful of death and more appreciative of life. Terminally ill people tend to go through several stages of dying—denial, anger, bargaining, depression, and acceptance—with considerable overlapping between the stages and with the stages sometimes out of this order. Each person experiences the dying process somewhat differently, however, depending on such factors as personality and type of illness.

BEREAVEMENT AND GRIEF

Some experts believe it is important for the bereaved to engage actively in grief work, a process that parallels the experience of dying and involves many of the same emotions. People who have not been able to resolve their grief may exhibit various symptoms, ranging from physical complaints to more persistent psychological symptoms. Those who live alone are especially likely to have difficulty working through their grief. Healthy grief consists of talking about our grief, sharing our feelings, and taking part in the rituals and activities that may eventually alleviate grief. Resilient individuals who use problem-focused coping and have social support are most likely to resolve their grief work in positive ways.

LIFE AND DEATH IN PERSPECTIVE

Now that people live longer, they are more apt to suffer from chronic and life-threatening illnesses and often die in a hospital. The increased use of lifesaving technology poses critical questions about prolonging life or letting someone die rather than suffer unduly. As a result, patients are being encouraged to express their own wishes through such instruments as the living will or health care proxy. The importance of providing terminally ill people with a humane and supportive community has led to the hospice movement, which is likely to expand in the coming years. It appears that a more realistic awareness of death as an inevitable companion of life, far from being morbid, may help each of us put our lives in better perspective and to live more fully.

SELF-TEST

1. Compared to young adults, older adults tend to
   a. become more fearful of death.
   b. think of death more often.
   c. become less religious.
   d. think of others' death, not their own.

2. Those who have experienced near-death generally
   a. become more spiritual.
   b. fear death more.
   c. become more self-centered.
   d. develop psychological problems.

3. According to Elisabeth Kübler-Ross, the second stage of dying consists of
   a. depression.   c. anger.
   b. bargaining for time.   d. denial.

4. The typical amount of time it may take a survivor of grief to overcome intense grief and depression is
   a. six months.   c. five years.
   b. one year.   d. never.

5. The group with a higher-than-average rate of death compared with others their age is
   a. widows over 40.   c. college graduates.
   b. married people.   d. widowed men over 55.

6. The constructive use of grief involves
   a. repressing one's grief.   c. talking out one's grief.
   b. avoiding thoughts of death.   d. trying to forget one's loss.

7. A living will almost always
   a. provides for organ donations.
   b. confers decision-making power on another individual.
   c. instructs doctors and families to stop life-sustaining procedures in cases of terminal illness.
   d. legally requests physician-assisted suicide.

8. A hospice is a supportive community that helps patients to
   a. live as long as possible.
   b. live and die with dignity.
   c. remain in the hospital to the end.
   d. die as quickly as possible.

9. Today's U.S. funeral ceremony is primarily for the benefit of the
   a. survivors.   c. larger community.
   b. the funeral director.   d. deceased.

10. In terms of personal growth, the realization that death is an inevitable companion of life
    a. usually hastens one's death. c. may give life new meaning.
    b. is a morbid idea.   d. generally leads to depression.

1. *Subjective life expectancy.* Simply knowing a person's age does not tell you how that person feels about his or her future. To discover this information, try the following exercise in subjective life expectancy. You may want your friends or other individuals to try it as well.

   1. I expect to live to age (circle your answer)

      30 35 40 45 50 55 60 65 70 75 80 85 90 95 100

   2. I want to live to age (circle your answer)

      25 30 35 40 45 50 55 60 65 70 75 80 85 90 95 100

   Are there discrepancies between your expressed desire and expectation? If so, what are the possible reasons? Usually, findings have shown that those past middle age expect and wish to live to a later age than younger people do. Did you find this to be true? When people expect to live less than the average life expectancy for their age, do they have a good reason? Did you find that some people were afraid to specify an age for fear it would somehow make death occur at that time?

2. *Your attitudes toward death.* Analyze your attitudes toward death. First, write down your actual experiences with death, such as the loss of a friend or loved one, the age and circumstances at which it occurred, and so forth. Then describe some of your feelings and attitudes toward death. Include your own responses to the subjective life expectancy exercise as well.

3. *Death as an altered state of consciousness.* Some people have observed a similarity between dying and the marginal state of awareness experienced just before sleep. Try to catch yourself in this state some night and make a mental note of your reactions. Was it a peaceful state? Did you find yourself naturally giving in to it? How did you feel after the loss of control or power?

4. *Reflections on the experience of bereavement.* Recall a personal experience of bereavement, whether the loss of a loved one or that of a friend. Then describe your experience in a page or so. To what extent did your experience include the grief work process described in the chapter? In what ways was your experience unique? Finally, how has your experience of grief affected your life? Has it made you more cautious and, perhaps, bitter toward life? Or has it eventually become "good grief," leading you to make the most of life and to reach out to others in a more meaningful way?

5. *Organ donation.* Have you thought about donating organs from your body before you die? After you die? If so, which organs? Are you interested in leaving your body for medical science? Why or why not?

6. *Write your own obituary.* This isn't as strange as it may seem. Major newspapers have a file of obituaries written while celebrities and national figures are still alive, and then they update these accounts at the time of death. Try writing your own obituary in two or three paragraphs. In addition to giving the standard information, such as your name, age, and position at work, point out some of your major accomplishments. Which community activities would you mention? Who are your survivors? In addition, list your funeral and burial plans. What day and time do you prefer to be buried?

Where is your service being held? Do you have any preferences regarding financial contributions to charities in lieu of flowers? Where do you want to be buried or have your ashes deposited?

QUESTIONS FOR SELF-REFLECTION

1. Do you occasionally think about the possibility of your own death?

2. Have you ever had a close brush with death?

3. Are you afraid of dying? Why? How do you cope with the thought?

4. How often do you think of someone who is dead?

5. Is there something you would especially like to do before you die? Why have you not done this thing?

6. Can you recall your first experience of grief? Whose death was it?

7. Have you experienced good grief?

8. Have you made a will? Do you have a health care proxy? Have you signed an organ donor card? Why or why not?

9. What kind of after-death service would you like, if any?

10. What do you believe happens to us after death?

FOR FURTHER INFORMATION

RECOMMENDED READINGS

KÜBLER-ROSS, E., & KESSLER, D. (2005). *On grief and grieving: Finding the meaning of grief through the five stages of loss.* New York: Scribner. Kübler-Ross's last "gift" to us before her own death, the book is an interdisciplinary approach to understanding grief.

UFEMA, J. (2006). *Insights on death and dying.* Philadelphia, PA: Lippincott, Williams, and Wilkins. This book is comprised of excerpts from columns written by a leading thanatologist.

WOODWARD, J. (2005). *At issue series—The right to die.* Chicago, IL: Greenhaven. A legal and ethical examination of both sides of the right to die issue.

WEBSITES AND THE INTERNET

http://www.hospice-america.org   A site that includes a consumer guide to hospice care.

http://nfcacares.org   A site dedicated to assisting family caregivers.

http://www.near-death.com   A site with much information on near-death experiences and the afterlife.

http://www.griefnet.org   A site started by a clinical psychologist offering information on grief and coping in the form of support groups, literature, etc.

http://www.mindspring.com/~scottr/will.html   A site with links to lots of information on living wills and related issues.

Answers to the Self-Tests

Chapter	Questions									
	1	**2**	**3**	**4**	**5**	**6**	**7**	**8**	**9**	**10**
1	b	d	c	c	a	a	b	a	a	c
2	b	d	c	c	b	a	b	b	d	a
3	d	d	a	a	d	a	b	c	d	b
4	b	c	c	d	b	d	c	b	d	a
5	b	a	c	d	a	d	a	c	c	d
6	a	b	d	c	c	c	a	d	c	b
7	d	a	a	d	a	c	b	d	a	d
8	c	a	b	d	a	a	b	a	b	a
9	a	a	b	d	c	c	a	c	a	b
10	c	a	b	d	a	a	c	c	a	b
11	d	d	b	b	a	c	a	c	d	b
12	c	b	a	a	b	a	b	c	d	a
13	a	d	a	c	a	c	a	d	c	a
14	b	a	b	c	d	a	b	c	b	a
15	c	a	b	a	c	a	a	c	a	a
16	b	a	c	b	d	c	c	b	a	c

Glossary

acceptance. The final stage of death and dying, in which dying people have somewhat accepted death and have disengaged themselves from others.

achievement motivation. The desire to accomplish or master something difficult or challenging as independently and successfully as possible.

acrophobia. An irrational fear of heights.

activity theory of aging. The belief that the more active a person remains, the more satisfied and better adjusted that person is likely to be, regardless of age.

actualization therapy. An approach that combines elements of the person-centered approach, therapy, and rational-emotive therapy (discussed under cognitive therapies) as a way of maximizing the individual's growth or self-actualization.

acute stress. Stress that is a momentary response to imminent danger and is relieved when the danger is over.

adherence to treatment regimens. The degree to which a person's behavior (e.g., taking medications, attending treatment sessions, etc.) coincides with medical or health advice.

adulthood. The period of life from physical maturity on, consisting of a sequence of physical and psychosocial changes throughout early, middle, and late adulthood.

affiliate. To be with others who are often similar to us or whom we like.

ageism. Negative attitudes toward and treatment of older Americans.

age-related changes. Changes that tend to occur at a given age, such as puberty.

agoraphobia. Classically known as "*fear of open spaces*," is typically the most severe phobic reaction and the one for which people most often seek treatment.

AIDS. Acquired immune deficiency syndrome, which is caused by a virus known as HIV and transmitted primarily through body fluids.

alarm reaction. Part of Selye's notion of the general adaptation syndrome of stress; the initial emergency response to stress-provoking agents when the body attempts to restore its normal functioning.

alcohol and drug abuse. Misuse or dependence on a psychoactive substance like alcohol.

allostasis. Achieving stability through changes via a process that maintains balance among the physiological factors essential for life.

allostatic load. Cumulative changes that reflect the cost to the body of adapting repeatedly to demands placed upon it.

altruism. A desire to help others at a cost to the helper.

Alzheimer's disease. A debilitating cognitive disorder that may, in fact, begin to develop in midlife but is often associated with old age.

amygdala. A part of the brain that directs signal traffic in the brain and triggers an all-systems alarm.

anal stage. According to Freud, the stage that occurs during the second year of life when the child's major source of physical pleasure becomes the releasing or retaining of feces.

anger. The feeling of extreme displeasure or resentment over (perceived) mistreatment.

anniversary reaction. An individual's response to unresolved grief resulting from significant losses.

anorexia nervosa. An eating disorder characterized by a severe loss of appetite and weight. The essential features of this eating disorder are a fear of becoming fat along with a disturbance in body image and a refusal to maintain normal weight.

anorexic disturbance. The way in which one's body weight or shape is experienced and includes undue influence of body weight or shape on self-evaluation or denial of the seriousness of the current low body weight.

antianxiety drugs. Drugs that are used primarily for alleviating anxiety; including minor tranquilizers.

antidepressant. Drugs that are used to treat depression and elevate mood, usually by increasing the level of certain neurotransmitters.

antipsychotic drugs. Drugs that are used primarily to relieve symptoms of psychoses, such as extreme agitation, hyperactivity, hallucinations, and delusions.

antisocial personality. A personality disorder characterized by long-standing habits of maladaptive thought and behavior that violates the rights of others.

anxiety. A vague, unpleasant feeling that serves as an emotional alarm signal, warning us of an impending threat or danger.

anxiety disorders. A group of disorders characterized by symptoms of excessive or inappropriate anxiety or attempts to escape from such anxiety.

anxious-ambivalent (attachment style). An attachment style in which the individual experiences emotional extremes such as jealousy but in which the individual also desires extreme closeness.

arbitrators. Neutral third parties who, using the same techniques as mediation, assist the parties with the conflict, hope that the parties can resolve their differences, but if they cannot, render a binding decision upon the parties.

archival method. Method in which scientists examine existing data such as historical documents that were fashioned before anyone knew they would be the subject of study.

assertiveness. The expression of one's rights and feelings in a direct way without violating the rights of others.

attachment. A close, emotional tie with another person.

attachment style. Our typical style of becoming involved with others. This includes the *secure attachment style,* in which individuals find it easy to trust and love others; the *avoidant style,* in which individuals feel uneasy about getting close to others; and the *anxious-ambivalent style,* which involves individuals who want to be attached but find it difficult to commit to others.

attribution. Searching for the causes of our own or someone else's behavior.

aversion to sex. Anxiety, disgust, repulsion, and other negative emotions toward sex.

avoidance (as related to illness). A pattern an individual utilizes to minimize or deny that there are symptoms of illness to notice.

avoidant (attachment style). An attachment style that results in the individual's feeling uneasy when other people get too close.

bargain for time. The third stage of death and dying in which individuals attempt to negotiate with others who might help them live longer.

basic needs. Needs that have a clear physiological basis and are related to survival.

battering. A pattern of behavior used to establish power and control over another person through fear and intimidation, often including the threat or use of violence. Battering happens when one person believes he or she is entitled to control another.

behavioral therapy. Therapy that involves discovering the factors that trigger and reinforce the problem behavior; specifying a target behavior to replace it; and then, by manipulating these factors, bringing out the desired behavior.

behaviorism. The view that psychology is an objective science that studies overt or external behavior.

bereavement. The process of adjusting to the experience of loss, especially the death of friends or loved ones.

binge eating. Eating an excessive amount of food within a discrete period of time and with a sense of lack of control over eating during the episode.

biological perspective. Many of our personal attributes and much of our personal development may be attributable to genetic and other biological influences.

biomedical therapies. Therapeutic strategies that rely on direct physiological intervention to treat the symptoms of psychological disorders.

bipolar disorder. An emotional disorder characterized by alternation of elated and depressive moods, popularly known as manic depression.

bisexual, bisexuality. Preference for sexual activity with partners of either sex.

blended families. Families created when remarried couples have children of their own in addition to children from previous marriages of both partners.

body image. Refers to the mental image we form of our own bodies.

body leakage. The leaking of the true emotion through body postures rather than the face.

body mass index. A measure of total body fat calculated from an individual's height and weight.

borderline personality disorder. A personality disorder in which the individual shows impulsive behavior and unstable social relationships as well as an unstable self-image.

bulimia nervosa. An eating disorder characterized by excessive overeating or uncontrolled binge eating followed by self-induced vomiting.

bullying. Repeated, unprovoked, harmful actions by one child or children against another.

burnout. A psychological syndrome of emotional exhaustion, depersonalization, and reduced personal accomplishment that occurs among individuals, especially those who do "people work."

calories. A measurement of energy produced by food when oxidized, or "burned," in the body.

career. The purposeful life pattern of work, as seen in the sequence of jobs and occupations held throughout life.

catharsis. Venting (releasing) anger.

centralized communication networks. Communication in groups in which one or two individuals control the flow of information.

charismatic leader. This type of leader inspires social change, is visionary, and appeals to followers' self-concepts and values.

child pornography. A visual depiction of a minor engaging in sexually explicit conduct, especially one lacking serious literary, artistic, political, or scientific value.

chlamydia. A bacterium that is spread by sexual contact and that affects both males and females.

chronic stress. The self-perception of "global" (or generalized and pervasive) stress in our lives.

claustrophobia. An irrational fear of closed places.

climacteric. The loss of reproductive capacity.

cognition. A general term for information processing, including a variety of processes such as attention, perception, and memory.

cognitive-behavioral therapies. A large and diverse group of therapies that characterize their orientation as either behavioral or cognitive or both and that attempt to modify faulty thinking or maladaptive behavior.

cognitive dissonance. An uncomfortable feeling caused when one's actions do not match one's attitudes or when one has made the wrong decision.

cognitive psychology. A theoretical perspective that assumes learning and behavior involve higher-level cognitive functions or thinking.

cognitive therapists. Focus on faulty cognitive processes as the crucial element in maladaptive behavior.

cognitive therapy. Therapy in which the central assumption is that the emotional and behavioral problems result from the individual's distorted thoughts and reactions to external events rather than from the events themselves. This approach encourages people to think more rationally about themselves and their problem.

cohabitation. The practice of unmarried persons living together, sharing bed and board.

cohabitation effect. An effect whereby couples that cohabit first have greater marital instability than couples that do not cohabit.

collectives. A large group that is unlikely to have a true leader or clear rules.

collectivist societies (cultures). Societies in which collective or societal gain is cherished over individual advancement.

coming out. When an individual accepts his or her sexual orientation as homosexual (or bisexual) and then tells others.

commitment. The pledge or promise to make something work, as in committing ourselves to a career or relationship. In love relationships, commitment is the cognitive aspect of love, which includes both a short-term affirmation of love and a long-term commitment to maintain love.

community-based service. The general term meaning that mental health services are located in the individual's own community or nearby.

community mental health center. A center designed to provide a variety of mental health services located in the patient's own community.

companionate love. A kind of loving but practical relationship based primarily on emotional closeness and commitment rather than physical, sexual intimacy.

compliance. A change in behavior in response to a direct request from another person to do so.

complicated grief. A psychological state in which a person's emotional reaction to loss remains repressed, often being manifested in unexplained physical or psychological symptoms.

compromise. When an adjustment is made by modifying opposing ideas or behaviors.

compulsion. An act that the individual feels compelled to repeat again and again, usually in ritualistic fashion or according to certain rules.

conditions of worth. The feeling most of us have that, instead of growing up in an atmosphere of unconditional acceptance, most of us feel we are loved and accepted only if we meet certain expectations and approvals.

confederates. Friends of the experimenter who have been told by the experimenter how to behave.

conformity. A change in behavior due to the real or imagined influence (pressure) of other people.

confrontation (as related to illness). A pattern an individual utilizes to directly note that there are symptoms of illness present.

consummate love. A complete and balanced love characterized by emotional closeness, sexual intimacy, and commitment between the partners.

contempt (in sexual relationships). A tactic in which insults are used to denigrate a partner's sexuality.

contingency theory of leadership. The theory identifies two attributes or styles of leaders known as people-oriented or task-oriented, which are effective at leading in different situations.

counselors. Professionals who receive training in personality theory and counseling skills, usually at the master's-degree level. Their counseling emphasis tends to reflect their respective professional affiliations, depending on whether they are doing marriage counseling, career counseling, pastoral counseling (clergy), or some other type.

couple adjustment. The changes and adjustments in a couple's relationship during the course of their committed or married life.

crisis intervention. A treatment for those who are in a state of acute crisis but do not need treatment for many sessions. Many cities offer these services in the form of telephone hotlines.

criticism (in sexual relationships). A response pattern related to human sexuality in which one partner attacks or criticizes the other partner's character.

crossdressers. Individuals who occasionally wear clothing of the opposite gender.

cultural diversity. The cultural pattern by which people from different cultural and ethnic backgrounds maintain in varying degrees both their national and their ethnic identities.

culture. The ideas, customs, arts, and skills that characterize a group of people during a given period of history.

culture-bound syndromes. Sets of symptoms much more common in some societies than in others.

cyberslacking. The overuse of the Internet in the workplace for purposes other than work.

date rape. Coercive sexual activity that occurs during a date.

day hospitals. Hospitals that provide part-time care for those with mental disorders during regular working hours and then allow them to return to their families in the evening.

death. The cessation of life as measured by the absence of breathing, heartbeat, and electrical activity of the brain.

decentralized communication networks. Communication in groups in which individuals can communicate relatively freely with one another.

decision making. The process of gathering information and relevant alternatives and making an appropriate choice.

defense mechanisms. Automatic unconscious mechanisms that protect us from the awareness of anxiety, thereby helping us to maintain a sense of self-worth in the face of threat.

defensiveness (in sexual relationships). A tactic in which we make excuses or refuse to take responsibility for our sexuality or use some other self-protective defense.

delusions. Beliefs that have no basis in reality.

denial of death. The first stage of death and dying, in which people characteristically feel that death cannot happen to them.

depression. An emotional state characterized by intense and unrealistic sadness that may assume a variety of forms, some more severe and chronic than others.

desensitization. The method of controlling anxiety by learning to associate an incompatible response, like relaxation, with the fear-provoking stimulus.

desire for success. The urge to succeed. A social motive in which the individual hopes for achievement and success; in some individuals this motive competes with another social motive, the fear of failure. Both of these motives contribute to overall need for achievement.

development. The relatively enduring changes in people's capacities and behavior as they grow older because of biological growth processes and people's interaction with their environment, including their social environment.

devil (horns) effect. Inferring uniformly negative traits from an appearance of a few negative traits.

diagnosis. The classification of a disorder within a set of recognized categories of abnormal behavior.

diathesis-stress hypothesis. A proposal that views schizophrenia as the interaction of a genetic vulnerability (the diathesis or predisposition) with environmental stressors.

discrimination. Applying unfair or negative treatment to groups on the basis of such features as age, sex, or race.

disengagement theory of aging. The theory that individuals tend to disengage from society with advancing age, with psychological disengagement usually preceding social withdrawal by about 10 years.

distress. Stress that has a harmful effect.

divorce. The legal dissolution of a marriage.

door-in-the-face effect. The requester first issues a large, unreasonable request. When the respondent answers "no," the requester makes the truly desired but smaller and more reasonable demand.

downward comparison (as related to health issues). A pattern of behavior individuals utilize to compare their own situation to others who are worse off.

early adulthood. The initial stage of adult development, from the late teens or early 20s through the 30s, characterized by the establishment of personal and economic independence.

ecological perspective. A perspective which emphasizes the influence of the contexts (i.e., settings) on development on the individual.

Electra complex. The sexual attraction of girls to their fathers and envy of their mothers.

electroconvulsive therapy (ECT). The administration of an electric current to the patient's brain to produce a convulsion; sometimes used in the treatment of severe depression.

emotion. A complex pattern of changes that include physiological changes, subjective feelings, cognitive processes, and behavioral reactions.

emotional intelligence (EI). The ability to regulate one's own emotions and to be empathic for others' emotions.

emotional self-regulation. The process by one inhibits or moderates one's emotional responses in order to remain engaged in thoughtful interaction.

emotion-focused coping. The attempt by the distressed individual to alter the emotional reaction to stress.

emotion-focused therapy (EFT). A cognitive therapy that provides a technique for changing basic thought and emotional patterns.

envy. Feelings of inferiority, longing, resentment, and disapproval.

e-recruiting. A process in which job candidates are screened by phone, video, or computer.

erectile inhibition. In sexuality, this is known as impotence or the inability of the man to experience erection.

eustress. Stress that has a beneficial effect.

evidence-based therapy. Therapy proven effective through rigorous research methodologies.

excitement (stage in the sexual response cycle). A stage of sexual arousal that causes increased muscle tension, engorgement of the genitals with blood, and increased heart rate.

exosystem. The social settings that the child is not part of, yet can still influence the child's development.

experience of dying. The sequence of physiological and psychological changes experienced by individuals who are dying, such as those with a terminal illness.

external locus of control. The belief by an individual that something outside of him- or herself, such as other individuals, fate, or various external situations, controls life events.

extrinsic motivation. The desire to engage in an activity because it is a means to an end and not because an individual is following his or her inner interests.

extroverts. Individuals who tend to be warm, outgoing, and involved in life.

face-saving. Saving one's own or someone else's image

false consensus effect. An assumption that others feel or believe as we do.

family therapy. An approach that includes the larger family unit, including children and adolescents, on the assumption that the disturbance of one family member reflects problems in the overall family patterns.

fear of failure. Fear that we will be humiliated by shortcoming.

female orgasmic disorder. Delay or absence of orgasm in a woman.

fight response (to stress). Confronting the stressor. (See also **flight response.**)

fight-or-flight response. Confronting the stressor or fleeing from the stressor.

first impression. The initial perception we form of others, in which we tend to judge them on the basis of very little information.

fixation. The emotional fixation of the personality at a particular anxiety-ridden stage that influences the individual to continue to act out symbolically any wishes that were overly inhibited or indulged.

flight response (to stress). Fleeing from the stressor. (See also **fight response.**)

forming (stage). The initial stage of group development, in which the members come together to form the group.

free association. Saying whatever comes to mind regardless of how trivial it sounds.

friendship. The affectionate attachment between two or more people.

fundamental attribution error. The tendency to overattribute people's behavior to their personality (traits) rather than to their circumstances or situations.

funerals. The ceremonies and rituals associated with the burial or cremation of the dead.

gender roles. Social and cultural expectations about what is appropriate for males and females.

gender stereotypes. Widely held generalizations about the characteristics and behavior of men and women that exaggerate the differences between the sexes.

general adaptation syndrome. According to Selye, nonspecific physiological mechanisms as a reaction to stress, which include three progressive stages—alarm reaction, stage of resistance, and stage of exhaustion.

generalized anxiety disorder. A chronic state of diffuse or free-floating anxiety.

genes. The biochemical units by which characteristics are inherited.

genital herpes. One of several herpes viral infections (human papillomavirus) that are primarily transmitted through sexual contact.

genital stage. The stage that begins with the onset of puberty and sexual maturation, from about 12 years of age on. In this period the individual's sexual interests are reawakened and focus on gratification through genital or sexual activity.

gestalt therapy. An approach that puts great value on the individual's responsibility in therapy but makes more use of here-and-now nonverbal behavior in the therapy session as a way of helping clients to unify their feelings and actions.

glass cliff. A situation where women may be set up for failure as a leader more often than are men.

global burden of disease. A measure of years of life lost to disability throughout the world.

gonorrhea. A common sexually transmitted bacterial infection that sometimes produces a cloudy, smelly discharge and a burning sensation upon urination.

good grief. Grief that leads to learning and growth in our bereavement.

great man theory (of leadership). A theory suggesting that great leaders are born with a certain common set of traits.

greenhouse gases. Gases that are naturally occurring or man-made and that trap heat in the earth's atmosphere.

grief. The intense emotional suffering that accompanies our experience of loss.

grief therapy. A form of therapy that assists the bereaved to cope with the death of a loved one.

grief work. The healthy process of working through emotions associated with loss and death; freeing ourselves emotionally from the deceased, readjusting to life without that person, and resuming ordinary activities.

GRIT (graduated and reciprocated initiatives in tension reduction). A conflict resolution technique in which each side gradually concedes something to the other side.

group polarization effect. Groups are likely to shift to either a more conservative or a riskier decision than individuals alone make.

groupthink. The tendency for groups to reach a consensus prematurely because the desire for harmony overrides the process of critical thinking and the search for the best decision.

guided imagery. A procedure that helps a person shut off the outside world and bypass the censor we call the brain, enabling the person to see, experience, and learn from an intuitive, feeling, unconscious nature. (See also **visualization**.)

halfway house. A residence in which newly released patients and ex-addicts can live under supervision for a short period of time while they make a crucial transition in their lives from a setting with close supervision and other restrictions. Also called group homes and board-and-care homes.

hallucinations. Sensory perceptions that occur in the absence of any appropriate external stimulus.

halo effect. Inferring uniformly positive traits from the appearance of a few positive traits.

happiness. A state with a preponderance of positive thoughts and feelings about one's life.

health psychology. A subfield of psychology that is concerned with how psychological and social factors affect health, wellness, and illness.

heterosexual, heterosexuality. Emotional and sexual preference for partners of the opposite sex.

heuristics. Mental shortcuts or guidelines for making complex decisions.

hierarchy of needs. According to Maslow, the hierarchical manner in which needs and motives function in relation to each other, so that the lowest level of unmet needs remains the most urgent.

hindsight bias. A biased representation of events or information once they have happened or after the fact.

homophobic. Term describing individuals who are afraid of homosexuals or hold negative attitudes toward homosexuals.

homosexual, homosexuality. Emotional and sexual preference for partners of the same sex.

hospice. A system of care that integrates a physical facility for the terminally ill with the patient's family and home to enable the patient to die with dignity.

humanistic psychology. A group of related theories and therapies that emphasize the values of human freedom and the uniqueness of the individual.

hyperstress. An excessive amount of stress.

hypoactive (inhibited) sexual desire. Lack of interest in sex.

hypochondriacs. People who habitually complain of unfounded ailments or exhibit an undue fear of illness.

hypostress. Insufficient stress.

hypothalamus. A small but important structure at the core of the brain that governs many aspects of behavior, such as eating and hormonal activity.

ideal body. The body we would like to have.

ideal self. The self we'd like to be including our aspirations, moral ideals, and values.

illusion of control. The mistaken belief that we can exercise control over chance-determined events.

illusion of invulnerability. A symptom of groupthink; the group members believe they are invincible and can do no wrong.

"I" messages. Honest but nonjudgmental expressions of emotions about someone whose behavior has become a problem.

immune system. A complex surveillance system, including the brain and various blood cells, that defends our bodies by identifying and destroying various foreign invaders.

incidence (of disorders). The number of new cases of disorders reported during a given period.

individualistic societies (cultures). Societies in which individual gain (needs, wants, and autonomy) is appreciated more than general societal gain.

infantilized. Treated like infants, as, for example, when other adults speak to older adults in baby talk.

ingratiation. Managing the impressions we leave on others so that they will like us and comply with our requests. An example is flattery.

in-group. The group with which we identify.

inhibited sexual arousal. Insufficient sexual arousal, such as the male's difficulty in sustaining an erection of his penis or the female's difficulty in generating sufficient vaginal lubrication.

inhibited vaginal lubrication. When insufficient vasocongestion and insufficient lubrication occur in women.

insight. Self-understanding.

insight therapies. Any therapy that aims to bring change by increasing self-understanding.

integrative solutions (for conflicts). Solutions that take into account the needs of both sides in a conflict such that both sides can win something.

interdependence. Mutual dependence among individuals in a given group or society.

internal locus of control. An individual's belief that something within him- or herself controls life events.

intersexed persons. People who are born with chromosomal or hormonal birth defects that cause them not to readily fit into "male" or "female" categories.

intimacy. The emotional aspect of love that includes closeness, sharing, communication, and support.

intimate relationships. Emotionally close relationships between two or more persons, such as friends or lovers, that may or may not include physical, sexual intimacy.

intrinsic motivation. Active engagement with tasks that people find interesting and that, in turn, promote growth and are freely engaged in out of interest.

jealousy. A complex emotion that occurs when we fear losing a close relationship with another person or have lost it already.

job. A position of employment; the set of work activities and responsibilities associated with a given position.

job satisfaction. People's feelings about different aspects of their jobs; how well one likes a given job, depending on such factors as pay and coworkers.

joint (shared) custody. Joint decision making by divorced parents about the child's care.

late adulthood. The final stage of adult development, from the mid-60s to death, characterized by adjustment to changing health, income, and social roles.

latency period. According to Freud, the period that takes place between 5 and 12 years of age. During this time the child's interests turn away from sexual satisfactions. Early sexual feelings are forgotten and sexual urges lie relatively dormant.

learned helplessness. Maladaptive passivity that frequently follows an individual's experience with uncontrollable events.

learned optimism. A learned way of explaining both good and bad life events that in turn enhances our perceived control and adaptive responses to them.

learning. A relatively permanent change in behavior.

learning theory. The systematic statement of principles that explains learning, defined as relatively permanent changes in behavior because of practice or experience.

leisure. Time free from work or duty that may be spent in recreational activities of one's choice.

libido. The psychic energy of the sex drive.

life review. A naturally occurring process of self-review prompted by the realization that life is approaching an end.

lithium. A natural mineral salt and mood stabilizer that is used to treat people with bipolar disorder.

living will. An instrument that instructs doctors and family members to stop using life-sustaining procedures in the event of a terminal condition.

locus of control. The source from which an individual believes control over life events originates—either within the person or outside of the person.

loneliness. A subjective state reflecting the fact that the quality of relationships wanted is lower than the quality and quantity of relationships available.

longitudinal studies. Research in which the same people are studied over a long period of time.

love. Deep and tender feelings of affection for or attachment to one or more persons.

macrosystem. The socio-cultural context in which development takes place, including cultural, sub-cultural, and social-class distinctions.

maintenance activities. Nonleisure and nonwork time spent in activities necessary for the maintenance of life, such as preparing meals and sleeping.

maladaptive behavior. Significant impairment in one or more areas of psychological functioning, especially the ability to work and to get along with others.

male impotence. The inability to experience an erection.

mania. A disorder in which the individual exhibits such symptoms as an expansive mood, increased social activity, talkativeness, sleeplessness, and reckless behavior.

marital satisfaction. The sense of gratification and contentment in a marriage, especially in the personal relationship between the partners.

marriage. The state of being married; usually the legal union between two people.

matching hypothesis. The tendency to settle for someone like ourselves, at least in regard to the level of physical attractiveness.

mediation. The intervention in a conflict by a neutral third party who assists the conflicting parties in managing or resolving their dispute.

mediators. Neutral third parties who intervene in conflict and who help the two disputing parties come to common agreements via communication, creative problem solving, and other techniques.

menopause. The period in a woman's life that includes the cessation of monthly menstrual cycles.

mesosystem. Refers to the linking of different microsystems (note, the child is in each setting, but at a different time).

microexpressions. Fleeting facial expressions that last only a fraction of a second.

microsystem. The setting that the child is currently in, such as the home or daycare center.

middle adulthood. The middle stage of adult development, from the late 30s to the mid-60s, characterized by the fulfillment of career and family goals.

midlife transition. The period of personal evaluation that comes sometimes with the realization that one's life is about half over.

mild cognitive impairment (MCI). An early form of Alzheimer's disease identified in a subgroup of people who have memory problems during the course of normal aging but are otherwise healthy and functional.

mindguards. A situation in groupthink in which individuals in the group take it upon themselves to censor dissenters in the group.

minority groups. Groups that are relatively small in number or that have less power as compared to majority groups. Any ethnic, racial, religious, or political group smaller than and differing from the larger, controlling group in a community or nation.

mistaken impression. The false or erroneous perception of others, often based on insufficient evidence.

mnemonic neglect. Poor recall (or forgetting) of negative feedback that is inconsistent with core aspects of the self-concept.

motherhood penalty. Refers to the fact that working mothers are viewed as less competent and less committed to work than non-mothers.

motivation. A general term referring to the forces that energize and direct our efforts toward a meaningful goal.

motive. Goal-directed activity that energizes and directs behavior.

motive targets. The people toward whom our attention or motives are directed.

mourning. The outward expressions of bereavement and grief, such as the wearing of black.

multiple orgasms. Experiencing two or more climaxes within a short period of time.

mutual-help groups. Groups whose members share a common problem and meet regularly to discuss their concerns without the guidance of professionals.

narcissistic personality. A personality disorder characterized by an undue sense of self-importance, often accompanied by a sense of inferiority.

near-death experience. The distinctive state of recall associated with being brought back to life from the verge of death.

needs. Tension states that arouse us to seek gratification.

negotiation. Making mutual concessions with another person.

networking. Using personal contacts to establish career opportunities.

neurotransmitter. Chemical substances that transmit neural impulses.

nicotine addiction. Difficulty giving up nicotine use, or smoking, when smoking has become habitual.

non-age-related changes. Events and influences that are unique to each of us and may occur at any age or not at all, such as divorce or the decision to change careers.

norm of reciprocity. An unwritten rule that guides reciprocal behavior related to the granting of favors.

norming (stage). The third stage of group formation in which the group comes to consensus about the rules under which it will operate.

norms. Unwritten standards or rules by which groups function and by which groups exert pressure on nonconforming members.

nutrition. Eating a proper, balanced diet to promote health.

obedience. Following a direct order or command.

obesity. An excessive amount of body fat, usually defined as exceeding the desirable weight for one's height, build, and age.

observational learning. The process in which people learn by observing other people and events without necessarily receiving any direct reward or reinforcement.

obsession. A thought or image that keeps recurring in the mind, despite the individual's attempts to ignore or resist it.

obsessive-compulsive disorder. The condition characterized by the involuntary dwelling on an unwelcome thought or the involuntary repetition of an unnecessary act.

occupation. The activities and responsibilities necessary to perform given work tasks in a particular line of work, such as nursing or marketing.

Oedipus complex. The sexual attraction of boys to their mothers and envy of their fathers.

oral stage. According to Freud, the stage that occurs during the first few years of life when the mouth becomes the primary means of gratifying desires of the id.

orgasm (stage in the sexual response cycle). The climax of sexual excitement that is pleasurable and releases tension.

out-group. Any group we perceive as being different from (outside of) our own group.

panic disorder, panic attacks. The type of anxiety disorder characterized by the occurrence of severe panic.

paralinguistics. Unspoken but important features of spoken communications, such as gestures.

paraprofessionals. Individuals who have two- or four-year degrees (or sometimes no degree at all) and work in the mental health field.

passion. The emotional or motivational aspect of love that involves physiological arousal and an intense desire to be united with the loved one.

passionate love. An intense emotional reaction to a potential romantic partner who may not even love you in return.

people- or **relationship-oriented leaders.** Leaders who concern themselves with their group members' feelings and relationships.

perceived control. The belief that we can influence the occurrence of events in our environment that affect our lives.

performing (stage). The final stage of group development, when the group functions better and performs its business.

personal control. The achieved amount of control we have over our lives; this term is often synonymous with perceived control.

personal distress. Intense or chronic negative self-awareness that interferes with one's sense of well-being or functioning.

personal growth. Personal change or development in a desirable direction, including the fulfillment of one's inborn potential.

personality disorders. When personality traits are so inflexible and maladaptive that they cause marked impairment in individual's social and occupational life.

personality traits. Enduring patterns of thinking, feeling, acting, and relating to others that we exhibit in a wide range of situations.

person-centered therapy. According to Carl Rogers, the view that the helper's genuineness, acceptance, and empathic understanding of the client are necessary and sufficient conditions for producing therapeutic change.

phallic stage. According to Freud, the stage that extends from the third to the fifth or sixth year is the period in which the child experiences sensual pleasure through handling of his or her genitals.

phenomenal self. An individual's overall self-concept available to awareness.

phobic disorders. The conditions characterized by a persistent and irrational fear of a specific object or activity, accompanied by a compelling desire to avoid it.

physical fitness. A human's ability to function efficiently and effectively, including both health-related and skill-related fitness components.

pituitary gland. The master gland of the endocrine, or hormonal, system.

plateau (stage in the sexual response cycle). The stage just before orgasm; in this phase, sexual arousal becomes more pronounced.

positive psychology. An umbrella term for the study of positive emotions, positive character traits, and enabling institutions.

positive regard. Acceptance by others.

postdecision regret. The regret that can be experienced shortly after we have finally made a particularly difficult choice or decision.

posttraumatic stress disorder. A severe anxiety disorder characterized by symptoms of anxiety and avoidance behavior; resulting from an unusually distressing event such as being assaulted.

power distance. The idea that people in groups accept the concept that people in an organization rightly have different levels of power and authority. The more status and privileges they ascribe to those in authority, the greater the power distance.

prejudice. An unfair, often negative attitude toward another person or group based solely on group membership.

premature ejaculation. Early orgasm in a man.

prevalence (of a disorder). The total number of active cases that can be identified in a given population at a particular time.

primary control. Actions directed at attempting to change the world to fit one's needs and desires.

primary (basic) emotions. The initial and direct emotional response to an experience.

primary group. This group is important because it is small, intimate, and interacts face-to-face.

problem-focused coping. The attempts by the distressed individual to change the environment or find a solution.

propinquity. Physical closeness.

psychiatric (clinical) social workers. Social workers who receive supervised clinical training as part of their master's degree program in the field of social work, and some earn a doctorate as well.

psychiatrists. Medical doctors who specialize in the treatment of mental illness.

psychoanalysis. Psychotherapy aimed at helping the person gain insight and mastery over unconscious conflicts. Also referred to as Freudian theory.

psychoanalysts. Psychiatrists or other mental health professionals who have received several years of additional training in personality theory and the therapeutic methods of one of the founding analysts.

psychodynamic theory. A group of related theories that view personality and behavior in terms of the dynamics, or interactions, of driving forces of personality and development such as desires, anxieties, conflicts, and defenses.

psychological absorption. A state of consciousness in which emotions, cognitions, and experiences related to the real-world are not consciously processed in the typical manner.

psychological disorder. A clinically significant behavioral or psychological pattern that is associated with (1) present personal distress; (2) disability or impairment in one or more important areas of functioning, e.g., maladaptive behavior; (3) significantly increased risk of suffering disability, pain, or death; and (4) an important loss of freedom or personal control.

psychological hardiness. The attitude that allows individuals to make the most of what are often bad situations. A characteristic of individuals who cope successfully with stress.

psychologists. Professionals who receive clinical training in the methods of psychological assessment and treatment as part of a program in clinical, counseling, or school psychology.

psychosexual stages. According to Freud, the sequence of critical stages in the developmental process; the way in which individuals handle the conflicts among their pleasure-seeking impulses, inhibitions, and environmental restrictions that becomes decisive for adult personality.

psychosurgery. Surgery designed to destroy or disconnect brain tissue in an attempt to regulate abnormal behavior.

psychotherapy. A helping process in which a trained, socially sanctioned therapist performs certain activities that will facilitate a change in the client's attitudes and behaviors.

psychotic symptoms. Symptoms that are signs of psychosis (e.g., schizophrenia) and that include hallucinations such as hearing voices, marked impairment in self-care and social relationships, and other signs of severe disturbance.

rape. Sexual intercourse under conditions of actual or threatened force that overcome the victim's resistance.

rational-emotive. A therapy in which the central assumption is that emotional and behavioral problems result from an individual's distorted thoughts and reactions to external events rather than from the events themselves. This approach encourages people to think more rationally about themselves and their problems.

reactance. An oppositional response that occurs when our personal freedom is restricted.

refractory period. The period of time following an orgasm when added stimulation will not result in orgasm.

reinforcement. The addition of something that increases the likelihood of a behavior.

relapse. A return to a previous state; in psychology, the return to a former problematic behavior.

reminiscence. Thinking about oneself and reconsidering past events and their meaning.

resentment. The second stage of death and dying, in which dying individuals resent those who are healthy.

resilience. Positive growth or adaptation following brief periods of stress after some stressful disruption or extreme adversity.

resistance. In therapy, when an individual hesitates or is reluctant to talk about some painful experiences.

resolution phase (stage in the sexual response cycle). The stage immediately following orgasm, in which the body returns to its normal, nonexcited phase.

responsibility diffusion. A phenomenon in which individuals in groups feel less responsible for the risk so are willing to make riskier decisions in groups.

retarded ejaculation. A delay or absence of orgasm in a man.

right to die. The legal and ethical view that competent individuals who are able to understand treatment choices and their consequences have the right to decide their own fate, such as the withholding of treatment that would delay death.

risky shift. A phenomenon in which groups coming to consensus make riskier decisions than individuals.

role. A set of rules that defines how an individual in a particular post in a group will behave.

romantic love. Consists of intimacy or closeness and passion. Strong emotional attachment to a person of the opposite or same sex, primarily on the basis of physical, sexual intimacy.

schizophrenia. A group of related psychotic disorders characterized by severe disorganization of thoughts, perceptions, and emotions; bizarre behavior; and social withdrawal.

seasonal affective disorder (SAD). A depression that is more likely to occur at certain times of the year, usually the winter months.

secondary control. Involves the individual's utilizing processes directed at making him- or herself fit into the world better.

secondary (complex) emotion. Emotional experiences that are reflective, involve evaluation of the self, and typically follow primary emotions.

secondary erectile inhibition. When a man has previously experienced erections but is consistently unable to have an erection of sufficient firmness to penetrate the woman's vagina.

secondary group. This group is usually larger than a primary group, has a formal or contractual reason for coming together, often disbands when the reason for its existence disappears; members are less likely to engage in regular face-to-face interaction.

securely attached. An attachment style by which people develop happy and trusting love relationships.

self-actualization/self-actualized. The process of fulfilling our inborn potential, involving a biological growth tendency as well as self-conscious efforts at growth.

self-alienation. The failure to acknowledge or accept certain aspects of ourselves; the feeling these qualities are foreign to us and we project them onto others, whom we then dislike.

self-clarity. The extent to which one's individual self-beliefs are clearly and confidently defined, internally consistent, and stable.

self-complexity. The extent to which one's self-concept is comprised of many differentiated self-aspects.

self-concept. The overall image or awareness we have of ourselves. It includes all those perceptions of "I" and "me," together with the feelings, beliefs, and values associated with them.

self-consistency. The tendency to perceive our experiences in a manner that is consistent with our self-concept; experiences that are not consistent with the self are distorted or denied to awareness.

self-direction. The need to learn more about ourselves and our world as a means of directing our lives more effectively.

self-disclosure. The sharing of intimate or personal information with others.

self-efficacy. The belief in one's capabilities to organize and execute courses of action required to produce give attainments.

self-enhancement theory. The tendency to try to get positive feedback that affirms their own ideas about our positive qualities.

self-esteem. The sense of personal worth associated with one's self-concept.

self-fulfilling prophecy. A prophecy that is fulfilled when people's expectations become a reality by virtue of their own behavior.

self-help groups. Groups whose members share a common problem and meet regularly to discuss their concerns without the guidance of professionals.

self-image. The personal evaluation of ourselves and the resulting feelings of worth associated with our self-concept.

self-immunization. The trivialization of threatening information, such as failure, by making the behavior seem less important.

self-recognition. A child's ability to differentiate him- or herself from others in the social environment.

self-serving attributional bias. Attributions that glorify the self or conceive of the self as causing the good outcomes that come our way.

self-verification theory. A theory about the tendency to want to preserve our own images (both positive and negative) of ourselves and therefore elicit feedback that verifies or confirms our own self-perceptions.

sensation-seeking motive. The tendency to seek out stimulating and novel experiences, partly because of biological factors.

serotonin. A neurotransmitter that has been linked to depression.

sexual dysfunction. A persistent problem that prevents the individual from engaging in or enjoying sexual intercourse.

sexual harassment. Any unwanted attention of a sexual nature occurring in the workplace that interferes with a person's ability to work.

sexual intercourse. The penetration of the vagina by the penis.

sexually transmitted diseases (STDs). Infections transmitted primarily by sexual intercourse.

sexual orientation. A component of sexuality and is characterized by enduring emotional, romantic, or sexual attraction to a particular gender.

sexual prejudice. Negative attitudes based on sexual orientation, whether the target is homosexual, bisexual, or heterosexual.

sexual response cycle. The basic sexual response patterns of men and women, as in sexual intercourse.

sexual victimization. Being coerced to engage in sexual acts under duress or force, such as rape.

shyness. The tendency to avoid contact or familiarity with others.

simple phobia. A most common type of phobia in which individuals are irrationally afraid of common objects such as dogs, snakes, insects, stairs, etc.

skill. The ability to perform a task well. It is usually developed over time through training or experience.

social anxiety/social phobia. An extreme form of shyness that can interfere with an individual's daily life and involves a chronic, irrational fear of and a compelling desire to avoid situations where others may scrutinize the individual.

social changes. Changes in the social patterns and institutions in society.

social–cognitive perspective. The view that human learning and behavior necessarily involve higher cognitive abilities as well as environmental influences.

social comparison. The process of using others to compare ourselves to in order to understand who we are relative to them.

social influence. Efforts on the part of one person to alter the behavior or attitudes of one or more others.

social loafing. Contributing less to a group effort than would be contributed to an individual effort.

social norms. The generalized expectations regarding appropriate behavior in a given situation or society.

social phobia. An extreme form of shyness that can interfere with an individual's daily life and involves a chronic, irrational fear of and a compelling desire to avoid situations where others may scrutinize the individual.

social self(selves). The way we feel others see us.

social support. A process whereby one individual or group offers comfort and advice to others who can use it as a means of coping.

spotlight effect. Refers to the situation in which we overestimate how prominent our own behaviors, appearance, and emotions are to others.

stage of exhaustion. Stage of Selye's notion of the general adaptation syndrome response to stress in which the body is unable to continue secreting hormones at an increased rate, so the organism can no longer adapt to chronic stress. Body defenses break down, adaptation energy runs out, and the physical symptoms of the alarm reaction reappear.

stage of resistance. Stage of Selye's notion of the general adaptation syndrome response in which the human organism develops an increased resistance to the stressor.

stereotypes. Widespread generalizations about people (based solely on their group membership) that have little if any basis in fact.

stigma. The use of negative labels to identify a person living with a mental disorder or with another distinguishing feature and whom you believe differs from you.

storming. The second stage in group formation in which group members disagree or often openly conflict when they learn about each other's opinions.

stress. The pattern of responses individuals make to stimulus events that disturb their equilibrium or exceed their coping abilities.

stressors. The collective label for the variety of external and internal stimuli that evoke stress.

stress-related illness. Any illness that is affected in an important way by one's emotions, lifestyle, or environment.

stress tolerance. The degree of stress you can handle or how long you can put up with a demanding task without acting in an irrational or disorganized way.

subjective well-being (SWB). A state with a preponderance of positive thoughts and feelings about one's life.

substitution. A conflict resolution strategy whereby we seek alternative goals with another person.

syphilis. A sexually transmitted and serious disease caused by a spiral-shaped bacterium, or spirochete.

tardive dyskinesia. A side effect of antipsychotic drugs, characterized by jerking movements around the neck and face and involuntary protrusions of the tongue.

task-oriented leaders. Leaders who are primarily concerned with getting the job done well and in a timely fashion.

technophobia. A fear of technology.

telecommuting. Periodic or regular work for one's employer performed at home or another remote location.

temperament. An individual's characteristic pattern of emotional response and behavioral reactivity to situations and stressors.

temporal memory. Memory for things related to time.

therapeutic alliance. The match or quality of fit between the client and the therapist.

therapist. A person trained to help people with psychological problems.

tobacco abuse. The abuse of tobacco to such an extent that heart, respiratory, and other health-related problems develop.

transference. The unconscious tendency of clients to project onto the therapist their feelings and fantasies, both positive and negative, about significant others in their childhood.

transformational leader. A leader who stimulates interest among colleagues and followers to view their work from a new perspective. The leader does this by generating awareness of the mission or vision of the organization and helps members to look beyond their own interests.

transinstitutionalization. The revolving-door syndrome in which mental patients find themselves housed in one institution after another, often including jails and prisons.

transition (stage in the sexual response cycle). The gradual shift from a nonsexual state to a sexual state of being and includes the awakening of sexual desire and a readiness for sexual arousal.

transitional objects. Objects that help the child transition from dependence on a caregiver for comfort and support to more independent forms of coping.

transsexuals. People who believe that they were born into the body of the wrong sex. They sometimes want to change this situation through hormone therapy and gender reassignment surgery.

transvestites. Individuals who dress to look like the opposite gender. Some transvestites wear other-gender clothing full-time and successfully pass as the opposite sex.

triangular theory of love. A theory of love that suggests there are three components to love—intimacy, passion, and commitment.

trust. People's abstract but positive expectations that they can count on friends and partners to care for them and be responsive to their needs, now and in the future.

Type A personalities. People who tend to be competitive, argumentative, time-urgent, ambitious, and impatient, and sometimes hostile. They are heart-attack prone.

Type B personalities. Individuals who are relaxed and easygoing, rather than competitive and impatient.

unconditional leisure. Any activity freely chosen, excluding work and maintenance activities.

unconditional positive regard. Unconditional positive acceptance; generally utilized in person-centered therapy.

underemployed. Working in a job beneath one's abilities or education.

unresolved grief. A psychological state in which a person's emotional reaction to loss remains repressed, often being manifested in unexplained physical or psychological symptoms.

visualization. A procedure that helps a person shut off the outside world and bypass the censor we call the brain, enabling the person to see, experience, and learn from an intuitive, feeling, unconscious nature. (See also **guided imagery**.)

voluntary marriage. The assumption that two people will remain married only as long as they are in love.

wellness. The positive ideal of health in which one strives to maintain and improve one's health.

withdrawal. To remove oneself physically or emotionally from an activity, organization, or person. In sexual relationships, a response pattern in which one partner ignores the other.

workplace. Place of paid employment outside the home.

work values. Those values that bring you the most enjoyment and satisfaction in a career or job.

References

AARP. (2002, November/December). Why we work. *Modern Maturity, 90.*

ABMA, J.C., & MARTINEZ, G.M. (2006). Childlessness among older women in the United States: Trends and profiles. *Journal of Marriage and Family, 68,* 1045–1056.

ABRAMOVITZ, M. (2002, February). Mirror mirror in your head: Your mental picture of your body can have a direct effect on your self-esteem and your behavior. *Current Health, 2,* 26–30.

ABRAMS, D.C., & LAMB, M. (2002, April). Father nature: The making of a modern dad. *Psychology Today,* 38–47.

ACKERMAN, J.M., GOLDSTEIN, N.J., SHAPIRO, J.R., & BARGH, J.A. (2009). You wear me out: The vicarious depletion of self-control. *Psychological Science, 20,* 326–332.

ADAMS, J., & ROSCIGNO, V.J. (2005). White supremacists, oppositional culture and the world wide web. *Social Forces, 84,* 759–778.

ADAMS, R.E., BOSCARINO, J.A., & FIGLEY, C.R. (2006). Compassion fatigue and psychological distress among social workers: A validation study. *American Journal of Orthopsychiatry, 76,* 103–108.

ADLER, J. (1999, June 14). Stress. *Newsweek,* 56–63.

Administration on Aging. (2009). *Aging statistics.* Retrieved May 9, 2009, from http://www.aoa.gov/AoARoot/Aging_Statistics/index.aspx.

ADRIANSON, L. (2001). Gender and computer-mediated communication: Group processes in problem solving. *Computers in Human Behavior, 17,* 71–94.

AHLFINGER, N.R., & ESSER, J.K. (2001). Testing the groupthink model: Effects of promotional leadership and conformity predisposition. *Social Behavior and Personality, 29,* 31–41.

AI, A.L., EVANS-CAMPBELL, T., SANTANGELO, L.K., & CASCIO, T. (2006). The traumatic impact of the September 11, 2001, terrorist attacks and the potential protection of optimism. *Journal of Interpersonal Violence, 21,* 689–700.

AINSWORTH, M. S., BLEHAR, M. C., WATERS, E., & WALL, S. (1978). *Patterns of attachment: A psychological study of the strange situation.* Oxford, England: Lawrence Erlbaum.

AJZEN, I. (2002). Perceived behavioral control, self-efficacy, locus of control, and the theory of planned behavior. *Journal of Applied Social Psychology, 32,* 665–683.

AKKIRMAN, A.D., & HARRIS, D.L. (2005). Organizational communication satisfaction in the virtual workplace. *Journal of Management Development, 24,* 397–409.

ALBANO, A.M., & HAYWARD, C. (2004). *Social anxiety disorder.* New York: Oxford University Press.

ALIMO-METCALFE, B., & ALBAN-METCALF, R.J. (2001). The development of a new transformational leadership questionnaire. *Journal of Occupational & Organizational Psychology, 74,* 1–27.

ALLOY, L.B., ABRAMSON, L.Y., & FRANCES, E.L. (1999). Do negative cognitive styles confer vulnerability to depression? *Current Directions in Psychological Science, 8,* 128–132.

ALLUMBAUGHT, D.L., & HOYT, W.T. (1999). Effectiveness of grief therapy: A meta-analysis. *Journal of Counseling Psychology, 46,* 370–380.

ALMEDOM, A.M. (2005). Resilience, hardiness, sense of coherence, and posttraumatic growth: All paths leading to "light at the end of the tunnel"? *Journal of Loss & Trauma, 10,* 253–265.

ALMEIDA, D.M. (2005). Resilience and vulnerability to daily stressors assessed via diary methods. *Current Directions in Psychological Science, 14,* 64–68.

ALTERMAN, J. (Speaker). (1999). The social/cultural dimension of the information revolution. Retrieved January 10, 2006, from http://www.cia.gov/nic/pdf_gif_research/html/cf154.chap6.html.

Alzheimer's Association. (2009). *2009 Alzheimer's disease facts and figures.* Retrieved July 10, 2009 from http://www.alz.org.

AMATO, P.R., & PREVITI, D. (2003). People's reasons for divorcing: Gender, social class, the life course, and adjustment. *Journal of Family Issues, 24,* 602–626.

AMATO, P.R., JOHNSON, D.R., BOOTH, A., & ROGERS, S.J. (2003). Continuity and change in marital quality between 1980 and 2000. *Journal of Marriage & the Family, 65,* 1–22.

American Psychiatric Association. (1994). *Diagnostic and statistical manual of mental disorders (DSM-IV) (4th ed).* Washington, DC: Author.

American Psychiatric Association. (2000). *Diagnostic and statistical manual of mental disorders, text revision (DSM-IV-TR).* Washington, DC: Author.

American Psychoanalytic Association. (1999). *Outcome studies on psychoanalysis.* http://www.apsa.org/pubinfo/IPAstudy.htm.

American Psychological Association. (1998, October). *How therapy helps.* http://helping.apa.org/therapy/psychotherapy.htm.

American Psychological Association. (2004a). *Answers to your questions about sexual orientation and homosexuality.* http://www.apa.org/pubinfo/orient.html.

American Psychological Association. (2004b). What lies behind the habit of 'tending and befriending' during stress. *Monitor on Psychology, 35,* 15.

American Psychological Association. (2006a). News release: Americans engage in unhealthy behaviors to manage stress. Retrieved May 30, 2006, from http://apahelpcenter.mediaroom.com/index.php?s=press_release&item=23.

American Psychological Association. (2006b). News release: Stress and emotions can negatively affect heart health. Retrieved May 30, 2006, from http://apahelpcenter.mediaroom.com/index.php?s=press_release&item=22.

American Psychological Society. (1999, July/August). Web assessments equally effective as interventions. *APS Observer, 19,* 37.

AMIRKHAN, J.H., RISINGER, R.T., & SWICKERT, R.J. (1995). Extroversion: A "hidden" personality factor in coping? *Journal of Personality, 63,* 189–212.

ANASTASIO, P.A., ROSE, K.C., & CHAPMAN, J. (1999). Can the media create public opinion? A social-identity approach. *Current Directions in Psychological Science, 8,* 152–155.

ANDERSON, C.A., & BUSHMAN, B.J. (2001). Effects of violent video games on aggressive behavior, aggressive cognition, aggressive affect, physiological arousal, and prosocial behavior: A meta-analytic review of the scientific literature. *Psychological Science, 12,* 353–359.

ANDERSON, C.A., GENTILE, D.A., & BUCKLEY, K.E. (2007). *Violent video game effects on children and adolescents: Theory, research, and public policy.* New York: Oxford University Press.

ANDERSON, C.J. (2003). The psychology of doing nothing: Forms of decision avoidance result from reason and emotion. *Psychological Bulletin, 129,* 139–168.

ANDERSON, S.M., & BERK, M.S. (1998). The social-cognitive model of transference: Experiencing past relationships in the present. *Current Directions in Psychological Science, 7,* 109–115.

Anonymous. (2005). Research says living wills won't guarantee patients' wishes: Michigan researchers say Patient Self-Determination Act a failure. *Medical Ethics Advisor, 21,* 1–4.

Anonymous. (2009). *Living with schizophrenia: Psychotherapy and schizophrenia recovery.* www.psychiatric-disorders.com/articles/schizophrenia/schizophrenia-recover.php.

Anred.com (2000, August). *Anorexia and related eating disorders.* http://anred.com.

ANTONIO, A.L. (2004). When does race matter in college friendships? Exploring men's diverse and homogeneous friendship groups. *Review of Higher Education: Journal of the Association for the Study of Higher Education, 27,* 553–575.

ARMOUR, S. (1999, November 2). Net peeves: Bosses police cyber-slackers. *USA Today,* 1B–2B.

ARNOLD, J.A. (2007). Influence of third party expertise on disputants' reactions to mediation. *Psychological Reports, 10,* 407–418.

ARNOLD, P., FLETCHER, S., & FARROW, R. (2002). Condom use and psychological sensation seeking by college students. *Sexual and Relationship Therapy, 17,* 355–366.

ARNTZ, A., VONCKEN, M., & GOOSEN, A.C.A. (2007). Responsibility and obsessive-compulsive disorder: An experimental test. *Behavior Research and Therapy, 45,* 425–435.

ARON, E.N., ARON, A., & DAVIES, K.M. (2005). Adult shyness: The interaction of temperamental sensitivity and an adverse childhood environment. *Personality and Social Psychology Bulletin, 31,* 181–197.

ARONOFF, J. (2006). How we recognize angry and happy emotion in people, places, and things. *Cross-Cultural Research: The Journal of Comparative Social Science, 40,* 83–105.

ASCH, S.E. (1951). Effects of group pressure upon the modification and distortion of judgments. In H. Guetzkow (Ed.), *Groups, leadership, and men.* Pittsburgh, PA: Carnegie Press.

ASHER, S.R., & PAQUETTE, J.A. (2003). Loneliness and peer relations in childhood. *Current Directions in Psychological Science, 12,* 75–78.

ASHMAN, O., SHIOMURA, K., & LEVY, B.R. (2006). Influence of culture and age on control beliefs: The missing link of interdependence. *International Journal of Aging & Human Development, 62,* 143–157.

ASPINWALL, L.G., & TAYLOR, S.E. (1992). Modeling cognitive adaptation: A longitudinal investigation of the impact of individual differences and coping on college adjustment and performance. *Journal of Personality and Social Psychology, 63,* 989–1003.

ATTWOOD, F. (2005). What do people do with porn? Qualitative research into the consumption, use, and experience of pornography and other sexually explicit media. *Sexuality & Culture, 9,* 65–86.

ATWATER, E. (1992). *I hear you: A listening skills handbook.* New York: Walker & Company.

AUSTENFELD, J.L., & STANTON, A.L. (2004). Coping through emotional approach: A new look at emotion, coping, and health-related outcomes. *Journal of Personality. Special Issue: Emotions, Personality, and Health, 72,* 1335–1363.

AVELLAR, S., & SMOCK, P.J. (2005). The economic consequences of the dissolution of cohabiting unions. *Journal of Marriage and Family, 67,* 315–327.

AYALON, L. (2008). Volunteering as a predictor of all-cause mortality: What aspects of volunteering really matter? *International Psychogeriatrics, 20,* 1000–1013.

AYMAN, R., KORABIK, K., & MORRIS, S. (2009). Is transformational leadership always perceived as effective? Male subordinates' devaluation of female transformational leaders. *Journal of Applied Social Psychology, 39,* 852–879.

AZAR, B. (2000, January). What's in a face? *Monitor on Psychology,* 44–45.

BAARS, B.J. (2003). I.P. Pavlov and the freedom reflex. *Journal of Consciousness Studies, 10,* 19–40.

BAGHURST, T., CARLSTON, D., WOOD, J., & WYATT, F.B. (2007). Preadolescent male perceptions of action figure physiques. *Society for Adolescent Medicine, 41,* 613–615.

BAGWELL, C.L., BENDER, S.E., ANDREASSI, C.L., KINOSHITA, T.L., MONTARELLO, S.A., & MULLER, J.G. (2005). Friendship quality and perceived relationship changes predict psychosocial adjustment in early adulthood. *Journal of Social and Personal Relationships, 22,* 235–254.

BAILEY, D.C., LARSON, L.M., BORGEN, F.H., & GASSER, C.E. (2008). Changing of the guard: Interpretive continuity of the 2005 Strong Interest Inventory. *Journal of Career Assessment, 16,* 135–155.

BAKER, K., & RANEY, A.A. (2007). Equally super? Gender-role stereotyping of superheroes in children's animated programs. *Mass Communication & Society, 10,* 25–41.

BAKER, S.R. (2004). Intrinsic, extrinsic, and amotivational orientations: Their role in university adjustment, stress, well-being, and subsequent academic performance. *Current Psychology: Developmental, Learning, Personality, Social, 23,* 189–202.

BALDAS, T. (2007). Age bias suits on the rise with older employees working longer. *The National Law Journal.* Retrieved June 15, 2009, from http://www.law.com/jsp/article.jsp?id=1173949426492.

BALSAM, K.F., BEAUCHAINE, T.P., MICKEY, R.M., & ROTHBLUM, E.D. (2005). Mental health of lesbian, gay, bisexual, and heterosexual siblings: Effects of gender, sexual orientation, and family. *Journal of Abnormal Psychology, 114,* 471–476.

BANDURA, A. (1965). Influence of models' reinforcement contingencies on the acquisition of imitative responses. *Journal of Personality and Social Psychology, 1,* 589–595.

BANDURA, A. (1973). *Aggression.* Englewood Cliffs, NJ: Prentice Hall.

BANDURA, A. (1986). *Social foundations of thought and action.* Englewood Cliffs, NJ: Prentice Hall.

BANDURA, A. (1997). *Self-efficacy: The exercise of control.* New York: W. H. Freeman.

BAR, M., & NETA, M. (2006). Humans prefer curved visual objects. *Psychological Science, 17,* 645–648.

BARBER, B.L. (2006). To have loved and lost . . . adolescent romantic relationships and rejection. In A. C. Crouter, & A. Booth (Eds.), *Romance and sex in adolescence and emerging adulthood: Risks and opportunities* (pp. 29–40). Mahwah, NJ: Lawrence Erlbaum.

BARBOUR, K.A., & BLUMENTHAL, J.A. (2005). Exercise training and depression in older adults. *Neurobiology of Aging. Special Issue: Aging, Diabetes, Obesity, Mood and Cognition, 26,* 119–123.

BARBUTO, J.E.J., & BURBACH, M.E. (2006). The emotional intelligence of transformational leaders: A field study of elected officials. *Journal of Social Psychology, 146,* 51–64.

BARGAL, D. (2004). Structure and process in reconciliation-transformation workshops: Encounters between Israeli and Palestinian youth. *Small Group Research, 35,* 596–616.

BARGAL, N., BEN-SHAKHAR, G., & SHALEV, A.Y. (2007). Posttraumatic stress disorder and depression in battered women: The mediating role of learned helplessness. *Journal of Family Violence, 22,* 267–275.

BARNES, B.L., & SRINIVAS, R. (1993). Self-actualization in different sex subgroups. *Journal of Personality and Clinical Studies, 9,* 19–24.

BARNETT, M.M. (2006). Does it hurt to know the worst?—Psychological morbidity, information preferences and understanding of prognosis in patients with advanced cancer. *Psycho-Oncology, 15,* 44–55.

BARON, R.A., & BYRNE, D. (1997). *Social psychology.* Boston: Allyn & Bacon.

BARSKY, A.J., PEEKNA, H.M., & BORUS, J.F. (2001). Somatic symptom reporting in women and men. *Journal of General Internal Medicine, 16,* 266–275.

BARTALOS, M.K. (2009). *Speaking on death: America's new sense of mortality.* Westport, CT: Praeger/Greenwood.

BARTHOLOME, A., TEWKSBURY, R., & BRUZZONE, A. (2000). "I want a man": Patterns of attraction in all-male personal ads. *Journal of Men's Studies, 8,* 309–321.

BASOW, S.A., & RUBENFIELD, K. (2003). "Troubles talk": Effects of gender and gender-typing. *Sex Roles, 48,* 183–187.

BASS, B.M., & RIGGIO, R.E. (2006). *Transformational leadership* (2nd ed.). Mahwah, NJ: Lawrence Erlbaum.

BATTLE, C.L., SHEA, M.T., JOHNSON, D.M., YEN, S., ZLOTNICK, C., & ZANARINI, M.C., et al. (2004). Childhood maltreatment associated with adult personality disorders: Findings from the collaborative longitudinal personality disorders study. *Journal of Personality Disorders, 18,* 193–211.

BAUER, J.J., McADAMS, D.P., & SAKAEDA, A.R. (2005). Interpreting the good life: Growth memories in the lives of mature, happy people. *Journal of Personality and Social Psychology, 88,* 203–217.

BAUM, D. (2004). The price of valor. *The New Yorker, 80,* 44.

BAUM, N. (2007). "Separation guilt" in women who initiate divorce. *Clinical Social Work Journal, 35,* 47–55.

BAUMEISTER, R.F., CAMPBELL, J.D., KRUEGER, J.I., & VOHS, K.D. (2003). Does high self-esteem cause better performance, interpersonal success, happiness, or healthier lifestyles? *Psychological Science in the Public Interest, 4*, 1–44.

BAUMEISTER, R.F., CAMPBELL, J.D., KRUEGER, J.I., & VOHS, K.D. (2005, December 20). Exploding the self-esteem myth. *Scientific American*, 292.

BAUMEISTER, R.F., DALE, K., & SOMMER, K.L. (1998). Freudian defense mechanisms and empirical findings in modern psychology: Reaction formation, projection, displacement, undoing, isolation, sublimation, and denial. *Journal of Personality. Special Issue: Defense Mechanisms in Contemporary Personality Research, 66*, 108–124.

BEARDSLEY, K.C., QUINN, D.M., BISWAS, B., & WILKENFELD, J. (2006). Mediation style and crisis outcomes. *Journal of Conflict Resolution, 50*, 58–86.

BEAUPRÉ, M.G., & HESS, U. (2005). Cross-cultural emotion recognition among Canadian ethnic groups. *Journal of Cross-Cultural Psychology, 36*, 355–370.

BEBETSOS, E., CHRONI, S., & THEODORAKIS, Y. (2002). Physically active students' intentions and self-efficacy towards health eating. *Psychological Reports, 91,* 485–495.

BECK, A.T. (1979). *Cognitive therapy and emotional disorders.* New York: American Library.

BECKER, A.E., BURWELL, R.A., HERZOG, D.B., HAMBURG, P., & GILMAN, S.E. (2002). Eating behaviours and attitudes following prolonged exposure to television among ethnic Fijian adolescent girls. *British Journal of Psychiatry, 180*, 509–514.

BECVAR, D.S. (2008). From the editor: The complexity of working with families. *Contemporary Family Therapy: An International Journal, 30*, 181–182.

BEDELL-AVERS, K.E., HUNTER, S.T. & MUMFORD, M.D. (2008). Conditions of problem-solving and the performance of charismatic, ideological, and pragmatic leaders. *Leadership Quarterly, 19*, 89–106.

BEE, P.E., BOWER, P., LOVELL, K., GILBODY, S., RICHARDS, D., GASK, L., & ROACH, P. (2008). Psychotherapy mediated by remote communication technologies: A meta-analytic review. *BMC Psychiatry, 8*, 60.

BEILOCK, S.L., KULP, C.A., HOLT, L.E., & CARR, T.H. (2004). More on the fragility of performance: Choking under pressure in mathematical problem solving. *Journal of Experimental Psychology: General, 133*, 584–600.

BEITEL, M., FERRER, E., & CECERO, J.J. (2005). Psychological mindedness and awareness of self and others. *Journal of Clinical Psychology, 61*, 739–750.

BELANTI, J., PERERA, M., & JAGADHEESAN, K. (2008). Phenomenology of near-death experiences: A cross-cultural perspective. *Transcultural Psychiatry, 45*, 121–133.

BELL, B.T., LAWTON, R., & DITTMAR, H. (2007). The impact of thin models in music videos on adolescent girls' body dissatisfaction. *Body Image, 4,* 137–145.

BENENSON, J.F., & ALAVI, K. (2004). Sex differences in children's investment in same-sex peers. *Evolution and Human Behavior, 25*, 258–266.

BENNETT, M.D.J., & MILLER, D.B. (2006). An exploratory study of the urban hassles index: A contextually relevant measure of chronic multidimensional urban stressors. *Research on Social Work Practice, 16*, 305–314.

BERDAHL, J.L., & MOORE, C. (2006). Workplace harassment: Double jeopardy for minority women. *Journal of Applied Psychology, 91*, 426–436.

BERGSTROM, R.L., NEIGHBORS, C., & LEWIS, M.A. (2004). Do men find "bony" women attractive?: Consequences of misperceiving opposite sex perceptions of attractive body image. *Body Image, 1*, 183–191.

BERNDT, T.J. (2002). Friendships' quality and social development. *Current Direction in Psychological Science, 11*, 7–10.

BESTE, S. A., BERGNER, R. M., & NAUTA, M. M. (2003). What keeps love alive? an empirical investigation. *Family Therapy, 30*(3), 125–141.

BEUTLER, L.E., MOLEIRO, C., & TALEBI, H. (2002). Resistance in psychotherapy: What conclusions are supported by research? *Journal of Clinical Psychology, 58,* 207–217.

BEVAN, J.L. (2003). Expectancy violation theory and sexual resistance in close, cross-sex relationships. *Communication Monographs, 70*, 68–82.

BIGLER, M., NEIMEYER, G., & BROWN, E. (2001). The divided self revisited: Effects of self-concept differentiation on psychological adjustment. *Journal of Social and Clinical Psychology, 20*, 396–415.

BING, N.M., NELSON, W.M., III, & WESOLOWSKI, K.L. (2009). Comparing the effects of amount of conflict on children's adjustment following parental divorce. *Journal of Divorce & Remarriage, 50*, 159–171.

BIPPUS, A.M. (2005). Humor usage during recalled conflicts: The effect of form and sex on recipient evaluations. In S.P. Shohov (Ed.), *Advances in psychology research, vol. 34* (pp. 115–126). Hauppauge, NY: Nova Science Publishers.

BJORNSEN, S. (2005). *The single girl's guide to marrying a man, his kids, and his ex-wife: Becoming a stepmother with humor and grace.* London: Penguin Books.

BJORNSTAD, R. (2006). Learned helplessness, discouraged workers, and multiple unemployment equilibria. *The Journal of Socio-Economic, 35*, 458–475.

BLANCHARD, A.L., & HENLE, C.A. (2008). Correlates of different forms and cyber-loafing: The role of norms and external locus of control. *Computers in Human Behaviour, 24*, 1067–1084.

BLANCHARD, E., & HICKLING, E.J. (2003). *After the crash: Psychological assessment and treatment of survivors of motor vehicle accidents.* Washington, DC: American Psychological Association.

BLANK, H., MUSCH, J., & POHL, R.F. (2007). Hindsight bias: On being wise after the event. *Social Cognition, 25*, 1–9.

BLATT, S.J., & SHAHAR, G. (2004). Psychoanalysis—with whom, for what, and how? Comparisons with psychotherapy. *Journal of the American Psychoanalytic Association, 52*, 393–447.

BLOCK, S.D., & BILLINGS, J.A. (2005). Learning from dying. *New England Journal of Medicine, 353*, 1313–1315.

BLUM, D. (1998, May/June). Finding strength: How to overcome anything. *Psychology Today, 32*–38, 66–73.

BOBROW, D., & BAILEY, M.J. (2001). Is male homosexuality maintained via kin selection? *Evolution and Human Behavior, 22*, 361–368.

BODENHAUSEN, G.V. (1990). Stereotypes as judgmental heuristics: Evidence of circadian variations in discrimination. *Psychological Science, 1*, 319–322.

BOELEN, P.A., & VAN DEN BOUT, J. (2007). Examination of proposed criteria for complicated grief in people confronted with violent or non-violent loss. *Death Studies, 31*, 155–164.

BOELEN, P.A., DE KEIJER, J., VAN DEN HOUT, M.A., & VAN DEN BOUT, J. (2007). Treatment of complicated grief: A comparison between cognitive-behavioral therapy and supportive counseling. *Journal of Consulting and Clinical Psychology, 75*, 277–284.

BOERNER, K., WORTMAN, C.B., & BONANNO, G.A. (2005). Resilient or at risk? A 4-year study of older adults who initially showed high or low distress following conjugal losses. *Journals of Gerontology: Series B: Psychological Sciences and Social Sciences, 60B*, 67–73.

BOGART, L.M., BIRD, S.T., WALT, L.C., DELAHANTY, D.L., & FIGLER, J.L. (2004). Association of stereotypes about physicians to health care satisfaction, help-seeking behavior, and adherence to treatment. *Social Science & Medicine, 58*, 1049–1058.

BOHART, A.C., & BYOCK, G. (2005). Experiencing Carl Rogers from the client's point of view: A vicarious ethnographic investigation. I. extraction and perception of meaning. *Humanistic Psychologist, 33*, 187–212.

BONANNO, G.A. (2004). Loss, trauma, and human resilience: Have we underestimated the human capacity to thrive after extremely aversive events? *American Psychologist, 59*, 20–28.

BONANNO, G.A. (2005). Resilience in the face of potential trauma. *Current Directions in Psychological Science, 14*, 135–138.

BONANNO, G.A., & KALTMAN, S. (2001). The varieties of grief experience. *Clinical Psychology Review, 21*, 705–734.

BONANNO, G.A., GALEA, S., BUCCIARELLI, A., & VLAHOV, D. (2007). What predicts psychological resilience after disaster? The role of demographics, resources, and life stress. *Journal of Consulting and Clinical Psychology, 75*, 671–682.

BONANNO, G.A., MOSKOWITZ, J.T., PAPA, A., & FOLKMAN, S. (2005). Resilience to loss in bereaved spouses, bereaved parents, and bereaved gay men. *Journal of Personality and Social Psychology, 88*, 827–843.

BONANNO, G.A., PAPA, A., LALANDE, K., WESTPHAL, M., & COIFMAN, K. (2004). The importance of being flexible: The ability to both enhance and suppress emotional expression predicts long-term adjustment. *Psychological Science, 15*, 482–487.

BONANNO, G.A., PAPA, A., LALANDE, K., ZHANG, N., & NOLL, J.G. (2005). Grief processing and deliberate grief avoidance: A prospective comparison of bereaved spouses and parents in the United States and the People's Republic of China, *Journal of Consulting and Clinical Psychology, 73*, 86–98.

BOND, C.F., Jr., & DEPAULO, B.M. (2008). Individual differences in judging deception: Accuracy and bias. *Psychological Bulletin, 134*(4), 477–492.

BOND, R. (2005). Group size and conformity. *Group Processes & Intergroup Relations, 8*, 331–354.

BOOKWALA, J., & JACOBS, J. (2004). Age, marital processes, and depressed affect. *The Gerontologist, 44*, 328–338.

BOUCHARD, T.J., Jr. (2004). Genetic influence on human psychological traits: A survey. *Current Directions in Psychological Science, 13*(4), 148–151.

BOWER, B. (2002). The social net: Scientists hope to download some insight into online interactions. *Science, 161,* 282–284.

BOWLBY, J. (1977). The making and breaking of affectional bonds: I. aetiology and psychopathology in the light of attachment theory. *British Journal of Psychiatry, 130,* 201–210.

BOYATZIS, C.J., MATILLO, G.M., & NESBITT, K.M. (1995). Effects of "The Mighty Morphin Power Rangers" on children's aggression with peers. *Child Study Journal, 25,* 45–55.

BRAUN, M., LEWIN-EPSTEIN, N., STIER, H., & BAUMGARTNER, M.K. (2008). Perceived equity in the gendered division of household labor. *Journal of Marriage and Family, 70,* 1145–1156.

BRAY, J.H., & JOURILES, E.N. (1995). Treatment of marital conflict and prevention of divorce. *Journal of Marital and Family Therapy. Special Issue: The Effectiveness of Marital and Family Therapy, 21,* 461–473.

BRAZIL, K., HOWELL, D., BEDARD, M., KRUEGER, P., & HEIDEBRECHT, C. (2005). Preferences for place of care and place of death among informal caregivers of the terminally ill. *Palliative Medicine, 19,* 492–499.

BRETT, J.M., & STROH, L.K. (2003). Working 61 plus hours a week: Why do managers do it? *Journal of Applied Psychology, 88,* 67–78.

BREWER, P.R., & WILCOX, C. (2005). The polls-trends: Same-sex marriage and civil unions. *Public Opinion Quarterly, 69,* 599–616.

BREWIS, A., & MEYER, M. (2005). Marital coitus across the life course. *Journal of Biosocial Science, 37,* 499–518.

BRODY, J.E. (2002, November 19). Adding some heft to the ideal feminine form. *The New York Times,* p. D7.

BRODY, L.R., & HALL, J.A. (1993). Gender and emotion. In M. Lewis & J.M. Haviland (Eds.), *Handbook of emotion* (pp. 447–460). New York: Guilford Press.

BROMAN, C.L. (1995). Leisure-time physical activity in an African American population. *Journal of Behavioral Medicine, 18,* 341–353.

BROWN, F.W., & MOSHAVI, D. (2005). Transformational leadership and emotional intelligence: A potential pathway for an increased understanding of interpersonal influence. *Journal of Organizational Behavior, 26,* 867–871.

BROWN, G.D.A., GARDNER, J., OSWALD, A.J., & QIAN, J. (2008). Does wage rank affect employees' well-being? *Industrial Relations: A Journal of Economy & Society, 47,* 355–389.

BROWN, K.T. (2004). The power of perception: Skin tone bias and psychological well-being for Black Americans. In G. Philogène (Ed.), *Racial identity in context: The legacy of Kenneth B. Clark* (pp. 111–123). Washington, DC: American Psychological Association.

BROWN, L.M., BRADLEY, M.M., & LANG, P.J. (2006). Affective reactions to pictures of ingroup and outgroup members. *Biological Psychology, 71,* 303–311.

BROWN, T.M., & RODRIGUEZ, L.F. (2009). School and the co-construction of dropout. *International Journal of Qualitative Studies in Education, 22,* 221–242.

BRUCH, M.A., & BELKIN, D.K. (2001). Attributional style in shyness and depression: Shared and specific maladaptive patterns. *Cognitive Theory and Research, 25,* 247–259.

BRUCH, M.A., HAMER, R.J., & HEIMBERG, R.G. (1995). Shyness and public consciousness: Additive or interactive relation with social interaction? *Journal of Personality, 63,* 47–63.

BRUNET, P.M., & SCHMIDT, L.A. (2008). Are shy adults really bolder online? It depends on the context. *CyberPsychology & Behavior, 11,* 707–709.

BUCHANAN, N.T., & FITZGERALD, L.F. (2008). Effects of racial and sexual harassment on work and the psychological well-being of African American women. *Journal of Occupational Health Psychology, 13,* 137–151.

BUCHER, D. (2009). *Diversity consciousness: Opening our minds to people, cultures and opportunities.* Upper Saddle River, NJ: Prentice Hall.

BUI, K., & TAKEUCHI, D.T. (1992). Ethnic minority adolescents and the use of community mental health care services. *American Journal of Community Psychology, 20,* 403–417.

BULLOCK, J.R. (2002). Bullying among children. *Childhood Education, 3,* 130–133.

BURKE, R.J., MATTHIESEN, S.B., & PALLESEN, S. (2006). Personality correlates of workaholism. *Personality and Individual Differences, 40,* 1223–1233.

Burst Media. (2009, May 7). *Nine of 10 women online seek health info via Web.* www.marketingcharts.com/interactive/nine-of-10-women-online-seek-health-info-via-web.

BURTON, C.M., & KING, L.A. (2008). Effects of (very) brief writing on health: The two-minute miracle. *British Journal of Health Psychology, 13,* 9–14.

BUTLER, A.C., CHAPMAN, J.E., FORMAN, E.M., & BECK, A.T. (2006). The empirical status of cognitive-behavioral therapy: A review of meta-analyses. *Clinical Psychology Review, 26,* 17–31.

BUTLER, D., & GEIS, F.L. (1990). Nonverbal affect responses to male and female leaders: Implications for leadership evaluations. *Journal of Personality and Social Psychology, 58,* 48–59.

BUYS, L.R. (2001). Life in a retirement village: Implications for contact with community and village friends. *Gerontology, 47,* 55–59.

BUZZI, G., COUPER, R.T.L., BARDY, A.H., & EVANS, J.M. (2002). Near-death experiences (Letter to the editor). *The Lancet, 359,* 2116.

BYBEE, J.A., & WELLS, Y.V. (2003). *The development of possible selves during adulthood.* New York: Kluwer Academic/Plenum Publishers.

CACIOPPO, J.R., HAWKLEY, L.C., & BERNTSON, G.G. (2003). The anatomy of loneliness. *Current Directions in Psychological Science, 12,* 71–74.

CADELL, S., REGEHR, C., & HEMSWORTH, D. (2003). Factors contributing to posttraumatic growth: A proposed structural equation model. *American Journal of Orthopsychiatry, 73,* 279–287.

CAMERON, A.F., & WEBSTER, J. (2004). Unintended consequences of emerging communication technologies: Instant messaging in the workplace. *Computers in Human Behavior, 21,* 85–103.

CAMPBELL-SILLS, L., COHAN, S.L., & STEIN, M.B. (2006). Relationship of resilience to personality, coping, and psychiatric symptoms in young adults. *Behaviour Research and Therapy, 44,* 585–599.

CANDERELLI, R., LECCESSE, L.A., & MILLER, N.L. (2007). Benefits of hormone replacement therapy in postmenopausal women. *Journal of the American Academy of Nurse Practitioners, 19,* 635–641.

CANLI, T., & GABRIELI, J.D.E. (2004). Imaging gender differences in sexual arousal. *Nature Neuroscience, 7,* 325–326.

CANN, A. & ETZEL, K.C. (2008). Remembering and anticipating stressors: Positive personality mediates the relationship with sense of humor. *Humor: International Journal of Humor Research, 21,* 157–178.

CAPPELLERI, J.C., BELL, S.S., ALTHOF, S.E., SIEGEL, R.L., & STECHER, V.J. (2006). Comparison between sildenafil treated subjects with erectile dysfunction and control subjects on the Self-Esteem and Relationship questionnaire. *The Journal of Sexual Medicine, 3,* 274–282.

CARBONELL, J. (2003). Baby boomers at the gate: Enhancing independence through innovation and technology. United States Department of Health and Human Services. Retrieved January 10, 2006, from http://www.hhs.gov/asl/testify/t030520.html.

CARDUCCI, B.J., & ZIMBARDO, P.G. (1995, November/December). Are you shy? *Psychology Today,* 34–40.

CAREY, A.R., & WARD, S. (2000, January 1). Thinking of retirement. *USA Today,* 1B.

CARLSON, E., & CHAMBERLAIN, R.M. (2004). Black-White perception gap and health disparities research. *Public Health Nursing, 21,* 372–379.

CARNAGHI, A., & MAASS, A. (2007). In-group and out-group perspective in the use of derogatory group labels: Gay versus fag. *Journal of Language and Social Psychology, 26,* 142–156.

CARRERE, R.A. (2008). Reflections on psychoanalysis conducted as a talking cure. *Contemporary Psychoanalysis, 44,* 400–418.

CARSTENSEN, L.L., & CHARLES, S.T. (1998). Emotion in the second half of life. *Current Directions in Psychological Science, 7,* 144–149.

CARTWRIGHT, D.S. (1956). Self-consistency as a factor affecting immediate recall. *The Journal of Abnormal and Social Psychology, 52,* 212–218.

CASERTA, M.S., & LUND, D.A. (1992). Bereavement stress and coping among older adults: Expectations versus the actual experience. *Omega Journal of Death and Dying, 25,* 33–45.

CASPI, A., & HERBENER, E.S. (1990). Continuity and change: Assortative marriage and the consistency of personality in adulthood. *Journal of Personality and Social Psychology, 58,* 250–258.

CASPI, A., & SILVA, P.A. (1995). Temperamental qualities at age three predict personality traits in young adulthood: Longitudinal evidence from a birth cohort. *Child Development, 66*(2), 486–498.

CASSIDY, C., O'CONNOR, R.C., HOWE, C., & WARDEN, D. (2004). Perceived discrimination and psychological distress: The role of personal and ethnic self-esteem. *Journal of Counseling Psychology, 5,* 329–339.

CASSIDY, G.L., & DAVIES, L. (2003). Explaining gender differences in mastery among married parents. *Social Psychology Quarterly, 66,* 48–61.

CASSIDY, J. (1999). The nature of the child's ties. In J. Cassidy & P. R. Shaver (Eds.), *The handbook of attachment theory and research (pp. 3–20).* New York: Guilford Publications.

CASSIDY, J., & SHAVER, P.R. (2008). *Handbook of attachment: Theory, research, and clinical applications* (2nd ed.). New York: Guilford.

Center for Mental Health Services (CMHS). (2003, April). *After a disaster: Self-care tips for dealing with stress.* http://www.mentalhealth.org/publications/allpubs/KEN-01-0097.

Centers for Disease Control and Prevention (CDC). (2001). *Youth risk behavior surveillance—United States, 2001.* http://www.cdc.gov/mmwr/preview/mmwrhtml/ss5104a1.htm.

Centers for Disease Control and Prevention (CDC). (2002a). *CDC Issues National Report Card on STDs.* http://www.cdc.gov/nchstp/dstd/Press_Releases/National_Report.

Centers for Disease Control and Prevention (CDC). (2002b). *43 percent of first marriages break up within 15 years.* http://www.cdc.gov/nchs/releases/01news/firstmarr.htm.

Centers for Disease Control and Prevention (CDC). (2002c). *New report sheds light on trends and patterns in marriage, divorce, and cohabitation.* http://www.cdc.gov/nchs/releases/02news/div-mar-cohab.htm.

Centers for Disease Control and Prevention (CDC). (2002d). *The burden of tobacco use.* http://www.cdc.gov/tobacco/overview/oshsummary02.htm.

Centers for Disease Control and Prevention (CDC). (2002e). *Trends in sexual risk behaviors among high school students—United States, 1991–2001.* http://www.cdc.gov/mmwr/preview/mmwrhtml/mm5138a2.htm.

Centers for Disease Control and Prevention (CDC). (2004). *Family health and fitness day: USA.* Retrieved August 7, 2006, from http://www.cdc.gov/omh/highlights/2004/hsept2504.htm.

Centers for Disease Control and Prevention (CDC). (2005). *Physical activity for everyone: The importance of physical activity.* Retrieved August 7, 2006, from http://www.cdc.gov/nccdphp/dnpa/physical/importance/index.htm.

Centers for Disease Control and Prevention. (2009). *Sexually transmitted diseases.* Retrieved July 2, 2009, from http://www.cdc.gov/std/.

CERRATO, P.L. (2001, February). Pollyanna may have been right after all. *Contemporary OB/GYN,* 1.

CHANG, E.C. (1996). Cultural differences in optimism, pessimism, and coping: Predictions of subsequent adjustment. *Journal of Counseling Psychology, 43,* 113–123.

CHAPMAN, K.L., KERTZ, S.J., & WOODRUFF-BORDEN, J. (2009). A structural equation model analysis of perceived control and psychological distress on worry among African-American and European-American young Adults. *Journal of Anxiety Disorders, 23,* 69–76.

CHAPMAN, M.A. (1999, September/October). Bad choices: Why we make them. How to stop. *Psychology Today,* 36–39, 71.

CHATZISARANTIS, N.L.D., HAGGER, M.S., BIDDLE, S.J., & KARAGEORGHIS, C. (2002). The cognitive processes by which perceived locus of causality predicts participation in physical activity. *Journal of Health Psychology, 7,* 685–699.

CHEN, G.M. (1995). Differences in self-disclosure patterns among Americans versus Chinese: A comparative study. *Journal of Cross-cultural Psychology, 26,* 84–91.

CHEN, I. (2009, June). The social brain. *Smithsonian,* 38–43.

CHEN, S., & FU, Y. (2008). Leisure participation and enjoyment among the elderly: Individual characteristics and sociability. *Educational Gerontology, 34,* 871–889.

CHIDAMBARAM, L., & TUNG, L.L. (2005). Is out of sight, out of mind? An empirical study of social loafing in technology-supported groups. *Information Systems Research, 16,* 149–168.

CHIVERS, M.L., RIEGER, G., LATTY, E., & BAILEY, J.M. (2004). A sex difference in the specificity of sexual arousal. *Psychological Science, 15,* 736–744.

CHO, C., & CHEON, H.J. (2005). Cross-cultural comparisons of interactivity on corporate web sites: The United States, the United Kingdom, Japan, and South Korea. *Journal of Advertising, 34,* 99–115.

CHO, H., & WILKE, D.J. (2005). How has the violence against women act affected the response of the criminal justice system to domestic violence? *Journal of Sociology & Social Welfare, 32,* 125–139.

CHOCHINOV, H.M., HACK, T., HASSARD, T., KRISTJANSON, L.J., McCLEMENT, S., & HARLOS, M. (2002). Dignity in the terminally ill: A cross-sectional, cohort study. *The Lancet, 360,* 2026–2030.

CHOI, I., & CHOI, Y. (2002). Culture and self-concept flexibility. *Personality and Social Psychology Bulletin, 28,* 1508–1517.

CHRISTENSEN, A.J., & JOHNSON, J.A. (2002). Patient adherence with medical treatment regimens: An interactive approach. *Current Directions in Psychological Science, 11,* 94–97.

CHRISTENSEN, T.C., WOOD, J.V., & BARRETT, L.F. (2003). Remembering everyday experience through the prism of self-esteem. *Personality and Social Psychology Bulletin, 29,* 51–62.

CHRISTIE-MIZELL, C.A., PRYOR, E.M., & GROSSMAN, E.R.B. (2008). Child depressive symptoms, spanking, and emotional support: Differences between African American and European American youth. *Family Relations, 57,* 335–350.

CHROBOT-MASON, D., RUDERMAN, M.N., WEBER, T.J., OHLOTT, P.J., & DALTON, M.A. (2007). Illuminating a cross-cultural leadership challenge: When identity groups collide. *International Journal of Resource Management, 18,* 2011–2036.

CHUNG, D. (2005). Violence, control, romance and gender equality: Young women and heterosexual relationships. *Women's Studies International Forum, 28,* 445–455.

CIALDINI, R.B., & GOLDSTEIN, N.J. (2004). Social influence: Compliance and conformity. *Annual Review of Psychology, 55,* 591–621.

CIVITARESE, G., FORESTI, G., & GIOVANNO, C.J. (2008). When our words disturb the psychoanalytic process: From resistance as a defense to resistance as an interactive process. *International Forum of Psychoanalysis, 17,* 82–90.

Clinical Psychiatry News. (2001, October). Psychiatrists call for overhaul of unwieldy DSM, *29,* 20.

COHAN, C.L., & KLEINBAUM, S. (2002). Toward a greater understanding of the cohabitation effect: Premarital cohabitation and marital communication. *Journal of Marriage and the Family, 64,* 180–192.

COHEN, A.B. (2009). Many forms of culture. *American Psychologist, 64,* 194–204.

COHEN, F., SOLOMON, S., MAXFIELD, M., PYSZCZYNSKI, T., & GREENBERG, J. (2004). Fatal attraction: The effects of mortality salience on evaluations of charismatic, task-oriented, and relationship-oriented leaders. *Psychological Science, 15,* 846–851.

COHEN, S., & PRESSMAN, S.D. (2006). Positive affect and health. *Current Directions in Psychological Science, 15,* 122–125.

COHEN-BENDAHAN, C.C.C., van de BEEK, C., & BERENBAUM, S.A. (2005). Prenatal sex hormone effects on child and adult sex-typed behavior: Methods and findings. *Neuroscience & Biobehavioral Reviews, 29,* 353–384.

COHN, M.A., FREDRICKSON, B.L., BROWN, S.L., MIKELS, J.A., & CONWAY, A.M. (2009). Happiness unpacked: Positive emotions increase life satisfaction by building resilience. *Emotion, 9,* 361–368.

COLLINS, R.L., ELLIOTT, M.N., BERRY, et al. (2004). Watching sex on television predicts adolescent initiation of sexual behavior. *Pediatrics, 114,* 280–289.

COLLINS, W.A., & van DULMEN, M. (2006). "The course of true love(s) ...": Origins and pathways in the development of romantic relationships. In A.C. Crouter & A. Booth (Eds.), *Romance and sex in adolescence and emerging adulthood: Risks and opportunities* (pp. 63–86). Mahwah, NJ: Lawrence Erlbaum.

CONE, A.L., & OWENS, S.K. (1991). Academic and locus of control enhancement in a freshman study skills and college adjustment course. *Psychological Reports, 68,* 1211–1217.

CONNOLLY, T., & ZEELENBERG, M. (2002). Regret in decision-making. *Current Directions in Psychological Science, 11,* 212–216.

CONNOR, K.M., & ZHANG, W. (2006). Resilience: Determinants, measurement, and treatment responsiveness. *CNS Spectrums, 11,* 5–12.

CONTRADA, R.J., ASHMORE, R.D., GARY, M.L., COUPS, E., EGETH, J.D., & SEWELL, A., et al. (2000). Ethnicity-related sources of stress and their effects on well-being. *Current Directions in Psychological Science, 9,* 136–139.

CONWAY, L.G., III, & SCHALLER, M. (2005). When authorities' commands backfire: Attributions about consensus and effects on deviant decision making. *Journal of Personality and Social Psychology, 89,* 311–326.

CONWAY, T.L., VICKERS, R.R., & FRENCH, J.R. (1992). An application of person-environment fit theory: Perceived versus desire control. *Journal of Social Issues, 48,* 95–107.

COOK, C.R., GRESHAM, F.M., KERN, L., BARRERAS, R.B., THORNTON, S., & CREWS, S.D. (2008). Social skills training for secondary students with emotional and/or behavioral disorders: A review and analysis of the meta-analytic literature. *Journal of Emotional and Behavioral Disorders, 16,* 131–144.

COOPER, H., OKAMURA, L., & McNEIL, P. (1995). Situation and personality correlates of psychological well-being, social activity, and personal control. *Journal of Research in Personality, 29,* 395–417.

COOPER, J. (2006). The digital divide: The special case of gender. *Journal of Computer Assisted Learning, 22,* 320–334.

CORNELIUS-WHITE, J.H.D., & CORNELIUS-WHITE, C.F. (2005). Reminiscing and predicting: Rogers's beyond words speech and commentary. *Journal of Humanistic Psychology, 45,* 383–396.

CORPUS, J. H., McCLINTIC-GILBERT, M. S., & HAYENGA, A. O. (2009). Within-year changes in children's intrinsic and extrinsic motivational orientations: Contextual predictors and academic outcomes. *Contemporary Educational Psychology, 34,* 154–166.

CORR, C.A. (1993). Coping with dying: Lessons that we should and should not learn from the work of Elisabeth Kübler-Ross. *Death Studies, 17,* 69–83.

CORRELL, S.J., BENARD, S., & PAIK, I. (2007). Getting a job: Is there a motherhood penalty? *American Journal of Sociology, 112,* 1297–1338.

COULSON, M. (2004). Attributing emotion to static body postures: Recognition accuracy, confusions, and viewpoint dependence. *Journal of Nonverbal Behavior, 28,* 117–139.

COULTAS, J.C. (2004). When in Rome . . . an evolutionary perspective on conformity. *Group Processes & Intergroup Relations, 7,* 317–331.

COURT, A. (2003, September 5–7). Out of Africa. *USA Weekend,* 5.

CRAMER, P. (2003). Defense mechanisms and physiological reactivity to stress. *Journal of Personality, 71,* 221–244.

CRAMER, P. (2006). *Protecting the self: Defense mechanisms in action.* New York: Guilford.

CRANDALL, C.S. (1994). Prejudice against fat people: Ideology and self-interest. *Journal of Personality and Social Psychology, 66,* 882–894.

CRANE, R.D., SODERQUIST, J.N., & GARDNER, M.D. (1995). Gender differences in cognitive and behavioral steps toward divorce. *American Journal of Family Therapy, 23,* 99–105.

CRAWFORD, M.T., McCONNELL, A.R., LEWIS, A.C., & SHERMAN, S.J. (2002). Reactance, compliance, and anticipated regret. *Journal of Experimental Social Psychology, 38,* 56–63.

CROCKER, J., & KNIGHT, K.M. (2005). Contingencies of self-worth. *Current Directions in Psychological Science, 14,* 200–203.

CROCKER, J., & PARK, L.E. (2004). Reaping the benefits of pursuing self-esteem without the costs? Reply to DuBois and Flay (2004), Sheldon (2004), and Pyszczynski and Cox (2004). *Psychological Bulletin, 130,* 430–434.

CROCKER, J., & WOLFE, C.T. (2001). Contingencies of self-worth. *Psychological Review, 108,* 593–623.

CRONE, D., SMITH, A., & GOUGH, B. (2005). 'I feel totally at one, totally alive and totally happy': A psycho-social explanation of the physical activity and mental health relationship. *Health Education Research, 20,* 600–611.

CROPLEY, M., & STEPTOE, A. (2005). Social support, life events and physical symptoms: A prospective study of chronic and recent life stress in men and women. *Psychology, Health & Medicine, 10,* 317–325.

CROSBY, F.J. (1991). *Juggling.* New York: Free Press.

CROSNOE, R., & ELDER, G.H. (2002). Successful adaptation in the later years: A life course approach to aging. *Social Psychology Quarterly, 65,* 309–328.

CROZIER, W.R. (2005). Measuring shyness: Analysis of the revised cheek and buss shyness scale. *Personality and Individual Differences, 38,* 1947–1956.

CSANK, P., & CONWAY, M. (2004). Engaging in self-reflection changes self-concept clarity: On differences between women and men, and low-and high-clarity individuals. *Sex Roles, 50,* 469–480.

CUIJPERS, P., VAN STRATEN, A., WARMERDAM, L., & ANDERSSON, G. (2009). Psychotherapy versus the combination of psychotherapy and pharmacotherapy in the treatment of depression: A meta-analysis. *Depression and Anxiety, 26,* 279–288.

CUSHNER, K. (2005). Conflict, negotiation, and mediation across cultures: Highlights from the fourth biennial conference of the international academy for intercultural research. *International Journal of Intercultural Relations. Special Issue: Conflict, Negotiation, and Mediation across Cultures: Highlights from the Fourth Biennial Conference of the International Academy for Intercultural Research, 29,* 635–638.

D'AUGELLI, A.R., HERSHBERGER, S.L., & PILKINGSTON, N.W. (1998). Lesbian, gay and bisexual youth and their families: Disclosure of sexual orientation and its consequences. *American Journal of Orthopsychiatry, 68,* 361–371.

DAHLEN, E.R., & MARTIN, R.C. (2005). The experience, expression, and control of anger in perceived social support. *Personality and Individual Differences, 39,* 391–401.

DALEY, A. (2008). Exercise and depression: A review of reviews. *Journal of Clinical Psychology in Medical Settings, 15,* 140–147.

DAMON, W., & HART, D. (1988). *Self-understanding in childhood and adolescence.* New York, NY, US: Cambridge University Press.

DANIELS, C. (2002). The last taboo: It's not sex. It's not drinking. It's stress—and it is soaring. *Fortune, 146,* 136–139.

DARLING, C.A., McWEY, L.M., HOWARD, S.N., & OLMSTEAD, S.B. (2007). College student stress: The influence of interpersonal relationships on sense of coherence. *Stress and Health: Journal of the International Society for the Investigation of Stress, 23,* 215–229.

DAVALOS, D.B., DAVALOS, R.A., & LAYTON, H.S. (2007). Content analysis of magazine headlines: Changes over three decades? *Feminism & Psychology, 17,* 250–258.

DAVIDSON, S. (2000, September–October). Jules & Tim. *Modern Maturity, 64–65,* 95–96.

DAVIS, G.F. (2001). Loss and the duration of grief (Letter to the editor). *The Journal of the American Medical Association, 285,* 1152.

DAVIS, K., & NEWSTROM, J.W. (1985). *Human behavior at work: Organizational behavior.* New York: McGraw-Hill.

DAVIS, M., MARKUS, K.A., WALTERS, S.B., VORUS, N., & CONNORS, B. (2005). Behavioral cues to deception vs. topic incriminating potential in criminal confessions. *Law and Human Behavior, 29,* 683–704.

DAVIS, S. (1996, July/August). The enduring power of friendship. *American Health,* 60–63.

DAVIS, S. (2003). Sex stereotypes in commercials targeted toward children: A content analysis. *Sociological Spectrum, 23,* 407–424.

DAY, A.L., & CHAMBERLAIN, T.C. (2006). Committing to your work, spouse, and children: Implications for work–family conflict. *Journal of Vocational Behavior, 68,* 116–130.

DE DREU, C.K.W. (2005). A PACT against conflict escalation in negotiation and dispute resolution. *Current Directions in Psychological Science, 14,* 149–152.

DEARBORN, K. (2002). Studies in emotional intelligence redefine our approach to leadership development. *Public Personnel Management, 31,* 523–530.

DEBERARD, M.S., & KLEINKNECHT, R.A. (1995). Loneliness, duration of loneliness and reported stress symptomatology. *Psychological Reports, 76,* 1363–1369.

DECI, E.L., & MOLLER, A.C. (2005). *The concept of competence: A starting place for understanding intrinsic motivation and self-determined extrinsic motivation.* New York: Guilford Publications.

DECI, E.L., & RYAN, R.M. (2008). Self-determination theory: A macrotheory of human motivation, development, and health. *Canadian Psychology/Psychologie Canadienne. Special Issue: Social Psychology and Self-Determination Theory: A Canadian Contribution, 49,* 182–185.

DEMAUSE, L. (1974). *The history of childhood.* New York: Psychohistory Press.

DEMOREST, A. (2005). *Psychology's grand theorists: How personal experiences shaped professional ideas.* Mahwah, NJ: Lawrence Erlbaum.

DENNERSTEIN, L., & HAYES, R.D. (2005). Confronting the challenges: Epidemiological study of female sexual dysfunction and the menopause. *Journal of Sexual Medicine, 2,* 118–132.

DENRELL, J. (2005). Why most people disapprove of me: Experience sampling in impression formation. *Psychological Review, 112,* 951–978.

DENTINGER, E., & CLARKBERG, M. (2002). Informal caregiving and retirement timing among men and women. *Journal of Family Issues, 25,* 857–879.

DERENNE, J.L., & BERESIN, E.V. (2006). Body image, media, and eating disorders. *Academic Psychiatry, 30,* 257–261.

DE-SOUZA, G., & KLEIN, H.J. (1995). Emergent leadership in the group goal-setting process. *Small Groups Research, 26,* 475–496.

DEYOUNG, R. (2005). Contingency theories of leadership. In N. Borkowski (Ed.), *Organizational behavior in health care* (pp. 187–208). Boston: Jones and Bartlett.

DI MATTEI, V.E., PRUNAS, A., NOVELLA, L., MARCONE, A., CAPPA, S.F., & SARNO, L. (2008). The burden of distress in caregivers of elderly demented patients and its relationship with coping strategies. *Neurological Sciences, 29,* 383–389.

DICKENSON, A. (2002, May). Dads and daughters: Strengthening this special relationship can strengthen a girl's self-esteem, too. *Time,* F9–F10.

DIEGUEZ, S. (2008). Skeptics need to reclaim, redefine and embrace near death experiences. *NDE Redux, 14,* 42–43.

DIENER, E., & SELIGMAN, M.R.P. (2002). Very happy people. *Psychological Science, 13,* 81–84.

DIGUISEPPE, R., & TAFRATE, R.C. (2003). Anger treatment for adults: A meta-analytic review. *Clinical Psychology: Science and Practice, 10,* 70–84.

DIMBERG, U., THUNBERG, M., & ELMEHED, K. (2000). Unconscious facial reactions to emotional facial expressions. *Psychological Science, 11,* 86–89.

DINAN, T.G. (2005). Stress: The shared common component in major mental illnesses. *European Psychiatry, 20,* 326–328.

DION, K.K., & DION, K.L. (1993). Individualistic and collectivistic perspectives on gender and the cultural context of love and intimacy. *Journal of Social Issues, 49,* 53–69.

DION, K.L., & DION, K.K. (2005). *Culture and relationships: The downside of self-contained individualism.* In R.M. Sorrentino, D. Cohen, J.M. Olson, & M.P. Zanna (Eds.), *Culture and social behavior: The Ontario symposium: Volume 10* (pp. 77–94). Mahwah, NJ: Lawrence Erlbaum.

DITOMMASO, E., BRANNEN, C., & BURGESS, M. (2005). The universality of relationship characteristics: A cross-cultural comparison of different types of attachment and loneliness in Canadian and visiting Chinese students. *Social Behavior and Personality, 33,* 57–68.

DOKA, L.K. (2005). Ethics, end-of-life decisions and grief. *Mortality. Special Issue: Ethical Concerns Involving End-of-Life Issues in the United States—Introduction: Ethics and End-of-Life Issues, 10,* 83–90.

DOLGIN, K.G., & KIM, S. (1994). Adolescents' disclosure to best and good friends: The effects of gender and topic intimacy. *Social Development, 3,* 146–157.

DOLGIN, K.G., MEYER, L., & SCHWARTZ, J. (1991). Effects of gender, target's gender, topic, and self-esteem on disclosure to best and midling friends. *Sex Roles, 25,* 311–329.

DONALDSON-EVANS, C. (2003, May 21). *Online dating is net success.* http://www.foxnews.com/story/0,2933,87256,00.html.

DONNELL, A.J., THOMAS, A., & BUBOLTZ, W.C. (2001). Psychological reactance: Factor structure and internal consistency of the Questionnaire for the Measurement of Psychological Reactance. *The Journal of Social Psychology, 141,* 679–687.

DONOVAN, R.J., & JALLEH, G. (2000). Positive versus negative framing of a hypothetical infant immunization: The influence of involvement. *Health Education and Behavior, 27,* 82–95.

DOSS, B. D., RHOADES, G. K., STANLEY, S. M., & MARKMAN, H. J. (2009). The effect of the transition to parenthood on relationship quality: An 8-year prospective study. *Journal of Personality and Social Psychology, 96,* 601–619.

DOUBLE, R. (1996). Three kinds of control. *PsyCritiques, 41,* 360–361.

DOVIDIO, J.F., & GAERTNER, S.L. (1999). Reducing prejudice: Combatting intergroup biases. *Current Directions in Psychological Science, 8,* 101–105.

DOVIDIO, J.F., GLICK, P., & RUDMAN, L.A. (Eds.). (2005). *On the nature of prejudice: Fifty years after Allport.* Malden, MA: Blackwell Publishing.

DOWNEY, L., & VAN WILLIGEN, M. (2005). Environmental stressors: The mental health impacts of living near industrial activity. *Journal of Health and Social Behavior, 46,* 289–305.

DOZOIS, D.J.A., FREWEN, P.A., & COVIN, R. (2006). *Cognitive theories.* Hoboken, NJ: John Wiley & Sons.

DRENTEA, P. (2002). Retirement and mental health. *Journal of Aging and Health, 14,* 167–194.

DRENTEA, P., & MOREN-CROSS, J.L. (2005). Social capital and social support on the web: The case of an internet mother site. *Sociology of Health & Illness, 27,* 920–943.

DREW, L.M., & SILVERSTEIN, M. (2007). Grandparents' psychological well-being after loss of contact with their grandchildren. *Journal of Family Psychology, 21,* 372–379.

DUFFY, K.G. (1991). Introduction to community mediation programs: Past, present, and future. In K.G. Duffy, J.W. Grosch, & P.V. Olczak (Eds.), *Community mediation: A handbook for practitioners and researchers* (pp. 21–34). New York: Guilford Press.

DUFFY, K.G., & THOMSON, J. (1992). Community mediation centers: Humanistic alternatives to the court system, a pilot study. *Journal of Humanistic Psychology, 32,* 101–114.

DUFFY, K.G., GROSCH, J., & OLCZAK, P.V. (1991). *Community mediation: A handbook for practitioners and researchers.* New York: Guilford Press.

DUNN, J., O'CONNOR, T.G., & CHENG, H. (2005). Children's responses to conflict between their different parents: Mothers, stepfathers, nonresident fathers, and nonresident stepmothers. *Journal of Clinical Child and Adolescent Psychology, 34,* 223–234.

DUNN, M.S. (2005). The relationship between religiosity, employment, and political beliefs on substance use among high school seniors. *Journal of Alcohol and Drug Education, 49,* 73–88.

DUNNE, G.A. (2000). Lesbians as authentic workers? Institutional heterosexuality and the reproduction of gender inequalities. *Sexualities. Special Issue: Speaking from a Lesbian Position: Opening up Sexuality Studies, 3,* 133–148.

DUNNING, D., HEATH, C., & SULS, J.M. (2004). Flawed self-assessment: Implications for health, education, and the workplace. *Psychological Science in the Public Interest, 5,* 69–106.

DUPRAS, A. (1994). Internalized homophobia and psychosexual adjustment among gay men. *Psychological Reports, 75,* 23–28.

DURRANT, J.E. (2008). Physical punishment, culture, and rights: Current issues for professionals. *Journal of Developmental & Behavioral Pediatrics, 29,* 55–66.

DWECK, C.S. (1999). Caution—praise can be dangerous. *American Educator, 23,* 4–9.

DWECK, C.S. (2008). Can personality be changed? The role of beliefs in personality and change. *Current Directions in Psychological Science, 17,* 391–394.

EAGLY, A.H. (2007). Female leadership advantage and disadvantage: Resolving the contradictions. *Psychology of Women Quarterly, 31,* 1–12.

EAGLY, A.H., & JOHANNESEN-SCHMIDT, M.C. (2001). The leadership styles of women and men. *Journal of Social Issues, 57,* 781–797.

EAGLY, A.H., & JOHNSON, B.T. (1990). Gender and leadership style: A meta-analysis. *Psychological Bulletin, 108,* 233–256.

EAGLY, A.H., KARAU, S.J., & MAKHIJANI, M.G. (1995). Gender and the effectiveness of leaders: A meta-analysis. *Psychological Bulletin, 117,* 125–145.

EAGLY, A.H., MAKHIJANI, M.G., & KLONSKY, B.G. (1992). Gender and the evaluation of leaders: A meta-analysis. *Psychological Bulletin, 11,* 3–22.

EASTON, J.A., SHACKELFORD, T.K., & SCHIPPER, L.D. (2008). Delusional disorder-jealous type: How inclusive are the DSM-IV diagnostic criteria? *Journal of Clinical Psychology, 64,* 264–275.

EATON, R.J., & GRAHAM, B. (2008). The role of gender and negative affectivity in stressor appraisal and coping selection. *International Journal of Stress Management, 15,* 94–115.

ECONOMOS, C.D., HILDEBRANDT, L.M., & HYATT, R.R. (2008). College freshman stress and weight change: Differences by gender. *American Journal of Health Behavior, 32,* 16–25.

EDWARDS, B.D., BELL, S.T., ARTHUR, W., Jr., & DECUIR, A.D. (2008). Relationships between facets of job satisfaction and task and contextual performance. *Applied Psychology: An International Review, 57,* 441–465.

EDWARDS, R. (1998). The effects of gender, gender role, and values on the interpretation of messages. *Journal of Language and Social Psychology. Special Issue: The Language of Equivocation, 17,* 52–71.

EDWARDS, W.J. (1996a). A sociological analysis of an invisible minority group: Male adolescent homosexuals. *Youth and Society, 27,* 334–355.

EDWARDS, W.J. (1996b). Operating within the mainstream: Coping and adjustment among a sample of homosexual youths. *Deviant Behavior, 17,* 229–251.

EFRATI-VIRTZER, M., & MARGALIT, M. (2009). Students' behaviour difficulties, sense of coherence and adjustment at school: Risk and protective factors. *European Journal of Special Needs Education, 24,* 59–73.

EGAN, D. (2005). Magical mystery cure: What would you do if a lobotomy was your only hope for happiness? *This Magazine, 38,* 14–23.

EGGERMONT, S. (2005). Young adolescents' perceptions of peer sexual behaviours: The role of television viewing. *Child: Care, Health and Development, 31,* 459–468.

EGGERMONT, S., & VAN DEN BULCK, J. (2006). Nodding off or switching off? The use of popular media as a sleep aid in secondary-school children. *Journal of Paediatrics and Child Health, 42,* 428–433.

EHRENSAFT, M. K. (2009). Family and relationship predictors of psychological and physical aggression. In K. D. O'Leary & E. M. Woodin (Eds.), *Psychological and physical aggression in couples: Causes and interventions.* (pp. 99–118). Washington, DC: American Psychological Association.

EKMAN, P. (1985b). *Telling lies.* New York: W. W. Norton.

EKMAN, P. (1993). Facial expression and emotion. *American Psychologist, 48,* 384–392.

ELIAS, M. (1999a, November 23). Culture affects choice on post-menopause estrogen. *USA Today,* D1.

ELIAS, M. (1999b, December 14). Mapping the mental-illness fight. *USA Today,* 7D.

ELIAS, M. (2002, September 12). Baby boomers' '70s mind-set has changed with the times; Back then, generation gap was greater, *USA Today,* D7.

ELICKER, J., ENGLUND, M., & SROUFE, L.A. (1992). Predicting peer competence and peer relationships in childhood from early parent-child relationships. In R.D. Parke, & G.W. Ladd (Eds.), *Family-peer relationships: Modes of linkage.* (pp. 77–106). Hillsdale, NJ: Lawrence Erlbaum.

ELIZUR, Y., & ZIV, M. (2001). Family support and acceptance, gay male identity, and psychological adjustment: A path model. *Family Process, 40,* 125–144.

ELLEVEN, R.K., & ALLEN, J. (2004). Applying technology to online counseling: Suggestions for the beginning E-therapist. *Journal of Instructional Psychology, 31,* 223–227.

ELLIOTTI, R., & FREIRE, E. (2007). Classical person-centered and experiential perspectives on Rogers. P*sychotherapy: Theory, Research, Practice, and Training, 44,* 285–288.

ELLIS, J.A., & SINCLAIR, R.D. (2008). Male pattern baldness: Current treatments, future prospects. *Drug Discovery Today, 13,* 791–797.

ENSARI, N., & MILLER, N. (2005). Prejudice and intergroup attributions: The role of personalization and performance feedback. *Group Processes and Intergroup Relations, 8,* 391–410.

EPSTEIN, M., & WARD, L.M. (2008). "Always Use Protection": Communication boys receive about sex from parents, peers, and the media. *Journal of Youth & Adolescence, 37,* 113–126.

EREZ, M., KLEINBECK, U., & THIERRY, H. (Eds.). (2001). *Work motivation in the context of a globalizing economy.* Mahwah, NJ: Lawrence Erlbaum.

ERIKSON, E.H. (1964). *Childhood and society* (2nd ed.). New York: W. W. Norton.

ERIKSSON, U., STARRIN, B., & JANSON, S. (2008). Long-term sickness absence due to burnout: Absentees' experiences. *Qualitative Health Research, 18,* 620–632.

EYAL, K., KUNKEL, D., BIELY, E. N., & FINNERTY, K. L. (2007). Sexual socialization messages on television programs most popular among teens. *Journal of Broadcasting & Electronic Media, 51*(2), 316–336.

EYSENCK, H.J. (1966). *The effects of psychotherapy.* New York: International Science Press.

FAGAN, J., & PRESS, J. (2008). Father influences on employed mothers' work-family balance. *Journal of Family Issues, 29,* 1136–1160.

FARQUHAR, J.C., & WASYLKIW, L. (2007). Media images of men: Trends and consequences of body conceptualization. *Psychology of Men & Masculinity, 8,* 145–160.

FAWCETT, J. (2004). Denial versus consciousness: Consideration of our own death can result in greater awareness and appreciation for life and all it entails. *Psychiatric Annals, 34,* 659.

FAY, N., GARROD, S., & CARLETTA, J. (2000). Group discussion as interactive dialogue or as serial monologue: The influence of group size. *Psychological Science, 11,* 481–486.

FEHR, B. (2004). Intimacy expectations in same-sex friendships: A prototype interaction-pattern model. *Journal of Personality and Social Psychology, 86,* 265–284.

FELDMAN, J., MIYAMOTO, J., & LOFTUS, E.F. (1999). Are actions regretted more than inactions? *Organizational Behavior and Human Decision Processes, 78,* 232–255.

FENWICK, P., LOVELACE, H., & BRAYNE, S. (2007). End of life experiences and their implications for palliative care. *International Journal of Environmental Studies, 64,* 315–323.

FERNANDEZ, A. M., VERA-VILLARROEL, P., SIERRA, J. C., & ZUBEIDAT, I. (2007). Distress in response to emotional and sexual infidelity: Evidence of evolved gender differences in Spanish students. *Journal of Psychology: Interdisciplinary and Applied, 141,* 17–24.

FERRARI, J.R., & DOVIDIO, J.F. (2000). Examining behavioral processes in indecision: Decisional procrastination and decision-making style. *Journal of Research in Personality, 34,* 127–137.

FIEDLER, F. (1978). The contingency model and the dynamics of the leadership process. In L. Berkowitz (Ed.), *Advances in experimental social psychology* (Vol. 11). Orlando, FL: Academic Press.

FIELD, D., & COPP, G. (1999). Communication and awareness about dying in the 1990s. *Palliative Medicine, 13,* 459–468.

FINCHAM, F.D. (2003). Marital conflict: Correlates, structure, and context. *Current Directions in Psychological Science, 12,* 23–27.

FINKELHOR, D., & JONES, L.M. (2004, January). Explanations for the decline in sexual abuse cases. *OJJDP Crimes Against Children Series: Bulletin,* 1–12.

FINN, M.A., BLACKWELL, B.S., STALANS, L.J., STUDDARD, S., & DUGAN, L. (2004). Dual arrest decisions in domestic violence cases: The influence of departmental policies. *Crime & Delinquency, 50,* 565–589.

FISCHER, C. S. (2008). What wealth-happiness paradox? A short note on the American case. *Journal of Happiness Studies, 9,* 219–226.

FISCHER, S. (1999, November 8). Stay fit, fend off breast cancer. *U.S. News & World Report,* 91.

FISK, A.D., & ROGERS, W.A. (2002). Psychology and aging: Enhancing the lives of an aging population. *Current Directions in Psychological Science, 11,* 107–110.

FISKE, S.T. (2002). What we know now about bias and intergroup conflict, the problem of the century. *Current Directions in Psychological Science, 11,* 123–128.

FITZSIMONS, D., MULLAN, D., WILSON, J.S., CONWAY, B., CORCORAN, B., DUMPSTER, M., GAMBLE, J., et al. (2007). The challenge of patients' unmet palliative care needs in the final stages of chronic illness. *Palliative Medicine, 21,* 313–322.

FLETT, G.L., HEWITT, P.L., BLANKSTEIN, K.R., & MOSHER, S.W. (1991). Perfectionism, self-actualization, and personal adjustment. *Journal of Social Behavior and Personality. Special Issue: Handbook of Self-Actualization. 6,* 147–160.

FLEURY-STEINER, R. E., BYBEE, D., SULLIVAN, C. M., BELKNAP, J., & MELTON, H. C. (2006). Contextual factors impacting battered women's intentions to reuse the criminal legal system. *Journal of Community Psychology, 34*(3), 327–342.

FLYNT, S.W., & MORTON, R.C. (2004). Bullying and children with disabilities. *Journal of Instructional Psychology, 31,* 330–333.

FOOTE, D., & SEIBERT, S. (1999, Spring/Summer). The age of anxiety. *Special Issue: Newsweek,* 68–72.

FOSTER, G. (2005). Making friends: A nonexperimental analysis of social pair formation. *Human Relations, 58,* 1443–1465.

FOX, S. (2008, August 26). *The engaged E-patient population: People turn to the internet for health information when the stakes are high and the connection fast.* www.pewinternet.org.pew-internet-&-american-life-project.

FRALEY, R.C. (2002). Attachment stability from infancy to adulthood: Meta-analysis and dynamic modeling of developmental mechanisms. *Personality and Social Psychology Review, 6,* 123–151.

FRANKEL, K.A., & BATES, J.E. (1990). Mother-toddler problem solving: Antecedents in attachment, home behavior, and temperament. *Child Development, 61,* 810–819.

FRANKL, V. (1978). *The unheard cry for meaning.* New York: Simon & Schuster.

FRAZIER, P., STEWARD, J., & MORTENSEN, H. (2004). Perceived control and adjustment to trauma: A comparison across events. *Journal of Social & Clinical Psychology, 23,* 303–324.

FREDRICKSON, B.L., TUGADE, M.M., WAUGH, C.E., & LARKIN, G.R. (2003). What good are positive emotions in crisis? A prospective study of resilience and emotions following the terrorist attacks on the United States on September 11th, 2001. *Journal of Personality and Social Psychology, 84,* 365–376.

FREUD, S. (1965). *New introductory lectures on psychoanalysis.* New York: W. W. Norton. (First German edition, 1933).

FRIEDMAN, M.J. (2005). Introduction: Every crisis is an opportunity. *CNS Spectrums, 10,* 96–98.

FRIES, J.F. (2002). Reducing disability in older age. *Journal of the American Medical Association, 288,* 3164–3166.

FROMM, E. (1963). *Escape from freedom.* New York: Holt.

FUDGE, A.K., KNAPP, M.L., & THEUNE, K.W. (2002). Interaction appearance theory: Changing perceptions of physical attractiveness through social interaction. *Communication Theory, 12,* 8–40.

FUNK, J.B., CHAN, M., BROUWER, J., & CURTISS, K. (2006). A biopsychosocial analysis of the video game playing experience of children and adults in the United States. *Studies in Media Literacy and Information Education (SIMILE).* Retrieved October 2, 2006, from http://www.utpjournals.com/simile/issue23/Issue23_TOC.html.

FURSTENBERG, A. (2002). Trajectories of aging: Imagined pathways in later life. *International Journal of Aging and Human Development, 55,* 1–24.

GABBARD, G.O. (2007). Psychotherapy in psychiatry. *International Review of Psychiatry, 19,* 5–12.

GABBARD, G.O., & LAZAR, S.G. (2004). *Efficacy and cost effectiveness of psychotherapy.* Report prepared for the APA Commission on Psychotherapy by Psychiatrists. http://www.psych.org/psych_pract/ispe_efficacy.cfm.

GALANTER, M., & KLEBER, H.D. (2008). *The American Psychiatric Publishing textbook of substance abuse treatment: Cognitive behavioral therapies.* Arlington, VA: American Psychiatric Publishing.

GAMINO, L.A., & SEWELL, K.W. (2004), Meaning constructs as predictors of bereavement adjustment: A report from the Scott & White grief study. *Death Studies, 28,* 397–421.

GARRICK, J. (2006). The humor of trauma survivors: Its application in a therapeutic milieu. *Journal of Aggression, Maltreatment & Trauma, 12,* 169–182.

GARY, F.A. (2005). Stigma: Barrier to mental health care among ethnic minorities. *Issues in Mental Health Nursing, 26,* 979–999.

GAVZER, B. (2000, July16). How can we help? *Parade,* 4–5.

GEDO, J.E. (2002, Spring). The enduring scientific contributions of Sigmund Freud. *Perspectives in Biology and Medicine,* 200–212.

GENOVA, P. (2003). Dump the DSM! *Psychiatric Times, 20,* 72.

GEORGE, H.R., SWAMI, V., CORNELISSEN, P.L., & TOVEE, M.J. (2008). Preferences for body mass index and waist-to-hip ratio do not vary with observer age. *Journal of Evolutionary Psychology, 6,* 207–218.

GIANAKOS, I. (2002). Predictors of coping with work stress: The influences of sex, gender role, social desirability, and locus of control. *Sex Roles, 46,* 149–158.

GIBBONS, M.B.C., CRITS-CHRISTOPH, P., & HEARSON, B. (2008). The empirical status of psychodynamic therapies. *Annual Review of Clinical Psychology, 4,* 93–108.

GIBBS, J. L., ELLISON, N. B., & HEINO, R. D. (2006). Self-presentation in online personals: The role of anticipated future interaction, self-disclosure, and perceived success in internet dating. *Communication Research, 33*(2), 152–177.

GIBSON, S. (2005). On judgment and judgmentalism: How counseling can make people better. *Journal of Medical Ethics, 31,* 575–577.

GILBERT, D.T., BROWN, R.P., PINEL, E.C., & WILSON, T.D. (2000). Three kinds of control. *Journal of Personality and Social Psychology, 79,* 690–700.

GILBERT, D.T., MOREWEDGE, C.K., RISEN, J.L., & WILSON, T.D. (2004). Looking forward to looking backward: The misprediction of regret. *Psychological Science, 15,* 346–350.

GILES, L.C., GLONEK, G.F.V., LUSZCZ, M.A., & ANDREWS, G.R. (2005). Effect of social networks on 10 year survival in very old Australians: The Australian longitudinal study of aging. *Journal of Epidemiology & Community Health, 59,* 574–579.

GILOVICH, T., & MEDVEC, V.H. (1995). The experience of regret: What, when, and why. *Psychological Review, 102,* 379–395.

GILOVICH, T., & SAVITSKY, K. (1999). The spotlight effect and the illusion of transparency: Egocentric assessments of how we are seen by others. *Current Directions in Psychological Science, 8,* 165–168.

GLANTZ, S.A. (2003). Smoking in movies: A major problem and a real solution. *Lancet, 362,* 258–259.

GLASER, R. (2005). Stress-associated immune dysregulation and its importance for human health: A personal history of psychoneuroimmunology. *Brain, Behavior and Immunity, 19,* 3–11.

GOBESKI, K.T., & BEEHR, T.A. (2009). How retirees work: Predictors of different types of bridge employment. *Journal of Organizational Behavior, 30,* 401–425.

GODFREY, J.R. (2004). Toward optimal health: The experts discuss therapeutic humor. *Journal of Women's Health, 13,* 474–479.

GOLDFRIED, M.R. (2007). From ABCT to evidence-based therapies: What's in a name? *The Behavior Therapist, 30,* 3–5.

GOLDIN-MEADOW, S. (2006). Talking and thinking with our hands. *Current Directions in Psychological Science, 15,* 34–39.

GOLDSTEIN, D.S., & KOPIN, I.J. (2007). Evolution of concepts of stress. *Stress: The International Journal of the Biology of Stress, 10,* 109–120.

GOLEMAN, D. (1998). What makes a leader? *Harvard Business Review, 76,* 92–102.

GOLEMAN, D. (2005). *Emotional intelligence: 10th Anniversary Edition.* New York: Bantam Books.

GOLOGOR, E. (1977). Group polarization in a non-sick-taking culture. *Journal of Cross-Cultural Psychology, 8,* 331–346.

GOODHEART, C.D., KAZDIN, A.E., & STERNBERG, R.J. (2006). *Evidence-based psychotherapy: Where practice and research meet.* Washington, DC: American Psychological Association.

GOODWIN, R., & ENGSTRON, G. (2002). Personality and the perception of health in the general population. *Psychological Medicine, 32,* 325–332.

GOODWIN, R., NIZHARADZE, G., LUU, L.A.N., KOSA, E., & EMELYANOVA, T. (1999). Glasnost and the art of conversation: A multilevel analysis of intimate disclosure across three former communist cultures. *Journal of Cross-Cultural Psychology, 30,* 72–90.

GORDON, K.C., FRIEDMAN, M.A., MILLER, I.W., & GAERTNER, L. (2005). Marital attributions as moderators of the marital discord-depression link. *Journal of Social & Clinical Psychology, 24,* 876–893.

GORDON, T., & SANDS, J.S. (1984). *P.E.T. in action.* New York: Bantam.

GOTTMAN, J., & CARRERE, S. (2000, September 23). Welcome to the love lab. *Psychology Today,* 42–47, 87.

GRABHORN, R., KAUFHOLD, J., MICHAL, M., & OVERBECK, G. (2005). The therapeutic relationship as reflected in linguistic interaction: Work on resistance. *Psychotherapy Research, 15,* 470–482.

GRAD, O.T., & ZAVASNIK, A. (1999). Phenomenology of bereavement process after suicide, traffic accident and terminal illness (in spouses). *Archives of Suicide Research, 5,* 157–172.

GRANBERG, E. (2006). "Is that all there is?" Possible selves, self-change, and weight loss. *Social Psychology Quarterly, 69,* 109–126.

GRAVES, S.B. (1999). Television and prejudice reduction: When does television as a vicarious experience make a difference? *Journal of Social Issues, 55,* 707–727.

GRAY, N. (2008). Health information on the internet: A double-edged sword. *Journal of Adolescent Health, 42,* 432–433.

GRAY-LITTLE, B., BAUCOM, D.H., & HAMBY, S.L. (1996). Marital power, marital adjustment, and therapy outcome. *Journal of Family Psychology, 10,* 292–303.

GREAVES, S. (2005). Happy hours: Stress and long hours are key contributors to a demotivated workforce with high levels of absenteeism and staff turnover. *Incentive Today, 20,* 25–28.

GREEN, B.C. (2005). Homosexual signification: A moral construct in social contexts. *Journal of Homosexuality, 49,* 119–134.

GREEN, K.E., GROVES, M.M., & TEGANO, D.W. (2004). Parenting practices that limit transitional object use: An illustration. *Early Child Development and Care, 174,* 427–436.

GREEN, S., & PRITCHARD, M. E. (2003). Predictors of body image dissatisfaction in adult men and women. *Social Behavior and Personality, 31*(3), 215–222.

GREENBERG, L.S., & WATSON, J.C. (2006). *The therapeutic relationship.* Washington, DC: American Psychological Association.

GREENBERG, M.T., CICCHETTI, D., & CUMMINGS, E.M. (1990). *Attachment in the preschool years: Theory, research, and intervention.* The John D. and Catherine T. MacArthur Foundation series on mental health and development. Chicago: University of Chicago Press.

GREENBERG, S., & SPRINGEN, K. (Fall/Winter 2001 Special Edition). Keeping hope alive. *Newsweek, 138,* 60–63.

GREENE, K., & FAULKNER, S.L. (2005). Gender, belief in the sexual double standard, and sexual talk in heterosexual dating relationships. *Sex Roles, 53,* 239–251.

GREENE, S.M., ANDERSON, E.R., DOYLE, E.A., & RIEDELBACH, H. (2006). Divorce. In G.G. Bear & K.M. Minke (Eds.), *Children's needs III: Development, prevention, and intervention* (pp. 745–757). Washington, DC: National Association of School Psychologists.

GREENHAUS, J.H., PARASURAMAN, S., & WORMLEY, W.M. (1990). Effects of race on organizational experiences, job performance evaluations, and career outcomes. *Academy of Management Journal, 33,* 64–86.

GREVE, W., & WENTURA, D. (2003). Immunizing the self: Self-concept stabilization through reality-adaptive self-definitions. *Personality and Social Psychology Bulletin, 29,* 39–50.

GREYSON, B. (2005). "False positive" claims of near-death experiences and "false negative" denials of near-death experiences. *Death Studies, 29,* 145–155.

GRIER, S.A., MENSINGER, J., HUANG, S.H., KUMANYIKA, S.K., & STETTLER, N. (2007). Fast-food marketing and children's fast-food consumption: Exploring parents' influences in an ethnically diverse sample. *American Marketing Association, 26*, 221–235.

GRIFFIN, J.M., FUHRER, R., STANSFELD, S.A., & MARMOT, M. (2002). The importance of low control at work and home on depression and anxiety: Do these effects vary by gender and social class? *Social Science and Medicine. Special Issue: Social and Economic Patterning of Women's Health in a Changing World, 54*, 783–798.

GROBANI, N., KRAUSS, S.W., WATSON, P.J., & Le BRITON, D. (2008). Relationship of perceived stress with depression. Complete mediation by perceived control and anxiety in Iran and the United States. *International Journal of Psychology, 43*, 958–968.

GROCKE, D. (2005). The role of the therapist in the Bonny method of guided imagery and music (BMGIM). *Music Therapy Perspectives, 23*, 45–52.

GROOPMAN, J. (2000, April 10). The doubting disease: When is obsession a sickness? *The New Yorker*, 52–57.

GROTH-MARNAT, G., & SUMMERS, R. (1998). Altered beliefs, attitudes, and behaviors following near-death experiences. *Journal of Humanistic Psychology, 38*, 110–125.

GROUZET, F.M.E., KASSER, T., AHUVIA, A., DOLS, J.M.F., KIM, Y., & LAU, S., et al. (2005). The structure of goal contents across 15 cultures. *Journal of Personality and Social Psychology, 89*, 800–816.

GRUENEWALD, T.L., KARLAMANGLA, A.S., GREENDALE, G.A., SINGER, B.H., & SEEMAN, T.E. (2009). Increased mortality risk in older adults with persistently low or declining feelings of usefulness to others. *Journal of Aging and Health, 21*, 398–425.

GUERRERO, L.K. (1997). Nonverbal involvement across interactions with same-sex friends, opposite-sex friends and romantic partners: Consistency or change. *Journal of Social and Personal Relationships, 14*, 31–58.

GUERRERO, L.K., & ANDERSEN, P.A. (1998). The dark side of jealousy and envy: Desire, delusion, desperation, and destructive communication. In B.H. Spirtzberg & W.R. Cupach (Eds.), *The dark side of close relationships* (pp. 33–70). Mahwah, NJ: Lawrence Erlbaum.

GUINTO, J. (2005, December). Time bandits. *Southwest Airlines Spirit, 143–144*, 153–154.

GUPTA, S. (2002, December 2). A hurry-up lifestyle can hurt the young: Even if you're only 18, impatience can mean hypertension later on. And that can be bad news for your heart. *Time*, 103.

Guttmacher Institute. (2004). Contraception in the United States: Current use and continuing challenges. Retrieved May 04, 2006, from http://www.guttmacher.org/presentations/contraception-us.html.

GUZZO, K.B. (2009). Marital intentions and the stability of first cohabitations. *Journal of Family Issues, 30*, 179–205.

HAAS, A., KOESTNER, B., ROSENBERG, J., MOORE, D., GARLOW, S.J., SEDWAY, J. et al. (2008). An interactive web-based method of outreach to college students at risk for suicide. *Journal of American College Health, 57*, 15–22.

HABERFELLNER, E.M. (2007). A review of the assessment of antidepressant-induced sexual dysfunction used in randomized, controlled clinical trials. *Pharmacopsychiatry, 40*, 173–182.

HADDAD, A. (2003). Ethics in action (acute care decisions). *RN, 66*, 27–29.

HAGGERTY, K., KOSTERMAN, R.F., CATALANO, R.F., & HAWKINS, J.D. (1999, July). Preparing for the drug free years. *Juvenile Justice Bulletin*, 1–11.

HAGIHARA, A., ODAMAKI, M., NOBUTOMO, K., & TARUMI, K. (2006). Physician and patient perceptions of the physician explanations in medical encounters. *Journal of Health Psychology, 11*, 91–105.

HAINES, M.P., BARKER, G.P., & RICE, R. (2003). *Using social norms to reduce alcohol and tobacco use in two midwestern high schools.* San Francisco: Jossey-Bass.

HAJJAR, I., GABLE, S.A., JENKINSON, V.P., KANE, L.T., & RILEY, R.A. (2005). Quality of Internet Geriatric Health Information: The Geriatric Web Project. *Journal of the American Geriatrics Society, 53*, 885–890.

HALEVY, N., BORNSTEIN, G., & SAGIV, L. (2008). "In-group love" and "out-group hate" as motives for individual participation in intergroup conflict: A new game paradigm. *Psychological Science, 19*, 405–411.

HALFORD, W.K., O'DONNELL, C., LIZZIO, K., & WILSON, A.L. (2006). Do couples at high risk of relationship problems attend premarriage education? *Journal of Family Psychology, 20*, 160–163.

HALL, C., & MOSEMAK, J. (1999, October 11). Making a successful marriage. *USA Today*, 1D.

HALL, J.A., ROTER, D.L., & MILBURN, M.A. (1999). Illness and satisfaction with medical care. *Current Directions in Psychological Science, 8*, 96–99.

HALPERN-FELSHNER, B.L., & MILLSTEIN, S.G. (2002). The effects of terrorism on teens; perceptions of dying: The new world is riskier than ever. *Journal of Adolescent Health, 30*, 308–311.

HAMILTON, M.C., ANDERSON, D., BROADDUS, M., & YOUNG, K. (2006) Gender stereotyping and under-representation of female characters in 200 popular children's picture books: A twenty-first century update. *Sex Roles, 55*, 757–765.

HANLEY, S.J., & ABELL, S.C. (2002). Maslow and relatedness: Creating an interpersonal model of self-actualization. *Journal of Humanistic Psychology, 42*, 37–56.

HANNAH, A., & MURACHVER, T. (1999). Gender and conversational style as predictors of conversational behavior. *Journal of Language & Social Psychology, 18*, 153–174.

HANSEN, J.C., & DIK, B.J. (2005). Evidence of 12-year predictive and concurrent validity for SII occupational scale scores. *Journal of Vocational Behavior, 67*, 365–378.

HANSON, M.S., FINK, P., SØNDERGAARD, L., & FRYDENBERG, M. (2005). Mental illness and health care: A study among new neurological patients. *General Hospital Psychiatry, 27*, 119–124.

HARDER, B. (2005). Potent medicine: Can Viagra and other lifestyle drugs save lives? *Science News, 168*, 124–126.

HARKLESS, L.E., & FOWERS, B.J. (2005). Similarities and differences in relational boundaries among heterosexuals, gay men, and lesbians. *Psychology of Women Quarterly, 29*, 167–176.

HARPER, G. (2004). *The joy of conflict: Transforming victims, villains, and heroes in the workplace and at home.* British Columbia, CA: New Society Publishers.

HARRELL, S.P. (2000). A multidimensional conceptualization of racism-related stress: Implications for the well-being of people of color. *American Journal of Orthopsychiatry, 70*, 42–57.

HARRIS, A.H.S., & THORESEN, C.E. (2005). Volunteering is associated with delayed mortality in older people: Analysis of the longitudinal study of aging. *Journal of Health Psychology, 10*, 739–752.

HARRIS, L. (1987). *Inside America.* New York: Vintage.

HARTER, S. (2006). The self. In N. Eisenberg, W. Damon, & R. M. Lerner (Eds.), *Handbook of child psychology: Vol. 3, Social, emotional, and personality development* (6th ed., pp. 505–570). Hoboken, NJ: John Wiley & Sons.

HARTMAN, M., & WARREN, L.H. (2005). Explaining age differences in temporal working memory. *Psychology and Aging. Special Issue: Emotion-Cognition Interactions and the Aging Mind, 20*, 645–656.

Harvard Health Letter. (2001, May). Doctors from Venus and Mars: How they differ, 4.

Harvard Health Letter. (2002, August). In brief—Heavenly experiences, 2.

Harvard Health Letter. (2004, July). Nine tips for patients, 1.

Harvard Health Letter. (2004, October). Staying the course, 1.

Harvard Health Letter. (2006, January). Patient, protect thyself? 1–2.

Harvard Mental Health Letter. (1998, November). Obsessive-compulsive disorder, 1–4.

Harvard Mental Health Letter. (2002a, January). General review—Disaster and trauma, 1–4.

Harvard Mental Health Letter (2005). Dysthymia. Psychotherapists and patients confront the high cost of "low-grade" depression. (2005). *The Harvard Mental Health Letter from Harvard Medical School, 21*, 1–3.

Harvard Women's Health Watch. (2002, March). Anxiety—When anxiety is overwhelming, 1–2.

Harvard Women's Health Watch. (2003, September). Research reveals biology of harmful stress, 1–2.

Harvard's Women's Health Watch, (2005, March). Not getting over it: Post-traumatic stress disorder, 1–2.

HASELTON, M.G. (2003). The sexual overperception bias: Evidence of a systematic bias in men from a survey of naturally occurring events. *Journal of Research in Personality, 37*, 34–47.

HATFIELD, E. (1988). Passionate and companionate love. In R.J. Sternberg & M.I. Barnes (Eds.), *The psychology of love* (pp. 191–217). New Haven, CT: Yale University Press.

HATFIELD, E., & RAPSON, R.L. (1993). Historical and cross-cultural perspectives on passionate love and sexual desire. *Annual Review of Sex Research, 4*, 67–97.

HATFIELD, J., & FERNANDES, R. (2009). The role of risk-propensity in the risky driving of younger drivers. *Accident Analysis & Prevention, 41*(1), 25–35.

HAVEREN, R.V., HABBEN, C.J., & KUTHER, T.L. (2005). New psychologists online: Changing the face of psychology through technology. In R.D. Morgan, T.L. Kuther, & C.J. Habben (Eds.), *Life after graduate school in psychology: Insider's advice from new psychologists* (pp. 321–327). New York: Psychology Press.

HAWKLEY, L.C., THISTED, R.A., & CACIOPPO, J.T. (2009). Loneliness predicts reduced physical activity: Cross-sectional & longitudinal analyses. *Health Psychology, 28*, 354–363.

HAZAN, C., & SHAVER, P. (1994). Attachment as an organizing framework for research on close relationships. *Psychological Inquiry, 5*, 1–22.

Health & Medicine Week. (2003, June 10). Role of chronic stress clarified, 3.

HÉBERT, R. (2005). Vacation: Not what you remember. *APS Observer, 18*, 12–19.

HEDGE, J.W., BORMAN, W.C., & LAMMLEIN, S.E. (2006). *Physical capabilities, cognitive abilities, and job performance.* Washington, DC: American Psychological Association.

HEIFETZ, A., & SEGEV, E. (2005). Escalation and delay in protracted international conflicts. *Mathematical Social Sciences, 49*, 17–37.

HEIMAN, J.R. (2008). Treating low sexual desire—new findings for testosterone in women. *New England Journal of Medicine, 359*, 2047–2049.

HEISER, N.A., TURNER, S. M., BEIDEL, D.C., & ROBERSON-NAY, R. (2009). Differentiating social phobia from shyness. *Journal of Anxiety Disorders, 23*, 469–476.

HELGESON, V.S. (1990). *The female advantage: Women's ways of leadership.* New York: Doubleday Currency.

HELGESON, V.S. (1994). Long-distance romantic relationships: Sex differences in adjustment and break-up. *Personality and Social Psychology Bulletin, 20*, 254–265.

HELGESON, V.S., & COHEN, S. (1996). Social support and adjustment to cancer: Reconciling descriptive, correlational, and intervention research. *Health Psychology, 15*, 135–148.

HELSON, R., & SOTO, C.J. (2005). Up and down in middle age: Monotonic and nonmonotonic changes in roles, status, and personality. *Journal of Personality and Social Psychology, 89*, 194–204.

HENDRICK, S.S. (2006). *Love, intimacy, and partners.* New York: Oxford University Press.

HENNINGSEN, D.D., HENNINGSEN, M.L.M., EDEN, J., & CRUZ, M.G. (2006). Examining the symptoms of groupthink and retrospective sensemaking. *Small Group Research, 37*, 36–64.

HEREK, G.M. (2000a). Sexual prejudice and gender: Do heterosexuals' attitudes toward lesbians and gay men differ? *Journal of Social Issues. Special Issue: Women's Sexualities, 56*, 251–266.

HEREK, G.M. (2000b). The psychology of sexual prejudice. *Current Directions in Psychological Science, 9*, 19–22.

HESS, U., SENECAL, S., KIROUAC, G., HERRERA, P., PHILIPPOT, P., & KLECK, R.E. (2000). Emotional expressivity in men and women: Stereotypes and self-perception, *Cognition and Emotion, 14*, 609–642.

HETH, J.T., & SOMER, E. (2002). Characterizing stress tolerance: "Controllability awareness" and its relationship to perceived stress and reported health. *Personality and Individual Differences, 33*, 883–895.

HEWSTONE, M., RUBIN, M., & WILLIS, H. (2002). Intergroup bias. *Annual Review of Psychology, 53*, 575–604.

HILBRECHT, M., SHAW, S.M., JOHNSON, L.C., & ANDREY, J. (2008). "I'm home for the kids": Contradictory implications for work-life balance of teleworking mothers. *Gender, Work & Organization, 15*, 454–476.

HILL, A., & MCKIE, R. (2008). Ten years on: It's time to count the cost of the Viagra revolution. *The Observer*, p. 30.

HILL, S. D., & TOMLIN, C. (1981). Self-recognition in retarded children. *Child Development, 52*(1), 145–150.

HINSHAW, S.P., & STIER, A. (2008). Stigma as related to mental disorders. *Annual Review of Clinical Psychology, 4*, 367–393.

HINSZ, V.B., & JUNDT, D.K. (2005). Exploring individual differences in a goal-setting situation using the motivational trait questionnaire. *Journal of Applied Social Psychology, 35*, 551–571.

HIRSCH, J.K., WOLFORD, K., LALONDE, S. M., BRUNK, L., & PARKER-MORRIS, A. (2009). Optimistic explanatory style as a moderator of the association between negative life events and suicide ideation. *Crisis: The Journal of Crisis Intervention and Suicide Prevention, 30*, 48–53.

HOBARA, M. (2003). Prevalence of transitional objects in young children in Tokyo and New York. *Infant Mental Health Journal, 24*, 174–191.

HOFFMAN, K.R. (2002, May 3). Are girls meaner than boys? *Time for Kids,* 4–5.

HOFSTEDE, G. (2001). *Culture's consequences.* Thousand Oaks, CA: Sage.

HOGARTH, R.M. (2005). Deciding analytically or trusting your intuition? The advantages and disadvantages of analytic and intuitive thought. In T. Betsch, & S. Haberstroh (Eds.), *The routines of decision making* (pp. 67–82). Mahwah, NJ: Lawrence Erlbaum.

HOGUE, M., & LORD, R.G. (2007). A multilevel, complexity theory approach to understanding gender bias in leadership. *Leadership Quarterly, 18*, 370–390.

HOHWY, J. (2004). The experience of mental causation. *Behavior and Philosophy, 32*, 377–400.

HOLLON, S.D., THASE, M.E., & MARKOWITZ, J.C. (2002). Treatment and prevention of depression. *Psychological Science in the Public Interest, 3*, 39–77.

HOLMBERG, D., & BLAIR, K.L. (2009). Sexual desire, communication, satisfaction, and preferences of men and women in same-sex versus mixed-sex relationships. *Journal of Sex Research, 46*, 57–66.

HOLMES, T.H., & RAHE, R.H. (1967). The social readjustment rating scale. *Journal of Psychosomatic Research, 11*, 213–217.

HONG, Y., WYER, R.S., & FONG, C.P.S. (2008). Chinese working in groups: Effort dispensability versus normative influence. *Asian Journal of Social Psychology, 11*, 187–195.

HOPKO, D.R., CRITTENDON, J.A., GRANT, E., & WILSON, S.A. (2005). The impact of anxiety on performance IQ. *Anxiety, Stress & Coping: An International Journal, 18*, 17–35.

HORGEN, K.B. (2005). Big food, big money, big children. In S. Olfman (Ed.), *Childhood lost: How American culture is failing our kids* (pp. 123–135). Westport, CT: Praeger Publishers/Greenwood Publishing Group.

HORNSEY, M.J., & JETTEN, J. (2005). Loyalty without conformity: Tailoring self-perception as a means of balancing belonging and differentiation. *Self and Identity, 4*, 81–95.

HORRIGAN, J.B. (2008). *Seeding the cloud: What mobile access means for usage patterns and online content.* www.pewinternet.org/~/media//Files/Reports/2008/PIP_Users .and.Cloud.pdf.pdf.

Hospice Foundation of America. (2003). *What is hospice?* http://www .hospicefoundation.org/pages/page.asp?page_id=47055.

Hospice Management Advisor. (2003). Innovative programs help stressed-out caregivers cope with problems: Alert systems, community nursing fill gaps, *8,* 73–75.

HOUCK, J.A. (2007). A comparison on grief reactions in cancer, HIV/AIDS, and suicide bereavement. *Journal of HIV/AIDS & Social Services, 6*, 97–112.

HOURAN, J., LANGE, R., RENTFROW, P.J., & BRUCKNER, K.H. (2004). Do online matchmaking tests work? An assessment of preliminary evidence for a publicized 'predictive model of marital success.' *North American Journal of Psychology, 6*, 507–526.

HOWLETT, D. (1999, November 9). Loving a good fright: It's in our nature. *USA Today*, 6D.

HUDD, S.S., DUMLAO, J., ERDMANN-SAGER, D., MURRAY, D., PHAN, E., SOUKAS, M., & YOKOZUKA, N. (2000). Stress at college: Effects on health habits, health status and self-esteem. *College Student Journal, 34*, 217–227.

HUDDY, L., KHATIB, N., & CAPELOS, T. (2002). The polls—trends: Reactions to the terrorist attacks of September 11, 2001. *Public Opinion Quarterly, 66*, 418–451.

HUESMANN, L.R. (2007). The impact of electronic media violence: Scientific theory and research. *Journal of Adolescent Health, 41*, S6–S13.

HUGENBERG, K. (2005). Social categorization and the perception of facial affect: Target race moderates the response latency advantage for happy faces. *Emotion, 5*, 267–276.

HUGENBERG, K., & BODENHAUSEN, G.V. (2003). Facing prejudice: Implicit prejudice and the perception of facial threat. *Psychological Science, 14*, 640–643.

HUNSLEY, J., & DI GIULIO, G. (2002). Dodo bird, phoenix, or urban legend? The question of psychotherapy equivalence. *The Scientific Review of Mental Health Practice, 1*, 11–22.

HUNTINGTON, S.P. (1999, June/July). When cultures collide. *Civilization,* 76–77.

HUPPERT, F.A. (2009). A new approach to reducing disorder and improving well-being. *Perspectives on Psychological Science, 4*, 108–111.

HYDE, J.S., & DELAMETER, J. (1997). *Understanding human sexuality.* New York: McGraw-Hill.

IIDAKA, T., NOGAWA, J., KANSAKU, K., & SADATO, N. (2008). Neural correlates involved in processing happy affect on same race faces. *Journal of Psychophysiology, 22,* 91–99.

INGRASSIA, M., & BECK, M., (1994, July 4). Patterns of abuse. *Newsweek,* 26–33.

INSKO, C.A., SCHOPLER, J., HOYLE, R.H., DARDIS, G.J., & GRAETZ, K.A. (1990). Individual-group discontinuity as a function of fear and greed. *Journal of Personality and Social Psychology, 58,* 68–79.

IYENGAR, S.S., WELLS, R.E., & SCHWARTZ, B. (2006). Doing better but feeling worse: Looking for the "best" job undermines satisfaction. *Psychological Science, 17,* 143–150.

JACCOBY, S. (1999, September/October). Great sex: What's age got to do with it? *Modern Maturity, 41*–45.

JACKSON, D., ENGSTROM, E., & HASSENZAHL, D.M. (2005). Effects of sex and seating arrangement on selection of leader. *Perceptual and Motor Skills, 100,* 815–818.

JACKSON, L.A., HUNTER, J., & HODGE, C.N. (1995). Physical attractiveness and intellectual competence: A meta-analytic review. *Social Psychology Quarterly, 58,* 108–122.

JACKSON, L.M., PRATT, M.W., HUNSBERGER, B., & PANCER, S.M. (2005). Optimism as a mediator of the relation between perceived parental authoritativeness and adjustment among adolescents: Finding the sunny side of the street. *Social Development, 14,* 273–304.

JACKSON, M. (2005). The limits of connectivity: Technology and 21st-century life. In D.F. Halpern, & S.E. Murphy (Eds.), *From work-family balance to work-family interaction: Changing the metaphor.* (pp. 135–150). Mahwah, NJ: Lawrence Erlbaum.

JACKSON, T., FLAHERTY, S.R., & KOSUTH, R. (2000). Culture and self-presentation as predictors of shyness among Japanese and American female college students. *Perceptual and Motor Skills, 90,* 475–482.

JACKSON, T., FRITCH, A., NAGASAKA, T., & GUNDERSON, J. (2002). Towards explaining the association between shyness and loneliness: A path analysis with American college students. *Social Behavior and Personality, 30,* 263–270.

JACKSON, T., WEISS, K.E., LUNDQUIST, J.J., & SODERLIND, A. (2002). Perceptions of goal-directed activities of optimists and pessimists: A personal projects analysis. *Journal of Psychology, 136,* 521–532.

JACOBSEN, C., & HOUSE, R.J. (2001). Dynamics of charismatic leadership: A process theory, simulation model, and tests. *Leadership Quarterly, 12,* 75–112.

JAMAL, M. (2005). Short communication: Personal and organizational outcomes related to job stress and type-A behavior: A study of Canadian and Chinese employees. *Stress and Health: Journal of the International Society for the Investigation of Stress, 21,* 129–137.

JAMES, V.H., & OWENS, L.D. (2005). 'They turned around like I wasn't there': An analysis of teenage girls' letters about their peer conflicts. *School Psychology International, 26,* 71–88.

JANIS, I.L. (1982). *Groupthink* (2nd ed.). Boston: Houghton Mifflin.

JANSZ, J., & MARTIS, R.G. (2007). The Lara phenomenon: Powerful female characters in video games. *Sex Roles, 56,* 141–148.

JAUHAR, S. (2003, March 16). When doctors slam the door. *The New York Times Magazine,* 32–35.

JENVEY, V.B. (2007). The relationship between television viewing and obesity in young children: A review of existing explanations. *Early Child Development and Care, 177,* 809–820.

JEWELL, K.S. (1993). *From Mammy to Miss America and beyond: Cultural images and the shaping of U.S. social policy.* London: Routledge.

JEWELL, R.D., & KIDWELL, B. (2005). The moderating effect of perceived control on motivation to engage in deliberative processing. *Psychology & Marketing, 22,* 751–769.

JOHNSON, C. (2005). Dating in cyberspace: Meeting the right person may be a click away. Retrieved April 02, 2006, from http://dnj.midsouthnews.com/apps/pbcs.dll/article?AID=/20051113/LIFESTYLE/511130301/1024.

JOHNSON, S. (2003, March). Fear. *Discover,* 33–39.

JOHNSON, S., & PATZ, A. (2003, March/April). Save your relationship. *Psychology Today,* 50–58.

JOHNSON, S.D., PHELPS, D.L., & COTTLER, L.B. (2004). The association of sexual dysfunction and substance use among a community epidemiological sample. *Archives of Sexual Behavior, 33,* 55–63.

JOHNSON, S.K., MURPHY, S.E., ZEWDIE, S., & REICHARD, R. (2008). The strong, sensitive type: Effects of gender stereotypes and leadership prototypes on the evaluation of male and female leaders. *Organizational Behavior and Human Decision Processes, 106,* 39–60.

JOHNSON, T., KULESA, P., CHO, Y.I., & SHAVITT, S. (2005). The relation between culture and response styles: Evidence from 19 countries. *Journal of Cross-Cultural Psychology, 36,* 264–277.

JOINER, T.E., WONDERLICH, S.A., METALSKY, G., SCHMIDT, N.B. (1995). Body dissatisfaction: A feature of bulimia, depression, or both? *Journal of Social and Clinical Psychology, 14,* 339–355.

JONER, A. (2005). Job satisfaction and job performance: Causal relationship or illusory correlation? *Nordisk Psykologi, 57,* 161–176.

JONES, D. (1995). Sexual selection, physical attractiveness, and facial neoteny: Cross-cultural evidence and implication. *Current Anthropology, 36,* 723–748.

JONES, S.M., & BURLESON, B.R. (2003). Effects of helper and recipient sex on the experience and outcomes of comforting messages: An experimental investigation. *Sex Roles, 48,* 1–19.

JONES, T., DEMORE, M., COHEN, L.L., O'CONNELL, C., & JONES, D. (2008). Childhood healthcare attitudes, and optimism as predictors of adolescent healthcare behavior. *Journal of Clinical Psychology in Medical Settings, 15,* 234–240.

JORM, A.F. (2005). Social networks and health: It's time for an intervention trial. *Journal of Epidemiology & Community Health,* 59, 537–538.

JOSEPHS, R.A., BOSSON, J.K., & JACOBS, C.G. (2003). Self-esteem maintenance processes: Why low self-esteem may be resistant to change. *Personality and Social Psychology Bulletin, 29,* 920–933.

JUDGE, T.A., EREZ, A., BONO, J.E., & THORESON, C.J. (2002). Are measures of self-esteem, neuroticism, locus of control, and generalized self-efficacy indicators of a common core construct? *Journal of Personality and Social Psychology, 83,* 693–710.

JUDGE, T.A., HURST, C., & SIMON, L.S. (2009). Does it pay to be smart, attractive, or confident (or all three)? Relationships among general mental ability, physical attractiveness, core self-evaluations, and income. *Journal of Applied Psychology, 94,* 742–755.

JUDGE, T.A., PICCOLO, R.F., & ILIES, R. (2004). The forgotten ones? The validity of consideration and initiating structure in leadership research. *Journal of Applied Psychology, 89,* 36–51.

JUMPER, S.A. (1995). A meta-analysis of the relationship of child sexual abuse to adult psychological adjustment. *Child Abuse and Neglect, 19,* 715–728.

KAHR, B. (2008). *Who's been sleeping in your head? The secret world of sexual fantasies.* New York: Basic Books.

KALMIJN, M. (2005). Attitude alignment in marriage and cohabitation: The case of sex-role attitudes. *Personal Relationships, 12,* 521–535.

KANEMASA, Y., & DAIBO, I. (2003). Effects of early adult attachment styles on intimate opposite-sex relationships. *Japanese Journal of Social Psychology, 19,* 59–76.

KAPLAN, R.E., & KAISER, R.B. (2003). Rethinking a classic distinction in leadership: Implications for the assessment and development of executives. *Consulting Psychology Journal: Practice and Research. Special Issue: Leadership Development: New Perspectives, 55,* 15–25.

KARAU, S.J., & WILLIAMS, K.D. (1993). Social loafing: A meta-analytic review and theoretical integration. *Journal of Personality and Social Psychology, 65,* 681–706.

KARAVIDAS, M., LIM, N.K., & KATSIKAS, S.L. (2005). The effects of computers on older adult users. *Computers in Human Behavior, 21,* 697–711.

KARK, R., SHAMIR, B., & CHEN, G. (2003). The two faces of transformational leadership: Empowerment and dependency. *Journal of Applied Psychology, 88,* 246–255.

KASSER, T., & RYAN, R.M. (1996). Further examining the American dream: Differential correlates of intrinsic and extrinsic goals. *Personality and Social Psychology Bulletin, 22,* 280–287.

KAYES, A.B., KAYES, D.C., & KOLB, D.A. (2005). Experiential learning in teams. *Simulation & Gaming, 36,* 330–354.

KAYES, D.C. (2005). The destructive pursuit of idealized goals. *Organizational Dynamics, 34,* 391–401.

KAZDIN, A.E. (2007). Mediators and mechanisms of change in psychotherapy research. *Annual Review of Clinical Psychology, 3,* 1–27.

KEERY, H., BOUTELLE, K., VAN DEN BERG, P., & THOMPSON, J.K. (2005). The impact of appearance-related teasing by family members. *Journal of Adolescent Health, 37,* 120–127.

KELLER, A., FORD, L. H., & MEACHAM, J. A. (1978). Dimensions of self-concept in preschool children. *Developmental Psychology, 14*(5), 483–489.

KELLER, M.C. (2008). The evolutionary persistence of genes that increase mental disorders risk. *Current Directions in Psychological Science, 17,* 395–399.

KELSEY, J. (1999, January). Up from depression. *Healthline*, 6–11.

KENNEDY, K.A., & PRONIN, E. (2008). When disagreement gets ugly: Perceptions of bias and the escalation of conflict. *Personality and Social Psychology Bulletin, 34*, 833–648.

KENSIT, D.A. (2000). Rogerian theory: A critique of the effectiveness of pure client-centered therapy. *Counseling Psychology Quarterly, 13*, 345–351.

KESSLER, R.C., MOLNAR, B.E., FEURER, I.D., & APPLEBAUM, M. (2001). Patterns and mental health predictors of domestic violence in the United States: Results from the National Comorbidity Survey. *International Journal of Law and Psychiatry, 24*, 487–509.

KIEFFER, K.M., CRONIN, C., & GAWET, D.L. (2006). Test and study worry and emotionality in the prediction of college students' reasons for drinking: An exploratory investigation. *Journal of Alcohol and Drug Education, 50*, 57–81.

KIERNAN, K. (2004). Redrawing the boundaries of marriage. *Journal of Marriage and Family, 66*, 980–987.

KIM, H.K., & McKENRY, P.C. (2002). The relationship between marriage and psychological well-being: A longitudinal analysis. *Journal of Family Issues, 23*, 885–911.

KIM, J., PARK, S., & EMERY, C.R. (2009). The incidence and impact of family violence on mental health among South Korean women: Results of a national survey. *Journal of Family Violence, 24*, 193–202.

KIM, J.L., COLLINS, R.L., KANOUSE, D.E., et al. (2006). Sexual readiness, household policies, and other predictors of adolescents' exposure to sexual content in mainstream entertainment television. *Media Psychology, 8*, 449–471.

KING, J.H., & ANDERSON, S.M. (2004). Therapeutic implications of pharmacotherapy: Current trends and ethical issues. *Journal of Counseling and Development. 82*, 329–336.

KINSEY, A.C., POMEROY, W.B., & MARTIN, C.E. (1948). *Sexual behavior in the human male*. Philadelphia: W. B. Saunders.

KIRCALDY, B., FURNHAM, A., & LEVINE, R. (2001). Attitudinal and personality correlates of a nation's pace of life. *Journal of Managerial Psychology, 16*, 20–34.

KIRK, J., & BELOVICS, R. (2006). Making e-working work. *Journal of Employment Counseling, 43*, 39–46.

KIRSCHENBAUM, H., & JOURDAN, A. (2005). The current status of Carl Rogers and the person-centered approach. *Psychotherapy: Theory, Research, Practice, Training, 42*, 37–51.

KIRSH, S.J. (2010). *Media and youth: A developmental perspective*. Oxford, UK: Wiley-Blackwell.

KIRSH, S.J. (2006). *Children, adolescents, and media violence: A critical look at the research*. Thousand Oaks, CA: Sage.

KITAYAMA, S., & UCHIDA, Y. (2005). Interdependent agency: An alternative system for action. In R.M. Sorrentino, D. Cohen, J.M. Olson, & M.P. Zanna (Eds.), *Ontario symposium on personality and social psychology*, June 2002, University of Western Ontario, London, Canada; an earlier version of this paper was presented at the aforementioned symposium (pp. 137–164). Mahwah, NJ: Lawrence Erlbaum.

KITO, M. (2005). Self-disclosure in romantic relationships and friendships among American and Japanese college students. *Journal of Social Psychology, 145*, 127–140.

KIVLIGHAN, D.M., MULTON, K.D., & PATTON, M.J. (2000). Insight and symptom reduction in time-limited psychoanalytic counseling. *Journal of Counseling Psychology, 47*, 50–58.

KLEESPIES, P.M. (2004). Life and death decisions: Psychological and ethical considerations in end-of-life care. In P.M. Kleespies (Ed.), *Life and death decisions: Psychological and ethical considerations in end-of-life care*. Washington, DC: American Psychological Association.

KLEIN, C.T.F., & HELWEG-LARSON, M. (2002). Perceived control and the optimistic bias: A meta-analytic review. *Psychology and Health, 17*, 437–446.

KLOHNEN, E.C. (1996). Conceptual analysis and measurement of the construct of ego-resiliency. *Journal of Personality and Social Psychology, 70*, 1067–1079.

KLONOWICZ, T. (2001). Discontented people: Reactivity and locus of control as determinants of subjective well-being. *European Journal of Personality, 15*, 29–47.

KLUGER, J. (2005). Vitamin sherpa. *Time, 166*, 93–94.

KLUGER, J., BRUNTON, M., & ROBINSON, S. (2005). Motorcycle riders. *Time, 166*, 97.

KNOX, D., & ZUSMAN, M.E. (2001). Marrying a man with "baggage": Implications for second wives. *Journal of Divorce and Remarriage, 35*, 67–79.

KOCH, S.C. (2005). Evaluative affect display toward male and female leaders of task-oriented groups. *Small Group Research, 36*, 678–703.

KOCHANSKA, G., COY, K. C., & MURRAY, K. T. (2001). The development of self-regulation in the first four years of life. *Child Development, 72*(4), 1091–1111.

KOERNER, B.I. (1997, March 31). Life after death? *U. S. News & World Report, 123*, 61–64.

KOGAN, N., & WALLACH, M.A. (1964). *Risk-taking: A study in cognition and personality*. New York: Holt.

KOHUT, A., & WIKE, R., (2008, Spring). Assessing globalization: Benefits and drawbacks of trade and integration. *Harvard International Review*, www.harvardir.org/index.php?page=article&id-1727.

KOLATA, G. (2002, November 19). Is frailty inevitable? Some experts say no. *The New York Times*, p. D5.

KOLDEN, G.G., CHISHOLM-STOCKARD, S.M., STRAUMAN, T.J., TIERNEY, S.C., MULLEN, E.A., & SCHNEIDER, K.L. (2006). Universal session-level change processes in an early session of psychotherapy: Path models. *Journal of Counseling and Clinical Psychology, 74*, 327–336.

KOMAN, E.S., & WOLFF, S.B. (2008). Emotional intelligence competencies in the team and team leader: A multi-level examination of the impact of emotional intelligence in team performance. *Journal of Management Development, 27*, 55–75.

KOMARRAJU, M., & KARAU, S.J. (2005). The relationship between the big five personality traits and academic motivation. *Personality and Individual Differences, 39*, 557–567.

KORNBLUSH, K. (2003, January–February). The parent trap: Working American parents have twenty-two fewer hours a week to spend with their kids than they did thirty years ago. Here's how to help the new "juggler family." *The Atlantic Monthly*, 111–112.

KORTE, S.M., KOOLHAAS, J.M., WINGFIELD, J.C., & McEWEN, B.S. (2005). The Darwinian concept of stress: Benefits of allostasis and costs of allostatic load and the trade-offs in health and disease. *Neuroscience & Biobehavioral Reviews. Special Issue: Individual Differences in Behavior and Physiology: Causes and Consequences, 29*, 3–38.

KOWALSKI, R. M., & LIMBER, S. P. (2007). Electronic bullying among middle school students. *Journal of Adolescent Health, 41*, S22–S30.

KRAAIJ, V., PRUYMBOOM, E., & GARNEFSKI, N. (2002). Cognitive coping and depressive symptoms in the elderly: A longitudinal study. *Aging & Mental Health, 6*, 275–281.

KRAUSE, N. (2005). God-mediated control and psychological well-being in late life. *Research on Aging, 27*, 136–164.

KRAUSE, N. (2006). Exploring the stress-buffering effects of church-based and secular social support on self-rated health in late life. *The Journals of Gerontology, 61*, 35–43.

KRESS, V.E.W., ERIKSEN, K.P., RAYLE, A.D., & FORD, S.J.W. (2005). The DSM-IV-TR and culture: Considerations for counselors. *Journal of Counseling & Development, 83*, 97–104.

KRUGER, J., EPLEY, N., PARKER, J., & NG, Z. (2005). Egocentrism over e-mail: Can we communicate as well as we think? *Journal of Personality and Social Psychology, 89*, 925–936.

KÜBLER-ROSS, E. (1975). *Death*. Englewood Cliffs, NJ: Prentice Hall.

KÜBLER-ROSS, E. (1987). *Working it through*. New York: Macmillan.

KÜBLER-ROSS, E. (1993). *On death and dying*. New York: Collier Books.

KÜBLER-ROSS, E. (1997a). *Death: The final stage of growth*. New York: Simon & Schuster.

KÜBLER-ROSS, E. (1997b). *On death and dying*. New York: Simon & Schuster.

KÜBLER-ROSS, E., & KESSLER, D. (2005). *On grief and grieving: Finding the meaning of grief through the five stages of loss*. New York: Scribner.

KUNKEL, D., EYAL, K., BIELY, E., Cope-FARRAR, K., DONNERSTEIN, E., & FANDRICH, R. (2003). *Sex on TV 3: A biennial report to the Kaiser Family Foundation*. Menlo Park, CA: Kaiser Family Foundation.

KURDEK, L. A. (2005). What do we know about gay and lesbian couples? *Current Directions in Psychological Science, 14*, 251–254.

L'ENGLE, K.L., BROWN, J.D., & KENNEAVY, K. (2006). The mass media are an important context for adolescents' sexual behavior. *Journal of Adolescent Health, 38*, 186–192.

LADD, G.W. (2005). *Children's peer relations and social competence: A century of progress*. New Haven, CT: Yale University Press.

LADISLAV, T. (2007). Identifying core categories of client-identified impact of helpful events in psychotherapy: A qualitative meta-analysis. *Psychotherapy Research, 17,* 310-320.

LAFRANCE, M., HECHT, M.A., & PALUCK, E.L. (2003). The contingent smile: A meta-analysis of sex differences in smiling. *Psychological Bulletin, 129,* 305-334.

LAGERFELD, S. (1999, February). Spending time: Do we have more or less today? *Current,* 10-16.

LAHEY, B.B., VAN HULLE, C.A., KEENAN, K., RATHOUZ, P.J., D'ONOFRIO, B.M., RODGERS, J.L., et al. (2008). Temperament and parenting during the first year of life predict future child conduct problems. *Journal of Abnormal Child Psychology, 36,* 1139-1158.

LAMB, D. (2009, June). Children of the dust. *Smithsonian,* 28-37.

LAMBERT, A.J., PAYNE, B.K., JACOBY, L.L., SHAFFER, L.M., CHASTEEN, A.L., & KHAN, S. (2003). Stereotypes as dominant responses: On the "social facilitation" of prejudice in anticipated public contexts. *Journal of Personality and Social Psychology, 84,* 277-295.

LANCE, L.M. (1998). Gender differences in heterosexual dating: A content analysis of personal ads. *Journal of Men's Studies, 6,* 297-305.

LANDY, S. (2009). *Pathways to competence: Encouraging healthy social and emotional development in young children* (2nd ed.). Baltimore, MD: Paul H. Brookes Publishing.

LANG, F.R., & CARSTENSEN, L.L. (1994). Close emotional relationships in late life: Further support for proactive aging in the social domain. *Psychology and Aging, 9,* 315-324.

LANGLOIS, J.H., KALAKANIS, L., RUBENSTEIN, A.J., LARSON, A., HALLAM, M., & SMOOT, M. (2000). Maxims or myths of beauty: A meta-analytic and theoretical view. *Psychological Bulletin, 126,* 390-423.

LANTZ, A. (2001). Meetings in a distributed group of experts: Comparing face-to-face, chat and collaborative virtual environments. *Behaviour and Information Technology, 20,* 111-117.

LARZELERE, R.E. (2008). Disciplinary spanking: The scientific evidence. *Journal of Developmental & Behavioral Pediatrics, 29,* 334-335.

LARZELERE, R.E., & KUHN, B.R. (2005). Comparing child outcomes of physical punishment and alternative disciplinary tactics: A meta-analysis. *Clinical Child and Family Psychology Review, 8,* 1-37.

LASALA, M. (2002). Walls and bridges: How coupled gay men and lesbians manage their intergeneration relationships. *Journal of Marital and Family Therapy, 28,* 327-339.

LASSER, J., THARINGER, D., & CLOTH, A. (2006). Gay, lesbian, and bisexual youth. In G.G. Bear, & K.M. Minke (Eds.), *Children's needs III: Development, prevention, and intervention* (pp. 419-430). Washington, DC: National Association of School Psychologists.

LAUZEN, M.M., & DOZIER, D.M. (2005). Recognition and respect revisited: Portrayals of age and gender in prime-time television. *Mass Communication and Society, 8,* 241-256.

LAVIE, C.J., MILANI, R.V., & VENTURA, H.O. (2009). Obesity and cardiovascular disease. *Journal of the American College of Cardiology, 53,* 1925-1932.

LAWRENCE, J.A., GOODNOW, J.J., WOODS, K., & KARANTZAS, G. (2002). Distributions of caregiving tasks among family members: The place of gender and availability. *Journal of Family Psychology, 16,* 493-509.

LAZARUS, R.S. (1993). From psychological stress to the emotions: A history of changing outlooks. *Annual Review of Psychology, 44,* 1-21.

LEARY, M.R. (1999). Making sense of self-esteem. *Current Directions in Psychological Science, 10,* 32-35.

LEDGERWOOD, A., & CHAIKEN, S. (2007). Priming us and them: Automatic assimilation and contrast in group attitudes. *Journal of Personality and Social Psychology, 93,* 940-956.

LEIBLUM, S.R. (2004). Gay marriage: Notes from North America. *Sexual and Relationship Therapy, 19,* 361-362.

LEMONICK, M.D. (2003, January 20). The power of mood. *Time. Special Issue,* 62-66.

LENDERKING, W.R. (2005). The psychology of quality of life. *Quality of Life Research: An International Journal of Quality of Life Aspects of Treatment, Care & Rehabilitation, 14,* 1439-1441.

LEPORE, L., & BROWN, R. (2002). The role of awareness: Divergent automatic stereotype activation and implicit judgment correction. *Social Cognition, 20,* 321-351.

LEVINE, R., SATO, S., HASHIMOTO, T., & VERMA, J. (1995). Love and marriage in eleven cultures. *Journal of Cross-Cultural Psychology, 26,* 554-571.

LEVITON, C.D., & LEVITON, P. (2004). What is guided imagery? The cutting-edge process in mind/body medical procedures. *Annuals of the American Psychotherapy Association, 7,* 22-29.

LEVY, B.R., DING, L., LAKRA, D., KOSTEAS, J., & NICCOLAI, L. (2007). Older persons' exclusion from sexually transmitted disease risk-reduction clinical trials. *Sexually Transmitted Disease, 34,* 541-544.

LEWIS, M. (1997). The self in self-conscious emotions. In J. G. Snodgrass, & R. L. Thompson (Eds.), *The self across psychology: Self-recognition, self-awareness, and the self concept.* (pp. 119-142). New York, NY, US: New York Academy of Sciences.

LEWIS, M., & BROOKS-GUNN, J. (1979). *Social cognition and the acquisition of self.* New York: Plenum Press.

LI, L.W. (2005). From caregiving to bereavement: Trajectories of depressive symptoms among wife and daughter caregiver. *Journals of Gerontology: Series B: Psychological Sciences and Social Sciences, 60B,* 190-198.

LIBBY, L.K., EIBACH, R.P., & GILOVICH, T. (2005). Here's looking at me: The effect of memory perspective on assessments of personal change. *Journal of Personality and Social Psychology, 88,* 50-62.

LILIENFELD, S.O. (2007). Psychological treatments that cause harm. *Perspectives on Psychological Science, 2,* 53-70.

LIND, M.R. (2001). An exploration of communication channel usage by gender. *Work Study: A Journal of Productivity Science, 50,* 234-240.

LINDGREN, A. (2002). Career development strategies for workers in their 60s. *Knight Ridder/Tribune News Service,* K4958.

LINDGREN, K.P., PARKHILL, M.R., GEORGE, W.H., & HENDERSHOT, C.S. (2008). Gender differences in perceptions of sexual intent: A qualitative review and integration. *Psychology of Women Quarterly, 32,* 423-439.

LINDSTROM, T.C. (1995). Anxiety and adaptation in bereavement. *Anxiety, Stress, and Coping: An International Journal, 8,* 251-261.

LING, K., BEENEN, G., LUDFORD, P., WANG, X., CHANG, K., & LI, X., et al. (2005). Using social psychology to motivate contributions to online communities. *Journal of Computer-Mediated Communication, 10,* (article 10).

LINLEY, P.A., & JOSEPH, S. (2004). Positive change following trauma and adversity: A review. *Journal of Traumatic Stress, 17,* 11-21.

LIPPKE, S., & ZIEGELMANN, J.P. (2006). Understanding and modeling health behavior: The multi-stage model of health behavior change. *Journal of Health Psychology, 11,* 37-50.

LITTLE, A.C., BURT, D.M., & PERRETT, D.I. (2006). Assortative mating for perceived facial personality traits. *Personality and Individual Differences, 40,* 973-984.

LIU, Y., & YUSSEN, S.R. (2005). A comparison of perceived control beliefs between Chinese and American students. *International Journal of Behavioral Development, 29,* 14-23.

LI-VOLLMER, M. (2002). Race representation in child-targeted television commercials. *Mass Communications & Society, 5,* 207-228.

LLERAS, C. (2008). Employment, work conditions, and the home environment in single-mother families. *Journal of Family Issues, 29,* 1268-1297.

LOCKWOOD, P., JORDAN, C.H., & KUNDA, Z. (2002). Motivation by positive or negative role models: Regulatory focus determines who will best inspire us. *Journal of Personality and Social Psychology, 83,* 854-864.

LOFSHULT, D. (2006). Caloric restriction is for the birds. *IDEA Fitness Journal, 3,* 79-80.

LOPES, P.N., BRACKETT, M.A., NEZLEK, J.B., SCHÜTZ, A., SELLIN, I., & SALOVEY, P. (2004). Emotional intelligence and social interaction. *Personality and Social Psychology Bulletin, 30,* 1018-1034.

LUBORSKY, L., & BARRETT, M.S. (2006). The history of empirical status of key psychoanalytic concepts. *Annual Review of Clinical Psychology, 2,* 1-19.

LUBORSKY, L., ROSENTHAL, R., DIGUER, L., ANDRUSYNA, T.P., LEVITT, J.T., SELIGMAN, D.A., BERMAN, J.S., & KRAUSE, E.D. (2003). Are some psychotherapies much more effective than others? *Journal of Applied Psychoanalytic Studies, 54,* 455-460.

LUCAS, R.E. (2005). Time does not heal all wounds: A longitudinal study of reaction and adaptation to divorce. *Psychological Science, 16,* 945-950.

LUCAS, T.W., WENDORF, C.A., IMAMOGLU, E.O., SHEN, J., PARKHILL, M.R., & WEISFELD, C.C., et al. (2004). Marital satisfaction in four cultures as a function of homogamy, male dominance and female attractiveness. *Sexualities, Evolution & Gender, 6,* 97-130.

LUCE, M.F. (2005). Decision making as coping. *Health Psychology. Special Issue: Basic and Applied Decision Making in Cancer Control, 24,* S23-S28.

Luszczynska, A., Benight, C.C., & Cieslak, R. (2009). Self-efficacy and health-related outcomes of collective trauma: A systematic review. *European Psychologist, 14,* 51–62.

Luszczynska, A., Scholz, U., & Schwarzer, R. (2005). The general self-efficacy scale: Multicultural validation studies. *Journal of Psychology: Interdisciplinary and Applied, 139,* 439–457.

Lyons, J.B., & Schneider, T.R. (2005). The influence of emotional intelligence on performance. *Personality and Individual Differences, 39,* 693–703.

Lyubomirsky, S., Sheldon, K.M., & Schkade, D. (2005). Pursuing happiness: The architecture of sustainable change. *Review of General Psychology. Special Issue: Positive Psychology, 9,* 111–131.

Ma, Y., & Qin, H. (2009). Regular and frequent sexual intercourse for elderly men could preserve erectile function. *Medical Hyphotheses, 72,* 370.

MacGeorge, E.L., Samter, W., & Gillihan, S.J. (2005). Academic stress, supportive communication, and health. *Communication Education, 54,* 365–372.

Maciejewski, P.K., Zhang, B., Block, S.D., & Prigerson, H.G. (2007). An empirical examination of the stage theory of grief. *Journal of the American Medical Association, 297,* 716–723.

MacKay, K.A., & Kuh, G.D. (1994). A comparison of student effort and educational gains of Caucasian and African-American students at predominantly white colleges and universities. *Journal of College Student Development, 35,* 217–223.

Mackie, D.M., Devos, T., & Smith, E.R. (2000). Intergroup emotions: Explaining offensive action tendencies in an intergroup context. *Journal of Personality and Social Psychology, 79,* 602–616.

MacNab, B., MacLean, J., Brislin, R., Aguilera, G.M., Worthley, R., Ravlin, E., Galperin, B. L., Tiessen, J. H., Jenner, S., Bess, D. Lituchy, T. R., & Turcotte, M. F. (2007). Culture and ethics management: Whistle-blowing and internal reporting within a NAFTA country context. *International Journal of Cross Cultural Management, 7,* 5–28.

Macneil, C.A., Hasty, M.K., Evans, M., Redlich, C., & Berk, M. (2009). The therapeutic alliance: Is it necessary or sufficient to engender positive outcomes? *Acta Neuropsychiatrica, 21,* 95–98.

Maddi, S.R. (2005). On hardiness and other pathways to resilience. *American Psychologist, 60,* 261–262.

Maher, B. (2003, January). Patching up the American family. *The World and I,* 56–58.

Main, M., & Solomon, J. (1990). Procedures for identifying infants as disorganized/disoriented during the Ainsworth strange situation. In M.T. Greenberg, D. Cicchetti, & E.M. Cummings (Eds.), *Attachment in the preschool years: Theory, research, and intervention.* (pp. 121–160). Chicago: University of Chicago Press.

Major, B., & Eccleston, C.P. (2005). Stigma and social exclusion. In D. Abrams, M.A. Hogg, & J.M. Marques (Eds.), *The social psychology of inclusion and exclusion* (pp. 63–87). New York: Psychology Press.

Major, B., Kaiser, C.R., & McCoy, S.K. (2003). It's not my fault: When and why attributions to prejudice protect self-esteem. *Personality and Social Psychology Bulletin, 29,* 772–781.

Mallikarjun, P. (2005, February). Understanding seasonal affective disorder. *The Practitioner, 249,* 116–124.

Malmberg, J., Miilunpalo, S., Pasanen, M., Vuori, I., & Oja, P. (2005). Characteristics of leisure time physical activity associated with risk of decline in perceived health—A 10-year follow-up of middle-aged and elderly men and women. *Preventive Medicine: An International Journal Devoted to Practice and Theory, 41,* 141–150.

Mandal, B., & Roe, B. (2008). Job loss, retirement and the mental health of older Americans. *Journal of Mental Health Policy and Economics, 11,* 167–176.

Mandell, B., & Pherwani, S. (2003). Relationship between emotional intelligence and transformational leadership style: A gender comparison. *Journal of Business and Psychology, 17,* 387–404.

Manger, T., Eikeland, O.J., & Asbjornsen, A. (2002). Effects of social-cognitive training on students; locus of control. *School Psychology International, 23,* 342–354.

Mansfield, A.K., Addis, M.E., & Courtenay, W. (2005). Measurement of men's help seeking: Development and evaluation of the barriers to help seeking scale. *Psychology of Men & Masculinity, 6,* 95–108.

Marano, H.E. (2005). What's a shy guy to do? *Psychology Today, 38,* 14.

Marazziti, D., Di Nasso, E., Masala, I., Baroni, S., Abelli, M., & Mengali, F., et al. (2003). Normal and obsessional jealousy: A study of a population of young adults. *European Psychiatry, 18,* 106–111.

Marcus, B. (1999). The efficacy of exercise as an aid for smoking cessation in women: A randomized, controlled study. *Archives of Internal Medicine, 159,* 1229–1234.

Markus, H., & Kitayama, S. (1991). Culture and the self: Implications for cognition, emotion, and motivation. *Psychological Review, 98,* 224–253.

Markus, H.R., & Kitayama, S. (2003). Culture, self, and the reality of the social. *Psychological Inquiry, 14,* 277–283.

Marques, J., Abrams, D., & Serodio, R.G. (2001). Being better by being right: Subjective group dynamics and derogation of in-group deviants when generic norms are undermined. *Journal of Personality and Social Psychology, 81,* 436–477.

Marshall, R.D., Bryant, R.A., Amsel, L., Suh, E.J., Cook, J.M., & Nerial, Y. (2007). The psychology of ongoing threat: Relative risk appraisal, the September 11th attacks, and terrorism-related fear. *American Psychologist, 62,* 304–316.

Martin, M. (1999). *Work and family: Today's juggling act.* http://www.uwyo.edu/CES/County_Info/Teton/News?feb99.htm.

Martin, R.A. (2001). Humor, laughter, and physical health: Methodological issues and research. *Psychological Bulletin, 127,* 504–519.

Martsch, M.D. (2005). A comparison of two group interventions for adolescent aggression: High process versus low process. *Research on Social Work Practice, 15,* 8–18.

Marzillier, S.L., & Davey, G.C.L. (2004). The emotional profiling of disgust-eliciting stimuli: Evidence for primary and complex disgusts. *Cognition & Emotion, 18,* 313–336.

Masche, J. G. (2008). Reciprocal influences between developmental transitions and parent-child relationships in young adulthood. *International Journal of Behavioral Development, 32,* 401–411.

Maslach, C., Schaufeli, W.B., & Leiter, M.P. (2001). Job burnout. *Annual Review of Psychology, 52,* 397–422.

Maslow, A.H. (1968). *Toward a psychology of being* (2nd ed.). New York: Van Nostrand Reinhold.

Maslow, A.H. (1971). *The farther reaches of human nature.* New York: Viking.

Mason, W.A., Conrey, F.R., & Smith, E.R. (2007). Situating influence processes: Dynamic, multidirectional flows of influence within networks. *Personality and Social Psychology Review, 11,* 279–300.

Masters, W., & Johnson, V. (1966). *Human sexual response.* Boston: Little, Brown.

Masters, W., & Johnson, V. (1979). *Homosexuality in perspective.* Boston: Little, Brown.

Masters, W.H., Johnson, V.E., & Kolodny, R.C. (1988). *Human sexuality* (3rd ed.). Boston: Little, Brown.

Masters, W.H., Johnson, V.E., & Kolodny, R.C. (1995). *Human sexuality.* New York: HarperCollins.

Mather, M., & Adams, D. (2007). The crossover in female-male college enrollment rates. Retrieved June 5, 2009, from http://www.prb.org/Articles/2007/CrossoverinFemaleMaleCollegeEnrollmentRates.aspx.

Mather, M., & Carstensen, L.L. (2005). Aging and motivated cognition: The positivity effect in attention and memory. *Trends in Cognitive Sciences, 9,* 496–502.

Matjasko, J.L., & Feldman, A.F. (2006). Bringing work home: The emotional experiences of mothers and fathers. *Journal of Family Psychology, 20,* 47–55.

Matlin, M.W. (1999). *Psychology.* Fort Worth, TX: Harcourt Brace.

Matsumoto, D. (2000). *Culture and psychology.* Pacific Grove, CA: Brooks/Cole.

Matsumoto, D. (2002). Methodological requirements to test a possible ingroup advantage in judging emotions across cultures: Comments on Elfenbein and Ambady and evidence. *Psychological Bulletin, 128,* 236–342.

Matsumoto, D. (2003). The discrepancy between consensual-level culture and individual-level culture. *Culture & Psychology, 9,* 89–95.

Matsumoto, D. (2004). Paul Ekman and the legacy of universals. *Journal of Research in Personality, 38,* 45–51.

Matsumoto, D. (2007). Culture, context, and behavior. *Journal of Personality, 75,* 1285–1320.

Matthews, K.A., Raikkonen, K., Sutton-Tyrrell, K., & Kuller, L.H. (2004). Optimistic attitudes protect against progression of carotid atherosclerosis in healthy middle-aged women. *Psychosomatic Medicine, 66,* 640–644.

Matud, P.M. (2004). Gender differences in stress and coping styles. *Personality and Individual Differences, 37,* 1401–1415.

MAU, W.C., & KOPISCHKE, A. (2001). Job search methods, job search outcomes, and job satisfaction of college graduates: A comparison of race and sex. *Journal of Employment Counseling, 38,* 141–149.

Mayo Clinic. (2002, September 4). *Women and depression: Understanding the gender gap.* http://www.mayoclinic.com.

Mayo Clinic. (2005). *Obesity.* Retrieved August 7, 2006, from http://www.mayoclinic.com/health/obesity/d500314.

MAYSELESS, O., & POPPER, M. (2007). Reliance on leaders and social institutions: An attachment perspective. *Attachment & Human Development, 9,* 73–93.

MCCABE, M.P. (2005). Boys want sex, girls want commitment: Does this trade-off still exist? *Sexual and Relationship Therapy, 20,* 139–141.

MCCARTHY, B., & MCCARTHY, E. (2009). *Discovering your couple sexual style: Sharing desire, pleasure, and satisfaction.* New York: Routledge/Taylor & Francis Group.

MCCONATHA, J.T., LIGHTNER, E., & DEANER, S.L. (1994). Culture, age, and gender as variables in expression of emotions. *Journal of Social Behavior and Personality, 9,* 481–488.

MCCONNELL, A.R., RENAUD, J.M., DEAN, K.K., GREEN, S.P., LAMOREAUX, M.J., & HALL, C.E., et al. (2005). Whose self is it anyway? Self-aspect control moderates the relation between self-complexity and well-being. *Journal of Experimental Social Psychology, 41,* 1–18.

MCCRAE, R.R., & COSTA, P.T. (1994). The stability of personality: Observations and evaluations. *Current Directions in Psychological Science, 5,* 173–175.

MCCRAE, R. R., & COSTA, P.T. (2003). *Personality in adulthood: A five-factor theory.* New York: Guilford Press.

MCDONALD-MISZCZAK, L., MAKI, S.A., & GOULD, O.N. (2000). Self-reported medication adherence and health status in late adulthood: The role of beliefs. *Experimental Aging Research, 26,* 189–207.

MCEWEN, B.S. (2005). Stressed or stressed out: What is the difference? *Journal of Psychiatry & Neuroscience, 30,* 315–318.

MCFARLAND, B.H. (2005). Introduction: Disaster dangers and decisions. *Community Mental Health Journal, 41,* 631–632.

MCGILLIS, D. (1997). *Community mediation programs: Developments and challenges.* Washington, DC: U.S. Department of Justice.

MCGREW, J.F., BILOTTA, J.G., & DEENEY, J.M. (1999). Software team formation and decay: Extending the standard model for small groups. *Small Group Research, 30,* 209–234.

MCGUE, M. (1999). The behavioral genetics of alcoholism. *Current Directions in Psychological Science, 8,* 109–115.

MCGUIRE, K.M.B., GREENBERG, M.A., & GEVIRTZ, R. (2005). Autonomic effects of expressive writing in individuals with elevated blood pressure. *Journal of Health Psychology. Special Issue: Psychological Interventions in Chronic Illness, 10,* 197–209.

MCNALLY, R.J., BRYANT, R.A., & EHLERS, A. (2003). Does early psychological intervention promote recovery from posttraumatic stress? *Psychological Science in the Public Interest, 4,* 45–79.

MEAGHER, D. (2007). How we die: Theory vs. Reality. *Death Studies,* 31, 266–270.

MEANA, M., & NUNNINK, S.E. (2006). Gender differences in the content of cognitive distraction during sex. *Journal of Sex Research. Special Issue: Scientific Abstracts, World Congress of Sexology 2005, 43,* 59–67.

MEDIATE, R., & FEINSTEIN, J. (2009). *Are you kidding me?: The story of Rocco Mediate's extraordinary battle with Tiger Woods at the US open.* New York: Little, Brown and Company.

MEHRA, B., MERKEL, C., & BISHOP, A.P. (2004). The internet for empowerment of minority and marginalized users. *New Media & Society, 6,* 781–802.

MEIJER, W.A., de GROOT, R.H.M., van GERVEN, P.W.M., van BOXTEL, M.P.J., & JOLLES, J. (2009). Level of processing and reaction time in young and middle-aged adults and the effect of education. *European Journal of Cognitive Psychology, 21,* 216–234.

MEINS, E. (1998). The effects of security of attachment and maternal attribution of meaning on children's linguistic acquisitional style. *Infant Behavior & Development, 21*(2), 237–252.

MEISSNER, W.W. (2007). Therapeutic alliance: Theme and variations, *Psychoanalytic Psychology,* 24, 231–254.

MEISSNER, W.W. (2008). Reply to commentary by M.H. Spero. *Psychoanalytic Psychology,* 25, 197–199.

MELLOR, D., HAYASHI, Y., FIRTH, L., STOKES, M., CHAMBERS, S., & CUMMINS, R. (2008). Volunteering and well-being: do self-esteem, optimism, and perceived control mediate the relationship? *Journal of Social Service Research, 34,* 61–70.

MENEC, V.H. (2003). The relation between everyday activities and successful aging: A 6–year longitudinal study. *The Journals of Gerontology, Series B, Psychological Sciences and Social Sciences, 58,* 74–83.

Mental Health Weekly. (2002). Caregivers at increased risk for depression, anxiety, *12,* 7.

Mentalhelp.net. (2000a, August). *Anxiety.* http://anxiety/anxietytoc.htm.

Mentalhelp.net. (2005). *Depression and women.* http://mentalhelp.net/poc/view_doc.php?type=doc&id=7983&cn=5. Accessed April 3, 2007.

Mentalhelp.net. (2010). *Women at greater risk for mental health problems.* http://www.mentalhelp.net/poc/view_doc.php?type=doc&&id=128&&cn=0&&clnt=clnt00001&&.

MESSMAN, S.J., CANARY, D.J., & HAUSE, K.S. (2000). Motives to remain platonic, equity, and the use of maintenance strategies in opposite-sex friendships. *Journal of Social and Personal Relationships, 17,* 67–94.

MEYER, D. (2006). Technology, job satisfaction, and retention: Rural mental health practitioners. *Journal of Rural Health, 22,* 158–163.

MEZULIS, A.H., ABRAMSON, L.Y., HYDE, J.S., & HANKIN, B.L. (2004). Is there a universal positivity bias in attributions? A meta-analytic review of individual, developmental, and cultural differences in the self-serving attributional bias. *Psychological Bulletin, 130,* 711–747.

MICHAEL, S., & SNYDER, C.R. (2005). Getting unstuck: The roles of hope, finding meaning, and rumination in adjustment to bereavement among college students. *Death Studies, 29,* 435–458.

MICHALOS, A.C. (1991). *Global report on student well-being (Vol. 1): Life satisfaction and happiness.* New York: Springer-Verlag.

MILGRAM, S. (1974). Obedience to authority. *Human Relations, 18,* 57–76.

MILLER, G.E., & WROSCH, C. (2007). You gotta know when to fold 'em: Goal disengagement and systemic inflammation in adolescence. *Psychological Science, 18,* 773–777.

MILLER, J.G. (1999). Cultural psychology: Implications for basic psychological theory. *Psychological Science, 10,* 85–91.

MILLER, J.K. (2008). Walk-in single session team therapy: A study of client satisfaction. *Journal of Systemic Therapies, 27,* 78–94.

MISRA, R., McKEAN, M., WEST, S., & RUSSO, T. (2000). Academic stress of college students: Comparison of student and faculty perceptions. *College Student Journal, 34,* 236–245.

MITCHELL, T. (2003, September 5–7). After 9/11. *USA Weekend,* 4.

MOEN, P., & ROEHLING, P. (2005) *The career mystique: Cracks in the American Dream.* Lanham, MD: Rowman & Littlefield.

MOHAN, J. (2006). Cardiac psychology. *Journal of the Indian Academy of Applied Psychology. Special Issue: Commemoration of the 10th International and 41st National Conference of IAAP, 32,* 214–220.

MOHR, R.D., & ZOGHI, C. (2006). Is job enrichment really enriching? Retrieved August 09, 2006, from bls.gov/ore/pdf/ec060010.pdf.

MONK, T.H., HOUCK, P.R., & SHEAR, M.K. (2006). The daily life of complicated grief patients—What gets missed, what gets added? *Death Studies, 30,* 77–85.

MONROE, S.M. (2008). Modern approaches to conceptualizing and measuring human life stress. *Annual Review of Clinical Psychology, 4,* 33–52.

MONROE, S.M., & REID, M.W. (2009). Life stress and major depression. *Current Directions in Psychological Science, 18,* 68–72.

MONTGOMERY, L.M. (2004). 'It's just what I like': Explaining persistent patterns of gender stratification in the life choices of college students. *International Journal of Qualitative Studies in Education. Special Issue: Conceptualizing Higher Education Students as Social Actors in a Globalizing World, 17,* 785–802.

MOORE, N. B., & DAVIDSON, J. K., SR. (2000). Communicating with new sex partners: College women and questions that make a difference. *Journal of Sex & Marital Therapy, 26*(3), 215–230.

MORAHAN-MARTIN, J.M. (2004). How internet users find, evaluate, and use online health information: A cross-cultural review. *CyberPsychology & Behavior, 7,* 497–510.

MOREAU, D. (2002, November). Payday: Sooner or later? *AARP Bulletin,* 26.

MORITSUGU, J., WONG, F.Y., & DUFFY, K.G. (2010), *Community psychology,* Boston, MA: Allyn & Bacon.

MORRIS, J.A., BROTHERIDGE, C.M., & URBANSKI, J.C. (2005). Bringing humility to leadership: Antecedents and consequences of leader humility. *Human Relations, 58,* 1323–1350.

MORRY, M.M. (2005). Allocentrism and friendship satisfaction: The mediating roles of disclosure and closeness. *Canadian Journal of Behavioural Science, 37,* 211–222.

MORRY, M.M., & GAINES, S.O. (2005). Relationship satisfaction as a predictor of similarity ratings: A test of the attraction-similarity hypothesis. *Journal of Social and Personal Relationships, 22,* 561–584.

MOTSCHNIG-PITRIK, R., & LUX, M. (2008). The person-centered approach meets neuroscience: Mutual support for C. R. Roger's and A. Damasio's theories. *Journal of Humanistic Psychology, 48,* 287–319.

MOYERS, T.B., MARTIN, T., CHRISTOPHER, PAULETTE, J., HOUCK, J.M., TONIGAN, J.S., & AMRHEIN, P.C. (2007). Client language as a mediator of motivational interviewing efficacy: Where is the evidence? *Alcoholism: Clinical and Experimental Research, 31,* 405–475.

MROCZEK, D.K., & SPIRO, A., III. (2005). Change in life satisfaction during adulthood: Findings from the Veterans Affairs normative aging study. *Journal of Personality and Social Psychology, 88,* 189–202.

MULAK, A., ERLANDSON, K.T., FARRER, J.W., HALLETT, J.S., MOLLOY, J.L., & PRESCOTT, M.E. (1998). "Un-huh. What's that all about?" Differing interpretations of conversational backchannels and questions as sources of miscommunication across gender boundaries. *Communication Research. Special Issue: (Mis)communicating Across Boundaries, 25,* 641–688.

MURRAY, S.L. (2005). Regulating the risks of closeness: A relationship-specific sense of felt security. *Current Directions in Psychological Science, 14,* 74–78.

MURRAY, S.L., HOLMES, J.G., & GRIFFIN, D.W. (2000). Self-esteem and the quest for felt security: How perceived regard regulates attachment processes. *Journal of Personality and Social Psychology, 78,* 478–498.

MUSGRAVE, C. (1997). The near-death experience: A study of spiritual transformation. *Journal of Near Death Studies, 15,* 187–201.

MYERS, D.G. (1993). *The pursuit of happiness.* New York: Avon Books.

MYERS, D.G. (1998). *Social psychology.* New York: McGraw-Hill.

MYERS, D.G., & ARENSON, S.J. (1972). Enhancement of dominant risk tendencies in group discussion. *Psychological Reports, 30,* 615–623.

MYERS, D.G., & DIENER, E. (1995). Who is happy? *Psychological Science, 6,* 10–19.

NAIL, P.R., MISAK, J.E., & DAVIS, R.M. (2004). Self-affirmation versus self-consistency: A comparison of two competing self-theories of dissonance phenomena. *Personality and Individual Differences, 36,* 1893–1905.

NAIR, E. (2001). The emperor has no clothes, or do you see individualist-collectivist societies? *International Psychology Reporter,* 18–20.

NAPLES, N.A. (2004). Queer parenting in the new millennium. *Gender & Society, 18,* 679–684.

NATHAN, P.E. (2007). Efficacy, effectiveness, and the clinical utility of psychotherapy research. In Hofmann, S. G. & Weinberger, J. (Eds.), *The art and science of psychotherapy.* New York: Routledge.

National Alliance on Mental Illness. (2006). *Grading the states: A report on America's health care system. National Alliance for the Mentally Ill.* http://www.nami.org/template.cfm?template=/contentManagement/contentDisplay.cfm&contentID=31181.

National Center for Chronic Disease Prevention and Health Promotion. (1999). *Physical activity and health: A report of the Surgeon General.* http://www.cdc.gov/nccdphp/sgr/summary.htm.

National Center for Chronic Disease Prevention and Health Promotion. (2000). *Statistics related to overweight and obesity.* http://www.niddk.nih.gov/health/nutrit/pubs/statobes.htm.

National Center for Chronic Disease Prevention and Health Promotion. (2005). *Adult cigarette smoking in the U.S.: Current estimates.* Washington, DC: Centers for Disease Control.

National Center for Health Statistics. (2002). *Environmental health.* http://www.cdc.gov/nchs/fastats/environ.htm.

National Center for Health Statistics. (2005). National health and nutrition examination survey. Retrieved August 7, 2006, from http://www.cdc.gov/nchs/nhanes.htm.

National Center for Health Statistics. (2006). Leading Causes of death: Number of deaths for leading causes of death. www.cdc.gov/nchs/fastats/lcod.htm.

National Center for Missing and Exploited Children. (2006). Child pornography—What is it? Retrieved May 11, 2006, from http://www.cybertipline.com/missingkids/servlet/pageservlet.

National Coalition Against Domestic Violence (NCADV). (2005). *The problem.* NCADV.org.learn/the problem-100.html.

National Family Caregivers Association. (2005). *Caregiving statistics.* Retrieved August 12, 2006, from http://www.Thefamilycaregiver.org.

National Institute of Diabetes and Digestive and Kidney Diseases. (2000). Statistics related to overweight and obesity. http://www.niddk.nih.gov/health/nutritlpubs/statobes.htm.

National Institute of Mental Health. (2001). *Facts about post-traumatic stress disorder.* Washington, DC: Author.

National Institute of Mental Health. (2002, September). *Depression.* http://www.nimh.nih.gov/publicat/depression.cfm.

National Institute of Mental Health. (2003). *Suicide facts.* http://www.nimh.nih.gov/research/suifact.htm.

National Institute of Mental Health. (2006a). *Depression: Diagnostic evaluation and treatment.* Retrieved July 06, 2006, from http://www.nimh.nih.gov/publicat.depression.cfm.

National Institute of Mental Health. (2006b). *Eating disorders: Facts about eating disorders and the search for solutions.* Retrieved July 05, 2006, from http://www.nimh.nih.gov/publicat/eatingdisorders.cfm.

National Institute of Mental Health. (2006c). *Medications: Antianxiety medications.* Retrieved July 06, 2006, from http://www.nimh.nih.gov/publicat/medicate.cfm.

National Institute of Mental Health. (2006d). *Mental disorders in America.* Retrieved July 2, 2006, from http://www.nimh.nih.gov/publicat/numbers.cfm.

National Institute of Mental Health. (2006e). *Reliving trauma: Post-traumatic stress disorder.* Retrieved July 05, 2006, from http://www.nimh.nih.gov/publicat/reliving.cfm.

National Institute of Mental Health. (2006f). *When someone has schizophrenia.* Retrieved July 05, 2006, from http://www.nimh.nih.gov/publicat/schizosoms.cfm.

National Institute of Mental Health. (2006g). *Women hold up half the sky: Women and mental health research.* Retrieved July 02, 2006, from http://www.nimh.nih.gov/publicat/womensoms.cfm.

National Institute of Mental Health. (2007a, January 17). *Science Update: U.S.-born children of immigrants may have higher risk for mental disorders than parents.* www.nimh.nih.gov/science-news/2007/us-born-children-of-immigrants-may-have-higher-risk-for-mental-disorders-than-parents. Retrieved June 8, 2009.

National Institute of Mental Health. (2007b, February 9). *Science Update: Study tracks prevalence of eating disorders.* www.nimh.nih.gov/science-news/2007/study-tracks-prevalence-of-eating-disorders. Retrieved June 8, 2009.

National Institute of Mental Health. (2007c, October 16). *Science Update: National survey tracks prevalence of personality disorders in U.S. Population.* www.nimh.nih.gov/science-news/2007/hational-survey-tracks-prevalence-of-personality-disorders-in-US-population.

National Institute of Mental Health. (2008a, May 7). *Science Update: Mental disorders cost society billions in unearned income.* www.nimh.nih.gov/science-news/mental-disorders-cost-billions-in-unearned-income. Retrieved June 8, 2009.

National Institute of Mental Health. (2008b, December 24). *Science Update: Study probes environment-triggered genetic changes in schizophrenia.* www.nimh.nih.gov/science-news/2008/study-probes-environment-triggered-genetic-changes-in-schizophrenia. Retrieved June 8, 2009.

National Institute of Mental Health. (2009, April 10). *Science Update: Black teens, especially girls, at high risk for suicide attempts.* www.nimn.nih.gov/science-news/2009/black-teen-especially-girls-at-high-risk-for-suicide. Retrieved June 8, 2009.

National Institute of Mental Health. (2009a). *How is depression detected and treated: Electroconvulsive therapy.* www.nimh.nih.gov/health/publications/depression/how-is-depression-detected-and-treated.shtml. Retrieved June 10, 2009.

National Institute of Mental Health. (2009b). *Treatment of anxiety disorders: - Cognitive behavioral therapy.* www.nimh.nih.gov/health/publications/anxiety-disorders/treatment-of-anxiety-disorders.shtml. Retrieved June 10, 2009.

National Institute of Mental Health (2009c). *Treatment of anxiety disorders: Medications.* www.nimh.nih.gov/health/publications/anxiety/treatment-of-anxiety-disorders.shtml.

National Institutes of Health. (2000). *Obesity: The practical guide: Identification, evaluation, and treatment of overweight and obesity in adults.* Washington, DC: National Institutes of Health.

National Mental Health Information Center. (2003). *The myth of the bad parent.* http://www.mentalhealth.org/publications/allpubs/Ca-0035/default.asp.

National Science Foundation. (2003). *Science and technology: Public attitudes and public understanding.* http://www.nsf.gov/sbe/srs/seind02/c7/c7h.htm.

NEFF, K.D. (2003). Self-compassion: An alternative conceptualization of a healthy attitude toward oneself. *Self and Identity, 2,* 85–101.

NEFF, L. A., & KARNEY, B. R. (2005). To know you is to love you: The implications of global adoration and specific accuracy for marital relationships. *Journal of Personality and Social Psychology, 88*(3), 480–497.

NEILI, R.K. (2008). Diversity's discontents: the "contact hypothesis" exploded. *Academic Questions, 21,* 409–430.

NELSON, C.A. (2006). Of eggshells and thin-skulls: A consideration of racism-related mental illness impacting Black women. *International Journal of Law and Psychiatry, 29,* 112–136.

NEMEROFF, C.B., BREMNER, J.D., FOA, E.B., MAYBERG, H.S., NORTH, C.S., & STEIN, M.B. (2006). Posttraumatic stress disorder: A state-of-the-science review. *Journal of Psychiatric Research, 40,* 1–21.

NESTER, S., BLANK, H., & von COLLIANI, G. (2008). Hindsight bias and causal attribution: A causal model theory of creeping determinism. *Social Psychology, 39,* 182–188.

NEUGARTEN, G.L. (1986). The aging society. In A. Pifer & L. Bronte (Eds.), *Our aging society.* New York: W. W. Norton.

NEUMARK-SZTAINER, D.R., WALL, M.M., HAINES, J.I., STORY, M.T., SHERWOOD, N.E. & VAN DEN BERG, P.A. (2007). Shared risk and protective factors for overweight and disordered eating in adolescents. *American Journal of Preventive Medicine, 33,* 359–369.

NEWMAN, M.G. (2004). Technology in psychotherapy: An introduction. *Journal of Clinical Psychology, 60,* 141–145.

NIELSEN, K., RANDALL, R., YARKER, J., & BRENNER, S. (2008). The effects of transformational leadership on followers' perceived work characteristics and psychological well-being: A longitudinal study. *Work & Stress, 22,* 16–32.

NIELSEN, M., SUDDENDORF, T., & SLAUGHTER, V. (2006). Mirror self-recognition beyond the face. *Child Development, 77*(1), 176–185.

NIETZEL, M.T., BERNSTEIN, D.A., & MILICH, R. (1991). *Introduction to clinical psychology.* Englewood Cliffs, NJ: Prentice Hall.

NIEUWENHUIZEN, A.G., & RUTTERS, F. (2008). The hypothalamic-pituitary-adrenal-axis in the regulation of energy balance. *Physiology & Behavior, 94,* 169–177.

NILSSON, L.G. (2008). Efficacy of the third wave of behavioral therapies: A systemic review and meta-analysis. *Behaviour Research and Therapy, 46,* 296–321.

NISHINA, A., JUVONEN, J., & WITKOW, M.R. (2005). Sticks and stones may break my bones, but names will make me feel sick: The psychosocial, somatic, and scholastic consequences of peer harassment. *Journal of Clinical Child and Adolescent Psychology, 34,* 37–48.

NOLEN-HOEKSEMA, N., PARKER, L.E., & LARSON, J. (1994). Ruminative coping with depressed mood following loss. *Journal of Personality and Social Psychology, 67,* 92–104.

NORRIS, J., STONER, S.A., HESSLER, D.M., ZAWACKI, T., DAVIS, K.C., GEORGE, W.H., et al. (2009). Influences of sexual sensation seeking, alcohol consumption, and sexual arousal on women's behavioral intentions related to having unprotected sex. *Psychology of Addictive Behaviors, 23,* 14–22.

NORTHEY, W.F. (2009). Effectiveness research: A view from the USA. *Journal of Family Therapy, 31,* 75–84.

NORUM, D. (2000). The family has the solution. *Journal of Systemic Therapies, 19,* 3–15.

O'CONNOR, D. (2008). *Arnie & Jack: Palmer, Nicklaus, and golf's greatest rivalry.* Boston, MA: Houghton Mifflin.

O'CONNOR, D.B., & SHIMIZU, M. (2002). Sense of personal control, stress and coping style: A cross-cultural study. *Stress and Health, 18,* 173–183.

O'DONOHUE, W., BUCHANAN, J.A., & FISHER, J.E. (2000). Characteristics of empirically supported treatments. *Journal of Psychotherapy Practice and Research, 9,* 69–74.

O'REILLY, K.B. (2009). Defective directives? *American Medical News, 52,* 7–9.

OETZEL, J.G., & TING-TOOMEY, S. (2003). Face concerns in interpersonal conflict: A cross-cultural empirical test of the face negotiation theory. *Communication Research, 30,* 599–624.

Office of the Surgeon General. (1999). *The Surgeon General's call to action to prevent suicide.* Washington, DC: Author.

OGDEN, C.L., CARROLL, M.D., CURTIN, L.R., McDOWELL, M.A., TABAK, C.J., & FLEGAL, K.M. (2006). Prevalence of overweight and obesity in the United States, 1999–2004. *Journal of the American Medical Association, 295,* 1549–1555.

OHTAKI, S., OHTAKI, T., & FETTERS, M.D. (2003). Doctor-patient communication: A comparison of the USA and Japan. *Family Practice, 20,* 276–282.

OISHI, S., HAHN, J., SCHIMMACK, U., RADHAKRISHAN, P., DZOKOTO, V., & AHADI, S. (2005). The measurement of values across cultures: A pairwise comparison approach. *Journal of Research in Personality, 39,* 299–305.

OLFSON, M., MARCUS, S.C., DRUSS, B., & PINCUS, H.A. (2002). National trends in the use of outpatient psychotherapy. *The American Journal of Psychiatry, 159,* 1914–1920.

OLSON, I.R., & MARSHUETZ, C. (2005). Facial attractiveness is appraised in a glance. *Emotion, 5,* 498–502.

ONG, A.D., BERGEMAN, C.S., & BISCONTI, T.L. (2005). Unique effects of daily perceived control on anxiety symptomatology during conjugal bereavement. *Personality and Individual Differences, 38,* 1057–1067.

ORANGE, L.M., & BRODWIN, M.G. (2005). Childhood sexual abuse: What rehabilitation counselors need to know. *The Journal of Rehabilitation, 71,* 5–11.

ORTIZ, S.Y., & ROSCIGNO, V.J. (2009). Discrimination, women, and work: Processes and variations by race and class. *Sociological Quarterly, 50,* 336–359.

OSBORNE, L. (2001, May 6). Regional disturbances. *The New York Times Magazine, 6.*

OSGOOD, C.E. (1962). *An alternative to war or surrender.* Urbana, IL: University of Illinois Press.

OSTBYTE, T., & TAYLOR, D.H., JR. (2004). The effect of smoking on years of healthy life lost among middle-aged and older Americans. *Health Services Research, 39,* 531–551.

OSTERBERG, L., & BLASCHKE, T. (2005). Drug therapy: Adherence to medication. *New England Journal of Medicine, 353,* 487–497.

OSWALD, D.L., & CLARK, E.M. (2003). Best friends forever?: High school best friendships and the transition to college. *Personal Relationships, 10,* 187–196.

OSWALD, R.F. (2000). Family friendship relationships after young women come out as bisexual or lesbian. *Journal of Homosexuality, 38,* 65–83.

OSWALD, R.F. (2002). Inclusion and belonging in the family rituals of gay and lesbian people. *Journal of Family Psychology, 16,* 428–436.

OVERHOLSER, J. (2007). The central role of the therapeutic alliance: A simulated interview with Carl Rogers. *Journal of Contemporary Psychology, 37,* 71–78.

OWEN, S.S. (2004). Corporal punishment experiences and attitudes in a sample of college students. *Psychological Reports, 94,* 348–350.

OXLEY, N.L., DZINDOLET, M.R., & MILLER, J.L. (2002). Sex differences in communication with close friends: Testing Tannen's claims. *Psychological Reports, 91,* 537–544.

OYSERMAN, D., COON, H.M., & KEMMELMEIER, M. (2002). Rethinking individualism and collectivism: Evaluation of theoretical assumptions and meta-analyses. *Psychological Bulletin, 128,* 3–72.

OZER, E.J., & WEISS, D.S. (2004). Who develops posttraumatic stress disorder? *Current Directions in Psychological Science, 13,* 169–172.

ÖZKAN, S., ALATAS, E.S., & ZENCIR, M. (2005). Women's quality of life in the premenopausal and postmenopausal periods. *Quality of Life Research: An International Journal of Quality of Life Aspects of Treatment, Care & Rehabilitation, 14,* 1795–1801.

PAAVONEN, E.J., PENNONEN, M., ROINE, M., VALKONEN, S., & LAHIKAINEN, A.R. (2006). TV exposure associated with sleep disturbances in 5- to 6-year-old children. *Journal of Sleep Research, 15,* 154–161.

PACE, B. (2001). Bullying. *Journal of the American Medical Association, 285,* 2156.

PACEY, S. (2005). Step change: The interplay of sexual and parenting problems when couples form stepfamilies. *Sexual and Relationship Therapy, 20,* 359–369.

PALMER, J.K., & LOVELAND, J.M. (2008). The influence of group discussion on performance judgments: Rating accuracy, contrast effects, and halo. *Journal of Psychology: Interdisciplinary and Applied, 142,* 117–130.

PAREKH, R., & BERESIN, E.V. (2001). Looking for love? Take a cross-cultural walk through the personals. *Academic Psychiatry, 25,* 223–233.

PARK, H., & ANTONIONI, D. (2007). Personality, reciprocity, and strength of conflict resolution strategy. *Journal of Research in Personality, 41,* 110–125.

PARK, H.S., LEE, H.E., & SONG, J.A. (2005). "I am sorry to send you SPAM": Cross-cultural differences in use of apologies in email advertising in Korea and the U.S. *Human Communication Research, 31,* 365–398.

PARK, L.E., CROCKER, J., & MICKELSON, K.D. (2004). Attachment styles and contingencies of self-worth. *Personality and Social Psychology Bulletin, 30,* 1243–1254.

PARKER, S., & DEVRIES, B. (1993). Patterns of friendship for women and men in same and cross-sex relationships. *Journal of Social and Personal Relationships, 10,* 617–626.

PARKER, S.M., CLAYTON, J.M., HANCOCK, K., WALDER, S., BUTOW, P.N., CARRICK, S., et al. (2007). A systematic review of prognostic/end-of-life communication with adults in the advanced stages of a life-limiting illness: Patient/caregiver preferences for the content, style, and timing of information. *Journal of Pain and Symptom Management, 34,* 81–93.

PARROTT, W.G., & SMITH, R.H. (1993). Distinguishing the experiences of envy and jealousy. *Journal of Personality and Social Psychology, 64,* 906–920.

PATTERSON, C.L., & SINGER, J.A. (2007). Exploring the role of expectancies in the mental and physical health outcomes of written self-disclosure. *Imagination, Cognition and Personality, 27,* 99–115.

PATTERSON, T.G., & JOSEPH, S. (2007). Person-centered theory: Support from the self-determination theory and positive psychology. *Journal of Humanistic Psychology, 47,* 117-139.

PAUL, G.L. (2007). Psychotherapy outcome can be studied scientifically. In S.O. Lilienfeld & W.T. O'Donohue (Eds.), *The great ideas of clinical science: 17 principles that every mental health professional should understand.* New York: Routledge.

PAWASKAR, M.D., & SANSGIRY, S.S. (2006). Over-the-counter medication labels: Problems and needs of the elderly population. *Journal of the American Geriatrics Society, 54,* 1955–1956.

PECCHIONI, L.L., & CROGHAN, J.M. (2002). Young adults' stereotypes of older adults with their grandparents as the targets. *Journal of Communication, 52,* 715–731.

PEDRO-CARROLL, J.L. (2005). Fostering resilience in the aftermath of divorce: The role of evidence-based programs for children. *Family Court Review. Special Issue on Prevention: Research, Policy, and Evidence-Based Practice, 43,* 52–64.

PEISAH, C., LATIF, E., WILHELM, K., & WILLIAMS, B. (2009). Secrets to psychological success: Why older doctors might have lower psychological distress and burnout than younger doctors. *Aging & Mental Health, 13,* 300–307.

PELL, M.D. (2005). Nonverbal emotion priming: Evidence from the 'facial affect decision task.' *Journal of Nonverbal Behavior, 29,* 45–73.

PERILLOUX, C., & BUSS, D.M. (2008). Breaking up romantic relationships: Costs experienced and coping strategies deployed. *Evolutionary Psychology, 6,* 164–181.

PERKINS, A.M., & CORR, P.J. (2005). Can worriers be winners? The association between worrying and job performance. *Personality and Individual Differences, 38,* 25–31.

PERLMAN, D. (1991). *Age difference in loneliness: A meta-analysis.* Vancouver: University of British Columbia. (ERIC Document Reproduction Service No. ED 326767.)

PERRY, P. (1997, July/August). Personality disorders: Coping with the borderline. *The Saturday Evening Post,* 44–52.

PERRY, P. (2005). New strategy for diagnosing bipolar disorder: Can diagnostic brain scans help identify patients with bipolar disorder? Interview with Dr. John D. Port. *Saturday Evening Post, 277,* 64–68.

PETER, R., HAMMARSTRÖM, A., HALLQVIST, J., SIEGRIST, J., & THEORELL, T. (2006). Does occupational gender segregation influence the association of effort-reward imbalance with myocardial infarction in the SHEEP study? *International Journal of Behavioral Medicine, 13,* 34–43.

PETERSON, C., & VAIDYA, R.S. (2001). Explanatory style, expectations, and depressive symptoms. *Personality and Individual Differences, 31,* 1217–1223.

PETERSON, K. (2002, July 8). Cohabiting can make marriage an iffy proposition. *USA Today,* D1–D2.

PETERSON, K.S. (1999a, September 29). A hostile start makes the argument for divorce. *USA Today,* pp. D1.

PETKOSKA, J., & EARL, J. K. (2009). Understanding the influence of demographic and psychological variables on retirement planning. *Psychology and Aging, 24,* 245–251.

PETTIGREW, T.F., & TROPP, L.R. (2008). How does intergroup contact reduce prejudice? Meta-analytic tests of three mediators. *European Journal of Social Psychology, 38,* 922–934.

PFAFF, D.W., MARTIN, E.M., & RIBEIRO, A.C. (2007). Relations between mechanisms of CNS arousal and mechanisms of stress. *Stress: The International Journal of the Biology of Stress, 10,* 316–325.

PFAFFENBERGER, A.H. (2005). Optimal adult development: An inquiry into the dynamics of growth. *Journal of Humanistic Psychology, 45,* 279–301.

PHILLIPS, J.A., & SWEENEY, M.M. (2005). Premarital cohabitation and marital disruption among White, Black, and Mexican American women. *Journal of Marriage and Family, 67,* 296–314.

PHILLIPS, L. (2005). Both specific functions and general ability can be useful: But it depends on what type of research question you ask. *Cortex, 41,* 236–237.

PHUA, V.C., HOPPER, J., & VAZQUEZ, O. (2002). Men's concerns with sex and health in personal advertisements. *Culture, Health and Sexuality, 4,* 355–363.

PIENTA, A.M., & HAYWARD, M.D. (2002). Who expects to continue working after age 62? The retirement plans of couples. *Journal of Gerontology: Series B: Psychological Sciences and Social Sciences, 57,* 199–208.

PIERSON, M.R., & GLAESER, B.C. (2002). Self-concept: Differences among adolescents by gender. *Academic Exchange Quarterly, 6,* 152–157.

PINQUART, M., & SCHINDLER, I. (2007). Changes of life satisfaction in the transition to retirement: A latent-class approach. *Psychology and Aging, 22,* 442–455.

PINQUART, M., & SÖRENSEN, S. (2005). Caregiving distress and psychological health of caregivers. In K.V. Oxington (Ed.), *Psychology of stress.* Hauppauge, NY: Nova Biomedical.

PLATOW, M.J., BYRNE, L., & RYAN, M.K. (2005). Experimentally manipulated high in-group status can buffer personal self-esteem against discrimination. *European Journal of Social Psychology. Special Issue: In Honour of Ken Dion, 35,* 599–608.

PLOMIN, R., & RENDE, R. (1991). Human behavioral genetics. *Annual Review of Psychology, 42,* 161–190.

PLONK, W.M., & ARNOLD, R.M. (2005). Terminal care: The last weeks of life. *Journal of Palliative Medicine, 8,* 1042–1054.

PLUTCHIK, R. (2001). The nature of emotions. *American Scientist, 89,* 344–350.

POLANSKY, J.R., & GLANTZ, S.A. (2004) *First-run smoking presentations in U.S. movies 1999-2003.* University of California San Francisco Center for Tobacco Control Research and Education. Retrieved May 15, 2008, from http://www.medscape.com.

POLIVY, J., & HERMAN, C.P. (2000). The false-hope syndrome: Unfulfilled expectations of self-change. *Current Directions in Psychological Science, 9,* 128–131.

POPOVICH, P.M., GULLEKSON, N., MORRIS, S., & MORSE, B. (2008). Comparing attitudes towards computer usage by undergraduates from 1986 to 2005. *Computers in Human Behavior, 24,* 986–992.

PORTER, S., & TEN BRINKE, L. (2008). Reading between the lies: Identifying concealed and falsified emotions in universal facial expressions. *Psychological Science, 19,* 508–514.

POTTER-EFRON, R.T. (2005). *Handbook of anger management: Individual, couple, family, and group approaches.* Binghamton, NY: Haworth Clinical Practice Press.

POUND, P., BRITTEN, N., MORGAN, M., YARDLEY, L., POPE, C., & DAKER-WHITE, G., et al. (2005). Resisting medicines: A synthesis of qualitative studies of medicine taking. *Social Science & Medicine, 61,* 133–155.

POWELL, A.D., & KAHN, A.S. (1995). Racial differences in women's desires to be thin. *International Journal of Eating Disorders, 17,* 191–195.

POWELL, G.N., BUTTERFIELD, D.A., & PARENT, J.D. (2002). Gender and managerial stereotypes: Have times changed? *Journal of Management, 28,* 177–193.

PRENTKY, R.A., KNIGHT, R.A., & LEE, A.F.S. (2006). Child sexual molestation: Research issues. In C.R. Bartol, & A.M. Bartol (Eds.), *Current perspectives in forensic psychology and criminal justice* (pp. 119–129). Thousand Oaks, CA: Sage Publications.

PREVITI, D., & AMATO, P.R. (2004). Is infidelity a cause or a consequence of poor marital quality? *Journal of Social and Personal Relationships, 21,* 217–230.

PRIEL, B., & DE SCHONEN, S. (1986). Self-recognition: A study of a population without mirrors. *Journal of Experimental Child Psychology, 41*(2), 237–250.

PRISLIN, R., & WOOD, W. (2005). *Social influence in attitudes and attitude change.* Mahwah, NJ: Lawrence Erlbaum.

PRITCHARD, M.E., & WILSON, G.S. (2006). Do coping styles change during the first semester of college? *Journal of Social Psychology, 146,* 125–127.

PUHL, R.M., & LATNER, J.D. (2007). Stigma, obesity, and the health of the nation's children. *Psychological Bulletin, 133,* 557–580.

PUTERBAUGH, D. (2005, May). Why newborns cause acrimony and alimony. *USA Today Magazine, 133,* 26–29.

PYSZCZYNSKI, T., & COX, C. (2004). Can we really do without self-esteem? Comment on Crocker and Park (2004). *Psychological Bulletin, 130,* 425–429.

QUIGLEY, D.G., & SCHATZ, M.S. (1999). Men and women and their responses in spousal bereavement. *Hospice Journal, 14,* 65–78.

QUILLIAN, L., & CAMPBELL, M.E. (2003). Beyond Black and White: The present and future of multiracial friendship segregation. *American Sociological Review, 68,* 540–566.

RACHMAN, S. (2008). Psychological treatment for anxiety: The evolution of behavior therapy and cognitive behavior therapy. *Annual Review of Clinical Psychology, 5,* 97–119.

RAIT, D.S. (2000). The therapeutic alliance in couples and family therapy. *Journal of Clinical Psychology, 56,* 211–224.

RANSON, K.E., & URICHUK, L.J. (2008). The effect of parent-child attachment relationships on child biopsychosocial outcomes: A review. *Early Child Development and Care, 178,* 129–152.

Rape, Abuse, & Incest National Network (RAINN). (2006a). *Statistics.* Retrieved May 17, 2006, from http://www.rainn.org/statistics.

Rape, Abuse, & Incest National Network (RAINN). (2006b). *Rape trauma syndrome.* Retrieved May 17, 2006, from http://www.rainn.org/effects-of-rape/rapetrauma-syndrome.html.

RATELLE, C.F., VALLERAND, R.J., CHANTAL, Y., & PROVENCHER, P. (2004). Cognitive adaptation and mental health: A motivational analysis. *European Journal of Social Psychology, 34,* 459–476.

RAUER, A.J., & VOLLING, B.L. (2005). The role of husbands' and wives' emotional expressivity in the marital relationship. *Sex Roles, 52,* 577–587.

RAYMOND, N. (2000, July/August). Mood: Blues around the world. *Psychology Today,* 12.

RAYNOR, D.A., PHELAN, S., HILL, J.O., & WING, R.R. (2006). Television viewing and weight maintenance: Results from the National Weight Control Registry. *Obesity, 14*(10), 1816–1824.

RAYNOR, D.A., WING, R.R., & PHELAN, S. (2007). Depression and adherence to medical advice. In A. Steptoe (Ed.), *Depression and physical illness.* Cambridge, UK: Cambridge University Press.

REGAN, P.C., & ATKINS, L. (2006). Sex differences and similarities in frequency and intensity of sexual desire. *Social Behavior and Personality, 34,* 95–102.

REGAN, P.C., DURVASULA, R., HOWELL, L., UREÑO, O., & REA, M. (2004). Gender, ethnicity, and the developmental timing of first sexual and romantic experiences. *Social Behavior and Personality, 32,* 667–676.

REID, A. (2004). Gender and sources of subjective well-being. *Sex Roles, 51,* 617–629.

REISBURG, L. (2000). Student stress is rising, especially among women. *The Chronicle of Higher Education, 46,* 49–50.

REISS, S., & HAVERCAMP, S.M. (2005). Motivation in developmental context: A new method for studying self-actualization. *Journal of Humanistic Psychology, 45,* 41–53.

RENNISON, C.M. (2003). *Intimate partner violence: Crime data brief.* Washington, DC: Bureau of Justice Statistics.

REYNOLDS, B.M., & REPETTI, R.L. (2006). *Adolescent girls' health in the context of peer and community relationships.* New York: Oxford University Press.

REYNOLDS, J.R., & TURNER, R.J. (2008). Major life events: Their personal meaning, resolution, and mental health significance. *Journal of Health and Social Behavior, 49,* 223–237.

RHOADES, G.K., STANLEY, S.M., & MARKMAN, H.J. (2009). The pre-engagement cohabitation effect: A replication and extension of previous findings. *Journal of Family Psychology, 23,* 107–111.

RHODES, G., YOSHIKAWA, S., CLARK, A., LEE, K., MCKAY, R., & AKAMATSU, S. (2001). Attractiveness of facial averageness and symmetry in non-Western cultures: In search of biologically based standards of beauty. *Perception, 30,* 611–625.

RICHARDS, J.M. (2004). The cognitive consequences of concealing feelings. *Current Directions in Psychological Science, 13,* 131–134.

RICHARDSON, J.D. (1991). Medical causes of male sexual dysfunction. *The Medical Journal of Australia, 155,* 29–33.

RITTER, B.A., & YODER, J.D. (2004). Gender differences in leader emergence persist even for dominant women: An updated confirmation of role congruity theory. *Psychology of Women Quarterly, 28,* 187–193.

ROBERTS, D.F., HENRIKSEN, L., & CHRISTENSON, P.G. (1999). *Substance use in popular movies and music.* Washington, DC: Office of National Drug Control Policy.

ROBERTS, S.T., & KENNEDY, B.L. (2006). Why are young college women not using condoms? Their perceived risk, drug use, and developmental vulnerability may provide important clues to sexual risk. *Archives of Psychological Nursing, 20,* 32–40.

ROBINS, R.W., & TRZESNIEWSKI, K.H. (2005). Self-esteem development across the lifespan. *Current Directions in Psychological Science, 14,* 158–162.

ROBINSON, H.M., & HOOD, S.D. (2007). Social anxiety disorder—A review of pharmacological treatments. *Current Psychiatry Reviews, 3,* 95–122.

ROBINSON, R.V., & JACKSON, E.F. (2001). Is trust in others declining in America? An age-period-cohort analysis. *Social Science Research, 30,* 117–146.

Rochford.org. (2000, August). *Suicide.* http://Rochford.org/suicide/resources/stats/us.

RODRIGUEZ-CALCAGNO, M., & BREWER, E.W. (2005). Job stress among Hispanic professionals. *Hispanic Journal of Behavioral Sciences, 27,* 504–516.

ROELOFS, J., MEESTERS, C., Ter HUURNE, M., BAMELIS, L., & MURIS, P. (2006). On the links between attachment style, parental rearing behaviors, and internalizing and externalizing problems in non-clinical children. *Journal of Child and Family Studies, 15,* 331–344.

ROESE, N.J., & SUMMERVILLE, A. (2005). What we regret most . . . and why. *Personality and Social Psychology Bulletin, 31,* 1273–1285.

ROFFE, L., SCHMIDT, K., & ERNST, E. (2005). A systematic review of guided imagery as an adjuvant cancer therapy. *Psycho-oncology, 14,* 607–617.

ROGERS, C.R. (1961). *On becoming a person.* Boston: Houghton Mifflin.

ROGERS, C.R. (1980). *A way of being.* Boston: Houghton Mifflin.

ROGGE, R.D., BRADBURY, T.N., HAHLWEG, K., ENGL, J., & THURMAIER, F. (2006). Predicting marital distress and dissolution: Refining the two-factor hypothesis. *Journal of Family Psychology, 20,* 156–159.

ROHNER, R.P. (1998). Father love and child development: History and current evidence. *Current Directions in Psychological Science, 7,* 157–161.

ROHRBAUGH, J.B. (2008). *A comprehensive guide to child custody evaluations: Mental health and legal perspectives.* New York: Springer.

ROKACH, A., & NETO, F. (2005). Age, culture, and the antecedents of loneliness. *Social Behavior and Personality, 33,* 477–494.

ROSARIO, M., SCHRIMSHAW, E.W., & HUNTER, J. (2009). Disclosure of sexual orientation and subsequent substance use and abuse among lesbian, gay, and bisexual youths: Critical role of disclosure reactions. *Psychology of Addictive Behaviors, 23,* 175–184.

ROSARIO, M., SCHRIMSHAW, E.W., HUNTER, J., & BRAUN, L. (2006). Sexual identity development among lesbian, gay, and bisexual youths: Consistency and change over time. *Journal of Sex Research. Special Issue: Scientific Abstracts, World Congress of Sexology 2005, 43,* 46–58.

ROSATO, J.L. (2006). Special issue on the evolution of marriage: Preface. *Family Court Review. Special Issue: The Evolution of Marriage, 44,* 31–32.

ROSEMAN, I.J. (2008). Motivations and emotivations: Approach, avoidance, and other tendencies in motivated and emotional behavior. In A. J. Elliot (Ed.), *Handbook of approach and avoidance motivation* (pp. 343–366). New York: Psychology Press.

ROSEN, R.C., SHABSIGH, R., KURITZKY, L., WANG, W. C., & SIDES, G.D. (2006). The efficacy of tadalafil in improving sexual satisfaction and overall satisfaction in men with mild, moderate, and severe erectile dysfunction: A retrospective pooled analysis of data from randomized, placebo-controlled clinical trials. *Current Medical Research and Opinion, 21,* 1701–1710.

ROSENTHAL, E.C. (2005). *The era of choice: The ability to choose and its transformation of contemporary life.* Cambridge, MA: MIT Press.

ROSS, C.E., & MIROWSKY, J. (2002). Age and the gender gap in the sense of personal control. *Social Psychology Quarterly, 65,* 125–145.

ROSS, M., & WILSON, A.E. (2003). Autobiographical memory and conceptions of self: Getting better all the time. (2003). *Current Directions in Psychological Science, 12,* 66–69.

ROSS, N. (2005). Health, happiness, and higher levels of social organization. *Journal of Epidemiology & Community Health, 59,* 614.

RÖSSLER, W., SALIZE, H.J., VAN OS, J., & RIECHER-RÖSSLER, A. (2005). Size of burden of schizophrenia and psychotic disorders. *European Neuropsychopharmacology. Special Issue: Size and Burden of Mental Disorders in Europe, 15,* 399–409.

ROTHAUPT, J.W., & BECKER, K. (2007). A literature review of Western bereavement theory: From decathecting to continuing bonds. *The Family Journal, 15,* 6–15.

ROTHERAM-BORUS, M.J., WALKER, J.U., & FERNS, W. (1996). Suicidal behavior among middle-class adolescents who seek crisis services. *Journal of Clinical Psychology, 52,* 137–143.

ROWE, D.C. (1990). As the twig is bent? The myth of child-rearing influences on personality development. *Journal of Counseling and Development, 68,* 606–611.

RUBIN, J.Z., PRUITT, D.G., & KIM, S.H. (1994). *Social conflict: Escalation, stalemate, and settlement.* New York: McGraw-Hill.

RUBIN, R. (1999, November 9). Pregnancy no longer pushes women to wed. *USA Today,* p. 1D.

RUDMAN, L.A., & GOODWIN, S.A. (2004). Gender differences in automatic in-group bias: Why do women like women more than men like men? *Journal of Personality and Social Psychology, 87,* 494–509.

RUSCHER, J.B., CRALLEY, E.L., & O'FARRELL, K.J. (2005). How newly acquainted dyads develop shared stereotypic impressions through conversation. *Group Processes & Intergroup Relations, 8,* 259–270.

RUSHTON, J.P., & BONS, T.A. (2005). Mate choice and friendship in twins: Evidence for genetic similarity. *Psychological Science, 16,* 555–559.

RUSSELL, D.P. (2007). Recruiting and staffing in the electronic age: A research-based perspective. *Consulting Psychology Journal: Practice and Research, 59,* 91–101.

RUSSO, F. (2005). Giving expertise: The new volunteers: More than just envelope stuffers. *Time Bonus Section, 166,* F18–F20.

RUSSO, N.F. (2008). Call to action: Reducing interpersonal violence across the lifespan. *American Journal of Orthopsychiatry, 78,* 383–385.

RYAN, M.K., HASLAM, S.A., & POSTMES, T. (2007). Reactions to the glass cliff: Gender differences in the explanations for the precariousness of women's leadership positions. *Journal of Organizational Change Management, 20,* 182–197.

RYAN, S., FRANZETTA, K., MANLOVE, J., & HOLCOMBE, E. (2007). Adolescents' discussions about contraception or STDs with partners before first sex. *Perspectives on Sexual and Reproductive Health, 39,* 149–157.

SAARDCHOM, N., & LEMAIRE, J. (2005). Causes of increasing ages at marriage: An international regression study. *Marriage & Family Review, 37,* 73–97.

SABINI, J., & SILVER, M. (2005). Ekman's basic emotions: Why not love and jealousy? *Cognition & Emotion, 19,* 693–712.

SAFDAR, S., FRIEDLMEIER, W., MATSUMOTO, D., YOO, S.H., KWANTES, C.T., KAKAI, H., et al. (2009). Variations of emotional display rules within and across cultures: A comparison between Canada, USA, and Japan. *Canadian Journal of Behavioural Science/Revue Canadienne Des Sciences Du Comportement, 41,* 1–10.

SAFREN, S.A., & PANTALONE, D.W. (2006). Social anxiety and barriers to resilience among lesbian, gay, and bisexual adolescents. In A.M. Omoto, & H.S. Kurtzman (Eds.), *Sexual orientation and mental health: Examining identity and development in lesbian, gay, and bisexual people* (pp. 55–71). Washington, DC: American Psychological Association.

SAGY, S. (2005). Chronic versus acute stress situations: A comparison of moderating factors. In K.V. Oxington (Ed.), *Psychology of stress* (pp. 101–112). Hauppauge, NY: Nova Biomedical Books.

SAKURAGI, T. (2004). Association of culture with shyness among Japanese and American university students. *Perceptual and Motor Skills, 98,* 803–813.

SALO, F.T. (2008). Letter from Melbourne. *International Journal of Psychoanalysis, 89,* 15–17.

SALOVEY, P., & GREWAL, D. (2005). The science of emotional intelligence. *Current Directions in Psychological Science, 14,* 281–285.

SANCHEZ, D.T., & CROCKER, J. (2005). How investment in gender ideals affects well-being: The role of external contingencies of self-worth. *Psychology of Women Quarterly, 29,* 63–77.

SÁNCHEZ-FRANCO, M.J. (2006). Exploring the influence of gender on the web usage via partial least squares. *Behaviour & Information Technology, 25,* 19–36.

SANTESSO, D.L., SCHMIDT, L.A., & FOX, N.A. (2004). Are shyness and sociability still a dangerous combination for substance use? Evidence from a U.S. and Canadian sample. *Personality and Individual Differences, 37,* 5–17.

SARGENT, J.D., WILLS, T.A., STOOLMILLER, M., GIBSON, J., & GIBBONS, F.X. (2006). Alcohol use in motion pictures and its relation with early-onset teen drinking. *Journal of Studies on Alcohol, 67,* 54–65.

SASSAROLI, S., GALLUCCI, M., & RUGGIERO, G. M. (2008). Low perception of control as a cognitive factor of eating disorders: Its independent effects on measures of eating disorders and its interactive effects with perfectionism and self-esteem. *Journal of Behavior Therapy and Experimental Psychology, 39,* 467–488.

SAUCIER, M.G. (2004). Midlife and beyond: Issues for aging women. *Journal of Counseling & Development, 82,* 420–425.

SAUNDERS, P.L., & CHESTER, A. (2008). Shyness and the internet: Social problem or panacea? *Computers in Human Behavior, 24,* 2649–2658.

SAVARD, J., LEDUC, N., LEBEL, P., BÉLAND, F., & BERGMAN, H. (2006). Caregiver satisfaction with support services: Influence of different types of services. *Journal of Aging and Health, 18,* 3–27.

SAVIN-WILLIAMS, R.C. (2006). Who's gay? Does it matter? *Current Directions in Psychological Science, 14,* 40–44.

SAYER, L.C. (2005). Gender, time and inequality: Trends in women's and men's paid work, unpaid work and free time. *Social Forces, 84,* 285–303.

SCARPA, A., HADEN, S.C., & HURLEY, J. (2006). Community violence victimization and symptoms of posttraumatic stress disorder: The moderating effects of coping and social support. *Journal of Interpersonal Violence, 21,* 446–469.

SCEALY, M., PHILLIPS, J.G., & STEVENSON, R. (2002). Shyness and anxiety as predictors of patterns of internet usage. *CyberPsychology and Behavior, 5,* 507–515.

SCHACHTER, S., & SINGER, J. (1962). Cognitive, social, and physiological determinants of emotional state. *Psychological Review, 69,* 379–399.

SCHEIER, M.F., & CARVER, C.S. (1993). On the power of positive thinking: The benefits of being optimistic. *Psychological Science, 4,* 26–30.

SCHINDEHETTE, S., CALANDRA, B., PODESTA, J.S., & WILLIAMS, K. (2004, April 5). Why did Julie take her life? *People,* 58–63.

SCHNEIDER, B. H., ATKINSON, L., & TARDIF, C. (2001). Child–parent attachment and children's peer relations: A quantitative review. *Developmental Psychology, 37*(1), 86–100.

SCHOOLER, D. (2008). Real women have curves: A longitudinal investigation of TV and the body image development of Latina adolescents. *Journal of Adolescent Research, 23,* 132–153.

SCHOOLER, D., WARD, L.M., MERRIWETHER, A., & CARUTHERS, A. (2004). Who's that girl: Television's role in the body image development of young White and Black women. *Psychology of Women Quarterly, 28,* 38–47.

SCHRAUFHAGEL, T.J., WAGNER, A.W., MIRANDA, J., & ROY-BYRNE, P.P. (2006). Treating minority patients with depression and anxiety: What does the evidence tell us? *General Hospital Psychiatry, 28,* 27–36.

SCHROF, J.M., & SCHULTZ, S. (1999, March 8). Melancholy nation. *U.S. News & World Report,* 56–63.

SCHULZ, R., & HECKHAUSEN, J. (1996). A life span model of successful aging. *American Psychologist, 51,* 702–714.

SCHUTTE, N.S., MALOUFF, J.M., BOBIK, C., COSTON, R.D., GREESON, C., JEDLICKA, C., & RHODES, E., et al. (2001). Emotional intelligence and interpersonal relations. *The Journal of Social Psychology, 141,* 523–536.

SCHÜTZWOHL, A. (2006). Sex differences in jealousy: Information search and cognitive preoccupation. *Personality and Individual Differences, 40,* 285–292.

SCHWARTZ, B. (2004). *The paradox of choice: Why more is less.* New York: Harper-Collins Publishers.

SCHWARTZ, P. (2002, May/June). Love is all you need. *Psychology Today,* 56–62.

SCHWARTZ, S.H., & RUBEL, T. (2005). Sex differences in value priorities: Cross-cultural and multimethod studies. *Journal of Personality and Social Psychology, 89,* 1010–1028.

SCHWINGHAMMER, S.A., STAPEL, D A., & BLANTON, H. (2006). Different selves have different effects: Self-activation and defensive social comparison. *Personality and Social Psychology Bulletin, 32,* 27–39.

SCOLLON, C.N., DIENER, E., OISHI, S., & BISWAS-DIENER, R. (2004). Emotions across cultures and methods. *Journal of Cross-Cultural Psychology, 35,* 304–326.

SCZESNY, S., BOSAK, J., NEFF, D., & SCHYNS, B. (2004). Gender stereotypes and the attribution of leadership traits: A cross-cultural comparison. *Sex Roles, 51,* 631–645.

SEDIKIDES, C., & KOOLE, S.L. (2004). In defense of the self. *Social Cognition, 22,* 1–3.

SEDIKIDES, C., GAERTNER, L., & VEVEA, J.L. (2005). Pancultural self-enhancement reloaded: A meta-analytic reply to Heine (2005). *Journal of Personality and Social Psychology, 89,* 539–551.

SEGERSTROM, S.C., & MILLER, G.E. (2004). Psychological stress and the human immune system: A meta-analytic study of 30 years of inquiry. *Psychological Bulletin, 130,* 601–630.

SELIGMAN, M.E.P. (1981). A learned helplessness point of view. In L.P. Rehm (Ed.), *Behavior therapy for depression.* New York: Academic Press.

SELIGMAN, M.E.P. (1992). *Learned optimism.* New York: Knopf.

SELIGMAN, M.E.P. (1994, May/June). What you can change and what you cannot change. *Psychology Today,* 34–41, 70, 72–74, 84.

SELIGMAN, M.E.P. (1995). The effectiveness of psychotherapy: The Consumer Reports study. *American Psychologist, 50,* 965–974.

SELIGMAN, M.E.P., STEEN, T.A., PARK, N., & PETERSON, C. (2005). Positive psychology progress: Empirical validation of interventions. *American Psychologist, 60,* 410–421.

SELYE, H. (1980). The stress concept today. In I.L. Kutash et al. (Eds.), *Handbook on stress and anxiety.* San Francisco: Jossey-Bass.

SELYE, H. (1991). History and present states of the stress concept. In A. Monat & R.S. Lazarus (Eds.), *Stress and coping: An anthology* (3rd ed., pp. 21–35). New York: Columbia University Press.

SENKO, C., & HARACKIEWICZ, J.M. (2005). Regulation of achievement goals: The role of competence feedback. *Journal of Educational Psychology, 97,* 320–336.

SETA, J.J., SETA, C.E., & McELROY, T. (2006). Better than better-than-average (or not): Elevated and depressed self-evaluations following unfavorable social comparisons. *Self and Identity, 5,* 51–72.

Sex Information and Education Council of the United States (SIECUS). (2001). *Lesbian, gay, bisexual and transgender youth issues.* http://www.siecus.org/pubs/fact/fact0013.html.

Sex Information and Education Council of the United States (SIECUS). (2002). *Sexuality in middle and later life.* http://www.siecus.org/pubs/fact/fact0018.html.

SHACKELFORD, T.K., & MOUZOS, J. (2005). Partner killing by men in cohabiting and marital relationships: A comparative, cross-national analysis of data from Australia and the United States. *Journal of Interpersonal Violence, 20,* 1310–1324.

SHACKELFORD, T.K., GOETZ, A.T., BUSS, D.M., EULER, H.A., & HOIER, S. (2005). When we hurt the ones we love: Predicting violence against women from men's mate retention. *Personal Relationships, 12,* 447–463.

SHAFIRKIN, A.V. (2003). Compensatory reserves of the human body and population health under conditions of exposure to chronic anthropogenic factors and prolonged psychoemotional stress. *Human Physiology, 29,* 12–22.

SHAH, A. (2007) Global computer usage, cell phone ownership jump. *The Pew Global Attitudes Project.* http://pcworld.about.come/gi/dynamic/offside.htm?=http://pewglobal.org/reports/pdf/258.pdf.

SHALALA, D. (1999). *Mental health: A report of the surgeon general.* http://www.surgeongeneral.gov/library/mentalhealth/home.html.

SHARMA, V., & ROSHA, J. (1992). Altruism as a function of self-actualization and locus of control of benefactor. *Psychological Studies, 37,* 26–30.

SHEAR, K., FRANK, E., HOUCK, P.R., REYNOLDS, C.F. (2005). Treatment of complicated grief: A randomized controlled trial. *Journal of the American Medical Association, 293,* 2601–2608.

SHEETS, V.L., & LUGAR, R. (2005). Sources of conflict between friends in Russia and the United States. *Cross-Cultural Research: The Journal of Comparative Social Science, 39,* 380–398.

SHEFFIELD, M., CAREY, J., PATENAUDE, W., & LAMBERT, M.J. (1995). An exploration of the relationship between interpersonal problems and psychological health. *Psychological Reports, 76,* 947–956.

SHELDON, K.M., ELLIOT, A.J., RYAN, R.M., CHIRKOV, V., KIM, Y., & WU, C., et al. (2004). Self-concordance and subjective well-being in four cultures. *Journal of Cross-Cultural Psychology, 35,* 209–223.

SHELDON, K.M., KASSER, T., HOUSER-MARKO, L., JONES, T., & TURBAN, D. (2005). Doing one's duty: Chronological age, felt autonomy, and subjective well-being. *European Journal of Personality, 19,* 97–115.

SHER, L. (2004). Light therapy for depressive disorders. *Psychiatric Times, 21,* 68.

SHERMAN, J.W., STROESSNER, S.J., CONREY, F.R., & AZAM, O.A. (2005). Prejudice and stereotype maintenance processes: Attention, attribution, and individuation. *Journal of Personality and Social Psychology, 89,* 607–622.

SHINEW, K.J., FLOYD, M.F., & PARRY, D. (2004). Understanding the relationship between race and leisure activities and constraints: Exploring an alternative framework. *Leisure Sciences, 26,* 181–199.

SHIOZAKI, M., MORITA, T., HIRAI, K., SAKAGUCHI, Y., TSUNETO, S., & SHIMA, Y. (2005). Why are bereaved family members dissatisfied with specialised inpatient palliative care service? A nationwide qualitative study. *Palliative Medicine, 19,* 319–327.

SHMOTKIN, D. (2005). Happiness in the face of adversity: Reformulating the dynamic and modular bases of subjective well-being. *Review of General Psychology, 9,* 291–325.

SHOCKETT, E.R., Teno J.M., Miller S.C., Stuart B.(2005). Late referral to hospice and bereaved family member perception of quality of end-of-life care. *Journal of Pain and Symptom Management, 30,* 400–407.

SHORT, S.E., ROSS-STEWART, L., & MONSMA, E.V. (2006). Onwards with the evolution of imagery research in sport psychology. *Athletic Insight: The Online Journal of Sport Psychology, 8,* 1–15.

SIEVER, M.D. (1994). Sexual orientation and gender as factors in socio-culturally acquired vulnerability to body dissatisfaction and eating disorders. *Journal of Consulting and Clinical Psychology, 62,* 252–260.

The Simon Wiesenthal Center. (2007). *Digital terrorism and hate.* Retrieved March 3, 2008, from http://www.wiesenthal.com/site/apps/s/content.asp?c=fwLYKnN8LzH&b=253162&ct=3876867.

SIMONS, J.S., GAHER, R.M., CORREIA, C.J., & BUSH, J.A. (2005). Club drug use among college students. *Addictive Behaviors, 30,* 1619–1624.

SIMONTON, D.K. (1987). *Why presidents succeed: A political psychology of leadership.* New Haven, CT: Yale University Press.

SINGH, A., & UPADHYAY, A. (2008). Age and sex differences in academic stress among college students. *Social Science International, 24,* 78–88.

SIVUNEN, A. (2006). Strengthening identification with the Team in Virtual Teams: The leaders' perspective. *Group Decision and Negotiation, 15,* 345–366.

SKYVING, M., BERG, H., & LAFLAMME, L. (2009). A pattern analysis of traffic crashes fatal to older drivers. *Accident Analysis & Prevention, 41,* 253–258.

SLATER, A., HOCKING, I., & LOOSE, J. (2003). Theories and issues in child development. In A. Slater & G. Bremner (Eds.), *An introduction to developmental psychology* (pp. 34–63). Malden, MA: Blackwell.

SLEEBOS, E., ELLEMERS, N., & DE GILDER, D. (2006). The carrot and the stick: Affective commitment and acceptance anxiety as motives for discretionary group efforts by respected and disrespected group members. *Personality and Social Psychology Bulletin, 32,* 244–255.

SLEEK, S. (1998, November). Better parenting may not be enough for some children. *APA Monitor, 30.*

SMITH, B.N., KERR, N.A., MARKUS, M.J., & STASSON, M.F. (2001). Individual differences in social loafing: Need for cognition as a motivator in collective performance. *Group Dynamics, 5,* 150–158.

SMITH, D.E., & COGSWELL, C. (1994). A cross-cultural perspective on adolescent girls' body perception. *Perceptual and Motor Skills, 78,* 744–746.

SMITH, P.B., & BOND, M.H. (1993). *Across cultures.* Boston: Allyn & Bacon.

SMITH, P.K., PEPLER, D., & RIGBY, K. (Eds.). (2004). *Bullying in schools: How successful can interventions be?* New York: Cambridge University Press.

SMITH, R.A., & WEBER, A. L. (2005). Applying social psychology in everyday life. In F. W. SCHNEIDER, J. A. Gruman & L. M. Coutts (Eds.), *Applied social psychology: Understanding and addressing social and practical problems.* (pp. 75–99). Thousand Oaks, CA, US: Sage Publications, Inc.

SMITH, T.J., & CAMPBELL, C. (2009). The relationship between occupational interests and values. *Journal of Career Assessment, 17,* 39–55.

SMITH, T.W. (2003). *American sexual behavior: Trends, socio-demographic differences, and risk behavior.* Chicago, IL: University of Chicago, National Opinion Research Center.

SMOCK, P.J., MANNING, W.D., & PORTER, M. (2005). "Everything's there except money": How money shapes decisions to marry among cohabitors. *Journal of Marriage and Family, 67,* 680–696.

SOLOMON, R.S. (2005). Name that feeling: Sabini and Silver on emotional names. *Psychological Inquiry, 16,* 41–44.

SOMECH, A. (2006). The effects of leadership style and team process on performance and innovation in functionally heterogeneous teams. *Journal of Management, 32,* 132–157.

SOMERS, C.L., & SURMANN, A.T. (2004). Adolescents' preferences for source of sex education. *Child Study Journal, 34,* 47–59.

SOMMER, K.L., & BAUMEISTER, R.F. (2002). Self-evaluation, persistence, and performance following implicit rejection: The role of trait self-esteem. *Personality and Social Psychology Bulletin, 28,* 926–938.

SONNENTAG, S., & ZIJLSTRA, F.R.H. (2006). Job characteristics and off-job activities as predictors of need for recovery, well-being, and fatigue. *Journal of Applied Psychology, 91,* 330–350.

SOOD, A., & TELLIS, G.J. (2005). Technological evolution and radical innovation. *Journal of Marketing, 69,* 152–168.

SOSIK, J.J. (2001). Self-other agreement on charismatic leadership: Relationships with work attitudes and managerial performance. *Group and Organization Management, 26,* 484–511.

SOUTHWICK, S.M., VYTHILINGAM, M., & CHARNEY, D.S. (2005). The psychobiology of depression and resilience to stress: Implications for prevention and treatment. *Annual Review of Clinical Psychology, 1,* 255–291.

SPECTOR, P.E. (2002). Employee control and occupational stress. *Current Directions, 11,* 133–136.

SPEK, V., CUIJPERS, P., NYKLICEK, I., RIPER, H., KEYZER, J., & POP, V. (2007). Internet-based cognitive behavior therapy for symptoms of depression and anxiety: A meta-analysis. *Psychological Medicine, 37,* 319–328.

SPIERS, A., & WALKER, G.J. (2009). The effects of ethnicity and leisure satisfaction on happiness, peacefulness, and quality of life. *Leisure Sciences, 31,* 84–99.

SPINDLER, S.R. (2001). Reversing the negative genomic effects of aging with short-term caloric restriction. *The Scientific World, 1,* 544–546.

SPOTTS, E.L., PEDERSON, N.L., NEIDERHISER, J.M., REISS, D., LICHTENSTEIN, P., & HANSSON, K., et al. (2005). Genetic effects on women's positive mental health: Do marital relationships and social support matter? *Journal of Family Psychology, 19,* 339–349.

SPRECHER, S., & HENDRICK, S.S. (2004). Self-disclosure in intimate relationships: Associations with individual and relationship characteristics over time. *Journal of Social & Clinical Psychology, 23,* 857–877.

SRIVASTAVA, S., & BEER, J.S. (2005). How self-evaluations relate to being liked by others: Integrating sociometer and attachment perspectives. *Journal of Personality and Social Psychology, 89,* 966–977.

SROUFE, L.A. (1996). *Emotional development: The organization of emotional life in the early years.* New York: Cambridge University Press.

STAINES, G.L., & CLELAND, C.M. (2007). Bias in meta-analytic estimates of the absolute efficacy of psychotherapy. *Review of General Psychology, 11,* 329–347.

STAMBOR, Z. (2006). Stressed out nation. *Monitor on Psychology, 37,* 28.

STANKIEWICZ, J.M., & ROSSELLI, F. (2008). Women as sex objects and victims in print advertisements. *Sex Roles, 58,* 579–589.

STANLEY, S.M., AMATO, P.R., JOHNSON, C.A., & MARKMAN, H.J. (2006). Premarital education, marital quality, and marital stability: Findings from a large, random household survey. *Journal of Family Psychology, 20,* 117–126.

STAPEL, D.A., & JOHNSON, C.S. (2007). When nothing compares to me: How defensive motivations and similarity shape social comparison effects. *European Journal of Social Psychology, 37,* 824–838.

STARCEVIC, V. (2005). *Anxiety disorders in adults: A clinical guide.* New York: Oxford University Press.

STASSEN BERGER, K. (2007). Update on bullying at school: Science forgotten? *Developmental Review, 27,* 90–126.

STEINER, A. (2001). Got time for friends? *Utne Reader,* 67–71.

STEPHENS, M.A.P., & FRANKS, M.M. (1999). Parent care in the context of women's multiple roles. *Current Directions in Psychological Science, 8,* 149–151.

STERN, J. (2006). A short introduction to psychoanalysis. *Psychoanalytic Psychotherapy, 20,* 65–68.

STERNBERG, R.J. (2004). *A triangular theory of love.* Philadelphia: Taylor & Francis.

STERNBERG, S. (2005, June 6) New use for Viagra: Treating lung disease. *USA Today,* p. 8D.

STERNGLANZ, R.W., & DEPAULO, B.M. (2004). Reading nonverbal cues to emotions: The advantages and liabilities of relationship closeness. *Journal of Nonverbal Behavior. Special Issue: Interpersonal Sensitivity, Part II, 28,* 245–266.

STEWART, G.L. (2006). A meta-analytic review of relationships between team design features and team performance. *Journal of Management, 32,* 29–55.

STICE, E., SHAW, H., & MARTI, C.N. (2007). A meta-analytic review of eating disorder prevention programs: Encouraging findings. *Annual Review of Clinical Psychology, 3,* 207–231.

STODOLSKA, M. (2005). A conditioned attitude model of individual discriminatory behavior. *Leisure Sciences, 27,* 1–20.

STOLZ, H.E., BARBER, B.K., & OLSEN, J.A. (2005). Toward disentangling fathering and mothering: An assessment of relative importance. *Journal of Marriage and Family, 67,* 1076–1092.

STRAUS, M.A., & STEWART, J.H. (1999). Corporal punishment by American parents: National data on prevalence, chronicity, severity, and duration, in relation to child and family characteristics. *Clinical Child and Family Psychology Review, 2,* 55–70.

STREICH, M., CASPER, W.J., & SALVAGGIO, A.N. (2008). Examining couple agreement about work-family conflict. *Journal of Managerial Psychology, 23,* 252–272.

STROEBE, M., SCHUT, H., & STROEBE, W. (2007). Health outcomes of bereavement. *Lancet, 370,* 1960–1973.

STROEBE, W., SCHUT, H., & STROEBE, M.S. (2005). Grief work, disclosure and counseling: Do they help the bereaved? *Clinical Psychology Review, 25,* 395–414.

STROEBE, W., ZECH, E., STROEBE, M.S., & ABAKOUMKIN, G. (2005). Does social support help in bereavement. *Journal of Social and Clinical Psychology, 24,* 1030–1050.

STROM, P., & STROM R. (2005). Parent-child relationships in early adulthood: College students living at home. *Community Journal of Research and Practice, 29,* 517–529.

STUPINSKY, R.H., RENAUD, R.D., PERRY, R.P., RUTHIG, J.C., HAYNES, T.L., & CLIFTON, R.A. (2007). Comparing self-esteem and perceived control as predictors of first-year college students' academic achievement. *Social Psychology of Education, 10,* 303–330.

Substance Abuse and Mental Health Services Administration (SAMHSA). (2006). Youth drug use continues downward slide older adult rates of use increase. Retrieved June 6, 2008, from http://www.samhsa.gov/news/newsreleases/060907_nsduh.aspx.

SUE, S., FUJINO, D., HU, L., TAKEUCHI, D., & ZANE, N. (1991). Community mental health services for ethnic minority groups: A test of the cultural responsiveness hypothesis. *Journal of Consulting and Clinical Psychology, 59,* 533–540.

SUH, E.J., MOSKOWITZ, D.S., FOURNIER, M.A., & ZUROFF, D.C. (2004). Gender and relationships: Influences on agentic and communal behaviors. *Personal Relationships, 11,* 41–59.

SUHAIL, K., & CHAUDHRY, H.R. (2004). Predictors of subjective well-being in Eastern Muslim culture. *Journal of Social & Clinical Psychology, 23,* 359–376.

SULLIVAN, A. (2003, August 11). Beware the straight backlash. *Time,* 35.

SULS, J., MARTIN, R., & WHEELER, L. (2002). Social comparison: Why, with whom, and with what effect. *Current Directions in Psychological Science, 11,* 159–163.

SUM, S., MATHEWS, R.M., HUGHES, I., & CAMPBELL, A. (2008). Internet use and loneliness in older adults. *CyberPsychology & Behavior, 11,* 208–211.

SUNNAFRANK, M., RAMIREZ, A.J., & METTS, S. (2004). At first sight: Persistent relational effects of get-acquainted conversations. *Journal of Social and Personal Relationships, 21,* 361–379.

SZABO, A., AINSWORTH, S.E., & DANKS, P.K. (2005). Experimental comparison of the psychological benefits of aerobic exercise, humor, and music. *Humor: International Journal of Humor Research, 18,* 235–246.

TAKANO, Y., & SOGON, S. (2008). Are Japanese men more collectivistic than Americans? Examining conformity in in-groups and the reference-group effect. *Journal of Cross-Cultural Psychology, 39,* 237–250.

TALBOT, L.A., & LUMDEN, D.B. (2000). On the association between humor and burnout. *Humor: International Journal of Humor Research, 13,* 419–428.

TALBOT, L.A., FLEG, J.L., & METTER, E.J. (2003). Secular trends in leisure-time physical activity in men and women across four decades. *Preventive Medicine: An International Journal Devoted to Practice and Theory, 37,* 52–60.

TALLIS, F. (2005). Crazy for you. *Psychologist, 18,* 72–74.

TAL-OR, N., & PAPIRMAN, Y. (2007). The fundamental attribution error in attributing fictional figures' characteristics to the actors. *Media Psychology, 9,* 331–345.

TANGRI, S.S., THOMAS, V.G., MEDNICK, M.T., & LEE, K.S. (2003). Predictors of satisfaction among college-educated African American women in midlife. *Journal of Adult Development, 10,* 113–125.

TAYLOR, S.E., & BROWN, J.D. (1994). Positive illusions and well-being revisited: Separating fact from fiction. *Psychological Bulletin, 116,* 21–27.

Techniques. (2000, March). Stressed out on campus, 9.

TEICHERT, N.W. (2002). *Nation faces inadequate care for seniors as baby boomers age.* Knight Ridder/Tribune Business News, Item 02333003.

THOBABEN, M. (2005). Defense mechanisms and defense levels. *Home Health Care Management & Practice, 17,* 330–332.

THOMAS, A., & CHESS, S. (1984). Genesis and evolution of behavioral disorders: From infancy to early adult life. *The American Journal of Psychiatry, 141*(1), 1–9.

THOMAS, A., CHESS, S., & BIRCH, H. G. (1968). *Temperament and behavior disorders in children.* Oxford, England: New York University Press.

THOMAS, J.L., PATTEN, C.A., DECKER, P.A., CROGHAN, I.T., COWLES, M.L., & BRONARS, C.A., et al. (2005). Development and preliminary evaluation of a measure of support provided to a smoker among young adults. *Addictive Behaviors, 30,* 1351.

THOMPSON, K.M. (2005). Addicted media: Substances on screen. *Child and Adolescent Psychiatric Clinics of North America, 14,* 473–489.

THOMPSON, K.M., & YOKOTA, F. (2004). Violence, sex, and profanity in films: Correlation of movie ratings with content. *General Medicine, 6.* Retrieved January 15, 2005, from http://www.medscape.com.

THOMPSON, S.C. (1999). Illusions of control: How we overestimate our personal influence. *Current Directions in Psychological Science, 8,* 187–190.

THOMPSON, V.S.S. (2002). Racism: Perceptions of distress among African Americans. *Community Mental Health Journal, 38,* 111–118.

TIGGEMANN, M. (2004). Body image across the adult life span: Stability and change. *Body Image, 1,* 29–41.

TIGGEMANN, M. (2005). Television and adolescent body image: The role of program content and viewing motivation. *Journal of Social & Clinical Psychology, 24,* 361–381.

TIRODKAR, M.A., & JAIN, A. (2003). Food messages on African American television shows. *American Journal of Public Health, 93,* 439–441.

TKACHUK, G.A., & MARTIN, G.L. (1999). Exercise therapy for patients with psychiatric disorders: Research and clinical implications. *Professional Psychology: Research and Practice, 30,* 275–282.

TOATES, F. (2009). An integrative theoretical framework for understanding sexual motivation, arousal, and behavior. *Journal of Sex Research, 46,* 168–193.

TOKER, S., SHIROM, A., SHAPIRA, I., BERLINER, S., & MELAMED, S. (2005). The association between burnout, depression, anxiety, and inflammation biomarkers: C-reactive protein and fibrinogen in men and women. *Journal of Occupational Health Psychology, 10,* 344–362.

TOLAN, P. H., GORMAN-SMITH, D., & HENRY, D. B. (2003). The developmental ecology of urban males' youth violence. *Developmental Psychology. Special Issue: Violent Children, 39,* 274–291.

TOMBERG, T., TOOMELA, A., PULVER, A., & TIKK, A. (2005). Coping strategies, social support, life orientation and health-related quality of life following traumatic brain injury. *Brain Injury, 19,* 1181–1190.

TOSEVSKI, D.L., & MILOVANCEVIC, M.P. (2006). Stressful life events and physical health. *Current Opinion in Psychiatry, 19,* 184–189.

TRAKHTENBERG, E.C. (2008). The effects of guided imagery on the immune system: A critical review. *International Journal of Neuroscience, 118,* 839–855.

TREAS, J., & GIESEN, D. (2000). Sexual infidelity among married and cohabiting Americans. *Journal of Marriage & the Family, 62,* 48–60.

TRIANDIS, H.C. (1999). Extending social psychology. *PsycCRITIQUES, 44,* 508–510.

TRIERWEILER, L.I., ELD, M., & LISCHETZKE, L. (2002). The structure of emotional expressivity: Each emotion counts. *Journal of Personality and Social Psychology, 82,* 1023–1040.

TSAI, J.L., KNUTSON, B., & FUNG, H.H. (2006). Cultural variation in affect valuation. *Journal of Personality and Social Psychology, 90,* 288–307.

TUCKER, P., DAHLGREN, A., AKERSTEDT, T., & WATERHOUSE, J. (2008). The impact of free-time activities on sleep, recovery and well-being. *Applied Ergonomics. Special Issue: Contemporary Research Findings in Shiftwork, 39,* 653–662.

TUCKMAN, B.W. (1965). Development sequences in small groups. *Psychological Bulletin, 63,* 384–399.

TUGADE, M.M., & FREDRICKSON, B.L. (2004). Resilient individuals use positive emotions to bounce back from negative emotional experiences. *Journal of Personality and Social Psychology, 86,* 320–333.

TURK, D.C. (1994). Perspectives on chronic pain: The role of psychological factors. *Current Directions in Psychological Science, 3,* 45–48.

TWENGE, J.M., & CROCKER, J. (2002). Race and self-esteem: Meta-analyses comparing Whites, Blacks, Hispanics, Asians, and American Indians and comment on Gray-Little and Hafdahl (2002). *Psychological Bulletin, 128,* 371–408.

U.S. Bureau of the Census. (1991). *Statistical abstract of the United States,* 1991 (111th ed.). Washington, DC: U.S. Government Printing Office.

U.S. Bureau of the Census. (2001). America's families and living arrangements. *Current Populations Reports.* Washington, DC: Author.

U.S. Bureau of the Census. (2006). *Selected social characteristics in the United States: 2006* (American Community Survey). Washington DC: Author.

U.S. Bureau of the Census. (2008). *U.S. Population projections.* Washington, DC: Author.

U.S. Bureau of the Census. (2008, August 14). *Press release: An older and more diverse nation by midcentury.* Washington, DC: Author.

U.S. Bureau of the Census. (2009). *Statistical abstract of the United States,* 2009 (128th ed.). Washington, DC: U.S. Government Printing Office.

U.S. Department of Agriculture. (2005). Johanna reveals USDA's steps to a healthier you. Retrieved August 7, 2006, from http://www.mypyramid.gov/global_nav/meida_press_release.html.

U.S. Department of Commerce. (2002). *A nation online: Executive summary.* http://www.esa.doc.gov/508/esa/ANationOnlineEXSFeb02.htm.

U.S. Department of Labor, Bureau of Labor Statistics. (2004). Job search methods. Retrieved April 6, 2006, from http://www.bls.gov/oco/oco20042.htm.

U.S. Department of Labor. (2007). Women in the labor force: A databook. www.bls.gov/cps/wlf-intro-2007.pdf.

U.S. Department of Labor, Bureau of Labor Statistics. (2009). Most frequent volunteer activities: Fundraising, tutoring, teaching. Retrieved August 26, 2009, from http://www.bls.gov/opub/ted/2009/jan/wk4/art01.htm.

U.S. Department of Labor, Bureau of Labor Statistics. (2009). *Occupational outlook handbook.* http://www.bls.gov.

U.S. Merit Systems Protection Board. (2005). Understanding job satisfaction. Issues of merit. Retrieved April 26, 2006, from http://www.mspb.gov/studies/newsletters/05septnws/05Septembernws.htm.

ULIJN, J., RUTKOWSKI, A.F., KUMAR, R., & ZHU, Y. (2005). Patterns of feelings in face-to-face negotiation: A Sino-Dutch pilot study. *Cross Cultural Management, 12,* 103–118.

UNDERWOOD, N. (2002a, January 21). The happy divorce. *McLean's,* 25–29.

UNDERWOOD, N. (2002b, January 21). Marital fixes. *McLean's,* 30–31.

VACCARO, J. (2004). The forgotten illness: Stigma still keeping many Americans from crucial mental-health treatment. (Opinions). *Modern Healthcare, 34,* 18.

VALKENBURG, P.M., PETER, J., & SCHOUTEN, A.P. (2006). Friend networking sites and their relationship to adolescents' well-being and social self-esteem. *CyberPsychology & Behavior, 9,* 584–590.

VALLERAND, A.H., HASENAU, S., TEMPLIN, T., & COLLINS-BOHLER, D. (2005). Disparities between Black and White patients with cancer pain: The effect of perception of control over pain. *Pain Medicine, 6,* 242–250.

VAN ASSEMA, P., MARTENS, M., RUITER, A.C., & BRUG, J. (2001). Framing of nutrition education messages in persuading consumers of the advantages of a healthy diet. *Journal of Human Nutrition and Dietetics, 14,* 435–442.

VAN DEN BULCK, J., BEULLENS, K., & MULDER, J. (2006). Television and music video exposure and adolescent 'alcopop' use. *International Journal of Adolescent Medicine and Health, 18,* 107–114.

VAN DIJK, E., & ZEELENBERG, M. (2005). On the psychology of 'if only': Regret and the comparison between factual and counterfactual outcomes. *Organizational Behavior and Human Decision Processes, 97,* 152–160.

VAN EMMENK, I.J., HETTY, E., MARTIN, C., & WENDT, H. (2008). Leadership behaviors around the world: The relative importance of gender versus cultural background. *International Journal of Cross Cultural Management, 8,* 297–315.

VAN ENGEN, M.L., & WILLEMSEN, T.M. (2004). Sex and leadership styles: A meta-analysis of research published in the 1990s. *Psychological Reports, 94,* 3–18.

VAN ENGEN, M.L., VAN DER LEEDEN, R., & WILLEMSEN, T. M. (2001). Gender, context and leadership styles: A field study. *Journal of Occupational and Organizational Psychology, 74,* 581–598.

VAN HARREVELD, F., VAN DER PLIGT, J., NORDGREN, L. (2008). The relativity of bad decisions: Social comparison as a means to alleviate regret. *British Journal of Social Psychology, 47,* 105–117.

VAN LOMMEL, P., VAN WEES, R., MEYERS, V., & ELFFERICH, I. (2001). Near-death experience in survivors of cardiac arrest: A prospective study in the Netherlands. *The Lancet, 358,* 2039–2045.

VANGELISTI, A.L., & YOUNG, S.L. (2000). When words hurt: The effects of perceived intentionality on interpersonal relationships. *Journal of Social and Personal Relationships, 17,* 393–424.

VEGG, P.R., SPIELBERGER, C.D., & WASSALA, C.F. (2002). Effects of organizational level and gender on stress in the workplace. *International Journal of Stress Management, 9,* 243–261.

VERMEIRE, E., HEARNSHAW, H., VAN ROYEN, P., & DENEKENS, J. (2001). Patient adherence to treatment: Three decades of research. *Journal of Clinical Pharmacy and Therapeutics, 26,* 331–342.

VITTENGL, J.R., & HOLT, C.S. (2000). Getting acquainted: The relationship of self-disclosure and social attraction to positive affect. *Journal of Social and Personal Relationships, 17,* 53–66.

VODANOVICH, S.J., & KASS, S.J. (1990). Age and gender differences in boredom proneness. *Journal of Social Behavior and Personality, 5,* 297–307.

VOGEL, D.L., WESTER, S.R., WEI, M., & BOYSEN, G.A. (2005). The role of outcome expectations and attitudes on decisions to seek professional help. *Journal of Counseling Psychology, 52,* 459–470.

VROOM, V.H., & JAGO, A.G. (2007). The role of the situation in leadership. *American Psychologist: Special Issue: Leadership, 62,* 17–24.

WAJCMAN, J. (2008). Life in the fast lane? Towards a sociology of technology and time. *British Journal of Sociology, 59,* 59–77.

WALDROP, D. P. (2007). Caregiver grief in terminal illness and bereavement: A mixed-methods study. *Health and Social Work, 32,* 197–206.

WALLER, G. (2009). Evidence-based treatment and therapist drift. *Behavioural Research and Therapy, 47,* 119–127.

WALLERSTEIN, J.S., & LEWIS, J.M. (2005). The reality of divorce. Reply to Gordon (2005). *Psychoanalytic Psychology, 22,* 452–454.

WALSH, J. (2002). Shyness and social phobia: A social work perspective on a problem in living. *Health and Social Work, 27,* 137–144.

WALTHER, J.B., VAN DER HEIDE, B., KIM, S., WESTERMAN, D., & TONG, S.T. (2008). The role of friends' appearance and behavior on evaluations of individuals on Facebook: Are we known by the company we keep? *Human Communication Research, 34,* 28–49.

WAMPOLD, B.E., MINAMI, T., TIERNEY, S.C., BASKIN, T.W., BHATI, K.S. (2005). The placebo is powerful: Estimating placebo effects in medicine and psychotherapy from randomized clinical trials. *Journal of Clinical Psychology, 61,* 835–854.

WANG, S., & WU, P. (2008). The role of feedback and self-efficacy on web-based learning: The social cognitive perspective. *Computers & Education, 51,* 1589–1598.

WARD, C., & SEARLE, W. (1991). The impact of value discrepancies and cultural identity on psychological and sociocultural adjustment of sojourners. *International Journal of Intercultural Relations, 15,* 209–225.

WARD, L.M. (2003). Understanding the role of entertainment media in the sexual socialization of American youth: A review of empirical research. *Developmental Review, 23,* 347–388.

WARD, R.A., & SPITZE, G.D. (2007). Nestleaving and coresidence by young adult children: The role of family relations. *Research on Aging, 29,* 257–277.

WARGO, E., (2009). Resisting temptation: Psychological research brings new strength to understanding willpower. *Observer, 22,* 10–15.

WARREN, N.A., (1997). Bereavement care in the critical care setting. *Critical Care Nursing Quarterly, 20,* 42–47.

WASSERMAN, I.M., & RICHMOND-ABBOTT, M. (2005). Gender and the Internet: Causes of variation in access, level, and scope of use. *Social Science Quarterly, 86,* 252–270.

WEINER, B., PANTON, S., & WEBER, M. (1999, April 28). *New study first to quantify illicit drug and substance use in movies and music popular among youth.* http://www.mediacampaign.org/inthenews/mediascope.html.

WEISS, M.G., & RAMAKRISHNA, J. (2006). Stigma interventions and research for international health. *Lancet, 367,* 536–538.

WESTERHOF, G.J., & BARRETT, A.E. (2005). Age identity and subjective well-being: A comparison of the United States and Germany. *Journals of Gerontology: Series B: Psychological Sciences and Social Sciences, 60B,* 129–136.

WESTMAN, A., HUNT, E., CICILLINI, V., & LEWANDOWSKI, L. (1999). Relationships among assisted suicide and religiousness, resources available, denial of dying, and autonomy. *Psychological Reports, 85,* 1070–1076.

WETHINGTON, E. (2000). Expecting stress: Americans and the "midlife crisis." *Motivation and Emotion, 24,* 85–103.

WHARTON, A.S., ROTOLO, T., & BIRD, S.R. (2000). Social context at work: A multilevel analysis of job satisfaction. *Sociological Forum, 15,* 65–90.

WHEELAN, S.A. (2009). Group size, group development, and group productivity. *Small Group Research, 40,* 247–262.

WHEELAN, S.A., & VERDI, A.F. (1992). Differences in male and female patterns of communication in groups: A methodological artifact? *Sex Roles, 27,* 1–15.

WHITE, K.S. (2008). Cardiovascular disease and anxiety. In M.J. Zvolensky & J.A.J. Smits (Eds), *Anxiety in health behaviors and physical illness.* New York: Springer Science.

WHITTY, M.T. (2008). Liberating or debilitating? An examination of romantic relationships, sexual relationships and friendships on the net. *Computers in Human Behavior, 24,* 1837–1850.

WHITTY, M.T., & CARR, A.N. (2006). New rules in the workplace: Applying object-relations theory to explain problem internet and email behaviour in the workplace. *Computers in Human Behavior, 22,* 235–250.

WICHMAN, A.L., RODGERS, J.L., & MACCALLUM, R.C. (2007). Birth order has no effect on intelligence: A reply and extension of previous findings. *Personality and Social Psychology Bulletin, 33,* 1195–1200.

WIERDA-BOER, H.H., GERRIS, J.R.M., & VERMULST, A.A. (2009). Managing multiple roles: Personality, stress, and work-family interference in dual-earner couples. *Journal of Individual Differences, 30,* 6–19.

WIGMAN, S.A., GRAHAM-KEVAN, N., & ARCHER, J. (2008). Investigating sub-groups of harassers: The roles of attachment, dependency, jealousy and aggression. *Journal of Family Violence, 23,* 557–568.

WILBURN, C. (2006). Mediation: A possible asset for EAPs: Though mediation is not always a good fit for workplace disputes, mediation services can provide EAPs with another tool to add to their repertoire of skills. *The Journal of Employee Assistance, 36,* 7–8.

WILDE, A., & DIEKMAN, A.B. (2005). Cross-cultural similarities and differences in dynamic stereotypes: A comparison between Germany and the United States. *Psychology of Women Quarterly, 29,* 188–196.

WILKINSON, S., & KITZINGER, C. (2005). Same-sex marriage and equality. *Psychologist, 18,* 290–293.

WILLIAMS, J.M.G., CRANE, C., BARNHOFER, T., VAN DER DOES, A.J.W., & SEGAL, Z.V. (2006). Recurrence of suicidal ideation across depressive episodes. *Journal of Affective Disorders, 91,* 189–194.

WILLOUGHBY, B.L.B., MALIK, N.M., & LINDAHL, K.M. (2006). Parental reactions to their sons' sexual orientation disclosures: The roles of family cohesion, adaptability, and parenting style. *Psychology of Men & Masculinity, 7,* 14–26.

WILLS, T.A., SARGENT, J.D., STOOLMILLER, M., GIBBONS, F.X., WORTH, K.A., & DAL CIN, S. (2007). Movie exposure to smoking cues and adolescent smoking onset: A test for mediation through peer affiliations. *Health Psychology, 26,* 769–776.

WILSON, J.M., STRAUS, S.G., & MCEVILY, B. (2006). All in due time: The development of trust in computer-mediated and face-to-face teams. *Organizational Behavior and Human Decision Processes, 99,* 16–33.

WILSON, K.G., CHOCHINOV, H.M., MCPHERSON, C.J., SKIRKO, M., GRAHAM, A.P., CHARY, S., et al. (2007). Desire for euthanasia or physician-assisted suicide in palliative cancer care. *Health Psychology, 26,* 314–323.

WILSON, R.S., BARNES, L.L., KREUGER, K.R., HOGANSON, G., BIENAS, J.L., & BENNETT, D.A. (2005). Early and late cognitive activity and cognitive systems in old age. *Journal of the International Neurological Society, 11,* 400–407.

WILSON, T.D., & GILBERT, D.T. (2005). Affective forecasting: Knowing what to want. *Current Directions in Psychological Science, 14,* 131–134.

WING, R.R., & RAYNOR, D.A. (2006). Lifestyle modifications in the obese patient with cardiovascular disease. In M.K. Robinson & A. Thomas (Eds.), *Obesity and cardiovascular disease.* New York: Taylor & Francis.

WINGFIELD, A., TUN, P.A., & MCCOY, S.L. (2005). Hearing loss in older adults: What is it and how it interacts with cognitive performance. *Current Directions in Psychological Science, 14,* 144–148.

WINNICOTT, D.W. (1953). Transitional objects and transitional phenomena; a study of the first not-me possession. *International Journal of Psycho-Analysis, 34,* 89–97.

WISEMAN, H., MAYSELESS, O., & SHARABANY, R. (2006). Why are they lonely? Perceived quality of early relationships with parents, attachment, personality predispositions and loneliness in first-year university students. *Personality and Individual Differences, 40,* 237–248.

WOJCIESZAK, M., & PRICE, V. (2009). What underlies the false consensus effect? how personal opinion and disagreement affect perception of public opinion. *International Journal of Public Opinion Research, 21,* 25–46.

WOLAK, J., MITCHELL, K., & FINKELHOR, D. (2007). Unwanted and wanted exposure to pornography in a national sample of youth Internet users. *Pediatrics, 119,* 247–257.

WOLPE, J. (1973). *The practice of behavior therapy.* New York: Pergamon.

Women's Way. (2006). Power skills: How volunteering shapes professional success. Retrieved August 9, 2006, from http://www.volunteermatch.org/volunteers/resources/surveyfnl.pdf.

WOOD, N.D., CRANE, D.R., SCHAALJE, G.B., & LAW, D.D. (2005). What works for whom: A meta-analytic review of marital and couples therapy in reference to marital distress. *American Journal of Family Therapy, 33,* 273–287.

WOODS, S., & WHITE, E. (2005). The association between bullying behaviour, arousal levels and behaviour problems. *Journal of Adolescence, 28,* 381–395.

WORKMAN, M. (2007). The effects from technology-mediated interaction and openness in virtual team performing measures. *Behaviour & Information Technology, 26,* 355–365.

World Health Organization. (2006). Women and mental health. Retrieved July 2, 2006, from http://www.who.int/mediacentre/factsheets/fs248/en/.

WorldatWork. (2009). *Telework trendlines 2009.* Retrieved July 15, 2009, from http://www.worldatwork.org.

WorldHeartFederation.org. (2007). *Children, adolescents and obesity.* Retrieved May 19, 2008, from http://www.world-heart-federation.org/press/facts-figures/children-adolescents-and-obesity.

WRIGHT, C.E., KUNZ-EBRECHT, S.R., ILIFFE, S., FOESE, O., & STEPTOE, A. (2005). Physiological correlates of cognitive functioning in an elderly population. *Psychoneuroendocrinology, 30,* 826–838.

WRIGHT, K. (2002, June). Six degrees of speculation. *Discover,* 19–21.

XIAO-PING, W. (2004). A comparison study of persons found not criminally responsible by reason of mental disorder between British Columbia, Canada and Hunan, China. *Chinese Journal of Clinical Psychology, 12,* 405–407.

XIE, G., & LEE, M.J. (2008). Anticipated violence, arousal, and enjoyment of movies: Viewers' reactions to violent previews based on arousal-seeking tendency. *Journal of Social Psychology, 148,* 277–292.

XIRASAGAR, S., SAMUELS, M.E., & STOSKOPF, C.H. (2005). Physician leadership styles and effectiveness: An empirical study. *Medical Care Research and Review, 62,* 720–740.

YAMAGUCHI, S., GELFAND, M., OHASHI, M.M., & ZEMBA, Y. (2005). The cultural psychology of control: Illusions of personal versus collective control in the United States and Japan. *Journal of Cross-Cultural Psychology, 36,* 750–761.

YARAB, P.E., & ALLGEIER, E.R. (1997, April). *Just don't have sex! Acceptability, disclosure, and forgiveness of extradyadic relationships.* Paper presented to the annual meeting of the Eastern Psychological Association, Washington, DC.

YAWAR, A. (2008). Time and humanity on psychiatric wards. *Lancet, 37,* 285–286.

YBARRA, O. (2001). When first impressions don't last: The role of isolation and adaptation processes in the revision of evaluative impressions. *Social Cognition, 19,* 491–520.

YODANIS, C. (2005). Divorce culture and marital gender equality: A cross-national study. *Gender & Society, 19,* 644–659.

YOSHIMURA, S.M. (2004). Emotional and behavioral responses to romantic jealousy expressions. *Communication Reports, 17,* 85–101.

YUEN, C.N., & LAVIN, M.J. (2004). Internet dependence in the collegiate population: The role of shyness. *CyberPsychology & Behavior, 7,* 379–383.

ZABRISKIE, P. (2004). Wounds that don't bleed: How severe stress is taking a toll on U.S. troops in Iraq. *Time, 164,* 40–42.

ZACCARO, S.J. (2007). Trait-based perspectives of leadership. *American Psychologist. Special Issue: Leadership, 62,* 6–16.

ZAUTRA, A.J., AFFLECK, G.G., TENNEN, H., REICH, J.W., & DAVIS, M.C. (2005). Dynamic approaches to emotions and stress in everyday life: Bolger and Zuckerman reloaded with positive as well as negative affects. *Journal of Personality. Special Issue: Advances in Personality and Daily Experience, 73,* 1–28.

ZEA, M.C., REISEN, C.A., POPPEN, P.J., BIANCHI, F.T., & ECHEVERRY, J.J. (2005). Disclosure of HIV status and psychological well-being among Latino gay and bisexual men. *AIDS and Behavior, 9,* 15–26.

ZEIDNER, M. (1995). Adaptive coping with test situations: A review of the literature. *Educational Psychologist, 30,* 123–133.

ZEIDNER, M., & MATTHEWS, G. (2005). Evaluation anxiety: Current theory and research. In A. Elliot & C. Dweck (Eds.), *Handbook of competence and motivation* (pp. 141–163). New York: Guilford.

ZHENG, H., LIU, Y., LI, W., YANG, B., CHEN, D., & WANG, X., et al. (2006). Beneficial effects of exercise and its molecular mechanisms on depression in rats. *Behavioural Brain Research, 168,* 47–55.

ZIEBLAND, S., ROBERTSON, J., JAY, J., NEIL, A. (2002). Body image and weight change in middle age: A qualitative study. *International Journal of Obesity & Related Metabolic Disorders, 26,* 1083–1091.

ZIMMERMAN, B.J., & SCHUNK, D.H. (2003). *Albert Bandura: The scholar and his contributions to educational psychology.* Mahwah, NJ: Lawrence Erlbaum.

ZIMMERMAN, C. (2004). Denial of impending death: A discourse analysis of the palliative care literature. *Social Science & Medicine, 59,* 1769–1780.

ZUCKERMAN, M. (2005). The neurobiology of impulsive sensation seeking: Genetics, brain physiology, biochemistry, and neurology. In C. Stough (Ed.), *Neurobiology of exceptionality* (pp. 31–52). New York: Kluwer Academic/Plenum Publishers.

ZUCKERMAN, M., KNEE, C.R., KIEFFER, S.C., & GAGNE, M. (2004). What individuals believe they can and cannot do: Explorations of realistic and unrealistic control beliefs. *Journal of Personality Assessment, 82,* 215–232.

ZUMMUNER, V.L., & FISCHER, A.H. (1995). The social regulation of emotions in jealousy situations: A comparison between Italy and the Netherlands. *Journal of Cross-Cultural Psychology, 26,* 189–208.

ZURBRIGGEN, E.L., & YOST, M.R. (2004). Power, desire, and pleasure in sexual fantasies. *Journal of Sex Research, 41,* 288–300.

ZURBRIGGEN, E.L., COLLINS, R.L., LAMB, S., ROBERTS, T.A., TOLMAN, D.L., WARD, L.M., et al. (2007). *Report of the APA task force on the sexualization of girls.* Washington, DC: American Psychological Association. Retrieved May 28, 2009, from http://www.apa.org/pi/wpo/sexualizationrep.pdf.

Photo Credits

Name Index

Subject Index